THINKING:
The Second
International Conference

THINKING:
The Second
International Conference

edited by

D. N. Perkins
Harvard Graduate School of Education

Jack Lochhead
University of Massachusetts, Amherst

John Bishop
The University of Auckland

LEA 1987
LAWRENCE ERLBAUM ASSOCIATES, PUBLISHERS
Hillsdale, New Jersey   Hove and London

Lawrence Erlbaum Associates, Inc., Publishers
365 Broadway
Hillsdale, New Jersey 07642

Library of Congress Cataloging in Publication Data

Thinking: the second international conference

   Papers presented at the 1984 International
Conference on Thinking, held at the Harvard Graduate
School of Education, Cambridge, Mass.
   Includes indexes.
   1. Thought and thinking—Congresses. 2. Thought and
thinking—Study and teaching—Congresses. I. Perkins,
David N. II. Lockhead, Jack. III. Bishop, John (John
Christopher) IV. International, Interdisciplinary
Conference on Thinking (2nd: 1984: Harvard Graduate
School of Education) V. Harvard University. Graduate
School of Education.
BF455.T533   1987   153   87-9165
ISBN 0-89859-805-2

Printed in the United States of America
10 9 8 7 6 5 4 3 2 1

Contents

PART II: CONTEXTS OF THINKING

PART III: THEORETICAL PERSPECTIVES ON THE TEACHING OF THINKING

Preface

Toward the end of August 1984, when most people were enjoying the last beaches and breezes of summer holidays, over 700 people gathered from all parts of the world at the Harvard Graduate School of Education, Cambridge, MA, to hear about, talk about, and *think* about thinking. Some 100 papers were presented on a variety of theoretical and empirical issues concerning thinking; plenary sessions addressed such themes as the nature of intelligence and national programs to enhance thinking; workshops were conducted in several contemporary approaches to fostering students' problem solving and learning abilities. The participants included psychologists, philosophers, and representatives of other academic disciplines concerned with thinking, and, just as importantly, administrators and practitioners concerned with the role of education in developing students' thinking.

The present volume offers a selection of papers from the many more presented at the 1984 International Conference on Thinking, continuing the tradition established by its predecessor volume, *Thinking: The Frontier Expands* (William Maxwell, editor, published by Lawrence Erlbaum Associates, Hillsdale, New Jersey). The editors, consulting with others as needed, chose with such criteria in mind as quality, provocativeness, cross-cultural relevance, accessibility, breadth of interest, and variety of fields represented. Even with these guidelines, we found ourselves pressed by space limitations to make a number of hard decisions and we regret that more of the insights brought to the conference could not be represented here.

The 1984 International Conference on Thinking was the second of a series beginning with the Fiji conference of January, 1982, organized by William Maxwell, then Dean of the School of Education at the University of the South Pacific, Suva, Fiji. Continuing his quest to draw attention to the topic of thinking, William Maxwell involved others in a committee to develop such conferences every 2½ years. The third in the series was held in Hawaii in January of 1987. The editors wish to thank Dr. Maxwell for his artful and dedicated efforts to make this series a reality. The 1984 conference was sponsored by three institutions who contributed capital and person-power to the project: the University of the South Pacific, the University of Massachusetts, and the Harvard Graduate School of Education. We thank these institutions for their enlightened commitment.

Finally, we wish to express our gratitude to Julia Hough, our editor for Lawrence Erlbaum Associates, for help well above and beyond the call of duty in planning this volume, responding editorially to authors, treating us editors with a good mix of pressure and patience, and in general greatly enhancing the book you have in your hands.

Foreword: The Right to be Intelligent*

Luis Alberto Machado

Over the past 10,000, 30,000, even 50,000 years, the human brain has possessed the same characteristics. There has been no biological evolution to explain history, civilization, or culture. The difference between a man or a woman of the caves and any one of us is not a biological difference. Our genetic code is exactly the same. The only contrasts lie in the information that our brain receives and in the processing of that information in our brain. And through all these years how much of our genetic intellectual capacity have we utilized? Some people say only 10%, a figure that cannot be exact because we do not really know what 100% of our brain capacity is. However, it may well be that we utilize a minimal portion of the genetic capacity of our brain.

Today we are witnessing, all over the world, a unique moment in human history. For the first time we have enough knowledge to permit us to develop our brain capacity in systematic ways. During the past 50 years there have been many studies demonstrating that people can learn to use their minds better. This means that every person—every woman, every child, and every man of every country—has the right to benefit from such

---

*This Foreword is a presentation given by Dr. Machado to open the *Conference on Thinking* upon which this book is based. As Minister for the Development of Human Intelligence in Venezuela from 1979 to 1984, Dr. Machado was instrumental in launching some dozen programs in Venezuela to improve the intelligence of various sectors of the Venezuelan population. As a minister of state, he also visited the governments of many nations to promote attention worldwide to the resource of human intelligence and its development. The title of this presentation is borrowed from Dr. Machado's book, *The Right to be Intelligent* (New York: Pergamon Press, 1980).

knowledge. One might say that this is a human right, a natural human right with which we are born. Consequently, society, in the person of its politicians, academicians, and other leaders, has the responsibility to do the best it can to put such knowledge into the hands of people all over the world.

What is some of this knowledge? For example, during the last 40 years we have developed early stimulation methods. We have had dramatic results, showing that the development of intelligence begins at the moment of birth, perhaps even before. Interventions with subnormal children have produced great improvements. Similar interventions with normal children also have produced accelerated development. Imagine what would happen if we were to give such techniques to all parents of the world so that they could improve the capacity of their children.

Unfortunately, the truth is that that knowledge is mainly within the confines of universities. How many parents in the United States know of their children's potential? Just a few. How many parents in India, in China, Australia, know of their children's potential? Just a few, though we have that knowledge. Is it possible to conceive of a more important program than to instruct and to motivate all mothers and all fathers—as well as all others who deal with children—about what science knows today concerning the development of the brain's capacity?

There are hundreds of books and articles concerning this matter. When children are born, they have all the neurons they are going to have for all the rest of their lives, but the neurons are immature, and they get to reach maturation by way of stimulation they receive through the senses. Only if the brain is stimulated in a proper way do those neurons reach maturation. So, if we stimulate a child's brain for the first 6 years of his life, that child will develop his or her capacity in a very dramatic way. We have to do our best to give this knowledge to all parents of this country and to all parents of the world.

Why don't all physicians attending women about to give birth instruct them about their child's potential intelligence? Why don't all nurses instruct women about their offspring's brain capacity? Why don't we utilize mass media for this purpose in the same way that we use it for commercial purposes? All mothers and fathers should be instructed about this. Why don't we start a project—an international collaboration?

I am a politician, and, as a politician, I think that there is not a more important aim for any government than to increase the possibility of realizing the potential mental capacity of all of its population; that is the best investment a country could make, the best investment of all. The richest resource of this country—and of China, India, South America, Europe—is not oil, nor is it gold. It is not industrialization. The richest source is the human brain. We will have to do the best we can to develop that resource, and this objective must be in the consciousness of the leaders of society. Chiefs of state, ministers, senators, deputies, all of them must be made aware of the importance of progress to develop human intelligence. Such programs should start at the moment of birth and even before, cover the first years of life, and continue throughout human life. There is much to be done.

Consider education as it usually is. In primary schools, secondary schools, and throughout college and university instruction, students receive information about diverse fields, but they are not taught how to process that information. The definition of a student is a person who studies, but are students taught how to become students? Are they taught how to study in a systematic way? We teach grammar, mathematics, biology, and chemistry. Does it result from our teaching that students learn to think in an effective way? This may occur indirectly, when our students are lucky and have an excellent teacher, but it does not happen in a systematic manner.

The purpose of teaching a subject is to teach the content of that subject, not to teach thinking. We have all been students in primary and secondary school. How much time did our teachers dedicate to the teaching of thinking? In primary school, how many hours were focused on the direct development of mental capacity? The greatest improvement imaginable for our educational system is the teaching of thinking in a systematic and specific way, rather than by accident.

Consider: In the classroom, students have to attend and to concentrate. But who has taught them how to attend and how to concentrate? Knowledge from the field of psychology shows us something about how to teach concentration. But when we use that in a systematic way, we only use it to teach teachers how to capture the audience and to teach better. During the past 40 years, innovations in our educational system may have created better teachers, but not better students. We teach how to teach, but we do not teach how to learn in a systematic way. A student learns how to learn incidentally. For another example, students have to analyze and synthesize, but where are students taught the processes of analyzing and synthesizing information? We teach students how to analyze a cell or the history of humanity, but we do not teach them the mental process of analyzing. For another example, there is a great deal of knowledge on how to solve problems, yet we do not teach students how to solve problems in effective ways.

For yet one more example, to think is to make relationships; to think creatively is to make new relationships; and intelligence is the capacity of making relationships among thoughts. In art and science no one has created anything wholly new. Creators such as scientists and artists are those who change the place of things by making new relationships among thoughts. It is not only a matter of knowledge but a matter of learning about how to process knowledge in order to discover new relationships. We have to teach that in a systematic way.

My dream is this: that in the future we will have a new subject introduced into educational system all over the world, that will teach thinking from kindergarten through college. We will incorporate this new subject specifically for the purpose of teaching students how to analyze information, solve problems, synthesize information, and find new relationships. Imagine that we have a million students who have studied traditional subjects throughout the educational system and are ending at the university level. Imagine that another million students have studied the same subjects, with the same teachers and textbooks, in addition to which they have studied the subject of thinking for 1 hour each day throughout their education. Could it be that those two groups would be the same? That is inconceivable. The second group would have a much greater capacity for thinking and creating than the first group. It is my conviction that we are able now to initiate the most significant transformation of education ever: teaching thinking as a proper subject. We can teach our children how to learn, how to solve problems, how to become more intelligent, by teaching them the same subjects but adding 1 hour daily on how to think.

Now, the development of the capacity to think does not end at the moment that we end our formal studies. Learning takes place throughout one's whole life, and an adult can cultivate his or her own intelligence and capacity for thinking. There is considerable knowledge about how to develop the capacity of thinking in the adult. Since intelligence is a faculty that can be developed as long as one lives, with proper attention to the matter a middle-aged adult should be more intelligent than a young adult. Accordingly, the transformation of society calls for developing everyone's intellectual capacity from the moment of birth and even before, continuing through the process of formal education, and extending throughout adult life. If we do this in all countries of the world, if we do this as a national aim for all nations of the world, coordinating actions all over the world, we will make the biggest revolution in history. Moreover, this revolution would be a peaceful one. You would not have to take from the hands of anyone, but only develop the potential that all of us possess.

What we must do—and I say this as a politician—is to take all of the knowledge contained in universities and put it in the hands of the people. We must utilize the mass media for this purpose. The transformation of the educational process, by teaching thinking throughout life, will yield a transformation of society. We have to dream about this transformation. It is in our hands, and we can create it. It depends on a decision, a decision mainly of the leaders of society, academic and political. The readers of this book may be mostly scientists, not politicians, but I ask for political action on the part of scientists.

In 1938, Albert Einstein wrote to President Roosevelt: Hitler can construct an atom bomb; you have to do something about that. Einstein was a scientist who decided to influence a politician. He chose to take action, to convince a politician about matters pertaining to a war and the making of an atom bomb. Now you have in your hands a more explosive bomb for the purpose of peace. If Einstein could act on his decision at that moment, I ask you to think of acting on another decision. I ask you to think about joining forces to convince political leaders that an educational transformation is necessary.

In sum, we have in our hands the possibility of a peaceful revolution. The potential for it lies in the human brain, and the possibility for it lies in our decisions. Can there be an objective more important than this one? We must do our best for the transformation of humanity. We must be aware that we are living in a pivotal moment of history. We must be conscious of the potential of all human beings of all races and of all countries of the world. We must recognize the possibility of a transformation of humanity, and through our love of humanity to help that transformation to take place.

I Philosophical and Conceptual Orientation

Contributions to the 1984 Conference on Thinking at the Harvard Graduate School of Education covered a very wide range of topics, and this breadth is reflected in the papers chosen for inclusion in this volume. Although doubtless alternative groupings would have been justifiable, the order in which we have presented the papers selected does indicate one useful way of exhibiting their interconnections.

All of our authors are in varying degrees concerned with thinking and its teaching, but some are more directly engaged with educational issues than are others. Accordingly, Sections C and D group contributions that belong primarily to educational psychology, philosophy of education, and the actual practice of training thinking skills. Sections A and B, by contrast, address issues that arise when we seek to understand what thinking is, how it is conditioned, and how it varies from context to context. Thus, these Sections deal with the psychology (and philosophical psychology) of thinking, and have their rightful place at the start, because we are unlikely to make much progress in understanding the *teaching* of thinking until we have considered the nature of thinking itself.

In Section A, we collect together a group of papers treating highly general questions about the nature of thinking. Although each paper is informed by empirical studies, the aim here is to provide a philosophical and conceptual

1

orientation on which to ground our understanding of thought. In Chapter 1, John Bishop surveys the development of modern physicalist philosophies of mind, whereas, in Chapter 2, Kenneth Gilhooly appeals against the tendency in psychology to compartmentalize different aspects of thinking, and suggests a unified account in terms of "mental modelling." In Chapter 3, Benny Shannon challenges the extent to which we can model mind as a matter of computations performed upon representations and proposes a dialectic between representational and nonrepresentational aspects of cognition.

A major focus of interest during the Conference were the two symposia on the nature of intelligence. Chapter 4 brings together the contributions of Richard Herrnstein, Arthur Jensen, Jonathan Baron, and Robert Sternberg on the prospects for developing human intelligence, whereas Chapter 5 contains Howard Gardner's talk on his Theory of Multiple Intelligences and an edited version of the discussion that followed. These two chapters provide valuable background against which we may consider some later contributions in Sections C and D that offer suggestions about how thinking skills might be developed.

The final three chapters in this opening section remind us, in very different ways, of the danger of delineating too narrowly the realm of real thinking. E. P. Brandon and C. A. Nolan, in Chapter 6, highlight the social and political dimensions of thinking with their study of the way in which our elliptical habits of reasoning provide room for a usually unnoticed ideological shaping of our thoughts. In Chapter 7, Victor Kobayashi renews Gregory Bateson's plea for including within the wider class of "thinking," not just deductive, inductive, and scientific reasoning generally, but also the intelligent use of metaphor. William Maxwell and Jack Lochhead provide us, in Chapter 8, with an example of just this type of metaphorical reasoning: they draw an analogy between some aspects of neural organization in the brain and the mechanisms they believe should motivate our thinking about organizations and groups. Thus, Section A ends in a fitting way with a personal statement of values, reminding us that our concern as thinkers and as teachers is not just with how things are, but with how they ought to be.

1 Thought, Action and the Natural Order

John C. Bishop
University of Auckland, New Zealand

No examination of recent research into the nature of thinking, however selective, could fairly omit reference to developments in Philosophy. This may surprise some, to whom Philosophy's institutional place as a specialised discipline within the humanities suggests that it can have little to contribute to empirical scientific research. Yet there should be no surprise because the philosophical task has always been to seek to unify human understanding. It is true, ironically enough, that the philosopher–synthesiser *has* been isolated within the academic community. Yet, although there may be many explanations for this, it is clear that one of the standard justifications for setting Philosophy apart is largely unwarranted. 'Purely conceptual' issues were thought to be essentially separate from empirical ones; and philosophers (generally by their own self-conception) operated in a division of labour in which their concerns were *to be defined* by "having nothing to do with mere facts." But the sharp distinction between the conceptual and the empirical has been challenged, partly on theoretical grounds (see Quine, 1951), and partly in the practice of recent philosophers who, adhering to the Socratic tradition of following the inquiry wherever it leads, have recognised the vital interrelationship of 'scientific' and 'philosophical' issues. This is not to say that now there are no distinctively philosophical questions but it is to say that any philosophical inquiry is now regarded as limited and self-stultifying if it ignores developments in the scientific disciplines.

The Monist Philosophy of Mind

Questions about the nature of thinking fall under the philosophy of mind, an area notable for its interconnection with empirical disciplines, such as cognitive psychology and the neurosciences. Some philosophers have even come to think that many issues in philosophical psychology are as Churchland (1984) states: "ultimately empirical in character; they will be decided by the comparative success and the relative progress displayed by alternative scientific research programs" (p. 6)[1]. There is now a concern that the interrelationship between philosophy and psychology at the research level should be reflected in a reorganisation of the curriculum, so that related questions about mind and behavior are no longer presented as if they belonged to the domains of two quite distinct disciplines[2].

But what *are* the distinctively philosophical problems about the nature of thought? The most fundamental is to understand how it is possible for there to exist, within the causal regularities of the natural order, systems capable of intentional action based on reasoning from their conscious awareness of their environments. Traditionally, this problem has been conceived as the question whether the universe must be more than purely material in order to accommodate conscious agents within it. The famous dualism of Descartes affirms that it must; consciousness and voluntary action are held to bear testimony to the existence of a nonphysical realm somehow (and problematically) related to the physical order. But Descartes' view can be regarded as a solution only at the cost of allowing that nature is radically split into an irreducibly mental and an irredeemably material order. This option does not strike many philosophers as attractive, for their ideal is to understand reality as a unity, and the faith that in principle this may be achieved is widespread. Accordingly, naturalistic or *monist* theories have been sought that will display the mind as part of a natural system that may be open to comprehension as a unified whole. Thus, what may be called the monist philosophy of mind is widely advocated. It may also be called 'physicalist', given that Physics investigates the basic 'stuff' of reality; the name 'materialism' is perhaps a little

---

[1]This book provides a most useful introduction to current debate in the philosophy of mind, as well as putting the case for a thoroughly scientific naturalism. For another useful overview, see Fodor, 1981.

[2]In 1981 the Council for Philosophical Studies offered a summer institute on curriculum development in philosophical psychology. A booklet, *Psychology and the Philosophy of Mind in the Philosophy Curriculum,* was subsequently published in 1983, and is available from the council at San Francisco State University, 1600 Holloway Avenue, San Francisco, CA 94132, U.S.A.

outdated because, for modern Physics, matter as popularly conceived is not as fundamental as once supposed. But, whatever its name, the central commitment is clear; nature is one and our understanding ought to aim to grasp it as one. It is the counsel of despair to adopt dualisms like Descartes'.

Tasks for the Monist

There are, I suggest, three focal tasks that philosophers of this monist persuasion need to accomplish.

First, an account is required of what mental states and events *are*, which will smoothly fit them into the ontology of our general science of nature. If, as is likely, mental items are not a basic feature of our natural ontology, it must be shown how they may be constructed from, or at least realised in, a system constituted of items that are ontologically basic.

Second, because reference to mental states is crucially important in the explanation of behavior, the monist must try to understand how such explanations are related to scientific explanations generally. When a mental and a physical explanation appear to apply to the same phenomenon, what account of their relationship is to be given? Do they compete, or are they compatible? If the former, which deserves to count as the 'real' explanation; if the latter, is their compatibility merely a matter of one's being reducible to the other, or are they distinct yet coapplicable? Of course, this second task is linked to the first because an account of what mental states are will have to allow for their causal roles—in being produced by environmental stimulation, as well as in producing behavioral responses.

The third task is to consider what implications a monist stance on the mind's place in nature has for our ethical perspective. Our practice of assigning moral responsibility seems to require that agents be answerable only for those occurrences that are under their control—in other words, only for their own actions. But an action is essentially a product of thought, though not necessarily conscious thought. So, to be responsible for our actions, it seems we must be responsible for the thoughts—the intentions and volitions—that produce them. (Indeed, some philosphers follow the Kantian tradition of supposing that this is the sole locus of our responsibility. For an interesting discussion of this view see Nagel, 1976.) Yet, if our intentions and volitions are items within the natural order, how can their occurrence genuinely be *our* responsibility? Will it not be the laws of nature, and their antecedent causes, which determine them? How, then, is responsible action possible? (For a presentation of this 'metaphysical problem of freedom,' see Chisholm, 1966.)

What Mental States Are and How They Explain: the Growth of Functionalism

Logical Behaviorism.   One celebrated means of satisfying the monist commitment to place the mind in the natural order is to 'dissolve' mental states into logical constructs out of behavioral dispositions, so that, for example, thinking that it's soon going to rain is understood as a complex disposition to behave in certain ways—seek shelter, bring in the washing, and so on. It was this *logical behaviorism* that that famous 'ghostbuster' Gilbert Ryle found himself left with as his positive theory of mind (see Ryle, 1949). But, as a positive account, it has some awkward features; can we really accept that to be in pain is simply to be disposed to cry out, rub the affected area, and so forth? Besides, if believing it's going to rain is just the disposition to seek shelter (among other things), how can reference to this belief *genuinely explain* any particular instance of shelter–seeking behavior?

The Mind–Brain Identity Theory.   The suggestion of the *central state materialists* was that such explanations have their force because the mental attribution (of belief, in this case) actually refers to certain states of the brain that produce the sheltering behavior. Mental states are thus held to be contingently identical with neural states, in much the same way, for example, that the temperature of a gas is identical with a certain excitation state of its molecules. Despite the obvious fact that pains, beliefs, hopes, and the like have strikingly different properties from brain states, proponents of this 'identity' theory, such as J. J. C. Smart, have been able to defend its coherence, and argue that, by familiar standards for judging hypotheses, the hypothesis that mental states are brain states is the best available theory of mind (Smart, 1959).

The Analogy with Computers: Functionalism.   Central state materialism has not, however, been able to sustain its original presumption that every distinguishable type of mental state might in principle be identified with a distinct type of neural state. It is here that cross fertilisation from computer science becomes evident. One favourite way to pose the question whether a physicalist theory of mind can be sustained is to ask whether machines can think. A.M.Turing's famous paper offered a suggestion about how to deal with this question, and so made way for the proposal that the mental states of a person might be understood on a strong analogy with the logical or functional states of a Turing-machine or general purpose computer (Turing, 1950). (Putnam, 1960, advances such a proposal, and gives an account of the notion of a Turing machine. See also Hofstadter, 1981.) This position retains one feature of logical behaviorism, namely, the goal of characterising mental states in terms of their causal role, yet it includes interrelationships with other mental states as part of this causal role, and so doesn't reduce the mental to a logical construct from behavior. On this *functionalist* view, just as the same computer program may be run in indefinitely many different types of machine, so the same type of mental functional organisation may have quite different physical embodiments. Because physically different systems may be functionally identical, the 'type–type' identity theory must be abandoned; there need not be a given neural condition correlated with each type of mental state. Nevertheless, functionalists remain within the monist philosophy of mind because no mental (functional) state can exist unless it is somehow physically realized. So there may be an identity between mental and physical states at the level of particulars, even if not at the level of general types. Functionalism has thus driven a wedge between two theses that were often supposed to be inextricably linked; the thesis of monism (or physicalism) that we have discussed, and the thesis of reductionism, which holds that what it means for a system to be in a mental state can be successfully analysed as a matter of the system's having certain physical characteristics. (For further discussion, and an account of the variety of functionalist views, see Block 1980b. For more on the relation between functionalism and reductionism, see Fodor 1974 and Boyd 1980.)

Functionalism and Cognitive Science: Difficulties for the Program.   Research into artificial intelligence has been directed towards developing computer programs whose operations mimic intelligent behavior. Modern cognitive science goes further, and treats as an empirical hypothesis about the mind the suggestion that its processes are computer-like. To quote Jerry Fodor (1983): "Contemporary cognitive theory takes it for granted that the paradigmatic psychological process is a sequence of transformations of mental representations and that the paradigmatic cognitive system is one which effects such transformations" (p. 29). Fodor has been influential in developing the notion of a "language of thought"—a system of language-like internal representations on whose syntactic features the procedural mechanisms of the brain operate (see Fodor, 1975). This approach to cognitive psychology seems naturally affiliated with functionalism. But this functionalist–cognitive-science program is not without its difficulties.

For one thing, there is the suspicion that functionalism has ignored what is arguably the most intransigent problem for any physicalist philosophy of mind, the problem of consciousness. As well as being open to characterisation in terms of their role in a system's functional economy, many (though not all) mental states have a qualitative 'feel' to them; it makes sense to ask *what it is like* to be in them. It is sometimes suggested that mental *qualia*, the 'raw feels' of experience, just cannot be fitted into a physicalist picture (see Nagel, 1974). Critics have argued that, in any case, functionalism doesn't explain how this can be done because it is conceivable that a system should instantiate the functional role of a certain type of mental state, yet not be *in* that mental state because it lacks the conscious component that it requires (see, for example, Block 1978). John Searle has even raised doubts about a functionalist interpretation of mental states that don't have any experiential component, such as the capacity to understand a natural language. Much debate has been provoked as to the significance of his 'Chinese Room' thought experiment, in which he describes a person who knows no Chinese, who implements, in a sealed room, a program (written, of course, in a language he does understand) whose functional role is to transform syntactic inputs (interpretable as questions in Chinese) into syntactic outputs (interpretable as sensible answers in Chinese to these very questions). (See Searle, 1980, and the peer discussion following.)

Another difficulty for cognitive science is the charge that its approach is fruitful only for certain "subdepartments" of mental function, and cannot be expected to unravel the mystery of thinking in general. Fodor has recently claimed that cognitive theory fits only those mental functions, like perceptual and linguistic analysis, which are 'modular', in the sense that they operate in restricted domains; are realised in innate, relatively automatic, neural systems; and exhibit "informational encapsulation" because the data on which they operate may include, as Fodor (1983) states, "considerably less than the organism may know" (p. 69). When it comes to the 'central' processors responsible for belief–fixation and general problem solving, Fodor (1983) argues that these systems must be holistic rather than modular, and observes (as his 'First Law of the Nonexistence of Cognitive Science') that "the more global . . . a cognitive process is, the less anybody understands it" (p. 107). His essay closes with the observation that "if someone—a Dreyfus, for example[3]—were to ask us why we should even suppose that the digital computer is a plausible mechanism for the simulation of global cognitive processes, the answering silence would be deafening" (p. 129).

The Eliminativist Alternative.   Though these objections may not be fatal to the functionalist program, they do make it worthwhile examining alternatives within the monist ideology. One recently canvassed option is *eliminative materialism*, which we may usefully explain by considering

---

[3]The reference is to Hubert L. Dreyfus. For a sample of his views, see, e.g., Dreyfus, 1972.

the second task noted earlier on the monist's agenda, namely providing a place for mentalistic explanations in the schema of natural science.

It is part of our socialisation that we acquire, in tandem, a language and a 'theory' for understanding the behavior of our fellows. This is our 'folk psychology', and we use it in everday interaction to make sense of our shared life by explanations that attribute a whole host of mental states to ourselves and others. As we have seen, one proposal is to understand these mental states as functional states. But the eliminativist urges a more radical means of giving effect to the monist commitment, namely to claim that a coherent natural science of behavior will have no need to make essential explanatory use of the concepts of our folk psychology. The mental, as we now conceive it, needs to be eliminated in much the same way that other entrenched concepts have been fruitfully dislodged and abandoned along the way in scientific history (see Churchland, 1984, Chapter 2, Section 5).

Eliminativism shares with dualism the common thesis that our concept of mind is not reducible to any physical concept that could properly be assimilated into an adequate natural science. But eliminativism contrasts completely with dualism in the moral it draws from this; rather than enshrining the mind in a nonphysical realm, it proposes that, from the point of view of theoretical science, if not of every day life, the concept of mind should be abandoned, and our folk psychology replaced by some more adequate theory. But how could such a replacement emerge? The eliminativists hope that it will eventually develop from the painstaking and gradual application of the "bottom-up" approach to an understanding of the mind, which begins by studying the basic machinery of the brain. Some impressive grasp of neural systems has already been obtained of course (see Churchland, 1984, Chapter 7, for an introductory review). But it is a long way up from the bottom! And the day is long to dawn when we may expect to understand, without the use of mental concepts, the complex human interactions that interest the historian, the political scientist or the psychologist. Although some may doubt the very conceivability of such a development, it has to be conceded that eliminativism has a powerful attraction, and there is a case for holding that it, rather than functionalism, is the philosophy of mind with which modern cognitive science ought to be harnessed (see Stich, 1983).

Yet there is something threatening (almost sinister!) in the eliminativist's vision. In the first place, the "qualia" objection might be renewed; are we not so directly certain of our experiences of sound, colour, pain, etc., that it is just absurd to suppose that we could ever come to agree that our concept of these mental items was "outmoded"? (It is instructive to consider an eliminativist reply to this question: see Churchland & Churchland, 1981.) But there is another aspect to the threat—the suspicion that eliminativism undermines the basis of our ethical perspective on human behavior.

Persons can be held morally responsible only for what they do. Thus, to apply the notion of moral responsibility, we must employ a distinction between a person's actions and events that merely happen to her or befall him. But we use our folk psychology to make this distinction because an action is essentially understood as behavior that issues from a certain sort of mental cause—as behavior that can be given an *intentional explanation* in terms of the mental states that constituted the agent's reasons for the action. Thus, if the whole folk psychological theory of mental causes gets abandoned, the concept of an action goes with it, and no further application can be made of the notion of moral responsibility.

Intentional Explanations—Are They Reducible?.   The status of intentional explanations has been much debated by philosophers. Opponents of physicalism characteristically maintained that 'reasons were not causes'; intentional explanations were not causal explanations at all, so the reductionist aim of accommodating them within the framework of scientific explanation was categorially impossible. A famous article of Donald Davidson's (Davidson, 1963) established once and for all that intentional explanations must be causal in some broad sense if they are to be distinguished from mere rational justifications of behavior in terms of the agent's beliefs and desires. But, interestingly enough, this doesn't do the trick of ensuring that folk psychology is of a piece with natural scientific explanatory theories. Davidson's own position, as it emerged in subsequent articles (see Essays 3, 11 and 12 in Davidson 1980), was to maintain that, though intentional explanations were causal, they possessed an autonomy relative to scientific explanation. His "anomalous monism" is the thesis that, although the causes referred to in an intentional explanation must be material (presumably neural) ones, there are no "bridge laws" that would enable a physical explanation to be inferred from the intentional one or vice versa. A further blow to reductionism about intentional explanations may be dealt by focussing on the problem of specifying the *way* in which mental states must cause matching behavior for an intentional explanation to apply. Davidson expresses pessimism about achieving this (Essay 4, Davidson, 1980), and I have myself argued that an examination of this problem shows that intentional explanations employ a primitive notion of "agent–causation" that is not at all at home in the realm of natural scientific explanation generallly (Bishop, 1983).

If these arguments are correct, intentional explanations don't belong in the same category as (other) scientific explanations. And that leaves us with a choice between eliminativism, which takes the attitude that what doesn't fit into natural science can have no explanatory value beyond the purely pragmatic, and an *explanatory dualism,* which maintains that certain phenomena (intentional actions) require a kind of explanation distinct from that applicable to phenomena generally.

It may fairly be asked whether this explanatory dualism is any less problematic than the ontological dualism of Descartes. If you reject the suggestion that some events might be caused by immaterial goings-on in a nonspatio–temporal substance (a 'soul' or 'spirit'), then will you not also, for similar reasons, reject the claim that some events are explicable as caused in a fashion quite distinct from ordinary causation? Perhaps so. However, explanatory dualism might be made more acceptable to the philosopher with monist sympathies if it can offer some way of *explaining* how an irreducibly distinct form of explanation can properly apply to (some) purely physical systems. If reduction of the mental to the physical isn't possible, then, to use Daniel Dennett's words, we must at least be able to 'legitimize' intentional descriptions of physical systems (see Dennett, 1978, Introduction, xvii). Dennett's own work on intentional systems is a pointer in the right direction here (see, e.g., Chapters 1 and 12, Dennett, 1978), although he is open to the charge that he legitimizes intentional explanations only by construing them purely instrumentally or pragmatically—as useful ways of describing certain systems from the point of view of one who interacts with them. Establishing this much evidently falls short of sustaining the claim that the real causes of a system's behavior can include mental events.

D. M. MacKay's 'Seeing the Wood and the Trees'.   What can be done to defend explanatory dualism? At the 1982 Suva Conference on Thinking, D. M. MacKay offered a defense of this view, entitled 'Seeing the Wood and the Trees' (published as MacKay, 1983). In the space remaining, I switch 'modes' and abandon the broad generalities of our discussion to date in order to focus on some particular features of MacKay's argument.

MacKay distinguishes in general between the physical analysis of a system (that explains 'the determination of one *force* by another *force*') and its informational analysis (that accounts for the 'determination of one *form* by another *form*') (p. 7). Both kinds of analysis may apply equally well to one physical system—and MacKay makes the same claim about the two perspectives on the conscious agent, which he calls the 'I-story' and the 'brain-story'. We cannot, he believes, reduce the mental account of human behavior to a physical account: rather, both accounts apply in a complementary fashion. Nevertheless, MacKay (1983) locates himself within the monist philosophy of mind, for he says: "I see no objection to describing these (different perspectives) as complementary aspects of a unity" (p. 8).

The defence of explanatory dualism requires two theses to be established. First, it must be shown that we do need to retain the 'folk psychological' perspective on human behavior. And, second, the autonomy or irreducibility of this perspective must be proved. (If the explanatory dualist wants to retain the monist commitment a third step is required; to give an account of how the kinds of states attributed in folk psychology may be realised in a physical system.)

MacKay's (1983) argument for the first thesis—the need to retain the 'I-story'—would not convince an eliminativist, though it does have the ring of good sense to it:

> I suggest that our most solid starting point is our immediate experience of what it is like to be a cognitive agent—the facts to which the "I-story" bears witness . . . What I am pointing to might be . . . labelled *obligated access:* for what I want to emphasize is that the facts of experience to which the I-story bears witness are facts we would be *lying* to deny. (p. 7)

Still, the eliminativist is right not to be convinced, for the question is here being begged against him. *Granted the concepts of our folk psychology,* we would indeed be lying if we claimed not to have the sensations, desires, emotions, etc. of which we are immediately aware. But the possibility the eliminativist raises is that *this whole system of concepts* could be replaced, in which case we would come to report what we know in introspection in alternative terms. From such a vantage point, we could look back on our past introspective reports, and regard them, not exactly as *lies*, but as falling short of the truth through the inherent inadequacy of the concepts they employed.

An alternative defence of the first thesis appeals, not to the allegedly self-evident facts of introspection, but to the values to which we are committed in our ethical perspective on human behavior. As already noted, these values seem to commit us to the folk psychological notion of an intentional action for which the agent may be held morally responsible. No doubt an eliminativist could insist that a revolution that sweeps away our folk psychology might appropriately trigger a revolution in our ethical thinking too. Although I cannot deny that we might end up with a more suitable replacement for our present notion of moral responsibility in this way, the *practical* conceivability of retaining a recognisably ethical perspective in the absence of the concept of an intentional action is so slight, that I am prepared to agree that we are stuck with our folk psychology (at least as it pertains to intentional action), and to turn to the further question of examining just how keeping these concepts can mesh with our scientific explanatory commitments.

MacKay's Argument for Irreducibility.

MacKay's Argument for Irreducibility.   MacKay offers an interesting argument for the second thesis needed to defend explanatory dualism. He expresses this irreducibility thesis as the claim that: "the I-story is no mere translation of the brain-story"; the mentalistic account of his experience to which the agent has access is not reducible to any "objective" physicalist story about his behavior. MacKay's main point is that explanations of behavior that may be available to 'detached nonparticipants' will always be 'systematically invalid' for the agent whose behavior is being explained. This claim is supposed to result from considerations about *predictions* of an agent's action as made from the two perspectives of the I-story and the brain-story because the material that provides an explanation of behavior typically could have supplied a prediction of its occurrence had it been known in advance. Predictions based on information about antecedent physiological states of the agent and the environment could in principle show that an agent *is certain* to perform a particular action—provided, that is, that the relevant causal laws are not merely probabilistic. MacKay's claim, however, is that, even if the causal laws are deterministic, no such 'brain-story' prediction of his behavior can be regarded *by the agent himself* as correct because from his perspective his future actions are not inevitable. Thus, whereas the brain-story could in principle provide an account of the agent's behavior under which it is completely determined by antecedent causes, the I-story could never admit such an account. So it follows that they are *not* the same story told in different words; the one does not 'translate' into the other. The crucial core of this argument is MacKay's (1983) claim that: "*there does not exist*, even unknown to the agent, a completely determinate specification of his immediate future, with an *unconditional* claim to his assent" (his emphasis, p. 9). Let us examine the 'simple' proof MacKay offers for this 'nonexistence theorem':

> assuming that conscious, cognitive processes and brain processes are correlated (not necessarily one-to-one, but so that *no significant change in cognitive state can take place without a correspondingly significant change in brain state*), then no complete specification of an immediately future brain state could be equally accurate, whether or not the agent himself believed it. If accurate only on the assumption that the agent would *not* know or believe it, it clearly has no claim to his assent, since it would be inaccurate if the agent were to believe it. If, however, we imagine a specification adjusted so as to become accurate if (and only if) the agent believed it, then, although the agent would (*ex hypothesi*) be correct to

believe this one, he would not be mistaken to disbelieve it (since it is inaccurate unless believed by the agent). (his emphases, p. 9)

MacKay emphasises that he takes this argument to establish more than just the distinctiveness of the agent's own perspective upon the prediction of his future action. He concludes:

We are saying that no prediction exists that can establish (even behind the agent's back) an unconditional belief worthiness-by-him. If calling the agent's future inevitable implies that it has one and only one specification, with an unconditional claim to the assent of all, including the agent if only he knew it, then the foregoing proves that his immediate future *is not competely inevitable* for a cognitive agent. (his emphasis, pp. 9-10)

I take it that "a prediction with an unconditional claim to the assent of all" is one such that anyone who knows the evidence for it ought, on pain of irrationality, to accept its truth. Now, let us grant MacKay's assumption that the evidence on which we make predictions of a person's behavior must include either the fact that she will believe the prediction true before she acts, or the fact that she will not believe it true. The rationale for this is that what an agent believes is correlated with her brain states, and a prediction of what an agent will do next must be based on information about her total antecedent brain state. MacKay argues that, whether she believes she will act as predicted or not, it is impossible to make a prediction that will have an unconditional claim to *her* assent.

Let us examine this argument. Suppose that the evidence that justifies the prediction that Sally will refuse to grant the loan at 2 p.m. this afternoon includes the fact that Sally does *not* come to believe this prediction before 2 p.m. Then, MacKay (1983) says: "the prediction clearly has no claim to (her) assent, because it would be inaccurate if the agent were to believe it." Now, *perhaps* it is true that the prediction would be inaccurate if Sally herself were to come to believe it; for, if, contrary to fact, she had believed it, the antecedent state of her brain before she makes her decision at 2 p.m. would have been different from what it actually is, and would have changed the total evidence on which the prediction of the outcome was justified—but it *need* not because perhaps the way Sally decides on loan applications isn't at all affected by any beliefs she may form in advance about what her decision will be (Certainly, if she's my bank manager, I'll expect her to consider my loan applications without prejudice!). But, even if we grant that this *would* have made a difference, MacKay's conclusion does not follow. All we require for the prediction to have an unconditional *claim* to Sally's assent is, not that she be able to agree to it, but that, if she comes to know the evidence that justifies the prediction, then *either* she agrees to it *or else irrationally* rejects it. Now, Sally *could* come to know the evidence about her brain states that justifies the prediction of her refusing the loan at 2 p.m. In doing so, given the correlation between brain- and belief-states, she will come to know that she will not believe the prediction of her refusal before 2 p.m. (for, remember, we are assuming that to be part of the evidence that nontrivially justifies the prediction). What cannot happen is that she *accepts* the evidence as justifying the prediction, for that would require it to be true both that she does and that she does not believe in advance that she will refuse the loan. So what must happen is that she *rejects* the prediction on the evidence, and, because *ex hypothesi* the evidence *does* justify the prediction, do so irrationally. Sometimes, then, it is impossible for agents to accept justified predictions of their own actions (namely, just in case the evidence for the prediction includes the fact that they do not come to accept it). But it was a stronger claim that MacKay wished to establish—that no specification of future behavior can exist with an unconditional claim to the assent of the agents themselves. And this has not been shown; from "they won't accept it" it does not follow that, on the evidence, they ought not to accept it.

Now consider the alternative supposition that the evidence justifying the prediction that Sally will refuse the loan includes her being in brain states correlated with coming to believe, before 2 p.m., that this prediction is true of her behavior at 2 p.m. (Maybe she knows enough about my financial history to be sure that she'll refuse my application, even though she will take that decision quite objectively and fairly.) Then it seems that this prediction *will* have an unconditional claim to Sally's assent because if Sally came to know the evidence justifying the prediction, there would be no obstacle to her accepting the prediction on the basis of it. Neither would there by any obstacle to her accepting the prediction for some other reason (such as the one suggested previously) and (irrationally) rejecting the brain-state justification for it. What couldn't happen is that Sally should reject the *truth* of the prediction because that would entail that she didn't believe in advance that she would reject the loan, and, *ex hypothesi*, she does believe this. Thus MacKay is right to allow that Sally "would be correct" to believe the prediction under these circumstances. Yet, puzzlingly, he goes on to maintain that Sally "would not be mistaken to disbelieve" the prediction because it is "inaccurate unless believed by (her)". Apparently, MacKay contradicts himself, for, if Sally would be correct to believe the proposition that p, it follows that she would be mistaken to disbelieve that p because to disbelieve that p is to believe that not-p (and not to have no beliefs on the question whether p). What MacKay must mean, presumably, is that, given that the evidence justifies the prediction only if it includes Sally's believing (in advance) the truth of the prediction, then, had Sally disbelieved this, the prediction would have been false, and the disbelief correct. This may be so, but it is not to the point; it does not show that, on this supposition, there is no specification of her future behavior with an unconditional claim to Sally's assent.

MacKay (1983) is right to claim that "no complete specification of an immediately future brain state could be equally accurate, whether or not the agent himself believed it" (p. 9). But this entails only that predictions of future brain states must, because beliefs are correlated with brain states, take account of the beliefs of the agent concerned, including his beliefs, if he has any, on the truth or falsity, justifiability or unjustifiability, of the prediction itself. Given the correlation hypothesis, the same is true for the prediction of future thoughts and actions, although it is likely that some matters for belief or disbelief don't make the sort of difference to the agent's brain states that could have any effect on the outcome of a given future choice (e.g., whether or not I believe there are seven consecutive sevens in the decimal expansion for pi probably has no effect whatsoever on whether I will choose a tomato or a cheese sandwich for lunch). Still, predictions of one's own future actions do provide a dimension of belief that will often be likely to affect those actions. No prediction of an agent's future behavior can compel her assent—for even rationally unassailable evidence for a prediction may be irrationally rejected. As well, it is open to an agent to seek to falsify a known prediction of her future action—though, as Alvin Goldman has clearly shown, such an intention is by no means bound to be achieved because a predictor may be able to take account of the precise effects that the agent's attempt to falsify it will have on her behavior, and adjust the prediction accordingly. (See Goldman, 1968). But neither of these truths establishes that there can be no complete specification of the agent's future that warrants her unconditional assent—that is such that, if she knew the evidence for it, she could reject it only on pain of irrationality.

Thus, *this argument of MacKay's* does not succeed in establishing the irreducibility thesis that is required to support explanatory dualism. It does not follow, of course, that explanatory dualism is false, or that there are no arguments that secure it. As so often, in Philosophy, results are modest; the best we get is a decision on the merits of a particular argument—and that decision is always open to revision because logical fallibility is a shared property of all thinkers. It may be that the subtlety of MacKay's argument has eluded me, and the criticisms I have offered miss their mark.

Conclusion

We have seen, then, some of the ways in which philosophers have tried to expound and defend a monist, or physicalist, philosophy of mind. The notion that mental goings-on and mental explanations for behavior belong to a class of their own proves remarkably resilient, however. The dualism of Descartes has never been decisively refuted—it is "just" faith in the unity of reality that keeps us from accepting it. The best response to this tension seems to be that of explanatory dualism, which retains the monist commitment by accepting that all reality is physical reality, but tries to make room for our irrepressible dualist tendencies by removing them from the ontological level, and locating them at the level of explanation. The proof that the 'mental–story' is not reducible to the 'physical–story' is not easily given. We have outlined—and criticised—one distinguished attempt to provide such a proof (MacKay's). But we have also noted some other attempts at the same goal (in our earlier section, "Intentional Explanations—are they Reducible?"). Perhaps these may succeed where MacKay's approach fails. Finally, we have noted that, even if irreducibility *can* be proved, the debate with the eliminativist still remains, and we may have to face the (exciting? disturbing?) thought that, in centuries to come, it will make as much sense to hold a conference on 'Thinking,' as it would now to gather chemists together to discuss recent progress in phlogiston theory, or to hold a conference for psychiatrists (nonfundamentalist ones anyway!) on trends in the control of demons.

REFERENCES

Bishop, J. (1983). Agent-causation. *Mind, 92,* 61–79.

Block, N. (1978). Troubles with functionalism. In C. W. Savage (Ed.), *Perception and cognition, issues in the foundations of psychology, Minnesota Studies in the philosophy of science, 9* (pp. 261–235). Minneapolis: University of Minnesota Press. Reprinted in Block, 1980a. (pp. 268–305)

Block, N. (Ed.). (1980a). *Readings in the philosophy of psychology,* Volume 1. Cambridge, MA. Harvard University Press.

Block, N. (1980b.) *What is functionalism?.* In Block, 1980a. (pp. 171–184)

Boyd, R. (1980). *Materialism without reductionism: What physicalism does not entail.* In Block, 1980a. (pp. 67–106)

Chisholm, R. M. (1966). Freedom and Action. In K. Lehrer (Ed.), (pp. 28-44). *Freedom and Determinism,* New York: Random House.

Churchland, P. M. (1984). *Matter and consciousness.* Cambridge, MA: M. I. T. Press.

Churchland, P. M., & Churchland, P. S. (1981). Functionalism, qualia and intentionality. *Philosophical Topics, 12,* 121–145.

Davidson, D. (1963). Actions, reasons and causes. *Journal of Philosophy, 60,* 685–700. Revised and reprinted in Davidson, 1980, pp. 3–19.

Davidson, D. (1980). *Essays on actions and events.* Oxford: Clarendon Press.

Dennett, D. C. (1978). *Brainstorms: Philosophical essays on mind and psychology.* Montgomery, VT: Bradford.

Dreyfus, H. L. (1972). *What computers can't do: The limits of artificial intelligence.* New York: Harper & Row.

Fodor, J. (1974). Special sciences, or the disunity of science as a working hypothesis. *Synthese, 28,* 97–115. Reprinted in Fodor, 1975, (pp. 9–25).

Fodor, J. (1975). *The Language of Thought*. New York: Crowell.

Fodor, J. (1981). The mind–body problem. *Scientific American, 244*, 124–133.

Fodor, J. (1983). *The modularity of mind, an essay in faculty psychology*. Cambridge, MA: M. I. T. Press.

Goldman, A. I. (1968). Actions, predictions and books of life. *American Philosophical Quarterly, 5*, 135–151.

Hofstadter, D. R. (1981). *The Turing Test: a Coffeehouse Conversation*. In Hofstadter & Dennett. (pp. 69–92).

Hofstadter, D. R., & Dennett, D. C. (1981). *The mind's I*. New York: Basic Books.

MacKay, D. M. (1983). Seeing the wood and the trees. In W. Maxwell (Ed.), *Thinking: the Expanding Frontier*. (pp. 5–12) Philadelphia: Franklin Institute Press.

Nagel, T. (1974). What is it like to be a bat? *The Philosophical Review, 83*, 435–450. Reprinted in Nagel, 1979, Chapter 12.

Nagel, T. (1976). Moral luck. *Proceedings of the Aristotelian Society*, Supplementary Volume *50*, 137–151. Reprinted in Nagel, 1979, Chapter 3.

Nagel, T. (1979). *Mortal questions*, Cambridge, UK: Cambridge University Press.

Putnam, H. (1960). Minds and Machines. In S. Hook (Ed.), *Dimensions of Mind*. (pp. 362–385). New York: New York University Press. Reprinted in Putnam, 1975.

Putnam, H. (1975). *Mind, language and reality: Philosophical papers, Volume 2*, Cambridge, UK: Cambridge University Press.

Quine, W. v. O. (1951). Two dogmas of empiricism. *The Philosophical Review, 60*, 20–43. Reprinted in *From a Logical Point of View*, (2nd edition). (pp. 20–46). Cambridge, MA: Harvard University Press.

Ryle, G. (1949). *The concept of mind*. London: Hutchinson.

Searle, J. (1980). Minds, brains and programs. *The Behavioral and Brain Sciences, 3*, 417–424.

Smart, J. J. C. (1959). Sensations and brain processes. *The Philosophical Review, 68*, 141–156.

Stich, S. (1983). From folk psychology to cognitive science. Cambridge, MA: M. I. T. Press.

Turing, A. M. (1950). Computing machinery and intelligence. *Mind, 59*, 433–460. Reprinted in Hofstadter & Dennett, 1981, (pp. 53–67).

2 Mental Modeling: A Framework for the Study of Thinking

K. J. Gilhooly
University of Aberdeen, Scotland

Although the study of thinking is receiving increased attention from psychologists, educationalists, and cognitive scientists, it is still widely perceived as a potpourri of isolated topics such as deductive reasoning, problem solving, concept learning, creative processes, undirected thinking, etc. Indeed, this point has been explicitly commented on in two recent textbooks in the field. Mayer (1983) states that readers of his survey of the thinking area "will need a fair tolerance for a lack of closure." Similarly, I have noted in my own text (Gilhooly, 1982) the lack of a general theory to tie together the distinct phenomena studied under the heading of "Thinking." Research on thinking is open to the accusation of being excessively "phenomenon–driven," as Newell (1973) charged of cognitive psychology in general, and it is easy to list a string of phenomena that have attracted research. The following short list provides some examples and is not intended to be exhaustive:

1. *Set Effects.* This work concerns failures to solve normally easy problems where the failures are brought about by particular prior experiences or by the layout of the problem. Thus, if subjects solve a series of anagram problems that all have "animal" word solutions then they will tend to be slowed down or even fail to solve an anagram that has a nonanimal word solution.

2. *Atmosphere Effects.* This research concerns the extent to which the conclusions that people draw from syllogisms are determined by a nonlogical impression or "atmosphere" formed by the presence or absence of negatives and by the quantifier "some" in the premises.

3. *Incubation Effects*. Does consciously setting a problem aside lead to better or faster solutions when the problem is tackled again? If so, is this effect due to unconscious work or to some beneficial form of forgetting?

4. *Introspective Accuracy*. To what extent and under what conditions can people give accurate reports of their own mental processes and contents?

5. *Training Creativity*. Can creativity be increased by training in special techniques such as brainstorming?

6. *Development of Expertise*. What processes mediate the transition from novice problem solver to expert problem solver in various task areas?

It might of course be argued that there is no compelling reason to suppose that all the activities intuitively classed as 'thinking' should be unifiable under a single overarching theory. Although accepting that there is no guarantee that such an overarching theory can be devised, I submit that the goal of developing such a theory is worth pursuing. Rather than having a number of unrelated 'minitheories' for each of the many subtopics in research on thinking it would be much more satisfactory to have a unifying theory that integrated the subtopics. As well as being desirable, I believe that the goal of a unified theory of thinking has some plausibility. This belief is strengthened by the successes obtained using single symbolic programming languages like Interlisp (Teitleman, 1976) to tackle a wide range of tasks such as language processing, expert diagnosis and game playing. The principles of the symbolic language may be regarded as constituting a general level theory, within which specific models can be devised for particular tasks. Indeed, Anderson (1983, p. 5) has argued that, by analogy to Interlisp, a single set of principles may underlie all of cognition, including thinking.

This chapter, then, aims to present a conceptual *framework* within which the hitherto disparate topics of thinking research may be interrelated, and within which a general theory may be developed. In common with Anderson (1983, p. 12), I view a "framework" as a general pool of concepts that can be sampled from to produce more specific theories (e.g., of deductive reasoning) and models (e.g., of syllogistic reasoning); that is to say, within a framework one can develop alternative theories and within a theory alternative models for particular phenomena can be devised. A framework cannot readily be assessed simply in terms of predictive accuracy (because different predictions may be derived from different models within the same framework). Instead, the fruitfulness of the framework must be judged on the extent to which it leads to new empirical work, yields fresh angles on old issues and generates new predictive models of particular phenomena.

Thinking as Mental Modeling

The basic notion of the present approach is that thinking is essentially *mental modeling*. To a large extent this view is derivative from the notion of man-the-scientist (Kelly, 1955): i.e., the idea that people seek to interpret and understand the world about them in a coherent fashion, and in that respect have similar goals to those of professional scientists. Scientists seek to understand the world in terms of symbolic models, which are symbol structures having some interpretation with respect to the external world. For example, an economist may propose that certain measures of money-supply are central in predicting economic growth, exchange rates and employment rates. In such a case, the economist will have identified variables and postulated interrelationships amongst them. The variables and the proposed relationships would be represented in a symbolic model that might be expressed in pencil-and-paper form or nowadays, more likely, in the form of a computer program. The program can then be run to predict future events or, by starting with data for a previous year, to check its fit to past results. Similarly, scientists have devised symbolic models of galactic evolution, continental drift, nuclear winters and other complex phenomena and the implications of these models can be explored by computer. I am suggesting, then, that computer models of the sort used by weather forecasters, astronomers, economists and other scientists, provide a concrete analogy for mental models; that is, mental models are like computer models in that they represent external reality and can be used to predict the future, explain the past and generate options for future actions. Unlike a scientist's computer model, however, a mental model may be implicit rather than explicit and so may be very difficult to communicate, whereas the scientist's model must be explicit and readily communicable to fellow specialists. Another likely difference is that the scientist's models are consciously constructed, tested, revised and replaced, whereas, outside of formal educational settings, mental models are more likely to be formed and modified by piecemeal learning processes rather than by conscious effort.

The mental modeling approach in psychology postulates that useful theories of cognitive processes will result if it is assumed that people interpret the world in terms of symbolic models. Because these models cannot be directly observed and, indeed, may well not be accessible even to the individuals "using" them, these hypothetical internal models are labelled "*mental* models." Mental models may be found in folk theories of all sorts and recent studies of laypeople's concepts of illness provide numerous examples. To take one such example, Fitzpatrick (1984) discusses a commonly held model for infectious illnesses. Laypeople tend to classify such illnesses as 'hot' illnesses (fevers) or 'cold' illnesses (e.g., colds and chills). For each type of illness there are associated lists of possible causes, likely courses, suitable treatments and degree of individual responsibility for becoming ill. Colds and chills are ascribed to low temperatures and especially to sharp transitions from hot to cold environments. Such temperature changes are held to affect particularly vulnerable areas of the body, such as the head and the feet. Treatment involves restoring the temperature equilibrium with hot drinks or by retiring to a warm bed. Fevers, on the other hand, are due to invisible entities ('germs' or 'bugs'), which are transmitted from person to person. Treatment usually involves taking some liquid medicine to flush out the germs. The individual is seen as less personally responsible for fevers than for colds on the grounds that infection is less avoidable than are adverse environments. Thus, we have here two illness models, one for 'hot' and one for 'cold' illnesses, with their own causes, courses and remedies. These particular models are widely shared within a given culture. Needless to say, trained physicians bring different models to bear on the same illnesses. Although the "official" biomedical models are epistemologically sounder, it is important for good doctor–patient communication that physicians be aware of typical lay models and the study of such models has become an important part of medical psychology.

Of course, this general approach is not entirely new, and antecedents of the view that thinking is mental modeling include Craik's (1943) pioneering analogies between physical models and mental models, as well as Johnson-Laird's (1975, 1983) analyses of mental modeling in reasoning and comprehension and the recent analyses of expert–novice differences in terms of mental model differences (Gentner & Gentner, 1983). What one rarely sees in the psychological literature is an attempt to apply the mental modeling notion consistently to a range of topics in the thinking area. Before going on to develop this idea, it will be useful to briefly characterize, or "model" the cognitive resources available for mental modeling.

Patterns of mental modeling activity will be constrained by basic information processing resources. For present purposes, the main aspects of resource to be considered are those of memory structure and content.

Memory structure may be usefully viewed as consisting of the two traditional main sections, viz., *long term memory,* and *working memory.* Long term memory is regarded, as usual, as a storage system of effectively unlimited capacity whereas working memory, on the other hand is relatively limited in capacity. In long term memory are stored already formed mental models and "building block" information from which new models may be formed. The stored information about already formed mental models roughly corresponds to Lachman's (1973) "encyclopae-dic" memory whereas the "building block" level equates with Tulving's (1972) "semantic" memory.

I now consider two main forms of mental modeling activity: Forming and using a model.

Forming Models

Model formation occurs during information gathering, whether it be by perception, reading, conversation, or some other route. An initial step is presumably to retrieve some basic level concepts and relationships on the basis of perceptual input and prior expectancies. For example, a brief glimpse at a newcomer to a room might yield basic level data that the person is male, wrinkled, has thinning long hair, and is wearing beads. These basic level data may serve to retrieve an already existing model consistent with the information available (e.g., 'aging hippy'). Essentially, this is a classification or categorization process.

So far I have described the rather routine model forming in which a new situation is categorized in terms of an existing model, but often enough no existing model will give a satisfactory fit and some modifications may be needed to the best fitting model to form a new (although derived) one that gives an improved fit. Sometimes, more drastic steps yet, may be needed: A novel model will be required, either built up from basic concepts, or by appropriately combining parts of existing models to make a new one (e.g., forming a 'microlight' model from 'propeller aeroplane' and 'hang glider' models).

The point at which an initially evoked model is judged so unsatisfactory that it must be modified or abandoned, is presumably the point at which the perceived costs of using the model (due to errors in prediction, say) outweigh, (a) the benefits of continuing to use it and, (b) the perceived costs of seeking a better one. For example, a computer user faced with yet another text editor might initially conclude that the new editor is very similar to one with which he or she is already familiar. This judgment might be based on similarity between the new and old command names. Depending on the degree of match between the old and the new editor a certain ratio of successes to errors will result as the user tries to operate the new editor as if it were the old one. Persistence with the "old model" for the new situation will presumably be greater the fewer the errors made using that model. Also, if the user manual for the new editor is reputed to be impenetrable then the user will persist longer with his or her inadequate model of the editor because the costs, in time, of forming a correct model are expected to be high. Thus, the perceived balance of costs and benefits of continuing with a less than perfect model as against seeking to form a better model, will determine whether a new model is sought, when the initial model does not completely fit the situation.

Using Models: Prediction and Problem Solving

Once a model for a current situation is established, or, at least, provisionally accepted, exploration can begin. This may be in the form of *prediction*, (What will happen next?) or *problem solving* (What should one do next?). In both prediction and problem solving there is a need for rules that can generate future states of a currently used model. Consideration of prediction and problem solving brings out the important idea that mental models contain "change-rules" within themselves that can be used to anticipate possible changes in the system being modeled whether the changes are time-based or are due to varying circumstances and actions. Mental models have a dynamic aspect and it is easy to appreciate their utility in prediction and "mental simulation" of alternative scenarios.

In contrast, other popular notions of mental representation based on the "schema" concept are more static. As Thorndyke (1984) points out, schema concepts have been almost wholly used in the context of information storage in and retrieval from long term memory, with little application to uses of stored information in problem solving. Schemas are essentially frameworks for encoding new inputs into preexisting categories and subcategories, and how further action is to be carried out on the schematized input is unclear (Anderson, 1983, p. 37). Possibly, "expected consequences" could be attached to schemas and predictions obtained from such a list of consequences. For example, if the current situation evokes a "wild animal loose" schema, an attached consequence might be, "you could be eaten." However, if the predictions depend heavily on the exact instantiation of the schema then many distinct instantiations and their expected consequences would need to be stored. This way of proceeding seems implausible in many cases. For example, in the case of predicting whether two aeroplanes will collide or not, exact heights, speeds and bearings must be taken into account. It seems implausible to suppose that there are ready made schemas for all possible combinations of heights, speeds and bearings. Rather it would seem more plausible to propose that a model is set up from which predictions are mentally computed.

Basically, the contrast between the mental modeling and the schema approaches reflects the general contrast between computation and storage in information processing. Which mix of storage and computation is optimal depends on the task and the architecture of the system carrying out the task. The two approaches should not be seen as mutually exclusive. An individual may use one approach for some tasks and the other approach for different tasks. However, especially when novel problems are to be considered, mental modeling would appear more plausible.

Ideally in *prediction*, there is no choice or uncertainty about which rules apply at any given state (cf. Laplace's notion of a clockwork universe), and "forward running" of the model can thus produce definite predictions.

However, in *problem solving*, and especially when the problem involves countering the actions of an adversary (e.g., in playing chess) then there are usually choices, or uncertainties, about which particular rule will, or should, be applied at any time. Thus, an expanding set of possible model developments quickly opens up, through which the solver must try to find the best path.

In principle, the solver could try to search forward mentally through a set of possible developments that expands rapidly with each step further ahead that the solver tries to explore from the current state. A complete look ahead to all possible end-states (e.g., wins, losses and draws in a game) would enable the solver to infer the best path to follow. However, such a complete look ahead is impossible for problems of any complexity. More limited forms of looking ahead to intermediate states have proven useful in computer programs that play games. These systems use some form of "evaluation function" that can assess the promise of states that could be reached a few moves ahead. That information, in turn, aids in selecting the best move to take in the immediate situation (e.g., making a first move in checkers). Even such limited forms of look ahead rapidly overload working memory and people generally use some forms of means–end analysis. In this approach, only actions that serve particular goals are examined, rather than all the actions that might be carried out in a given situation. Means–ends analysis places less demand on working memory and does ensure that efforts are directed to promising directions.

The "work" of model exploration and modification is assumed to occur in working memory, and to be governed by relevant rules stored in long-term memory. Certain rules will be specific to the current model (the 'change-rules' of that model), whereas others will be of a more general character and correspond to broad strategies (such as means–end analysis) that can be applied to a wide range of problems.

Models of complex situations will be inherently incomplete, because the 'grain' of reality is finer than any conceivable model. So, a car mechanic's mental model of an engine that he is working on will not normally include representation of minor scratches, dirt deposits, etc. Because working memory is severely limited, probably only a part of a complex model can be encoded in working memory at any given time, e.g., the spark plug system in the car mechanic case. Thus, given the limitations on models generally, and the further limitations imposed by working memory constraints, there is always the risk that a critical aspect of a problem situation will *not* be represented in the model, leading to a representation within which the problem is unsolvable. The opposite difficulty may also arise, of course, in which restrictions are imported into the model of the problem that do not apply. This seems to be a part of the difficulty of the nine-dot problem, for instance. In this task subjects are presented with a pattern of 9 dots arranged in a square three-by-three array. The subjects are then asked to draw four straight lines, without lifting their writing implement from the paper, in such a way that all the dots are connected. Typically, this task is found to be very difficult, largely because subjects tend only to consider line patterns *within* the square array of dots. However, no solution is possible unless one of the lines is continued beyond the square array. The restriction to the square array is a self imposed one and does not form part of the instructions.

An erroneous model of a problem may be induced by experience with superficially similar problems that are actually structurally different. The 'water jars' type of set effect (Luchins, 1942) seems to display an automatized evocation of a misleading model, within which solution is impossible. In the 'water jars' task, Luchins asked subjects to decide how one could obtain a specified amount of water using three jugs of fixed capacities and an unlimited source of water. For example, given three jugs (A, B, and C) of capacities 18, 43 and 10 units, how could you obtain exactly 5 units of water? The solution can be expressed as B-A-2C. After a series of problems with that same general solution, subjects had great difficulty with the following problem. Given jugs A, B and C of capacities 28, 76 and 3 units respectively, how could you obtain exactly 25 units of water? The solution is simply A-C; but, when the problem is given after a series of problems involving the long solution, B-A-2C, many subjects fail to solve or are greatly slowed down compared to control subjects.

Applications to Other Aspects of Thinking

Some other areas of application of the mental modeling approach are now discussed.

Logical Reasoning Tasks.   For consistently successful performance in typical deductive reasoning problems, such as syllogisms, abstract models corresponding to those devised by formal logicians are required. In practice, subjects seem to develop models of the situation to be reasoned about that deviate from the patterns of formal logic. This is at least partly because three of the four standard premises (e.g., 'some As are Bs') are consistent with multiple states of affairs, which may well not be fully represented in any single model. A recent example of a model-based approach in reasoning is found in Johnson-Laird and Steedman's (1978) successful analysis of syllogistic reasoning in terms of analogical model making. In this theory it is assumed that the premises are represented by relationships among a small number of typical exemplars of the categories entering into the premises. For instance, given the premise, 'All the artists are beekeepers', subjects are assumed to form a mental model incorporating an arbitrary number of elements representing artists each of which is related to a separate beekeeper element. Additionally there are represented beekeeper elements *not* related to artist elements. A second premise, such as "Some beekeepers are drivers," would be represented in a similar way and combined with the first to give and overall model. The way in which the overall model is formed is such as to make it very likely that the conclusion, "Some artists are drivers," will be invalidly drawn. This model, in addition to fitting much well established data, also accounts for the recently uncovered "figural bias" effect.

An example of this effect is that the premises, "Some of the parents are scientists; all of the scientists are drivers," tend to elicit the conclusion, "some of the parents are drivers," rather than the equally valid conclusion, "some of the drivers are parents." On the other hand, premises of the form, "some of the scientists are parents; all of the drivers are scientists," tend to elicit the invalid conclusion "some of the parents are drivers." Johnson-Laird's (1983) mental modeling analysis predicts this bias, whereas earlier approaches to syllogistic reasoning do not.

Concept Learning

In the typical laboratory concept learning task, the subject has to discover a classification rule over a set of stimuli on the basis of information about the class membership of individual stimuli (e.g., Bruner, Goodnow & Austin's classic 1956 study). This task may be regarded as requiring the formation and revision of models in the light of basic level data. It seems from the studies that direct tests of current models are generally preferred; that is to say, that if the current model is "red squares are positive examples of the rule," people prefer to ask about red square stimuli rather than green squares, red circles or green circles. Whereas this bias serves the need for economy of cognitive effort because the subject need not decide which of the many possible nonexemplars of the model to test, it can easily lead to overrestrictive hypotheses. (For example, all red squares might be positive examples, but the rule could be "red *or* square" rather than "red square" stimuli). Many subsequent studies explored the parameters of the concept learning task, varying numbers of dimensions (Walker & Bourne, 1967), numbers of values per dimension (Gilhooly, 1974, 1975) and rule complexity (Neisser & Weene, 1962), among other aspects. Although this area has somewhat fallen from fashion, it may merit reanalysis from the mental modeling point of view. The effects of rule complexity and stimulus dimensionality, in concept learning, for instance, may have a bearing on the complexity of model structures that can be readily dealt with in working memory.

Daydreaming. Daydreaming may be seen as the running of models in which the "change–rules" applied are only weakly constrained by realistic considerations whereas wish-fulfilling changes are given free rein. In contrast, during directed thinking aimed at problem solving, I assume strong goal control, which would maintain a given model as the basis for exploration and constrain the "change–rules" explored to the plausible and safe. During daydreaming, the model being worked with tends to change quite frequently (approximately once every 5-10 seconds, according to thought sampling studies carried out by Klinger, 1978). These changes appear to be due to evocation of competing models in response to data placed in working memory as a result of current model activity. For example, daydreaming about playing golf, I might think of the ball being carried away by a bird and placed in a nest that I then discover to contain a hoard of jewelry. In turn, this thought could evoke a 'rich-lifestyle' model, which would furnish material for the next daydreaming phase, and so on. It has been suggested (Singer, 1975) that daydreaming involves attending to normally unnoticed flows of activity in a continuously active long term memory. This could be interpreted in the current context as proposing that a continuous model using process is always going on unconsciously in long term memory, whereas only changes in working memory have a conscious effect. This notion does offer a way of handling incubation phenomena (should such truly exist) and posttrauma intrusive thoughts, as resulting from unconscious work; both these topics are now briefly explained.

The notion of incubation in thinking derives from introspective reports by artists and scientists and was popularized by Wallis (1926) in his four stage analysis of problem solving. In this analysis, an initial stage of conscious work (Preparation) is followed by a period in which the problem is not consciously worked on (Incubation). If all goes well, incubation is followed by Inspiration, the occurrence of a useful idea that arises unbidden and which must be developed further in a final stage of Verification. Singer's notion of unconscious model using would fit in the idea of unconscious work during the incubation period.

Posttrauma intrusive thoughts are thoughts about a distressing experience that occur even although the individual tries to suppress them. Such thoughts are commonly reported by people who have experienced real life traumas such as fires or aeroplane crashes. Laboratory analogues of such thoughts have been reported in studies of mild stresses induced by watching films that have disturbing contents, e.g., Becker, Horowitz and Campbell's (1973) study of the effects of a film showing aboriginal circumcision rituals. As with incubation, these intrusive thoughts may reflect unconscious work, in this case, perhaps, aimed at adjusting the individual's models of human behaviour to adapt to the disturbing input.

Creative Processes.   On the current approach, creative processes are seen as involving the construction of new mental models. This may be done from basic level concepts upwards, by recombining elements of existing models, or by modifying existing models. Clearly, analogies may play a role in this process, in that existing models ("base" models) might be modified to provide new models for some target area. Thus, the model of the "pump" provided a new and useful model for the operations of the heart in the 18th century physiology. Many technological advances seem to involve combining elements of existing models. For example, the combining of the internal combustion engine with a carriage produced the early automobile; the combining of propeller engines with hang gliders gives us the microlight flying machine. Also, many mythological creatures represent combinations of elements from existing models, e.g., centaurs and unicorns. These examples point up the decomposability of complex mental models into submodels and sub-submodels, . . . (a process that may be continued quite far by those expert in a given field). This process of decomposing models and recombining the resulting submodels seems to be fundamental to much creative thinking; however, it appears not to have attracted much research attention.

Concluding Comments: Future Directions

This chapter has sought to indicate the plausibility of the mental modeling framework for the study of thinking. A framework has a shaping effect on research and I conclude by noting a few directions suggested by the framework proposed here.

1. The study of "insight" may be revived. In the current approach, "insight" may be interpreted as the point when the model with which the problem solver is working undergoes a revision (or replacement) that permits solution in a very few steps. Perhaps it is when the number of

steps is so small that the sequence can be run through easily in working memory that solvers have the experience of "insight." Suitable tasks for studying insight will probably be ones in which an inappropriate model tends to be adopted initially but which is then (usually) revised or replaced (perhaps with the aid of hints), at least eventually. The nine-dot task or some of the classic Gestalt problems (Duncker, 1945) may be suitable material for such studies.

2. From the educational point of view one might ask: What would be the effects of training students to be more aware of the model-using nature of their thinking? Increased awareness may promote flexibility in model revision and replacement. Informal discussions that I have had with science teachers at the Scottish equivalent of high school level, indicate that students at that level are rarely exposed to the notion of science as a model making and revising enterprise. Rather, they tend to be taught that Newton's theory is "how things really are," or that atoms really are little balls with hooks. This may be easier to understand initially, but surely can only lead to confusion when more sophisticated concepts are introduced at a later stage. Also, of course, this approach fails to train students to think like scientists. An approach in which students are encouraged to create, test and modify models is surely needed.

3. Age effects in thinking might be profitably examined in the light of the "modeling" approach. Increased age may bring an increased number of models in long term memory that could be used for interpreting new situations; but, this may also lead to a reduction in the likelihood of forming new, possibly more appropriate models, because, with a larger stock of models, there is a greater chance of locating one that offers an acceptable degree of fit to the new situation. Also, it might be that given a particular degree of fit, older subjects may be less ready to abandon initially formed models and develop new ones. Perhaps there is an additional factor of decreasing ability to decompose models and recombine resulting submodels with age. Lehman's (1953) classic study of age effects on creative achievement is consistent with such a possibility; but, more detailed investigations of age effects on model using and forming processes would be needed to test this hypothesis.

To conclude, I suggest that the mental modeling approach to thinking is currently useful and should be fruitful in the future.

ACKNOWLEDGMENTS

Thanks are due to Jack Lochhead and John Bishop for their insightful comments on an earlier version of this chapter.

REFERENCES

Anderson, J. R. (1983). *The architecture of cognition.* Cambridge, MA: Harvard University Press.

Becker, A., Horowitz, M., & Campbell, L. (1973). Cognitive response to stress: Effects of changes in demand and sex. *Journal of Abnormal Psychology, 82,* 519–522.

Bruner, J. S., Goodnow, J. J., & Austin, G. A. (1956). *A study of thinking.* New York: Wiley.

Craik, K. J. W. (1943). *The nature of explanation.* Cambridge: Cambridge University Press.

Duncker, K. (1945). On problem solving. *Psychological Monographs, 58,* (270).

Fitzpatrick, R. (1984). Lay concepts of illness. In R. Fitzpatrick, J. Hinton, S. Newman, G. Scambler, & J. Thomson (Eds.), *The experience of illness* (pp. 11–31). London and New York: Tavistock Publications.

Gentner, D., & Gentner, D. R. (1983). Flowing waters or teeming crowds: Mental models of electricity. In D. Gentner & A. L. Stevens (Eds.), *Mental models* (pp. 99–130). Hillsdale, N.J.: Lawrence Erlbaum Associates.

Gilhooly, K. J. (1974). Response times and inspection times in n–value concept learning. *Acta Psychologica, 38,* 99–115.

Gilhooly, K. J. (1975). Latencies and confidence in n–value concept learning. *Acta Psychologica, 39,* 105–118.

Gilhooly, K. J. (1982). *Thinking: directed, undirected and creative.* London: Academic Press.

Johnson–Laird, P. N. (1975). Models of deduction. In R. C. Falmagne (Ed.), *Reasoning: Representation and process* (pp. 7–54). Hillsdale, NJ: Lawrence Erlbaum Associates.

Johnson–Laird, P. N. (1983). *Mental models.* Cambridge, England: Cambridge University Press.

Johnson–Laird, P. N., & Steedman, M. (1978). The psychology of syllogisms. *Cognitive Psychology, 10,* 64–99.

Kelly, G. A. (1955). *A theory of personality,* New York: Norton.

Klinger, E. (1978). Models of normal conscious flow. In K. S. Pope & J. L. Singer (Eds.), *The Stream of consciousness* (pp. 225–258). New York: Wiley.

Lachman, R. (1973). Uncertainty effects on time taken to access the internal lexicon. *Journal of Experimental Psychology, 99,* 199–208.

Lehmann, H. C. (1953). *Age and achievement.* Princeton, NJ: Princeton University Press.

Luchins, A. W. (1942). Mechanization in problem solving: The effect of Einstellung. *Psychological Monographs, 54,* (10), 248.

Mayer, R. E. (1983). *Thinking, problem solving, cognition,* San Francisco: W. H. Freeman.

Neisser, U., & Weene, P. (1962). Hierarchies in concept attainment. *Journal of Experimental Psychology, 64,* 644–645.

Newell, A. (1973). You can't play 20 questions with nature and win. In W. G. Chase (Ed.), *Visual Information Processing* (pp. 283–302). London & New York: Academic Press.

Singer, J. L. (1975). Navigating the stream of consciousness: Research in daydreaming and related inner experience. *American Psychologist, 30,* 727–738.

Teitleman, W. (1976). *INTERLISP reference manual.* Xerox, Palo Alto Research Center.

Thorndyke, P. W. (1984). Applications of schema theory in cognitive research. In J. R. Anderson & S. M. Kosslyn (Eds.), *Tutorials in learning and memory* (pp. 167–191). New York: Freeman.

Tulving, E. (1972). Episodic and semantic memory. In E. Tulving & W. Donalson (Eds.), *Organisation of memory.* London: Academic Press.

Walker, C. M., & Bourne, L. E. Jr. Concept identification as a function of amount of relevant and irrelevant information. *American Journal of Psychology*, 74, 410–417.

Wallas, G. (1926). *The art of thought*. London: Jonathon Cape.

Weisberg, R. W., & Alba, J. W. (1981). An examination of the alleged role of 'fixation' in the solution of several 'insight' problems. *Journal of Experimental Psychology: General*, *110*, 169–192.

3 On the Place of Representations in Cognition

Benny Shanon
The Hebrew University of Jerusalem, Israel

The characterization of human knowledge by mental semantic representations and of human thinking by computational operations performed on these representations is discussed. Several limitations of the representational–computational characterization are noted. It is concluded that representations are the products of cognitive work, and that they cannot serve as the basis for it. Representational patterns are encountered in particular contexts, defined by the relative autonomy of the organism from the environment in which one lives, from one's biological substrate, from the external and internal environment, and from the medium of one's message. Cognition, in turn, is characterized as a dynamic process between the representational and the nonrepresentational, or presentational.

Practically all of contemporary cognitive science—both natural and artificial—is conducted within the representational–computational framework. This perspective may be defined by the following three tenets:

1. Man behaves by virtue of knowledge.
2. Knowledge consists of mental representations, i.e., of well-defined symbols organized in well-formed semantic structures. [Symbols, it may be noted, are entities defined by the coupling of two levels—the medium and the message; the medium lacks intrinsic significance and its sole import is that it enables one to express or communicate the latter.]
3. Cognitive activity consists of the manipulation of these symbols, i.e. of computations.

The purpose of the following discussion is to mark the limitations of this representational–computational view of mind. I argue that representations cannot offer a full account of human cognitive activity. Rather than constituting the basis for such activity, representations are the products of it. Thus, whereas there are aspects of cognition that may very well be characterized as representational and computational, there are others that cannot be so characterized. These other aspects, I argue, are actually both primary and more general than the representational ones. Given that those aspects of mind that may be characterized as representational constitute only a particular facet of cognitive reality, the role and place of representations in cognition have to be examined and redefined.

Underlying the following critique of mental semantic representations is a distinction between the three tenets noted previously. Specifically, it seems to me that the three tenets are of two different kinds. The first consists of an epistemological postulation, whereas the second and the third present the two facets of a particular psychological characterization. The epistemological postulation of representation is based on the following line of reasoning: Human behavior manifestly exhibits systematic well-ordered patterns; man must, therefore, be in possession of information that makes these patterns possible, that is, he has to have it mentally represented in his mind. This postulation is fundamental to any mentalistic investigation of cognition. Its most famous expression is encountered throughout Chomsky's psychological writings (1965, 1972, 1975, 1980): Human verbal behavior, Chomsky notes, is manifestly in accordance with rules; man must, therefore, possess, even if in a latent, tacit fashion, knowledge of these rules. Fundamental as the first tenet is from a philosophical point of view, psychologically it is empty. The tenet endows cognitive entities with an epistemological status, but it specifies no more. Cognitive–psychological substance is specified by the second and third tenets, that define—albeit in a general manner—what representations are and what are the psychological operations that are associated with them.

The arguments put forward here are based on the appraisal that the philosophical and the cognitive–psychological characterizations of representation are not coextensive. Specifically, the knowledge that is exhibited by human behavior and that is referred to by the first tenet may not be fully accounted for by the theoretical constructs referred to by the second and third tenets. Following this appraisal a series of arguments marking the limitations of representations are presented. None of these offers a demonstrative proof, nor are they, taken together, conclusive. Yet, in its entirety the discussion, I hope, draws a certain perspective on the structure of mind and marks new lines for future cognitive research. My stance is not that representations or computations do not play a role in the workings of the cognitive machine, and it is not my intention to call for a return to a behavioristic psychology. My aim, rather, is to point out that those aspects of mind that are characterized as representations constitute a very particular facet of psychological reality. Consequently, the role and place of mental representations in the workings of the mind and in cognitive theory has to be examined and redefined.

The Argument from Context

The argument from context may be considered in reference to various domains of human behavior. The one most studied is the linguistic, and it is the focus of the discussion here.

For the representational account to be complete, it should be possible to offer a formulation coded in an underlying conceptual language that fully captures the meaning of any word. Investigators from different quarters have shown this not to be possible. Winograd (1980) (see also Fodor, Garrett, Walker, & Parkes, 1980; Kripke, 1972; Putnam, 1975) has demonstrated that no matter how specified a definition of a word may be, a context can always be found for which this definition is not sufficient. By way of example Winograd considers the word "bachelor", perhaps the most famous case of a compositional semantic definition. As pointed out by Katz and Fodor (1963), a "bachelor" is an adult, unmarried, human male. Yet, there are contexts in which these conditions are met and the label "bachelor" is not appropriate, and others where the conditions are violated but the label is nonetheless employed. Examples of these two types are the case of a member of a steady homosexual couple, and the case of an independent career woman, respectively. To be sure, one could add up features and alter the definition, but for any set of features a context could be found in which the new definition would still be lacking.

The unconstrained variability of context rendering fixed semantic definitions in principle impossible is markedly demonstrated by contextual expressions. These expressions consist of novel verbal usages to which speakers could not have been exposed beforehand; they have been studied by Clark and his associates (Clark, 1983; Clark & Clark, 1979; Clark & Gerrig, 1983). Remarkably, people have no difficulty in either producing or comprehending such expressions. Thus, consider the following expression as uttered by an employee of the phone service in response to a person who called for directory assistance: (1) You'll have to ask a zero. What is meant by this expression is that the hearer has to approach that employee of the phone service who is reached by dialling 0. It is totally unlikely that the meaning of "zero" employed here is represented in any speaker's mental lexicon. Rather than retrieve it from a set of entries that are specified in semantic representation, one has to generate the meaning in question; this process involves an appraisal of the entire context at hand.

Clark and his associates have also studied new derivations of words such as nouns turned into verbs. Here are two examples: (2) He porched the newspaper. (3) He houdinied his way out of the trunk. The meanings of these expressions are "He threw the newspaper to the porch," and "He managed to escape in the manner classically attributed to Houdini." In both cases the interpretation is clear even though the particular linguistic form has not been previously known to the hearer (or even to the speaker who uttered it).

Further still, the contribution of the context is such that at times it is possible to employ words to refer to items other than the ones actually defined by their extension. In other words, contextual considerations may sometimes override the lexical information associated with words. By way of example, note the following cases: (4) *A* is tapping *B* on the shoulder, addressing him as *C*, although it is clear to all concerned that the addressee is really *B*. (5) *A* presents *B* with a tray of candies and says "Have a cookie." This particular phrasing will not hinder *B* from helping himself to a candy. (6) A common expression is "Do you have a paper and pencil?" Yet, nowadays pencils are seldom used and most often what is offered is a pen instead.

The cases considered so far indicate that the meanings of words cannot be captured in fixed semantic representations and that in order to compute them context has to be taken into consideration. To this one may respond by invoking a distinction between literal and nonliteral readings. The former are the simple cases that allow for straightforward semantic analysis, whereas the latter require the further consideration of context. Specifically, given that the literal reading does not apply, it is subject to operations that alter meaning and derive the nonliteral reading; these operations apply by reference to context. This analysis assumes, then, that the distinctions between literal and nonliteral meanings is well demarcated, that the former is basic and semantically determined whereas the latter is derived and involves the consideration of context. A priori, such an analysis is parsimonious: it characterizes simple cases in a context-free manner and leaves contextual considerations to the complex cases only. Such a two-fold analysis is encountered in the literature with both metaphors and speech acts. Yet, further inspection reveals that the assumptions on which the analysis is based simply do not hold.

Let us start with metaphors. As a preliminary argument against the two-stage analysis of metaphor it will be noted that it is not at all clear that a sentence can be characterized as metaphorical in itself, out of context. The sentence "All men are animals" is literal when uttered by a biology teacher but metaphorical when uttered by a professor of ethics or, alternatively, by an embittered feminist.

Further, the distinction between literal and metaphoric expressions is not well demarcated. This is shown by the following two sentences, originally discussed by Rumelhart (1979): (7) The policeman raised his hand and stopped the car. (8) Superman raised his hand and stopped the car.

First, this pair of sentences indicates that the distinction between literal and nonliteral meaning is not clear-cut. The two sentences are different, but which one is the literal one? If it is the one referring to the more concrete state of affairs, then (8) is the literal one, but if it is the one that pertains to the more standard state of affairs, then (7) is the more literal. Indeed, the particular labeling is not important. Different as these two sentences may be, both require for their interpretation the general evaluation of context. Both require, in other words, the more complex cognitive processes that the standard analysis would associate with the nonliteral, metaphorical reading only. Coupled with the appraisal that the so-called literal reading is itself dependent on contextual evaluation, this observation suggests that the standard analysis of metaphor is of no avail, and that nonliteral readings are not derived from corresponding literal ones. Given that the distinction between literal and nonliteral readings is not categorical and that both involve the evaluation of context, and because the metaphorical interpretation is the more general one, then by considerations of parsimony one might as well say (with Lakoff & Johnson, 1980) that all language is metaphorical.

An analogous state of affairs is encountered with speech acts. Standardly, speech acts are differentiated into ones that are direct and ones that are not. The former, according to Searle (1975), are "the simplest cases of meaning in which the speaker utters a sentence and means exactly and literally what he says," whereas the latter are ones "in which one illocutionary act is performed indirectly by way of performing another." Thus, consider the following expression as it is uttered around a dinner table: (9) Can you pass the salt?

Interpreted directly, (9) is a question, and the answer to it is either "yes" or "no." Usually, as in the context noted, however, it is indirectly interpreted as a request, in which case the appropriate response is rather the passing of the salt. The standard analysis of this phenomenon is analogous to that noted previously in conjunction with metaphor; namely, given that the direct reading is not appropriate, the indirect reading is derived from it by reference to contextual considerations. The analysis is based on Grice's (1975) cooperative principle according to which participants in conversations are maximally cooperative and they say only what is pertinent. But then, uttered at dinner and interpreted as a question, (9) constitutes a violation of the cooperative principle. The speaker knows that the hearer can, in fact, pass the salt, and the hearer knows that he does. When the speaker poses question (9), then, he is not abiding by the assumed conversational contract. Rather than drawing this undesirable conclusion, the hearer concludes that (9) does not mean what it appears to and he interprets it (by means of a transformation called conversational implicature) in an indirect fashion. Although this analysis has been the basis for both linguistic (Gordon & Lakoff, 1971) and psychological research (Clark & Lucy, 1975), it seems to me to be conceptually flawed. In order to conclude that the cooperative principle is violated, the hearer has to arrive at a global interpretation of the context. In our example, he would have to realize that the participants in the conversation are engaged in eating behavior, that there is a salt shaker that is closer to him than to the speaker, his interlocutor, and that he (the speaker) is in need of it. What this amounts to is that the very mechanism that assumedly detects the violation of the cooperative principle is the one that constitutes the comprehension of the so-called indirect reading of the speech act in question. In other words, not only is the so-called indirect reading not dependent on the so-called direct one (cf. Clark, 1979), but in fact the former, pragmatic reading is primary and the latter, semantic one is secondary or derived.

The foregoing argument was conceptual; it is supported, however, by recent empirical findings. Against the two-stage model of metaphor are findings by Glucksberg and his associates (Gildea & Glucksberg, 1983; Glucksberg, Gildea, & Bookin, 1982) that, in context, the processing of metaphor does not require more time than that of literal expressions and that, in fact, metaphoric readings are processed automatically even when there is no need for this to be done. Analogously, Gibbs (1984) found that, when the appropriate context is given, indirect speech acts do not take longer to process than the corresponding direct ones and that indirect processing does not depend on direct processing.

Let me summarize. The argument from context was two-fold. First, the inherent limitations of the semantic characterization of so-called literal meaning was noted. Second, it was pointed out that such a characterization cannot even be taken as a first, simple account, to be amended, when necessary, according to pragmatic, contextual considerations; such considerations cannot be dispensed with in general. Thus, literal meaning cannot be characterized as primary, nor can nonliteral meaning be characterized as derived from it. Taken together, the two facets of the argument indicate that representations in the specified psychological sense cannot serve the epistemological requirement, i.e. the full specification of knowledge.

The Argument from the Medium

Consider the sentence: (10) The cat is on the mat. What is the underlying semantic representation of this sentence? The standard answer would be:

(11) THE CAT IS ON THE MAT, which is an expression in an abstract propositional form that encodes the meaning of (10): It specifies the two arguments, CAT and MAT, and the relationship that holds between them.

But, then, consider (12), the French translation of (10): Le chat est sur le tapis. Standardly, the semantic representation of (12) would, again, be said to be (11). Yet, the very fact that (10) is an English sentence whereas (12) is French makes them different. There can always be contexts in which this difference in language may be relevant, just as is the difference between (10) and (13): The dog is on the mat.

An example for such a context is that of two novels written in English, the texts of which are identical except for one sentence. In one novel the sentence is (10) whereas in the second it is (12). The literary effect, hence the meaning in the particular context, of the two novels is clearly different. An actual literary case in which the language distinction is of utmost significance are the opening pages of Tolstoy's *War and Peace*.

If the language of expression contributes to the meaning of sentences, and if underlying representations should incorporate all relevant distinctions of meaning, then the underlying semantic representation should be modified so as to incorporate the language distinction in it. In the modified representation each proposition will be amended by a tag indicating what the language of expression is. The language of expression is, however, just one aspect of the medium. To it one could add, in verbal communication, tone of voice, intonation, rhythm, and the like. With the increasing number of relevant aspects of the medium the tagging method becomes cumbersome and nonparsimonious, and its usefulness is, therefore, to be questioned. Not only are the relevant aspects of the medium numerous, they are unconstrained. Thus, the tagging strategy presents one with a problem analogous to the one presented by semantic features. Given that the aspects of the medium are not constrained, and because there is no principled way to select between them, the tagging procedure is of no avail because for any tagging that one would specify another aspect of the medium might loom.

A possible retort to this argument is to differentiate between the potential and the actual. Not all potentially relevant aspects of the medium must be specified in the modified formal representation. In each actual instance the number of distinctions to be specified is limited; hence, in effect, the problems noted earlier may be dissolved. The point of the matter is, however, that the relevant distinctions are seldom marked as such, nor are they known beforehand. Thus, distinctions that were not deemed particularly significant at the time of utterance may appear so later. On Sunday, for example, you may be told that the person who said "The cat is on the mat" during the party Friday night was Lady Chatterley's lover, whereas the person who said "Le chien est sur le tapis" was the great-grandson of Marie Antoinette. Although there may be times in which you will fail to make the identification, to successfully achieve it is clearly a common human performance. One's memorial representation, then, has to incorporate the medium distinction.

Given the richness of the medium one might propose another account, namely, a dual, two-part representation: One part will specify the propositional content and the other, the medium. The problem with this account is that the medium and the contentual message are not clearly demarcated. Indeed, what pertains to medium and what pertains to message is context-dependent. An example may be a detective novel in which sentence (10) has been uttered on several occasions. The reader then arrives at the last chapter and notes that the sentence is uttered by Lady Feline. It is only now that the reader realizes that in all the previous instances the sentence was uttered by a man. The medium distinction may thus be taken as a significant clue: what has been a characteristic of the medium may turn out to be an aspect of the message.

Let us take stock. Our discussion of the medium started with the observation that medium distinctions may be significant and meaningful. If semantic representation encodes all meaningful distinctions of sentences, it has to incorporate the medium distinctions as well. Two particular proposals for such encoding were considered and rejected. The first proposal was to encode the medium distinctions in the standard semantic fashion and to amend the propositional representations with tags specifying these various distinctions. Given that the tagging account presents problems analogous to those presented by semantic features in general, the second proposal was considered. By this account a dual representation is employed of which one part is propositional and codes for the message, whereas the second part is nonpropositional and codes for all medium distinctions in full. The problem with this account, however, is that the distinction between message and medium is not well demarcated, and that, further, it may vary with context. Given the basic observations regarding the significance of the medium and the discarding of the two proposals considered, one is left with the conclusion that the medium has to be encoded in full and in a manner that is neither propositional nor separate from the encoding of the message. This lack of separation between medium and message is tantamount to saying that the encoding is not symbolic.

The foregoing discussion has been conceptual. Against it one may invoke experimental results that show that people are not sensitive to medium distinctions. A classical study is by Sachs (1967): It shows that information regarding phonological structure is rapidly lost and with time people maintain only semantic information. Yet, there are reasons to suspect this conclusion. The Sachs study was conducted in a controlled laboratory situation, whereas recent naturalistic studies of actual conversations in which subjects participated indicate that people have remarkably good memory and detection ability for parameters of the medium: identities of speakers, their voice and location, as well as semantically nonsignificant variations in surface structure such as variations between nouns and anaphoric pronouns (Keenan, MacWhinney, & Mayhew, 1977; Kintsch & Bates, 1977; Masson, 1984).

The foregoing discussion was confined to language, but surely the maximal relevance of the medium and the meaninglessness of the distinction between medium and message is much more apparent in the case of nonverbal expressions. In a painting, the brushstrokes are no less "meaningful" than the forms that are being depicted. The case of music is, evidently, even more striking, for in this form of expression medium and message seem to fully converge.

The Argument from Expression, Emotion, and Action

The consideration of medium naturally leads to the consideration of expression. A person exhibits a facial expression: Is this expression the manifestation of an underlying state of mind? Several indications hold against this characterization.

First, the postulation of an underlying state does not seem to add anything by way of explanation. In the case of linguistic expressions the decomposition to an underlying semantic code is a priori motivated by the reduction—in the manner of a chemical analysis—of the many lexical items in the language into a small number of elementary primitives, a reduction that enables one to account for orderly relations and systematic patterns between seemingly different phenomena. Not so in the case of facial expressions. Thus, consider a particular facial composition said to express a state of mind, A, and a modification of it (e.g., one in which the lips are stretched) said to express another state of mind, B. Does the specification of the two underlying states add anything to the variation in the expressions noted? I think not. Facial expressions can be changed ad infinitum and with each change a new underlying state will be postulated. Such a postulation will serve an epistemological function in the weak sense noted at the beginning of our discussion. Specifically, it may satisfy one's ideological view of psychological order, namely, that human expressions are the manifestation of underlying mental reality. Substantively (i.e., from the perspective of the psychologist, not the philosopher), however, nothing has been gained. A is a state associated with one facial expression, whereas B is a state associated with another. Except for the epistemological labeling no understanding has been achieved.

An argument can also be made from the converse direction. As any student of literature knows, the human face cannot be fully captured by words. For the painter this is elementary: A painting that can be rendered into a verbal description is generally not a true piece of art. In art, as in facial expression, the medium is not just a very important dimension: The medium is what there is.

That this is indeed so is more pronounced in the case of bodily expressions. Consider, for example, the cat. It moves in a way that embodies not only specific cat behavior but also a definite cattish character. Surely, if the cat had the body of a dog it would move in a totally different manner, and the character one would associate with it would be different as well. This character, then, is part and parcel of what the cat is. It cannot be separated from whatever is present on the surface, from the feline medium so to speak, and there is no sense searching for it on any covert level.

The consideration of facial and bodily expressions leads directly to the consideration of psychological faculties that are intimately tied to them; I refer to emotions and motor behavior. Conceptually, it is not at all difficult to come up with a representational account of affective states. Such accounts have actually been offered both in cognitive psychology (Bower, 1981) and in artificial intelligence (Lehnert, 1981). According to these accounts, affective states are propositionally characterized as gradedly modified predicative states. Such a characterization leaves out, I think, precisely what is particular to emotions, what distinguishes them from cognitive states, namely, their being associated with the body.

With motor behavior the situation is more acute. Phenomenologically, conscious knowledge not only does not help, but often interferes with motor performance. Indeed, attributing motor behavior to underlying representations will eventually result in the absurd. Extending the case of facial expressions, one may eventually arrive at a lopsided state of affairs in which the seemingly simple world presently in front of us is founded on enormous covert structures of representation. In the extreme, this covert world may reach immense dimensions indeed. The attribution of underlying representations to motor behavior will lead to the attribution of knowledge in cases that blatantly defy our intuitions: to any bodily function that proceeds in an orderly manner, and to nonhuman organisms whose behavior is manifestly in accordance with rules. A telling demonstration to this effect is given in a cartoon in Boden (1983). A kingfisher is shown whose preying behavior is in accordance with Snell's law. Would we say that Snell's law is mentally represented in the bird's mind?

The Argument from the Unbridgeable Gap

The argument from the unbridgeable gap is more philosophical than the other arguments noted here; given that it bears on general metaphysical considerations I only mention several cases associated with the argument, and do not consider it in full. The cases are various but they all present the same basic underlying patterns: Specifically, two domains or realms of reality are noted. The two are, de facto, related, but the representational account fails to capture this relationship.

The first case to be noted has to do with the fundamental characteristic of representations, that is, their referential power. Standardly, in the philosophical literature, representations, and semantics in general, are defined by the relationship between linguistic or conceptual entities and objects or states of affairs in the world. As pointed out by Winograd (1975), however, in the context of cognitive science semantics is taken from a different perspective: Analyses in cognitive psychology and artificial intelligence examine the structure and relationships of entities whose referentiality is taken for granted, but they fail to account for the reference relation itself. The representational model, then, ignores the relationship between the cognitive agent and the world. In this respect it assumes what Fodor (1980) calls "methodological solipsism."

Failures of the representational model to account for the relationship between organisms and the world in which they live are abundant. One case has already been noted previously with regard to emotion, where the model fails to capture the involvement of the body. A celebrated case is that of perception. A fundamental observation of the nonorthodox Gibsonian theory of direct perception (see, e.g., Gibson, 1979) is that perception cannot be divorced from the organism's movement and action in the world. The representational account of perception, however, opposes the world outside to the psychology of the organism within: The former is taken as given and the latter is said to perceive it as if internally recording it in its mind. The entire Gibsonian enterprise marks aspects in which such a characterization is not tenable. It should be added that analogous observations have been made in the context of biological cognitive function (i.e., with regard to immunology and evolution) by the proponents of the theory of autopoiesis (Maturana, 1978; Maturana & Varela, 1980; Varela, 1979). Finally, there is the case of consciousness. A fully specified representational account is equivalent to a computer program. Such an equation marks the greatest limitation of the representational account, namely that it fails in principle to capture precisely those aspects of human psychology that distinguish man from a computer.

The Argument from Development

The argument from development is concerned with two problems. The first is the problem of origin and the second that of sequencing.

The problem of origin has already been noted in the case of the kingfisher earlier. If all knowledge is constituted by semantic representations and all psychological activity by computational operations, then one is led to the conclusion that early stages in development are characterized by well-specified representations. This paradoxical conclusion should hold in both the ontogenic and the phylogenic domains. Indeed, such an extreme nativistic view is the basic tenet of one central treatise in contemporary theoretical cognition, Fodor's *Language of Thought* (1975). This is not the place to examine Fodor's argument in detail; rather, I take his argument as an extreme case demonstrating the unnatural conclusions to which the representational account leads.

Second, let us consider the problem of sequencing. It appears that, quite generally, the representational account entails characterizations that from a developmental perspective are unnatural. Specifically, the representational account imposes orders of complexity opposite to those marked as natural by independent considerations, such as temporal order.

First, the order of ontogenetic development. As noted previously, according to the standard representational account context-independent semantics is basic and context-dependent pragmatic analysis is derived from it. The sequencing of the child's acquisition of language, however, exhibits an opposite order: in its earlier stages children's language is more tied to action in context (Bates, 1976; Bruner, 1975), and it tends to be metaphorical (Gardner & Winner, 1978). Clearly, this order is natural: Linguistic behavior that is contextually tied with action is, intuitively, closer to preverbal behavior; the order, in other words, is the following:

$<*>$ nonverbal behavior—pragmatic verbal behavior—semantic verbal behavior.

According to the representational account, however, the predicted order is:

$<**>$ nonverbal behavior—semantic verbal behavior—pragmatic verbal behavior,

an order that both defies intuitive naturalness and is not in line with the actual order of phenomena.

Another sequence is associated with primary and secondary processes. Following Freud (1900), the former govern primitive, irrational thinking, including the workings of the unconscious, whereas the latter govern rational, conscious thinking. The primary processes precede the secondary ones in development, and unlike secondary processes they are encountered in uncontrolled states, of which dreaming is paradigmatic. It is evident that both phenomenologically and from the theoretical perspective of psychoanalysis the primary processes are simpler than the secondary ones. But note: The former are metaphorical, whereas the latter are not. A natural order would therefore be one that characterizes the primary processes as precedent to the secondary ones; as noted in the first section of this discussion, such a sequence is opposite to the one entailed by the standard representational account.

Analogous observations may be made with respect to other sequences, of which I mention two encountered on two extremes of the time scale. On the small-scale order of processing are the progressions marked in microgenetic studies (see Flavell & Draguns, 1957; Werner, 1948); these suggest that the metaphorical, multifaceted and fuzzy aspects of meaning are appreciated before those that are literal, fixed and well defined. On the large scale there is cultural development. It is no accident, I think, that poetry developed before prose: it is a direct correlate of the primacy of metaphor—again, a phenomenological order that runs counter to the order entailed by the semantic representational account.

CONCLUSION

Taken together, the foregoing arguments show that the representational–computational perspective is fundamentally limited. The arguments from context and medium indicate that accounts based on this perspective may never be complete; the arguments from expression, action and emotion indicate that very important facets of human psychology cannot be accounted for by the representational–computational approach; the arguments from development as well as the comments on metaphor and speech acts indicate that the representational facets of mind are not primary or basic but rather secondary or derived. Thus, it appears that representations define particular facets of human psychology: ones that are associated with later stages of development—ontogenic, phylogenic, cultural, and procedural. These facets, it appears, evolve from ones that are not representational. Specifically, a progression may be noted from the unidimensional level, which does not distinguish between medium and message, to the symbolic level, whose essence is the bidimensional distinction between the signifier and the signified—from that which is ill defined, undifferentiated, and multifaceted to that which is well defined, differentiated, and articulated; from activities that are part and parcel of one's being in the world to ones that attest to the increasing autonomy of the individual. Following Langer (1942), I refer to the earlier, nonrepresentational patterns as presentational.

The foregoing comments suggest the viewing of cognition as a dynamic movement between two poles, the presentational and the representational. One turns to the representational pole when one wants to achieve autonomy, and this in several respects:

1. Autonomy from the *biological substrate* of which one is built. The representational facets of mind are not directly reducible to brain activity (see Dennett, 1978), nor are they intertwined in bodily function as perception, action or emotion might be.

2. Autonomy from the external *environment*. Representations allow the organism not to fully depend on the environment in which one is immersed. As pointed out in the various critiques of behaviorism (Chomsky, 1957; Fodor, 1971; Pylyshyn, 1980), people's behavior cannot be characterized as responses to stimuli in the environment. People respond to stimuli in terms of their meaning, and the coupling between stimuli and responses is not forced upon them but is determined by the interpretation of the situation at hand. Furthermore, people behave even when stimuli are not present and can refrain from action even when they are. Indeed, people are also able to mentally dissociate themselves from the present, to return to the past, to entertain alternative possibilities and to plan for the future.

3. Autonomy from other *information*. Representations allow one to shelter information one entertains and to free it from the influence of other activity in one's mind. On the one hand, one can fix particular information and dissociate it from other information; on the other hand, one can abstract information, thus disregarding the medium in which it is couched. In enabling these dissociations, representations may be regarded as instruments for the establishment of local central modularities in the mind (see Fodor, 1983, and the discussion in Shanon, 1984). It is noted that one ramification of this dissociation is the creation of internal objects in one's mind, a creation that offers the basis for reflection upon one's own cognitions.

The foregoing discussion emphasized the overall long-term and functional progression from the presentational to the representational, but in the actual course of psychological activity the converse course may also be taken. When autonomy is needed one draws towards the representational pole; this is advantageous when one would like to ignore one's body, to isolate oneself from the environment in which one lives, to act (or not to act) arbitrarily; to shelter information, to create a mental world of one's own, to focus on the solution of problems or the execution of particular tasks, and to reflect. There are, however, other contexts: ones in which one would like to get in touch with one's biological existence, to organically immerse oneself within the world, to digest what one knows and to integrate various pieces of information in a meaningful fashion, to bring together the different aspects on one's self so as to actualize the individual personality one is. In all these cases one draws to the presentational pole.

Surely, both movements are important. Without representations, neither precise human communication nor conscious reflection could have been achieved. Yet, states of existence that are often considered more integrated, more mature, perhaps even more wise, as well as expressions of art, seem to be associated with presentations. Clearly, it is the ability to operate in accordance with either pole as well as the ability to move from one to the other—not the perfection of one polar performance or the other—that is the crucial aspect of mental activity, what makes us, in point of fact, human. That this is the case is marked by the consideration of the extreme cases associated with each of the two poles. On the representational pole the case in point is the computer. The computer is the representational–computational machine par excellence: hence its impressive achievements and its enormous potentialities, hence also its ever-present limitations. On the presentational pole the case in point is the harmonious existence of organisms in the world. A fish in the water, a wild deer on the prairie, are in their own ways the actual manifestations of perfect being. (This, note, is not a metaphysical or even mystical claim; it is simply the basic tenet of the theory of evolution.) Some people have advocated the returning of man to this naturalistic condition as the cure for all societal evils; I do not doubt their intentions, but I am certain that if this path had been taken, no culture would have been created. Indeed, the moral of this entire discussion is that cognition itself would not have been possible.

In closing, let me consider the general view of mind that emerges from the foregoing discussion. This view regards action in the world, not symbolic reference, as the basis for cognition. Man acts in the world and in so doing he produces actions, utterances, and expressions. These are not the overt expressions of covert underlying representational structures, and their meaning is not a function of such representations. Rather, these productions are the crystalization of dynamic activity that does not have the characteristics of semantic representation—well-definedness, symbolism, and abstractness. (The recent work in neoconnectionism may be viewed as a particular application of such a model; see Hinton & Anderson, 1981.) In turn, these products serve as the substrate for further cognitive work, that may be taken from either the representational or the presentational perspective.

Cognitive scientists have so far focused their attention on the representational perspective. Rather than confining his attention to only one pole, however, the student of mind should study the two-way dynamics between the representational and the presentational, the processes that enable movement between the two poles as well as the maintenance operations that keep them apart, and the differential functional contexts associated with them. All this will surely require the development of an alternative conceptual framework in cognition, but this is a topic that extends beyond the scope of the present discussion.

REFERENCES

Bates, E. (1976). *Language and context*. New York: Academic Press.
Boden, M. (1983). Artificial intelligence and animal psychology. *New Ideas in Psychology, 1*, 11–33.
Bower, G. H. (1981). Mood and memory. *American Psychologist, 36*, 129–148.
Bruner, J. S. (1975). The ontogenesis of speech acts. *Journal of Child Language, 2*, 1–19.
Chomsky, N. (1957). Review of B. F. Skinner's "Verbal Behavior." *Language, 35*, 26–58.
Chomsky, N. (1965). *Aspects of the theory of syntax*. Cambridge, MA: MIT Press.
Chomsky, N. (1972). *Language and mind*. New York: Harcourt, Brace, Jovanovich.
Chomsky, N. (1975). *Reflections on language*. New York: Pantheon.
Chomsky, N. (1980). *Rules and representations*. New York: Columbia University Press.
Clark, E. V., & Clark, H. H. (1979). When nouns surface as verbs. *Language, 85*, 797–811.
Clark, H. H. (1979). Responding to indirect speech acts. *Cognitive Psychology, 4*, 430–477.
Clark, H. H. (1983). Making sense of nonce sense. In G. B. Flores d'Arcais, & R. J. Jarvella (Eds.), *The process of language understanding*. Chicester: Wiley.
Clark, H. H., & Gerrig, R. J. (1983). Understanding old words with new meanings. *Journal of Verbal Learning and Verbal Behavior, 22*, 591–608.
Clark, H. H., & Lucy, P. (1975). Understanding what is meant from what is said. *Journal of Verbal Learning and Verbal Behavior, 14*, 56–72.
Dennett, D. C. (1978). *Brainstorms*. Sussex: Harvester.
Flavell, J., & Draguns, J. (1957). A microgenetic approach to perception and thought. *Psychological Bulletin, 54*, 197–217.
Fodor, J. A. (1971). Could meaning be an rm? In R. C. Oldfield, & J. C. Marshall (Eds.), *Language*. Penguin.
Fodor, J. A. (1975). *The language of thought*. New York: Thomas J. Crowell.
Fodor, J. A. (1980). Methodological solipsism considered as a research strategy in cognitive psychology. *The Behavioral and Brain Sciences, 3*, 63–71.
Fodor, J. A. (1983). *The modularity of mind*. Cambridge, MA: MIT Press.
Fodor, J. A., Garrett, M. F., Walker, E. C. T., & Parkes, C. H. (1980). Against definitions. *Cognition, 8*, 263–368.
Freud, S. (1900/1954). *The interpretation of dreams* (Trans. J. Strachey). London: Allen & Unwin.
Gardner, H., & Winner, E. (1978). The development of metaphorical competence: Implications for humanistic disciplines. In S. Sachs (Ed.), *On metaphor*. Chicago: University of Chicago Press.
Gibbs, R. W. (1984). Literal meaning and psychological theory. *Cognitive Science, 8*, 275–304.
Gibson, J. J. (1979). *The ecological approach to visual perception*. Boston: Houghton–Mifflin.
Gildea, P., & Glucksberg, S. (1983). On understanding metaphor: The role of context. *Journal of Verbal Learning and Verbal Behavior, 22*, 577–590.
Glucksberg, S., Gildea, P., & Bookin, H. B. (1982). On understanding nonliteral speech:

Can people ignore metaphors? *Journal of Verbal Learning and Verbal Behavior, 21*, 85–98.

Gordon, D., & Lakoff, C. (1971). Conversational postulates. *Papers from the 7th regional meeting of the Chicago Linguistic Society*, 63–84.

Grice, H. P. (1975). Logic and conversation. In P. Cole & J. L. Morgan (Eds.), *Syntax and semantics 3: Speech acts*. New York: Academic Press.

Hinton, G. E., & Anderson, J. A. (Eds.). (1981). *Parallel models of associative memory*. Hillsdale, NJ: Lawrence Erlbaum Associates.

Katz, J. J., & Fodor, J. A. (1963). The structure of a semantic theory, *Language, 39*, 170–210.

Keenan, J. M., MacWhinney, B., & Mayhew, D. (1977). Pragmatics in memory: A study of natural conversation. *Journal of Verbal Learning and Verbal Behavior, 16*, 549–560.

Kintsch, W., & Bates, E. (1977). Recognition memory for statements from a classroom lecture. *Journal of Experimental Psychology: Human Learning and Memory, 3*, 150–159.

Kripke, S. A. (1972). Naming and necessity. In D. Davidson, & G. Harman (Eds.), *Semantics of natural language*. Dordrecht: Reidel.

Langer, S. (1942). *Philsophy in a new key*. Cambridge, MA: Harvard University Press.

Lakoff, G., & Johnson, M. (1980). The metaphorical structure of the human conceptual system. *Cognitive Science, 4*, 195–208.

Lehnert, W. G. (1981). Affect and memory representation. *Proceedings of the third annual conference of the Cognitive Science Society*, 77–83.

Masson, M. E. J. (1984). Memory for the surface structure of sentences: Remembering with and without awareness. *Journal of Verbal Learning and Verbal Behavior, 23*, 579–592.

Maturana, H. R. (1978). Biology of language: The epistemology of reality. In G. A. Miller & E. Lenneberg (Eds.), *Psychology and biology of learning and thought*. New York: Academic Press.

Maturana, H. R., & Varela, F. J. (1980). *Autopoiesis and cognition*. Dordrecht: Reidel.

Putnam, H. (1975). *Mind, language, and reality. Philosophical papers, Vol. 2*. Cambridge: Cambridge University Press.

Pylyshyn, Z. W. (1980). Computation and cognition: Issues in the foundation of cognitive science. *The Behavioral and Brain Sciences, 3*, 111–169.

Rumelhart, D. R. (1979). Some problems with the notion of literal meanings. In A. Ortony (Ed.), *Metaphor and thought*. Cambridge: Cambridge University Press.

Sachs, J. D. S. (1967). Recognition memory for syntactic and semantic aspects of connected discourse. *Perception and Psychophysics, 2*, 437–442.

Searle, J. R. (1975). Indirect speech acts. In P. Cole, & J. L. Morgan (Eds.), *Syntax and semantics 3: Speech acts*. New York: Academic Press.

Shanon, B. (1984). *Remarks on the modularity of mind*. Working paper, The Rothman Center for Cognitive Science, The Hebrew University of Jerusalem.

Varela, F. J. (1979). *The principles of biological autonomy*. New York: North Holland.

Werner, H. (1948). *Comparative psychology of mental development*. Chicago: Follet.

Winograd, T. (1975). Frame representations and the declarative–procedural controversy. In D. G. Bobrow & A. Collins (Eds.), *Representation and understanding: Studies in cognitive science*. New York: Academic Press.

Winograd, T. (1980). What does it mean to understand language? *Cognitive Science, 4*, 209–241.

4 Symposium: Can Intelligence Be Improved?

Richard Herrnstein, Arthur Jensen, Jonathon Baron, and
Robert Sternberg

INTRODUCTION, AND THE VENUZUELAN
EXPERIMENT—RICHARD HERRNSTEIN

How we answer our question, "Can intelligence be improved," obviously
depends on how we define intelligence, and it would be possible at the
outset to spend much time quarrelling about definitions. Because I think
that this would be just about the least productive thing we could do, let us
start with a very broad understanding of intelligence as that relatively
enduring trait (or set of traits) that differentiates people's capacities for
intellectual behavior. And, to avoid any further definitional problem, let
us just adopt our ordinary common sense understanding of what "intellectual behavior" means. This will then leave plenty of room for the
participants in this symposium to argue for their preferred notions of what
intelligence is.

In this section, I describe the Venezuelan project I was associated with
from 1979 until 1983. The study used approximately 900 seventh-graders
in a provincial capital in Venuzuela called Barquisimeto, some 300 kms
from Caracas. The children were divided into experimental and control
groups, approximately matched for initial ablity as measured by standardized tests adapted for use in Venuzuela. The experimental course was
taught mostly by local teachers, recruited and given some training in
Barquisimeto during the year preceding the study. The course was taught
in the 1982-1983 academic year to classes of between 30 and 40 students in
three 45-minute sessions per week, integrated into the normal school
timetable. To give some idea of the magnitude of the course, the teachers'

51

manual (available in both Spanish and English versions) consisted of twenty 100-page volumes, with every student receiving a workbook almost as long as the teachers' manual. At the start of the year, the students were given a battery of tests involving over eight hours of actual testing time. An equally lengthy set of tests was given at the end of the year, and less extensive testing took place at intervals during its course. We estimated that well over two million test-item responses were collected, graded and analyzed from this sample of children. The course itself was organized into six general topics: foundations of reasoning; understanding language; verbal reasoning; problem solving; decision making and inventive thinking. In all, a total of almost one hundred 45-minute lessons were produced, with a core of 60 lessons that we aimed to have taught as a first priority, in the hope of using as many of the remaining forty as possible as well. But, in the event, only just over half (56) of the lessons produced were used.

The results were, briefly, as follows. Three standardized tests were administered; the Otis–Lennon Scholastic Abilities test, suitably adapted with Venuzuelan content; a version of Cattell's culture-fair test; and a test adapted from existing United States tests called General Abilities Tests. Because these were 12-14 year old children, who would normally show substantial mental growth during an academic year, the effectiveness of the experimental course had to be measured against a moving baseline. Thus, the proper comparison here is between the extent of the gains made by the two groups. The improvement shown by the experimental group was indeed greater than that shown by the control—highly significantly so on the Otis–Lennon and the General Abilities Tests, and less dramatically (but still significantly) so on the Cattell test. We also administered some tests specifically tailored to the course itself, to assess the degree to which the students had learned to do the kinds of problems in foundations of reasoning, understanding language, etc. that were the subject matter of the course (though never using the precise course material). On these target abilities tests, an even larger enhancement of performance was found among the students in the experimental group. (The effect sizes for the standardized abilities tests were of the order of .3 or .4 of one standard deviation of gains; for the target abilities tests, the effect sizes were approximately twice as large.) So, on our evaluation criteria, the program may be judged to have produced a moderate to large improvement.

What we do not know, because we have had no chance to measure it, is the extent to which the effects of the course persist, and whether the improved abilities generalize to other kinds of performances. Anecdotal evidence from students and teachers suggests that the experimental group students did do better in their regular courses, but anecdotal evidence like this must be substantiated before it can be taken very seriously.

Let me conclude by saying that a program of this sort has an effect, not just on students and teachers, but also on the experimenters. On the whole, we were more optimistic about the potentialities for enhancing intelligence after the experiment than before it. The change in behavior that resulted from this really rather modest intervention into the lives of youngsters (just 45 minutes, three times a week, for a year) was profound and dramatic, which should give some encouragement to those searching for techniques to enrich conventional education. Of course, conducting experiments such as this is extremely costly, but the investment may be fully justified, not just in terms of advancing our understanding of the development and improvement of intelligence, but also because they may produce new instruments for educational intervention.

TEACHING INTELLIGENCE: A TRIARCHIC MODEL

Robert J. Sternberg
Yale University

A TRIARCHIC MODEL FOR TEACHING INTELLIGENCE

Can intelligence be taught? Without a doubt. Parents do it; teachers do it; friends do it; one does it oneself. Certainly, no one believes that intelligence develops solely as a function of heredity or maturation. Experience must play a role, and experience is mediated by people (Feuerstein, 1980). But if intelligence is purposefully to be taught, just how is this teaching to be accomplished? There are now available a wide variety of approaches, but most of these approaches are of one of three kinds. I argue that two of these three kinds of approaches to teaching intelligence are misguided.

ALTERNATIVE APPROACHES TO
TEACHING INTELLIGENCE

One kind of approach seems to derive from nowhere at all except, perhaps, the desire of the originators of these approaches to make money. One can find at airport counters and in corner book stores any number of books on improving one's intelligence, or becoming a supergenius in 10 easy lessons. Most of these approaches are wrong headed, and some of them are downright dangerous.

When I refer to some of the approaches as "dangerous," I do not do so as a manner of speech, or because I believe that hyperbole makes communication of points more effective. One of these books, that I found at an airport counter, had as its first technique the increment of the level of carbon dioxide in one's body. One is exhorted to exhale into a brown paper bag, and then to breathe in deeply the gaseous contents of the bag. The idea is that increasing the level of carbon dioxide in the blood stream will somehow raise one's level of intellectual functioning. I know of no evidence to suggest that increased carbon dioxide will increase one's intelligence. But it can undermine one's health, and even render one unconscious.

Other books do not necessarily lead one to undermine one's health, but they may lead one to waste a great deal of one's time. The books often contain various kinds of games or gamelike puzzles that may be challenging in their own right but that have no clear relation to increasing one's intelligence. Such games may be fun to do, and have value if one enjoys playing such games, but one should not expect from them that they will lead to an increase in one's intelligence. These books are most worthwhile if they are simply viewed as providing enjoyment for its own sake, if, indeed, they do provide such enjoyment. If not, it is unclear that there is any benefit at all to using them.

Teaching to the Tests

A second kind of approach involves teaching to IQ tests, in other words, providing exercises that are intended directly to improve scores on such tests. Such an approach would be useful if it were indeed the case that intelligence tests truly measured intelligence, or at least, the most significant aspects of it. But I would argue that teaching to intelligence tests can in some ways be counterproductive, even to the point of generating elements of stupidity rather than of intelligence (Sternberg, in press). Consider some principles that would follow from teaching intelligence to the tests:

1. Work as quickly as you can.
2. Read everything carefully.
3. Memorize a lot of new vocabulary.
4. Learn the best strategy for solving each problem.
5. Get lots of practice on various tests and test-like items.
6. Use all of the information in the problem.
7. When you don't find your answer in the answer options, pick the option with the best answer and move on.
8. Try to "psych-out" the test constructor.
9. Intelligence is the same thing for everyone.
10. Intelligence is what IQ tests measure.

In Sternberg (in press), I show that each of these principles is, in fact, incorrect, if one's goal is to teach intelligence rather than IQ. Teaching intelligence to the tests is at best an incomplete way of improving people's intelligence, and at worst, a seriously misguided way of improving intelligence. Some other kind of approach is needed that better reflects what intelligence really is.

Theory-Based Approaches

Theory-based approaches to teaching intelligence start with a theory of intelligence, and then derive the training program from that theory. A well-known example of such a program is Feuerstein's (1980) Instrumental Enrichment Program, which is based upon Feuerstein's theory of deficits in intellectual functioning. Programs such as Feuerstein's tend to be somewhat broader in scope than do IQ-test-based programs, and also to work better in practice than do the test-based programs. They encompass a broader conception of the nature of intelligence, and also a more refined conception of how intelligence can and should be taught. The fact that a training program is based upon a psychological theory does not, of course, guarantee either that the training program is any good or that the theory on which it is based has any validity. Hence, it is necessary to be every bit as scrupulous in evaluating these programs as it is to be in evaluating any other kind of program. But I view theoretical basis as a necessary, although not sufficient, condition for the success of a training program, and thus programs that are based upon psychological theories have taken at least one step in the right direction (Sternberg, 1983).

Teaching Intelligence

I would like to give two examples of intelligence training from our own research based on the *triarchic* theory of intelligence. The three processes in the triarchic theory are: selective encoding, selective combination, and selective comparison. The selective encoding process involves distinguishing relevant from irrelevant information. For example, if one is studying for a test or trying to learn something from a book or a lecture, one cannot memorize or learn everything; one has to selectively decide what information is relevant, and focus on encoding that in preference to the rest. The second process is selective combination. Once the selective encoding is complete, the information must be integrated in an optimal way so that it fits together. For example, people who study for an exam on difficult and complex material often find that all of a sudden they see the way the subject fits together into a coherent whole. The third process is selective comparison. This process concerns the relationship between the new knowledge and what you already know.

First, consider an application of the triarchic theory to verbal comprehension training. We picked that topic because psychologists have found vocabulary to be one of the best single indicators, if not the very best indicator, of a person's overall level of intelligence. Why is vocabulary such a good measure of intelligence? I suggest that it is because vocabulary tests measure indirectly people's ability to learn meanings of words as they encounter the words in context, and this ability to acquire information from context is essential to function intelligently in a wide variety of domains. Sternberg and Powell (1983) have proposed a theory of how people learn words from context, and the unit of *Intelligence Applied* (Sternberg, 1986) dealing with knowledge acquisition focuses upon the skills involved in learning words from context.

According to the theory, three general processes are involved: knowledge-acquisition components, use of these components on context cues, and effective handling of mediating variables that render application of the components to the cues more or less difficult.

The training starts with an exposition regarding three processes of knowledge acquisition: (1) selective encoding, by which information relevant to deciphering the meaning of the word is separated from information irrelevant to that purpose; (2) selective combination, by which relevant information is combined; and (3) selective comparison, by which old information is brought to bear upon the learning of the new word.

Context cues are kinds of information to which the knowledge-acquisition components can be applied. There are eight types of context cues: (1) setting cues, (2) value—affect cues, (3) static property cues, (4) active property cues, (5) causal–functional cues, (6) class membership cues, (7) antonymic cues, and (8) equivalence cues. Students receive exercises on the application of the three processes to each of these kinds of cues.

Mediators are the variables that make application of the knowledge-acquisition processes to the contextual cues either easier or more difficult. Seven mediators that have been identified as particularly important in learning words from context are (1) the number of occurrences of the unknown word, (2) the variability of the contexts in which multiple occurrences of the unknown word appear, (3) the importance of the unknown word to understanding the context in which it is embedded, (4) the helpfulness of the surrounding context to understanding the meaning of the word, (5) the density of unknown words in the passages you are reading, (6) the concreteness of the unknown word and of the surrounding context, and (7) the usefulness of previously known information in understanding the passage or in understanding the meaning of the unknown word.

Each of the concepts in this theory is explained and illustrated through the use of passages that require learning of words from context. Consider an example of one of the 17 passages used to illustrate these concepts:

Although the others were having a marvelous time at the party, the couple on the blind date was not enjoying the merry-making in the least. A *pococurante*, he was dismayed by her earnestness. Meanwhile, she, who delighted in men with full heads of hair, eyed his substantial *phalacrosis* with disdain. When he failed to suppress an *eructation*, her disdain turned to disgust. He, in turn, was equally appalled by her noticeable *podobromhidrosis*. Although they both loved to dance, the disco beat of the music did not lessen either their ennui or their mutual discomfort. Both silently vowed that they would never again accept a blind date.

The meanings of the unknown words are:

pococurante—a nonchalant or indifferent person;

phalacrosis—baldness; a bald spot;

eructation—a belch;

podobromhidrosis—smelly feet.

Through the use of the aspects of the theory, it becomes possible to improve one's ability to learn meanings of words from context, and thereby to improve one's vocabulary.

We gave such a training program to a group of adults, with only 45 minutes for the training condition. We used pre- and posttests and appropriate controls. The critical result was this: the people in the control group who got irrelevant training didn't improve; the people who just got practice didn't improve either. The ones who got the theory-based practice improved fairly dramatically, up 30% of the way from the scores they had to the maximum on the test, basically from about 28 to 36 on a 50-point scale.

Second, consider an experiment involving insight training (Davidson and Sternberg, 1984). The treatment lasted 5 weeks and stressed selective encoding, selective combination, and selective comparison, but this time in a very different context. For example, a typical problem stated that you have black socks and brown socks in a drawer mixed in a ratio of 4 to 5. It asked how many socks you have to take out of the drawer to be assured of having a pair of the same color. In that problem, the ratio of 4 to 5 is irrelevant; people who tend to get the problem wrong focus on the ratio information and try to use it. Other selective combination problems include a dinner party where there are 5 people sitting in a row at a table. Scott is seated at one end of the row and Ziggy is seated next to Matt; Joshua is not sitting next to Matt or Scott. Only one person is sitting next to Walter. Who is it? The training over the 5 weeks included 4 types of exercises. The first type was training in the 3 processes. We showed specific examples in a variety of problem contexts. The second type involved group exercises where students would work together in groups solving problems and talking about how they solved them. The third kind of training had students perform the exercises independently and then later talk about what they had done. The last type of training involved games, that were used largely for motivation. We got significant gains, again about 30%, for the experimental relative to the control group. Furthermore, there was transfer. We had in the pretest and the posttest some mystery stories. These were problems where the task was to figure out how Detective Fordney knew who committed a crime. These problems were not covered in the treatment, yet students showed significant gains relative to the control group. This result proved durable a year later in a posttest.

I have given two examples of how theory-based training can improve intellectual skills. Let me draw some conclusions from these two experiments. The first is that intelligence can be trained; that is the main conclusion that I want to draw. However, in order to get substantial effects there are certain things you ought to do. The first is that you should start with a theory.

The second thing is that the theory should specify mental processes to train—both basic processes and executive or metaprocesses.

The third thing is that there should be some kind of link to the students' world. It's very hard to get transfer of training even in problems that look similar. Unless you have some kind of links built into what the person is actually going to do, you may get significant gains in your test problems but nothing at all when the person really has to use what has been taught.

Fourth, make sure that the training is appropriate for the population to whom it is given.

Fifth is motivation. If the people don't care, it doesn't matter how good the cognitive training is, they're not going to learn.

Finally, you should be able to evaluate progress on the specific components you expect to train, so that afterwards you will know what worked and what didn't work. One of the problems with many evaluations is that they show gains on some things and lesser gains or no gains on others, but one can't go back and say what exactly in the program was successful and what needs change. If you have a theory-based program and a theory-based test, then you may be able to say what was good and what wasn't.

Other Features of the Intelligence Applied Program

I have given two examples from the *Intelligence Applied* program, but it has other features worth noting. For example, the first chapter of the student text reviews previous theories of intelligence and programs for training intelligence, thereby giving the students an orientation to the field. The second chapter presents the triarchic theory, that has evolved from these past theories of intelligence and intellectual-skills training, and is the theory on which the program is based. The theory is presented in a nontechnical way so that students can understand why they are doing what they are doing in the program. The last chapter of the student text is entitled, "Why intelligent people fail (too often)," and discusses emotional and motivational blocks to the utilization of one's intelligence, such as lack of motivation, lack of impulse control, capitalization on the wrong abilities, inability to translate thought into action, and lack of product orientation. The idea is to make students aware of how often very intelligent people fail to capitalize upon their intelligence because of emotional and motivational obstacles to putting intelligence into practice.

Although the text can be used on its own, it is better used in conjunction with the teacher's manual, which has a number of features to enhance instruction. For example, it is strongly recommended that the reading and problem solving of each chapter be accompanied by a subset of the class-discussion questions, paper topics, and supplementary projects that are suggested for each chapter in the teacher's manual. In this way, students get a richer exposure to the material than they would get solely through the use of the student text.

The *Intelligence Applied* program is based on a validated theory of human intelligence specifying components of intelligence, (metacomponents, performance components, knowledge-acquisition components), the experiential base upon which these components operate (coping with novelty and automatization), and the functions to which these processes apply, through experience, in the everyday world (adaptation, selection, and shaping in practical intelligence). The program does not represent merely another attempt to improve IQ scores. Rather, it represents what I believe will be the wave of the future in the enterprise of intellectual-skills training: helping students increase their intelligence in a broadly defined, enriched, and enjoyable way.

ACKNOWLEDGMENTS

Preparation of this chapter was supported by Contract N00014-85-K-0589 from the Office of Naval Research and Contract MDA903-85-K-0305 from the Army Research Institute.

REFERENCES

Feuerstein, R. (1980). *Instrumental enrichment: An intervention program for cognitive modifiability*. Baltimore: University Park Press.

Davidson, J. E., & Sternberg, R. J. (1984). The role of insight in intellectual giftedness. *Gifted Child Quarterly, 28,* 58–64.

Sternberg, R. J. (1983). Criteria for intellectual skills training. *Educational Researcher, 12,* 6–12, 26.

Sternberg, R. J. (1986). *Intelligence applied: Understanding and increasing your intellectual skills.* San Diego: Harcourt, Brace, Jovanovich.

Sternberg, R. J. (in press). Teaching intelligence: The application of cognitive psychology to the improvement of intellectual skills. In J. B. Baron, & R. J. Sternberg (Eds.), *Teaching thinking skills: Theory and practice.* New York: Freeman.

Sternberg, R. J., & Davidson, J. E. (1982). The mind of the puzzler. *Psychology Today, 16,* June, 37–44.

Sternberg, R. J., & Powell, J. S. (1983). Comprehending verbal comprehension. *American Psychologist, 38,* 878–893.

AN HYPOTHESIS ABOUT THE TRAINING OF INTELLIGENCE

Jonathan Baron
University of Pennsylvania

I wish to offer a "best guess" hypothesis, consistent with the evidence I know of, which, if it is correct, implies that those of us who want to teach people to be more intelligent will have to be aware of some limitations on what we can do. I conceive of teaching intelligence as training of certain abilities in substantial generality, that is, so that they are broadly useful.[1]

In brief, some abilities can be trained this way and others cannot. Skills, narrowly conceived, cannot be trained in general. Methods or strategies can be trained in general, but there are few at best that are powerful enough to count as parts of intelligence. The abilities that can be trained most usefully may be called styles. I have in mind things like thoroughness in searching for evidence, willingness to consider alternative possibilities, and fairness in the way one goes about searching for evidence and using it. To some extent, these styles may be taught as habits, the way one teaches good manners. But I think a more productive way to teach them is by instilling appropriate goals and beliefs. Just as we

---

[1]Without this stipulation, we would not be training intelligence, but rather some specific piece of knowledge or skill. I would further stipulate that there ought to be essentially no limit on the domains where a component might prove useful. This stipulation follows from my view (Baron, 1985a) that intelligence should be defined so as to help people achieve their rational goals *whatever these goals might be.*

may teach good manners by instilling a concern for others, we may teach good thinking by instilling a concern for the truth and a belief that it is possible to get to the bottom of things through our own efforts. In essence, the teaching of intelligence, like the teaching of moral behavior, involves the enforcement of certain *standards of conduct*.

The question of whether *any* aspects of intelligence can be taught is not one we can answer definitively now. It is like the question, "Can diet prevent heart disease?" What we want is a best guess for practical purposes, not a conclusive scientific demonstration—although that would always be nice. Thus, it is inappropriate to argue that the burden of proof is on one side or the other. The practical issue before us involves the probable costs and benefits of various proposals, not scientific certainty.

There are a few facts that make me think that the teaching of intelligence *is* possible. First, there is the cross-cultural evidence about the effects of schooling. In many countries, it is unfortunately still possible to do experiments on children who seem to differ only in that some of them go to school and others do not. In every study I know in which this has been done, (e.g., Stevenson et al., 1978) schooling has been found to have substantial beneficial effects on the performance of problem-solving and memory tasks. The tasks in question are not directly taught in school, so it appears that the children have learned something general.[2]

Another type of study looks at the overall effect of extended training programs, particularly those for preschool children. The best guess about why these programs often succeeded in improving school achievement is that they instilled the goals and beliefs associated with good school work. The preschool programs in question had only short lasting effects, at best, on IQ scores (Lazar et al., 1982; Scarr & Carter-Saltzman, 1982; Zigler & Seitz, 1982). It should be noted, however, that these programs were not generally designed to increase intelligence as such, and certainly made no attempt to teach good thinking. Rather, they seem to resemble the programs designed to improve achievement motivation in older children, that have also been successful (e.g., Kolb, 1965). I know of only one of these studies, that of Blank (1973), that has directly set about to teach good thinking in the sense I think would work, and to my knowledge it has not been followed up. What the studies we have do indicate, however, is that character can be changed through explicit interventions.

Aside from these special interventions, there is a great deal of evidence (e.g., Jencks et al., 1972; Scarr & Carter-Saltzman, 1982) that children's family background has a large influence on their IQ scores, beyond the

Baloney !

---

[2]It might be argued that no further improvement in general abilities is possible once a child attends school. There is no reason to think this is true, and some reason—specifically, the other evidence I shall cite—to think it is false.

More below (handwritten)

influence of heredity. Family background has an even larger influence on school achievement and on worldly success. I have argued (Baron, 1985a) that IQ tests underrepresent the personality components of intelligence. Hence, the effect of family background on school achievement suggests that these components are indeed malleable to a considerable degree and that the home conditions of many children could stand improvement.

Another source of evidence for the trainability of good thinking comes from observations of the errors that people make in problem-solving tasks. Many workers have noticed that mistakes in problem solving seem not to be the result of forgetting or lack of speed but rather the result of a kind of unreasonableness in the way the subject approaches the problem (Bloom & Broder, 1950; Selz, 1935; Whimbey & Whimbey, 1975). Errors are caused by sticking to the wrong approach even when it is obviously leading nowhere, by guessing without checking, and by giving an answer that could easily be seen not to meet the requirements of the task. For example, many workers have noticed that errors in analogy problems are often associates of the third term, with no attention given to whether the relation between terms one and two is preserved in terms three and four. In my own observations of people solving problems in Raven's Progressive Matrices, a test often given without a time limit, I have seen subjects frequently guess about the answer without being sure and without bothering to check. Further, several studies (e.g., Baron, Badgio, & Gaskins, 1985; Galotti, Baron, & Sabini, 1986) have now shown that successful problem solvers often spend more time per problem than less successful ones. It seems likely that such stylistic factors as the amount of time one spends is under control, and therefore teachable. (Further evidence on this point is presented later.)[3]

Now for my long promised hypothesis about the training of intelligence. It is that intelligence cannot be trained at all by training skills—in a narrow sense of the term—but it can be trained by training styles and their associated beliefs and goals.

First, consider skills. In the narrow sense of the term "skill," the way to improve a skill is to practice it. As a result of practice, skills increase in speed and accuracy. For this to happen, it is not necessary for the subject to do anything in a different way; that would be counted as a change in method or strategy. The evidence is that skills can be improved with

---

[3]It may be argued that variation in style is small compared to variation in more basic properties of performance such as mental speed. However, when speed is important in life, there is often an opportunity to improve one's speed at a specific task through practice, and practice effects may be large compared to individual variation. In many of the important things in life, such as decision making of the sort that extends over days or weeks, speed is not really an issue at all, but styles such as one's openness to alternatives and to evidence may well be important.

practice; indeed, they can become essentially automatic. However, when such improvment occurs, it does not transfer to stimuli in a different category. This was the conclusion of Thorndike and Woodworth (1901) and it is fully consistent with more recent data as well (see Baron, 1985b, and Woodworth, & Scholsberg, 1954, ch. 24, for reviews). To take a dramatic recent example, Eriksson, Chase, and Faloon (1980) gave a normal undergraduate extensive practice at memorizing strings of numbers. The subject's span increased from about 7 digits to about 79. The improvement was apparently the result of changes in method, but there was also a clear opportunity to practice the task itself. Despite this opportunity, the subject's span for letters was unchanged; it remained about 6. Consistent with earlier conclusions, one does not build one's memory ability *in general* by practice at specific kinds of memorization.

This conclusion about skills, if true, has a broader implication for the teaching of intelligence. In some writing about teaching—and perhaps in some teaching—it is claimed that the way to teach something is to set up a goal for the student and provide practice at achieving that goal, with corrective feedback. Thus, if we want to teach creativity, we give exercises in creativity; if we want to teach people to understand the main point of a text, we ask them to read texts; if we want to improve the ability to discriminate visual forms, we provide practice at it; and if we want to teach intelligence, we give children practice at test items like those on the IQ test. Such training may sometimes work, for the students may discover new methods that help them in the tasks where they are trained and even in a few related tasks. The students may also change their style, for example, they may learn to become more cautious; and they may become more motivated, more concerned about achieving certain kinds of goals. But our best guess is that they are not improving because of increases in skills. If there appears to be such improvement, it is limited to the tasks on which the training is given.

It has been suggested that much of intelligence consists of strategies or methods, and these can be taught (Baron, 1978; Brown, 1974; Flavell, 1970). This discussion was inspired by demonstrations that the memory deficiencies of retardates (in particular) could be partially remediated by teaching the subjects strategies for memorizing. Recently, a number of studies have shown that transfer to new situations will occur when pains are taken to provide the training in a generalizable, transferrable way (e.g., Brown, Campione, & Barclay, 1979). Although this work seems promising, I have a couple of questions about it. First, although the teaching of strategies may be worthwhile, a strategy seems more like a specific piece of knowledge rather than a component of intelligence. Few if any strategies are sufficiently general to meet the criterion of generality I proposed earlier, and those that are seem very much like styles (Baron,

1985b). Second, it seems likely that many of these successful training studies actually change the subjects' styles as well as their specific strategies. In most training studies involving memory strategies, the trained strategy takes longer to use than what the subject was doing before, and extra time is required in transfer as well. Training children to be less impulsive and more self critical might suffice to produce the same results even in the absence of strategy training. In this case, I argue that there has been a true change in intelligence, for such style changes are substantially general in the sense I described.

A number of training studies have been directed more explicitly at the kind of styles I have alluded to. In an important paper by Otto Selz (1935) a few of these studies are reviewed. One of the most revealing of these studies was a thesis done by Jakob Andrae under Selz's supervision. In this study, an experimental and control group of students, age 11–13, were given an intelligence test consisting of completion tests (stories with words left out), word ordering, verbal analogies, and number-series completions. The experimental group was given training on only the completion test for one hour on two successive days. The training was designed to make students take into account the requirements of the task, checking each possible answer to see if these requirements were met. Subjects were taught both to explain why answers did not meet the requirements and to justify answers when they seemed to fit. The training was done in the form of what seemed to be a lively competitive exercise in which students were called on to defend their answers at the blackboard, whereas other students in the group chimed in with criticisms and explanations. After the training, a second intelligence test was given. The experimental group showed substantial improvement not only on the completion test but also on all the others, to roughly the same extent. For example, on one of the completion tests, the experimentals improved from 60% to 78% correct while the controls improved from 60% to 63%, and on the analogy test, the experimentals went from 28% to 69% while the controls went from 33% to 41%. Of great interest, I think, is the finding that the experimental group was more than twice as likely as the control group to scratch out an answer and correct it in the posttest (244 times vs. 103), although the experimentals were less likely to do this in the pretest (22 times vs. 41). Again, this finding held to a roughly equal extent over all tasks. Although these results were from a short term study with an immediate posttest, there is no reason to think that they would change qualitatively with more extensive training and a more delayed posttest. Selz's explanation of these effects is very much in the spirit of my own theorizing, although he uses the term *Verhaltungsweisen*—roughly, modes of conduct—where I use the term styles.

In a more recent attempt, Irene Gaskins and I conducted an eight month training study in her school for reading-disabled children, the Benchmark School (Baron et al., 1985). The teachers in the school (including Gaskins) identified three styles that they felt were holding many children back from academic success, even when their initial reading problems had been largely corrected. We called these styles impulsiveness, rigidity, and nonpersistence. Impulsiveness consists of failing to think sufficiently on an individual problem or when answering a question. Rigidity consisted of an unwillingness to consider alternatives to one's initial hypothesis about how something should be done or about the truth of some issue. Nonpersistence was the failure to complete extended activities, such as seat-work assignments; it can be taken as a sign of lack of motivation. Our training program tried to overcome these biases by emphasizing three slogans: "Take time to think," "Consider alternatives," and "Keep at it." The value of these new styles was explained in terms of hypothetical examples; exercises were done; children were given feedback about their actual classroom behavior.

The program was a success according to teacher ratings of the styles we tried to train; the experimental group improved considerably and the control group hardly at all. The training also affected ratings of academic performance given by teachers of children who had graduated Benchmark and gone to other schools. In addition, children did slow down and take more time to think in a few different laboratory measures using tasks other than those used in training. Those children who had been rated as particularly impulsive also improved in their overall accuracy on these tasks. Tasks that showed these effects included a test of arithmetic word problems and a test of syllogisms. Because syllogisms have been used on IQ tests, we have some reason to think that training of this sort would help performance on IQ tests, at least those on which speed is not an important element in scoring. But this is not an important point for my argument, for I suspect that IQ tests are in general relatively insensitive to the stylistic components of intelligence. One informal observation of our study was that it was quite easy to teach children to go through the motions of spending more time on the task, checking their work, and so on, as long as the teacher was standing over them with the proverbial whip. What was more difficult was to instill the goals and beliefs that would insure that they would maintain their new styles, or *Verhaltungsweisen*, outside of the training sessions.

It is my hunch that the inculcation of these goals and beliefs is the most important aspect of any effort to teach intelligent thinking. Good thinkers, I think, are those who believe that intuition is often not the last word, that a considered judgment or answer is more likely to be correct than an unconsidered one, and that individuals can often figure things out for themselves. Good thinkers also have the goals of wanting to be correct or to make the best decision, rather than the goal of having been right all along, and the goal of being prudent in the service of long-term interests of themselves and others rather than the pursuit of immediate satisfactions. I would thus argue that the teaching of intelligence is part of the teaching of character. In teaching people to think well, we are trying to maintain and extend certain intellectual standards, much in the way we maintain moral standards in teaching other kinds of conduct.

REFERENCES

Baron, J. (1978). Intelligence and general strategies. In G. Underwood (Ed.), *Strategies in information processing* (pp. 403–450). New York: Academic Press.

Baron, J. (1985a). *Rationality and intelligence*. Cambridge, MA: Cambridge University Press.

Baron, J. (1985b). What kinds of intelligence components are fundamental? In S. F. Chipman, J. W. Segal, & R. Glaser (Eds.), *Thinking and learning skills. Vol. 2: Research and open questions* (pp. 365–390). Hillsdale, NJ: Lawrence Erlbaum Associates.

Baron, J., Badgio, P., & Gaskins, I. W. (1985). Cognitive style and its improvement: A normative approach. In R. J. Sternberg (Ed.), *Advances in the psychology of human intelligence* (Vol. 3). Hillsdale, NJ: Lawrence Erlbaum Associates.

Blank, M. (1973). *Teaching learning in the preschool*. Columbus, OH: Merrill.

Bloom, B., & Broder, L. (1950). *Problem-solving processes of college students*. Chicago: University of Chicago Press.

Brown, A. L. (1974). The role of strategic behavior in retardate memory. In N. R. Ellis (Ed.), *International review of research in mental retardation* (Vol. 7). New York: Academic Press.

Brown, A. L., Campione, J. C., & Barclay, C. R. (1979). Training self-checking routines for estimating test readiness: generalization from list learning to prose recall. *Child Development, 50*, 501–512.

Ericsson, K. A., Chase, W. G., & Faloon, S. (1980). Acquisition of a memory skill. *Science, 208*, 1181–1182.

Flavell, J. H. (1970). Developmental studies of mediated memory. In H. W. Reese & L. P. Lipset (Eds.), *Advances in child development and behavior* (Vol. 5). New York: Academic Press.

Galotti, K. M., Baron, J., & Sabini, J. (1986). Individual differences in syllogistic reasoning: Deduction rules or mental models. *Journal of Experimental Psychology: General, 115*, 16–25.

Jencks, C., Smith, J., Ackland, H., Bane, M. J., Cohen, D., Gintis, H., Heyns, P., & Michelson, S. (1972). *Inequality: A reassessment of the effect of family and schooling in America*. New York: Basic Books.

Kolb, D. A. (1965). Achievement motivation training for underachieving high school boys. *Journal of Personality and Social Psychology, 2*, 783–792.

Lazar, I., Darlington, R., et al. (1982). Lasting effects of early education: a report from the consortium for longitudinal studies. *Monographs of the Society for Research in Child Development, 47*, Serial No. 195.

Scarr, S., & Carter-Saltzman, L. (1982). Genetics and intelligence. In R. J. Sternberg (Ed.), *Handbook of human intelligence*. New York: Cambridge University Press.

Selz, O. (1935). Versuche zur hebung des intelligenzniveaus: Ein Beitrag zur Theorie der

Intelligenz und ihrer erziehlichen Beeinflussung. *Zeitschrift für Psychologie, 134,* 236–301.

Stevenson, H. W., Parker, T., Wilkinson, A., Bonnevaux, B., & Gonzalez, M. (1978). Schooling, environment, and cognitive development: a cross cultural study. *Monographs of the Society for Research in Child Development, 43,* Serial No. 175.

Thorndike, R. L., & Woodworth, R. R. (1901). The influence of improvement in one mental function upon the efficiency of other functions. *Psychological Review, 8,* 247–261.

Whimbey, A., & Whimbey, L. S. (1975). *Intelligence can be taught.* New York: Dutton.

Woodworth, R. S., & Schlosberg, H. (1954). *Experimental psychology.* New York: Holt.

Zigler, E., & Seitz, V. (1982). Social policy and intelligence. In R. J. Sternberg (Ed.), *Handbook of human intelligence.* New York: Cambridge University Press.

THE PLASTICITY OF "INTELLIGENCE" AT DIFFERENT LEVELS OF ANALYSIS

Arthur R. Jensen
University of California, Berkeley

My present position regarding the degree to which human intelligence can be improved by psychological and educational means is that the answer will depend largely on the level of analysis accepted as representing "intelligence."

My study of the research literature concerning experimental attempts to raise the intelligence of children leads me to several conclusions in which I have varying degrees of confidence. First, I feel most confident that there is no compelling or convincing evidence, as yet, that training techniques have any effect on intelligence conceived of as Spearman's g in the broadest sense. The small and usually transient effects on g that have been claimed for some studies can be explained more parsimoniously in terms of certain psychometric artifacts. It has been possible, certainly, to demonstrate gains on specific tests, including certain standard IQ tests. What has not been demonstrated, however, is that the individuals in the treated groups whose IQs have been raised relative to an untreated control group will show comparable gains on other, superficially dissimilar, g-loaded tasks or that they will perform like untreated persons of the same IQ in those "real life" pursuits that make intellectual demands. Virtually all of the evidence I have seen, from numerous compensatory education programs and from small but intensive studies

such as the Milwaukee Study of Heber and Garber (1979) or the Abecedarian Project in North Carolina (Ramey, et al., 1976), is consistent with
the hypothesis that it is the specificity, and possibly certain small group
factors, of the IQ tests, that have been trained up, rather than the g factor
itself. Such results are discouraging to people interested in raising IQ, as it
is the g factor that represents the "active ingredient" of IQ in terms of its
broad predictive validity and the breadth of transfer of the effects of
training.

Training and structured learning can undoubtedly enhance achievement in the form of knowledge and skills. That is mainly what education is
about. Effective and efficient performance in virtually all tasks of at least
moderate complexity depends upon a store of knowledge or skills gained
by learning, practice, and experience. And all biologically normal persons
are able to achieve through learning, practice, and experience. Traditional
IQ tests are fairly broad samples of achievement. The problem is that
persons differ widely in achievement even when their opportunity and
motivation for achievement are highly similar. Such variation implies that
something more than the quantity and quality of experiential inputs is
involved in human variation in ability. The persistence of this great
variation in the face of our best attempts to equalize opportunity and
maximize motivation for learning and intellectual development is one of
the factors that makes the study of human intelligence so fascinating,
problematic, and controversial. The clear perception that something more
than inequalities of experiential input is involved in inequalities of
achievement, a perception unchallenged for centuries by all but a few
psychologists, is largely the basis for the notion of mental ability, or
aptitude, that is independent of achievement, and in some sense more
basic. Hence, educators and policy makers in recent years have shown as
much or even more concern with improving children's intelligence as with
improving education in the traditional sense. And yet, although there
seems little doubt that we can improve education and the general level of
achievement in the traditional school subjects, there is considerable
doubt, at present, that we are able to improve people's intelligence in the
sense of aptitude, independent of achievement.

Future attempts to improve children's intelligence, not with guaranteed results, but as an experiment, will probably be directed at a different
class of psychological variables than those we now generally think of as
intellectual achievement. Current information processing models of intelligence view a number of elementary cognitive processes (ECP) and
metaprocesses (MP) as the basic underpinnings of intellectual achievement. One central question in this line of research concerns the trainability of the ECPs and MPs and the plasticity of individual differences
therein.

The relationship of the ECPs and MPs to the domain of psychometric intelligence can be represented by the simple hierarchical model shown in Fig. 4.1.

The horizontal dashed line in Fig. 4.1 separates the behaviorally or psychologically measurable variables (above the line) from those that are measurable only physiologically, such as evoked brain potentials, or from those that are less directly measurable, by means of inferred physiological processes, such as cortical conductivity (Klein & Krech, 1952), synaptic errors (Hendrickson, 1982), neural oscillation (Jensen, 1982), and the like. The physiological level is represented as one general factor, g_B (B for "biological"), although, given our present state of knowledge, this level could just as well be represented as several distinct physiological processes or as correlated processes, due to their sharing one common process, i.e., g_B. The nature of this physiological underpinning of human abilities is a major focus of Eysenck's (1982) theorizing about the findings of correlations between features of the average evoked potential and psychometric g, or g^p, which is depicted in the hexagon at the top of the hierarchy in Fig. 4.1. All the solid lines in the figure represent correlations.

The various elementary cognitive processes (P) are correlated through their sharing of common physiological processes. Different parts of the brain or different neural assemblies are presumably specialized for various aspects of information processing. These processes are described by terms such as stimulus apprehension, iconic memory, stimulus encoding, short-term memory (STM), rehearsal of encoded STM traces, memory scanning, retrieval of information from long-term memory (LTM), transfer, discrimination, generalization, transformation of encoded information, mapping of relations, visualization and mental rotation of figures in 2- or 3-dimensional space, and response execution. The *processes* (P) in this model, depicted here as being closely connected with some biological substrate, can all be measured by means of chronometric tasks, either directly or through derived scores. By subtraction of response latencies of simple tasks from those of more complex tasks, one can measure individual differences in the additional processes involved in the more complex tasks. Various processes can also be identified by the use of partial correlations or by a factor analysis of a combination of various tasks intended to tap different processes.

Different sets of elementary processes, P, can be utilized by a given *metaprocess* (*MP*). Because metaprocesses are further removed from the biological substrate and are probably mainly products of learning and practice, their connection to the biological substrate is via the elementary processes that enter into the metaprocesses. Metaprocesses consist of strategies for selecting, combining, and using elementary processes,

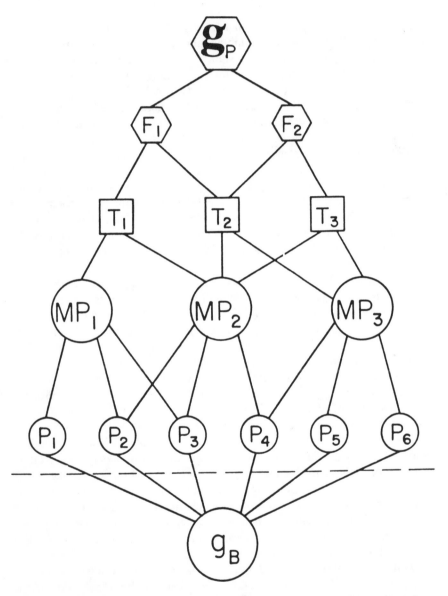

FIG. 4.1. Simplified representation of relationships among processing and psychometric variables. See text for explanation.

problem recognition, rule application, planning, allocation of resources, organization of information, monitoring one's own performance, and the like. Different metaprocesses are intercorrelated because they share certain elementary processes in common and also because the experiential factors that inculcate metaprocesses are correlated in the educational and cultural environment. It is probably at the level of metaprocesses that cultural differences have their primary impact.

Both processes and metaprocesses enter into performance on complex *psychometric tests* (*T*). Even a single complex test item may well depend on a number of *P*s and *MP*s for successful performance. Various tests are intercorrelated, moreover, not only because they share certain common *P*s and *MP*s but also because they may share common information stored in long-term memory. Note that at each level in this hierarchy, something new is added in terms of environmental inputs. The cumulative impact of these acquired elements is at its maximum at the level of single items in psychometric tests. Item variance is largely specificity, a technical term in factor analysis, referring to a source of variance that is peculiar to a particular item (or a particular test) and not shared in common with other variables. Specificity may arise from individuals' idiosyncratic experiences, making for unique and uncorrelated bits of information, or from complex and unique interactions among the *P* and *MP* demands and the informational content of a particular test item. In fact, all primary psychological measurements are saturated with task-specific variance. Chronometric measurements of elementary processes are no exception. Specificity, which is the bane of individual differences research, can be reduced only by using composite scores or factor scores (which are a particular weighted composite of the component scores) derived from a number of varied tasks or tests, thereby "averaging out" the specificity of the individual tasks.

The top part of the hierarchy in Fig. 4.1, including *T*, *F*, and g_p, encompasses the realm of traditional psychometrics, including various test scores and hierarchical factors extracted by factor analysis. Here, for the sake of simplicity, are represented only two first-order factors (F_1 and F_2) and one second-order factor, psychometric *g*, or g_p. The most general factor, of course, may emerge as a third-order or other higher order factor. Each successively higher factor level excludes some source of variance. The primary factors, for example, exclude the test-specific variance, and the second-order factors exclude the variance that is peculiar to each primary factor, and so on. The most general factor, g_p, is the variance common to all the sources below it in the hierarchy.

Some homogeneous tests, such as Raven's Progressive Matrices, contain relatively little specificity and are therefore quite good measures of g_p. Other tests, like the Wechsler scales, although containing quite heterogeneous items and subtests with considerable specificity, yield composite scores from which, in effect, the specificity is averaged out, providing a good measure of g_p.

Superficially very different tests, such as Verbal Analogies, Digit Span, and Block Designs, are intercorrelated presumably not because of common content or correlated educational experiences, but because they have a number of elementary processes and metaprocesses in common. Because the more superficial differences between tests contribute mainly to their specificities, these differences are not reflected in g_p. Hence it has been found that g factor scores are more highly correlated with chronometric measures of elementary processes than are any particular types of tests. Vernon (1983), for example, found that all of the correlations between the Wechsler Adult Intelligence Scale (WAIS) and a number of reaction time (RT) measures (from several elementary cognitive tasks) were due to the general factor of the WAIS. When the g factor was partialled out, none of the WAIS subtest scores correlated in the least with the RT measures. Thus, although g_p and P_1, P_2, etc., appear widely separated in the schematic hierarchy, they actually seem to have greater variance overlap, as shown by the correlation, than do some of the more proximal variables. This picture may also help to elucidate the otherwise surprising finding that, although g_p is derived from factor analysis of psychometric tests that bear virtually no superficial resemblance in format, content, or method of administration to the RT techniques used in elementary cognitive tasks (ECTs), g_p shows correlations almost as large with ECTs as with the psychometric tests from which g_p is derived.

One of the crucial theoretical questions, with reference to Fig. 4.1, regarding that there is presently little consensus, is whether more of the variance in psychometric g (g_p) is attributable to the processes (P) or to the metaprocesses (MP). The learned information content in the psychometric tests (T) can already be virtually ruled out as an important source of g variance, because tests that differ markedly in their information content, such as vocabulary and matrices, are nevertheless highly saturated with one and the same g. The multiple correlation of several simple ECTs with g_p has been so substantial in some studies as to suggest that perhaps 50% or more of the g_p variance is accounted for by individual differences in elementary cognitive processes (e.g., Vernon, 1983). If task specificity were further minimized in such studies, by using at least three or four different techniques for measuring each of the elementary processes that have already been shown to yield substantial correlations, it seems likely that even as much as 70% of the g variance would be associated with the elementary processing variables. Also, the existing studies have not taken sufficient account of the reliability of these processing measures. Proper corrections for attenuation might appreciably raise the correlations between ECTs and g_p. Split-half or other internal consistency estimates of the reliability of ECTs usually overestimate the test–retest reliability, and it is the test–retest reliability that should be used in correcting correlations for attenuation when the correlated measurements have been obtained in different test sessions, on different days, for example, or even at different times of the same day, such as before and after lunch. Some of the ECT measurements are so highly sensitive to an individual's fluctuating physiological state from morning till night and from day to day as to have quite low test–retest reliability as compared with most psychometric tests. Theoretical interest, of course, focuses on the *true-score* multiple correlation between the elementary cognitive processes and g_p. One feasible goal of this research would be to determine the relative proportions of variance in g accounted for by each of a number of clearly identifiable processes and metaprocesses.

It is my conjecture that most of the present attempts at training up intelligence have their greatest observable effects, in terms of the hierarchy in Fig. 4.1, at the level of specific psychometric tests (T_1, T_2, etc.). Training effects will fade at the higher levels of the hierarchy—the primary factors (F) and the general factor (g_p). Because a treated group will possibly show gains in the specificity of a number of tests, and because these specificities will therefore be correlated within a group composed of treated and untreated individuals, any apparent gains in the primary and general factors will be artifactual; that is, the g factor extracted from a battery of tests given to a sample of treated individuals will not be entirely the same g as the g obtained in a sample of untreated individuals. The g of the treated group would be predicted to show correlations with various nonpsychometric criteria that differ from the correlations found in untreated groups. In terms of Fig. 4.1, the chain of causality between the level of T and the lower levels of the hierarchy will have been disrupted. Treatment gains at level T and above that are not reflected in gains in the measurements at the levels of metaprocesses and elementary processes are most likely subject to fade-out within a year or two and would show little transfer effect to "real life" achievements. This is the condition we have most often observed in programs aimed at training up intelligence.

How and to what extent training can be focused on metaprocesses and elementary processes remains to be explored, although there are already some signs of success for types of performance with inferred connections to certain metaprocesses (Detterman & Sternberg, 1982). But there is little evidence, to my knowledge, of training effects on elementary cognitive processes.

What is still most unclear is the relative amounts of variance in psychometric g that are associated with individual differences at the levels of elementary processes and metaprocesses. Although it seems more plausible that the metaprocesses should carry the larger source of variance, certain recent findings make me wonder. In a number of elementary cognitive tasks so simple that individual differences can be reliably measured only in terms of reaction times or response latencies, we have found average between-group performance differences that are almost as large, in terms of standard deviation units, as the group differences in IQ itself. Nor is it at all clear that any kind of training could appreciably influence performance on elementary cognitive tasks. Practice effects on these tasks are almost negligible.

One of the most surprising findings comes from a study of academically gifted children, that I have done in collaboration with Sanford Cohn of the Johns Hopkins University and Jerry Carlson of the University of California at Riverside. A group of manifestly gifted children, succeeding in university courses in math and science at 12 to 14 years of age, was compared with a same-age group of average and bright junior high school pupils on a battery of elementary cognitive tasks, all based on reaction times to simple stimuli. The tests are so simple that if performance were merely scored in terms of number of right and wrong responses, instead of in terms of response latencies, the true-score variance would be absolute zero. These tests have minimal intellectual content and some have none at all—such as simply removing one's index finger from a pushbutton when a light flashes on. Yet on every one of these tasks, even the simplest, with response latencies around 250 milliseconds, the gifted and nongifted groups differ significantly beyond the .001 level—differences ranging from about one to three standard deviations. They did not differ any more than that on Raven's Matrices, a high-level test of g. Scores from a reaction time test based on the Hick paradigm, in which the subject simply lifts his or her finger from a pushbutton when one light in a panel of anywhere from one to eight light bulbs goes on, were subjected to a discriminant analysis. This analysis correctly classified 87% of the subjects as gifted or nongifted. The few errors in classification were pupils in the "nongifted" group. Evidently, academically gifted children differ from their more average age-mates not only at the level of academic knowledge and high-level scholastic skills that might be accounted for by certain metaprocesses. They differ also in speed and efficiency at the level of the most elementary cognitive processes. Indeed, it seems reasonable to believe that the direction of causality in individual differences goes from the elementary cognitive processes (and their physiological basis) to the relatively high-level knowledge and cognitive skills involved in successful performance on IQ tests and in academic achievement. Certainly, it is much harder to imagine how possession of the knowledge content of

IQ tests and scholastic achievement tests could possibly confer any advantage in the speed or efficiency of performing the elementary cognitive tasks.

If there is a practical implication of these findings for developing nations that want to develop the intellectual, technical, and scientific resources latent in their populations, it is this: If financial and educational resources are limited, count on selection more than on training per se for most quickly and efficiently increasing the amount of manifest talent from which the nation can benefit. Develop suitable techniques for discovering those individuals for whom the investment of limited educational resources will pay the greatest dividends. And apply these techniques far and wide in every sector of the population, regardless of class, caste, or race. The distribution of talent cuts across all such classifications. If such advice may sound elitist and does not sit well with dyed-in-the-wool egalitarians, I can only say it is the most predictably safe bet that psychology is now able to offer.

REFERENCES

Detterman, D. K., & Sternberg, R. J. (Eds.). (1982). *How and how much can intelligence be increased.* Norwood, NJ: Ablex.

Eysenck, H. J. (1982). The psychophysiology of intelligence. In C. D. Spielberger & J. N. Butcher (Eds.), *Advances in personality assessment* (Vol. 1). Hillsdale, NJ: Lawrence Erlbaum Associates.

Heber, R., & Garber, H. (1979). The Milwaukee project: A study of the use of family intervention to prevent cultural-familial mental retardation. In B. Z. Frielander, G. M. Sterritt, & G. E. Kirk (Eds.), *Exceptional infant* (Vol. 3). New York: Brunner/Mazel.

Hendrickson, A. E. (1982). The biological basis of intelligence. Part I: Theory. In H. J. Eysenck (Ed.), *A model for intelligence.* Heidelberg: Springer-Verlag.

Jensen, A. R. (1982). Reaction time and psychometric *g.* In H. J. Eysenck (Ed.), *A model for intelligence.* Heidelberg: Springer-Verlag.

Klein, G. S., & Krech, D. (1952). Cortical conductivity in the brain-injured. *Journal of Personality, 21,* 118–148.

Ramey, C. T., Collier, A. M., Sparling, J. J., Loda, F. A., Campbell, F. A., Ingram, D. L., & Finkelstein, N. W. (1976). The Carolina Abecedarian Project: A longitudinal and multidisciplinary approach to the prevention of developmental retardation. In T. Tjossem (Ed.), *Intervention strategies for high risk infants and young children.* Baltimore: University Park Press.

Vernon, P. A. (1983). Speed of information processing and general intelligence. *Intelligence, 7,* 53–70.

5 Symposium on the Theory of Multiple Intelligences

The second of the conference symposia dealt with the Theory of Multiple Intelligences, which Howard Gardner, of Project Zero, Harvard University, developed in his book, *Frames of Mind* (Gardner, 1983). Dr. Gardner began with an exposition of his Theory; Jonathan Baron, of the University of Pennsylvania, and Robert Sternberg, of Yale University, then engaged with him in a critical discussion, that was moderated by David Perkins, of Project Zero, Harvard University. An edited version of these proceedings follows, with a bibliography of references at the end. It should be noted that some of the questions that were directed to the participants by Dr. Perkins were based on submissions from members of the audience.

A: DR. GARDNER'S INTRODUCTORY TALK

I thought I'd begin with a demonstration of something I've recently taken up—mind reading. You will first have to allow me some premises: that you come from the west, grew up using a western language, and were acculturated in a region influenced by Western civilization. Now, if all this is true, you are likely to believe two things—and I'm going to suggest that both these things are wrong. In fact, even if you have read *Frames of Mind,* and believe all of it (and now we are getting to a very circumscribed set!), you are likely to hold these two wrong beliefs. I have come to call them the "two dogmas of intelligence," even though I have to admit that I often hold to them myself.

The first dogma says: there's a single thing called intelligence, and people vary in how much they have of it—in the vernacular, they are either "smart" or "stupid." All western languages have cognates for these terms. The second dogma is that intelligence can be measured; that one or another IQ test gives an adequate approximation of a person's intelligence; and that it is a worthwhile educational and social goal to try to devise some kind of instrument that can quickly tell you how intelligent somebody is. And such instruments might include, not just IQ tests, but reaction time tests, and possibly even brain wave measures or chemical assays.

Now that I've read your mind, I'm going to try a new sport called mind changing. I want to challenge these two dogmas. In order to do so, make your mind as much of a blank slate as possible on the subject of intelligence. In fact, try to pretend that you have never heard much about the term *intelligence;* you've never heard about Binet and what he did; you've never heard about the work of the many speakers at this conference who have studied intelligence; and you haven't even heard of "*g*," the notion of general intelligence. (For reviews see Block & Dworkin, 1976; Gould, 1981; Spearman, 1927; Sternberg, 1984; Thurstone, 1938.)

Let me explain why I'm asking you to engage in this suspension of belief by providing a little autobiography. My original training was remote from issues to do with intelligence: I began studying history, then moved to developmental psychology, and then to the psychology of the arts, that is how I came to meet David Perkins, with whom I've worked for nearly 20 years at Harvard on Project Zero. I also carried out post-doctoral research in the area of neuropsychology. As a student, I was specially impressed by the thinking of Piaget, and so, as a neophyte Piagetian, I subscribed to the notion that people are capable of very general mental operations, such as sensorimotor operation, concrete operations, and formal operations. On this view, operations are content neutral—equally applicable to quite different types of content. So if, for example, you are at the concrete operational level, you are there with respect to time, space, language, and so on. Now, at the time I was a Piagetian, it is fair to say that I believed the two dogmas, although in the nonreflective kind of way in which I imagine most people who are not students of educational psychology believe them. I casually assumed, that is, that some people were smart and some were dumb and that there were tests you could use to assess this. Frankly, these beliefs made me feel good, because I used to do well in those tests and so I figured I must be smart. In case I seem to be bragging, I should also admit that I did much better on those tests that I did in most other things, and this really gave me a sense of security, that is interesting because many people experience anxiety about tests, whereas I always felt very much at home when taking them. But, as I say, these were unreflective thoughts, and I remained an outsider to the "Educational Psychology Establishment," that was probably a good thing, because I would have been less likely to challenge the dogmas if I had been heavily trained in that area. One tends to fall in love with those topics one knows a great deal about: thus, because I wasn't so well versed in the intricacies of Intelligence Theory, *g*, and so on, I had a certain latitude for speculation on these subjects.

Once I was duly licensed to be a psychologist, I proceeded to my own research, working primarily with two groups: studying the cognitive, and particularly artistic, development of normal and gifted children at Harvard Project Zero; and working with various kinds of brain-damaged patients at the Veterans Hospital in Boston. These individuals tend to have quite specific disabilities: If they have problems with language, for example, they do not necessarily have problems with other areas, such as logical reasoning, musical performance, or drawing. A similar message seemed to emerge from my work with normal and gifted children: we often found children who were extremely good in one area of study, but quite ordinary or less than ordinary in others. Thus, although I continued to be a card-carrying Piagetian, and espoused the two dogmas if anyone asked me, my research was, almost without my realizing it, steadily undermining these two dogmas. For I was seeing, time and again, that individuals' abilities in one area were not good predictors of their abilities in other areas I was studying.

I might well have continued with this latent schizophrenia, had it not been for an interesting event that happened in the late '70s. Some representatives of the Van Leer Foundation of the Hague approached a group of colleagues at Harvard with a proposal for a project seeking to understand the notion of human potential. Despite the wideness of the topic, the challenge was intriguing. A number of us agreed to take part, and it fell to me to investigate human cognitive potential. (Ultimately, the Van Leer Project issued four books: Gardner, 1983; Levine & White, 1986; Scheffler, 1985; and White & Pollak, 1986.) Interestingly enough, this Van Leer Project on Human Potential was conceived at the same time as Project Intelligence in Venezuela. That may not be a complete coincidence: the *Zeitgeist* was at work.

This opportunity enabled me to explore more deeply the idea that I was beginning to form that there are really different kinds of intellectual faculties—or, as I said to myself more colloquially, different kinds of minds. I also sought to deepen my understanding of what is known about the organization of cognition in the nervous system, and found, through the Project, an opportunity to discover more about how mental skills are used in other cultures. In this connexion, I performed a "thought" experiment, in which I imagined going into many different cultures and trying to identify, in each, its developed roles or "end-states"—abilities highly prized in that culture, and really important for its survival. As part of the experiment, I thought about religious leaders, shamans, seers, mothers, fathers, dancers, surgeons, sculptors, hunters, businessmen, and so forth. I put myself to the challenge of coming up with a notion of cognition, that could give a better account of how the human organism can become highly competent in these very diverse kinds of capacities.

For the sake of simplification, I picked out three end-states: the first, was a sailor in the South Seas in the Pulawat Islands, who can navigate among hundreds of islands simply by looking at the configuration of stars in the sky, by remembering occasional land marks, and having a sense of how the boat moves over different kinds of surfaces and terrains. The second end-state was a young Islamic scholar who has mastered the Koran (that requires memorizing it), and is now studying with a mullah in a holy city, learning how to debate the merits of his scriptures against those of others. The third end-state was a young woman living in Paris, who has a microcomputer on which she composes avant-garde music. Keep these three different end-states in mind, as I describe the Theory of Multiple Intelligences.

In developing this Theory, I did not start with an examination of existing tests and their correlations with one another, as someone with a more traditional psychometric background might have done. I was not interested in predicting success and failure in school (that is what led to Binet's pioneering work). Instead, my initial intuition that there were different kinds of minds led me to sample the range of cognitive end-states as thoroughly as I could, and then to seek a model that might help us to progress in explaining how these different competences develop.

In my provisional definition of 'an intelligence,' I speak of an ability to fashion products, or to solve problems, that are of significance within one or more cultural settings. Thus, my definition has nothing to do with the two dogmas of intelligence, because I do not take intelligence to be a *single* capacity at all. Of course, I need criteria for ascribing an intelligence to a subject, and to obtain these I used a large number of sources. I considered what we know about development in both the normal and the gifted child, and about patterns of breakdown after brain damage. This was probably the single most important source of information. Data about which sorts of things break down together, and which can be either broken down or spared in isolation, are helpful in providing some sense of how to build a model of the workings of the central nervous system. I looked at exceptional individuals, especially children, prodigies, idiot–savants, autistic children, children with learning disabilities—groups that all show unusual kinds of (jagged, rather than flat) cognitive profiles. I considered what is known about the evolution of cognition, and cognitive capacities in different species. I also looked at psychological evidence, both from psychometrics (which kinds of tests correlate and which don't), and from psychological experimentation that shows whether or not training for a specific task yields a capacity that is transferrable to other kinds of tasks.

I then performed what I candidly term *a subjective factor analysis*. I didn't enter a bunch of scores into the computer and see which factors were extracted; I eyeballed the data for a long time, testing for plausibility various ways of classifying "intelligences," and thus arrived at a provisional list of seven different kinds:

Linguistic intelligence. that is the intelligence of a poet or an orator;

Logical Mathematical Intelligence. that is the intelligence found in a mathematician or a scientist.

I always mention these two intelligences first, because they are the ones most prized in the west; the ones most important for schooling, and that, by and large, standardized tests exist to assess. I accept that these tests do a reasonable job in assessing linguistic and logical mathematical intelligence. But where I begin to depart from my colleagues is in my claim that there are five other intelligences that deserve to be placed on their own pedestals along with the other two:

Musical Intelligence. found in the composer;

Bodily Kinesthetic Intelligence. the ability of the dancer, and of the athlete; the person who works with the hands, the craftsperson or surgeon;

Spatial Intelligence. found in the sculptor, surveyor, and the person skilled in topology.

Many psychologists, swallowing hard, can accept the five intelligences so far given: it is the last two, which are the 'personal' forms of intelligence, which are the most controversial, except, interestingly enough, amongst clinicians:

Interpersonal Intelligence: the concerns knowledge of other people, how they work, and how to work with them: salesmen and women, politicians and religious people usually have high interpersonal intelligence;

Intrapersonal Intelligence: this is the skill correlative to the previous one, and turned inward: it has to do with self-knowledge, and culminates in a developed sense of self, that includes an accurate notion of what you can and cannot do, an ability to plan and the like.

Let me now offer some remarks about the kind of approach this Theory represents. As the human species has evolved over the millenia, it has developed high degrees of skill in these seven areas. People do differ in the level of their abilities in these areas, but every normal human being can do quite well in each, and, usually, quite well in several. But there are seven different competences here: according to the Theory, a certain level of competence in one area is no predictor of how competent a person will be in another. Each factor has what I call an *autonomous core:* a psychological process that is *sui generis,* and that is not tied to any particular sense organs, but operates at a somewhat higher level of abstraction. There is no necessary correlation between skill in one intelligence and skill in another.

In fact, skills that are culturally recognised as such usually involve a *blend* of intelligences: only *freaks* (and I use the term technically), can 'make it' simply by having one intelligence. Furthermore, there is no one-to-one mapping between having certain intelligences and adult vocational or avocational expertise and activity: being strong in a particular intelligence doesn't predict what a child will do as a grown up, but it does predict the *kinds* of things he or she is likely to do well. Note also, however, that people may decide to work in an area in which they are not particularly strong.

So far, then, I have argued against the first dogma by claiming that there's a plurality of intelligences. I want now to challenge the second dogma. I do not claim that testing is necessarily bad, nor even that tests couldn't be devised for each of the seven intelligences. But, whereas for language and logic, the sort of testing we do now is probably adequate, when it comes to the other intelligences, testing becomes less and less appropriate, at least in the ways we usually think of as testing. I think we need to talk about *means of assessment,* that is a more neutral term for discovering a person's profile of intelligences. And I reject what I think has been the standard tendency in psychology: if you can't devise a test for it, then it can't have anything to do with the realm of intelligence. I think we must try to avoid what I call, perhaps in too sloganeering a manner, "the Westist-Testist Bias," and try to broaden our notion of means of assessment so that all the intelligences I have mentioned can come within its scope. I doubt whether short pencil and paper tests, or measures of brain waves, are going to tell us very much about the five intelligences I have added to the original two.

There are some similarities between my theory and traditional 'faculty' theories, going back to the phrenology of Franz Joseph Gall, or, in psychometrics, to Thurstone's seven vectors of the mind. Yet there are significant differences too. I believe that all of the intelligences are what a philosopher would call "natural kinds," and thus that the Theory of

Multiple Intelligences can in principle be rooted in biology. Of course, Gall believed that his theory could be grounded in the biology of his day too, so perhaps that is not a signficant difference. My theory, however, is culturally sensitive, because it seeks to account for a broad range of culturally recognized end-states. To return, briefly, to the three end-states mentioned earlier: The Pulawat sailor is strong in spatial and bodily skills; the Koranic student is extremely strong in linguistic skills (because he has memorized the entire Koran), and has logical mathematical skills also, though perhaps of a circumscribed type in as much as certain conclusions are proscribed. He will also have interpersonal skills, because the right kind of relationship with his mullah is required if he is to advance. (The modern secular school, incidentally, has emphasized logical mathematical and linguistic intelligences. Now, interpersonal intelligence has been downgraded in importance, whereas intrapersonal skills are perhaps emphasized more). In a computer-based school of the future, in which our computing composer would be at home, language may become less important, logical mathematical skills more important, and intrapersonal skills extremely important. For the computer environment demands planning, a correct assessment of your own skills and ability to use those of others.

A further significant distinguishing mark of my theory is that it is vertically rather than horizontally based. Psychology textbooks typically have a chapter on memory, a chapter on perception, a chapter on learning, and so on—and the implied assumption is that there are mechanisms of memory, perception and learning, which apply equally to any kind of material. A vertical theory disagrees. It holds that, in different content domains (like language, music or logic), there are special forms of memory, perception and learning, proper to each domain. And it becomes a completely empirical question whether the way memory works in music is the way it works in language, whether the way perception works in art is the way it works in mathematics, and so on. This is a very controversial claim, which is rejected by many psychologists but has been vigorously argued by Jerry Fodor (1983). Indeed, if you draw but one message from my remarks, I hope it will be that it is possible to have a theory of intelligence, and a theory of thinking, which is content based—which allows that the way thinking occurs in one area may be different from the way it occurs in others.

Similarly, I do not believe that there is a single thing called *creativity*, and I am very dubious about creativity tests. The ability to do something novel, which will ultimately be socially recognised as important and of lasting value, in one particular area (say music) has no predictive value as to creativity in other areas—no more so than being intelligent in one area predicts intelligence in another. Even Leonardo da Vinci, who is often held out as the epitome of the universal genius, was creative in some areas but not notably so in such areas as music or personal understanding.

The Theory of Multiple Intelligences does purport to be a developmentally based theory. I believe that each intelligence has its own biological trajectory—times when certain potentials arise, sensitive periods, if you will. I would like to think that, some day, researchers will study the differing life trajectories of the different intelligences. It is also important that we think about each intelligence relative to its manifestations at different ages. Thus, pattern-recognition skills in infancy may evolve into symbol-using skills in early childhood, which then produce in our culture the ability to handle different kinds of notations, which are exploited in various different vocational and avocational cultural roles. Thus, intelligence at different stages in life cannot be discerned with a single tool: We need tools appropriate to each age.

I also advocate an ethological approach to intelligences. It is very important that, at certain ages, children come into contact with materials that will engage their intelligences in what I call *crystallizing experiences*. Educators ought to develop a sense of which materials fulfil this role, and when they should be made available. My approach, then, to each of the intelligences, is an organismic, developmental one.

At present, my theory has more implications for assessment than it does for teaching or training. Yet, although I don't have strong views on this topic, I do want to say that I am sceptical about massive promises for the rapid training of thinking in any area. I suspect that theories about how intelligence can be trained are often unduly sanguine about the possibility of the trained skills transferring across what I understand to be distinct intelligences. I would, however, like to push the whole educational establishment charged with assessment towards more of a concern with products—not products that can be fashioned in a few seconds, but things like writing essays, telling stories, making paintings, carrying our scientific experiments and devising mathematical proofs. This will involve a very different time scale from the one assessors are used to dealing with, and the standardized type of test will become increasingly redundant.

It is, of course, very easy just to have opinions about intelligence and education. So I should emphasize that I do intend in the next four years to try out some of these notions. With my colleague David Feldman at Tufts University, and a staff we are now assembling, I shall be working in a preschool in the Boston area in order to try to develop a new means of assessing intellectual propensities in young children. We believe that, as early as 3 or 4 years of age, children have different cognitive profiles, and we hope to find unobtrusive ways of figuring out what these are. We will provide experiences that will illuminate the children's strengths, including such things as going to a museum, seeing a play, or simply finding one's way round the neighborhood. After assessing each child, we want to produce a two- or three-page "Propensities Report," for parents and teachers. This report will suggest the child's strengths and weaknesses, and the combination of abilities we think the child has. But each report will also recommend certain activities, in school, at home and in the community, which should enable the child to pursue the development of his or her abilities. The schools have a hard enough time developing the two intelligences on which they currently focus: it would no doubt be too much to ask them to suddenly take on training in five more. But I believe that the schools can be much better assessors of students' abilities than they have been until now, and that they can serve as brokers to help effect connections between the child and his or her family, and opportunities in the community.

I began by suggesting that most of us unreflectively accept two dogmas about intelligence. The first was that intelligence is a single thing, and I hope that it has now become clear that it isn't simply an infelicity of language to say that there are many 'intelligences.' The second dogma was that intelligence can be measured in short tests, and I hope I have opened your minds to the need for other means of assessment, particularly when it comes to the nontraditional intelligences. Having tried to repudiate two dogmas, I now want to close with two dreams. The first dream (that I hope doesn't cause anyone nightmares) is that eventually there will be much less of a need for testing. Marx said that the state should eventually fade away: well, I would like to think that testing will eventually fade away, and that children will be able to let us know in more naturalistic ways, which sorts of things they are good at and like to do. In a society where there is greater fit between the kinds of abilities and skills people have, and the activities and roles that are available, formal testing would be almost unnecessary. I know this is utopian—almost as utopian, even, as Ambassador Machado's (1980) notion of making everyone an Einstein—but I believe you do have to dream.

My other dream follows closely from my conviction that all of us have some control over the future, so that, if we think something is a good idea, we can move in the direction of its fulfilment. In my ideal society, where the full range of talents and abilities and intelligences would be recognized, not only would people feel better about themselves, but the society would function more productively. When you have only one train—the language–logic train—and everybody is being forced to travel on it, you're inevitably going to have a lot of casualties.

To my slogan of "Westist and Testist," I recently added a new rhyme, "Bestest." You will perhaps remember David Halberstam's book, *The Best and the Brightest,* whose theme, suggested by its ironic title, concerns how we sent the highest IQ types to Washington, and got the

Vietnam War and other catastrophes as a result. My serious point here is that we have bet very heavily on this one form of intelligence, and, although many wonderful things have no doubt thereby been achieved, we have also got ourselves into lots of quandaries. There are tremendous problems facing our world, including (as I think we should remember each day) the very question of its survival. Although I know that paying attention to more intelligences will not by itself ensure survival, I do believe that there are abilities, and combinations of abilities, which people have, which have not been sufficiently appreciated in the society with which we are most familiar. If we paid more attention to these abilities, we might move a little further in the direction of surviving—even in the direction of thriving!

DISCUSSION

Perkins: In discussing Howard Gardner's Theory of Multiple Intelligences, we should realize that the debate is not "Gardner versus *g*," for there are lots of theories of intelligence. Some posit many different components—not just seven, as Gardner does, but 120 (see Guilford & Hoepfner, 1971); the classic theory posits one—*g*; there are theories that posit about three, and so forth. All such theories might be called *power* or *hardware* theories because they presume that there are hardware mechanisms corresponding to the various posited components. Theories differ on the question whether practice can improve the efficiency of these mechanisms, thereby increasing intelligence—but, in any case, it's all a question of mechanics. Then there are alternative approaches that provide a metacognitive perspective on intelligence, according to which intelligence is really a matter of acquiring a repertoire of very general skills of various sorts: skills of memory, skills of strategic problem solving, and so forth. Then there are theories like Jonathan Baron's, which view intelligence as 'cognitive style' (see Baron's contribution to previous chapter). And some people, yet again, believe that intelligence is a very differentiated thing, very specific to a multitude of subject matters. Thus, we do well to keep in mind the great range of views of intelligence, although in this chapter we can only discuss a few.

I suggest four questions for us to explore. In common with theories in any area, every theory of intelligence focuses on a certain range of phenomena that it seeks to explain, and may have little to say about other kinds of phenomena that are central to the concerns of other theories. Thus, as our first question, we may ask how the Theory of Multiple Intelligences (MI Theory) differs from other theories of intelligence in the sort of phenomena that it seeks to explain.

A second question is this: what could constitute evidence against MI Theory? How could it, in principle, be disconfirmed? What logical or evidential reservations might one have about it?

Third, let us consider what MI Theory has to say about the prospects of improving mental functioning through education. Dr. Gardner has expressed some tentative reservations about holding out high hopes here—but perhaps there is more to be said.

Fourth, let us set aside the question of the soundness of MI Theory, and consider why it is so attractive to many people. Some theories have much popular appeal: Sometimes a person's enthusiasm seems to have more to do with a theory's appeal than with any analytical penetration or evidential support it may possess. Thus, if, for instance, you prefer MI Theory to Arthur Jensen's view of intelligence (see contribution by Jensen in previous chapter), it is worth asking whether this is because the evidence for MI Theory is superior or whether it is because you simply "like" the theory better.

To start with the first question: What is MI Theory about? What phenomena does it most centrally seek to illuminate?

Sternberg: Dr. Gardner invited us to try to erase from our minds the assumptions we derive from our knowledge of the history of educational psychology. For my part, I think this may be a mistake, because, although such an exercise may lead to a genuinely novel insight, there is also the risk that we shall merely repeat past mistakes. And I do have the impression that Gardner is to some extent placing old wine in new bottles. He speaks of doing 'subjective factor analysis,' and mentions Thurstone as a possible intellectual antecedent, and it does seem to me that MI Theory is really about what factor theories were about. For, consider, does MI Theory say what the processes of intelligence are? No. Does it say what mental representations are? Not really. Does it say, as Piaget's theory does, what the mental structures are? No. Does it give the nature of the executive or metastrategic operations? No. What it says is that there are latent somethings—musical intelligence, spatial intelligence, logical–mathematical intelligence, and so on—that generate appropriate performances. And these 'somethings' are very similar to the factors of factor theory. Now, I think that there is nothing terribly wrong with such a theory, but it does leave a lot of questions unanswered.

Another problematical feature of MI Theory is its reliance on subjectivity: if you are going to do factor analysis, you are better off, I think, doing it objectively rather than subjectively. Perhaps a lesson can be learnt from Thurstone, who originally took a position very similar to Gardner's in claiming that the abilities constituting each factor were primary and distinct. By the end of his career, because of overwhelming objective data from correlations among tests, he had to admit that the factors were not distinct after all, and he was even prepared to allow that they yield to a second-order *g* factor.

The phenomena that MI Theory seeks to explain, I think, are what Gardner calls *end-states,* or careers in people's lives. And Gardner's notion of intelligences is similar to what others have called talents. If you look at the list of talents in the Marland Report, or at the list given by Piechowski, you find lists very similar to Gardner's list of intelligences (Marland, 1971; Piechowski, 1979). So MI Theory is really a theory of talents, that lead into different kinds of job streams, like those of poets, mathematicians, dancers, salesmen, and so on.

Perkins: You seem to be suggesting that MI Theory is somehow retrogressive in harking back to factor analysis. But do you admit that it says something about talents or intelligences which other theories have neglected?

Sternberg: Yes, I do see MI Theory as progressive in certain respects. In the '70s, there was a real need for research to be done into the processes of intelligence. But what was actually investigated were the processes that generate responses to IQ tests, and the suspicion arose that IQ tests may not measure all we want to measure when we seek to understand intelligence. Thus, one goal for the '80s, to which Gardner's theory contributes, is better to define the total domain of intelligence. Thus, although I don't necessarily agree with the way Gardner does it, I think it is very important to expand the domain of what we classify as intelligent activity.

Perkins: Howard, perhaps I can ask you to respond. In particular, is Dr. Sternberg correct to say that MI Theory essentially seeks to explain what jobs people do?

Gardner: Well, the Theory is certainly not just about jobs: it is about the range of roles that are valued in a culture. Intelligence is what permits the solving of problems the culture regards as important, and the production of valued products. So it's a basis for much more than just jobs (that is why I always speak of intelligence as emerging in 'vocational and avocational' activity and expertise).

This point provides a good start for a wider answer to Dr. Sternberg's questions. Every theory must have a point of departure, and mine is to survey those competences that have been valued by cultures over a long period of time in different parts of the world. This has not been the point of departure for most other theorists of intelligence. If my view might be caricatured as a "jobs" view, the standard view, that Sternberg seems to have been defending, might be caricatured as a "tests" view. For the standard departure point is to begin with the tests psychologists have developed, and consider how they do and do not correlate with one another.

I agree with Sternberg that objective analysis is preferable to subjective: when I described what I did as "subjective" factor analysis, I didn't intend the term as one of approbation! The problem is, though, that there seems to be some inescapable subjectivity required if we are to say just what it is that any theory of intelligence ought to explain. Consider the kinds of things that, on the "tests" approach, are correlated with one another: they are short-answer, switch-from-one-context-to-another-as-quickly-as-you-can, do-it-in-half-an-hour instruments that Educational Testing Service and others have developed to an extremely high degree of finesse. Competence in performance on such tests may, of course, be used as the input in a factor analysis. But I will not be convinced that a factor analysis can really uncover intelligence unless it is based on what is culturally valued as an important area of expertise. The problem with any factor analysis is the quality of the input—the "garbage in, garbage out" principle clearly applies. Thus, I see myself as trying to improve the quality of the input, and not holding too many preconceived ideas about what the output may be. (Indeed, let me emphasize that it *may* turn out in the end that there is something to the notion of g or general intelligence, and that there are metacomponents that extend from music to spatial coordination, and so on.) To give an example, suppose we give the Seashore Test, and find it correlates 0.2 with something else and conclude that there is a correlation between musical ability and, say, Raven's Matrices. My complaint would be that we should not just assume that the Seashore Test gets at what is important about being a person who can analyze music, and think musically. Indeed, the musicians I have talked to agree that it doesn't even scratch the surface of what is really important here. My goal, then, is to perform factor analyses only when the psychologists and the experts in the relevant domain have satisfied themselves that they have really identified capacities that are genuinely important and valuable. I believe that this can be done only if we consider, not just brief performances, but the products of more long-term activity, such as stories, compositions and theories. So I am all in favor of objective factor analysis, but I am not in favor of accepting that this requires us to accept as our point of departure the results of the current standardized tests.

Baron: May I suggest an analogy that I find helpful between the study of intelligence and the study of economic systems? The question, 'what is the concept of intelligence?,' may be compared with the question, 'what is the concept of a nation's economic strength?.' We might answer the latter by considering the products of a country's industries, and then considering those features that encourage particular forms of production rather than others. As well, we should have to attend to general aspects of an economy that affect all industries—the so-called infrastructure of transport facilities, financial conditions, levels of education, and so on. On this analogy, Gardner's theory is entirely about the products of intelligence, and the capacities that yield them—it is radical because it repudiates any possible general or central system (any 'infrastructure'). I am concerned that it may be quite unwarranted to neglect these general features (as it surely would be in considering the analogous concept of economic strength). But I do believe that Gardner's theory is valuable because it broadens the range of what we look at in investigating intelligence—something that I think all three of us agree to be necessary. An inquiry into intelligence ought to consider the whole range of things that it is worthwhile to do, and not just performance on tests. Once we do this, there is much less evidence for a general intelligence, or g, factor, because the correlations that have been used to argue for such a factor all have to do with the same kinds of short item tests that Gardner has just described. There are hints of evidence that, once we admit this broader notion of intelligence, there is no longer any basis for postulating g. Just to give one example, Dörner and Kreutzig (1983) ran a test in which the subject had to manage a simulated African country for several weeks. Some subjects succeeded in preventing the simulated citizens from starving, others did not, and ability in this respect was totally uncorrelated with IQ, as measured by standardized tests.

Gardner: Let me briefly comment on Dr. Baron's concern that my theory leaves out the infrastructure of intelligence and neglects important general factors. I was impressed by Baron's notion of intelligence as *style* in the previous seminar (see Baron's contribution in previous chapter), although I have been accustomed to understanding the capacities he mentions—caring about a task, attending to detail, being willing to stick with it, and so on—as a matter of character development. These things are general and transferable—but I would not class them as purely cognitive or computational. Furthermore, having such capacities is no substitute for being able to "think in a certain medium" (be it musically, kinesthetically, logically, or whatever), although, of course, they do enhance such thinking: if you can think logically, and also have developed attention to detail (say), then you will no doubt be better, for example, at producing intricate proofs of complicated theorems than you would be if you lacked this "style." Although I think there are limits beyond which people cannot go in the different intelligences, in practice, the development of appropriate styles may enormously enhance the products of intelligence.

Sternberg: To respond to Dr. Gardner's reply to my earlier comments, let me say first that I was not defending what he caricatures as the "tests" view. I do agree (and I have tried to make this clear in my writings e.g., Sternberg, 1977, 1985) that the point of departure must be theory rather than tests. Second, it seems to me that Gardner's emphasis on MI Theory as dealing with the range of roles and products that are culturally valued is little different from understanding the Theory as concerned with the range of jobs, which are essentially social roles. Now, there is nothing wrong with a theory that will explain how these social roles emerge. But there are surely questions, that are independent of social values, that a theory of intelligence ought to address: How do our mental processes operate?; how are different skills, factors, or intelligences coordinated in performing a task? Finally, I agree that the traditional tests of intelligence are far from fully adequate. But the question does remain: Why do these rudimentary instruments produce such highly correlated results? If spatial intelligence is indeed separate from mathematical intelligence, as Gardner proposes, why do tests scores in these areas correlate almost as highly as the reliabilities? Why is it so hard to separate these two capacities in terms of performance?

Perkins: Let me interpose a metacomment. Notice that we are not anywhere near dealing with a neat theory here whose truth can be straightforwardly checked against an array of data. Rather, our theories of intelligence seem to be constructions, complicatedly connected with data and observations. And this, it may be noted, is not an unusual, but a typical situation with theories in general. Yet Dr. Sternberg's last point does seem to present clear counterevidence against MI Theory: Howard, how do you explain the high correlation between success in mathematical and spatial intelligence tests?

Gardner: In my view, the tests used in establishing such correlations are not pure measures of the intelligences involved.

Perkins: But doesn't that response not make MI Theory immune to disconfirmation? It seems that, whenever there appear to be correlations contrary to the predictions of the Theory, the tests used will, just for that very reason, be dismissed as impure measures!

Gardner: No. I have no wish to trivialize the evidence by such an ad hoc move. Ideally, I would like to tease apart the capacity to be a good test taker from strengths in each of the ingelligences. If there is, indeed, such a thing as a *general* test-taking ability, then the observed correlations might reflect *that* common factor, and not the kind of relationships between intelligences that would disconfirm MI Theory.

Sternberg: I think, nevertheless, that certain tests might still be more reflective of some intelligences than of others. However, I agree that a fair tests of the Theory would have to start with an agreed-on measure of each particular intelligence that did not simply measure general competence in test taking. Provided such tests are possible, MI Theory is disconfirmable, and would, of course, be disconfirmed if the correlations persisted under such tests.

Perkins: On this question of correlations, what does Dr. Gardner have to say on the frequently claimed connection between logical mathematical and musical intelligence? Do you simply deny it, Howard?

Gardner: In *Frames of Mind,* I came to a point of view on this, but it's only fair to point out that the evidence doesn't range far above the anecdotal. People who are mathematically talented often show considerable interest in music (perhaps music presents itself as an extremely interesting field for the mathematical mind with its fascination for patterns of any sort). But many musicians I have talked to maintain that a mathematician's interest in music does not necessarily amount to true musicality—knowing how to perform a piece of music to bring out its structure or mood. We must be cautious, then, about confusing interest with expertise: it may just be an interest in music that is correlated with mathematical intelligence.

I am very interested in prodigies, incidentally, and I think noteworthy that most prodigies, though good in everything, are normally extremely good in just one thing. (The omnibus prodigy, such as a Goethe or a Leonardo, is extremely rare.) This offers some support, I think, for a more factorial theory as against a theory of general intelligence.

Baron: There is perhaps a third possibility: it may be that prodigies develop because they form unusually high levels of interest that motivate them to practice a specific skill to an extraordinary degree. The psychological literature (e.g., Hayes, 1985) does suggest that the effect of differential levels of practice on the development of a skill is very great. Thus, it may be that prodigies can be explained without any appeal to innate gifts—for the unusual interest that motivates the practice could be culturally determined or even quite accidentally triggered.

Perkins: This raises an important point, not yet discussed: does Dr. Gardner consider his seven kinds of intelligences to be innate?

Gardner: I do believe that there is a genetically set limitation on a person's ultimate level of possible attainment in each intelligence, and, perhaps, on the rate at which progress will be made in each. But, of course, this determination still leaves enormous degrees of freedom: Dr. Baron is quite right, for example, to point out that what you start with is a predisposition only, which has to be "triggered" in some way—for example, by an interest.

It is more important, I think, to say what it is I want to reject—namely, the idea that people come with exactly equivalent predispositions in each area. Benjamin Bloom (1984), who has worked recently with people who are the "best" in six different fields, makes the kind of claim that I reject—that the important determinant of ability is training. And Samuel Johnson epitomized the view I oppose when he said, "true genius is a mind of large general talents, accidentally determined to some particular direction." I do not say there are *no* people like that, but I do say that it is the exception. It is no accident that individuals develop strengths in one area or another, and that parents cannot just arbitrarily decide what to bring their children up to be.

Perkins: Let me return to a question Dr. Sternberg raised: the issue of an executive. Most contemporary theories of cognition hold that there is an overriding, organizing element in intelligence, which holds procedures and strategies together across different domains. Does MI Theory avoid the need for such an executive? Or is it possible to draft one from among the seven intelligences? If Intrapersonal Intelligence is what serves to promote self-knowledge, can it function as a higher order intelligence, as an executive process?

Gardner: In the book, I do discuss the sense of self, which I think develops out of the Intrapersonal Intelligence, and one could indeed understand an executive processor as developing from there. But it is important to recognize that there might be metacomponents and strategic abilities that are highly honed in one area without being especially transferrable to others. Perhaps all or most of these higher order abilities are as vertically organized as the lower order ones? It is also possible to have what Fodor and others term a *dumb executive,* which makes sure the wires don't get crossed, and maybe arranges a pecking order amongst various mental functions, but doesn't really make the strategic decisions that belong to a true executive.

Note also that we belong to a society that strongly emphasizes individual agency, and so we have a lot riding on the notion (intrinsic to our 'folk psychology') that there is an internal mental decision maker. Our society is a "particle society," that understands individuals as atoms: other cultures may be more typically "field societies," where it is 'the others' or 'the tradition' that makes decisions about what individuals do. In such a society there would be less of a proclivity to postulate an inner executive. For a concrete example, consider the child prodigy, whom we might naturally suppose to have highly developed mental executive capacities. In fact, in the prodigies David Feldman (1986) studied, what executive processes there are that govern the child tend to reside in a parent, usually the mother. And this interestingly illustrates how strategic metacomponents can work very well without being located in the individual's own head!

Sternberg: But is it not important, in proposing a theory of intelligence, to have the evidence of truly scientific research, rather than just relying heavliy on anecdotes and observational evidence? Surely we need to see how we could *test* these claims Dr. Gardner makes about how executive mental functions might be either accommodated or explained away by his Theory?

Gardner: I am certainly not opposed to doing researach on this aspect or any aspect of MI Theory—indeed, as I have already mentioned, now that the Theory has been propounded, I am trying to find evidence about the intelligences in the preschool years. But, because my Theory is a new one, if it has any validity, we must expect it to take many years to assess where that validity lies: that is what has been necessary for previous theories of intelligence, after all.

Earlier, Dr. Sternberg was urging that I really need to be interested in the processes and structures that are involved in each of my postulated intelligences. And I want to say that he is absolutely right! Sternberg, indeed, has himself been a leader in bringing a much finer-grained analysis to traditional intelligence tests, and I accept that we need to bring the same degree of care to thinking about what it means to be spatially skilled, musically skilled, or bodily skilled, as we have to the solving of analogies or the ability to remember digits. Thus, I am not against process and structural analysis of each of the intelligences, and would wish to bring to bear on this expanded Theory of Multiple Intelligences the sophisticated psychological resources developed by others in more traditional areas.

Baron: On the particular question of an executive or central processor, it seems to me that there are three kinds of evidence for positing such a thing, over and above the Intelligences that Dr. Gardner recognizes.

First, there is evidence for the existence of the self, which is not so much "an" intelligence, but rather the person, who decides what to pay attention to, and who has beliefs and intentions that direct the organism's behavior. As I understand it, the evidence from neuropsychology is that it is very hard to destroy this self with brain lesions: In fact, a person will usually find means of circumventing specific disabilities caused by brain lesions.

Gardner: I wish that were true, but, in general, I don't think it is. One of the remarkable things about frontal lobe damage, is that the patient can absolutely lose the sense of who he is, what has happened to him, how to plan, and so on, and yet retain an IQ of 140. Thus, people can be 'computationally intact' in the psychometric areas, yet altogether lose this executive sense (which, incidentally, is one reason why frontal lobotomies were discontinued—because the person retains his previous IQ yet becomes almost inert). Now, I agree that this provides evidence for accepting the existence of an executive: but I would want to locate it within Intrapersonal Intelligence, and would resist the idea that it somehow stands beyond and above the seven Intelligences and controls their operations.

Baron: What, then, do you make of the second sort of evidence, that suggests that there are processing systems that cut across the content areas as your Theory differentiates them? Memory ability and mental speed are cases in point. And the evidence that the processes involved here do cut across your different "intelligences" comes not just from correlations in degrees of skill, but from certain ways of manipulating the brain. For example, when you give people dextroamphetamines, they perform more quickly *every*sort of task requiring mental energy, no matter what "system" it is in (Gupta, 1977). And there is a third type of evidence for admitting some over-arching structure, and that is the evidence for the significance of style and character in mental performance, which I discussed in the previous seminar (see contribution by Baron, previous chapter).

Gardner: What's most valuable in MI Theory can, I believe, be retained even if this type of evidence does require us to admit that there are quite general aspects of mental function. I am quite open, for example, to the notion that there are general speed factors affecting the operation of all of the intelligences. (Although, as we know from studies of reflectivity and impulsivity, greater speed doesn't necessarily lead to success in a task; Kagan & Kogan, 1970). I am more skeptical about the claim that memory operates in a way that is blind to content. There is considerable neurophysiological evidence for the separation of linguistic memory from spatial, facial, bodily, or musical memory (Gardner, 1976). (It is instructive to realize that, normally, when we say a person has a good memory we mean that he or she is good at using memory in certain kinds of linguistic skills. We tend just not to think of a good memory for a piece of music, or the steps of a dance.)

Perkins: Now that we have had a chance to discuss the logic of MI Theory, and the problems of squaring it with the (often ambiguous) evidence, let's change gears, and consider what the theory may have to say about the educational goal of enhancing thinking skills. Many people have thought that, if you can improve a person's executive processes and style, then you can enhance mental efficiency considerably. I take it that you are somewhat dubious about that, Howard?

Gardner: I think we all agree that executive abilities are important. My point is, however, that enhanced executive skills in no way compensate either for having a propensity in the relevant intelligence or for having had a lot of practice in the relevant skill. Thus, I'm suspicious of teaching the executive skills—unless the subjects already have a lot going for them. If they do, of course, then interventions to improve executive functions can be very powerful. But they do not have a power that transcends subject domains.

Sternberg: Well, then, what *should* the teacher try to do to enhance skill in thinking? Could Dr. Gardner draw out some of the positive implications of his Theory for training?

Gardner: The most important implication is that, for each intelligence, we may expect to find, first, different kinds of "markers" for the presence of special strengths, and, second, different sorts of behaviors, strategies, and skills that promote the development of such strength. Because this sounds so general, let me mention an example that I discuss at some length in *Frames of Mind* (Chap. 14): the Suzuki method of training musical performance. This method works because of the brilliant analysis done by Suzuki of what factors matter in developing musical skill in early life. What Suzuki did for musical performance can, I think, be done for every other intelligence: indeed, each intelligence may require its own specific educational theory. Such a theory would to some extent be developmental (concerned with crystallising experiences, and so on), and to some extent would prescribe modelling and other more agressive interventions familiar from educational psychology generally. We must not just assume—and this is my point—that what techniques are going to work at what ages will be uniform across each of the intelligences.

Perkins: Can you explain your reference to the developmental aspect of such an educational theory? What exactly are "crystallising experiences," and how can they be promoted?

Gardner: A crystallizing experience is one specified by three results: First, it produces an instant affective affinity with a certain domain that previously had not held much significance for the individual. Second, it produces a decision to invest more energy and time (at least in the short run) in the area concerned. And third, it causes a redefinition of the self to emerge: "Now I am an X," "now here is something I do well in." Such experiences are likely to occur at quite different ages, depending on the area concerned: In music, I believe, they occur rather earlier than in other domains, for instance. The developmental theory also employs the notion of *mentorship:* a close involvement over a significant period with an expert in an area, that is not purely intellectual but also mutual and personal. Often crystallizing experiences are triggered in relationship with such a mentor—but this need not be so. And mentors may play roles other than to catalyse crystallising experiences (Mozart's father, for example). (See Walters & Gardner, 1986.)

Sternberg: Let me be a bit provocative here about the range of skills that MI Theory seems to count as intelligent. Does gym class train intellectual skills? If bodily kinesthetics is one of the intelligences, then surely the answer is that it does? And that seems odd.

Gardner: Well, I don't see why it should. Recall that my Theory starts with the identification of products and problems that matter. And very often performances in sport, dance, and the like, *do* matter. It is quite sensible to speak of the intelligent exercise of control over one's body, especially when almost instant adjustments can be made in a complex bodily movement to fit in appropriately with what another player or dancer may unexpectedly do. This is the kind of skill that coaches seek to enhance.

Sternberg: But wouldn't such a view imply that *bodily* defects (such as those resulting from cerebral palsy, for example) were forms of *mental* retardation?

Gardner: I don't think so. My Theory does imply, of course, that a person who lacks certain skills—who is physically rather uncoordinated, or tone deaf, for example—is weak in one or other of the intelligences. But whether such weakness counts as *retardation* is highly culturally relative. For those who have been culturally conditioned, like ourselves, into thinking of mental retardation almost solely in terms of weakness in linguistic and logical mathematical intelligence, it is rather salutary to realise the possibility of a culture in which people are primarily evaluated for their musical or artistic skill. In fact, just because societies change, evaluations of skills do too. What reason would we now have for valuing highly the massive feats of linguistic memory so prized before books were widely available? And, perhaps, if computers do absorb more and more of the domain in which linguistic and mathematical skills are exercised, our own society may evolve into one where artistic skills *are* the most highly valued because computers handle everything else!

Perkins: Finally, let us consider our fourth question: What makes Dr. Gardner's theory interesting to people. For some, the Theory resonates with an existing concern or agenda; for example, to decrease the use of conventional testing in schools. For others, the theory may create dissonance because it is not consistent with a view of the world to which they are committed. These reactions to the Theory seem to be independent of any considered, "scientific," assessment of the its logical coherence and evidential support. What view should we take of such reactions?

Baron: I have two observations to make here. One reason why Gardner's Theory appeals is that it allows everyone too be good at something. (This is a feature of any theory that doesn't postulate a strong general intelligence, *g*, factor.) Yet Gardner's Theory also has significant nativist components: it postulated a predisposed potential in each of the seven areas that cannot be altered (though, of course, it can be elicited) by environmental features. And, for some people, that is threatening. If intelligence, or the intelligence*s*, are significantly innately constituted, people suspect that it really doesn't matter what teachers do, and a kind of fatalism results.

Perkins: Is there anything wrong with promoting a theory because you find it appealing, or neglecting it because it makes a hypothesis you dislike?

Sternberg: There is nothing at all wrong with being interested (or uninterested) in a theory for such reasons. But I think it very important to recognise that these are not scientific, but popular, grounds for interest in a theory. This distinction has to be made—but it does not follow that one kind of interest is inherently superior, for they may both have to work together. Theories that are grounded purely in scientific interest obviously risk having no genuine impact, whereas theories that capture the popular imagination for some reason, without having any basis in a scientific concern for evidence and internal coherence, may be seriously misleading and damaging. For example, people may test or train skills irrelevant to intelligence. I think we should be open to the possibility that Gardner's theory is more responsive to popular than to scientific concerns.

Baron: I think we need to consider what we want a theory of intelligence *for.* Sometimes a theory of intelligence functions as an ideology for educational practice. If this is what a theory is to be used for, it may be wise to be cautious in drawing conclusions about innate capacities and the ages when they become apparent. For example, consider a hypothesis that holds that unless a certain talent is manifest by the age of two, it isn't there. If this theory is acted on, *and it's mistaken,* then not only will some children with the talent be deprived of the opportunity to develop it, but the evidence that would falsify the theory will never have the chance to emerge. On the other hand, acting on a mistakenly generous assumption about how long the talent may take to appear, will at worst mean wasted effort—that might, anyway, be counterbalanced by the fact that this course of action may generate the kind of evidence that may be used to improve the theory. Thus, a cost-benefit analysis needs to be done if a theory is held for this purpose. Then there are other purposes: A theory of intelligence might be wanted to enable the selection of people for different educational tracks, and then a more "scientific" theory will be needed. Or the point of the theory might be to find out how intelligence can be taught. And a theory developed for this purpose might be quite different, placing emphasis on discovering what processes can be controlled. Indeed, I myself have tried to develop such a theory (Baron, 1985), without wanting to claim that it can serve any of the other purposes at all.

Perkins: Let me give Dr. Gardner the last word on this issue of what makes theories attractive. Howard, do you like your theory?

Gardner: I'll try not to be too self-serving! One thing that has, I think, attracted people to *Frames of Mind* is that it is rich in examples drawn from many different parts of the world. People were ready, I think, for a book that brings in a very diverse range of evidence: many of the cases from other cultures intrigued people, such as that of the Pulawat sailors, for instance. And perhaps the fact that the Theory is seriously rooted in Biology also gives it a certain *éclat.*

Perkins: How about the fact that it's nonmathematical?

Gardner: Perhaps that is a factor—but I didn't have it in mind. I was going to mention Margaret Mead's remark that; "every 10 years the American community needs a new educational plaything, and it doesn't really matter what it is." A cynical view might be that my book is just such a plaything. But I do think it hasn't been a *mere* plaything: there has been a helpful aspect to it that surprised me. Of all the groups who showed interest in the book, those who showed the most have been people with connections in the independent schools, where teachers aren't quite so pressured, where there's sometimes a little extra money for projects, and where there is an *idiographic* interest—an interest in responding more to each individual student's abilities and going beyond the basic skills that have so mesmerized the public schools. For MI Theory itself is idiographic: It allows room for lots of individual intelligence profiles, and enables people to make connextions with their existing grasp of just how widely the people they know differ in their skills and potential.

REFERENCES

Baron, J. (1985). *Rationality and intelligence*. New York: Cambridge University Press.
Block, N., & Dworkin, G. (1976). *The IQ controversy*. New York: Pantheon.
Bloom, B. (Ed.). (1984). *Developing talent in young people*. New York: Bantam.
Dorner, D., & Kreutzig, H. (1983). Problemlosefahigkeit und intelligenz. *Psychologische Rundschau, 34*, 185–192.
Feldman, D. (1986). *Nature's gambit*. New York: Basic Books.
Fodor, J. A. (1983). *The modularity of mind*. Cambridge, MA: MIT Press.
Gardner, H. (1976). *The shattered mind*. New York: Vintage.
Gardner, H. (1983). *Frames of mind*. New York: Basic Books.
Gould, S. J. (1980). *The mismeasure of man*. New York: Norton.
Guilford, J. P., & Hoepfner, R. (1971). *The analysis of intelligence*. New York: McGraw–Hill.
Gupta, B. S. (1977). Dextroamphetamines and measures of intelligence. *Intelligence, 1*, 274–280.
Halberstam, D. (1972). *The best and the brightest*. New York: Random House.
Hayes, J. R. (1985). Three problems in teaching general skills. In S. F. Chipman, J. W. Segal, & R. Glaser (Eds.), *Thinking and learning skills, Vol. 2, Research and open questions* (pp. 391–405). Hillsdale, NJ: Lawrence Erlbaum Associates.
Kagan, J., & Kogan, N. (1970). Individual variation in cognitive process. In P. H. Mussen (Ed.), *Carmichael's manual of child psychology* (Vol. 1). New York: Wiley.
LeVine, R., & White, M. (1986). *Human conditions: the cultural basis of educational development*. Boston: Routledge & Kegan Paul.
Machado, L. A. (1980). *The right to be intelligent*. New York: Pergamon Press.
Marland, S. P., Jr. (1971). *Education of the gifted and talented* (2 Vols.). Washington, DC: U.S. Government Printing Office.
Piechowski, M. M. (1979). Developmental potential. In N. Colangelo & R. T. Zaffrann (Eds.) *New voices in counselling the gifted* (pp. 25–57). Dubuque, Iowa: Kendall-Hunt.
Scheffler, Israel. (1985). *Of human potential*. Boston: Routledge & Kegan Paul.
Spearman, C. (1927). *The abilities of man: Their nature and measurement*. New York: Macmillan.
Sternberg, R. J. (1977). *Intelligence, information processing, and analogical reasoning: The componential analysis of human abilities*. Hillsdale, NJ: Lawrence Erlbaum Associates.

Sternberg, R. J. (1985). *Beyond IQ: A triarchic theory of human intelligence.* New York: Cambridge University Press.

Thurstone, L. L. (1938). Primary mental abilities. *Psychometric Monographs, 1.*

Walters, J., & Gardner, H. (1986). Crystallizing experiences. In R. Sternberg, & J. Davidson (Eds.), *Conceptions of giftednesses.* New York: Cambridge University Press.

White, M., & Pollak, S. (Eds.). (1986). *The cultural transition: Human experience and social transformations in the third world and Japan.* Boston: Routledge & Kegan Paul.

6 Ellipsis and Ideology

E. P. Brandon
University of the West Indies, Jamaica

> *The* periphrasis, *or circumlocution, is the peculiar talent of country farmers; . . . the* ellipsis, *or speech by half-words, of ministers and politicians.*[1]

The study of thinking, and of how to improve thinking, sometimes focuses on fairly technical, formalizable issues such as have been studied by logicians, and, at other times, on extremely diffuse problems raised by ordinary argument, propaganda, advertizing, or ideology. There are few bridges between these kinds of concern. I lay the foundations for one such bridge in this chapter. I try to show that the notion of ellipsis as used in philosophical analysis can be fruitfully applied in the sociological study of ideology. Ideology is not only to be studied; it is, I believe, to be exposed. I hope that sensitizing people to ellipses can contribute to this exposure of ideological obfuscation, but I do not show this now—my examples may, however, suggest some of the possibilities.

Ellipsis

The notion of ellipsis is in fact something of a dark horse in the philosophical stable. It is used by various authors in different contexts, but no one, to be best of my knowledge, has ever examined it carefully and thor-

---

[1]"Martinus Scriblerus" *The Art of Sinking in Poetry* (ch. XIII).

oughly.[2] It would appear that philosophers have borrowed it from grammar and stylistics without much attention either to its use there or to the ramfications of its philosophical employment. But it can be made philosophically respectable, at least for the purposes of critical logical analysis.

Very roughly, one could say that traditional examples of ellipsis fall into two distinct groups, with a more contentious set of cases that fall between the two main groups. I label the two main sorts of ellipsis *grammatical* and *semantic*, the contentious kind will be called *structural*. In all cases, the root idea of ellipsis is of "words understood," components of a sentence that have been omitted but that must be understood to be there. One difference between the three groups lies in the motivation for supposing that something has been left out. It should be obvious that the root idea of words understood is very unspecific, but I think some uses of the notion can be illuminating.

Examples of grammatical ellipses arise from two main sources: dialogue, and some compressed grammatical structures. Thus if I ask *How did you get here?* you might well reply simply by saying *By bus*, which would have to be understood as elliptical for something like *I got here by bus*. In general it is clear that a context of dialogue allows, indeed often requires, a certain amount of such rule-governed ellipsis, in which what would otherwise not be counted as grammatical sentences can stand as complete utterances.

What I am calling compressed grammatical structures are a mixed bunch whose members depend in part on one's grammatical theory. A few examples should give a feel for this sort of ellipsis, though different authorities might not accept all of the following (I indicate the position of the elided component by writing / /): *Mary's car is faster than John's / /; He said / / I might stay; No one can / / or will refuse;* or, for a literary example, *The court of Arcadius indulged the zeal / /, applauded the eloquence / /, and neglected the advice, of Synesius.*[3]

Another type of ellipsis that I want to group along with these grammatical cases, although it is in fact a question of semantics, arises from the dropping of an obvious qualification. Thus *a daily* is in origin and in meaning *a daily newspaper;* and a group of lawyers would naturally interpret talk of *an action* in a way different from a group of philosophers.

I want to group all these types of ellipsis together as grammatical because they are philosophically uninteresting. Talk of ellipsis here is motivated largely by appeal to paradigmatic sentence types that can be

---

[2]The discussion in this section draws on ideas and material documented in my paper, "Ellipsis: History and Prospects," to appear in *Informal Logic.*

[3]Edward Gibbon *The Decline and Fall of the Roman Empire,* ch. XXX. The ordinary examples were suggested by the article on ellipsis in Fowler (1983).

deformed or *contracted* (Matthews' term for my *compressed*, 1981, p. 42) in various circumstances. In general the omissions are obvious, that is why it is often pedantic to draw attention to them. This is not to say that these kinds of ellipsis are uninteresting for linguistics; the pity is that they are of limited extralinguistic concern—they are not likely to reveal very much in the study of thinking or of value formation or indeed of the semantic side of language itself. And so the focus on these types of ellipsis detracts from the value, for our purposes, of, for instance, Lyons' survey of semantics (1977) or Sandell's studies of linguistic style and persuadability (1977).[4]

Besides noting grammatical ellipses, the traditional study of language has also stressed the fact that people leave a lot unsaid, that the context of utterance contributes a very great deal to the meaning of what is said. In logic, Aristotle noticed that people often leave whole premises unstated, yielding enthymemes; in stylistics, Quintilian observed that many incomplete sentences (such as *If you don't stop talking, I'll. . . .*) require detailed knowledge of the context of utterance to be deciphered. Coming to more recent times, Jespersen (1924) can speak for many in his discussion of what he called *suppression:*

> As in the structure of compounds, so also in the structure of sentences much is left to the sympathetic imagination of the hearer, and what from the point of view of the trained thinker, or the pedantic schoolmaster, is only part of an utterance, is frequently the only thing said, and the only thing required to make the meaning clear to the hearer. (p. 309)

It is this tradition that philosophers have taken over, without noticing how far it diverges from the sort of grammatical ellipsis the stricter grammarians were prepared to accept, and without trying to pin it down by specifying how one should find or fill in this sort of ellipsis and what its boundaries might be (cf. Goffman, 1981, p. 67, for a similar criticism from another viewpoint—the whole of Goffman's first chapter is a lucid demonstration of the complexities of contextual and grammatical ellipsis in conversation).

Before showing what I think is the viable component in the philosophers' appropriation of semantic ellipsis, let me mention the category I labelled *structural* ellipsis because it too may have inspired some of the philosophical adaptations. Very roughly, many different grammatical

---

[4]In his experiments Sandell takes ellipsis simply to be grammatical ellipsis but in his discussions he notes that "style may be conducive to persuasion by confusing the cognitive powers of the receiver" (p. 154) and refers to work by Hansen, in Danish and unavailable to me, on the way in which a standard of comparison is often left unstated: points that cohere with the characterization I use of semantic ellipsis.

theories have wanted to analyze certain constructions as involving more or less obligatory deletions of grammatical units. So some have wanted to see *What I said was true* as reflecting an underlying *That which I said was true,* or again *I want to visit Paris* as involving something like *I want that I visit Paris.* One obvious danger in such approaches is to evade the falsification of grammatical claims: If you really want all sentences to have a subject or a finite verb, it can be too easily arranged by appeal to this sort of ellipsis. But despite the dangers, grammarians cannot seem to do without some appeals to ellipses of this kind. (Thus Jespersen 1924, pp. 103–4 is critical of Sweet, but is prodigal with his own kind of structural ellipsis in what he calls a *nexus,* p. 143; for more recent discussion see Allerton, 1975, and Matthews, 1981, ch. 8.) Although these kinds of analysis have close links with logical analyses, in linguistics they are inspired by grammatical theory, not logical theory, and so, despite their fascination, they do not often raise philosophically interesting issues.

What, then, are the philosophers getting at when they talk of ellipsis? It is not, I think, any and every omission from what is said. Indeed, any attempt to capture those would lead to chaos because there is always something more that could be said. A useful notion of ellipsis must be kept distinct from the general idea of lack of specificity. The useful notion focuses on those items that have not been stated and that are not part of the ordinary workings of proper names or token-reflexives but that are necessary for the truth-value of what is said to be determined. Filling in such an ellipsis allows us to give a determinate sense, true or false, to what was previously an indeterminate claim. Such a view can be found in the following two representative quotations from philosophers, Keynes (1921) and Platts (1979), who have explicitly talked about ellipsis:

> When in ordinary speech we name some opinion as probable without further qualification, the phrase is generally elliptical. We mean that it is probable when certain considerations, implicitly or explicitly present to our minds at the moment, are taken into account. We use the word for the sake of shortness, just as we speak of a place being three miles distant, when we mean three miles distant from where we are then situated, or from some starting-point to which we tacitly refer.(Keynes, 1921, p. 7)

> Until we know, or form beliefs about, the appropriate filling, we have no complete understanding of these sentences. We know (up to a point) the meanings of the words they contain, and (perhaps) their syntactic structure; but we have no idea *which* conditions would make the sentences true or false. (Platts, 1979, p. 168)

As may perhaps be obvious, these brief characterizations do not settle everything. I am, for instance, inclined to disagree with Platts about one of his examples, *Rudy is attractive*. As he says, Rudy may be attractive as a ballet dancer or as a dinner guest, and the bare sentence does not tell us how. But rather than see this as ellipsis, I would see it as closer to a kind of lack of specificity created by attaching an existential quantification to a predicate: *Rudy is married* is perfectly determinate because *married* means *married to someone,* and similarly one might wish to analyze *attractive* as *attractive in some respect*. But it is not peculiar to judgments of ellipsis that they depend on one's wider theoretical framework.

In semantic ellipsis something is left out that must be replaced for anything determinately true or false to be said. In many cases the elided element is very obvious and can be easily recovered. If your car chugs to a halt with the fuel gauge reading 'empty' and you say *It needs some gas,* it does not take much perspicacity to realize that it needs gas to start going again. In other cases the elided element may be so taken for granted that it is unobvious: Swinburne (1968) argues that a claim like *Kingston is 60 miles from Ocho Rios* omits mention of a frame of reference that is necessary for measuring distance and for identifying places. It takes an Einstein to reveal some of our ellipses.

But the kind of case that most concerns me is different from either of the previous. In those cases there is something quite definite elided, something that is either immediately available to the people concerned or deeply hidden in a shared framework of assumptions. But the cases of ellipsis that are most important for proponents of clearer thinking do not necessarily involve anything definite; rather the elliptical sentences accurately reflect an indeterminate meaning. Their users do not have anything definite in mind, although the language appears to keep them afloat. In such a context the philosopher's appeal to ellipsis is more a critical move than a description of what people have in mind. As Sloman (1970) said, it is "less important here to give a strictly accurate account of what people actually do say than to suggest what they might say if only they knew how" (p. 394). So when, for instance, educators say that we need to encourage creativity, no one has a clear idea of what end this might achieve (if indeed they have any clear idea of the means being advocated). Whereas in the case of the empty gas tank language allows us not to be pedantic, here the same linguistic resources allow the perpetuation of intellectual smog.[5]

---

[5]See my 1980 for a detailed discussion of the verb *to need*. Because I have mentioned the possiblity that there can be implicit existential quantifications, it might be worth spelling out why that solution will not work here. Very simply it is because *A needs X for some end or other* (instead of the elliptical analysis *A needs X for Y*) will always be true, whereas we treat claims about needs as easily falsifiable. But for *I need a bottle of Lafite every day* to be false, we must be assuming some restrictions on the possible fillers of the *Y* slot; to live in the manner I aspire to it is true that I need Lafite in virtually endless amounts.

Ellipsis and the Reproduction of Ideology

Although the topic of ellipsis may not have received much attention from philosophical logicians, discussions of ideology could fill libraries. Rather than enter into debates about the most useful notion of ideology, I simply record the conception I use, as Mackie (1975) states it:

> An ideology is a system of concepts, beliefs, and values which is character-
> istic of some social class (or perhaps of some other social group, perhaps
> even of a whole society), and in terms of which the members of that class
> (etc.) see and understand their own position in and relation to their social
> environment and the world as a whole, and explain, evaluate, and justify
> their actions, and especially the activities and policies characteristic of their
> class (etc.). (p. 185)

It is essential to this conception that "at least some of the beliefs and concepts in the system are false, distorted, or slanted" (ibid.) although this certainly does not mean that everything in an ideology is false or distorted; indeed, as Mackie argues, there are good reasons to think that a fair amount will be simply true. It is also essential that an ideology be in some group's interests; it will in general contribute somehow to the group's flourishing. In the primary case, the group in question will be the group that subscribes to the ideology, but it is also possible for other groups to adopt an ideology that is contrary to their own interests although supporting the interests of some other group.

The question I ask of ideologies as Mackie portrays them is how they persist. They are cognitive systems, value systems, in some respects false or distorted, that are expressed and transmitted, in part at least, in language. They give an account of reality, but they also conceal it; they promote partial interests, but they have an air of obviousness or natural-ness about them. How is the trick played?

There is of course no reason to expect a single answer to this question. Ideologies are made up of diverse elements, as are their false or distorted parts, and the mechanisms whereby they are appropriated are almost certainly going to be diverse too. Mackie (1975) suggests, for instance, that the way facts and values are intertwined in much of our language contributes a great deal to the transmission and reception of ideology:

> A system of concepts, beliefs and values will be more stable and more
> effective in controlling and justifying conduct if the evaluative aspect is
> wrapped up in the concepts and beliefs, if those who have the ideology see
> things-as-they-are as exerting certain pressures on them. Slanting the news
> reports is a more potent form of propaganda than printing a rousing editorial
> alongside a neutral and objective report. (p. 195)

And in a famous phrase, Stevenson has pointed to the way "persuasive definitions" can exploit the semantic lack of specificity of many widely used terms while retaining their emotional or evaluative aura (1963, ch. 3). I suggest that semantic ellipsis is another and often distinct route for the transmission of ideology.

Before looking at some possible examples, let us review the proposed mechanism of ideological reproduction. Elliptical sentences (as always from now on, these are cases of what I have labelled *semantic ellipsis)* are perfectly grammatical. They therefore do not call attention to themselves. As has been noted, such sentence types are very often unambiguous and determinate in context because everyone in that context knows perfectly well how to bridge the gap that has been elided. They therefore look like perfectly meaningful sentences. Even when participants are unable to specify precisely what has been omitted, they can often think of possible plausible fillings, or of particular instances in which the claim seems true, or they may merely suppose that there must be some such cases. I label these attempts to restore some of the elided content "particularizations." They might be exemplified in the case of the earlier sentence *We need to encourage creativity* by thoughts such as *If we want more interesting television shows, we should encourage creativity,* or remembering a relative's child, *If John's urge to draw abstract designs hadn't been frustrated by his teacher, he might not have dropped out of school,* or utterly unspecifically, *We're sure to have a better society if there was more creativity.* None of these help to specify what the original claim might mean, nor do they confirm or disconfirm it, but I suggest these, or thoughts like them, can help people think that they really have understood something definite in the original claim, and something moreover that is true. With such particularizations to back them up, the elliptical claims are easily accepted as part of one's stock of "knowledge." But because, as we shall soon see, what is elided is very often the main bearer of evaluative weight, agreement and commitment can be obtained for the speaker's values and aims without him ever having to specify what these are, much less defend them.

Let us see how this is meant to work. Take a typical child at school. People can be easily persuaded that woodwork or plumbing (or designing computer software) is relevant for him (if not for her), although playing the piano or studying Tacitus is irrelevant. But a little reflection reveals that *X is relevant/irrelevant for A* is semantically elliptical: to decide whether a subject is relevant to a person (these are the givens of this example) we have to add some kind of end or purpose. Plumbing is relevant if you want to be able to fix the toilet or if we want to cut down on professional plumbers, but almost certainly not if you want to be a classical philologist. When we specify to what something is relevant, we have a question of truth or falsehood (though it might be difficult to answer or still be somewhat vague). Before we specify the end, we are floundering, although many people seem blissfully unaware of their predicament.

Although the full claim, *X is relevant for A to achieve F,* expresses a matter of fact, there is often also an evaluative issue waiting in the wings. Typically, we would only be asking whether X is relevant for A in the light of our commitment to some values of F. Our values, our aims, fit into the F slot, but it is this slot that is normally elided. Even if we do use the full form, we are not thereby stating that F is to be pursued; the evaluation is implicit in the context of utterance—I would not normally waste your time telling you what is relevant to achieving F, G, and H unless there were a live issue of whether you should aim for them, but a value position is not part of what the claim means.

The factors that are in fact valued tend to be omitted. Claims are accepted because particularizations can be found. Thus, given the present situation of our pupil, there is a fair chance that he will need to fix the toilet or a tap, so learning how to do so is relevant for him; whereas he is not likely to want, or to be called on, to play a piano. As far as likely present roles go, the one is relevant, the other irrelevant. So the claims, thus particularized, are plausible. But because the particularization is tacit, it is not brought out into the open so that people can recognize that it refers to present roles rather than to the likely, or merely possible, roles a person may play several years or decades down the line. Nor can it be seen to ignore the various other aims a person concerned for education might set the school system.

I have tried to show how talk of relevance is elliptical in a potentially damaging way (in general agreement with Barrow, 1981, pp. 34–7, although we differ on the precise place of the evaluations). Elsewhere I have done the same for talk of needs (1980) and equality (1984), and I have shown that the quantificational indeterminacy which language permits can wreak havoc even with very careful thinking (1982a). Talk of responsibility (cf. Mackie, 1955) or opportunity is equally elliptical, with the result that much time and energy is wasted pursuing indeterminate issues couched in these terms. Perhaps the importance both of the issue and of ellipsis as I see it will permit us to glance at one more area, that of freedom.

The abstract noun *freedom* allows us to note an important source of lack of specificity that is related to the grammarian's structural ellipsis. Such abstract nouns are best understood as transformations from their related predicate expressions, in this case *is free.* Semantically this predicate is elliptical for *is free to V,* and such an infinitive phrase can quite easily be inserted when the predicate is used. But although it is still possible, it is not so natural to insert the infinitive phrase when one moves to the abstract noun. One can talk of freedom to *V* or of the freedom to *W,* but neither are so quick off the tongue as the simple *freedom.*

But if this suggested analysis is on the right lines, all talk of freedom or of a free society is elliptical; determinate sense can only be given to *freedom to V* or *freedom to W.* This ellipsis permits political rhetoric to try to conceal the facts that these specific freedoms are often not widely shared, perhaps not obviously beneficial, nor obviously compatible with other desirable goals (including other freedoms); it tries to restrict us to virtually empty but rousing talk of freedom *simpliciter.* It is amazing, for one with a faith in rational argument, to observe the endless debate about the supposed incompatibility of freedom and equality, when both these terms are full of holes and there are only determinate (and often easily answerable) questions about whether the freedom to *V* on the part of *A* is compatible with an equality between *A* and *B* with respect to *F* (for generally good sense here see Carritt, 1940, and Norman, 1982).[6]

The political ideology of freedom exploits an obvious ellipsis. But there is also a more diffuse ideology of metaphysical freedom, which can be illuminated by reference to ellipsis. For this, I suggest we dig a little deeper into talk of being free to uncover the negative skeleton of all talk of freedom, ability, and its simple associate, the modal auxiliary verb *can.* The point of talking of a negative skeleton is that a claim like *I can drive a car* is to be understood as saying that *There is no obstacle to my driving a car.* Some such analysis is by now fairly popular (cf. Graham, 1977, pp. 254–255). To find the ellipsis, we have to notice that obstacles come in various kinds—there are sheer physical obstacles (our anatomy is such that we cannot fly like birds; we cannot have breakfast in London and lunch on Mars; etc.); there are obstacles created by normal, though not invariable patterns of behaviour; there are legal obstacles; there are moral obstacles; there are logical obstacles. Usually when we talk about what we can or cannot do, about our freedoms, we presume that we are talking with reference to some such obstacle field. Perhaps, given that field, there was no obstacle to my doing what I did nor to my doing any number of

---

[6]Keith Graham, to whom I am endebted for comments on this chapter, has suggested that the standard issue of freedom *from* ought to be mentioned here. I am inclined to see *John is free from X* as a way of saying that *X* is not an obstacle to John's doing whatever it is. All talk of freedom involves agents, actions (types or tokens), and obstacles. In stressing freedom *from* one stresses particular obstacles instead of generalizing about them as one does in talking of freedom *to.* But in focusing on obstacles, one typically glosses over the actions in question. My point in the text is that the only determinate questions for politics are about specifiable sets of obstacles, agents, and actions. Both our normal ways of talking about freedom (*to* or *from*) typically leave at least one of these three constituents unspecified.

other things—I could well have done otherwise. But when the determinist affirms that in fact I couldn't have done otherwise (which apparently contradicts our ordinary belief), he invokes a quite unusual obstacle field, viz. the sum of all obstacle fields, the whole universe. With respect to all the obstacles there might be, the determinist may be right, but his claim is compatible with our ordinary common sense when this is interpreted as elliptically referring to some much more homely field of obstacles (cf. Mackie, 1982, p. 167). Dr. Johnson's assurance that our will is free is thus sustained by the generally elliptical invocation of a limited range of obstacles.

I have concentrated on pointing to ways in which ellipsis helps to perpetuate error or acquiescence; but very little in this world is that simple. The lack of specificity due to elision can be exploited on behalf of the poor and the oppressed. Not only are fillings opposed to the dominant fillings possible, but the mere elliptical notion can contain a standing invitation to find such fillings; it has, as it were, some power of its own that can be used in the fight of truth and justice against the deadweight of unthinking privilege. Thus, although admitting that an ideological appeal to equality can gloss over practically any situation, Corbett (1965) adds that to use it at all:

> is to accept a point of substance; it is to accept, at least, the relevance of asking, in any practical situation, whether there may not be some respect in which the people in question should not be treated more similarly than they are; it is to be prompted to look for respects that have been overlooked, and others that are new. (p. 181)

Rationality and the Persistence of Ideology

Many students of society have written at great length on ideology. I am not alone in thinking that these students have not in general paid much attention to the precise mechanisms whereby ideologies are perpetuated. In a fairly recent discussion Kellner (1978) said that "the sociology of knowledge . . . showed astoundingly little interest in any detailed study of the structure and mechanisms of social communication" (p. 325), and Garland's (1981) forthright claim, "there are two central questions one can ask of ideology: what are its origins?; what are its effects?" (p. 128), suggests that sociologists are not going to be overly concerned with my worry about how an ideology manages to stay alive. Although sociolinguistics and sociology are now alive to linguistic problems, they do not seem to pay much attention to the more strictly logical issues I am pointing to. Perhaps the artificiality and formalism of much work in logic has falsely suggested that it has little bearing on how people actually think or on the mechanisms whereby their confusions are perpetuated.

But questions of transmission are, however, of some interest, not only in their own right, but also, in the context of social explanation, because the easy reproduction of ideology seems to clash with the rationality assumptions built into such explanations. The whole question of the degree and kind of rationality implicit in social explanation is too large and controversial to tackle here, but I think it would be generally agreed that we assume other people share with us a physical environment, some of whose ways of working they grasp as well as we do, and that we assume they act, in general, to achieve their purposes. However weird and wonderful some of their ideas and practices may be, there must be some such core (not necessarily the same in every case) of shared world and minimal rationality. This further implies that people can, in some measure, distinguish truths from falsehoods and better from worse arguments or reasons. But of course it does not mean that they must be able to pontificate in the second-order style of logical appraisal, although in fact many people can do so. More needs to be said to square these remarks with the truths contained in talk of "theory-laden" observations and elsewhere that beckon the unwary into the quagmire of a general relativism, but this is not the place to say it. All I need now is agreement that we must attribute some minimal good sense and rationality to our fellows in order to understand them at all. How much more we attribute seems as much a matter of temperament as of empirical evidence—it may be worth remembering here that good sense in one area is compatible with utter credulity in another—so I only note that the problem this chapter addresses arises more insistently the more rationality one accords people. It is perhaps only worth raising if one thinks people fairly sensible.

Outside the religious area, or rather the theological portion thereof, beliefs are within reach of evidence, proposals can be seen to have consequences. So falsehood, gross distortion, and gross partiality ought not to survive, especially when their contents have a central importance in people's lives. But error, distortion, and partiality are precisely the raison d'etre of secular (and of course also religious) ideologies. There is a strong temptation to see people who wholeheartedly accept such ideologies as radically incapacitated, dupes of a false consciousness from which they can only be awakened, if at all, by the stern voice of a miraculously clear-sighted authority. But if it can be shown that the beliefs in question are held in accordance with general principles of evidence and inference, then we can perhaps hope that a man who cannot, in the miasma of ideology, tell a hawk from a handsaw, could yet do so when the hidden is made visible, and do so on the basis of intellectual skills he already possesses.

The task is, then, to give a certain amount of logical respectability to our normal dealings with elliptical claims, our normal talk about needs, equality, responsibility, and so on. Semantic ellipsis permits fallacies of equivocation, but the mere fact that it is semantic ellipsis—so that the sentences used are perfectly grammatical—allows such shifts of meaning to be hidden. Because one can reason quite happily with symbols or nonsense words or approximations to grammatical sentences, elliptical claims can figure in arguments without appearing to malfunction.

Elliptical claims are protected by another pervasive feature of our thinking: the tacit qualification of often tacit general principles. Even when we do rise to explicitly saying something of the form *All A are B,* we rarely mean it: *everyone* usually conveys a much less straightforward quantification, everyone in our kind of society, perhaps, or most people we have met, or typical people, or everyone except children, idiots, and peers of the realm (cf. Hodges, 1977, pp. 191–197). Similarly, principles or maxims are not usually to be taken literally. Given that one can infer from *Some A are B* to *All AX are B,* where the *X* slot stands ready to receive enough qualifications to make the inference valid, qualifications of the sort that would normally be left unsaid, the fact that one can very often find what I earlier called particularizations to support elliptical claims means that one can much too readily assume that such particularizations have validated the general elliptical claim.

Although one must admit that these general, and inescapable, features of our thinking may sometimes excuse what might appear fallacious, it must also be acknowledged that people do not do very well on the overall consistency of their beliefs, nor do they recognize simple fallacies as well as they can follow valid arguments (cf. Ennis, 1981; Nolan & Brandon, 1984). But the point remains that semantic ellipsis, and its errors, trade on generally acceptable thinking strategies. The resulting confusions need not be a sign of irremediable incapacity; one might even hope that they can be recognized for what they are with a little mental therapy.

The Contribution of Ellipsis to Ideological Explanations

In the preceding section I claimed that the persistence of ideology needs explaining, preferably as a quasirational process, and that the prevalence of semantic ellipsis can assist us in that task. To substantiate those abstract claims, I propose now to take a few remarks about ideology and to indicate briefly how ellipsis could help to round them out. In taking these examples, I am not necessarily endorsing their accuracy; I am only concerned with them now as typical of remarks made by students of ideology.

My first examples come from some recent essays by Michael Apple (1979), which typify much recent work in the sociology of education. At one point he claims that hegemony requires fundamental agreements at a tacit level, which are transmitted by his version of the "hidden curriculum":

> The controversies usually exhibited in schools concern choices *within* the parameters of implicitly held rules of activity. Little attempt is made to focus on the parameters themselves. The hidden curriculum in schools serves to reinforce basic rules surrounding the nature of conflict and its uses. It posits a network of assumptions that, when internalized by students, establishes the boundaries of legitimacy. This process is accomplished . . . by nearly the total absence of instances showing the importance of intellectual and normative conflict in subject areas. The fact is that these assumptions are obligatory for the students, since at no time are the assumptions articulated or questioned. (p. 87)

Although Apple's own example concerns the routinization of subjects as uncontentious bodies of knowledge by the school system, his way of talking and his later references to "social norms" learnt "by coping with the day to day encounters and tasks of classroom life" clearly suggest the relevance of the kind of insinuation of values by means of ellipsis that we looked at earlier. The factors that carry the evaluative weight, that set the terms of the debate, tend to be elided and so are imposed without being noticed. They thus easily become natural or obvious, exemplifying once again what Bourdieu and Passeron (1977) style the traditionalism of most schooling, its refusal to enunciate its own ground rules.

In several other places Apple notices the prevalence of tacit assumptions (cf. p. 34, p. 83, p. 125f) and our resulting tendency not to question the framework of debate (cf. my account of our moral thinking in similar terms, 1979, 1982b), but he does not tell us how the cognitive resources we use aid and abet these restrictions. Semantic ellipsis surely helps. It contributes to an explanation of his claim that: "The orientations which so predominate curriculum and educational theory . . . effectively obscure and often deny the profound ethical and economic issues educators face" (p. 149). It also helps to explain, and make consistent with the stress on the tacit nature of ideology, another point Apple makes: ideological rhetoric is fairly explicit and systematic about what *can* be agreed on (p. 21f). Ellipsis allows an audience to particularize claims so that each person can accept them, but no one need ever ask whether my way of accepting them is consistent with yours; we all subscribe to the same elliptical claim unaware of the yawning chasms that separate what we have in fact accepted. Semantic ellipsis can be added to the list of ways in which, "where claims are vacuous, vague, imprecise, ambiguous and generally unclear, conflicts are likely to be minimized and go unnoticed" (Naish, Hartnett, & Finlayson, 1976, p. 99).

One other point Apple makes is that ideological categories tend to be "essentializing" (p. 135). This seems analogous to the way in which ellipsis can encourage false belief in absolutes when the realities are relative. Apple's examples, "slow learner," "discipline problem," may not all involve ellipsis, and his point may not be exactly the same as mine, but there are parallels; and it is perhaps worth noting that a slow learner is presumably a slow learner of A and B but not necessarily of everything the school might have on offer.

One writer who has focused on the transmission of ideology is Trevor Pateman (1980). One of his more controversial suggestions is that many people simply lack the conceptual structure required to handle political or social debate (ch. V). One might hope to sidestep the general question of who has what conceptual resources by noting that many of the interrelated terms in question (freedom; responsibility; authority; . . .) are usually used elliptically. The result is a very diffuse conceptual foam, in which these terms connect with each other but with many gaps. It is not surprising that people easily get lost and find it hard to hold onto occasional insights. (I have already adverted to the sorry state of debate about equality and liberty among people who are not obviously among Pateman's incapacitated workers or children.)

The fluidity of the standard terms of political debate is a constant theme in Nigel Harris' discussion of ideology (1971). His metaphors and comments continually invite a gloss in terms of semantic ellipsis, as I have explained it previously. Thus in talking of the move from equality to equality of opportunity he says:

> Very little remains of a concept thus subject to the acid of political debate in which at least one side finds it useful to redefine the other side's basic demands so that they become unobjectionable. What does remain is a blur, in which anyone can identify with the concept on nearly any grounds, even though the grounds on which two people identify with the same concept are mutually contradictory. (p. 24)

But one cannot in general redefine someone's words and get away with it—whatever Humpty Dumpty might have said—though in politics it keeps happening. I suggest that it is not so much that equality is redefined into submission, but that it is elliptical from the start, so that it only retains its force when people remember to specify which respects they are really interested in; if that happened, and also if one remembered to ask which opportunities were in question, people might not find themselves so easily driven into what are often emasculated notions of equal opportunities.

Again, in discussing the intellectual sin of taking remarks out of context, Harris (1971) adverts to the very features that encourage both grammatical ellipsis at one level and ideologically powerful semantic ellipsis at another:

> The logic of debate disciplines, reshapes and, indeed, creates the positions of an ideology, even though the essence of those positions derives from a given social situation. That social situation is also crucial for understanding the ideology, for people do not at all have the same perception of events: a flat disc may appear circular from one position, but a thin strip from another. (p. 54)[7]

But a remark can only be credibly abused out of context if it leaves a crucial part of its meaning in the context; that is precisely what semantic ellipsis encourages. I suggest that semantic ellipsis provides a plausible answer to the question that frequently arises of how it is possible for ideology, as Harris and others characterize it, to flourish among normally intelligent people. No doubt there is much more to be said, but at least we have one important part of the answer.

Conclusion

I have tried to show that a fairly precise logical notion has a part to play in explaining the workings of ideology. The phenomena to which ellipsis gives a name have been widely noted in philosophical discussions, if not always carefully distinguished from a general lack of specificity; the fact that ideologists trade on confusions, indeterminacies, and other semantic faults is also well known. Semantic notions have indeed been brought to the analysis of ideology before (as in Naish et al., 1976), but I do not know of this precise pairing elsewhere.

One point of stressing this particular mechanism, as indeed of stressing mechanisms at all, is to be better able to counteract ideology. There is a danger that students of ideology and its transmission will characterize it in ways that do not leave any obvious room for common sense to respond critically. How to take arms against mystification so arcanely described? But ordinary people only have common sense, so if that can't provide the intellectual tools, they will not be able to defend themselves intellectually. I stress ellipsis because it is a very simple (no doubt from the standpoints of logic and linguistics, an absurdly oversimple) explanation of the workings of the language in which much potent ideology is embodied. It

---

[7]Lacking the tools I have offered here, Harris' intuitions sometimes let him down—the slide to relativism suggested in the quotation here is endorsed in his final chapter. But it might be worth noting his remarks on Burke (p. 210) for another example of ellipsis allowing one to omit what is evaluatively fundamental—in this case, saying that something served a function but without having to specify what function.

therefore suggests itself as a valuable tool in the promotion of critical rationality.

REFERENCES

Allerton, D. J. (1975). Deletion and proform reduction. *Journal of Linguistics, 11*, 213–237.
Apple, M. W. (1979). *Ideology and curriculum.* London: Routledge & Kegan Paul.
Barrow, R. (1981). *The philosophy of schooling.* Brighton: Wheatsheaf Books.
Bourdieu, P., & Passeron, J. C. (1977). *Reproduction in education, society and culture* (R. Nice, Trans.). London: Sage.
Brandon, E. P. (1979). The key of the door. *Educational Philosophy & Theory, 11*, 23–34.
Brandon, E. P. (1980). O reason not the need. *Education for Development, 6*, 18–25.
Brandon, E. P. (1982a). Quantifiers and the pursuit of truth. *Educational Philosophy & Theory, 14*, 50–58.
Brandon, E. P. (1982b). Radical children. *Access, 1*, 26–32.
Brandon, E. P. (1984). The philosophy in the philosophy of education. *Teaching Philosophy, 7*, 1–15.
Carritt, E. F. (1940). Liberty and equality. *Law Quarterly Review, 56*, 61–74.
Corbett, P. (1965). *Ideologies.* London: Hutchinson.
Ennis, R. H. (1981). A conception of deductive logic competence. *Teaching Philosophy, 4*, 337–385.
Fowler, H. W. (1983). *A dictionary of modern English usage* (rev. ed.). Oxford: Oxford University Press.
Garland, D. (1981). Review of *Marx and Engels on law* by M. Cain & A. Hunt, *Reading ideologies: an investigation into the Marxist theory of ideology and law* by C. Sumner, and *On law and ideology* by P. Hirst. *Sociology, 15*, 127–130.
Goffman, E. (1981). *Forms of talk.* Oxford: Blackwell.
Graham, K. (1977). *J.L. Austin: a critique of ordinary language philosophy.* Atlantic Highlands, NJ: Humanities Press.
Harris, N. (1971). *Beliefs in society.* Harmondsworth: Penguin Books.
Hodges, W. (1977). *Logic.* Harmondsworth: Penguin Books.
Jespersen, O. (1924). *The philosophy of grammar.* London: George Allen & Unwin.
Kellner, H. (1978). On the cognitive significance of the system of language in communication. In T. Luckmann (Ed.), *Phenomenology and sociology.* Harmondsworth: Penguin Books.
Keynes, J. M. (1921). *A treatise on probability.* London: Macmillan.
Lyons, J. (1977). *Semantics* (2 vols.). Cambridge: Cambridge University Press.
Mackie, J. L. (1955). Responsibility and language. *Australasian Journal of Philosophy, 33*, 143–159.
Mackie, J. L. (1975). Ideological explanation. In S. Körner (Ed.), *Explanation.* Oxford: Blackwell.
Mackie, J. L. (1982). *The miracle of theism.* Oxford: Clarendon Press.
Matthews, P. H. (1981). *Syntax.* Cambridge: Cambridge University Press.
Naish, M., Hartnett, A., & Finlayson, D. (1976). Ideological documents in education: Some suggestions towards a definition. In A. Hartnett & M. Naish (Eds.), *Theory and the practice of education* (Vol. 2). London: Heinemann.
Nolan, C., & Brandon, E. P. (Aug. 1984). *Conditional reasoning in Jamaica.* Paper to be presented at the Conference on Thinking, Harvard.

Norman, R. (1982). Does equality destroy liberty? In K. Graham (Ed.), *Contemporary political philosophy*. Cambridge: Cambridge University Press.

Pateman, T. (1980). *Language, truth and politics* (2nd. ed.). Lewes: Jean Stroud.

Platts, M. (1979). *Ways of meaning*. London: Routledge & Kegan Paul.

Sandell, R. (1977). *Linguistic style and persuasion*. London: Academic Press.

Sloman, A. (1970). "Ought" and "better." *Mind, 79*, 385–394.

Stevenson, C. L. (1963). *Facts and values*. New Haven, CT: Yale University Press.

Swinburne, R. (1968). *Space and time*. London: Macmillan.

7 Metaphor and Thinking about Living Systems: Exploring Gregory Bateson's "Men Are Grass" Syllogism

Victor N. Kobayashi
University of Hawaii at Manoa

We live in an unprecedented time in history when the whole world is threatened by destruction. It is not only man who is endangered, but most of the forms of life that we are familiar with, and on which we are dependent for our well-being. The dangers come not only from the threat of a nuclear holocaust, but also from the damage to natural ecological systems through the introduction of new chemicals, and through the widespread destruction of forests and aquatic systems that might escalate into a large scale breakdown of what we know to be an interrelated network of life that constitutes our world environment.

It is because of this crisis that a suggestion of Gregory Bateson needs to be taken seriously. He has proposed that the way we ordinarily think, the way many scientists, businessmen, and political leaders usually think, coupled with the enormously powerful technology that man has developed, has within it fundamental error. Conventional ways of thinking, he has argued, are part of the problem of widespread human alienation and of the breakdown of the world biological ecosystem.

Part of Bateson's criticism of conventional thinking involved questioning logic, which emphasizes subjects, rather than predicates.

In one of his last statements before his death in 1980, Bateson argued that a "syllogism" of the form

> Grass dies.
> Men die.
> Men are grass.

should not be easily dismissed (Bateson, July 1980). We know why such a syllogism would be generally considered invalid; any freshman course in logic would teach us its unreasonableness. This chapter does not pursue the standard arguments for the unacceptability of this "syllogism," but instead takes Bateson's view seriously, and attempts to answer the question, "From what perspective might there be some validity to Bateson's 'grass syllogism'?"

To Bateson the "glass syllogism" reflects the way poets and schizophrenics speak. He admits that he has argued in terms of this "Affirming the Consequent" type syllogism, and then proceeds to defend its use. A conventionally acceptable syllogism would be:

> Men die.
> Socrates is a man.
> Socrates will die.

It involves classes and membership in classes. It identifies Socrates as a member of a class, men, which belongs to a class of those who will die.

Although all of this reasoning is neatly correct, Bateson argues that the "grass syllogism" concerns the relationships of predicates, and that it is not at all concerned about the classification of subjects. When read this way, he asserts, it focuses on the relationships between predicates and as such offers a healthier way of thinking about biological systems, than a view that is preoccupied with subjects and their membership in classes. For Bateson, the grass syllogism comes closer to the "logic" on which the biological world is grounded, as well as on which mental processes are structured. Conventional logic, he suggests, is part of the profound error in man's thinking that has led to the deterioration of the environment upon which we depend for our livelihood.

Metaphor

For Bateson the grass syllogism affirms and embraces metaphor. To say that men are *like* grass in that both forms of life die is not the same as to say that men *are* grass. The former is called a *simile*, the latter a *metaphor*. If we restate the grass syllogism in the form of the simile, where the "metaphor" is pegged down as an analogue, thus annihilating its status as a metaphor, we would all agree that the conclusion is valid:

> Men die.
> Grass dies.
> Men are like grass (in that they both die).

However, it is clear that Bateson means for the "syllogism" to be in metaphoric form, that the conclusion is that "men are grass," and not, "men are like grass."

Metaphoric thinking seems to characterize the way in which prelinguistic mammals think. By this, Bateson means that if we could attribute a statement to what is being communicated by one nonhuman mammal to another, it would take the form of a metaphor. When a cat "meows" and looks up at us when we open the refrigerator door, the cat's communication can be stated as something like "You are mother"—a metaphor, a statement of the cat's relationship to us, which we might then translate into a more conventionally linguistic form, "Give me milk." This translation is pragmatically correct in the sense that giving the cat milk will confirm our interpretation of the cat's meow, but it might be considered presumptuous because we are anthropomorphizing the cat's thinking process and its communicative behavior by attributing to them characteristics that presume that a "meow" and the particular behavior of the cat in this particular context can be directly regarded as having a linguistic structure stripped of metaphor. Bateson argues that the cat's meow is more accurately to us perceived as an invitation to enter into a relationship of being a "mother" to the cat, and we can respond, because we and cats share the common experience of being nurtured by a "mother" figure during our childhood.

Metaphoric thinking also characterizes the way many other animals "think." Bateson (1972) describes the communication of birds as having metaphoric characteristics.

> when a grown-up bird makes like a baby bird in approaching a member of the opposite sex, he's using a metaphor taken from the relationship between child and parent. But he doesn't have to peg down whose relationship he is talking *about*. It's obviously the relationship between himself and the other bird. They're both of them present. (p. 57, emphasis in original)

EMPATHY

As noted previously, *presence* of the two birds in the relationship is part of the context of the metaphoric message. The same would be noted in our relationship to the cat in our earlier example. The meow is in the context of our moment of encounter with the cat, our being in each other's presence. This suggests that the grass syllogism acknowledges its author's "voice," that is, the statement, "Men die" involves people including the author of the statement, and we readers who are invited to participate in its meaning at the moment of our reading or hearing the statement. This point leads me to argue that the truth of the "grass syllogism" seems also to be concerned with the importance of a deep sense of empathy for other forms of life. The meaning of "men are grass" is not that men are "literally" grass, but that the statement expresses a deep empathy for other forms of life; it affirms man's relationship to grass.

Bateson considers empathy, that is seeing what an animal does and comparing it with what it feels like to do the same, an important state of mind, in that it affirms a sense of our kinship with other animals, and an awareness of the "aesthetics of being alive." Such a sensibility and awareness expresses a kind of truth in its assertion of our connectedness to all of life, and to the rest of nature. Bateson's concern for such empathy is revealed in his discussion of totemism in *Mind and Nature*.

Primitive man practiced totemism, which is a religion that is based on an analogy between the social system and the natural world, the world of plants and of animals. Bateson considers totemism as related to this sense and awareness. Bateson (1982) states: "Perhaps the attempt to achieve grace by identification with the animals was the most sensitive thing which was tried in the whole bloody history of religion" (p. 64). Bateson (1980) also states:

> For many peoples, their thinking about the social system of which they are the parts is shaped (literally in-formed) by an analogy between that system of which they *are* the parts and the larger ecological and biological system in which the animals and plants and the people are all parts. The analogy is partly exact and partly fanciful and partly made real—validated—by actions that the fantasy dictates. The fantasy then becomes morphogenetic; that is, it becomes a determinant of the shape of the society. (p. 140, emphasis in original)

The "partly exact" aspect of totemism is for Bateson what is scientific because human relations in totemism are organized to resemble the relationship found in nature, and as biologists today affirm, all living things are connected in an interdependent ecosystem of which man is a part. Note also that Bateson is aware that totemism is also "partly fanciful" and more importantly is "morphogenetic" in that it influences the evolution of a culture: The way human beings perceive the world and their relationship to it has consequences on their actions on the world, and these effects become part of the cultural environment. Because of its "partly exact" aspect, Bateson considered totemism a better way of organizing societal relationships than the modern way, which often uses nineteenth-century machines as the analogue for the way people pattern their social relationships (Bateson, 1980, p. 140). Totemism involved a more holistic view of man's place in the natural environment.

According to Bateson (1980), the degradation of man's relationships to the biological ecosystem began in Europe when totemism degenerated into heraldry. "We can see how ego displaced enlightenment, how the family animals became crests and banners, and how the relations between the animal prototypes in nature got forgotten" (pp. 141–142). The transition to heraldry involved a kind of secularization, a change from the sacredness of man's relationship to the animal world to "a shift of attention away from the relationship to focus [on] *one end* [of the relationship], on the objects or persons who are related" (p. 141, emphasis in original). There is, in other words, a shift from the relationship of predicates to the emphasis on subjects. Man loses the sense that he is one with grass and other animals in abandoning a system of beliefs that invokes that sense. Similarly, Bateson seems to be saying that in the case of conventional logic empathy and its context (presence) are stripped away, because the subjects, rather than the relationship of the predicates, become the focus. Man gains distance from other forms of life (including himself), a gain in a more "objective" view of the world, that becomes a world of things; but there is a corresponding loss of empathy and connectedness and a sense of presence and of "being in the world."

Abduction as Metaphorization

Bateson also considers all human thought ultimately to have its basis in metaphor through a process that he calls *abduction*, which he defines in the following way.

We are so accustomed to the universe in which we live and to our puny methods of thinking about it that we can hardly see that it is, for example, surprising that abduction is possible, that is possible to describe some event or thing (*e.g.*, a man shaving in a mirror) and then to look around the world for other cases to fit the same rules that we devised for our description. We can look at the anatomy of a frog and then look around to find other instances of the same abstract relations recurring in other creatures, including, in this case, ourselves. According to Bateson (1980): "This lateral extension of abstract components of description is called *abduction*, and I hope the reader may see it with a fresh eye. The very possibility of abduction is a little uncanny, and the phenomenon is enormously more widespread than he or she might, at first thought, have supposed" (pp. 157–158).

The "very roots" of science, as well as art and religion "are instances or aggregates of instances of abduction, within the human mental sphere" (p. 158). Both the structure of thought, and thought itself, are metaphoric analogues of what we are thinking about: "all thought would be totally impossible in a universe in which abduction was not expectable" (p. 158).

At one level, then, Bateson is saying that the kind of thinking exemplified by the form of the grass syllogism is basic to all thought, not to mention basic as a form that describes the manner in which mammals (including man) communicate with each other. Some form of the grass syllogism is at the root of the sciences, and therefore cannot be dismissed without putting all science into question. Science is after all a product of the human mind, and it always maintains a connection with persons, with subjects involved in observation and participation.

Logic itself is also ultimately dependent on metaphor in its claiming to be some kind of analogue of "reality," although it may not be the same kind of metaphor involved in the grass syllogism.

Empathy can be also regarded as an awareness that the physiology and anatomy of our bodies have abductive relationships with that of other forms of life. When we see the "legs" of a crab, we somehow perceive that they have a relationship to the rest of the body, in the same way as our legs have a relationship to our own bodies. Intuitively, unconsciously, abduction pervades our thought processes.

At another level, Bateson is also arguing that logic through its emphasis on distinctions and classes of things, tears apart the basic unity of living systems.

"I hold to the presupposition that our loss of the sense of aesthetic unity was, quite simply, an epistemological mistake. I believe that the mistake may be more serious than all the minor insanities that characterize those older epistemologies which agreed upon the fundamental unity" (Bateson, 1978, p. 14).

Today's pathologies, including the possibility of nuclear disasters, are all aspects of such an "epistemological mistake" that have been for a long time in man's history, and ordinary logic and "objective" language are part of the error.

In one of his "metalogues," Bateson says that although it is not scientific to be anthropomorphic, science cannot be completely "objective" in the sense of being not human, not aesthetic (Bateson, 1972, p. 47). In Bateson's (1972) metalogue the Daughter (D) and the Father (F) discuss "objectivity" and its limitations:

D: What are the really big differences between people and animals?
F: Well—intellect, language, tools. Things like that.
D: And it is easy for people to be intellectually objective in language and about tools?
F: That's right.
D: But that must mean that in people there is a whole set of ideas of whatnot which are all tied together. A sort of second creature within the whole person, and that second creature must have a quite different way of thinking about everything. An objective way.
F: Yes. The royal road to consciousness and objectivity is through language and tools.

D: But what happens when this creature looks at all those parts of the person about which it is difficult for people to be objective? Does it just look? Or does it meddle?

F: It meddles.

D: And what happens?

F: That's a very terrible question.

D: Go on. If we are going to study animals, we must face that question.

F: Well . . . The poets and artists know the answer better than the scientists. (pp. 48–49)

The father then quotes some lines from one of Bateson's favorite poets, William Blake, and explains that Blake was aware of the split created in man by the kind of "thought" made possible by language and tools. " 'Thought' should remain a part of the whole but instead spreads itself and meddles with the rest," and ". . . slices everything to bits," the first slice being "between the objective thing and the rest." More of the connectedness of the world is split up, "because the intellect is always classifying and dividing things up." Thus, the father points out, "It's easy to be objective about sex but not about love." Sex is about the bits, whereas love involves being in the larger whole (Bateson, 1972, pp. 49–50).

Ordinary logic, then, deals with the world split up by human intellect and language, and the relationship involved in that world of language. It evolved along with the development of tools that man uses to accomplish his conscious purpose. Logic is useful in this kind of universe. And, for Bateson, conscious purpose, coupled with complex technology, is what has led to the rapid destruction of nature. Logic itself is an abductive system that corresponds to the structure of modern society besides being an artifact of that society. The use of logic as an abductive system with regards to nature is however dangerous. According to Bateson (1978): "logic and quantity turn out to be inappropriate devices for describing organisms and their interactions and internal organization" (p. 15).

Logic and Language

Bateson considers the Grass Syllogism as having the same formal structure as man's thought before speech was invented. As discussed earlier, other animals communicate metaphorically. With the evolution of language, it became possible for subjects to become, both in conscious thought and in the culture that language helped to shape, separable from predicates.

"You see, if it be so that the grass syllogism does not require subjects as the stuff of its building, and if it be so that the Barbara syllogism (the Socrates syllogism) does require subjects, then it will also be so that the

Barbara syllogism could never be much use in a biological world until the invention of language and the separation of subjects from predicates. In other words, it looks as though until 100,000 years ago, perhaps at most 1,000,000 years ago, there were no Barbara syllogisms in the world, and there were only Bateson's kind, and still the organisms got along all right" (Bateson, 1980, p. 11).

Perhaps another step was taken with the invention of the alphabet in splitting the world into subjects and predicates. According to Walter Ong, the development of formal logic is related to the development of literacy.

"We know that formal logic is the invention of Greek culture after it had interiorized the technology of alphabetic writing, and so made a permanent part of its noetic resources the kind of thinking that alphabetic writing made possible. In the light of this knowledge, Luria's experiments with illiterates' reactions to formally syllogistic and inferential reasoning is [sic] particularly revealing. In brief, his illiterate subjects seemed not to operate with formal deductive procedures at all—which is not the same as to say that they could not think or that their thinking was not governed by logic, but only that they would not fit their thinking into pure logical forms, which they seem to have found uninteresting. Why should they be interesting? Syllogisms relate to thought, but in practical matters no one operates in formally stated syllogisms" (Ong, 1982, p. 52).

According to Ong, literacy marked an important departure away from a consciousness that was tuned to the immediate, personal, and interactive world of direct relationships fostered by an oral, nonliterate culture. It became possible to make statements that were not regarded as involving the author's voice and to present material that could be received with a sense of distance. The message could be regarded as being "objective," less related to the subjective presence of its author. As man evolved from orality to literacy, he took another step, away from a Buberian I-Thou world to a more I-It world. (In fact, Buber's *I and Thou* can be read as calling us away through his writing from a universe created by literacy to return to the consciousness of orality, and even to a world of prelinguistic consciousness.)

Literacy also enabled men to communicate with each other without the communicants being bodily present before each other, or even after the author had died or denied what had been written. In written prose the author's voice tends to disappear (except in the case of those forms of literature, especially poetry, where the written language is used artistically) with the author's voice made present.

Zen Buddhism in particular, influenced by Taoism, invites us to return to prelinguistic consciousness, to an emphasis on presence and being-in-the world, so as to find our "true place" in relationship to the world where there is no "I" separate from the "other." Buber (1970) seems to use the Grass Syllogism, by turning the grass into a tree when he writes:

I contemplate a tree.
. . .
I can assign it to a species and observe it as an instance, with an eye to its construction and its way of life.
. . .
I can dissolve it into a number, into a pure relation between numbers, and eternalize it.
. . .
But it can also happen, if will and grace are joined, that as I contemplate the tree I am drawn into a relation, and the tree ceases to be, an It. (pp. 57–58)

Poetry and Prose

Bateson (1972) asserts: "Poetry is not a sort of distorted and decorated prose, but rather prose is a poetry that has been stripped down and pinned to a Procrustean bed of logic" (p. 136). Poetry uses language, but can free itself from logic, to make such statements as "men are grass." Bateson argues that poetry, and other forms of art, are correctives to the overly I-It purposive rationality we find ourselves in today, because they return us to the vision of the "grass metaphor."

"Mere purposive rationality unaided by such phenomena as art, religion, dream, and the like, is necessarily pathogenic and destructive of life; and that its virulence springs specifically from the circumstance that life depends upon interlocking *circuits* of contingency, whereas consciousness can see only such short arcs of such circuits as human purpose may direct" (Bateson, 1972, p. 146).

Bateson concludes that poetry, in the end, involves saner thinking than logic, because poetry (and all good art, for that matter) reflects the way in which the biological world is structured. Although logic distorts, it is through logic that we today act, with an increasingly powerful technology, on the world of nature.

"And it became evident that metaphor was not just pretty poetry, it was not either good or bad logic but was in fact the logic on which the biological world had been built, the main characteristic and organizing glue of this world of mental process that I have been trying to sketch for you in some way or another" (Bateson, July 1980, p. 11).

The Snakes Bite Its Tail

Of course, my discussion here as well as Bateson's arguments are written in prose and hangs on a framework of logic. It takes the logical frame to enable us to comment on a relationship, and to establish a distance, or a separation from the consciousness of being totally in the present, a kind of consciousness that approaches madness. Distance provides certain advantages, but also leads to ecological madness by introducing another kind of error. Men are snakes.

ACKNOWLEDGMENTS

I wish to thank Dr. Frank Tillman, professor of philosophy, Hawaii Loa College, Hawaii, Dr. Herbert Simons, professor of speech, Temple University, Philadelphia, and Dr. Jack Lochhead, professor of physics, University of Massachusetts, for providing helpful criticisms and comments to earlier drafts of this chapter. They are not necessarily in agreement, of course, with any or all of the contents of this chapter.

REFERENCES

Bateson, G. (1975). Ecology of mind: The sacred. In Fields (Ed.), *Loka: A journal from Naropa Institute* (pp. 24–27). Garden City: Anchor Books.

Bateson, G. (1980, July). *Men are grass: Metaphor and the world of mental process. Lindisfarne letter.* Stockbridge: Lindisfarne Association.

Bateson, G. (1980). *Mind and nature: A necessary unity.* Toronto, New York, and London: Bantam.

Bateson, G. (1978, Summer). The pattern which connects. *Coevolution Quarterly, 5–15.*

Bateson, G. (1972). *Steps to an ecology of mind.* New York: Ballantine Books.

Bateson, G. (1982, Winter). They threw God out of the garden: Letters from Gregory Bateson to Philip Wylie and Warren McCulloch. Edited by R. E. Donaldson, *Coevolution Quarterly, 62–67.*

Buber, M. (1970). *I and thou.* (Trans. Walter Kaufmann). New York: Scribner.

Kobayashi, V. (1983). Mind and nature: Teaching and thinking. In William Maxwell (Ed.), *Thinking: The expanding frontier.* Philadelphia: The Franklin Institute Press, 255–259.

Ong, W. J. (1982). *Orality and literacy: The technologizing of the word.* London and New York: Methuen.

8 The Human Brain as a Model for Decision Making*

William Maxwell
The IQ Foundation, Inc.

Other chapters in this book focus on intelligence within individuals, but none of us is a sovereign drop undisturbed by the surrounding sea. Each is immersed in a network of organizations that influence what and how she or he thinks. Today that sea is becoming increasingly polluted by the difficulty organizations have in wisely and promptly making the complex decisions demanded by a rapidly changing environment (Peters & Waterman, 1982). The entire world faces organizational crises brought on in part because we have no model, or theory, for how large organizations should function in the modern age.

In 1982 the first international thinking conference met in Fiji, one of a few places left on this planet where the rate of technological change is slowed and a little of the old organizational integrity is preserved. In the preface to the report on that conference (Maxwell, 1983), Jerome Bruner (1983) states:

> For while this volume is not in any conventional sense a treatise on education but a treatise on mind, it approaches mind in a proper spirit of instruction: It is concerned with its perfectibility, the shape it imposes on knowledge, the prosthetic devices (like language) to which it can be linked or must be linked in order to achieve effectiveness, the manner in which it expresses, not only its own inherent form, but the form of the culture that nurtures it.

---

* This chapter is based on a talk of the same title given by William Maxwell at the Conference on Thinking, with additional argument from cybernetics added by Jack Lochhead.

We wish to address here the perfectibility of human organizations; how they can be reshaped to achieve greater effectiveness, and how they can be recultured to nurture the development of each human mind within.

First, let us briefly consider the modern organization and how it came to its present form. Of the living models for "ideal" organizational behavior, the most familiar is that of Max Weber; this is generally called the bureaucratic or rational model. Weber offered bureaucracy as a clean, rational, i.e. nonemotional, alternative to the regally corrupt systems of governance that characterized both church and state in 19th Century Europe. He replaced the single executive decision maker with many bureaus staffed with bureaucrats, each expert in the domain of that bureau. Once a potential decision was directed to the correct bureau, it could be handled in a cool, rational, and expert manner. Because each bureaucrat was a specialist he (and in rare cases she) would be uninfluenced by the many "irrational" factors that might otherwise distract one from the optimal course of action.

Bureaucracy was a response to increasing complexity. When a single individual could no longer handle all the information necessary for effective administration, problems could be broken into separate parts each of which would be manageable. But the cost of this solution was that there were inadequate mechanisms for preserving the big picture.

From Moscow to Washington critiques of bureaucracy and its bureaucrats form a large fraction of today's humor. These jokes give vent to two frustrations: Bureaucracy is slow and uncaring; its decisions often ignore essential factors. We usually blame the bureaucrats for these failures but Steinbruner (1974) suggests it may be the system of bureaucracy itself that is at fault.

> From history one gains an appreciation that established paradigms are neither lightly nor quickly displaced—even by challengers of clear superiority. . . . Nevertheless, the conditions for a major challenge to the established paradigm of rational decisions are unmistakably present. . . . These conditions obviously require a more sophisticated understanding of decision processes than that which prevailed in less demanding times. Beyond that, the internal logic of rational theory is under strain, particularly from accumulating experimental evidence on basic decision processes which is difficult to reconcile with central assumptions of the theory. Such internal strain has generally preceded a successful challenge to a paradigm. Most important, however, is the fact that a set of assumptions about the decision process distinctly different from those of rational theory is beginning to emerge from research in a number of disciplines on the fundamental processes of the human mind. These developments are quite unlikely to culminate in anything as dramatic as a scientific revolution in which one dominant paradigm is replaced by another. They do suggest, however, that

the theory of decision is in for a major adjustment and that rational assumptions will not continue the degree of dominance they now have.

Assumptions, which promise ultimately to compete with rational theory, as a basis for policy analysis, have been developed by people concerned with the way human beings process information. . . . This pertinent work has taken place in a wide variety of fields—the psychology of learning and of perception, linguistics, logic, epistemology, and information theory, to name the most rigorous of the disciplines involved. . . . In brief, cybernetics provides an analysis of extremely simple decision-making mechanisms which are nonetheless highly successful in the proper environments. (pp. 12–13)

What is cybernetics and what can it offer that bureaucracy cannot? Wiener (1948) called cybernetics the study of "control and communication in the animal and the machine." A critical aspect of this study is the nature of feedback control loops. What is revolutionary here is the function of causality. When the output of a system is feedback as input it is no longer possible to rely on simple models of the form A causes B. The very notion of input and output is blurred. Powers stressed this in his work, *Behavior: The Control of Perceptions.* The bureaucratic model is based on a simple machine analogy, information is fed in and decisions are put out. Cybernetics draws its analogies from living systems (See Kobayashi, this volume); cybernetic systems stabilize their "inputs" to fit certain internally set reference values. This concern with controlling input makes them sensitive to their environment and focused on their future. They are what von Foerster (1968) calls Purposive Systems.

Bateson (1979) and Wiener (1950) and many others have argued for application of the cybernetic perspective to human organizations. We can add little to their insights, instead we propose to step back and consider other ways in which the human brain furnishes a powerful alternative model to the bureaucratic model of efficient decision making.

The search for models of decision-making appears to have followed or paralleled a pattern identified by Comte (1798–1857), one of the founders of sociology, to describe the evolution of scientific enquiry: First, mankind studied that which is most remote, astronomy; then physics; then chemistry. Then, the race developed biology, then sociology, and finally, man began to study man's inner workings.

One model that mankind invented to study that which Aristotle termed *politics* but which ought to be termed in this context as the art of making decisions in social organizations, was abstract logic, something, again metaphorically speaking, away out there in space, beyond time and place and person. Then, man sought his theories, his models, especially those who followed Darwin and Count de Gobineau, from biological species and began to speak of territory, aggression, and dominance and alliance and kinships, class, and hundreds of other concepts literally borrowed whole cloth from the jungle.

Now of late, an increasing number of writers have tentatively led us to the frontier that is the human brain where we propose to look for the next sources of models for decision making.

Jean Piaget, for one, with over 20 papers published in zoology before his 21st birthday, argued that biological principles could help us to understand epistemological problems (Sprinthall, 1981).

Steinbruner (1974) similarly points out the obvious in making his case for a cybernetic approach to decision making. "Presumably," he writes, "there is no one who would seriously contest that the human brain is the ultimate focus of decision making. When we speak of such things as organizational process, political bargaining and rational calculations, we tacitly know that in the final analysis that phenomena involved are based upon human mental operations" (p. 91).

If we examine the processes whereby decision-making information is transmitted from neuron to neuron or to and from other types of cells, we discover several concepts that, by analogy, help build a model for organizational decision making. The units of the human brain function in a way that they offer the powerful force of example to anyone interested in strengthening any human organization.

Metaphor does not pretend to be the Truth. Thus, we can allow a metaphor to entertain or enlighten us as if it were a part of a game going on in our heads. Zen Buddhists offer us puzzles such as a calm drop in an agitated sea. In that spirit we offer five metaphors deriving from how the human brain works and perhaps how human organizations ought to.

First, there is no autocrat in the brain, no "executive" neuron; no supervising neuron. Rather, thousands of neurons appear to *coach* each other.

We use the term *coach* for its metaphorical clarity. The process whereby neurons reach a consensus as to what signal will go to a given muscle is far more complex and, according to Evarts, is an area of brain studies "now uppermost" in priority (Evarts, 1979).

Not only does the brain lack autocratic neurons, it itself does not act as an autocrat. According to Wiener (1948):

The central nervous system no longer appears as a self-contained organ, receiving inputs from the senses and discharging into the muscles. On the contrary, some of its most characteristic activities are explicable only as circular processes, emerging from the nervous system into the muscles, and re-entering the nervous system through the sense organs, whether they are proprioceptors or organs of the special senses. (p. 15)

The richness of this relationship was described by the cybernetician Victor Gurfinkel paraphrased here by Evarts (1979):

> Gurfinkel noted that an essential characteristic of a marksman is his ability to stabilize the gun. Studies of the electromyographic and kinematic characteristics of the army marksmen showed that although many parts of their bodies moved, the pistol was virtually immobile. All kinds of reflex mechanisms stabilized the position of the marksman's hand in space: the vestibulo–ocular system, the vestibulospinal system and so on.

From these examples we conclude that the ideal human organization need not be highly centralized or autocratic.

Second, the brain is a very widespread communication network. The interconnections between neurons are not in the ratio of 1 to 6 or 1 to 24, as assumed optimal by some organizational theories, but on the order of 1:10,000. Each neuron directly relates to, shares information with, is coached by, and coaches up to 10,000 other neurons. Furthermore, these interconnections reach all across the brain, as stated by Hubel (1979): "If a particular part of the brain is destroyed and the brain is stained by the Nauta method a few days later and then examined under a microscope, the presence of selectively stained fibers in some second and quite distant part means that the second region receives fibers from the destroyed part" (p. 48).

"The incredibly complex interconnections among neurons are not random, as has sometimes been supposed, but rather are the very antithesis of random: highly structured and specific" (p. 47).

The picture one receives of the living brain is 100,000,000,000 active cells, each listening to thousands of others and sending signals to thousands of others. The word "beehive" is far too mild to convey the true picture, as Hubel continues:

> Almost every neuron receives input from many terminals, usually many hundreds and sometimes thousands, some of which are excitatory and some inhibitory. At any instant, some inputs will be active and some quiescent, and it is the sum of the excitatory and inhibitory effects that determines whether or not the cell will fire and, if it does fire, the rate at which it does so. In other words, the neuron is much more than a device for sending impulses from one place to another. Each neuron constantly evaluates all the signals reaching it from all other cells and expresses the result in its own rate of signaling. (p. 49)

We believe that in the ideal organization individuals would be encouraged to share and seek information from the largest possible network of other people.

Peters and Waterman describe how Hewlett and Packard encourages each of its employees to share his or her ideas. The picture they paint of engineers being encouraged to leave their work uncovered on their desks for anyone to peek at is the very antithesis of bureaucracy.

The third metaphor is this: In the brain, communication proceeds at a rate of 150 to 200 ion exchanges per second. One index of the efficiency of organization is its communication time or intervals. How long does it take a secretary to answer the telephone or the office to respond to a letter? Peters and Waterman argue that such indices are also inverse measures of organizational pathology—pathologies easily remedied. One of the great organizers of all time, Muhammed, expressed a similar idea when he said "pay your workers before their sweat is dry."

Fourth, all information, both stored and incoming, is continuously under review, is reflected on. Revision is the norm; that is, the changing of perceptions and interpretations is built into the mechanism.

There is perhaps a great analogical truth that dragons are seen out of the corner of the eye. If one cell whistles, "wolf, wolf" the other cells take a close hard look and send a signal that we can read as "sheep" or "shadow" or "sunset silhouette" or whatever.

The organizational analog is that because the environmental inputs are never constant, responses can never be constant. Perhaps the most frustrating and destructive aspect of the bureaucratic mind is that reluctance to reconsider decisions and modes of operation. Were our brains to work that way we would be in constant flight from imaginary monsters.

The fifth and last metaphor follows: Each cell acts as if the survival of the entire organism depended on its diligence and efficient functioning. Kandel (1979) argues:

> The first major question that students of simple systems of neurons might examine is whether the various neurons of a region of the nervous system differ from one another. This question, which is central to an understanding of how behavior is mediated by the nervous system, was in dispute until recently. Some neurobiologists argued that the neurons of a brain are sufficiently similar in their properties to be regarded as identical units having interconnections of roughly equal value.
>
> These arguments have now been strongly challenged particularly by studies of invertebrates showing that many neurons can be individually identified and are invariant in every member of the species. (p. 67)

In other words, we are but a few steps away from giving every neuron its individual name! Kandel (1979) goes on to say, "The first finding to emerge from these studies is that the individual cells exert a control over behavior that is specific and surprisingly powerful" (p. 67). Somewhere in Genesis, the individual human is promised a dominion. Organizations that harmonize their structures with the human brain are likely to give every member a degree of sovereignty that would be threateningly alien to the bureaucratic mentality.

Conclusion

Analogies and metaphors can inspire and even guide, but they are not the detailed prescription from which one can fashion or orchestrate the workings of large organization. And at the present time few areas and functions of the brain are understood in the detail necessary for the design of serious simulations. We are quite far from having such models for the entire brain. Nevertheless, our meager knowledge of the brain offers evidence that alternatives to the bureaucratic system exist and that they often function well. Now that we have intimations of solutions, we must increase our searching behavior. Perhaps we can do so before it is too late, before total chaos wipes out the possibility of continuing the evolution of mankind.

REFERENCES

Bateson, G. (1979). *Mind and nature: A necessary unity.* New York: Dutton.

Bruner, J. (1983). Preface. In William Maxwell (Ed.), *Thinking: The expanding frontier.* Philadelphia: Franklin Institute Press.

Evarts, E. V. (1979, September). Brain mechanisms of movement. *Scientific American, 21* (3).

Hubel, D. H. (1979, September). The brain. *Scientific American, 21* (3).

Kandel, E. R. (1979, September). Small systems of neurons. *Scientific American, 21* (3).

Maxwell, W. (Ed.). (1983). *Thinking: The expanding frontier.* Philadelphia: Franklin Institute Press.

Nauta, W. J. H., & Feirtag, M. (1979, September). The organization of the brain. *Scientific American, 21* (3).

Peters, T. J., & Waterman, R. H., Jr. (1982). *In search of excellence.* New York: Warner Books.

Powers, W. T. (1973). *Behavior: The control of perception.* Chicago: Aldine.

Sprinthall, R. C., & Sprinthall, N. A. (1981). *Educational psychology.* Reading, MA: Addison-Wesley.

Steinbruner, J. H. (1974). *The cybernetics theory of decision.* Princeton: Princeton University Press.

von Foerster, H., White, J. D., Peterson, L. J., & Russel, J. K. (Eds.). (1968). *Purposive systems.* New York: Spartan Books.

Wiener, N. (1948). *Cybernetics: Control and communication in the animal and the machine.* New York: Wiley.

Wiener, N. (1950). *The human use of human beings.* Boston: Houghton Mifflin.

II CONTEXTS OF THINKING

Several contributions to the Conference involved studies of how people think in particular contexts. A central concern here is with the role cultural differences may play in determining variations in the way people think. In Chapter 9, José Buscaglia examines the influence of the Spanish language and of the Latin-American culture on thought; Robert Stewart, in Chapter 10, examines various hypotheses for explaining the apparent ethnic differences in academic achievement in Fiji. Of course, cultures need not be purely ethnically defined: science and business, for example, both arguably count as cultures that cross ethnic barriers. Thus, in Chapter 11, Daniel Isenberg reports on his studies of the ways in which business managers think, and, in Chapter 12, Carol Smith and Arthur Millman seek to throw light on the innovative thinking of scientists by means of their case study of Charles Darwin's early thought. This section concludes in Chapter 13 with Herb Koplowitz's fictitious case study illustrating various levels of cognitive development beyond the formal operations stage described by Piaget and demonstrating how each level creates a type of mental culture with ethnic barriers to communication. George Forman then investigates in Chapter 14 how children play in the "electronic theater" of computer graphics and considers the implications of this context for our understanding of cognitive development.

9 The Development of Thinking Skills Within the Cultural Identity of Latin America

José Buscaglia

During the period 1979 to 1984, the author participated in a collaborative project involving the government of Venezuela, Harvard University, and the Cambridge, Massachusetts consulting firm Bolt Beranek and Newman. In the course of the 5-year effort, we designed, implemented, and evaluated a course to teach thinking skills at the 7th-grade level in Venezuela. The detailed and generally positive results of this experiment appear in the Final Report for "Project Intelligence."[1] What follows is an exercise in reflection, an attempt to address the specific issue of cultural differences, how these affect certain cognitive functions, and what this implies for education as a means of fostering the development of third world countries.

Inevitably, every culture or particular social structure at any given moment promotes the development of a series of dominant intellectual abilities in keeping with the particular structure of that society. By the same token, any given culture or particular social structure tends to inhibit the development of other sets of skills. The survival value of and level of reinforcement for each particular skill or subset of skills is, in general, what determines the overall traits in the cognitive profile.

Using the Latin American cultural context as an example and, more specifically so that of Venezuela, we try to analyze the multidimensional aspects of this phenomenon focusing, primarily, on the following conditioning factors:

---

[1]*Project Intelligence: The Development of Procedures to Enhance Thinking Skills*, Final Report, October 1983, prepared by: Harvard University and Bolt Beranek and Newman Inc., Cambridge, Mass.

141

- Historical Background: the impact of social, economic, and political development
- Language
- Value System and Beliefs
- Environment

For each of these categories we will single out a number of particular skills or behaviors and attempt to point out how these are adversely or positively affected by the aforementioned factors.

Secondly, we try to bring together these factors and establish the relationship between that particular culture and intellectual development.

Thirdly, we comment on the particular issue of how a course designed to enhance thinking skills fits into that framework.

Finally, we derive some general conclusions and ancillary recommendations from the overall analysis.

In focusing on the issues addressed in this chapter, it seems strategically necessary to focus first on some negative cultural trends that might interfere with the goal of promoting new mental attitudes. This does not imply a disregard or undervaluation of other intellectual skills that characterize some of the more positive aspects of the Latin American cultural identity. We use this approach only to target our analysis and insure a more objective assessment of the present conditions.

HISTORICAL BACKGROUND: THE IMPACT OF SOCIAL, ECONOMIC AND POLITICAL DEVELOPMENT.

There are a number of recurring and salient aspects in the historical development of Latin America that can be closely related to the evolution of specific mental attitudes. We briefly comment on several of these and point out to what extent these could have, or still do, inhibit or promote the development of specific thinking skills.

The Autocratic Tradition, "Caudillismo" and Dictatorship

Between 1000 A.D. and the coming of the Spaniards, the dominant Amerindian civilizations of the Aztecs in Mexico and the Incas in the Andes consolidated their spheres of influence. They provided continuity to the theocratic form of government of the Mayas that were well established as far back as the 4th century B.C. and the Chibchas that were integrated in the Inca empire circa 2000 years ago. The inhabitant of

Venezuela, Northern Colombia, and the Caribbean, although never fully incorporated into the previously mentioned highly structured aristocratic theocracies, were nonetheless influenced by their concepts of the sacredness of the ruler and the stratification of society. By comparison, the level of development of the circum-caribbean indians can be roughly compared to the neolithic societies of Europe, where the tribal ruler and shaman jointly represented two aspects of authority. The Aztec and Inca theocracies, on the other hand, are in many ways comparable to the Egyptian Middle and New Empires or the Sumer and NeoBabylonian Empires, where "Universal States" were founded based on autocratic theological systems that controlled fundamental aspects of cultural, administrative and social behavior.

What landed in America with the Spaniards were the symbols, institutions and concepts of a European feudal society that had evolved by the time of the conquest of America into a centralized monarchical system. The symbols of the "Sacra y Real Magesta" with the mysterious and unchallengeable authority of a Pantocrator Tetramorphos came from beyond, from the unknown (from heaven or its equivalent) to replace, in the manner of a second coming, the indigenous symbols of authority.

By comparison to the development of European civilization, one thing was different; there was no Hellenic humanism, no Roman republic, no Renaissance in between. It is no coincidence, then, that the colonial empire in America mainly centered around the three main viceroyalties: the Viceroyalty of New Spain, the Viceroyalty of New Granada, and the Viceroyalty of Peru. These were the three great centers of the theocratic universal empires of Pre-Columbian America.

Whether in the context of more centralized and larger social structures of the great Amerindian empires or the less populous parochial states ruled by the "caciques" or "curacas," the autocratic character of these societies was equally evident. The rulers normally represented an unchallengeable authority whose power was basically sacred and whose defiance was a heresy. The inflexible chain of command and social strata provided the pyramidal structure through which these paternalistic systems worked. In Spanish colonial America, the Sacra Magesta similarly came to hold absolute power, and his authority flowed down the highly structured system of the viceroys "visitadores" - "provincial governors" - "audiencias" "intendencias" - "cabildos" - "corregidores" and "alcades" down to the land owners or "hacendados." As the state officials were expected to serve blindly or execute the chain of command, those who owned no land and had no official position basically belonged, at first, to the encomendado or the state, and later, to the hacendado under whose protection they were allowed to survive. "La vara del rey" (the king's staff) carried by the alcaldes, or the "mazo real" (royal mace) of the cabildo were visual symbols of the source of power from which their authority derived.

In a dominant-dependent sociopolitical structure where rank order is kept in check by an authoritarian aggressive attitude, rational dialogue with the authorities is generally an ineffective means toward producing change. "La razón del poder y no el poder de la razón" (the reason of power and not the power of reasoning) permeates the psychological attitude and sets the grounds for the only possible mechanism of instrumenting change: by open defiance or violent means; that is, by power usurped.

At the first level of defiance, we find the classic Spanish formula used during colonial times by disobedient officials—"Obedezco pero no cumplo" (I obey but do not implement). This act of defiance was usually accompanied by the symbolic gesture of the official in placing the royal edict or command over his head, thus displaying a sign of respect for the "Sacra Magesta" whereas ignoring its content. At this level in the hierarchy, the degree of disobedience could be counterbalanced by the degree of local power held by the official. But, when things came to worse, as was the case in the events leading to the war of independence, it was no longer the individual official's defiance, but a power struggle within the system itself. This struggle was led mainly by a highly educated minority of "criollos" (sons of wealthy Spaniards born in America) who were romantically enamoured by the avant-garde republican ideas of justice and equality espoused by Rousseau in his *Social Contract* and *Emile* and by the writings of Voltaire, Raynal, Montesquieu, and others. Open rebellion was met with violence, and violence itself was to be the only effective way of instrumenting change. The "Decreto de Guerra a Muerte" (the Decree of War till Death) issued by Bolívar on June 15, 1813 set the stage for his "Campaña Admirable" that established the second republic.

Yet again, even in the pandemonium that followed, new symbols replaced the old ones, whereas the mechanism for asserting power remained basically the same. Violence, repression, and open rebellion continued in turn by and between the liberals and the conservatives, the "pipiolos" and the "pelucones," the Bolivarians and the anti-Bolivarians or regional caudillos as they struggled against each other for dominance, not by using rational dialogue but again by imposing *their* "right" with might. In some instances, oligarchies replaced the old aristocracy. In others, caudillos or dictators climbed to the top of their self-built or borrowed pyramids of absolute power. The degree of illiteracy and the strong tradition of autocratic rule did not provide any other means for establishing authority.

It is not surprising that the caudillos were for the most part generals or self-made generals whose right to command was typically determined by their success in the battlefield and their strong charismatic personality. The caudillo's principles or ideas were second to his style or ability to command and his overall manly personality. When it was the case that the caudillo was basically or totally illiterate, he was seen as an exemplar of the men from the lower classes that personified the character of a region and on whose behalf he had taken over. His style and personality in a way was to represent the alter ego or libido of those conditioned to milleniums of serfdom. He ruled the land as a super hacendado and made no distinction between the wealth of his parochial state and his own private fortune. Loyalty to him was a matter of deep personal loyalty or attachment and a willingness to die for him rather than a matter of philosophical or political conviction.

Local caudillos gradually gave way to the rise of dictatorships, as the cunningness of one caudillo was able to eliminate, discredit, or assert dominance over others with the backing of the armed forces and the secret police. In some cases, the outer appearance of a constitutional regime was kept for strategic reasons or to insure foreign aid.

The present democratic systems in Venezuela and Latin America, in general, have inherited at least some modified characteristics of these deeply rooted historical traditions. It remains to be discussed how these modes of behavior influence the development of specific mental skills and, in particular, skills related to decision making, problem solving, productivity, and scientific and objective rationality. In the sections to follow, we try to indicate how learning in and out of school works within these parameters.

Decision Making

Paternalism and censorship tend to inhibit the full exercise of decision making. Because of these factors, an individual's freedom to participate and contribute to the decision-making process in his daily life, his work environment, his community and public affairs, are greatly reduced as is his ability to develop an analytical approach and the skills to generate and evaluate alternatives and consider consequences.

Moreover, if the individual is persistently discouraged from making his own decisions and even reprimanded when he ventures to do so, his overall capacity to develop the skills related to decision making will be consistently impaired. When the individual does not fulfill an adequate role in the decision making process, he cannot share any major sense of responsibility for the decisions taken by others. To the extent that the system for the most part only allows for compliance, the individual cannot fully feel the need to measure the consequences of his actions.

Problem Solving

The lack of participation determines a special attitude of the individual toward the establishment. Just as his level of participation in the decision-making process is reduced, so too must be his share in participating creatively in the problem-solving process. If the individual is merely given the guidelines to perform according to a problem-solving plan that has been thought out and designed by others, he tends to operate unaware of how his actions contribute or not to the solution. The superficial understanding he might have of what he is doing or how what he is doing fits in with the general scheme, does not allow him to relate his fragment of the solution to the solution of the problem as a whole.

No problem can be solved without first understanding thoroughly what the problem is about. This fact tends to negate the possibility of effective problem solving in a social context where all participants should share in the analytic–synthetic cycle only according to their specific, designated role in implementing a solution. Moreover, the skills required to conceptualize a problem and relate its solution to a real world situation would receive little exercise under such circumstances.

When the corporate or civil servant sees himself as merely serving or servicing a dominant minority and as practically sharing nothing from the benefits of his productivity, he cannot be properly motivated to contribute in a meaningful and imaginative way. He tends to limit himself to fulfilling his limited role more out of fear of being left out if his degree of servitude is not judged to be adequate, than out of a sense of moral or intellectual commitment.

Contrary to meritocracy, in this type of palingenetic autocratic system, the individuals survive and rise to higher positions in accordance to their degree of personal loyalty to the interest of the dominant minority. Flattery and praise given to the higher ranking official is, in most cases, the most valid strategy for obtaining a reward. No deep intellectual involvement or analysis of the situation is required as long as the individuals contribute to maintaining the power of the higher official who guarantees their positions in the rank order.

To present even valid arguments is very seldom viewed as being in the interest of the establishment if they suggest that the higher officials or the ruler, party or government in power might not have a clear understanding of the problem at hand or should consider a different strategy. Moreover, it can be seen as disrespectful, disloyal, and offensive. To question the judgment of the higher official or the appropriateness of the official policy is usually viewed as a threat. To attempt to bring to reason or to prove wrong whomever represents the authority, is offensive to his honor and dignity. Honor and right judgment overlap and, therefore, it is dishonorable to be proven wrong.

To the degree that the individual is conditioned to inhibit his judgment and his objective assessment, his ability to become an effective problem solver is greatly discouraged while at the same time his development of nonrational and nonobjective survival skills is encouraged.

Scientific and Objective Rationality

Basic affective response is, for the most part, a nonconditioned involuntary behavior. Whereas the style, channels, and degree of expression of affect are indeed conditioned by the sociocultural environment, the basic drives are inherent in the individual. On the other hand, objectivity and rationality are, for the most part, learned behaviors that often come in conflict with the affective response.

Objectivity and rationality can indeed be considered survival skills, especially in highly developed societies. Nevertheless, the right conditions must be present for them to develop to the level where they can produce scientific and technological development.

Venezuela and Latin America in general are certainly not underdeveloped in the fields of art, music, literature, and the like, which derive their vitality from the affective elements of human nature. The latin "élan vital" for creativity and productivity in these fields is impressive indeed. Moreover, the three main cultures that contributed most of the present cultural character of Latin America, the Hispanic, and Amerindian, and the African stand out for their strong identity and expressive capacity.

Unfortunately, the same cannot be said for scientific and technological development. What there is in the technological field in Latin America is mainly borrowed technology. What there is in regards to scientific productivity is mainly the product of training received abroad. What, then, are the right conditions required to develop the scientific and technological capacity? Why is the inclination towards scientific thinking not clearly evident in the population as a whole?

Objective judgment is most of all required for sound scientific analysis. Objective judgment should be unprejudiced, unbiased, not subjective, and basically unemotional. The object of analysis must be viewed with a certain sense of detachment without passing judgment on its nature and innermost mechanism until an adequate level of information has been considered and evaluated. The persuasiveness of emotional and illogical evidence that nourishes a confirmation bias must be disregarded. The analyst must be able to recognize and even seek out contradictions and inconsistencies.

These and other related fundamental characteristics typify the scientist's attitude and his view of the world. The tight and orderly style of thinking that fosters objective and scientific reasoning is not generally speaking a natural product of the present Latin American sociocultural tradition, nor for the most of third world countries.

LANGUAGE

The Royal Academy of the Spanish Language

The *"Real Academia Española"* (The Royal Academy of the Spanish Language) establishes for all the Spanish-speaking people the correct and accepted way of using Spanish. All new words incorporated into the language must be presented, defended, and voted on by this institution before they become part of the Spanish language. Every Spanish-speaking country has an Academy of the Language (Academia de la Lengua) that send delegates to Madrid to define the acceptable boundaries of the Spanish language. Since 1965 the *"Comisión Permanente de la Asociación de Academias de la Lengua Española"* (Permanent Commission of the Association of Academies of the Spanish Language) was established to work together in maintaining the *unity* of the Spanish language. Together they publish the "Diccionario de la Lengua Española." The motto of the Academy *"Limpia, Fija y Da Esplendor"* (cleanses, sets, and gives splendor) characterizes its function.

The "Real Academia Española" is mentioned because the Spanish language itself is the main instrument of maintaining cultural unity in the Spanish-speaking world. In doing this, the academy sustains a fundamental element that conditions both the affective and thinking processes throughout the Spanish-speaking world.

We try to point out some of the essential characteristics in the structure and use of the Spanish language that we feel directly influence the thinking process:

1. Highly descriptive with a strong emphasis on the visual and sensorial elements.

2. Pictorial and emotive in character with stronger emphasis on the aesthetic use of the language rather than the concreteness of the ideas.

3. In Spanish usually one is *moved* to accept the veracity of what is being said by the way it is expressed rather than by the weight of the evidence.

4. Adjectives, adverbs, and frequently divergent clauses modify the noun and the character of the verb to a greater degree than they do, for example, in English.

5. For the aforementioned reason, sentences tend to be longer and more elaborate in detail, usually bridging over several interrelated ideas within the structure of the same sentence.

6. Dedre Gentner (1981) states on her research on relational concepts,[2] that in English, the *manner* of motion is conflated into the verb; in Spanish, the *direction* of motion is conflated. Compare the English and Spanish descriptions: The bottle *floated into* the cave. "La botella *entró* a la cueva *flotando*."

> In English we conflate the *manner* of motion ("floating") into the verb, leaving the direction of motion of the bottle relative to the cave ("into") as a separate word. In Spanish, the *direction* of motion relative to the cave ("entering") is incorporated into the verb, but the manner of movement ("flotando") is left out. (p. 166)

It may well be that the most significant cross-cultural variation in meaning is to be found among verbs and other relational terms. Note that the mental image one would derive from the Spanish and English sentences is different. Also in the Spanish sentence one would tend to add adjectives or a clause after the "botella" and an adverb before or after the word "flotando," or a descriptive clause. One could also begin the sentence with the verb "enter" and rearrange, like in Latin, the rest of the sentence in a number of ways.

7. The logical sequence of subject-verb-object, that is typical of the English language, is not so in Spanish. One does not "paint a picture" or "react to an impression" in three-component units when using Spanish as a vehicle of expression.

8. The Spanish metaphor, as in poetry, tends to be more image oriented, whereas in English it tends to be more meaning oriented. Meaning in Spanish is again more a question of "it is that way because I feel it is that way" rather than "it is that way because it seems reasonable that it should be that way."

Characteristic Trends of the Spanish Language

One can list a number of words to describe the character of the Spanish language all of which relate to distinctions often made by psychologists in classifying thinking styles, such as:

---

[2]Gentner, Dedre, (1981). Some interesting differences between verbs and nouns. *Cognition and Brain Theory, 4* (2), 161–178.

iconic	*divergent*	*affective*
field-oriented	gap-filling	supra-rational
telluric	lateral	surrealistic
peripheral	unpredictable	dramatic
descriptive	structurally fluent	sensationalistic
multi-dimensional	left-handed (Bruner)	dynamic
impressionistic	generative	energetic
visually-oriented	non-sequential	impulsive
sensorial	longer & complex sentences	emotional
substantive	panoramic	lyrical

We do not mean, of course, that these inherent tendencies in the Spanish language dominate to such an extent that one cannot "think" with the language structure of Spanish in directions opposite to those pointed, nor do we mean to say that these characteristics imply that other languages, such as English, cannot be stirred in similar directions. They should only be interpreted as prevailing tendencies of the Spanish language.

We have grouped these prevailing tendencies under three categories that we believe mutually reinforce each other. The iconic trend increases the affective stimulation that in turn fosters the divergent diaspora.

Language and Objective Reality

It is perhaps these aforementioned characteristics of the Spanish language that, for the most part, influence the meaning of what is considered to be objective reality and, therefore, what is considered to be true or real within the boundaries of that objective reality.

In properly using the Spanish language to its full lyrical potential, reality can very easily be transformed into an iconography that merely represents or symbolizes a more permanent conceptual world beyond the limits of the concrete. This particular approach to reality is further reinforced by the deep magical–religious concept that the ultimate "objective" reality lies beyond empirical truth and that the everyday "real" world is in fact a nonpermanent transitory state that attains fulfillment only in the transcendental.

By asserting the primacy of the emotive and transcendental over the material and empirical, the very nature of the Spanish language establishes an a priori condition to knowing and experiencing that places fundamental reality beyond what could or should be rationally explained. Perception then becomes a bridge to intuition where the objective analysis of perception is seen as secondary to the apprehension of meaning. This visionary idealism tends to create a schism between body and soul where reality and ideational consciousness are always confronting each other in the decisive battle of Armageddon.

The Spanish language itself was born in what was seen as a decisive battle between Christianity and "the infidels." Antonio de Nebrija presented his grammar to the Catholic Queen so that the Spanish language would always accompany the (Christian) empire. Even Franco and his Falange, who considered themselves as the successors of Isabella I, constantly referred to Spain as "the spiritual reservoir of the West" whereas labeling republicans and democrats as infidels and forbidding the use of other Hispanic languages and dialects.

In Latin America where, in general, true republicanism and participatory democracy is not so deeply rooted and the Spanish language has preserved the same fundamental characteristics, the same conflict continues between objective reality and reality as expressed through the Spanish language. Beginning with José Enrique Rodó's *Ariel* in 1900, the struggle between the winged spirit "Ariel" and the forces of materialism represented by "Calibán" has been repeatedly referred to in Latin American literature as the conflict between the northern and southern hemispheres. The need, therefore, to substantiate reality is often looked at with disdain as an attempt to reduce nature to structural definitions that detract from its aesthetic and expressive potential.

In whatever way, the social and political structure and the use of the Spanish language mutually reinforce each other and indeed can be seen as having other potentially positive effects. What seems apparent is that the Spanish language as used nowadays is not the most practical instrument to foster the development of an objective scientific mentality nor administrative pragmatism. The very essence of its conceptual nature comes into conflict with the systematic and down-to-earth approach.

Further research might indicate that similar problems could be found in most languages as presently used in other third world countries.

VALUE SYSTEM AND BELIEFS

Nothing preconditions more the development of specific mental skills than the values embedded within a given culture. As a consequence, the areas of achievement of a given sociocultural group mirror its scales of values.

The Use of Language

The Spanish language has not developed an adequate scientific–technological vocabulary because very little value is placed on what it represents or is capable of producing. Moreover, there is a persistent and deliberate attempt to "protect" the Spanish language from neologisms as if, in doing so, we were keeping away a formidable enemy and thus protecting the "purity" of a value system that in itself is considered incompatible with whatever the free trade of the contemporary technological jargon implies.

Foreign or transliterated words from other technologically developed languages, specifically English, are uncomfortably used, and with some embarrassment, within the inner circle of special activity groups because there is no other alternative than to do so, but they do not circulate naturally or freely as an integral part of the Spanish language. Their usage tends to remain limited to the small professional groups who have been educated abroad in each particular discipline.

To be scientifically and technologically creative is inevitably limited under such conditions. Technological and scientific thinking requires a clear assessment and highly defined references to reality. To reason concretely about reality, halfway in one language and halfway in another, frequently leads to a distortion of meaning and syntax and, therefore, to a confused verbal reasoning process. Whatever values and objectives underline each language, they naturally come into conflict with each other.

The common grounds for effective communication depend on the degree of knowledge or source of the imported jargon. This tends to be substantially different among members of the scientific community. Dissemination of information outside the ingroups who share common grounds for communication is awkward and difficult. To keep abreast of recent developments in any given technological or scientific field requires an easy access to sources of information, most of which are not available locally nor in Spanish. (The need to be aware and to be able to acquire advanced specialized equipment compounds the difficulty.) This situation requires frequent travelling, sufficient resources to do so, and, in the long run, is not an effective way of keeping in touch with the state of the art. Neither does it provide for the serene atmosphere required to do uninterrupted research. The constant changes in the cultural and linguistic setting required "to keep in touch" also adds to the level of anxiety under which research is normally conducted.

Empirical Truth and Absolute Truth

Reinforcing the aforementioned language issue, the long-standing conflict between empirical truth and absolute truth still remains very much a part of Hispanic culture. The unchallenged dogmatism that prevailed in Europe throughout the Middle Ages became the authoritarian dogmatism of the Spanish crown with Isabella I and the Inquisitor General of Castille, and the crown of Aragon, Fray Tomás de Torquemada, who enacted the rules and regulations for the Sacred Tribunals and enforced compliance with extreme severity. Philip II, the champion of catholicism and leader of the counterreformation, isolated and protected his empire against the winds of the reformation and, in doing so, against the new ethics and the new scientific outlook. Whereas in most of Europe and North America the nature of truth and knowledge and how one discovers and acquires them, was heading in the direction of self-reliance and freedom of conscience, truth and knowledge in the Hispanic world remained as the interpretative domain of the official authorities.

Although changes in the types of government in Spain and Latin America have occurred, and significant revisions to the enclosed dogmatic attitudes within the catholic church have been made recently, such progressive trends cannot easily diminish centuries of deep conditioning. Latin America has fallen behind in the development of a truly objective scientific rationale because that in itself has been for centuries considered a threat to its "spiritual" values, religious beliefs, and political interests.

Anarchism

The inherent tendency toward anarchism evident in all Hispanic cultures is the direct consequence of the longstanding and persistent efforts by the government and the ecclesiastical power structures to maintain control by deliberately suppressing the degree to which an individual is allowed to reason freely or against what has been established or reasoned out officially. Because empirically based truth or compelling evidence is for the most part disregarded when commands or principles are presented as unchallenged statements, reasoned out logical arguments prove to be ineffective ways for changing the established viewpoint or policy. Repression may force compliance but simultaneously builds on the psychological attitudes that breed anarchy.

The Paradox of Opposing Attitudes

Contradictory as it may seem, the aforementioned scenario fosters the simultaneous presence of opposing attitudes such as docile and rebellious, aggressive and loving, cooperative and indifferent, and structured and unstructured. This phenomenon, that can be called *the paradox of opposing attitudes,* tends to make Hispanic culture almost incomprehensible to the outsider. The ultimate expression of this paradox could be the cry of "¡Viva la muerte!" (Long live death!)

If this principle is to be considered an outstanding characteristic of Hispanic culture, objective rationality would be predominantly at the losing end of the spectrum, whereas a high degree of tolerance for contradiction would foster alogical reasoning patterns and reaction formation behavior. Moreover, alogical rhetoric is often not only considered to have a highly aesthetic and expressive value, but also to reflect "reality" in a more accurate way than if it were to be analyzed under strict logical premises. The Spanish philosopher, Miguel de Unamuno, characterized this inherent tendency in the Hispanic temperament in stating: "I believe we could attempt the Holy Crusade of rescuing the sepulcher of the Knight of Madness from the power of the Noblemen of Reason."

Yet, the complexity of contradictions of the Hispanic scale of values goes beyond the phrenastenic attitudes of Don Quixote. Truth and reality are viewed by Don Quixote from an anachronistic, unobjective, and morally idealistic perspective. Sancho's reaction formation is diametrically opposed to Don Quixote, yet they walk together as a symbol of the schism of the soul that permeates the Hispanic culture.

Arnold Toynbee argues that these alternative ways of behavior, feeling, and life, exemplify the schism of the soul in societies that are in the process of desintegration.[3] This cannot be said of Hispanic culture. It originated in this way and has grown, expanded, and survived to the present day. It is precisely the constant confrontation between opposing extremes of the scale of values that provide most of the "élan vital" in Hispanic cultures.

Generally speaking, the lack of organizational skills in Hispanic culture can account for the traditional deficiency in the organizational structures and, for the most part, can be viewed as one reason why authoritarian regimes have been persistently required to impose a sense of order. Yet, just this lack of self-control and hyperactive expressiveness accounts for much of its creative potential, from life style and folklore to the arts and the humanities. This is not technological creativity, that requires the opposing or complementary element of controlled objectivity, but it is, nonetheless, creativity that can be harnessed potentially for other ends. Moreover, creativity and expressivity tend to be obsessive, having a built-in reinforcing mechanism that can, in principle, more than compensate for whatever passive abandonment, truancy, or sense of drift, decadent societies show according to Toynbee.

---

[3]Toynbee, Arnold J., *A Study of History*, Abridgement by D. C. Somervell, Oxford University Press, 1946, Vol. I, Ch. VII.

ENVIRONMENT

Two interrelated aspects of the environment influence the development of cultural identity: The *physical* environment and the *human* environment. How these two formidable forces interplay with one another accounts for much of the drama of development, success or failure of a given culture. Let us first consider the challenge of the physical environment.

The Physical Environment

Arnold J. Toynbee illustrates in "The Challenge of the Environment"[3] how the stimulus of "hard countries" fosters the success of civilizations by presenting an adequate degree of challenge that, in the process of being overcome, ensures success. Too much of a challenge, on the other hand, can cause failure, as very little challenge can be insufficient to promote significant prosperity.

By comparison to his examples of the civilizations that originated in the Yellow River, Attica, Byzantium, Israel, Scotland, and New England, one must consider subtropical Venezuela as an example of a culture originating in a benign environment. We must of course set aside from this environment–culture interrelationships, most of the "Amazonas" state and the Waicas cultures, the areas surrounding the Caroni and the Pemones culture, and the Motilones culture south–west of the Maracaibo Lake, where the voraciousness of nature's metabolism shows no sign yet of being domesticated. In general, in the rest of the country, where most of the population lives (the north–west triangle), nature is bountiful and the climate requires no great foresight to allow survival.

The Human Challenge

In this environment, human beings can basically survive and reproduce with minimum effort, minimum protection from the inclemency of the weather and very little planning ahead. The climate and the land is, therefore, in this and similar subtropical areas of the world, not such a strong mechanism of natural selection for promoting the set of skills that result in cooperative effort and foresight, with all its by-products. The great challenge then, in the absence of a strong direct challenge from nature, is man himself. It is the human challenge that influences some of the dominant characteristics of the Venezuelan cultural personality and the cultures of other equally plentiful and benign environments.

When the land itself, basically on its own, can provide, it is the ownership of the land that becomes the top priority. Power is then translated into ownership of the land and the control over its resources, and the establishment of power and control over those who own no land nor what it sustains or produces.

When industrialization and modern capitalism started, only the land-owners (latifundistas) had the resources to develop other sources of income and invest in the future. For the most part, the landed aristocracy became the industrial entrepreneurs. They not only had the capital required, but also the power, level and quality of education, and the administrative experience to do so.

Even today the old inherited right of ownership and control over the land by a dominant minority transfers to the new sense of ownership of the resources in the present capitalist system. The ruling class establishes dominance basically in the style of the old hacendados. Even political power is deep down considered as something one owns or inherits, together with the right to use it. The old overdeveloped territorial instinct of the "latifundistas" and the caudillos, with their style of exercising control, still remains as a reinforcing agent in the present-day human environment. Likewise, the class struggle between the few that "have" and the many that "have not" also remains the same.

A COURSE TO ENHANCE THINKING SKILLS: CULTURAL GROWTH VERSUS TRANSCULTURATION

We have focused mainly on elements in the cultural identity of Latin America that seem to arrest the development of an objective scientific–technological mentality and administrative efficiency. Yet, the intrinsic values of the Latin American civilizations clearly manifest outstanding humanistic qualities, surprising artistic, musical, and literary achieve-ments, and a potential strength that, above all, must be preserved and stimulated.

The confrontation between societies that have developed high technol-ogy and organizational efficiency and most of the third world countries does tend to create in the latter a schism of the soul and of the social body; however, this does not imply a negative verdict. The *ethos* of these cultures, after all, represent most of the world population and in many instances the defense of some of the highest spiritual, moral, and cultural values of the human race. Moreover, we cannot rightfully state that technological societies are to be the ultimate goal of human accomplish-ment, nor that the type of human behavior these societies have produced through natural selection is to be considered as the final stage of human evolution.

In view of this fact, and from an educational point of view, one has to think in terms of what specific skills should be directly taught or enhanced to allow a society, such as the Venezuelan, to develop the necessary level of technological and organizational competence vis a vis first world countries. In doing so one must focus on the objective of *adding to* or *widening the scope of* the students' intellectual resources rather than substituting, changing the nature of or interfering with their identity or self-determination.

What follows is a brief description of some of the target skills addressed in The Teachers' Manual for Project Intelligence[4] and why they should be further developed within and in keeping with the Venezuelan cultural identity.

Teaching Foresight

In terms of the skills most appropriate to teach in the kind of *physical* environment of a country such as Venezuela, we find the skills relating to foresight as being most relevant. The more survival depends on foresight, the more it is necessary for the individual to exercise inductive and deductive reasoning. This, in turn, leads to a more structured analytic thinking process and a clearer understanding of the sequential ordering of reality in time and space. To be left out in the open or caught unprepared carries a more real meaning in environments where you have seasonal changes or where the particular characteristics of the environment require more constant prevision. When the physical environmental circumstances in the near or far future anticipate no major changes, tomorrow is just as good as today. Whatever action is taken to insure survival might be as sufficient today as it is tomorrow.

Given these premises, one could deduce that further emphasis on the direct teaching of inductive and deductive reasoning beyond the level we address this issue in our course would be advisable. Foresight is what allows the individual to be able to plan ahead and, therefore, to develop organizational skills. In furthering the teaching of deductive and inductive reasoning as applied to predicting future outcomes and as an instrument for problem solving, we would be promoting organizational skills and a more sequential assessment of reality.

---

[4]*Teachers' Manual—Project Intelligence*, Harvard University, Bolt, Beranek, and Newman Inc., Republic of Venezuela—Ministries of Education and Intelligence, 20 volumes, October 1985.

See also:

*Manual del Profesor—*Proyecto Inteligencia, published by Ministry of Education, Rep. of Venezuela, Vols. 1–3, 1986–

Odyssey—A Curriculum for Thinking, Mastery Education Corp., Pub., Watertown, Mass. 1986–

Teaching Participatory Skills

We also find participatory skills to be most relevant. In this respect the overall methodology of the course hinges on the highest degree of participation and effective interaction between teachers and students. The free exchange of ideas make it possible for every student to actively contribute to classroom activities. The teachers' traditional role of being the proprietor and provider of the information that the students must, for the most part, passively receive is completely altered. Both students and teacher enter into a new participatory kinship that eventually should transfer to community affairs.

The microcosm of the school environment reflects the power structure of society. Either society takes the lead and, as it changes, alters the school environment, or, the school system, by a deliberate attempt at doing so changes the school environment and, in so doing, accelerates the process of social transformation. In whatever direction the process of change becomes more active, what seems evident in the present structure of the Venezuelan society is an increasing development in the direction of students' participation in classroom activities and citizens' in community affairs.

The Language Issue

Our course introduces a number of key concept words that are mainly used as tools to organize and generate thinking. More to this effect should be done to provide a continuity to this effort.

The descriptive richness of the Spanish language should be used to further the development of new ideas based on these concept words in order to further their meaning and usage while preserving in parallel the expressive potential of the Spanish language. Analogical reasoning, for example, is a most adequate instrument to create relational bridges and promote concept formation.

Verbal reasoning centers on the analysis of the structure of meaning in language and how accurately it can be made to refer to reality. As such, the further development of lessons in this area, beyond those included in this course, would train students to use language with the precision required for its use in science and technology.

The Organizational Issue

Again, to deliberately teach students the basic principles of organization of ideas, concepts, arguments, plans of action, and the like seems like the most transferable process-oriented strategy to develop in them the kinds of skills that would foster administrative efficiency.

In teaching problem-solving strategies we directly teach the kinds of skills required to implement specific objectives and to deal with real world situations in an expedient and effective manner.

Teaching inventive thinking by using as an instrument the analysis of designs furthers the development of structural planning and valid assessment.

With these approaches we are not superimposing any alien cultural element into the Venezuelan culture but simply promoting a more structured use of its creative potential. Growth in this direction would facilitate a more adequate framework for its development.

Towards a Process-Oriented Curriculum

Any new fashion or mode of behavior implies a transformation, but when new fashions or modes are simply borrowed and not culturally adapted, they become another form of subjugation that tends to deform the existing identity rather than foster the development of a new one. Educational innovation should aim at producing a new synthesis based on creative adaptation and not on products of other successful cultures.

In teaching a process-oriented course, we directly promote cultural growth and creative adaptation. By training the students to be rationally selective we better prepare them to discriminate between what is useful and meaningful and what is merely superficial and futile. We are not confronting the students with the predefined shapes and manners of a new reality, but rather, giving them the mental skills to adequately process whatever stimulus they might encounter. Moreover, we present students with strategies to analyze designs, arguments, relationships and the like so that they can use these strategies in other situations where their own judgment would determine what value, usefulness or truth is there to that which they are investigating.

In terms of the right attitude, what we aim at is to cultivate intellectual initiative. Thinking is a habit fomented by the stimulus of ideas. The precision and effectiveness of the ideas resulting from the process of thinking improves the quality of further thinking. By focusing our attention on the process of thinking itself we strive towards a dual objective: to make the students aware of the value of the ideas they can produce; and, in doing so, awaken the students' confidence in the fact that they themselves can generate valid concepts, arguments, and evidence to support their claims.

Self-determinism sets as a prerequisite that the individuals belonging to any given society be able to productively think for themselves. The degree thereof of self-determinism depends on how well a given culture and, particularly, the educational system within the framework of that given culture are able to promote the kind of thinking skills that would be conducive to a more independent and successful social, organizational, economic, and political structure.

CONCLUSIONS AND ANCILLARY RECOMMENDATIONS

1. There are evident cultural and linguistic barriers in the present social structure of Latin America and, it's suggested, in third world countries generally, which prevent the desired level of scientific and technological development. Some of these impediments are long existing characteristics of these cultures in general, whereas others are the result of extrinsic pressures.

2. A principal force, under present global conditions, for promoting an integrated well-balanced development in third world countries is for implementation of a comprehensive educational program to directly train students and teachers at all levels in the kinds of skills and thinking processes required to promote the scientific, technological, and creative capacities of the population.

3. The nature of these programs should be carefully evaluated and adapted to insure changes in those specific attitudes and values that are considered to be the key inhibiting factors, and nourish those that can promote significant gains.

4. In the process of adding new thinking skills to the intellectual repertoire of the population, careful consideration should be given so as not to inhibit those skills that form part of the natural reservoir of their intellectual competence. Moreover, these should be used to acculturate the incorporation of the new skills in keeping with the positive elements in the cognitive profile of the population.

5. Particular attention should be given to vocabulary and the use of language. A special international commission should be set up to prepare and maintain updated versions of the dictionaries presently used in third world countries incorporating all the words and concepts used at present in science and technology. Simplified and illustrated editions should be made available for primary and secondary school levels. The new comprehensive program should directly and indirectly, and at every level, aim at incorporating the new concept words and their usage to the students' vocabulary.

6. A Permanent International Assembly of Graduate Schools of Education and Psychology should be set up to foster more rational educational approaches to bridge the inequalities of development at the international level. This assembly should maintain a global and unprejudiced perspective on education, guarantee the free-flow of information and pedagogical materials, and provide financial and logistic support to acculturate and implement programs.

10 Ethnic Differences in Academic Achievement in Fiji

Robert A. C. Stewart, Ph.D.
The University of the South Pacific
Suva, Fiji

INTRODUCTION

All around the world there is growing concern, often demonstrated through legislative action, with affirmative action: The need to provide equal opportunity regardless of ethnicity, sex, or other factors. At a time when the countries of the Western World seem to be reconsidering the paths they have chartered toward these desirable goals, it may be useful to consider how Fiji, with its 600,000 population spread across the vastness of the South Pacific ocean, is coping with its biethnic nature.

The University of the South Pacific (USP) is truly international serving 11 separate countries, ranging from Tokelau with a population of 1,600 to Fiji with 500,000 inhabitants. These 11 countries cover a geographic area three times that of Europe, but have a total land mass equivalent to Denmark. They extend from the Cook Islands in the East to the Solomon Islands in the West and encompass Western Samoa, Tokelau, Niue, Tonga, Fiji, Gilbert Island, Tuvalu, Nauru and Vanuatu. The region includes an estimated 60 cultures, 300 languages, and ranges across Melanesia, Polynesia and Micronesia.

The main campus of USP is in Suva, the largest city in Fiji, the largest and wealthiest of the eleven countries. Fiji contributes the bulk of the students attending USP. In terms of its per capita Gross National Output, Fiji is an "upper middle income" country on the World Scale, comparable, for example, to Costa Rica.

Fiji's largest export is sugar; tourism is also a major source of revenue. The country has been independent since 1970. One hundred years ago

163

Indians were brought by the British to work as indentured laborers. After surviving great hardships, most of the Indians remained to settle permanently in Fiji. They have been joined by others from India, and nowadays, Indo-Fijians (50%) outnumber the indigenous Fijian people (45%) whose roots in Fiji go back into the mists of time. Other groups in Fiji make up the remaining 5% and include Europeans, Part-Europeans, Rotumans, Chinese and other Pacific Islanders. The coexistence of these cultures in a single relatively small country is the source of "the Fijian education problem." Although the indigenous Fijians live quite comfortably, by South Pacific standards they are often at a disadvantage when compared with Indo-Fijians. Fearing the long term consequences of such competition, the British placed several affirmative action articles in the new country's constitution. For example, the vast proportion of the land on Fiji is owned by the indigenous Fijian people, and these land-owning rights are insured through the Fijian Land Trust Board and the Nation's Constitution. Seats in the Parliament are allocated to maintain proportionate representation of each group. Currently, the party in power is predominantly composed of the indigenous Fijian people, whereas the opposition parties presently have more Indo-Fijian members.

The So-Called "Fijian Education Problem"

Since independence there has been a massive expansion of secondary education. However, a source of concern to successive governments has been the fact that indigenous Fijians make proportionately less use of the educational system at the higher levels and accordingly do not qualify to the same degree for entry to professions and highly skilled occupations.

The Government is determined to have nearly equal participation rates at all levels of education for the two main ethnic groups. It prescribes a 50:50 admission policy for the University. In fact, the University is not involved in selecting individual students, and specifies only minimum standards for admission. Although an equal proportion of indigenous Fijians are admitted to the University they come with lower levels of academic performance; thus it is no surprise that they generally do not do well as the Indo-Fijians.

In 1979, the Fijian Teachers Association, the USP Institute of Education and the Suva Institute of Educational Research organized a seminar to define precisely the alleged "Fijian Education problem." A research officer was appointed (Mr. Joeli Nabuka), and the Fijian Education Achievement Project was launched.

Reports on the Fijian Education Achievement Project by both Mr. Nabuka (1982, 1984) and Dr. Warwick Elley (1979, 1982) provide a clear assessment of the present status of Fijian Education.

The Fijian Education Achievement Project used a random sample of 41 secondary schools—with separate samples for the analysis of Fiji Junior and New Zealand School Certificate (NZSC) results.

The major conclusions summarized here are from Elley (1982) and Nabuka (1982 & 1984).

(i) Fijian students to as well as or better than non-Fijians in English and Social Science. In fact Fijians do considerably better in English in the primary school (perhaps because they face no problems in transferring from vernacular script, as is the case for Hindi and Urdu). The advantage is maintained up to the University Foundation level, though this statistic is distorted by the Fijians greater school drop-out rate.

(ii) Fijian students do not perform as well as Indians in Science and Math subjects at any level. Science pass rates for the Fiji Junior certificate in 1980 were 36% (Fijian) and 44% (Indian). On the more difficult New Zealand School Certificate exam twice as many Indians (30%) passed as did Fijians (15%).

The Fijian Education Achievement Project sent two questionnaires to a random sample of 44 schools ($\frac{1}{3}$ of the total number of secondary schools). Of the 22 Fijian schools, 21 responded; and of the 22 Indian schools, 18 responded. One questionnaire was sent to school principals. Its conclusions were that Fijian schools are: (a) Smaller; (b) More remote; (c) Directed by less experienced principals; (d) Poorly equipped in science laboratories, libraries, furniture and office equipment.

On the other hand Fijian schools tended to have smaller classes perhaps in part because a greater proportion of indigenous Fijians live in remote rural areas. By correlating the information from the principals' questionnaire with school performance on the Fiji Junior Certificate exam four factors were identified that contributed to higher test performance: (1) Number of library books ($r = +0.39$); (2) Number of ancillary staff ($r = +0.37$); (3) Adequate science labs ($r = +0.32$); (4) Large classes ($r = +0.31$).

This last factor seems to contradict conventional educational wisdom but may really reflect rural vs. urban settings.

A second questionnaire was completed by nearly 3,000 pupils (1,055 Fijian and 1,895 Indian). It reveals the following differences between the two ethnic groups.

1. *Books in Home*. Indian pupils have access to more story books in English (33% Fijian pupils have over 20 books; 52% Indian pupils do.)

2. *Boarders*. Nearly $\frac{1}{3}$ of Fijian pupils in Form 4 (grade 10) attend boarding schools, whereas no Indian students are boarders.

3. *Living with Parents*. Another 20% of Fijian 4th formers live away from home with relatives and friends. Thus only 48% live with their parents, whereas 89% of Indian students live with their parents.

4. *Absence from School*. Approximately 13% of Fijian students admitted to being absent for more than 10 days in the first 2 terms of 1981. Only 8.7 % of Indian students said they were absent this often.

5. *Electricity in the Home*. There was no difference between ethnic groups in access to electricity in the home—there was a figure of 52% for both groups.

6. *Help with Homework*. There was a small reported difference in the amount of help with homework, as reported by both ethnic groups. Thus 31% of Fijians receive help 'often' compared with 38% of Indians.

Students at the University Level

Elley and Thomson (1978, 1979) used Progressive Achievement Tests to test USP Foundation students on three general skills: reading comprehension, general vocabulary and listening comprehension. (Note: USP "Foundation" is equivalent to North American High School grade 13 or USA first year University level.) On these language related skills Fijian students out performed most other groups. These results are partially consistent with Naidu's (1981) report on the academic performance of the different ethnic groups at USP. Here Fijians were found to outperform Indians in English, but not in the nine other disciplines. Table 10.1 (Naidu 1981) describes the relative performance of ethnic groups in ten different disciplines.

TABLE 10.1
Performance by Discipline of Ethnic Groups at USP for 1979

Discipline	First	Second	Third
Economics	Indians	Others	Fijians
Sociology	Others	Indians	Fijians
Geography	Others	Indians	Fijians
Admin. Studies	Indians	Others	Fijians
Maths	Indiana	Others	Fijians
English	Others	Fijians	Indians
Education	No marked differences		
Chemistry	Indians	Others	Fijians
Physics	Indians	Fijians	Others
Biology	Both Indians and Fijians equal		

A similar picture emerges from Gibbs (1981) study of student performance between 1976 and 1980 in the Fiji School of Medicine. Of the 64 Fijian students admitted, only 19 passed their medical course. By contrast, of the 47 overseas who were admitted, 24 passed; and of the 82 Indians admitted, 63 passed.

Overall we have a picture that doesn't quite add up. Indian students have a clear advantage in mathematics, but Fijians are better in English. These differences do not seem sufficient to explain the higher performance found among Indians at the university level. In fact, research in areas such as general ability (or intelligence) and language competence has shown that Fijian and Indian scores are not significantly different (cf. Bennett, 1970, 1971, 1972; Chandra, 1975A & B; and Elley & Thomson, 1978, 1979). Nutrition and pre-school education are two other factors that are roughly equalized for both groups. It seems that factors other than academic potential must be of crucial importance.

Such factors have been considered by Dr. Tupeni Baba (1979 & 1982) who has provided a useful framework of categories that may explain the level of Fijian education achievement in relation to other groups.

(a) *Psychological Factors*
Motivation–aspiration
Need Achivement
Locus of Control
Cognitive Style

(b) *Socio–Cultural Factors*
Individualism–cooperation
Cultural conflict
Tradition of academic scholarship

(c) *Institutional Factors*
Urban–rural
Facilities
Teacher quality

Since Baba's paper, both Basow (1982) and Kishor (1982a, 1982b) have found lower levels of self-esteem in Fijians as compared to Indians. Teachers know the importance of a healthy sense of self-esteem in students for successful achievement in the classroom. Students are more able to take risks (of exposing their possible ignorance or coming up with original solutions) if they have a basic sense of confidence.

Also significant is the finding by both the aforementioned authors, of a more *external* locus of control among Fijian than Indians. This represents a tendency to attribute one's successes and failures (say on a class test) to external factors such as luck or favoritism of the teacher. With an *internal* locus of control one would see oneself as dependent on one's *own* efforts rather than external factors over which one has no control. Thus it is possible that Fijian with strong University potential drop out simply because they do not recognize their own ability.

But the motivational picture is not quite that simple. Basow (1982) using a 4-factor measure of achievement motivation showed that Fijians score *higher* than Indo-Fijians on "competitiveness," particularly among males. Questions on this scale emphasize the importance of winning, doing better than others and enjoyment of competing. Fijians also score higher than Indo-Fijians on "work orientation" but this effect is only significant for females and for university students. Basow suggests that, "only Fijian students with exceptionally high work orientation scores make it to university." In other research it has been shown that high "work orientation" is important to actual educational achievement, but that high competitive scores do not necessarily facilitate this. Stewart (1980 & 1983) has shown that Fijians have a lower level of belief in the general trustworthiness of people than do Indo-Fijians. However, studies in the Solomon Islands (Stewart, 1983) show large differences in trust between people seen as "close" as compared to people seen as "distant." If this applies to Fijians as well it might explain why students tend to drop out as their schools get farther from home.

We have been focusing on Fijian education, but we should perhaps remind ourselves of what Fijian youngsters share with other youngsters, of whatever race. The psychologist, Abraham Maslow, has suggested that we can think of *universal* human needs in the following way: (a) The most basic are the physical needs (food, water, shelter, etc.); (b) Next are needs for a sense of love and esteem from others, and then finally; (c) A person needs to find meaning and purpose in life.

I would like to emphasize the psychological need of people to "feel good about themselves" or to have a positive sense of self-esteem. We have already noted the research studies that suggest that there may be lower levels of self-esteem in Fijians as compared to Indo-Fijians. An effort in this area may well have enormous benefit for all children, Fijian and non-Fijian alike. The more sure an individual feels about himself and his abilities the more willing he is to place himself in potential learning situations that may involve taking a risk.

There is much that teachers, parents and educational administrators can do to build a sense of confidence, competence and self-esteem in the young people with whose care they are charged. Canfield and Wells (1976) and Wertime (1979) have linked the amount of a pupil's self-esteem to a stack of poker chips. Some start out the learning game with more "chips," so to speak, than others; because of self-confidence they can take the bigger risks. Teachers have a particular responsibility to make sure each child has enough "chips" to stay in the learning game, and maintain a "you can do it" attitude. Reluctance to risk failure (because of lack of self-esteem) can be manifested in withdrawn silence on the one extreme to mischievous and disruptive behavior on the other.

What are the Alternatives in Fijian Education?

There are at least three options for Fijian Education: The first option is of course to do nothing. This is a perfectly respectable option for some problems, but I feel that many in Fiji would argue that this option is not possible in this case. In fact the existing affirmative action policies are a rejection of this option.

The second is to induce change at the psychological level. A number of the psychological factors listed *are* amenable to change through training. A child with a low sense of self-esteem can learn confidence; an individual can shift from an external locus of control to a somewhat more *internal* locus of control. Change of this variety requires training of teachers and parents.

A third is to try change at the socio–cultural and institutional levels. The socio–cultural factors listed by Baba may be somewhat less amenable to modification. However, such change is possible, if it is desired. It may be useful to remember that any living, dynamic culture is also continually changing. It is in the ability to blend the best from the past with the best from the future that a culture shows its vibrancy and vitality. Some observers (e.g. Davis, 1980, and Griffin, 1983) have argued that the message reaching Fijians is ambiguous—"stick with custom"/"change your ways." Both are necessary; the critical question is which to do when.

Conclusion

The *choice* of options rests primarily with the people of all races in the independent nation of Fiji. Fiji, like other nations will need to carve its own solutions to the problems of equalizing educational opportunity for *all* its citizens. Perhaps this chapter has provided a window on how these concerns are being addressed in Fiji, and the South Pacific. The long-term importance of such concerns is reflected in an old Chinese proverb:

"Those who plan one year ahead should grow crops.
Those who plan 10 years ahead should grow trees.
Those who plan 100 years ahead should take care of young people."

REFERENCES

Baba, T. L. (1979). A Challenge to the Nation: The Fijian Education Problem, *Directions, 2,* 15–19.

Baba, T. (1982). *Some Research Problems Worth Pursuing in Fijian Education,* 6.1 in Stewart, R.A.C. (Ed.)

Basow, S. A. (1982). Cross-Cultural Patterns in Achievement Motivation—Ethnic Group and Sex Comparisons in Fiji, 6.2 in Stewart, R.A.C. (Ed.)

Bennett, M. (1970). Reasoning Test Response in Urban & Rural Fijian and Indian Groups in Fiji, *Australian Psychologist, 5* (3) 260–266.

Bennett, M. (1971). Some Problems of General Ability Testing in Fiji, in Cross-Cultural Ability Testing: Report of a Research Workshop, Hamilton: University of Waikato.

Bennett, M. (1972). Predicators and Determinants of Educational Performance in the South Pacific, *Journal of Social Psychology, 88* (1), 145–146.

Canfield, J. & Wells, H. C. (1976). Self-Concept in Teaching and Learning, in *100 Ways to Enhance Self-Concept in the Classroom: A Handbook for Teachers and Parents,* Englewood Cliffs, NJ: Prentice Hall.

Chandra, S. (1975A). Some Patterns of Response on the Queensland Test, *Australian Psychologist, 10,* 185–192.

Chandra, S. (1975B). Cognitive Development of Indians and Fijians, in Berry T. & W. Lonner (Eds.) *Applied Cross-Cultural Psychology* Amsterdam Swets and Zeitlinger, BV, 248–253.

Davis, M. M. (1980, May). *Buccaneers and Chiefs: Muckers and the City—Crime and Delinquency Among Young Fijians.* Paper presented to 50th ANZAAS Congress, Adelaide, South Australia.

Elley, W. B. (1979). *Summing up Address at Research Seminar on Fijian Education,* sponsored by USP Institute of Education, Fijian Teachers Association and Suva Institute of Educational Research. Suva: USP.

Elley, W. B. (1982). *Progress Report on Project on Fijian Education Achievement.* Suva: University of the South Pacific Institute of Education.

Elley, W. & Thomson, J. (1978). *The English Language Skills of USP Foundation Studies.* Unpublished Report to the School of Education Board of Studies, University of the South Pacific.

Elley, W. & Thomson, J. (1979). *The English Language Skills of USP Foundation Studies.* Unpublished Report to the School of Education Board of Studies, University of the South Pacific.

Gibbs, W. T. (1981). The Performance of Fijian Medical Students. *Fijian Medical Journal, 9* (1 & 2) 19–22.

Griffin, C.C.M. (1983). Social Structure, Speech and Silence: Some Fijian Reactions to the Problems of Social Change. In Maxwell, W., et al. (Eds.) *Thinking: The Frontier Expands.* Philadelphia: Franklin Institute Press.

Kishor, N. (1982a). *Self Perception Among Adolescents in Fiji: Ethnic Comparisons.* Unpublished manuscript, University of the South Pacific, School of Education.

Kishor, N. (1982b). *The Effect of Self-Esteem and Locus of Control in Career Decision Making of Adolescents in Fiji,* 11.3 in Stewart, R.A.C. (Ed.)

Nabuka, J. (1982). *Progress Report on Project on Fijian Education Achievement.* Suva: Fijian Teachers' Association.

Nabuka, J. (1984). Influence of Home Background on the Achievement of Fijian and Indian Studies in Fiji. Unpublished MA Thesis. Australia: Macquarie University.

Naidu, R. (1981). *Success rate of ethnic groups in programmes and courses offered at the*

University of the South Pacific. Unpublished paper, School of Education, The University of the South Pacific.

Stewart, R.A.C. (with H. Laidlaw & M. Mulipola-Lui) (1980). Beliefs about Human Nature held by Adolescents in Fiji: Some Preliminary Ethnic and Sex Comparisons. *Social Behavior and Personality: An International Journal, 8* (1) 125–128.

Stewart, R.A.C. (1982). (Ed.) *Human Development in the South Pacific: A Book of Readings,* Second Edition. Suva: USP Extension Services.

Stewart, R.A.C. (1983). Us and Them: Beliefs about Human Nature held by Young People in the South Pacific. In Maxwell, W. (Ed.) *Thinking: The Frontier Expands.* Philadelphia: Franklin Institute Press.

Wertrine, R. (1979). Problems and Courage Spans, Lochhead, J. & Clement J. (Eds.) *Cognitive Process Instruction,* pp. 191–200. Philadelphia: Franklin Institute Press.

11 Inside the Mind of the Senior Manager

Daniel J. Isenberg
Harvard Graduate School of Business Administration
Boston, MA

Imagine the following situation: A man is sitting at a desk in an office, in front of him a tape recorder and a stack of seven index cards. He is told that on the seven cards is a short business case that has been cut up, pasted on the cards, and the cards randomly shuffled. He is told to work through the case to understand what if any are the problems facing the protagonist, and what if anything he should do. While working through the case he will be allowed to rearrange the cards in any way that he wants to, to take notes, and in general to perform the task in the way that he feels is best. The only constraint is that he is to think out loud while working on the case, reporting all of his thoughts, reactions, and ideas just as they occur to him. The man performs his task in the following way:

1. First, he reads the cards through once, and rearranges them in what seems to be chronological order.

2. Next, he goes through each card in detail, analyzing it systematically and thoughtfully for meaning.

3. His reported thoughts are fairly abstract, and he does not linger long over details, pausing primarily to ask many clarifying questions. To the observer he appears to flail about aimlessly, with no clear purpose or method for understanding the information he is studying.

4. The man postpones positive or negative evaluation of the protagonist, until late in the task.

5. He also postpones generating action steps until he has finished analyzing the whole case in detail and most facets of the case have been explored.

6. As the man proceeds with his task he is verbal and introspective, reporting his thoughts unhesitatingly as they occur. Yet despite his own introspectiveness, he does not "get into the shoes" of the case actors.

7. The end result of the task is an action plan that is simple, clear, and tied closely to the data in the case.

Now imagine an almost identical situation: a different man and a different office, yet the same cards, recorder, and instructions. This second man performs his task in the following way:

1. Rather than arranging the cards in sequence and then studying them, this man takes each card in its original sequence, studies it in depth, and then goes on to the next.

2. Rather than studying the cards in chronological order, this man glances frequently back and forth between cards, reconsidering and reinterpreting already processed information.

3. As he works through the cards, this second man pays attention to the details, hovering over specific facts, mulling possible interpretations.

4. In processing the information in the case, this second man interprets wildly, going way beyond the surface meaning of the facts to develop hunches several steps of inference removed from the data.

5. The man is quite critical of the protagonist early on in the task, using such terms as "crazy," "baloney," "stupid," "dumb."

6. The man intermingles diagnosis and action planning, generating action steps as early as the third card. When he is finished with his task, the action plan has several distinct steps and one or two contingency plans.

7. Finally, the second man empathizes with the case actors, frequently putting himself into their shoes.

One of these men is the general manager of a $1 billion division of a *Fortune* 100 company, with 16,000 divisional employees, profit and loss responsibility for the division, plus responsibility for strategy formulation; he is over 50 years old, and has six years' experience as a division general manager. The other is a very bright Harvard-Radcliffe college senior, 20 years old, planning a business career after first earning an MBA degree. Which man is the manager, and which man is the student?

Managerial Thinking

The fact that the answer to the previous question comes to us hesitatingly, and with limited confidence, is just one indication that our knowledge of managerial thinking is far from complete. A systematic search of the literature confirms that academic research on the internal workings of the managerial mind has been sporadic and unsystematic (e.g., Simon, 1976; Srivastva, 1983). On the face of it, the subject of managerial thinking seems to hold obvious importance to the study of management and organizational behavior, as well as to our more general understanding of human cognition in real-life situations. Yet there are several less obvious reasons, both practical and theoretical, for why the study of managers' thought processes is important. For one, we know a fair amount about the outward behavior of managers at various levels (e.g., Kotter, 1982; Mintzberg, 1973; Stewart, 1982), thus a complementary inside view that describes how managers think could be directly linked to these data. For example, Sproull (1984) has studied how low-level supervisors allocate their attentional resources. But we do not yet know what more senior managers spend their time thinking about, and how this resource allocation compares with the observations of discontinuous, spontaneous, and even frenetic behavior that have appeared in the literature (e.g., Mintzberg, 1973).

Second, we really know very little about the actual problem-solving and decision-making processes that executives use in their work. On the one hand, prescriptive models give the impression that managerial thinking should and can be systematic and rational (e.g., Kepner & Tregoe, 1965). Although much of this work is sophisticated and rich, it often is not grounded in an empirical, descriptive understanding of the actual thinking processes used by real executives. On the other hand, descriptive research on managerial thinking is frequently based upon speculation, unburdened by systematic data collection (e.g., Weick, 1983), although there are some exceptions (e.g., Argyris, 1982; Burgoyne & Hodgson, 1983; Staw, 1980). Do empirical observations of managerial thinking support, qualify, or contradict the more speculative views of how managers really think?

A third reason for studying the thought processes managers use in their job is in order to develop more effective managers. There is presently a burgeoning body of evidence from nonmanagerial professions (e.g., computer programming, medicine, physics, professional writing, chess playing, circuitry design, radiology, and so on) that suggests that expertise depends primarily upon the way professional knowledge is cognitively organized during and after training, and how this knowledge base is accessed during performance (e.g., Bouwman, 1981; Chase & Chi, 1981; Glaser, 1984). It is becoming increasingly clear, for example, that skillful performance is dependent upon an interaction between how professional knowledge is organized, the professional's cognitive abilities, and how the information is accessed (e.g., Glaser, 1984). Can we begin to piece together a cognitive profile of the skillful manager, a profile that takes into account the content of his or her knowledge, the organization of such knowledge, as well as how it is accessed? If so, can that profile then be used to better train aspiring managers and improve the performance of practicing ones? (These applied questions will not be addressed in the present chapter, but see Isenberg, 1984; 1985).

The Current Research Project

To begin to address the previous questions, an ongoing series of empirical field investigations of the thinking processes of very senior executives, primarily general managers, has been conducted (Isenberg, 1982, 1983, 1984, 1985, 1986, in press, in preparation). The research has drawn upon concepts from administrative theory (e.g., Axelrod's (1976) use of the concept of cognitive maps); nonlogical processes (Barnard, 1938), cognitive psychology (e.g., cognitive heuristics, Tversky & Kahneman, 1974), microeconomics (e.g., procedural rationality, satisficing, Simon, 1978b), artificial intelligence (e.g., plausible reasoning, Gentner & Collins, 1981), opportunistic planning (Hayes–Roth & Hayes–Roth, 1979), and organizational behavior (e.g., enactment and sensemaking, Weick, 1979). Each of these literatures has contributed in a piecemeal way to the conceptualizations that are now beginning to emerge.

Methodologically, the research has been heterodox, incorporating at various stages and with varying degrees of success in-depth interviewing, unstructured observation, multidimensional scaling and cluster analysis (e.g., Kruskal & Wish, 1978), verbal protocol analysis (Ericsson & Simon, 1984; Hayes, 1981b), questionnaire data, and a technique called "thought sampling," to be described later. (The opening examples are drawn from the collection and interpretation of verbal protocols, Isenberg, in press.)

By now the ongoing research project has involved over thirty managers, including five chief executive officers (CEOs), one president, thirteen division general managers, one chief financial officer (CFO), and fifteen middle managers ranging from functional vice president to junior market analyst. The results from a study of six of the most senior managers in the sample (Isenberg, 1984), as well as preliminary findings from a study of 12 division general managers in six companies, are summarized and illustrated later.

SIX SENIOR MANAGERS: STUDY ONE

The participants in the first study were three CEOs, one president, one CFO, and one division general manager. These managers worked in four companies ranging in size from $10 million and several hundred employees, to $1.4 billion and 16,000 employees.

Method

The methods in this first study consisted of:

1. a two hour initial interview to explore decision-making and problem-solving techniques, the use of rational analysis and intuition, the manager's historical development of managerial skills, as well as to collect background information about the company and the manager's role in it;

2. two days of passive, unstructured observation during which time attempts were made to infer what must be taking place inside the manager's mind in order to explain his on-line behavior;

3. a follow-up interview during which clarifying questions were asked and inferences presented from the previous two days of observation. Frequently, the feedback session uncovered additional thoughts relevant to the research topic.

Clearly, these methods were not systematic and left much room for the introduction of the researcher's own biases and assumptions. Nevertheless, the purpose at this stage of the research was primarily to generate plausible hypotheses, as well as to lead to the development of more rigorous and appropriate techniques for future data collection.

Results

The findings from Study One are summarized in Tables 11.1 and 11.2 (for a detailed description see Isenberg, 1984). They are categorized into observations of *what* the senior managers seemed to spend their time

TABLE 11.1
What the Six Senior Managers Thought About

The senior managers rarely made substantive decisions

The senior managers usually thought about business or technical issues off-line

The senior managers frequently thought about organizational and group processes on-line

The senior managers thought about individual people in great depth and on-line

Certain senior managers thought about one or a very few overriding concerns

TABLE 11.2
How the Senior Managers Thought

The senior managers relied heavily on intuition for
  - Sensing problems
  - Synthesizing data
  - Checking sustained analysis
  - Action–planning
  - Rapidly performing routine "programs"

The senior managers managed problem/opportunity/theme networks
  - Problem framing
  - Problem "networking"

The senior managers worked the ladder of abstraction

The senior managers thought and acted in tandem

The senior managers utilized surprises to further their understanding

---

thinking *about,* and *how* they thought when they paid conscious attention to those topics. The findings about what topics seemed to occupy the senior managers' attention stand in contrast to a common stereotype that students, junior managers, and many laypeople possess, namely, that managers spend their time thinking about important business issues— should we expand, maintain, or contract our product offerings? Should we build another manufacturing facility? If so, where? What should our long-term business plan be? How should we change our competitive strategy? Should we acquire company C or divest division D? More accurately, however, it appeared that during the course of the day these senior managers tended to think about people and processes. How can we implement our strategy? How can we encourage the kind of necessary cooperation between divisions within our company? Is Jack doing well in his new position? Who are the up-and-coming junior managers, and how can we encourage them to take initiative? The managers *did* think about the business, but that thinking tended more often than not to be off-line— driving in the car, flying to another city, during specially convened meetings to deal with business issues, and at home while listening to music or watching TV. Furthermore, instead of making discrete deci- sions, they often avoided or postponed pronouncing their own stance, preferring instead to wait for opportune moments to take incremental and reversible actions, or to help their subordinates perform the analyses and reach conclusions on their own (see Corbin, 1980; Weiss, 1980; Wrapp, 1967). On the occasions when these managers did announce decisions, it was very hard to pin down either *who* actually made the decision or *when* the decision itself was made. Much more attention was paid to defining the problem and initially framing the decision in the first place.

Identifying thinking *processes* that the senior managers used to deal with their tasks was more elusive, partly because many real-life cognitive processes are either automatic, inaccessible to introspection, or both. Nevertheless, it was possible at the end of the study to hypothesize five general characteristics of how these senior managers were thinking (see Table 11.2). Rather than exclusively using either intuition *or* rational analysis, the senior managers seemed to use the two in various combinations in order to (a) sense the existence of problems or issues that required further attention, (b) synthesize data into more complete and encompassing patterns, (c) check the results of sustained analysis (a "belt-and-suspenders" approach), (d) rapidly chart a course of action or generate possible solutions to problems, and (e) rapidly perform routine activities (e.g., sorting through their in-basket).

A second observation was that these senior managers did not spend their time solving isolated problems, rather they seemed to manage a "portfolio" of problems, opportunities, and issues, all of which were interconnected in the manager's mind, similar to an associative or semantic network (e.g., Collins & Quillian, 1969). Thus, when dealing with a production control problem, for instance, the manager may have been simultaneously cognizant of and dealing with career development issues in the production control group, the fact that the production control function was the scapegoat for unresolved conflict between manufacturing and the divisional controller's office, and the corporation's unwillingness to consider purchasing production control systems from a company other than IBM. Part of the process of problem management, then, was forming mental connections and more general and encompassing categories among the various problems and issues that the manager faces. A second part of the process was that of problem framing or problem defining, in which the problems or issues were cast in terms that made them more amenable to direct solution.

A third observation in Study One was that these managers worked the ladder of abstraction very vigorously, dealing with very specific and very general information in close juxtaposition. When examining a financial statement, for example, a manager might have identified a specific number to dwell upon, ask about, and try to understand, and may have used that one number as the underpinning for a hypothesis about an emerging industry trend. This rapid "recycling" between the general and specific was a very economic way of combining years of experience and general rules of thumb with each specific situation that arises.

Fourth, these senior managers appeared to think and act in close tandem. For them, the process of thinking through a problem involved attempting to solve it, and only through its solution could anything approximating true understanding emerge.[1]

A fifth characteristic of these senior managers' thought processes was the utilization of surprise to further their understanding. Numerous instances were observed in which the executives allowed themselves to be surprised, and instead of suppressing the surprising evidence they used it in order to test and advance their own understanding of their situation. Implicit in this approach seemed to be an attitude that the facts were friendly, although they may be frustrating at times.

Discussion

Several questions emerged from the first study of the six senior managers. For one, how specific were the findings to the level of chief executive officer? At this level we might suppose that managers' thinking tends to be very long term, somewhat removed from the responsibility of making operating decisions on a daily basis. Perhaps one would observe more of the stereotypical decision making if one were to observe lower-level general managers. Second, how close were the data to the actual thought processes used by the managers' being observed, or were they due more to the researcher's and managers' own inferences about their thinking? Recent research in psychology has led researchers to question interview data that asks respondents to introspect (Nisbett & Wilson, 1977). Third, are the emergent hypotheses descriptive of senior managers, or *effective* senior managers? Implicit in the study is the assumption that these managers are at least effective enough to have passed many tests of their effectiveness in comparison with their peers, yet the assumption of effectiveness needs to be more explicitly studied before strong confidence can be placed in the resulting prescriptions and implications of this research (Isenberg, 1985).

HOW GENERAL MANAGERS THINK: STUDY TWO

The questions raised in Study One led directly to the design of Study Two. Preliminary findings from Study Two are reported later. The participants

---

[1]Weick (1983), observing that managers appear to act thoughtfully yet spend little time thinking, has argued that:

> . . . thinking is inseparably woven into and occurs simultaneously with action. When managers tour, read, talk, supervise, and meet, those actions contain managerial thought, they do the thinking for managers, they are substitutes for thinking, and they reduce the necessity for separate reflective episodes. (p. 222)

Weick's picture conforms closely with the findings from Study One.

in Study Two were 12 general managers—division heads who managed no other general managers, had profit and loss responsibility, and had at least heavy input into, if not total responsibility for, the business strategy of their own division. The 12 general managers worked in six multidivisional corporations, and two managers per company participated in the study. One of the managers in each pair had been chosen by the senior human resource manager as an "outstanding" general manager with "great potential, one of our very best." The other had been chosen as an "average general manager, or one who had been experiencing some difficulty." All data collection was conducted blind. The six companies included three mature or declining companies (metals, industrial equipment, consumer durables) and three high-growth companies (electronics, communications, component distribution). The divisions ranged from small to large in both dollar volume and numbers of people employed.

Method

Five methods of data collection were used in an attempt to improve on Study One by being more systematic and getting closer to the actual thought processes the managers used in their work. As in Study One, three of the methods included an initial interview, two days of observation and inference, and feedback and discussion. In addition, two other methods were used.

Verbal protocol analysis.   As described in the introduction to this chapter, each manager spent anywhere from 20 to 45 minutes reading, analyzing, and coming up with an action plan for the Dashman Company case while thinking aloud and talking into a tape recorder. The recordings were transcribed carefully and subjected to a content analysis. This method is called verbal protocol analysis and is one of the most widely used methods for studying problem-solving in cognitive psychology (Ericsson & Simon, 1984; Hayes, 1981b). The Dashman case was chosen for its shortness (713 words), for its lack of technical detail, and for its proven subtlety and richness through its use as a teaching case since 1947. Instead of the case being presented in its typical format, the case was divided into its seven major paragraphs and each paragraph was typed on an index card. Before each session, the cards were shuffled. This was done in order to better study how managers cope with nonsequential information processing.

A subsidiary study was conducted comparing the first four general managers' Dashman protocols with those of three Harvard–Radcliffe seniors interested in business careers. The purpose of the subsidiary study was both to help develop the content coding scheme and also to begin to isolate the "managerial" components of the thinking that the general managers used while responding to the Dashman case.

Thought sampling.   A second method labelled "thought sampling" was developed in conjunction with this research. Like verbal protocol analysis, it is a thinking aloud method, but rather than thinking aloud while analyzing a case or while engaged in a problem-solving task determined by the researcher, the managers were asked approximately ten times during a day that they were observed to either "Tell me what is going through your mind right now," or "Tell me what was going through your mind when [the meeting/phone conversation/spontaneous interaction] occurred a few minutes ago," depending upon whether the manager was engaged in interaction or was alone at the time. The answers to the questions were tape recorded, transcribed, and analyzed.

Preliminary Findings[2]

Observations and interviews.   A number of tentative patterns are beginning to emerge from preliminary analyses of the data from Study Two. It appears that the hypotheses that emerged from Study One are being confirmed, with some important qualifications. The division heads in Study Two do not seem to make a greater number of substantive decisions than did the first six executives from Study One, but there does seem to have been more on-line thinking about the technical issues, particularly in the smaller divisions (less than $100 million). For example, two managers of $40 million divisions were studying product blueprints and project projections in detail. The managers still seemed to devote the bulk of their attention to thinking about implementation, particularly people and organizational processes.

Second, although these managers relied, if anything, more heavily on intuition than did the managers in Study One, some of them have used systematic decision-making techniques such as decision trees and linear programming. Nevertheless, they expressed skepticism about the value of such methods unless supported by their gut feelings. Furthermore, there was some individual variation. One of the managers considered himself to be a very rational and disciplined manager and had introduced planning of various kinds into his division. At least some of his thinking seemed to be heavily influenced by the model of rationality prescribed in Kepner and Tregoe (1965).

Third, there seemed to be greater variation in the treatment of surprise.

---

[2]These findings are based on the first six general managers whose data have been analyzed. More complete reports are currently in progress (Isenberg, 1985b; in press (b)).

The same "rational" manager described earlier tended to suppress surprise, reacting to its occurrence with anger rather than treating surprise as instructive. Most of the managers however, showed great interest when surprising events arose and used them as opportunities to learn something new.

The findings vis-à-vis thinking–acting cycles, working the ladder of abstraction, and problem management appear at this stage to be replicated.

Protocol analyses. The comparison of students' and general managers' responses to the Dashman case has led to the profiles presented in the introduction to this chapter. Tables 11.3 and 11.4 present two examples, and Table 11.5 presents a summary profile of the students' and general managers' analytic strategies (see Isenberg, in press). The first example is taken from the protocol of a division head, the second taken from the protocol of a student. In the manager's protocol one can see the early emergence of action ideas, critical evaluation, a process of fitting the various pieces together in his mind, and the suggestion that Mr. Post follow an incrementalist approach to his situation. The student's protocol illustrates a greater amount of information seeking, and a very intelligent, in-depth analysis of Post's situation that sticks closely to the facts of the case. However, it also displays a distant, or nonempathic understanding

TABLE 11.3
General Manager's Protocol

Well, what, yeah, what I'm trying to do is I'm trying to figure out, I'm trying to sort out, I, I'm supposed to be Mr. Post and ah, I guess, you know you—have a hard time here with that because I don't identify very well with this guy, but ah and I don't know why, you know, as Mr. Post, one of my first decisions was to begin immediately to centralize the company's purchasing procedure. Ah, it ah, e-e-, I know why, but, I mean, says here, it was *experienced* person executive in charge of purchasing, and then it says raw materials are going to become increasingly difficult supply, and so, and this is late in 1940, so we could see the war's comin', and so that I, I can see the advantage of centralizing the ah ah purchasing ah ah but, knowing what I know about history, you know, I, I might not go at it this way, I'd say, hey, what are, what are the things that might become difficult, you know, i-i-i-i its, it's says the company would face increasing difficulty in securing certain essential raw materials. Well, what are those certain essential raw materials, and why don't I focus on that problem rather than on trying to centralize the company's purchasing procedure which I don't, I can see, that I could centralize certain essential raw material purchases very quickly, whereas if I try to centralize the whole damn purchasing thing, I can't do it as quickly, and then I could, well I don't see why I can't move in a step-wise fashion into the whole thing, that's what bothers me, I think, right now, I mean this is what I'm what, I'm gettin' out of it, and then I don't like the idea of people who try to move in without a lot of, without a lot of, of background and try to centralize things. And then secondly, . . .

TABLE 11.4
Student's Protocol

Well, uhm, I don't know if they would understand, although it does sound like if they are going to coordinate all the different offices, they'll need to centralize in some way, or somehow be aware of what each head is doing. Um, but I wonder what the alternatives were? This procedure should give us in the central office the information that we need to see that each plant secures the optimum supply of materials. In this way the interest of each plant and the company as a whole will best be served. Now—on the one hand he's just saying that uh, all they want is information, in this first paragraph, that the purchasing executive in the several plants, notify the central office of these larger contracts. But then in the second paragraph there's the implication that there's more is going to happen than just information, that in fact the ability of the separate plants to go ahead and make purchases will uh, actually be overseen, and subject to the approval of the central authorities. Uhh (short pause) so, the central office will use this information, and they will make sure that each plant secures the optimum supply of materials and they will tell the plants what the optimum materials are instead of the plants themselves, who probably know the uh, buying, the needs of the plants better, uhm, are going to be told what to buy. So—or what the optimum supply is. Uhm, I'm wondering how Mr. Post knows that the central authorities are going to know what the optimum amount is, uh, if he hasn't even visited the central plants? And I wonder how much he knows about the purchasing procedures of each of the plants? Uhm, although from the company's, if in some way, each of the plants has to, and and and I wonder why there's an optimum supply that the central plant, that the central location would be able to figure out that each of the separate ones wouldn't? Uh, now did the separate ones work together in relation to the central office?

---

of Mr. Post's situation. The student's protocol is fairly neutral in its evaluation of Mr. Post.

Thought sampling—illustrative examples. Tables 11.6 and 11.7 show examples taken from the thought sample protocols of two division heads, and are included primarily to illustrate the data generated by the thought sampling procedure. It is clear from these two examples that these two general managers were very evaluative and were quite concerned with people and processes. Furthermore, we can see an example of problem management in the protocol of the head of the industrial equipment division in that he perceived a number of connections between the visit of the corporate task force and his own longer term interests. This is the kind of opportunistic thinking by the general managers that seemed so prevalent and that is consistent with their strategy for responding to the Dashman case (Isenberg, in press).

DISCUSSION

At this stage of the research one must resist the temptation to overinterpret the findings. However, it is possible to identify several theories

TABLE 11.5
Case Problem Solving Strategies: Managers versus Students

Students	Managers
Read all cards at once	Study cards one at a time
Rearrange cards sequentially	Do not rearrange cards
Then systematically study each card	Go back and forth through cards
Remain abstract (gloss details)	Stick on details, interprets
Ask many clarifying questions	Ask some clarifying questions
Flail about unsystematically, aimlessly	Appear purposeful, guided
Are not critical early on	Are very critical early - "crazy" "stupid" "bullshit"
Postpone generating action ideas	Intermingle action planning and diagnosis
Expressive, reflective, introspective	Not reflective
Action plans are simple, tied to analysis	Action plans are complex, somewhat tied to diagnosis
Show nonempathic understanding	Show empathic understanding

that are consistent with the data, and that appear to be helpful in conceptualizing about the general domain of inquiry. Three such theoretical positions are discussed later, namely, the phenomenon of *ill-structured problems* (e.g., Taylor, 1974), *cognitive models of action planning* (e.g., Hayes-Roth and Hayes-Roth, 1979), and *natural reasoning process* (e.g., Collins, Warnock, Aiello, & Miller, 1975).

Ill-structured problems.   Assuming the reliability and validity of the findings reported thus far, we want to begin to explain why senior managers think the way they do. One source of explanation is the task environment that these senior managers work within. Although there are risks associated with invoking the environmental imperative too freely, it is nevertheless a common and often fruitful starting place when a researcher attempts to place a set of findings in perspective (e.g., Homans, 1950). Just what is the operating environment of the senior manager? For our purposes, four of Kotter's (1982) six characteristics of the job of general manager are important:

1. Setting goals, policies, and strategies despite great uncertainty;

TABLE 11.6

GM Industrial Equipment Division

Context	Thoughts
Meeting with HR staff and Communications consultant. Plant closure announcement.	"Concerned that they are focusing on communicating this one subject and not addressing communication total status of where our business is at . . ."
Similar meeting, 1 month later, reacting to detailed action plan for communicating plant closing to work force.	"It's hygienic, not personal . . . need to recognize the blending of personal and business needs . . . bothers me that this is getting too (sterile) . . . There's got to be some better way to do this procedure . . ."
	"(Simulates plan in his mind; this generates criticism of plan) Christ, what you think you're going to tell them has already been told to them, so let's get everybody together . . ."
	"I was trying to say, let's get everybody, all our managers, into our confidence at the same time as the union . . . then address the concern of having some way of asking questions and giving feedback . . ."
Meeting with corporate (R&D) task force on involvement with product standards	"Planting a seed . . . about funding . . . we may be able to qualify for some money . . . and a seed about engineering not going to be a separate function long after the (business group) reorganization . . . engineering and manufacturing ought to merge . . ."
	"Let them know that what they're working on is important . . . make them receptive in case you come up with ideas . . . they're all in a position to really help if you've got an emergency."

2. Balancing resource allocation among functions, business units, and various time frames;

3. Controlling an extremely diverse set of activities in order to identify and solve problems rapidly;

4. Managing a network of relationships that includes hundreds of people who can either offer support or provide resistance to the manager.

TABLE 11.7
Consumer Durables

GM Division

Context	Thoughts
General manager's staff meeting. Publicizing changing of suppliers.	"What *is* our position? I can't sit here and say we're not going to communicate . . ." "Participative management says communicate but shop chairman wants his name in the papers . . ."
General manager's staff meeting. Discussion of trip to competitor/possible partner in venture.	"I'm planting the seed (for possible cooperation) . . ." "Let's look at it, no emotion . . . think it out, know whether it fits strategic plan going forward . . ."
New product presentation. Total project team attending.	"What the hell is he bringing all these people in for? . . . what are they gonna do . . . something I don't expect . . . (engineer) should have set special meeting . . . I'm playing catch-up . . ."
Staff meeting. Discussion of shop chairman.	"I'm ready to puke . . ." "Jesus Christ, here we go again, waste some more time . . . we're not going to solve anything, just play with ourselves until we get it out of our system . . ."

Emphasizing that the dominant issue in understanding the general management task is "understandable complexity," Kotter (1982) comments that the task:

. . . show[s] a level of complexity which even the general managers themselves had difficulty consciously understanding. Indeed, as we shall see, these very successful general managers often had great difficulty explaining what it was they did, why, and why that worked as well as it did. (p. 9)

The great degree of uncertainty, combined with the strenuous information processing demands associated with the general management task, are characteristic of what are variously called ill-structured problems (e.g., Taylor, 1974), wicked problems (e.g., Rittel & Webber, 1973), ill-defined problems (Hayes, 1981a), or nonprogrammed activities (March & Simon, 1958). Table 11.8 systematically summarizes several factors that contribute to the ill-structured nature of the senior management environment. Fig. 11.1 hypothesizes several effects of ill-structured task environments upon the cognitive functioning of senior managers. Specifically, we can begin to see how ill-structuredness might lead to the increased importance of problem definition (Lyles & Mitroff, 1980) and the increased ability to cope with surprising events. The increase in cognitive construction and thinking–acting cycles are described well by Hayes (1981a):

> It is easy enough to create an ill-defined problem. If you sit down at your local lunch counter and order a "milk shake, please, any flavor," you will have presented the counter people with an ill-defined problem. They may refuse to accept it . . . or they may accept the problem enthusiastically, reveling in the creative freedom you have provided them . . .
>
> Since each problem solver may make different "gap-filling" decisions in solving the same ill-defined problem, each may, as a result, arrive at a different solution . . . [which] may differ considerably in quality. Our skill in solving ill-defined problems, then, depends in an important way on our ability to make good gap-filling decisions.
>
> The second action we may have to take to define an ill-defined problem is to jump into the problem before we fully understand it. Very often the real nature of a problem is hidden from us until we actually try to solve it. (p. 22)

TABLE 11.8
Characteristics of Unstructured Problems

	Problem Definition	Problem Causes
THE PROBLEM	Experts disagree on definition Problem symptoms shift Multiple, interrelated symptoms Imprecise, unreliable information on symptoms	Multiple causes Causes are interrelated Imperfect cause-relations Causes are unique
THE GOALS	Goal Properties Multiple goals Conflicting goals with inherent trade-offs	
THE SOLUTIONS	Solution Properties Multiple paths Solution not identifiable	Solution-Cause Links Attempted solutions change causes Long-linked feedback Ambiguous–imprecise feedback

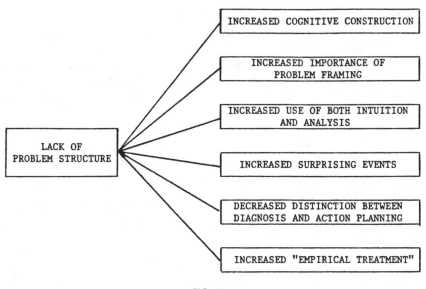

FIG. 11.1

What Hayes refers to as "gap-filling" is the same as "cognitive construction" in Fig. 11.1 and closely related to Weick's (1979) concept of "enactment," that is, using the degrees of freedom inherent in the plethora of data to construct an understanding that loosely fits, but an understanding that is one of many possible understandings. Hayes' notion of "jumping in" to work on a problem prior to its definition is the same as what is here identified as "thinking–acting cycles" (Isenberg, 1984; 1985). It is also similar to "empirical treatment" in medicine, and "empirical design" in engineering, namely, that when faced with a complicated or poorly understood disease or design problem, treatment or design is embarked upon in the absence of a complete understanding of all of the causes. In medicine, the problem may be cured without the physician ever knowing exactly what the problem was, or knowing only after the cure is complete. Thus we often observe senior managers acting before they think very much, all the while using intuition to determine exactly where to being the thinking–acting cycle.

Cognitive models of action planning.   The senior manager's world is laden with action, yet very little is understood about how senior managers formulate specific action steps. Our preliminary observation earlier is that various categories of intuitive processes partially describe the process of action planning. Recent work in artificial intelligence provides some insight into these elusive processes. For example, Hayes-Roth (Hayes-Roth & Hayes-Roth, 1979; Hayes-Roth, 1983a, 1983b) contrasts two models of the action planning process, the *hierarchical* model and the *opportunistic* model. The hierarchical model we recognize as that of managerial rationality, in which general goals are initially stated and are successively refined into subgoals until some minimal level of action specificity is reached, at which point the planning stops and execution begins. At each stage of the action planning process, more general goals are accepted as givens, and subgoals are established only in order to achieve the more general ones (see March & Simon, 1958, for a similar discussion of means–ends analysis).

A second, more complex and more realistic cognitive model is the opportunistic model, that allows for new opportunities to arise for better action planning and action taking at various points in the implementation process. At these points, the plans are modified in ways that were impossible to foresee when planning initially began. "This view of the planning process suggests that planners will produce many coherent decision sequences, but some less coherent sequences as well. In extreme cases the overall process might appear chaotic" (Hayes-Roth & Hayes-Roth, 1979, p. 276).[3] The opportunistic model has been developed and tested in experimental situations in which a person has ten hypothetical errands to plan out and run in a hypothetical town, given a map of the town and a time frame. These are the kinds of problems, commonplace for senior managers, in which there is too much to do in too little time, and thus the amount of information that the planner needs to hold in working memory is excessive. In these situations, according to Hayes–Roth, the plan develops incrementally, there is a jumping around within the planning space, several unrelated specific sequences are planned without linking them together, specific sequences are planned disregarding the overall plan, priorities may be ignored at any one point, and each decision produces a new situation, thus influencing subsequent decisions.

What are the cognitive skill requirements of opportunistic thinking? For one, a very active memory that allows the planner to be flexibly matching needs with opportunities, as can be seen in the thought samples of both general managers as they "plant seeds" for future cooperation

---

[3]Hammett's *Red Harvest* (1929) portrays numerous examples of opportunistic action planning, such as the following dialogue shows:

"Is that what you were up to when you uncooked the fight?"

"That was only an experiment—just to see what would happen."

"So that's the way you scientific detectives work. My God! For a fat, middle-aged, hard-boiled, pig-headed guy, you've got the vaguest way of doing things that I ever heard of."

"Plans are all right sometimes," I said. "And sometimes just stirring things up is all right—if you're tough enough to survive, and keep your eyes open so you'll see what you want when it comes to the top."

"That ought to be good for another drink," she said. (p. 79).

(Tables 11.6 and 11.7). Second, opportunistic thinking requires the ability to make connections among different problems and opportunities, an ability that is directly related to the concept of the problem network that is part of the process of problem management. Third, it requires an *attitude* of taking advantage of every opportunity as it arises, which is consistent with the observation that the general managers in Study Two tended to fully take advantage of the information present on each card as it appeared. Fourth, opportunistic thinking requires a certain attitude towards surprise; for the manager to think opportunistically, he must continually entertain the expectation that expectations will change due to unplanned and unpredictable events and information. The fifth cognitive requirement of opportunistic thinking is the ability to mentally simulate action–result sequences during implementation because these sequences cannot all be planned out in advance and new action planning takes place during the process of implementation.

Given the previous discussion, it seems likely that the opportunistic model of action planning captures an important portion of the variance in managerial thinking, a belief that is strengthened by opportunistic-like concepts that have appeared in the administrative literature (e.g., muddling through, Lindblom, 1959; logical incrementalism, Quinn, 1980; and garbage can processes, Cohen, March, & Olsen, 1972). Nevertheless, the opportunistic model has both descriptive and prescriptive problems. For one, many senior managers do in fact engage in long-term planning, which should not occur in a purely opportunistic mode. Second, many senior managers do in fact forego opportunities because they are in conflict with plans, policies, or strategies. Prescriptively, opportunistic action planning and implementation runs the risk of the "local maximum." In other words, it is possible by planning in purely opportunistic terms to paint oneself into a corner by painting in those areas that are easiest to get to and ignoring an overall plan.

In a recent paper Hayes–Roth (1983a) has introduced the concept of "strategic opportunism," and although undefined, the term is evocative and suggests an answer to the shortcomings of opportunistic thinking. Strategic opportunism connotes an interaction between general goals, policies, and strategies on the one hand, and on the other hand specific emergent opportunities that can only be determined by the unique characteristics of each situation. The interaction takes place in the form of a bottom-up flow of information about the specific opportunities inherent in each situation, and a top-down flow of goals, constraints, and rules.

How consistent is the model of strategic opportunism with the findings from the current research? The observation that senior managers vigorously work back and forth between general and specific information is quite consistent with strategic opportunism. Strategies, goals, and policies are all very general and abstract, whereas thoughts about people and organizational processes, and the ability to empathize with people observed in the Dashman protocols, are very specific. The ability to connect specific actions and information to general policies and strategies is a major component of strategic opportunism; as one executive vice president put it:

> One rule of thumb that I have learned is to know to the bottom of your soul what it is you are trying to accomplish so you can take advantage of the opportunities as they come up. It is impossible [while you are managing] to continue to look at a written reference source, a piece of paper, [e.g., a strategic plan] to take advantage of opportunities which need to be responded to instantly.

Natural reasoning: plausible versus logical. Understanding the thinking processes that senior managers use on the job requires us to understand the reasoning processes that they use in order to comprehend the problems, issues, and opportunities that confront them. One model that is helpful in understanding this aspect of managerial thinking is sometimes called "plausible" reasoning (e.g., Collins, et al., 1975; Gentner & Collins, 1981). To sum up years of research on human reasoning processes, it has become quite clear that humans do not typically reason in strictly logical terms. The concept of plausible reasoning as distinct from logical reasoning is both descriptively accurate and prescriptively helpful. For example, in response to the following question: "Have you ever met Ronald Reagan?", most people answer in the negative after a few seconds thought. How do they arrive at the answer? It is both impractical and impossible for people to survey every experience they have had in which they had met a person, and ask themselves, was that person Ronald Reagan or not? Instead, people reason, "If I had met a president of the United States, I would have remembered it. Ronald Reagan is a president of the United States. I don't remember meeting him, therefore, I did not meet him." Plausible? Yes. Logical? No, because it is founded on a likely premise, not a sound premise.

Plausible reasoning does a tolerably good job at arriving at probable conclusions in most circumstances, yet not always. When asked if San Diego is east or west of Reno, Nevada, most people conclude that San Diego is west of Nevada based on the argument that California is west of Nevada (true), and therefore all places in California are west of all places in Nevada (false).

Plausible reasoning is useful in explaining many of our observations of senior managers, such as the working back and forth between general and specific information in order to develop models of the situations they are faced with. In this process, managers develop hunches that make sense given the limited information at hand, and then selectively search for information to support or disconfirm those hunches (although they tend to look more for confirming than for disconfirming information). This can be seen quite clearly in the Dashman protocols, as well as in the on-line observations and thought samples. For example, one division head received a phone message that he had been called by a product expediter from another division that purchased products from the manager's division. The division general manager surmised that the expediter could have been calling for one of two reasons, either price or delivery time on a specific production run. Walking by his marketing manager's office, the general manager asked a subordinate why might the expediter be calling, and immediately received the answer, "Price." Notice that the plausible reasoning process used in this case rapidly limited the number of possibilities to be tested for. Note also that although this answer obviously constituted a very weak test of his hypotheses, the answer boosted his confidence in one of the hypotheses from moderate to almost total. Thus, one of the benefits of the plausible reasoning process is that it sharply increases the incremental value attached to each new datum, more so than if plausible hypotheses had not been generated. Plausible reasoning also raises the incremental value of surprises, because a surprise in other terms is a signal that what the manager thought was plausible might in fact be implausible, and the manager's "map" of the situation may require changes.

The fallacy of decision discreteness.   The suggestion from this research program is that managers seldom make discrete decisions that are substantive in nature, but rather emerge in a multiperson, multitopic, ongoing process that eventuates in incremental actions taken by different individuals, not the manager alone. Opportunistic thinking supports such a process because it facilitates the manager's flexible response to new information, new perspectives, and unanticipated obstacles and opportunities. In fact, when problems are ill-structured, avoiding discontinuous, "large" decisions is probably an optimal strategy. If one of the characteristics of problems is the impossibility of identifying all of the relevant factors in advance with certainty, the chances of ignoring an important variable and creating unintended consequences are great. Furthermore, developing a plausible understanding of the situation may be helped when the manager takes a series of small, incremental steps, making modest changes on a small number of variables at a time and maximizing learning from each step by reflecting on the consequences.

Nevertheless, our stereotype of managers as quintessential decision-makers, which I call the fallacy of decision discreteness, is a resilient one. Perhaps this is because the belief in discrete, substantive decisions helps us to parse, interpret, and communicate about the ongoing stream of activity that exists in organizations. "Making a decision" then becomes a term of convenience for simplifying a complex, relatively undifferentiated mass of actions. In other words, the fallacy serves more of a function for the observer of managers and organizations, and less of a function for managers themselves. This argument suggests, therefore, that rather than being a blueprint for future managerial action ("I should make decisions"), the concept of decision is more useful for retrospective reflection on events that have already occurred. The major drawback for thinking in terms of discrete decisions occurs when we confuse the *concept* of decision making with organizational *reality* itself. Thus, believing that managers make decisions, inexperienced managers ignore the subtlety of all of the processes that in actuality represent the work of the manager, and tend towards pronouncements of policy and strategy that are ultimately ineffective (Weiss, 1980; Wrapp, 1967).

CONCLUSION

To summarize the research findings and explanatory theory to date, it has been suggested that senior managers rarely make discrete, substantive, business decisions, spend the bulk of their on-line attention thinking about organizational and interpersonal processes as opposed to technical aspects of the business, and pay attention to a small number of overriding concerns. The process by which they move the organization forward is characterized by several types of intuition, the management of a cognitively connected portfolio of problems and issues, recycling back and forth between general and specific information, paying attention to the phenomenon of surprise, and cycles of thinking and acting in close concert. On a more general level, their thinking takes place in the form of plausible reasoning, seems to be characterized by "strategic opportunism," and is adapted to dealing with ill-structured problems. It is also argued that discrete decision making by managers is somewhat of an inaccurate term that serves a function for the observer more than for the manager.

REFERENCES

Argyris, C. A. (1982). *Reasoning, learning, and action*. San Francisco: Jossey–Bass.
Axelrod, R. (ed.) (1976). *The structure of decision*. Princeton, NJ: Princeton University Press.
Barnard, C. I. (1938). *The functions of the executive*. Cambridge, MA: Harvard University Press.

Bouwman, M. (1981). The use of accounting information: Expert versus novice behavior. In G. Ungson & D. Braunstein, *Decision-making: An interdisciplinary inquiry,* pp. 134–167. Boston, MA: Wadsworth.

Burgoyne, J., & Hodgson, V. (1983). Natural learning and managerial action: A phenomenological study in a field setting. *Journal of Management Studies, 20,* 387–399.

Chase, W., & Chi, M. (1981). Cognitive skill: Implications for spatial skill in large-scale environments. In J. Harvey (ed.), *Cognition, social behavior, and the environment,* pp. 111–136. Hillsdale, NJ: Lawrence Erlbaum Associates.

Chase, W., & Simon, H. (1973). Perception in chess. *Cognitive Psychology, 4,* 55–81.

Cohen, M., March, J., & Olsen, J. (1972). A garbage can model of organizational choice. *Administrative Science Quarterly, 17,* 1–25.

Collins, A., Warnock, E., Aiello, N., & Miller, M. (1975). Reasoning from incomplete knowledge. In D. Bobrow & A. Collins (eds.), *Representation and understanding: Studies in cognitive science,* pp. 383–415. New York: Academic Press.

Collins, A., & Quillian, M. (1969). Retrieval time from semantic memory. *Journal of Verbal Learning and Verbal Behavior, 8,* 240–247.

Corbin, R. (1980). Decisions that might not get made. In T. Wallsten (ed.), *Cognitive processes in choice and decision behavior,* pp. 47–68. Hillsdale, NJ: Lawrence Erlbaum Associates.

Ericsson, K., & Simon, H. (1984). *Verbal protocol analysis.* Cambridge, MA: MIT Press.

Gentner, D., & Collins, A. (1981). Studies of inference from lack of knowledge, *Memory and Cognition, 9,* 434–443.

Glaser, R. (1984). Education and thinking: The role of knowledge. *American Psychologist, 39,* 93–104.

Hammett, D. (1929). *The complete Dashiell Hammett.* New York: Knopf, 1942 (1929).

Hayes, J. (1981a). *The complete problem solver.* Philadelphia: Franklin Institute Press.

Hayes, J. (1981). Issues in protocol analysis. In G. Ungson & D. Braunstein (eds.), *Decision-making: An interdisciplinary inquiry,* pp. 61–77. Boston, MA: Wadsworth.

Hayes–Roth, B. & Hayes–Roth, F. (1979). A cognitive model of action planning, *Cognitive Science, 3,* 275–310.

Hayes–Roth, B. (1983a). *The blackboard architecture: A general framework for problem-solving?* Unpublished manuscript, Stanford University Computer Science Department.

Hayes–Roth, B. (1983b). *A blackboard model of control.* Unpublished manuscript, Stanford University Computer Science Department.

Homans, G. (1950). *The human group.* New York: Harcourt Brace.

Isenberg, D. J. (1982, August). *Managers' knowledge structures.* Paper presented at the Academy of Management Annual Meetings, New York, August 1982.

Isenberg, D. J. (1983). *Drugs and drama: The effects of two dramatic events in a pharmaceutical company on managers' cognitions.* Harvard Business School Working Paper.

Isenberg, D. J. (1984). How senior managers think. *Harvard Business Review,* November-December, 80–90.

Isenberg, D. J. (1985). Some hows and whats of managerial thinking: Implications for future army leaders. In J. Hunt & J. Blair (Eds.), *Leadership on the future battlefield.* New York: Pergamon.

Isenberg, D. J. (1986). The structure of process of understanding: Implications for managerial action. In H. Sims & D. Gioia (Eds.), *The thinking organization.* San Francisco: Jossey-Bass.

Isenberg, D. J. (in press) Thinking and managing: A verbal protocol analysis of managerial problem solving. *The Academy of Management Journal.*

Isenberg, D. J. (in preparation). *Managerial thinking: Toward strategic opportunism.* Book manuscript.

Kepner, C., & Tregoe, B. (1965). *The rational manager.* New York: McGraw–Hill.

Kotter, J. (1982). *The general managers.* New York: Free Press.

Kruskal, J., & Wish, M. (1978). *Multidimensional scaling.* Beverly Hills, CA: Sage.

Kuhn, T. (1962). *The structure of scientific revolutions.* Chicago: University of Chicago Press.

Lindblom, C. (1959). The science of "muddling through." *Public Administration Review, 19,* 79–88.

Lyles, M., & Mitroff, I. (1980). Organizational problem formulation: An empirical study. *Administrative Science Quarterly, 25,* 102–119.

March, J., & Simon, H. (1958). *Organizations.* New York: Wiley.

McCaskey, M. (1982). *The executive challenge: Managing change and ambiguity.* Boston: Pitman.

Mintzberg, H. (1973). *The nature of managerial work.* New York: Harper & Row.

Nisbett, R., & Wilson, T. (1977). Telling more than we can know: Verbal reports on mental processes. *Psychological Review, 84,* 231–259.

Quinn, J. (1980). *Strategies for change.* Homewood, IL: Irwin.

Rittel, H., & Webber, M. (1973). Dilemmas in a general theory of planning. *Policy Sciences, 4,* 155–169.

Schon, D. A. (1963). *The displacement of concepts.* London: Tavistock Press.

Simon, H. (1976). *Administrative behavior.* New York: Free Press. (3rd edition).

Simon, H. (1978a). On how to decide what to do. *Bell Journal of Economics, 9,* 494–507.

Simon, H. (1978b). Rationality as process and product of thought. *American Economic Review, 68,* 1–16.

Sproull, L. (1984). The nature of managerial attention. In L. Sproull & P. Larkey (eds.), *Advances in information processing in organizations,* pp. 9–28. Greenwich, CT: JAI Press.

Srivastva, S. (ed.) (1983). *The executive mind.* San Francisco: Jossey–Bass.

Staw, B. (1980). Rationality and justification in organizational life. In B. Staw & L. Cummings (eds.), *Research in organizational behavior: Volume 2,* pp. 45–80. New York: JAI Press.

Stewart, R. (1982). The relevance of some studies of managerial work and behavior to leadership research. In J. Hunt, U. Sekaran, & C. Schriesheim (eds.), *Leadership: Beyond establishment views,* pp. 11–30. Carbondale, IL: Southern Illinois University Press.

Taylor, R. (1974). Nature of problem ill-structuredness: Implications for problem formulation and solution. *Decision Sciences, 45,* 632–643.

Tversky, A., & Kahneman, D. (1974). Judgement under uncertainty: Heuristics and biases. *Science, 185,* 1124–1131.

Weick, K. (1979). *The social psychology of organizing.* Reading, MA: Addison–Wesley.

Weick, K. (1983). Managerial thought in the context of action. In S. Srivastva (ed.), *The executive mind,* pp. 221–242. San Francisco: Jossey–Bass.

Weiss, C. (1980). Knowledge creep and decision accretion. *Knowledge: Creation, Diffusion, Utilization, 1,* 381–404.

Wrapp, G. (1967). Good managers don't make policy decisions. *Harvard Business Review, 5.*

12 Understanding Conceptual Structures: A Case Study of Darwin's Early Thinking

Carol L. Smith
University of Massachusetts, Boston
and

Arthur B. Millman
University of Massachusetts, Boston

Historians of science have done important work recently on the development of the ideas of several outstanding individual scientists such as Galileo, Newton, and Darwin. This work, often using the scientist's unpublished writings, is of interest not only to historians but also to philosophers, psychologists, and educators. Topics of general interest include: (1) methodological issues about identifying and characterizing concepts and conceptual structures; (2) issues about how to characterize the conceptual structures that guide the discovery of a theory and the similarities and differences between them and later, or mature, conceptual structures; and (3) the nature of the cognitive processes that lead to discovery. One of our aims in the larger project of which this chapter is a part is to use a detailed study of Darwin's work in reasoning to the discovery of the theory of natural selection to shed some light on these general issues. In this chapter we provide a new interpretation of one important phase of Darwin's work and suggest some implications of this case study of creative thinking in science for science education and the teaching of thinking.

An especially valuable resource for understanding the development of Darwin's thought in one of his most creative periods is the first transmutation notebook, or B Notebook, begun in July 1837.[1] The Notebook is, of course, very far from a finished text, polished for publication. The very sketchiness, ambiguity, and tentativeness of the Notebook entries, al-

---

[1]The transmutation notebooks were first published in De Beer, Rowlands, & Skramovsky, 1960–67.

though making it difficult to attribute a precise doctrine to Darwin, provide evidence about the processes of his thought and the intellectual constraints under which he operated. Because Darwin did not need to worry about having his ideas in a form suitable for communication to others, he did not need to make definitive choices or censor himself as strictly as would otherwise have been necessary. We are left with a partial record of his tentative thinking from which, along with other sources, we can try to build up analyses of the concepts, hypotheses, and systems of ideas he worked with, as well as his style of inquiry.

Darwin's notebooks were used by Howard Gruber in preparing *Darwin on Man* (1981), his pioneering study of Darwin's creative scientific thinking. Gruber rightly stresses that ideas need to be understood in context and that the development of ideas involves the reorganization of existing structures. Before Gruber's work the prevailing view had been that the natural selection theory, which Darwin initially hit upon in 1838, about 15 months after beginning the B Notebook, was Darwin's first distinctive theory—in contrast to theories, such as traditional creationism or Lyell's theory, which Darwin adopted from others. We are particularly interested in the assumption, made by Gruber (as well as Kohn 1980 & Perkins 1981), that Darwin's early thinking is well characterized as the holding of a succession of theories, each of which is internally consistent. Gruber argues that in the B Notebook Darwin held an early distinctive theory prior to the natural selection theory. Gruber calls this early theory the "monad theory" (and also finds a slightly later variant of the monad theory that he calls the theory of "perpetual becoming"). David Kohn (1980) agrees with Gruber that Darwin had an early theory, but disagrees about what the theory was. Kohn believes that Darwin never held a monad theory, and offers an alternative account of the theory Darwin held before the natural selection theory. In one section of his wide-ranging study, Hodge (1983) tries to mediate between Kohn and Gruber on the question of the centrality of the concept of "monad." In order to organize his account of Darwin's early work and its relation to Lyell's, Hodge also deploys the notions of an "explanatory tradition" (setting out fundamental problems and resources for solving them) and an "explanatory program" (an agenda of problems). Hodge adapts these notions from current work in the philosophy of science (Lakatos, 1978; Laudan, 1977).

We agree with Hodge that the characterization of Darwin's views requires reference to a rich body of features and a unit (or units) of analysis different from, and larger than, the traditional notion of "theory." We suggest an additional way of characterizing Darwin's early thinking in the B Notebook that provides further understanding of it, complementing the analysis stressing explanatory problems. Our approach also reveals important aspects overlooked by the search for a consistent theory. Our view stresses that, in this early phase, Darwin was engaged in a process of *exploratory thinking* guided by a *concept cluster* (along with background assumptions and other features).

In contrast, Gruber and Kohn describe Darwin as *holding* an early *theory* or a succession of early theories in the B Notebook. Holding a theory involves being committed over time to a coherent body of *propositions*. Being committed to a concept cluster involves assuming that a set of partially specified concepts can be used to illuminate a domain of phenomena through considering—whether simultaneously or successively—rival or alternative hypotheses about how the concepts are related, i.e., entertaining a variety of very different theories within the framework of the cluster. We think the description of Darwin as holding an early theory or succession of early theories may be misleading for two reasons. First, it suggests that Darwin is firmly committed, even though briefly, to these early theories when, instead, he is engaged in a more fluid process of formulating tentative theories and exploring their implications. Second, the search for a sequence of specific theories overlooks a level of theoretical commitment on Darwin's part, lasting throughout the course of the transmutation notebooks. This is his commitment to a concept cluster as the route to a satisfactory theory. Thus, on our analysis Darwin is sometimes simultaneously considering several rival theories rather than holding any single theory.

Exploratory thinking can be characterized by a number of differences from the holding of a finished theory. Exploratory thinking is much less rigid. (1) It is less committed to specific interrelationships among concepts. As a result there can be a play with concepts in which the thinker entertains different possibilities for the hypotheses relating central concepts and explores their implications. (2) The concepts themselves are not fully specified. Rather they are partially–specified placeholders. (3) The argumentation is not organized into a coherent, fully-consistent whole; instead, there are many local arguments exploring particular assumptions and their implications.

Our chapter is in two parts. First, we sketch our characterization of Darwin's thinking in the early part of the B Notebook. Second, we consider some of the implications of this case study of Darwin's route to the discovery of the theory of natural selection for science education, specifically for the design of a conceptually-guided discovery approach to teaching evolutionary biology.

Exploratory Thinking in the B Notebook

Darwin opened the B Notebook in July 1837 in order to help himself think through and organize a range of problems related to the transmutation of species. Before starting the B Notebook, Darwin had already accepted the plausibility of the idea of the transmutation of species; that is, that there are relationships of descent between some fossil species and living species. His problem was both to prove the transmutation of species and to explain it using universal laws of life. He thought that he needed a theory of variation and its causes if he was to make any progress in understanding the transmutation of species.

We argue that at the outset of the B Notebook Darwin is committed to a central core of concepts consisting of *adaptive variation, reproduction, life span,* and *changing conditions of life.* Our first argument that these four concepts constitute a central concept cluster comes from a close examination of the first fifteen pages of the B Notebook: Darwin opens the Notebook with an argument relating all four concepts, in an attempt to construct a theory of the transmuation of species.

Darwin begins by asking himself what the purpose is of the life cycle of birth, reproduction, and death. He raises two fundamental questions: "Why is life short, why such high object—generation.—" (B2). He goes on to answer his questions, making the following argument:

First, Darwin *knows* that the geological world is changing. It is an established principle of Lyellian geology that the world varies continuously and cyclically. This changing world necessitates that organisms change if they are to remain adapted.

Second, Darwin works with the assumption that the changing environment directly induces adaptive variation. He further assumes that the young of living organisms are more plastic than adults, more capable of responding to environmental change, because the young are both simpler and less fixed in organization. That form of reproduction that starts with new individuals at the simplest stage of organization and has them develop through a series of stages of organization allows the most flexibility for change in response to changing environmental conditions. Darwin thinks that adult organisms cannot modify sufficiently from some "unknown difficulty." So new organisms need to be produced as successors. Hence, he concludes, ("ordinary") reproduction is a means for organisms to vary adaptively.

Finally third, Darwin argues that death destroys the effect of accidental injuries, "which if animals lived for ever would be endless" (B4). So there is a reason why life is short, for organisms with indefinite life would accumulate a mass of injuries and they would also presumably become extremely inflexible (from the "unknown difficulty"). Therefore a life cycle with the processes of both death and reproduction is required if organisms are to remain adapted to their changing environments.

The passages (B5-B15) that come after this opening argument show that Darwin thinks he has found a source of a tremendous amount of adaptive variation that is enough, moreover, to produce transmutation of species.

A second argument for regarding this concept cluster as central for Darwin's theory construction is provided by a somewhat conjectural reconstruction of the process that led to Darwin's choice of these four concepts. This reconstruction considers the logical relations among the concepts as well as methodological principles Darwin sought to follow in his search for a satisfactory scientific theory. According to this reconstruction, the outlines of Darwin's first theorizing, and ultimately of his natural selection theory, emerged out of what is in effect a metaphysical research program concerning life. This reconstruction, supported by the opening pages of the B Notebook, is as follows: Darwin is concerned with adaptive variation capable of leading to transmutation of species. This seems to require death (or limited life span) to eliminate the no longer well-adapted organisms. Death in turn requires reproduction or some form of replacement (creation), if life is not to disappear. Both death and reproduction are universal and observable in the individual life cycle.[2] A theory based on the concepts of death and reproduction would be consistent with methodological principles that governed Darwin's search for a theory: he was looking for universal laws of life and causes that are observable or analogous to observable causes. So far, so good. But are death and reproduction sufficient to account for adaptive variation and ultimately for the transmutation of species? This sets Darwin off on the series of explorations that constitute the B Notebook.

A third reason is that the B Notebook can be seen as centered on the exploration of the relationships among the partially specified concepts in the cluster. Darwin is more committed to holding that there are some illuminating relationships among these concepts than he is to any specific relationship. He plays around with these relationships in several ways, one of the most salient of which is this: he considers relationships that are drastically opposed to one another. Often he considers both a hypothesized relationship and its opposite, that is, its contrary or contradictory. This process of exploratory thinking involves shifts in the concepts and alternative specifications of their exact nature. It is part of the power and fruitfulness of this cluster of concepts that they have the potential for a variety of diverse specifications. His immediate problem, then, becomes how to get clear about the relationships among these concepts.

One strategy Darwin uses is to draw analogies between individual organisms, species, and superspecies entities. These analogies suggest to

---

[2]It might be objected that death may not be a feature of the asexual reproduction of single–cell organisms. Darwin's concern with asexual reproduction, however, was largely about plants, and there he thought that grafting, say, could not be continued forever.

Darwin many of the shifts that he makes in the concepts in the cluster. A fuller discussion of how Darwin generates his alternative hypotheses and conceptual specifications would need to deal also with (1) cross-cutting conceptual distinctions or classifications, (2) background assumptions that constrain the possibilities that Darwin regards as worth considering, and (3) dimensions along which the partially-specified concepts can be further specified.

We now illustrate what we mean by Darwin's play with hypotheses about how the concepts in the primary concept cluster are related. Two important examples concern (1) opposite hypotheses relating reproduction and adaptive variation and (2) opposite hypotheses relating life span and reproduction. As a backdrop to these hypotheses, in both examples, Darwin also considers the relationships to changing conditions of life.

Let us begin with the pair of concepts: reproduction and adaptive variation. On the opening page of the B Notebook Darwin distinguishes between two kinds of reproduction: the "coeval kind" such as by fissioning or budding and the "ordinary kind." What is the principle that for Darwin distinguishes between the two kinds of reproduction? Is he simply drawing a distinction between asexual and sexual reproduction? In the coeval kind of reproduction all the descendent individuals are "absolutely similar" (B1). They do not vary at all. In the ordinary kind of reproduction there is variation: "Hence we see generation here seems a means to vary or adaptation" (B3). But the most important difference for Darwin is this: In the coeval kind the new individuals are not simple forms that pass through a series of stages of increasing complexity; instead, they are already multicellular, complex forms that grow in size or fill out missing parts, but that do not unfold from a simple origin through stages. On the other hand, in the ordinary kind "the new individual pass[es] through several stages" (B1). Darwin wonders parenthetically whether this latter sort of development of the individual is not a recapitulation of what "the original molecule has done" (B1). Note that in explaining the difference between these two kinds of reproduction Darwin does not appeal to the characteristic of sexual reproduction that it allows for something like genetic recombination and, for that reason, increases variation. Instead, it is the point about development from the simplest form through stages that is significant for Darwin. He believes it is the latter feature of the ordinary kind of reproduction that gives it its great potential for the production of variation.

He seems to think that the changing environment causes or "induces" variation and that this variation will be adaptive or directed towards restoring the adaptation of the organism to its new environment. On the other hand, Darwin recognizes that some variations that the environment induces in individuals count as "accidental injuries." Their accumulation would be endless and undesirable. So Darwin is trying to establish a contrast between (1) induced (and beneficial) variations that can accumulate to form a change of species in the appropriate circumstances, and (2) accidental injuries that would accumulate to a worsening series of defects. He persuades himself that death prevents the accumulation of harmful variations. Hence he is able to think of variations as beneficial.

Thus at the outset of the B Notebook, Darwin assumes that reproduction of the ordinary kind is a means to produce adaptive variation. But having obtained a clue to the source of the needed supply of variation, Darwin immediately recognizes a problem: "With this tendency to vary by generation, why are species are [sic] constant over whole country" (B5). He needs to have change but also the stability and real existence of species. This problem leads him to consider different relations between reproduction and the production of variation and to search for the conditions under which ordinary reproduction leads to adaptive variation.

Darwin's solution to this problem is to call on a law of inheritance that will see to it that there is blending or averaging among the various characteristics of parents so that the constancy of the species can be preserved: "Beautiful law of inter-marriages partaking of characters of both parents /and then infinite in number" (B5). There is evidence for this blending of opposites. For example, "In man it has been said, there is instinct for opposites to like each other" (B6). Note that on this view reproduction, i.e., crossing, is seen as a means to insure constancy of species, not variation. But then this seems to go too far in the direction of suppressing the accumulation of variation for the sake of preserving the constancy of the species over a range. Darwin then considers a principle of intermarriage that, given some distinguishing conditions, goes in the other direction and enhances the maintenance of variation: "Aegyptian cats and dogs, ibis—same as formerly, but separate a pair and place them on fresh island, it is very doubtful whether they would remain constant; is it not said that marrying-in *deteriorates* a race, that is alters it from some end which is good for man.-" (B6). Apparently Darwin thinks that close inbreeding of a small population, especially when it is in a different environment from the rest of the population, will produce significant variation that can accumulate to a change of species. "According to this view animals on separate islands, ought to become different if kept long enough apart, with slightly differ[ent] circumstances" (B7). Thus Darwin almost simultaneously considers two quite different hypotheses: (1) that crossbreeding of two individuals with different characters produces blending in the offspring, and (2) that inbreeding, or the crossing of two closely similar individuals may produce rather large changes (B7).

Inbreeding over a long period of time, he thinks, may be the condition that leads to adaptive variation, but the exact mechanism is not clear to him. Inbreeding may prevent the effects of blending. And having the long time allows the characters to be acquired slowly, which he thinks is necessary for them to become hereditarily fixed. But he is not sure if the facts support his view about the effects of inbreeding. In the initial passage (B6) he considers that it is said that inbreeding deteriorates a race, but then he glosses this saying as meaning that inbreeding makes the organism less useful for man. As part of the wide network of observations he draws upon, he also later refers to the fact that incestuous marriages of Tahitian kings led to a loss of viable young. Similarly, inbreeding in dogs leads to loss of desire. At the end he reiterates that inbreeding is a means to vary quicker—but with a question mark.

Outbreeding is seen as a means of insuring constancy. But the effects of outbreeding might vary with the differences in the groups being outbred. Earlier he had noted that hybridization sometimes leads to loss of fertility. And he also later considers that in crosses involving large differences in characters, blending may not occur. Rather, there may be a reversion to the type of one parent (atavism). He was very concerned throughout the B Notebook with exploring the conditions under which both blending and atavism would occur. And at the end he thought that the existence of blending might entail only a limited mutability of species that would be a problem for his theory: "Those species which have long remained are those—? Lyell?—which have wide range and therefore cross and keep similar. But this is difficulty: this immutability of some species" (B170). On these issues there is tentative exploration rather than adherence to fixed doctrine on Darwin's part.

Now let us consider a second pair of concepts: life span and reproduction. Embedded in Darwin's discussion of the ordinary kind of reproduction (of individuals) is the suggestion that reproduction somehow uses up a fixed supply of energy and so shortens life. Darwin immediately finds a counterargument: "Yet eunuch, nor cut stallions, nor nuns are longer lived" (B2).

Having set up analogies between individual, species, and superspecies entities (or "monads"), Darwin then moves to consider whether some relationship holds between species life span and the production by a species of descendent species. He conjectures that those species that have changed the most have the shortest life, i.e., that those species that have the greatest number of species as descendants in a single line of descent have the shortest life span (B22-23). The idea seems to be that reproduction may be exhausting. This conjecture is set in the context of the supposition that a monad has a fixed life span. Here it is clear that a monad is not only a simple life form, arising by spontaneous generation in accordance with natural laws, but is also the group of species it becomes through transmutation and the multiplication of forms. Then, if all

monads have the same fixed life span, those that have changed the most—
that have developed through the greatest number of changes of species—
must have species with the shortest life span. (The average lifetime of a
species times the number of species must equal a constant, the monad life
span.) But the supposition that a monad has a fixed life span leads to
difficulty, though Darwin recurs to this supposition twice (B29, B35). The
second time he writes, "If we grant similarity of animals in one country
owing to springing from one branch, and the monucle has definite life,
then all die at one period, which is not .: MONUCULE NOT DEFINITE
LIFE" (B35).

Having run into a snag in his attempt to find an entity—in this case,
monads—with a fixed life span and thereby an explanation of species
extinction in terms of internal causes, Darwin considers an explanation of
death as the result of external causes: Perhaps "death of species is a
consequence . . . of non-adaptation of circumstances" (B38-39).

Then Darwin tries a variant of his original idea but with a twist.
Suppose that the entity with a fixed life span is the species (rather than the
monad) and that the entity with the variable life span is not the species but
rather a superspecies unit, namely a branch of the monad. He considers a
possible law that "existence definite without change, superinduced or
new species. Therefore animals would perish if there was nothing in
country to superinduce a change?" (B61). Again, "They die, without they
change, like golden Pippins" (B63). Whereas earlier Darwin had enter-
tained the hypothesis that *shortness* of life is associated with more
reproduction, now he entertains the hypothesis that *length* of life is
associated with more reproduction; that is, here Darwin entertains the
possibility that length of life (for a branch of a monad) is related positively
to change of species or the production of one species by another. Note
that in this case reproduction instead of being exhausting is revivifying.

Part of what Darwin is struggling with here is the distinction between
two forms of extinction: (1) death of a species because each individual of
that species eventually dies without leaving offspring, and (2) death of a
species because it eventually transmutes into a different species. A
species can live on even though it is no longer extant, if it leaves other
species as progeny. Thus reproduction for species, even more literally
than for individuals, can be a middle way between life and death.

In brief, Darwin entertains both the hypothesis that more reproduction
is associated with shorter life (B22-23) and the hypothesis that more
reproduction is associated with longer life (B61). As Darwin considers
these different relationships he fills out the specifications of the concepts
in different ways. (1) He varies the entity whose death or reproduction is
being considered. In this example, Darwin first assumes that monads have
a fixed life span and that species that reproduce the most have the

shortest life span. Darwin then tries a variant of his original idea. He now supposes that the entity with a fixed life span is the species (rather than the monad); the entity with a variable life span is a superspecies unit, namely a branch of the monad. Therefore, those species that reproduce have in a sense longer life. (2) Another way Darwin fills out the concepts is by picking alternative specifications for a component dimension. In the example, reproduction changes from being seen as exhausting to being seen as revivifying. Species life span moves from being variable to being fixed.

From Exploration to Theory

We have argued that Darwin's thinking in the B Notebook is well characterized as a search for how to conceptualize the relations between four primary concepts: reproduction, lifespan, adaptive variation, and changing conditions of life. What guided Darwin's thinking, then, was not a specific theory about the relations of these four elements, but rather the fundamental assumption that any successful theory of transmutation of species must relate these elements. We have tried to show that he played around with different characterizations of these relations by focusing on different specifications of these general concepts. We have also tried to show how this play led him to a deeper understanding of the theoretical problems he faced.

We would argue further that this concept cluster was a particularly rich and rewarding one. It oriented him to viewing adaptive variation as occurring gradually over the course of many generations (with reproduction as part of the causal mechanism), rather than as occurring within the lifespan of any individual. The concept cluster had only to be modified, not totally abandoned, to accommodate his natural selection theory. In his natural selection theory, death and adaptive variation still figure prominently. However, adaptation and variation are articulated as distinct concepts, thus allowing for a different overall pattern of interrelations among these concepts.

We think our characterization of Darwin's early thinking as exploratory thinking guided by a concept cluster (along with background assumptions) is illuminating. Darwin later sometimes (but not always) described his route to the natural selection theory as a purely inductive one, in keeping with then-current ideas about sound scientific method. A careful examination of the B Notebook (as well as other Darwin materials) proves otherwise, as is now generally recognized by scholars. Darwin hypothesized. But further, part of Darwin's success is attributable to his concern with conceptual exploration and the solution of theoretical problems, not simply his diligence in searching for generalizations that would link all the known facts. This sensitivity was reflected in his choice of a particularly revealing concept cluster.

Gruber and Kohn would agree, of course, that Darwin was not a simple inductivist. But they have each described Darwin as holding an early theory in the B Notebook, a characterization we think is misleading. If one is looking for an early *theory* as the core guiding research, then one is led to look for a set of propositions that have some coherence and are stable over time. This leads one to overlook many important elements in the core. Thus Kohn concludes that only Darwin's beliefs about reproduction and variation are at the core of his early theoretical concern. Kohn considers Darwin's thinking about death not to be a part of his early theory because Darwin was not consistent on the topic. But, if one takes a concept cluster to be guiding thinking in the early phases, then constancy of specific propositions is no longer so important. Rather, constancy at a more abstract level and the consideration of deeper regularities underlying the exploratory thinking become paramount. Attending to this more abstract level not only allows us to recognize that the concept of death is integral to Darwin's early thinking, it also allows us to see the importance of conceptual play in Darwin's style of thinking.[3]

Implications for Science Education

Science teachers frequently share two goals: (1) getting students to internalize the specific content of their subject and (2) getting students to engage in scientific thinking. Our case study of Darwin suggests some new ways of achieving both goals. In this section of our chapter we will describe some implications of our case study for science education.

First, let us consider the goal of getting students to internalize the specific content of scientific disciplines. The current science education literature stresses the importance of engaging students' naive theories. (See Driver & Easley, 1978; McCloskey, 1983; Minstrell, 1982; Posner, Strike, Henson, & Gertzog, 1982; Resnick, 1983.) According to this view, students have naive theories that they bring into the science classroom. Learning depends on prior knowledge, and instruction requires confrontation with alternative conceptions in the form of naive theories; the teacher needs to identify students' conceptions and take them seriously by challenging students with arguments and evidence to revise them or give them up. This view, which we call the "alternative conceptions" or "naive theories" view, very valuably brings out how achieving the goal of

---

[3]We are extending our concept cluster analysis to other phases of Darwin's work in another paper in progress. We uncover greater continuity between Darwin's early theorizing and his mature theory than is generally thought.

helping students think scientifically is directly useful in helping students master scientific content. Such a view has led to attempts to characterize these naive theories. Further, some investigators have even taken it as a working hypothesis that students' naive theories may frequently be similar to some of the discarded theories or paradigms in the history of science. For example, Michael McCloskey (1983) has called attention to the similarities between students' theories about motion and the impetus theory of medieval physics.

Although we agree with many of the assumptions of work done from the "alternative conceptions" perspective and find the notion that students hold naive theories a powerful one, such work does not always suggest systematic ways to help students *change their ideas* to develop the sophisticated theory being taught. A teacher may discover, for example, in characterizing students' naive theories that they are radically different in form from the mature theory to be taught. There may also be areas like geology and evolutionary theory where students do not even have a well worked out naive theory. Experimental demonstrations may be much less feasible in some subjects such as evolutionary biology than in mechanics, where the alternative conceptions view has been most fully developed.

Our work suggests a new approach in these cases, one that preserves the basic insight that it is important to engage students at an intuitive level. We think that studies (such as we have done of Darwin) of the early history of *currently accepted theories* rather than of discarded theories may suggest ways to help students change their ideas in order to develop the sophisticated theory being taught.

We can illustrate our main suggestions with a specific example related to our historical case study. What is the best way to draw students into engagement with evolutionary theory and mastery of its fundamentals? The traditional way of introducing students to the theory of evolution starts by posing the questions: Where do different species come from? How did life begin? These are perhaps rather foreign to students.

We suggest that it is worth considering the hypothesis that Darwin's own route into the theory of evolution by natural selection may have some lessons for biology education. Parallelism with the history of science suggests that some geological ideas may be an important preliminary preparation for assimilation of the theory of evolution. It may be useful to prepare the way by discussing the fossil evidence for the history of life on earth—with its record of extinct species—as well as the arguments for the age of the earth. It may be then both more gripping and ultimately more illuminating to ask: Why death? Why do organisms including human beings die? Why is there reproduction of new individuals? These questions appeal to facts from the individual life cycle that are familiar and deeply interesting. It is probably natural for students to look for answers related to purpose and adaptation. The four basic concepts in Darwin's concept cluster can thus be produced from a relatively natural starting point.

Some of the difficulties that students reportedly have (Brumby, 1979; Brumby, 1984; Deadman & Kelly, 1978) are similar to difficulties that Darwin initially had. Students have particular difficulty understanding the idea of natural selection; so did Darwin. Students see adaptation as a directed response to environmental change—thus not acknowledging that some variations may not be adaptive; so did Darwin. One advantage of beginning with this particular concept cluster is that it does not presuppose that students have an understanding of selection or distinguish between adaptation and variation.

Students, however, also have difficulty with many things with which Darwin did not have difficulty. For example, students tend to think of adaptation as occurring only during the lifetime of the organism. They do not see the role of reproduction in adaptation (Brumby, 1979; Brumby, 1984; Deadman & Kelly, 1978). Hence, a second advantage of introducing students to this particular concept cluster is that it may help students to see that there is a connection between reproduction and adaptation.

The teacher can then begin to have the students play with these ideas and their interrelationships. What are the ways in which death and adaptation are related? What are the ways in which reproduction and adaptation are related? The teacher could also suggest particular types of relations to look for (such as quantitative relations, causal relations, and conditional relations) as well as heuristic strategies for formulating these relations. Three useful strategies are (1) considering relations that are opposite to the one first formulated, (2) trying out the same relation between different items, and (3) looking for analogies. We suggest that this kind of play with concepts can serve an important role in aiding in their mastery and make some concepts (e.g., natural selection) more accessible.

This brings us to our second implication for science education, regarding how to get students engaged in scientific thinking. Current approaches that stress inquiry in science primarily have students collect data and generalize from the data. But we argue that for students to think in a scientific way they must be concerned with conceptual and theoretical problems as well as observational problems (cf. Laudan, 1977). A sound inquiry approach to science education should also allow for conceptual exploration and the solution of theoretical problems, rather than presuppose a narrowly inductive approach to scientific inquiry. Similarly, adequate concepts and theories are necessary if students are to interpret observations and demonstrations correctly.

In sum, a case study of Darwin's early thinking is not only illuminating about the processes of scientific discovery but may also have novel lessons for helping students engage in scientific thinking.

SELECTED BIBLIOGRAPHY

Brumby, M. N. (1979). Problems in learning the concept of natural selection. *Journal of Biological Education* 13, 119–122.

———. (1984). Misconceptions about the concept of natural selection by medical biology students. *Science Education, 68,* 493–503.

Carey, S. (1984). Cognitive development: The descriptive problem. In M. Gazzaniga (Ed.). *Handbook of cognitive neuroscience.* New York: Plenum Press.

Clement, J. (1982). Students' preconceptions in introductory mechanics. *American Journal of Physics, 50,* 66–71.

Deadman, J. A., & Kelly, P. J. (1978). What do secondary school boys understand about evolution and heredity before they are taught the topics? *Journal of Biological Education, 12,* 7–15.

De Beer, G., Rowlands, M. J., & Skramovsky, B. M. (eds.) (1960–67). Darwin's notebooks on transmutation of species. *Bulletin of the British Museum (Natural History),* Historical Series, 2 (1960–1), 23–200, 3 (1967), 129–76.

Driver, R., & Easley, J. (1978). Pupils and paradigms: A review of literature related to concept development in adolescent science students. *Studies in Science Education* 5, 61–84.

Driver, R., & Erickson, G. (1983). Theories-in-action: Some theoretical and empirical issues in the study of students' conceptual frameworks in science. *Studies in Science Education* 10, 37–60.

Gruber, H. E. (1981). *Darwin on man: A psychological study of scientific creativity.* 2d ed. Chicago: University of Chicago Press.

———. (1983). History and creative work: From the most ordinary to the most exalted. *Journal of the History of the Behavioral Sciences* 19, 4–14.

Hodge, M. J. S. (1983). Darwin and the laws of the animate part of the terrestrial system (1835–1837): On the Lyellian origins of his zoonomical explanatory program. *Studies in History of Biology* 6, 1–106.

Kohn, D. (1980). Theories to work by: Rejected theories, reproduction, and Darwin's path to natural selection. *Studies in History of Biology* 4, 67–170.

Kuhn, T. S. (1970). *The structure of scientific revolutions.* 2d ed. Chicago: University of Chicago Press.

Lakatos, I. (1978). *Philosophical papers.* 2 volumes. Cambridge: Cambridge University Press.

Laudan, L. (1977). *Progress and its problems.* Berkeley: University of California Press.

Mayr, E. (1982). *The growth of biological thought: Diversity, evolution and inheritance.* Cambridge, MA: Harvard University Press.

McCloskey, M. (1983, April). Intuitive physics. *Scientific American* 248, 122–130.

Minstrell, J. (1982, January). Explaining the 'at rest' condition of an object. *The Physics Teacher.*

Minstrell, J., & Smith, C. (1983). Alternative conceptions and a strategy for change. *Science and Children, 21,* 31–33.

Perkins, D. (1981). *The mind's best work.* Cambridge: Harvard University Press.

Posner, G. J., Strike, K. A., Hewson, P. W., & Gertzog, W. A. (1982). Accommodation of a scientific conception: Toward a theory of conceptual change. *Science Education* 66, 211–227.

Resnick, L. B. (1983). Mathematics and science learning: A new conception. *Science* 220, 477–478.

Shapere, D. (1984). *Reason and the search for knowledge.* Dordrecht, Holland: Reidel.

Smith, C. L., Carey, S., & Wiser, M. (1985). On differentiation: A case study of the development of the concepts of size, weight, and density. *Cognition in 21,*177–237.

Toulmin, S. (1972). *Human understanding.* Princeton: Princeton University Press.

13 Post-Logical Thinking

Herb Koplowitz, Ph.D.
The Longwoods Research Group Limited
Toronto, Canada

INTRODUCTION

The past 5 years have witnessed an accelerated awareness that college students and other adults cannot or do not think rigorously. There has also been an accelerated effort to improve adult thinking skills and habits. Many of the programs initiated out of these concerns are designed to foster logical thinking. In Piagetian terminology, they are designed to bring adults into the formal operations stage.[1]

I am heartened to see the development of these programs because I share the awareness that adults do not, in general, think logically, and, for reasons that I explain later, I too am concerned about the quality of adult reasoning. However, I do not believe that logical critical thinking is the highest form of thought, nor that formal operations is the final stage of adult cognitive development. In this chapter, I describe a theory of adult cognitive development that includes two post-formal operational stages. I have three reasons for doing so:

First, I have found this to be a useful theory. Knowing an adult's level

---

[1]The theoretical foundations of my theory are Piagetian. In his terms, I am dealing with two stages he described as "concrete operations" and "formal operations" (Piaget 1973), and two post-formal stages that he did not describe, which I have labelled "general system theory" and "unitary" (Koplowitz 1984). In order to avoid technical jargon in the discussion of my theory, I am here writing about these four stages as "pre-logical," "logical," "post-logical," and "unitary."

I thus use the word "logical" in two senses. In the technical sense, "logical" is used as a synonym for "formal operational," the fourth of Piaget's stages. In the more general sense, I also use the word to refer to reasoning that deals appropriately with propositional logic. (See Inhelder & Piaget 1958).

213

of cognitive development helps me to determine how to inform that person, what level of analysis he or she is capable of working at, and whether it is appropriate for me to intervene by working to raise the individual's cognitive level.

Second, the theory provides a context in which to examine critical thinking and programs designed to foster it. The theory provides a perspective on where and how it is appropriate to teach critical thinking, and what the limits of critical thinking are.

Third, and most important, the theory is inspiring. In the context of this theory, logic is not seen as an abstract standard against which thinking can be measured. Rather, logical thinking is seen as being characteristic of one stage in human development that can go much further. Focussing on human development tends to lift us out of the dispassionate stance that scientists tend to live in. Although it is important for us to be dispassionate (in the sense of unbiased) in examining the results of our research, it is also important for us to be passionate (that is, enthusiastic and committed to action) about thinking and improving thinking. Throughout this chapter I explore the importance of striving toward out potential, and also explore the role of cognitive development within human development. I return to this point at the end of the chapter.

Background for Discussion of the Theory

I am most concerned here with explaining the theory and showing how it manifests itself in daily work life rather than in presenting evidence of the theory's viability. (Readers interested in such evidence are referred to Koplowitz 1978, 1984.) One major example, concerned with a troubled organization, is used throughout to demonstrate thinking characteristic of each stage. I describe the organization and then explain how employees at different levels of cognitive development would analyze the problem. The characteristics of thinking at all stages are summarized in Table 13.1.

The organization we are concerned with gets its funding from the government. Within the organization is a department that provides consulting services to organizations in both the public and private sectors.

Mike has just taken over as head of the department and is assessing the situation he has inherited. He has a reputation as a good listener. Before he took the job, Mike spoke with his new supervisor, Betty. She feels it is time for the department to become more visible and to find ways of serving more clients. She believes that the department is doing some creative work, but she indicated that she has never clearly understood what the department has been doing. The official reports are all filed on time, but management still does not have a feel for the department's activities and achievements. Mike also spoke with the three consultants working for him, Ed, Chris and Wilma. They told him that the department's greatest problem is low morale.

TABLE 13.1
Stages in Adult Cognitive Development

	Pre-logical	*Logical*	*Post-logical*	*Unitary*
Cause	One-step	Linear	Cyclical	All-pervading/ Cause and effect as manifestations of one dynamic
Logic	Emotion over logic/Process not separate from content	Logical	Logic in context	One communications tool out of many
Relation among variables	Unrelated	Independent	Interdependent	Constructed
Blame/ problem location	Others	Where problem starts	In the system	Problems as opportunities/ Boundary constructed
Intervention site	Others	Where the problem is	Where there is leverage	Where appropriate
Ability to deal with the abstract	Concrete	Abstract	Relationships	Spiritual– Nonmaterial
Boundaries	Closed	Closed	Open	Constructed

Ed and Wilma feel overworked and underappreciated. Ed senses that middle and upper management are not happy with the department's work, but he cannot point a finger at hard evidence to substantiate the feeling, and he has never confronted Mike's predecessor or Betty to find out what, if anything, is wrong.

As I explore this organization and the thinking of its employees, you might reflect on similar individuals and organizations that you are familiar with to see how they fit the patterns I present.

Pre-Logical Thought

Ed is generally a pre-logical thinker.[2] In exploring the cause of problems, he tends to make one-step analyses.

---

[2]I am characterizing individuals as being within particular stages of cognitive development only for purposes of illustration. It would be more accurate to characterize particular concepts or strategies as being within given stages. Any given individual will tend to use concepts and strategies from several stages although he or she may function predominantly in one mode. An adult may, for example, tend to think logically, in some areas think post-logically, and occasionally slip into pre-logical thinking.

When asked why managers give no feedback about the department's work, Ed says that middle management does not know what the staff has been doing. Unless probed, however, he will not explore why middle management does not understand the department. He does not look at the pressures on middle management that might keep its attention away from the department's work and he does not explore how the department might act differently so as to get feedback from management.

For a pre-logical thinker like Ed, any state of affairs is conceived of as the consequence of the state immediately preceding it, and the analysis ends there.

The absence of logical reasoning in the pre-logical thinker appears in several ways. Pre-logical thinkers tend to respond emotionally to statements rather than to analyze them logically.

Mike told Ed that he thought that the department had not organized its work efficiently, and that it was therefore important for the department to explore how it carried out its work. Ed replied "You're wrong. We've been working as hard as we can."

Note the syllogism imbedded in Mike's statement.

Major Premise: We should examine inefficient aspects of the department.
Minor Premise: The organization of our work is inefficient.
Conclusion: We should examine how we organize our work.

Logically, Ed can disagree with the conclusion only by disagreeing with one or both of the premises. Ed, however takes the statement personally, understanding it only as an attack on himself and his work. Mike never accused the department of not working hard. In defending himself, Ed acts emotionally and, typical of pre-logical thinkers, changes the subject instead of dealing with it rationally.

Pre-logical thinkers tend not to relate effects of one variable to those of another.

Ed suggested the department take a consulting skills course. He mentioned another department in the organization that had taken the course and which was outperforming their department, citing that as proof of the value of the training. "That doesn't prove anything," Wilma said. "Ed, you know that their morale is so much better than ours that they're bound to outperform us."

Ed lacks the strategy that Inhelder and Piaget (1958) called "separation of variables." He focusses on only one variable at a time, in this case, skill level. He does not relate this variable to other variables, such as morale, which also affect the outcome.

Wilma thought that the arrival of a new manager, especially one who is a good listener, might be a good time for department members to meet to discuss the department's problems. When Wilma convened the meeting, Ed showed another limit to pre-logical thinking, the inability to separate form or method from content.

> Wilma opened by saying, "Let's start off by getting clear about just what the problems are." Ed's response was, "Well, I think someone needs to tell management to get off our backs."

Pre-logical thinkers like Ed have difficulty setting agendas and sometimes abiding by them. They have trouble separating talk about how they will work on a problem from the problem solving itself.

Ed has also shown two other characteristics of pre-logical thinkers. They tend to locate blame for problems in others, and they tend to believe that it is these others who must be changed if problems are to be solved. It is clear to Ed that management is to blame for the morale problem, and that the solution to the problem lies in management's changing its ways.

Pre-logical thinkers tend not to think abstractly, and the boundaries they draw around parts of the world they know tend to be solid, closed boundaries. It is clear to Ed who is a manager and who is not, and it is clear to him that problems in management can be solved only by helping or forcing managers to change. And when Ed talks about the management of the organization, he means the *people* at Mike's level and above (and is likely to use the singular noun "management" as plural as in "We must give management what they want"). Management is not an abstract function within the organization, but a collection of concrete individuals. In Ed's view, the boundary around this collection is closed; any individual in the organization is either inside the boundary or outside of it.

The poor quality of Ed's thinking puts him at a disadvantage in the world, and also disadvantages groups of which he is a member. Because he does not analyze logically, he is open to manipulation by others. Because his causal analyses are one-step and because he does not separate method from content, he is limited in his abilities to understand situations he is in and devise solutions for his problems. He responds illogically, and often defensively to criticism and cannot follow agendas, and so is a distraction to groups he works with. His tendency to react emotionally and to not analyze arguments logically leaves him ill-suited to make reasonable choices. He will detract from any democracy, whether on a national or a work–place scale.[3]

It is not just every human's democratic right to be intelligent, to use

---

[3]For a more detailed look at pre-logical thinking among adolescents and adults, see Lochhead 1977, 1979 & 1980, Renner & Paske 1977, and Wertime 1984.

Machado's (1980) phrase, but also every democracy's need to develop the intelligence of its members.

Logical Thinking

Both Wilma and Chris are logical thinkers. In exploring the cause of problems, they look for linear causal chains.

> Wilma agrees with Ed that the management's lack of feedback about the department's work is due to its lack of knowledge about the department. She has looked further to see that department members do keep a low profile that leaves management without knowledge of the department. She understands that this is why management does not give feedback (Fig. 13.1a). Wilma also tried to understand the department's morale problem. It occurred to her that the staff members are not sure of the value of their work. Further thought showed her that staff members had no measure of the value of their work. This led to their uncertainty, which caused the morale problem (Fig. 13.1b).

Wilma's analysis does not stop at the situation immediately preceding the one to be explained, but rather is carried out to the construction of a causal chain (Fig. 13.1) that could, theoretically, be extended back indefinitely.

Logic plays an important role in Wilma's and Chris's thinking.

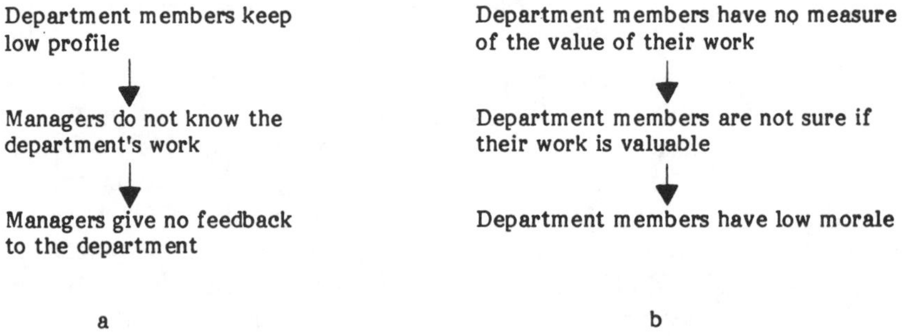

Department members keep low profile

↓

Managers do not know the department's work

↓

Managers give no feedback to the department

a

Department members have no measure of the value of their work

↓

Department members are not sure if their work is valuable

↓

Department members have low morale

b

FIG. 13.1.   Logical linear concept of causality

Chris did not agree with Mike when he said that the department should examine how it organized its work because work was being done inefficiently. She thought for a moment about why she disagreed. It was clear to her that the department's work could be better organized, but she realized that there was no consensus about which work should be done, and that the focus of discussion should be on strategic planning. She told Mike that she disagreed with him because she felt it was not important at the moment to examine inefficiencies in the department. It was more important to develop consensus around departmental goals.

Chris was able to separate out from Mike's syllogism exactly which premise it was that she disagreed with. This is a critical ability of logical thinking.

As was shown before, Wilma, as a logical thinker, was able to relate the effect of department members' skills, as one variable, to the effect of their morale, as another variable. She sees them operating independently to affect the department's performance.

When the meeting began, another ability of logical thinkers appeared.

Wilma suggested that the group begin its meeting by clarifying what the department's problems were, and then proceed with discussion of each problem separately. After Ed jumped in and said that he felt what was needed was to get someone to tell management to get off the group's backs, Chris said she was not happy with Wilma's proposed agenda. She suggested that the meeting begin not as Wilma proposed but with a discussion of how each of the group members felt about working in the department.

Ed, as a pre-logical thinker, was unable to separate the content of the meeting from the process by which the content would be addressed. He began talking about the problems before it was settled how those problems would be discussed. Chris, as a logical thinker, knew that the topic was the agenda, and she addressed that topic. She was able to separate content from process.

When the meeting progressed to a discussion of problems and their solutions, two other characteristics of logical thought were manifested.

The group members felt that some of the department's work was not of a high enough quality, and that this was because they themselves were unskilled at organization development. However some of their work entailed developing organizations. They decided that they should get training in this area. They also felt that they were not getting the clear feedback they needed from management, and that this was because managers were uncomfortable and unskilled at giving feedback. They decided that managers should be given training in communication skills.

In analyzing problems, logical thinkers construct a causal chain to discover what the origin of that chain is. That is where they locate the blame for the problem, whether that puts the blame on themselves or on others. The site for intervention, the place where changes should be made in order to solve the problem, is the very place where blame was located. The department's low quality work was seen, ultimately, as being the result of consultants' poor skills, so those skills should be improved. The lack of feedback was seen, ultimately, as being the result of managers' poor communications skills, so those skills should be improved. In this regard, logical thinkers differ from pre-logical thinkers who more rigidly locate blame and intervention sites in others (or in themselves if they have low self-esteem), and from post-logical thinkers who, as will be seen later, take a yet more flexible view.

Logical thinkers are capable of much more abstract thought than are pre-logical thinkers, but they still draw closed boundaries in separating one part of the world they know from another. Wilma and Chris can separate "management," the function, from "managers," the people. However, it is clear to them that management is the job that managers do, that they themselves are not managers, and that Betty and Mike are managers. There is no ambiguity in that distinction. Also, they propose improving management by improving managers.

Wilma and Chris are at a definite advantage over Ed because of their abilities to think logically. They make more sophisticated causal analyses and are capable of correctly analyzing situations in which they themselves are at fault. They can run more productive meetings because they can discuss how to structure the meeting before going on to discuss its content. They are less liable than pre-logical thinkers to be verbally manipulated by others because they can analyze arguments logically. In their problem solving they are more flexible than pre-logical thinkers, and better able to consider others' points of view. However, they are not as flexible in their thinking as post-logical thinkers are.[4]

Post-Logical Thought

Mike is a post-logical thinker.[5] A characteristic of post-logical thinkers is that they see cause as happening not only linearly but also cyclically.

---

[4]For a more detailed view of logical thinking as a psychological phenomenon, see Inhelder and Piaget 1958, Perry 1968, and Commons, Richard, & Armon 1984.

[5]What I am here calling "post-logical thought" follows the structure of general system theory. General system theory (G.S.T.) is usually defined as a discipline "whose subject matter is the formulation and derivation of those principles that are valid for 'systems' in general" (Von Bertalanffy 1968, p. 32). I find it unsatisfactory to consider G.S.T. a study of something external. Such a definition leads to arguments as to whether a particular entity such as an automobile engine is or is not a system, when G.S.T. itself holds that anything can be regarded as a system. It is more useful to consider G.S.T. to be a way of thinking, or as a stage in the development of thinking.

After the employees' meeting, Wilma talked with Mike about management's lack of feedback to the department and how it was ultimately caused by the department's low profile (Fig. 13.1a). She said she was also concerned about the staff's low morale (Fig. 13.1b). Mike showed her that these two problems were interrelated, and that the low morale and the lack of feedback caused each other (Fig. 13.2). She was able to follow each of the steps as Mike traced around the causal cycle with her. Still, she found it difficult to understand how her low morale caused her lack of knowledge about the value of her work when it was so clear to her that the lack of knowledge of the value of her work caused her low morale.

Mike also asked Wilma about a few things that were puzzling him. "Why is it that this office never advertises or promotes its services? Any private sector consulting organization would do some sort of promotion." Wilma replied that there was no need for promotion because the department was always busy and probably could not handle any more clients. Mike also wondered about some of the department's inefficiencies and asked Wilma about making changes so that the department could expand its service capabilities. "There's no need for that," she replied. "We have always been able to handle any requests for service that we get." Mike was puzzled. Somehow, the capabilities of the department happened exactly to equal the demands for service from it without the department's ever acting to control the balance by hiring or firing staff, generating new business, or shunting business it could not handle elsewhere. He understood the situation better when he compared Wilma's causal picture (Fig. 13.3a) with his own (Fig. 13.3b). He saw that the low demand for service resulted from the lack of promotion. It seemed likely that the department was underworking itself

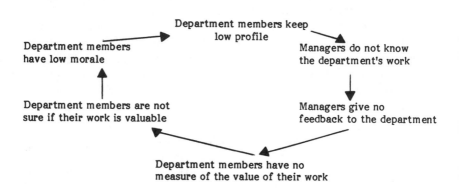

FIG. 13.2. Post-logical cyclical concept of casuality

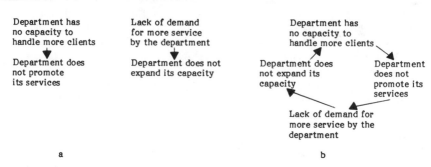

FIG. 13.3.   Linear causal chains combined into causal cycle

and that when consultants had extra time on their hands they probably put extra unneeded time into existing clients rather than into generating new business. But if the department were to become more efficient, it could serve more clients, it would be able to afford to promote, and demand for service would increase.

Logical thinkers, with their concept of causality, tend to see themselves as reacting to given aspects of their realities. In this case, Wilma saw her low morale as a reaction to managers' lack of appreciation of her work. She saw the department's not expanding its capacity as a reaction to a low level of demand for its services. Post-logical thinkers with a cyclical concept of causality, understand that we often produce those "givens" in our reality to which we react. Mike could see that Wilma not only reacted to the managers' lack of appreciation of her work but also, through her low profile, caused it. He could see that the department not only reacted to low demand but also, through its lack of promotion, caused it.[6]

The cyclical view of causality enables post-logical thinkers to view

---

[6]The post-logical view of causality differs from the logical view in another important way. The logical thinker believes that if applying a small force will result in a small effect, then applying a large force will result in a large effect, and that the effect will be in the same direction as that of the force applied. The post-logical thinker understands that a small force can also result in a large effect if a positive feedback cycle is involved, a large force can result in a small effect if a negative feedback cycle is involved, and, in paradoxical interventions, a force can result in an effect in the opposite direction. For further exploration of the post-logical concept of causation, see Koplowitz 1976, Watzlawick, Beavin, & Jackson 1967, and Watzlawick, Weakland, & Fisch 1974.

things in context, and one thing they tend to view in context is logical argument. Wilma made implicit use of two syllogisms:

1. We should not promote our services if we have no capacity to serve more clients than we have now. We have no capacity to serve more clients than we have now. Therefore, we should not promote our services.

2. We should not expand our capacity if there is no excess demand for our services. There is no excess demand for our services. Therefore, we should not expand our capacity.

To Wilma, both major premises and minor premises are true, and the conclusions are valid. Mike, however, looks not only at Wilma's arguments, but also at the context in which they are made. Looking at the arguments alone (Fig. 13.3a), he would agree with all premises and both conclusions. When he looks at them in context (Fig. 13.3b), however, his opinion changes. He now disagrees with the first minor premise that his department has no excess capacity because he recognizes that an increase in demand will stimulate his staff to become more efficient. He also disagrees with the minor premise of the second argument. He believes there is excess demand for the department's services, but that the department has not yet tapped it.

Note that Mike can still make logical arguments and is still convinced by others' logical arguments. The difference between him as a post-logical thinker and Wilma as a logical thinker is that Mike, unlike Wilma, looks at the context in which a logical argument is made in order to see whether the context changes the judgement of the truth of the premises.[7]

We have seen how Wilma, as a logical thinker, was able to relate the effects of one variable, e.g. staff members' skills, to the effects of another variable, e.g. staff members' morale. Although logical thinkers see that there is a relation between variables, they tend to think of them as acting independently of each other. Post-logical thinkers see variables as interdependent.

Wilma told Mike about her conversation with Ed regarding the course on consulting skills. "The other department Ed was talking about does well because its morale is high, not because of its skill level," she repeated. Mike was taken back by her definiteness and challenged her. "How can you

---

[7]The arms buildup represents another example of this kind of reasoning. It is reasonable for the U.S. to build up its arms in the face of expanding Soviet military strength. It is reasonable for the U.S.S.R. to build up its arms in the face of expanding American military strength. It is only when these reasonings are viewed in context of each other that their fallaciousness becomes apparent.

determine which is more important, skill or morale?" he asked. "I suppose you could do something to improve skills at another time and see which brought about the greater improvement in performance," she replied. "How can you improve skill level without at the same time affecting morale?" Mike asked. "How can you improve morale without affecting skill level, say, at the very least, the skill of approaching clients cheerfully?" Wilma was confused by Mike's questions. They made sense to her to some extent, but she was sure there had to be a way to find out whether morale or skill was more important in a department's performance.

Wilma, as a logical thinker, understands morale and skill to operate independently of each other. She therefore believes it must be possible to separate the effects of morale from the effects of skill. Mike, as a post-logical thinker, understands morale and skill to operate interdependently. Each provides the context in which the other operates and neither can be varied without affecting the other.

Because post-logical thinkers look not only at objects and events but also at their contexts, and because they view causality as cyclical rather than linear, they conceptualize problems differently and intervene to solve them differently from how logical thinkers do.

Mike thought about his staff's morale problem. Unlike Wilma, he did not blame the problem on management. Rather, he saw there was a self-sustaining cycle that needed to be stopped. He could think of several ways of improving the unsatisfactory situation, including improving top managers' communications skills and increasing his staff's visibility. He realized it would be very difficult for him to convince top managers that they needed training in communications. In fact, their very inability to listen would likely prevent them from understanding his message and acting on it. However, he could raise his staff's visibility by inviting top managers into departmental meetings and by encouraging his consultants to train other members of the organization in techniques that the department had developed.

He believed that if he did this, upper managers would become familiar with the department's work and comment favorably about it to his staff members, thereby improving their morale.

He also thought about the department's efficiency. He held numerous department meetings to develop and implement a plan for expanding the department's capacity, but he could see that his staff was not motivated in the process. He then switched tactics and involved his staff in some easy and enjoyable promotional activities. When his consultants saw that the promotion was working and that they soon would have more clients than they could service, they became very interested in increasing the department's capacity.

Mike, as a post-logical thinker, put the blame for problems in the dynamics of systems rather than in individuals or in events that initiate the problems. A circle has no beginning. Because he views cause as being cyclical, Mike sees no beginning to the causal process that results in the problem. He understands his staff's morale problem to be the result of an unfortunate dynamic in the system. He does not blame top management for his staff's morale problem. Post-logical thinkers do not find the concept of blame, in the sense of blaming individuals, to be useful at all in understanding how situations arise or how problems can be solved.

As a post-logical thinker, Mike is not restricted to intervening at the site of the cause of the problem for three interrelated reasons. First, as we have just seen, he does not see a problem as having a cause. Second, a causal cycle has no beginning, but it can be broken at any point. Third, post-logical thinkers understand any action as a reaction to a context; if they decide to change a particular action, they have the choice of changing the action directly or changing the context to which it is a reaction. Instead of intervening at "the cause" of a problem, post-logical thinkers intervene where they have leverage, that is, where they can effect the greatest change with the application of the least effort.

Wilma wanted to change top managers' behavior of not giving feedback about the department's performance. As a logical thinker, she chose to consider the cause of the problem to be management's behavior, and so she decided to intervene there. Mike, as a post-logical thinker, understood that there was no one cause of the problem, that the causal cycle underlying the problem could be broken at any point, and that the managers' behavior could be changed by altering the context to which they were reacting. His point of greatest leverage was his staff's behavior. By altering his staff's visibility, which he could control, he could change the managers' behavioral context. They would now have to respond to a high visibility group instead of to a low visibility group, and they would likely respond to it by noticing it and giving it attention and feedback.

Similarly, Mike found it difficult to get his staff to increase the department's efficiency when he tried to do it directly. He had more leverage in getting the staff to promote the department's services. His staff was then working in the context of high demand for services, and it reacted to that context by increasing the department's capacity.

Post-logical thinkers are capable of more abstract thought than are logical thinkers. Although logical thinkers locate cause in concrete objects and their actions, post-logical thinkers locate cause in such abstract entities as "systems dynamics." And whereas logical thinkers must directly intervene exactly where they want change to happen, post-logical thinkers, with their more abstract understanding of causality, can change a pattern by changing its context.

Post-logical thinkers draw open boundaries around entities and events.

In discussions of management's responsibilities, Mike has difficulty in deciding whom he would consider to be a manager and whom he would consider not to be a manager. To him, a manager is anyone who performs management functions, such as ensuring that staff members are given feedback and setting goals for organization. When his staff members raise their visibility so as to get feedback and when they participate in goal setting sessions, they perform management functions and are managers. Beyond that, Mike understands that the boundary around the people whom the organization considers to be managers is itself open in that energy and information pass across it. Therefore, a problem in management is a problem for the whole organization, and the solution to the problem might come from intervention anywhere in the organization, not just in what is called "management." Mike was concerned about two of management's problems: Not knowing enough about the department's performance and not giving the department feedback. He solved them not by intervening in management but by intervening in his staff. By making his staff more visible, he solved two of management's problems.

The boundaries drawn by post-logical thinkers are open in two senses. First, they do not clearly separate inside from outside but allow leakage. Second, they allow energy and information to pass across them. As a result, problems inside a boundary can be solved by intervening outside of the boundary.

Mike, as a post-logical thinker, is at an advantage over logical thinkers like Wilma and Chris. Whereas he can make and analyze logical arguments as well as they can, he can also look at their contexts and see whether that affects his judgement of the truth of their premises. He understands the interdependence of roles and can therefore analyze events more clearly. And he is more flexible in his solution of problems, directing his interventions not only at situations he wants to change but also at their contexts and at linked events where he has leverage. However, he still lacks the freedom of unitary thinkers.[8]

Unitary Approach

The unitary approach[9] knows and acts on the world as a unit. In the unitary approach, one understands that although it is possible and often useful to draw boundaries that break the world into separate entities and events, the world itself is undifferentiated. Unitary concepts are most commonly found in modern physics and in spiritual disciplines. Although

---

[8]For a more detailed view of post-logical thinking, see Koplowitz 1976, 1978 and 1984, Watzlawick, et al. 1967, and Commons et al. 1984.

[9]Thought is a mental process of working out how different things relate to each other and how mental images are affected by transformations. I believe that individuals who operate at a unitary level do not work out their answers but rather have a direct or observational access to them, and that there is, therefore, no "unitary thought." There are, however, unitary concepts and unitary consciousness.

very few individuals are capable of sustaining a unitary consciousness, there are more who are able to achieve momentary unitary perspectives of situations. Such a person is Wilma's Aunt Maude.

> Wilma talked about the morale problem at work with her Aunt Maude, and she tried to explain what Mike had said about causal cycles in the organization. As Wilma talked about the situation, Maude understood it as human nature and as part of a much larger causal picture. Maude related how Wilma had learned to keep a low profile in her family when she was not feeling good about herself, and to assume she was not doing well if she did not have specific evidence to the contrary. Maude added that she could see Wilma's children learning the same habits.
>
> Wilma described turning down an invitation to speak about her work to other employees in the organization because she felt nervous. Earlier she had complained about Mike's boss planning her week without including any time to give Wilma and her colleagues feedback about their work. Maude tried without success to show Wilma that these were not two events but one. In Maude's view, Wilma's declining the invitation to speak invites lack of feedback.

Maude's unitary concept of causality differs in two important ways from the logical and post-logical concepts. First, to logical thinkers, the causes and effects of a given event are confined to a line. To post-logical thinkers, they are confined to a cycle. To Maude, they have no boundary; causality is all-pervading. Wilma's low morale is caused not only by management's lack of feedback and Wilma's own low profile, but also by events in her own family, events in others' families, and so on. Her low profile has effects not only on her own morale but also on her children's habits as they watch and learn from their mother's behavior.

Second, Maude understands cause and effect not to be different events but different manifestations of one underlying phenomenon. It is like the way the existence of the north pole of a magnet implies the existence of a south pole, even if the south pole is not visible. The occurrence of the cause implies the occurrence of the effect, even if it has not yet manifested. As north and south poles are different aspects of one phenomenon, neither existing in isolation of the other, so too cause and effect are different aspects of one dynamic and not separately existing events.

It is important to note that Maude can draw a boundary line and call what is inside of it a causal event. She can focus on a line or on a cycle of causality. She can also draw a separation between cause and effect. She can talk with Mike at his level and to Wilma at her level. But she understands that the boundary is not one that she has noticed out in the world, but one that she herself constructed.

Like logical thinkers, Maude is able to reason making use of syllogisms. Like post-logical thinkers, she understands that in applying logical reasoning, one must consider the context in which one reasons. But Maude's use of logic is tempered by more considerations.

Maude could see that Wilma was not at all convinced by Mike's statement that low morale was caused by low profile. Wilma understood each step in Mike's argument, but she could not grasp his conclusion. Maude knew that she could not convince her niece of Mike's argument. So she steered the conversation to how uncertain Mike must feel of his welcome in his new position. "Wilma," she said, "where are your manners? You really ought to have an office party to welcome Mike." She convinced Wilma to hold the party and to invite Mike's boss as well. Maude knew that in the course of the party, Wilma would talk with Mike and with his boss. She believed that out of that, some rapport might develop that would lead to Wilma's getting the feedback she needed. That would at least solve Wilma's problem. If she learned from it how her morale was connected with her profile, so much the better.

Maude did not restrict herself to using logic to convince Wilma. If Wilma could learn her lesson indirectly, that would suffice. And Maude did not confine herself to changing Wilma's belief in order to change her behavior and solve her problem. If she could raise Wilma's profile subtly, without convincing her of the need to raise her profile, that also would suffice.

As a reserve strategy, Maude might have taken what would appear to be an illogical approach. She might have devised an argument to convince Wilma to keep her profile even lower, if in so doing Wilma would realize how she prevents management from getting the information it needs.

Maude can think logically, but she uses logic as only one of a number of a communication tools to change others' ideas and behaviors.

In her unitary moments, Maude differs from both logical and post-logical thinkers in her understanding of how variables relate to each other.

Wilma told Maude about her discussion with Mike regarding skills and morale. Mike had talked about the skill of being cheerful with clients. Wilma said, "Being cheerful isn't a skill. When you are feeling good about yourself, when your morale is up, then you are cheerful. It's not a question of skill." Maude smiled, knowing that her point would be difficult to describe. "You seem to think that morale and skill are distinct, separate things. Really, they're part of the same thing, and how you define them is what makes them different." As expected, the point was lost on Wilma.[10]

---

[10]The concept of variable as construct appears in modern physics in the Heisenberg uncertainty principle. The physicist cannot measure both position and momentum with total accuracy. The process of measuring a variable such as momentum is more akin to creating the variable than it is to discovering or noticing it.

The concept of variable as construct appears in spiritual traditions as well. In the Hindu tradition, the word "maya" is used to refer to the illusion that the diversity we perceive is real. The undifferentiated world is considered to be real, but the boundaries that break it into separate variables, entities, and events are not real.

Although Maude, as a logical thinker, understands variables to operate independently of each other and Mike, as a post-logical thinker, understands them to operate interdependently, Maude understands that the very boundary between variables to be constructed. When she needs to in conversation, Maude can talk of 'morale' as separate from 'skills,' but she understands that to be an artificial construction of two separate variables from what is essentially undifferentiated.

> Wilma took her aunt's advice and had the party for Mike. In the following weeks, she found herself making more opportunities to talk with Mike's boss. "You may find yourself becoming more assertive in other situations now as well," said Maude. "Your 'problem' provided you with an opportunity to develop yourself and overcome some barriers that had been holding you back." "That could be," replied Wilma, "but how did you figure out that my having a party would solve the problem?" "I just found myself making a suggestion to you. But what makes you think your 'problem' is solved? Do you think that it consisted only of your low morale?"

To the unitary mind, problems are not problematic. Both Wilma and Mike saw in the low morale a problem to be solved, a situation that needed correction. To Maude, however, a "problem" is an opportunity to develop one's potential rather than a situation that is somehow mistaken or in need of correction. A problem occurs when the approach of an individual or an organization meets the limits of its applicability, and this provides the opportunity to improve the approach.

Also, to the unitary mind, a problem is not bounded. To a logical thinker like Wilma, the problem began with the lack of measure for the value of the department's work, and ended with low morale. To a post-logical thinker like Mike, there is a problematic dynamic in the system bounded by a causal cycle. Maude, however, understands the lack of feedback and the low morale in the department to be essentially inseparable from dynamics in other systems. For purposes of conversation she can separate "the problem event" from its context, but she understands that separation as an action committed by her.

Finally, to the unitary mind, there is usually no problem solver sitting outside of a problem situation. Therefore, there can be no intervention. Maude understood herself to be a part of her niece's situation. She therefore did not necessarily understand herself to be deliberately "solving" a problem or "intervening" in a situation, but rather, simply to be present and receptive.

It should be clear by now that the unitary mind operates at a high level of abstraction. The world is understood to be essentially continuous and without boundaries. An individual constructs boundaries, breaking the world into entities and events in order to talk about them and manipulate them. In its most developed phase, the unitary mind is concerned with a nonmaterial reality.

In the unitary level, one develops a depth of understanding that allows one to both accept situations as they are given, and to bring about the most appropriate changes with the least disturbance.[11]

A Critical Look at Critical Thinking

As I indicated in the introduction, a developmental theory such as the one presented here provides some perspective on critical thinking and on programs designed to teach it.

Most obviously, a theory that posits post-logical thinking suggests that there is a need to teach not only logical thinking but also post-logical thinking. There are adults both in college and in the workplace who do not think logically, and they need to learn how to do so. But there is a need for other adults, particularly those in management positions, to learn to think post-logically. It is the responsibility of their mentors to teach them to pay attention to causal cycles and to interdependencies among roles, and to learn to intervene where they have leverage rather than just where problems surface.

One must be able to think logically before being able to think post-logically, and on these grounds, I am in agreement with the movement to teach critical thinking. But the theory, presented here and in particular the General System Theory aspects of it, indicates some cautions that must be observed in teaching critical thinking.

General System Theory cautions us to look at phenomena in the contexts in which they occur. We should look not just at the absence of logical thinking skills and at programs to teach logical thinking, but also at the context that creates the absence of critical thinking skills. What factors in our educational system and our society at large prevents the natural development of thinking skills? Piaget's developmental theory indicates that logical thinking is something that should naturally develop in individuals. If it does not, we should look at what we are doing to hold it back. Because adults do not think logically, there is now a need for programs to teach them to do so. But there should not be a need for such programs, and we should put some effort into finding what factors in our educational system inhibit the development of logical thinking and work to eliminate them.

Also, there is a tendency in logical thinking while solving problems to look for factors that are missing or insufficient, and to solve the problem by increasing these factors. Often, this leads to the creation of another problem when these factors are introduced to excess. General System Theory, on the contrary, seeks to bring factors into balance. Three balances in particular must be maintained in the training of critical thinking.

---

[11]For a further look at the unitary stage see Koplowitz 1978 and 1984 and references in them to spiritual texts and concepts in modern physics, and Wilber 1981.

First, a balance must be maintained between thought and action. It is important to make a sufficient search for evidence, possibilities and goals, and it is important that thought not be impulsive. But it is also important that the thinker know when to stop thinking and when to take action. (This is why Jonathon Baron 1984 calls for an "optimal" amount of search rather than a "sufficient" or "maximal" amount of search.) Although impulsive thinking is a problem both in school and in the workplace, there is a problem in both settings of individuals thinking too long and not taking action. Indeed, one of the findings of Daniel Isenberg's (1984) study of C.E.O.'s is that top managers tend to make decisions before they have had the opportunity to amass all possible evidence and come to definite conclusions.

Second, although it is important to be unbiased in use of evidence, it is also important to have some trust in one's preconceptions or hunches and to be particularly careful in examining evidence contrary to them. Another of Isenberg's findings was that C.E.O.'s are not completely rational in their decision making, but tend to use a number of intuitive processes. Whereas many adults have problems in fair use of evidence, many also have lost touch with their own intuition. We must find ways of teaching people correct use of evidence without losing access to intuition.

Third, although adults need to learn to think abstractly, this should not be at the cost of their ability to think concretely and emotionally. Richard Wertime (1984) laments students' inability to move beyond the emotional level of analysis represented by the following. "Personally, I don't like it when people test or challenge you. I just think it's *rude.*" He would like them to be able to compare the concept of testing with the concept of challenging. My concern is only that the latter analysis not be taught at the cost of the ability to produce the former. Whereas many adults cannot think abstractly, many also cannot identify and own their own feelings. It may take many adults years of Gestalt therapy to arrive at the ability to move from "Confrontation is rude" to "I get embarrassed when confronted."

The Importance of Cognitive Development

Pre-logical thinkers are liable to be manipulated by others who use arguments that would not stand up to logical analysis. They are liable to make illogical choices and to detract from the effectiveness of groups they are members of. In matters of verbal argument and analysis they are not able to serve themselves or others skillfully.

Post-logical thinkers have a flexibility in their thinking that enables them to intervene in situation in a most powerful way. They tend not to get stuck in situations that trap less sophisticated thinkers. However, there is an incompleteness in their approach that is resolved only in unitary thought.

In the past 20 years, the human potential movement has worked to raise awareness of our emotions and of our bodies. It is only recently that we have come to give due attention to mental development. The danger lies in our taking a dispassionate view of our subject. There is no more important task, nothing that will more help fulfill the potential of human beings than to improve the thinking skills of ourselves, our students, and of the population in general.

BIBLIOGRAPHY

Baron, J. (1984, August). *What is good thinking?* Paper presented at Conference on Thinking. Harvard University.

Bateson, M. (1972). *Our own metaphor.* New York: Alfred A. Knopf.

Commons, M., Richard, F., & Armon, C. (Eds.). (1984). *Beyond formal operations: Late adolescent and adult cognitive development.* New York: Praeger.

Inhelder, B., & Piaget, J. (1958). *The growth of logical thinking from childhood to adolescence.* New York: Basic Books.

Isenberg, D. (1984, November). How senior managers think. *Harvard Business Review.*

Koplowitz, H. (1976). *The college classroom as organism: A general system theory approach to understanding and changing the college classroom.* Doctoral thesis, University of Massachusetts, Amherst.

———. (1978). *Unitary thought: A projection beyond Piaget's formal operations stage.* Unpublished manuscript. Available from the author at The Longwoods Research Group Limited, Suite 200, 2161 Yonge Street, Toronto, Ontario, Canada M4S 3A6.

———. (1984). A projection beyond Piaget's formal operations stage: A general system stage and a unitary stage. In Commons, M., Richards, F., & Armon, C. (Eds.). *Beyond Formal Operations: Late adolescent and adult cognitive development.* New York: Praeger.

Lochhead, J. (1977, August). *A profile of the cognitive development of freshman engineering students.* Paper presented at American Psychological Associates Convention, San Francisco.

———. (1979). On learning to balance perceptions by conception: A dialogue between two science students in Lochhead, J., & Clements, J. (Eds.). *Cognitive Process Instruction.* Philadelphia: Franklin Institute Press.

———. (1980). *The confounding of cause and effect, change and quantity.*

Machado, L. (1980). *The right to be intelligent.* Elmsford, NY: Pergamon.

Perry, W. (1968). *Forms of intellectual and ethical development in the college years.* Cambridge: Harvard University.

Piaget, J. (1973). *The child and reality: Problems of genetic epistemology.* New York: Viking.

Renner, J., & Paske, W. (1977, May). Quantitative competence of college students. *Scientific American* (283–292).

Von Bertalanffy, L. (1968). *General system theory.* New York: George Brasiller.

Watzlawick, P., Beavin, J., & Jackson, D. (1967). *The pragmatics of human communication.* New York: Norton.

Watzlawick, P., Weakland, J., & Fisch, R. (1974). *Change: Principles of problem formation and problem resolution.* New York: Norton.

Wertime, R. (1984, August). *Slowing language down: A heuristic for systematically getting at the issue.* Paper presented at Conference on Thinking, Harvard University.

Wilber, F. (1981). *No boundary.* Boulder: Shambala.

14

Computer Graphics as a Medium for Enhancing Reflective Thinking in Young Children

George E. Forman
University of Massachusetts, Amherst

Interactive video is now available to millions of children. Is it better than anything it replaces? Can we identify unique aspects of the video medium itself that represents an advantage over previous media?

By interactive video I mean any television image that can be controlled by the viewer; common examples include the games, puzzles, and adventures that children play on computers by manipulating joysticks, keyboards, light pens, touch tablets, and touch screens. Our emphasis is on pictorial representation, so we are not talking about word processing or for that matter, computer programming, in this chapter. The primary example is a product called Paint and Play Workshop (by Coleco Industries) that allows a child to animate his/her own cartoon by manipulating a joystick and a few simple push buttons on the joystick chassis. In some sense it is an electronic equivalent to both a doll's house and a coloring book.

We contrasted the child's play with the electronic doll's house to play with ordinary doll figures and furniture. Each medium lends itself to a particular form of symbolic play. This chapter discusses how the physical aspects of each media constrain and elicit what children chose to symbolize in their play. These observations were made in the spirit of Gardner (1983), Olson (1977), and Salomon (1979). A nontrivial comparison between two media requires that one identifies media differences that can not be eliminated. For example, only the video medium can give the child a replay of his or her past action. Salomon (1979) calls these unique aspects *codes of the medium.*

Yet looking at the inherent codes might draw our attention away from the interface between the user and the medium. Therefore I prefer to add the term *affordances,* borrowed from J. J. Gibson (1979). Gibson was concerned with what meanings are inherent in an object because of a type of user–object compatibility, e.g. the size of the hand vis-a-vis the size of the object. The user directly calculates that compatibility and makes tactical decisions about object manipulation based on those calculations. Although Gibson was referring to calculations made at the sensory level, the concept of affordance is a useful addition to the study of symbolic media. What affordances characterize each medium, and how do these affordances suggest symbolic content? With miniature objects the child picks up the little doll physically. Thus it's affordance for lifting makes it more probable that the child will think to symbolize a pretend jumping of the doll. The affordance of picking up and moving is itself assimilated into the child's intention to symbolize something. A close look at affordances of a medium should yield a better understanding of the relation between mind and media (see Greenfield, 1984).

I have not mentioned how symbolic play can increase a child's knowledge. Not every symbolic act leads the child to new discoveries. In fact a majority of a child's symbolic acts are over-learned rituals or merely an instrumental response to obtain some immediate objective. New knowledge generally results from something that gives the child enough pause to cause reflection. The following sections identify how interactive video encourages children to pause and reflect.

The Video Medium

At the University of Massachusetts Child Development Laboratory, we have been comparing the inventiveness children exhibit on the video game compared to their inventiveness on a three dimensional mock up of the video microworld. First I describe the video software so you can better visualize the examples to follow.

One or two children sit in front of a color television set and use a controller to move characters, select or paint objects, and select or paint scenes. Each child has a controller with a keypad of 12 buttons, a joystick, and two fire buttons on the side. Initially the child sees a Smurf character that can be moved anywhere on the screen by use of the joystick. The right fire button makes the character jump, the left makes the character drop, with appropriate noise effects as accompaniments. The keypad buttons allow many additional functions. Four buttons allow the child to shift the background scene among two indoor and two outdoor settings. Another button allows the child to use the joystick to paint in any of a dozen colors. The painted lines can be easily erased. The child also has a button that calls up four blank screens that can be used to construct animated cartoons. The animation is created by making slight position changes of an object across the four blank screens, then hitting the record button on the keypad, then calling up the four screens, followed by hitting the replay button to see the sequence animate. The child can also use the record and replay operations to play back many minutes of moving the character icons through the four scenes. Children can choose from three menus of predrawn objects such as furniture, trees, and letters, and children can choose to direct any one of four different characters in the Smurf family.

The Medium of Miniature Objects

A three dimensional version of the Paint and Play Workshop world was made inside a shallow walled box four feet by six feet. It was divided into quadrants, each a mock up of the background as presented in the four scenes in the Coleco product. The miniature landscape included such features as a mezzanine platform, a Lego block fireplace, a hill and stream made of wood and felt, and four doors that made it possible for the child to enter any quadrant from any other quadrant. The children were also supplied with three plastic Smurf figures, about 2 inches tall, along with assorted ladders, tables, chairs of propropiate size and near replicas to those presented in the Paint and Play menus.

A three dimensional medium makes an interesting contrast with the video medium for several reasons. Because children can animate both miniature objects and video icons, the differences between the two media are more subtle than kinetics vs. nonkinetics. The video icon can be manipulated on line in real time or in a video replay. The miniature object can be manipulated only in real time. The video icon can be moved but not touched, whereas the miniature object can be touched, grasped, and squeezed. The video icons are recognizable Smurfs, as are the miniature objects; therefore any differences in symbolization can not be reduced to something as obvious as meaningfulness.

Enhanced Thinking through Reflectivity

The importance of reflection has been stressed at least since 1938 when John Dewey (1963) admonished: not all experience is educational. Experiences upon which a person reflect have the potential of yielding knowledge more general than the specific experience itself. Out attempts to help students reflect range from slogans such as "Think about what you're doing," to elaborate schemes to have students write down or map out their thoughts. Reflection, according to Piaget's revised theory of equilibration (Piaget, 1975) results from a mismatch between the self and the object. It is this mechanism that offers great promise in comparing the video and three-dimensional media.

The video icon moves across a screen several feet away from the hand actions that produces the movement. The miniature object moves only when the hand contacts the object itself. Thus inherent in the video medium we have a unique relation between self and object. Does this disjointed relation between self and object increase reflectivity in the user? After observing 10 preschool age children for three months, we have identified several ways that the video medium heightens reflectivity.

Procedures Needed to Make Selections

If a child wants to add a bed to an indoor scene, she or he must call up the furniture menu, move the cursor arrow via the joystick to the bed, push a button to shift the object from menu to scene, and then move the object via the joystick to the selected location. Compare this with the ease of putting a bed into the three dimensional doll house. The electronic medium makes choices much more deliberate because the procedures for selecting an object must be activated in a particular sequence. We hear the following comments often in the video medium.

Laura to herself, "Let's see, I think I want a tree now, that little tree, yes that little tree."

Dae San to his friend Mathew, "Let's get a bed, one for you and one for me."

In the three dimensional model of Paint and Play world, children seldom announce in advance what they are going to select from the box of toys, they just reach in and take the object they want. Furthermore children seem to decide what to do with a toy after they have removed it from the box. This was evident in the following activity. Children would pick up, say a ladder, inspect it, perhaps noticing that it can be joined to another ladder section, and then they would lean it against a wall somewhere in the doll house space. One child even used the ladder as a magic wand for a few seconds before using it as a climber. Thus it seems that ideas for the use of miniature objects flow from the physical manipulations, whereas ideas for use of the video icons come full blown from premeditation, often announced to others.

If it is true that children deliberate more about choices in the video medium than in the three dimensional model, there is the corollary chance that the video medium encourages greater planfulness, perhaps at the cost of playfulness. The affordance of the medium itself slows the children down and creates distance between self-action and object placement.

Procedures Needed to Create Movement

If a child wants the icon character to jump over a stream, two button operations are required. The child pushes the jump button as the icon approaches the left bank and then pushes the drop button to arch the jump down to the right bank. A continuous flow is further assisted by subtle pressure on the joystick to establish direction and momentum.

In the three dimensional model the child simply holds on to the little doll and jumps his/her own hand over the stream while focusing attention on the doll in the hand. The manual skill of an arching action is so overlearned that no reflection is needed to execute the symbolic effect of jumping. Yet when the child executes jumping in Paint and Play, the child for the first time realizes that a jump is really the coordination of two actions, an up move and a down move. This is true because both moves have to be executed by the child, rather than leaving the second movement to the automatic force of gravity. As you might predict, our preschoolers found it difficult to understand the need for two button presses to effectuate an arching jump. Their attempts to have Smurf jump up and down on the bed often lead to a one way trip to the ceiling.

Incongruous Positions

Because a video icon can be moved anywhere on the CRT children were constantly creating arrangements that not only violated gravity but also violated the usual. A T.V. set icon might land in bed, thus creating laughter and much conversation about how to both sleep and watch T.V. in bed. The number "2" might be added to a chair yielding laughter about how two can be one arm of the chair. Then there was Dae San who cloned a single bed into a bunk bed, thereby discovering the world of composite objects.

The three or four year old child approaches three dimensional objects in terms of the many affordances between hand, object, and surface. Stacking one bed on another does not flow from this set of affordances. Thus it takes an exceptional four year old to discover the bunk bed relation with the miniature toys. The flexibility of the video medium makes these happy accidents more probable, and when they occur in all their unexpected splendor, they give the child pause to reflect, laugh, and to think about what this strange object could be in a sensible world.

No doubt there are different relations more likely discovered in the three dimensional medium than the video medium. Themes about supporting bridges, people gathering, and changing speeds are more common in symbolic play with the three dimensional model. These themes emerge because physical support, clustering dolls, and varying speed are physical variations afforded by the three dimensional objects. It would take an exceptional preschool age child to go beyond the constraints of the video medium and conjure these themes without medium support. The point is simply this: Symbolization is prepped by the affordances of the physical medium itself.

A Shared Surface

The video screen is the whole playspace. It is like a common stage or easel for two children. The three dimensional model has four defined spaces, the four rooms. The two children can be in different rooms at the same time, something that is impossible with Paint and Play. This constraint of the video medium has several effects on symbolic play.

For one the children talk to each other more with the video medium. Even though children do not necessarily make direct negotiations about use of space, their symbolizations incorporate this concern. Mathew uses his Smurf to talk to his somewhat more dominant playmate, "Let's be friends." Children often announce, "Let's go outside now," an implicit request for permission to change the scene on the shared surface. These negotiations are not necessary in the three dimensional model. There parallel play prevails over interactive play.

With video the characters themselves can literally share the same space, as when the two children each have placed their respective characters on the same spot on the CRT. The characters can even walk, fall, or jump through another Smurf. Detours are not necessary. Children do not get their own body in another child's workspace. So themes of territoriality and aggression emerge less often in the video symbolic play. There are great games of chase, but no catching. And these games are light hearted given the absence of physical consequences to being chased. The following episode occurred between two girls each using the video paint brush.

> Laura, age 4 years 8 months, was painting on the screen. Jenny, age 5 years 4 months, was also painting, but in a different color.
> Laura, "Don't paint over the tree, O.K." Jenny does not acknowledge Laura immediately, so Laura adds, "I'll paint around you," as if this would box Jenny in.
> Jenny, "I'll paint a T.V." and proceeds to make a rectangle figure.
> Now Laura is exploring how to make the biggest enclosure possible by moving her cursor brush around the outside edge of the screen. At one point Jenny moves her strip of paint over one just laid down by Laura.

Laura, "Hey you're painting me." They both laugh and then Laura moves in behind Jenny's active brush. "I'm painting you." Jenny, "I'm painting you."

Now there is much laughter and more comments about how both are painting each other. The joy seems to come in the fun of doing unto others as they are doing unto you, and at the same time! So the chaser is also the chasee in an interesting reciprocal relation collapsed into a single time frame. The video screen as a shared interactive surface seems to elicit a great deal of this type of coordinated symbolization.

Of course these two girls coordinate their play somewhat in the three dimensional model, but the form is quite different. The cooperative acts in the model consist of assigning character identities ("You be Papa Smurf and I'll be Gargamel."), deciding who gets the limited supply of ladders, or taking turns fleshing out the details of a story in progress. Thus it seems that the visual pattern sets the context in the video medium whereas character identity and motive are more the context in play with miniature objects.

This media difference calls to mind something that Wolf and Gardner (1979) term *patterners* vs. *dramatists* in their discussion of individual differences. The orientation to patterns vs. drama may be due to inherent aspects of each medium or simply due to greater fluency with miniature toys. This difference needs further study. But the possibility remains that the video medium is primarily a graphic medium driven by concern for good visual form, whereas play with small toys is primarily a temporal medium driven by concern for a sensible flow of acts. This division between the graphic and temporal should break down as computers make animation easier and icons more object-like. As computer memory gets cheaper, icons will be able to diminish in size, occlude each other, and cast realistic shadows. These visual effects will provoke new forms of symbolization that are more expressive and replete to use Goodman's language of art (Goodman, 1976). Still, it will be important for children to use even powerful computer graphics as tools to construct realism and expressivity. Reflectivity would not be increased if articulate and replete images were made available to the child ready made.

Discrete Changes

The Paint and Play medium does not scroll from one scene to another. The changes are discrete changes. First you are in the kitchen, then you are outside in a park. The child first walks his or her Smurf to the door on the left side of the screen. When the scene change button is pushed, the Smurf instantly appears in a new scene on the right edge of the screen.

Although this filmic device is understood by even the three year olds, same Smurf, new scene, it is obviously quite different from scene shifts executed in the three dimensional model.

In the three dimensional model the child moves the plastic toy from one scene to the next, seeing both at once, and seeing the landscape pass from left to right as the child moves his or her body forward to the right. The four quadrants in the model have a fixed position even though the child can chose to go from any one to any other. The video scenes have no fixed position among themselves because there is no reference frame that includes all four scenes. The "position" of the four scenes is embodied only in the position of the four buttons on the controller keypad.

What effect does this media difference have on symbolization. We were attentive to the children's comments about going to a new scene. On Paint and Play children would announce the name of the room or outdoor space. "Let's go to the kitchen." Or one child, who had placed his Smurf at the window in the kitchen, said "Let's go outside," pretending that he had seen the outside from his kitchen window.

The comments in the three dimensional model were often the same, but with less frequency. Children would simply move their Smurf to a new quadrant of the model, or would say something like, "Come in here with me," or "I'm going over there." With the three dimensional model children spoke ambiguous sentences that were clarified by pointing or placing objects. This was not possible with Paint and Play. The video medium requires more explicit language and quite possibly more reflection on just where one was about to go. Thus we see once again that the increased distance between self action and object manipulation heightens the need to make specific reflections on performance.

Video Replay

The record and replay function of Paint and Play was by far the most significant difference with the three dimensional model. Children might re-enact a routine recently performed in the three dimensional model, but at no point could they watch that action happen again, exactly as before, without their hands being in the scene.

It was interesting to watch children witness the replay of something they had just completed. Several of the three year olds did not quite understand that the action they were seeing was the same as what they had just controlled. Therefore they treated it as an interference to their own play rather than a review of their play. Slightly older children were initially confused but figured it out in a short time.

Auburn, 4 years, 6 months, watches the replay and says, "Who's making my Smurf move? I'm not doing it, she's (playmate) not doing it, and you're (teacher) not doing it, so who's doing it?" Notice that even though Auburn is confused about the agent of action, she does not dispense with the idea that an agent is necessary.

After a second cycle through record and replay, Auburn then says, "Now let it do it by itself," indicating that she knows the computer is making the characters move. Later she understands that the movement is a replay of what she had done earlier.

To the teacher's question, "Do you remember what happens next?" Jenny answers, "I remember something but it's not going to happen now." Later, after a brief wait, she predicts "Now I'm gonna watch T.V., I think." At that point the Smurf sits on the bench to watch T.V. Jenny not only remembered the form of a particular event, she had a fair sense of its temporal position.

Play in the three dimensional model may involve review from time to time, as when a child tells an adult what he had just done out of view. But there is no confirmation of that review one way or the other. The child's reconstructive memory goes unchallenged by an objective replay. With the video, reflection is heightened when a child's prediction is challenged by immediate replay.

The self record and objective replay is yet another means of increasing self–object distance. In another study recently completed at the University of Massachusetts (Forman, Fosnot, Edwards, & Goldhaber, 1982) children from 4 to 7 years watched instant replays of their attempts to balance unsymmetrically weighted blocks. Some children watched a replay that would freeze the frame just prior to their placing the block on the fulcrum. As the frame was frozen they were asked to predict what they were about to do. After their prediction the tape continued. These children showed progress in formulating a more consistent theory about why blocks balance or fall. Other children were shown a replay in which the frozen frame and question came just at the point that the block was placed on the fulcrum. Here the children were asked what the block was about to do. These children did not progress in their theory building, the reason being that this replay technique did not heighten the difference between self and object. The first condition called on children to think about their own hypotheses and then see its objective consequence, whereas the second condition called on children to think about the block's position and then see its objective consequence.

The point is that the replay can increase the distance between self and object. In Paint and Play children gradually learn about the special status of the record mode. While the scene is being recorded children begin to think about their screen effects in a different way. They begin to explore unusual effects so that this will be seen during replay. Their attention is divided between making the present script and viewing it later. They are both watching the action and watching themselves watching it later. This type of distance between the present actions of the self and the video clip as a future object, is essentially a new level of reflection, premeditation, and planning. Although we did not see editing in our four and five year olds, I am sure that editing would occur with the older children and would represent yet another level of reflection and objectification of the current action. The form and structure of the animated script would become a concern and children would edit to add a sensible flow, dramatic tension, a beginning, middle and end. Obviously this use of computer replay allows children to go far beyond the perennial teacher's slogan, "Think about what you're doing.

Summary

Many procedures indigenous to interactive video seem to enhance reflectivity by creating distance between self and object. Some forms of reflectivity emerge from the affordances of the physical medium, such as the physical distance between the controller and the moving icon. Other forms of reflectivity are determined by software constraints, such as the discrete shift between scenes. Record and replay is certainly one of the most unique procedures that heightens reflectivity. Through the power of the computer the child, in effect, plays with a trace of his or her own action and gains a perspective impossible with on line manipulation of three dimensional toys (see Forman, 1985).

We are only in the beginning stages of understanding the advantages of interactive video media. The concepts of self–object distance, affordance, and reflectivity can generate new uses of computer graphics to stimulate thinking in young children. Children one day will literally be able to play with their own shadows, say through a life-size television image with replay capability. How interesting it would be for children to see a rerun of their own shadow as cast in profile or with their face to the light source. They could slow it down or speed it up to gain a better understanding of how their own body moves when kicking, batting, or doing a cartwheel. These are but a few derivations from self–object distancing that have implications for the education of young children.

REFERENCES

Dewey, J. (1963). *Experience and education*. London: Colliers Books.
Forman, G., Fosnot, K., Edwards, G., & Goldhaber, J. (1982). *The use of stopped-action video replay to heighten theory testing in young children solving balancing tasks*. Final Report, National Institute of Education, Grant NIE G-81-0095.

Forman, G. (1985). Kinetic print in computer graphics for young children. In E. Klein (Ed.) *Computers and children*. San Francisco: Jossey-Bass.

Gardner, H. (1983). *Frames of mind, the theory of multiple intelligences*. New York: Basic Books.

Gibson, J. J. (1979). *The ecological approach to visual perception*. Boston: Houghton Mifflin.

Goodman, N. (1976). *Languages of art: An approach to a theory of symbols*. Indianapolis: Hackett.

Greenfield, P. (1984). *Mind and media: The effect of television, video games, and computers*. Cambridge: The Harvard University Press.

Olson, D. (1977). From utterance to text: The bias of language in speech and writing. *Harvard Education Review, 47*, 257–82.

Piaget, J. (1975). *The development of thought, equilibration of cognitive structures*. New York: Viking Press.

Salomon, G. (1979). *Interaction of media, cognition, and learning*. San Francisco: Jossey-Bass.

Wolf, D., & Gardner, H. (1979). Style and sequence in symbolic play. In N. Smith & M. Franklin, (Eds.), *Symbolic functioning in childhood*. Hillsdale, NJ: Lawrence Erlbaum Associates.

III

THEORETICAL PERSPECTIVES ON THE TEACHING OF THINKING

This section brings together papers that provide theoretical perspectives for understanding how we should teach thinking.

The enhancement of critical thinking skills is the goal of many an educational program, and so it is useful to consider, as Jonathan Adler does in Chapter 15, just what these skills consist of. Adler's contention is that it is as much epistemological and dialectical skills that the critical thinker needs, as the logical skills on which traditional courses have often focused.

Those who seek to promote good critical thinking face the problem of deciding whether to advocate the addition of general "critical thinking" programs to the standard curriculum, or whether to seek to integrate a suitable critical dimension into each separate discipline of the curriculum. One factor in deciding this issue is settling the "problem of transfer": can thinking skills acquired in one subject domain (or at some high level of abstraction) be expected to transfer to other areas? Or will they tend to remain relatively restricted in application to the subject area in which they were developed? Robert Swartz argues in Chapter 16 that, although there are quite general thinking skills, their development will not satisfactorily be achieved just by "add-on" programs in critical thinking. Rather, *all* curriculum teaching needs to be re-oriented so that it promotes critical skills and attitudes. In Chapter 17, David Perkins and Gavriel Salomon offer a general model of transfer of learning that explains why transfer commonly does not occur and specifies conditions for the teaching of thinking that would foster transfer.

In Chapter 18, Delores Gallo argues that it is an important educational goal to promote empathy, since empathy fosters not just imagination, but also the more "convergent" rational skills. Sharon Bailin takes up the topic of teaching for creativity in Chapter 19, in which she argues that the teaching of standard skills is not inimical to creativity, as some may suppose, but is actually a necessary precondition for its possibility.

D. Midian Kurland, Catherine Clement, Ronald Mawby, and Roy Pea offer in Chapter 20 a close look at the cognitive demands of learning to program and the prospects for transfer from programming experience to other contexts of cognition. Continuing the focus on programming in Chapter 21, Ronald Mawby examines the exceptional demands of attaining high proficiency in programming with its attendant prospects for transfer to other domains. In Chapter 22, Richard Paul turns to the problem of critical thinking in the classroom, reviewing how the institutions of education have persistently slighted it and exploring ways to restore attention to critical thinking in school contexts. Oscar van Leer concludes the section in Chapter 23 with an exploration of the powers of "ascendent thinking" that breaks rigid disciplinary boundaries by generalizing ideas from one context and applying them to another.

15 On Resistance to Critical Thinking

Jonathan E. Adler
Brooklyn College of the
City University of New York

Educators concerned with critical thinking have two distinguishable objectives: to teach a set of skills and to offer an ideal for a liberally educated citizen.[1] Either objective requires focus on the development of the person, not simply the teaching of methods. Positive attitudes and dispositions toward critical inquiry must be encouraged. With such lofty and valuable goals, attention must be devoted to the prospects for success.

The critical thinker will apply to himself or herself the same critical scrutiny that he or she applies to others. But our own beliefs share a need for self-preservation or protection that ill disposes us toward self-criticism. Similarly, the act of putting forth a claim opens a person up to objections, some of which are likely to be unanticipated or unanswerable by that person. So we put ourselves at risk too.

Teaching critical thinking challenges students personally and socially and intellectually. Consequently, educating for the development of a critical intelligence, if it is done well, faces singularly difficult hurdles. The first part of this chapter elaborates on some obstacles to critical thinking, dividing them into cognitive, motivational or personal, and methodological obstacles. Part two develops an example that illustrates some of these themes, whereas exploring the suggestion that the teaching of critical thinking should be viewed as an epistemological enterprise. Epistemology is actually much richer in content and more complex in

---

[1]For the former see Ennis (1962). Critical thinking as an educational ideal is a view well articulated by Scheffler (1960, 1973) and Siegel (1980).

247

principles than one is led to believe from the conception typically invoked in discussions of critical thinking. This enriched conception of epistemology is brought to bear on the difficulties set out in Part One.

SOME DISTINCTIVE DIFFICULTIES
IN THINKING CRITICALLY

The teaching of reasoning, thinking skills, or critical thinking is usually promoted as a single topic, understandably, because all involved inferences and higher cognitive processes of wide applicability. In this section, I isolate some of the more distinctive and intractable problems of critical thinking.

Reasoning as a cognitive process is rapid, nonconscious, and ubiquitous. It underlies such pervasive activities as comprehension, perception, and the explanation of action.[2] These activities are dependent on our memory capacities, whose limitations impose a severe need for economy on all our cognitive processes. Short-term memory capacity is limited to retaining the "magic number" of seven items. An enormous amount of information is rapidly forgotten. Long-term memory, though its storage capacity is comparatively vast, evidences the pressures of economy in the pervasive organizational structuring and "chunking." These pressures are also said to account for the "short-cuts" and "heuristics" that play a central role in reasoning and information processing.

As we try to avoid informational overload, we continually seek bold theories and explanations to help us understand the natural and social world. We can harmonize these opposed pulls by facilitating inferences so that, from a little data, a lot of information can be extracted.[3]

A host of examples can be developed out of H. Paul Grice's theory of conversational reasoning (see Grice 1967, 1975). Thus the response that "John is either in the kitchen or in the backyard" is taken by the hearer to implicate what is not said namely, that the speaker does not know which of these two places John is in. Thus more information is found than is said. Inferences such as these are facilitated by strong biases that absorb new phenomena into the persons' explanatory system of beliefs. In Grice's theory the central bias is one of a presumption by the hearer that the speaker is trying to be cooperative. (Hence, informative, so if the

---

[2]See Lance Rips (in press).

[3]For a useful survey of the literature on heuristics and biases see Nisbett and Ross (1981). Doubts might be raised about my use of evidence from nonconscious reasoning processes. First, unconscious reasoning patterns clearly influence and set important constraints on our conscious reasoning abilities. Second, I appeal to aims in nonconscious inferences (e.g., gaining information) that are paralleled in conscious reasoning.

speaker did indeed know John's whereabouts he would say so. As he did not say so, he therefore does not know.)[4]

By contrast, critical thinking must be careful, slow, and highly selective. Our reasoning is astonishingly quick when there is information to be gained. But to be critical is often to block inferences by moving to a more neutral, more objective level of inquiry. Criticism frequently diminishes the capacity to offer explanations—rejection is not followed by a better view. When we are thinking critically, we step back from the forward-looking inferential path to reflect, analyze, question, and doubt. Biases must be scrutinized; implicit assumptions must be brought to the fore. The price of the greater objectivity is time, effort, information, and conflict with other cognitive aims.

In matters of personal concern, the critical thinker must overcome pulls toward self-deception and other forms of "motivated irrationality." Studies in social psychology, beginning with cognitive dissonance research, reveal that these pulls are powerful and pervasive.[5] Moreover, there appears to be little (subjective) access to information that would distinguish between the operation of cognitive dissonance and the normal course of reasoning and belief formation (see Nisbett & Wilson, 1977). Presuming that we desire to appear correct to ourselves and others, if a person is placed in a position that *insufficiently justifies* an action he or she has taken or a judgment he or she has made, that person has an *investment* in proving that act's worth. A famous study of this phenomenon required participants in an experiment to lie to other prospective subjects about the value of that experiment, in order to induce their participation. Those who received only $1 for their efforts tended to rate that experiment as much more worthwhile than other subjects who received the obviously greater compensation (justification) of $20.

Because the assessment of the value of a personal action or judgment is not readily susceptible to (intersubjective) verification, we are likely to bend in the direction of higher valuation where it suits us. Other beliefs can then be marshalled to further support. Counterevidence is selectively heard, giving salience to what supports our position, and diminished importance to what threatens it. This cycle is pervasive. So innocent and common an act as understanding another person demands our effort and time, and a presumption of cooperation and charity in interpretation that prejudices us, albeit minimally, toward the truth and virtue of what that person says or writes.[6]

---

[4]The psychological literature is replete with further examples. An especially dramatic finding is Brown and Fish (1983). See also Fodor's (1983, pp. 94–97) discussion of the research on natural categories by Rosch and others.

[5]For a clear presentation see Aronson (1976). See also Paul (1982).

[6]Davidson (1974) has done most with the Principle of Charity.

Consider the bias toward dividing information into foreground and background, a distinct advantage in argumentation and conversation. Assumptions are put aside or left implicit as presumed shared background knowledge, so that the precise point of the disagreement stands out sharply. But the devious arguer can exploit this division of labor. He or she will try to get some of the actual points of disagreement into the background. The hearer (reader) is manipulated to accept, or at least to pay less attention to, a point that he or she initially is reluctant to believe.

One famous use of this manipulative device is Antony's funeral oration in *Julius Caesar*. Antony never states anything *directly* negative against Brutus. On the contrary, he repeatedly asserts, "For Brutus is an honourable man." Consequently, the evolving disgust with Brutus' action becomes stronger than the evidence merits. Consonance is maintained by increasing faith in the nobility of Antony correlative with mounting anger at Brutus.

Critical thinkers in an analogous situation must explicitly bring forward for examination what all have accepted. They act unsociably; what they want to question, their peers take for granted. They question the value of an opinion or judgment to which they have already committed themselves. So they are forced to admit *collaborating* in their own deception. They have gone along with a discourse whose claims and presuppositions they now disagree with. Yet, as they go further on, they implicitly commit themselves—by that very engagement—to more and more of the beliefs they want to challenge. When they finally do take a critical stance, they question what appears to all to be what they have already accepted.

Teaching critical thinking would be a lighter load if it were simply a matter of imparting substantive general directives such as: take the other person's point of view; offer reasons for your claims; do not generalize from a sample unless you have considered the total evidence. But a memorizable and usable list of such rules is not forthcoming. Earlier I offered crucial evidence for this apparently bold claim. I noted the deep-rooted nature of cognitive biases, but I sought to highlight not only the negative features that attend the pejorative "bias"; rather, I emphasized the cognitive *gains,* especially informational, that require, and are furthered by, biases.[7] If this is so, even so simple a methodological rule as "Beware of biases, attempt to overcome if found," will be in many contexts self-defeating. A similar claim applies to demands that we treat the evidence fairly and modify or reject our hypothesis with (putative) conflicting evidence. Our conservativeness (resistance to modifying be-

---

[7]Here I differ with the heuristics approach to problem solving. I disagree with Perkins' (1982) harsh denigration of a "makes sense epistemology" in comparison to a "critical epistemology."

liefs with new evidence) and confirmation bias (giving higher weight and attention to positive cases, at the expense of negative ones) are a persistent feature of human belief formation.[8] But conservatism is also required by the good (lay) scientist. Hypotheses or beliefs must not immediately yield to contrary evidence lest we lose our foothold in a domain, becoming subject to rather accidental findings of inquiry. Hasty generalization is not a formal failure, but a failing in a domain where boldness is likely to lead to error, given background knowledge. The methodological rules or values we propose to teach must either be devoid of content such as "Do not be *too* biased"; "Do not be *too* resistant to contrary evidence," or they must be stated and studies so that the overcoming of bias or conservatism takes place within a framework that permits (other) biases and conservativeness.

Consider the fundamental demand for impartiality in moral reasoning, common to the Golden Rule, the Principle of Equal Interests, universalizability, role reversal, and similar principles. There is a wide range of alleged counterexamples that have been offered to the impartiality demanded by such principles of moral reasoning. For example, if you can save one of two persons, one of whom is your child, it is ludicrous to even weigh, let alone weight equally, the other child's interests. Partiality is morally demanded.[9]

Consider the basic demand of practical reasoning for consistency between thought and action. In the opening chapter of *Middlemarch,* Dorothea renounces her share of the mother's jewelry, giving it all to her sister Celia, who cares more for such worldly trinkets. Dorothea finally consents to take two of the items, and here her sister feels triumphant in Dorothea's lack of consistency: "either she should have taken her full share of the jewels, or, after what she had said, she should have renounced them altogether." I assume that we are meant to accept the sister's diagnosis while yet maintaining the appropriateness of Dorothea's behavior. It shows a morally reflective person, who courts the charge of practical inconsistency in her resistance to a sanctimonious adherence to abstract principles.

Insistence on impartiality or practical consistency in these examples is inappropriate. It is a foolish scientism or moralism or legalism. I do not deny that we should always conceive impartiality or practical consistency as applicable constraints. Given their essential generality, they could

---

[8]See the recent collection Kahneman, Slovic, and Tversky (1982).

[9]See Williams' (1982) essays 1–3. For a reply to such alleged counterexamples see Hare (1983). The plausible suggestion that family bonds constitute relevant differences must be developed very carefully to avoid the well-known danger of trivializing universalizability by allowing too many ways for cases to fail to be morally similar.

apply to virtually any moral reasoning. This becomes apparent as one imagines variants of these examples where the charge of bias or hypocrisy would be precisely to the point. In the example on saving one of two drowning children, let us imagine that you have a job to offer, rather than the saving of a life. If your relationship to one of the two applicants is much weaker than parent to child, you should start to wonder whether your defiance or universalizability has moved from sound loyalty to prejudice. We diminish the force of these constraints or principles only with good common sense, social intelligence, and worldly experience.

Four related conclusions can be drawn from these examples: First, it these basic principles are going to be so ridden with exception, there is little hope that critical thinking can depend in large part on the inculcation of correct principles. Second, we cannot construe the exceptions or inconsistencies as applied to particular cases as refutations of these principles. The point is that they remain in force (to different degrees) even while we justifiably disobey them. Third, even if ultimately one can formulate versions of these principles or higher order principles that mitigate these as counterexamples, the resulting modified and, presumably, more complex principles may be overly sophisticated for the main body of students (a critical example, role reversal, is not followed by most adults).[10] Fourth, observe that the counterexamples offered are realistic enough so that we cannot expect students to avoid them.

AN EXTENDED ILLUSTRATION

I now further illustrate the obstacles of Part I, in order to state something positive about directions for teaching critical thinking. I do not attempt a resolution—a means to overcome all these obstacles. Critical thinking does have costs and represents only one—one very important—perspective on reasoning or argumentation.

The analysis and criticism of arguments, the central focus of courses and programs in critical thinking, highly favor only those arguments that can be stated explicitly and certified in terms of our current knowledge and evaluative methods as good reasons. A whole range of good, though often dangerous, argumentative support is thereby eliminated or denigrated, including arguments that play on metaphor, or allusion, or the possibility of future connections and associative support. The tacit and rhetorical dimensions of argument are downplayed. Faith in the emphases of critical thinking programs should not blind one to the admission of their limitations.

---

[10]Kohlberg (1982).

My illustration involves two contrasting cases presented next.

Case 1.   A teenage boy tells his parents that he intends to try heroin. His parents tell him of recent statistics indicating "that a majority of teenage first-time heroin users run into drug-related difficulties later" (Kahneman & Tversky, 1983, 509–510). The son dismisses these statistics claiming he knows himself well enough to be confident that these difficulties will not happen to him.[11]

Case 2.   A teenage girl informs her parents that she wants to have sex with her boyfriend. The parents point out to her the high rate of teenage pregnancy. She dismisses these statistics claiming she knows herself (and her boyfriend) well enough to be confident that they will take the necessary precautions. It will not happen to her.

Here is an analysis of the first example: The question at issue is the probability of this boy's running into drug-related difficulties if he tries heroin. There are two relevant pieces of evidence: individuative (his estimation of his own strength of character) and base rate (the statistics of what happens to first-time heroin users). To judge the overall probability we must use both pieces. Even though the boy's confidence may be high, when we integrate it with the base rates there is not a high probability that the boy will be able to end his experiment unscathed. The boy, in judging on the basis solely of the individuative information, is reasoning badly; he is dismissing good data that runs counter to his own desires.

Should we view the second example in the same way? Many readers will have different initial judgments on these two cases; wherein lies the difference between the two? Are judgments on behalf (presumably) of the girl's case over the boy's an unfair bias, given the structural similarity of the two problems? In both cases we have individuative and base-rate data that conflict.

A student might question the details of the example: Do we know enough about the boy and the girl in the respective problems?; are we reading in assumptions about them that are not given?; are we comparing the right reference classes?; should we compare teenage heroin users with teenagers engaging in sex, or first-time teenage heroin users who discuss the matter with their parents, compared to the corresponding class for teenage pregnancy? One way to respond to these questions is to claim that the teacher supplies the problem and the student must simply take it as is, provided that there is sufficient information to be determinative of

---

[11]The example is taken from Kahneman and Tversky (1983), who introduce it as a response to Cohen (1981). See succeeding issues of the *Behavioral and Brain Sciences* for Cohen's reply.

an answer. From this point of view, which Piaget and Kohlberg share, further assumptions about the boy or girl (e.g., she is trustworthy), or debates about the various reference classes that may be proposed as of greater pertinence, show a poorer ability to handle abstract, well-circumscribed problems.

On the other hand, real critical reasoning frequently involves a refusal to accept a problem in the form in which it is given, (e.g., Has the boy already tried marijuana and did his parents consent?). Carol Gilligan (1982), in presenting Kohlbergian dilemmas to females, found a characteristic refusal on the part of some women to accept moral dilemmas in the presented form. We can dismiss their responses because they show a change of the subject. Or we can admire their refusal to see moral problems as akin to artifactual word problems of algebra.

Some students might see inconsistency in our differing judgments. The proper analysis is the same in both cases, so that our judgments should be the same. Other students might hold that the differing judgments turn on differences in values, not on formal matters: drug-related difficulties are more threatening than pregnancy. How can they translate this felt difference into one that makes a proper justificatory difference, while avoiding the charge of inconsistency? Notice that the students who rest their argument on consistency based on the formal analysis have a ready answer that ends debate. Students who do not find the results of that formal analysis satisfactory are left with uncertainty but reason to search further.

Prominent in this pair of examples is a conflict between different ways an individual can assess the possible outcomes of his or her actions: from a personal perspective (one's self-knowledge) and from the perspective of himself or herself as members of a given class (e.g., teenagers). To what extent are the boy and the girl in these respective examples correct in claiming to distinguish themselves from other teenagers—to know themselves better than those other teenagers, whose behavior is represented in the worrisome statistics? This theme is similar to the one in moral reasoning alluded to earlier: How does one give fair weighting to the interests of others, and maintain the loyalties and personal projects that are essential to realizing one's own life plans or more simply, living one's own life?

Some students will focus on the egocentric and self-deceptive dangers: e.g., the boy should not presume himself able to extricate himself from the biochemical pulls (etc.) that harmed so many of his peers. Respect for others, and humility with respect to his own powers, should direct the boy to listen to his father. Justification secures objectivity only by meeting standards of evidence that go outside oneself. The pertinent question is: What evidential value do others place on these statistics for decisions about experimenting with drugs or sex? A social conception of knowledge, with its attendant values of mutual respect, fairness, and objectivity, suggests itself as the concept to guide the critical thinker.

If the mutual respect promoted by a social conception of knowledge guides the critical thinker, it must not overwhelm him or her. One cannot always allow oneself to be absorbed into the reference classes for which solid correlations exist. The teenage girl, and those sympathetic to her, will want to say that they do have reasonable confidence that she will not get pregnant. This may not be completely justified. She can adduce evidence of her own strength of character and good sense, but ultimately she is taking a stance. Philosophers of education have overemphasized justification in critical thinking, at the expense of personal integrity.

Strangely, there is a convincing, yet ignored, corollary within epistemology: Justification must end with a decision or judgment, not with certain grounds. We try to make the decisions as reasonably as possible, mitigating arbitrariness by keeping ourselves open to further refinement. Nonetheless, unjustified elements enter. The conflict between the need for justification and the impossibility of continually finding it shows the student the riskiness of critical thinking. You must take a stand, though you are unable to answer all reasonable doubts. You must be open to criticism, while—not instead of—preserving your own commitment.

Finally, note that the objectivity gained by giving dominance to the base rates is at the cost of increasing information. We rely on the statistics in both preceding cases at the cost of accepting the beliefs of the boy and girl. We fail to increase the fund of mutual belief when we doubt the worth of the teenagers' self-confidence. On the other hand, agreement with individuative data, at the cost of the conflicting message of the base rates, invites severe error.

A similar theme is debated by contemporary epistemologists. A traditional view is that the aim of knowledge is truth alone, and that judgments of evidential confirmation or support are *global* judgments, permitting comparisons between disparate fields. On a more recent, though not predominant, view, inquiry is a local enterprise governed by (valuative) assumptions peculiar to a domain. In particular, a variety of cognitive aims (or interests) must be balanced and weighted, including the aims of reducing error, increasing information, and maximizing simplicity. On this conception, differing methodological judgments are to be expected. Inquirers must attempt to optimize these multiple, possibly conflicting, aims without benefit of a decision procedure or firm principles to adjudicate disputes.[12]

---

[12]Such diverse philosophers as Levi (1965) and Habermas (1971) both conceive knowledge in these terms.

EPISTEMOLOGICAL APPROACH
TO CRITICAL THINKING

Our focus has been on resistance to critical thinking—personal, social, cognitive, and methodological. Recognizing such resistance should give us a basis for a realistic determination of the proper standards for successful instruction. The depth, naturalness, and pervasiveness of this resistance should drive home that we must not aim to eliminate it. Rather, instruction for critical thought must respect an essential tension within the complex of factors that constitute the critical thinker.[13]

We can list on one side a set of attitudes or actions that we consider virtues of the critical thinker. But I suggest that there are also attitudes, listed on the other side in tension with these, that are both resistant to and required for good critical thinking.

Critical Thinking

Supportive Attitudes or Actions	Complementary Attitudes or Actions
1. Open to opposing viewpoints	Dogmatic, committed
2. Accepts fallibility	Confident
3. Universalizes, impartial, abstracts[14]	Personalizes and particularizes; contextual sensitivity
4. Humble	Bold
5. Critical	Supportive
6. Literal	Charitable, imaginative, metaphorical
7. Detached (objective)	Engaged
8. Serious	Playful
9. Honest	Persuasive
10. Autonomous	Deferential (to authority)
11. Skeptical	Cooperative and accepting
12. Insistent on clarity and precision	Tolerant of ambiguity and vagueness
13. Practically consistent, i.e. actions conform to principles	Practically inconsistent, hypocritical
14. Seeks criticism; alters behavior accordingly.	Integrity and tenacity in preserving projects and self-conception.

When I say these are attitudes in tension, I mean that they are likely to give rise to conflicting judgments. This leaves open the possibility of mutual dependence. Conflicting judgments will be specific contrary assessments, e.g., "I should accept that p is true" versus "I should continue to test whether p is true." I do not give examples as to how each

---

[13]For a criticism of the standard texts on related grounds, see Finnochario (1981).
[14]See Adler (1984) on some limits and costs of abstraction.

member of the underappreciated right side is involved in developing critical thinking. I assume extrapolation is possible on the basis of previous examples and discussion.

Why is the list on the right downplayed? Failings on the left side are the more glaring. But ignoring the right side is unfortunate in three ways. First, illustrations used are simplistic, so that the curricula and exercises are impoverished. Second, instruction becomes directed to the development solely of methods that define institutional reasoning (e.g., science), neglectful of the fact that we are attempting to develop *persons* who have needs, desires, goals, and commitments that cannot be suspended at will. Third, we underestimate the difficulties of thinking critically.

Because attitudes listed in the two columns are in tension and because there will often not be any adjudicating principles when problems for critical thought occur, *practical wisdom* is required to give guidance. So part of the teaching of critical thinking must involve extensive practice. It is only be considering many cases that call for subtle discriminations and by giving students opportunities to use a variety of possibly disharmonious skills that a solid foundation of experience can be developed.

Extensive practice is also required for related Aristotelian reasons. Aristotle tells us that to be virtuous one should do what the virtuous man does. Becoming virtuous is a matter of discerning and acting according to the correct models, not primarily of discovering the right principles or methods. Attitudes and beliefs can adapt to actions, not, as commonsensically conceived, always determining actions. Our attitudes and beliefs can shift after an action, making that action appear more defensible.[15] The importance of practical wisdom lies in its facilitating the difficult movement from right thought to right action.

Practical wisdom allows the critical thinker to be highly selective in his skepticism. He is discerning and judicious in deciding when to adopt the critical stance. A much neglected skill is *knowing when* to think critically. What topics, forms of communication, or methods are most likely to require special caution and effort? What clues might the audience in *Julius Caesar* use to prick them to a critical attention that would normally be wasteful effort?

The selectivity extends beyond simply shunning the role of the radical philosophical skeptic. The limits on appropriate doubting in everyday life are so great that they lead to the judging of apparently like cases unlike; or at least, not being able to say how the cases, that we judge differently, are different. For example, a legitimate response to the first case aforementioned is that the parents should insist that their son not take heroin. They still may and perhaps should engage in dialogue on the subject, but unlike

---

[15]See Elster (1982).

prior discussions this one will not permit a serious possibility of a shift in view for all participants. Despite their having taught and modeled the value of open and mutually respectful dialogue, the parents must now break abruptly from that value, not even allowing the suggestion that an affirmative answer is a live option.

One more familiar example: Everyone looks forward to the ideal of equal opportunity for hiring and promotion. Yet many believe in "Affirmative Action" programs that seek to promote, though not determine, increased opportunities for minorities suffering from a history of discrimination. Because such benefits are not directly for those discriminated against, nor against those who so discriminated, nor solely an attempt at just compensation, it is hard to be dismissive of those who claim inconsistency between the ideal and the practical consequences of Affirmative Action programs. We can defend the position in a number of ways: e.g., insisting that guidelines are not quotas and are to be used only for the purposes of justifying reassessment of policies that have led to severe disproportionate representation of some groups at the expense of others. But I do not find that this completely disarms the charge of inconsistency (sometimes under the phrase *reverse discrimination*), especially when backed by examples in which guidelines appear to have slipped into quotas.

If these examples are as typical of those that face critical thinkers as I assume, they show the need for tolerance of the gap between one's own strong judgments and quite limited ability to justify them. The critical thinker must respect the charge of practical inconsistency, whereas yet refusing to be incapacitated by it. Unfortunately, there is a powerful tendency for instruction in critical thinking to enforce an expectation that justification of all beliefs is usually necessary, and that resources are always available for discharging this epistemic responsibility. Thereby a rigid demand for resolution is encouraged, which, being impossible to fulfill, undermines the most basic goals of the instruction.

I have alluded to the connection between my overall themes and contemporary epistemology. Many educators and philosophers of education have made the suggestion that critical thinking is an epistemological enterprise. Even critics of critical thinking courses such as McPeck (1981) conceive it this way.

The epistemological approach to critical thinking instruction emphasizes the importance of giving reasons and being open to objections. This approach is often contrasted with those that identify critical thinking instruction with some combination of studies in formal methods of logic, probability theory, or statistics. This conception of epistemology is quite pallid compared to the substantive findings of contemporary epistemology relevant to critical thinking. Simply finding reasons in favor of our position is too easy and can just be a spur to avoid serious criticism. On the other hand, the welcome mat for criticism cannot always be out. As the late philosopher Alan Ross Anderson once quipped: we must be open-minded, but not so open that our brains fall out.

Epistemology is a branch, arguably the central branch, of philosophy. It is concerned with exhibiting fundamental problems and perplexities in our conception of knowledge, especially in our judgments of the scope of our knowledge. Perplexity encourages inquiry, Socrates famously observes in the *Meno,* because it moves one from a position of certainty to one of doubt. Although we attempt to test imaginative responses to these perplexities with rigorous and self-reflective argumentation, we do not expect resolution. Students are left without final answers. Our hope is that their disquiet inspires a self-consciousness about, perhaps even a reexamination of, fundamentals—the kind of virtue that explains why critical thinking, like philosophy, is, as Iris Murdoch observes, "a thing which it is not easy to do."[16]

ACKNOWLEDGMENTS

I want to thank L. Jonathan Cohen, Catherine Z. Elgin, and John Bishop for comments.

REFERENCES

Adler, J. E. (1984). Abstraction is uncooperative. *Journal for the Theory of Social Behavior, 14,* 165–182.

Aronson, E. (1976). *The social animal* (2nd ed.). San Francisco: W. H. Freeman.

Brown, R., & Fish, D. (1983). The psychological causality implicit in language. *Cognition, 14,* 237–273.

Cohen, L. J. (1981). Can human irrationality be experimentally demonstrated? *Behavioral and Brain Sciences, 4,* 317–370.

Davidson, D. (1974). On the very idea of a conceptual scheme. *Proceedings and addresses of the American Philosophical Association.*

Elster, J. (1982). Sour grapes—utilitarianism and the genesis of wants. In A. Sen & B.A. O. Williams (Eds.), *Utilitarianism and beyond.* Cambridge: Cambridge University Press.

Ennis, R. (1962). A concept of critical thinking. *Harvard Educational Review.*

Finnochario, M. A. (1981). Fallacies and the evaluation of reasoning. *American Philosophical Quarterly, 18,* 13–22.

Fodor, J. A. (1983). *The modularity of mind.* Cambridge, MA: Bradford Books/The M.I.T. Press.

Gilligan, C. (1982). *In a different voice.* Cambridge, MA: Harvard University Press.

Grice, H. P. (1967). *Logic and conversation.* Unpublished manuscript of the William James Lectures, Harvard University.

---

[16]Murdoch (1970, p. 1).

Grice, H. P. (1975). Logic and conversation. In D. Davidson & G. Harman (Eds.), *The logic of grammar* (pp. 64–75). Belmont, CA: Dickenson.

Habermas, J. (1971). *Knowledge and human interests.* London: Heinemann Educational Books, LTD.

Hare, R. M. (1983). *Moral thinking.* Oxford: Oxford University Press.

Kahneman, D., Slovic, P., & Tversky, A. (Eds.). (1982). *Judgment under uncertainty: Heuristics and biases.* Cambridge: Cambridge University Press.

Kahneman, D., & Tversky, A. (1983). Can irrationality be intelligently discussed? *The Behavioral and Brain Sciences, 6,* 509–510.

Kohlberg, L. (1982). *The philosophy of moral development (Vol. 1).* Cambridge, MA: Harvard University Press.

Levi, I. (1965). *Gambling with truth.* New York: Knopf.

McPeck, J. (1981). *Critical thinking and education.* New York: St. Martin's Press.

Murdoch, I. (1970). *The sovereignty of good.* Boston: Routledge & Kegan Paul.

Nisbett, R. E., & Ross, L. (1980). *Human inference: Strategies and shortcomings of social judgment.* Englewood Cliffs, NJ: Prentice–Hall.

Nisbett, R. E., & Wilson, T. D. (1977). Telling more than you can know: Verbal reports on mental processes. *Psychological Review, 84,* 231–259.

Paul, R. (1982). Teaching critical thinking in the "strong sense": A focus on self-deception, world views, and a dialectical mode of analysis. *Informal Logic Newsletter, iv,* 2–7.

Perkins, D. N. (1982). *Difficulties in everyday reasoning and their change with education.* Final report to the Spencer Foundation, Project Zero, Graduate School of Education, Harvard University.

Perkins, D. N., Allen, R., & Hafner, J. (in press). Difficulties in everyday reasoning. In W. Maxwell (Ed.), *Thinking: An interdisciplinary report.* Philadelphia: Franklin Institute Press.

Rips, L. J. (in press). Reasoning as a central intellective ability. To appear in R. J. Sternberg (Ed.), *Advances in the study of human intelligence (Vol. 2).* Hillsdale, NJ: Lawrence Erlbaum Associates.

Scheffler, I. (1960). *The language of education.* Springfield, IL: Charles C. Thomas.

Scheffler, I. (1973). *Reason and teaching.* New York: Bobbs–Merrill.

Siegel, H. (1980). Critical thinking as an educational ideal. *Educational Forum, 45,* 7–23.

Williams, B.A.O. (1982). *Moral luck.* Cambridge: Cambridge University Press.

16 Critical Thinking, the Curriculum, and the Problem of Transfer

Robert J. Swartz

Consumerism has become part of the fabric of 20th-century western society. There is a form of consumerism, which, although not unique to the west, finds an especially extreme manifestation here. We have all become, in one way or another, avid consumers of information. It is no longer just word-of-mouth that we rely upon to gain our stock of basic knowledge. We now have *Reader's Digest*, The CBS Evening News, textbooks, *The New York Times, The National Enquirer,* and the best sellers.

This merely scratches the surface. The free market of ideas contrasts sharply with situations in other countries in which the flow of information is curtailed and manipulated for uniformity in attitude and belief. In our society almost anyone can say something and be believed. The forceful speaker or writer still has the capacity to hold his or her audience spellbound. The imagery of language is captivating, and when we add to it the visual and auditory imagery of contemporary media, we must acknowledge that the power of the word has become one of the greatest forces in human history.

We do try to reckon with this force. There are editorial boards and there are critics. But even the most well meaning of these endorse ideas for consumption that the next group of editors reject. We are virtually inundated with information, and most of us sort through it and accept what we do simply because of its appeal or because of an affinity we have to what is being conveyed, or worse, to the way it is being conveyed. In our pluralistic society there is not just a pluralism of values. There is a pluralism of what we take as fact as well.

A pluralism of ideas has, of course, been endorsed by our best thinkers: Thomas Jefferson, Horace Mann, and John Dewey, reflecting an older tradition that includes John Locke and goes back to Plato. But a second piece of this ideal is missing. What these thinkers endorse is free expression to lay ideas before us, and also the use of our good sense and reason in sorting through these ideas and accepting only the best of them. It is the latter that we often endorse but rarely realize.

Once again, we are moving to bring critical thinking back into school classrooms. It is right to think that in these classrooms lies the hope of these thinkers. Here we have a chance to give the youth in our society what they need to put this second piece in place. It is crucial that, if this attempt is to succeed this time, it be based on a firm conceptual foundation and that it impact on children in ways that they do not leave behind when they leave these school classrooms. What they learn must *transfer and become a part of their lives*. In this chapter I examine two basic approaches to bringing critical thinking into classroom teaching: the *subject-specific skills approach*, and the *general skills approach*. I argue that both of these approaches can be enhanced by explicitly teaching for transfer. I make some suggestions about how to do this directed at those who will ultimately bring critical thinking into their classrooms, schools, and school systems—educational practitioners.

A DIRECT APPROACH TO BRING CRITICAL THINKING INTO THE CLASSROOM

There is an approach to this problem that many teachers have been practicing for years: to bring examples of the claims about that which we want our students to be more discriminating directly into the classroom and to spend the time thinking through the issues that they generate. This approach is now supported by some special curriculum materials that are issue oriented: materials on the arms race, for example, or on poverty, or on the prison system (see Bender, 1982; Wright, 1980). Although how individual teachers handle these issues, with or without these materials, is often quite exciting, this approach has severe limitations. It usually finds its way into only a small corner of the curriculum, e.g., in high school current events courses, chosen only as electives in most school systems. Although the impact of thinking through these issues in many cases has been quite dramatic, it is far too isolated a practice to do the job we want. The challenge is to find ways of bringing teaching for critical thinking into *mainstream* instruction, K–12, in ways that maximize our chances of achieving this goal for all students.

This challenge necessitates an *indirect* approach. We cannot add consideration of all the items we ultimately want to help our students think about to an already crowded curriculum. Perhaps we can split off the ingredients of critical thought from *these* items of content and focus on these processes in mainstream instruction, helping students develop the tools that they will be using when they come against the barrage of information that they face in contemporary society.

Putting the challenge of bringing critical thinking into the classroom in this way, of course, underscores the necessity of thinking through to what extent and how we can teach to maximize the transfer and integration of critical thinking into the lives of our students.

CRITICAL THINKING WITHIN TRADITIONAL SUBJECTS

The ferment of ideas set in a framework in which they are subject to commonly accepted critical standards is not an unfamiliar phenomenon in human history. It recurs again and again in the great intellectual traditions represented by the academic disciplines. It is not surprising, therefore, to find the methodology and research traditions of separate fields of study the basis for bringing an emphasis on critical thinking into the classroom. Teaching practices that emphasize giving facts to students, and that rely on stimulating memory and recall to a great degree, make teaching in subjects like science and history ripe for rethinking, in order to put more of an emphasis on higher judgmental skills. The research traditions of these fields provides a ready-made basis for this rethinking.

This is an approach typified by the *Amherst Project,* a project of the early and mid-1970s. It brought together a group of high school history teachers and university faculty who were dissatisfied with the way a textbook and fact-oriented approach to history left students uncritical thinkers, all too ready simply to accept what they read or are told as fact. Source books on major events in American History are the fruits of this project, and they provide the American History teacher with what is needed for critical thinking oriented teaching in this subject. These source books are designed to include a good sampling of the raw materials of which history is made. Through much of this material, the ferment of contrasting interpretations of historical events, their upshot, and a critical reading of historical writing can be generated. Topics that are covered include the Korean War, myth and reality concerning the American West, and freedom and authority in Puritan New England, just to name a few.

To give the flavor of the contents of these booklets, and how they can provide raw material for critical thinking oriented instruction included in teaching mainstream American History, I now turn to some of the selections included in the lead issue in the series, *What Happened on*

Lexington Green?: An Inquiry into the Nature and Methods of History (Brown, 1970). The first is from a typical American history textbook, *The United States: A Story of Free People* (Steinberg, 1963). Steinberg says:

> In April, 1775, General Gage, the military governor of Massachusetts, sent out a body of troops to take possession of military stores at Concord, a short distance from Boston. At Lexington, a handfull of 'embattled farmers', who had been tipped off by Paul Revere, barred the way. The 'rebels' were ordered to disperse. They stood their ground. The English fired a volley of shots that killed eight patriots. It was not long before the swift-riding Paul Revere spread the news of this new atrocity to the neighboring colonies. The patriots of all New England, although still a handfull, were now ready to fight the English. Even in faraway North Carolina, patriots organized to resist them. (p. 92)

Teaching from books like Steinberg's generally leads students to accept uncritically what is written as fact and carries layers of attitude along with it through the use of such terms as *atrocity* and *patriots*. So here we have prime material for critical thought.

Winston Churchill (1957), also quoted in *What Happened on Lexington Green?*, says the following of the same incident:

> At five o'clock in the morning the local militia of Lexington, seventy strong, formed up on the village green. As the sun rose the head of the British column, with three officers riding in front, came into view. The leading officer, brandishing his sword, shouted, 'Disperse you rebels, immediately!' The militia commander ordered his men to disperse. The colonial committees were very anxious not to fire the first shot, and there were strict orders not to provoke open conflict with the British regulars. But in the confusion someone fired. A volley was returned. The ranks of the militia were thinned and there was a general *mêlée*. Brushing aside the survivors, the British column marched on to Concord. (Vol. 3, pp. 180–181)

There are differences in tone and style in these two passages that can be exploited in looking at the writing of history as the writing of literature. But there are also *factual* differences. Steinberg comes right out and says that the British fired the first shot; Churchill clearly implies that it was the colonists.

In the hands of a skillful teacher this should be enough for a start. Though this is not any longer a big issue (nor even if it were, would it tell us much about the causes of the Revolutionary War) it is interesting enough to prompt curiosity about who is right, and low keyed enough to allow quick distance for a more dispassionate investigation. Yet, it is not just the raw material for an academic exercise, as we see later. So where can the skillful teacher move after exposing students to those conflicting texts?

If we are troubled by this difference, we might be reluctant to go to another history text. They may all be prone to the same sort of difficulties. A look at what is behind these texts (the primary sources these historians use) may put us in a better position. The skillful teacher will allow students to suggest looking at these sources by raising the right questions. But here some high school teachers will be at a loss. What primary sources? And who has time to look for them?

Taking this into account the Amherst Project tries to include primary sources in their booklets. There are testimonials, newspaper articles, and other written reports of the same incident by witnesses. For example, this is one by Sylvanus Wood, a colonial witness:

> The British troops approached us rapidly in platoons with the General officer on horse-back at their head. The officer came up to within two rods of the center of the company where I stood—the first platoon being about three rods distant. They there halted. The officer then swung his sword and said 'Lay down your arms, you damned rebels, or you're all dead men— fire!' Some guns were fired by the British at us from the first platoon but no person was killed or hurt, being probably charged only with powder. Just at this time Captain Parker ordered every man to take care of himself. The company immediately dispersed; and while the company was dispersing and leaping over the wall, the second platoon of the British fired, and killed some of our men. There was not a gun fired by any of Captain Parker's company within my knowledge. (p. 36)

What better than a firsthand account of this incident will settle this question? But will it? This booklet provides us with enough to move into another level of critical discussion. Does a detailed account like this suffice? Despite the details, most students have enough experience to know that it doesn't suffice, although the teacher may have to prompt them to make the connection between this question and their own experience. Our decision about whether this account is credible can be based on our judgment about whether the author is reliable, and there are criteria we use to make this sort of judgment everyday. What can we discover about Sylvanus Wood? He indeed was a member of Captain Parker's company. He must have been running and running with some panic. Can we trust his account fully in these circumstances? The clincher, though, comes when we ask about the date of this account, for according to the records Sylvanus made this statement in 1826, about 50 years after the incident! In 1826 it clearly becomes subject to all the faults that time imposes on our memories. Perhaps, though, we should not stop here. What other criteria are there for judging the reliability of such accounts of witnesses? Maybe some others are satisfied that resurrect the credibility of this account.

Here we have a sketch of how material from one of the Amherst Project source books can be used by skillful teachers to structure some important critical thinking activites into the teaching of American History. The framework of these activities is the research framework of historical investigation. Once we open this door, it is a quick and easy step to bring students into a fuller range of historical research. Examining artifacts, looking at documents, and historical interviewing are at our service. These can be put at the service of students by bringing such primary material into the classroom, or using the community as the classroom. Local museums, historical societies, and, for more recent history, community records and recollections, set in a good critical framework, can make history come alive for our students. Other critical skills in the use of evidence in historical interpretation and explanation can be introduced in the same way that skills related to the reliability of sources of information were introduced using Amherst Project material. The activities just described relating to the Battle of Lexington can serve as a breakthrough, serving as a model that can be applied to other examples that may help students uncover the riches—or poverty—of other kinds of historical detective work.

Finally, this can be a route to realizing one of the basic goals of the Amherst Project: a look at the nature of history and historical knowledge itself. A look at all the eyewitness reports of the Battle of Lexington reveals the same kind of breakdown along party lines as we find in many of the textbooks. Were Winston Churchill and Samuel Steinberg gilding the lily? Were they speculating? Is all history speculation? Can we ever gain knowledge of the past? These, indeed, are the philosophical questions about history that the Amherst Project suggests we raise with our students, questions that are integrated into the very study of history. It is certainly appropriate, meaningful, and important to raise these questions in the history classroom.

CRITICAL THINKING IN HISTORY AND THE TRANSFER OF CRITICAL THINKING SKILLS

There is a danger that a close look at the Battle of Lexington will engage students in using some good critical thinking about the eyewitness reports about the battle and not impact much on the critical thinking they do about other issues in history where eyewitness accounts are relevant. The teaching here may be too particularized. Even just within history we want students to acquire skills that they apply to other relevant issues as part of their normal cognitive activity in the field.

This is the most natural way that the issue of teaching for the *transfer* of critical thinking skills arises in fields like history. How can the critical thinking skills used by historical researchers be taught in order to maximize transfer, and what is the scope of the transfer that we can expect? The latter question is a theoretical issue to which I turn in the next section of this chapter. The former requires some comment here.

The problem of transfer is not unique to the teaching of critical thinking skills. Indeed, our very earliest learning exemplifies our abilities at transfer, and the very earliest teaching helps accomplish it. I refer to the learning of a natural language. In whatever ways we help children to speak our language, the linguistic skills developed transfer quickly and early. We extract the principles of syntax and transfer this knowledge to new situations to which we apply them.

It is clear that successful transfer is viewed as an essential goal of the learning process when teaching is aimed at helping students grasp general principles and develop general skills. The conventional method of testing for the development of a skill is to see if the student can use that skill in new, unfamiliar problem situations. We test students' computational skills development when we give them new problems that they can solve only by employing the skills for which we are testing. Such testing clearly contrasts with testing aimed at recall of information that is, by its very nature, particularized to that information.

There are components of the activity I have just described that are designed to move students beyond the Battle of Lexington in just these ways. These enhanced techniques were often lacking in earlier discovery-oriented instruction in education. They involve two things: standing back from the particular example and reflecting on the standards of, and general principles of, the reliability of eyewitnesses, and of sources of information in general; and, secondly, giving students guided practice in extending their application of these principles to other examples in history. This is a critical thinking oriented version of a not unfamiliar methodological tool used in good skill-oriented instruction to bring about the broadest possible range of application of the skills taught. In cases in which practice in using the same skills to work through many other examples is not feasible, even simply pointing out analogies—or having the students themselves come up with analogies—will enhance transfer. In the critical thinking activities I described about the very specific incident of the Battle of Lexington, the seeds of incorporating good critical thinking skills that are useful in the field into the way students deal with historical questions in general are ready for mature growth.

Earlier, I commented on the fact that, in our consumer-oriented society, information has become as much a product for our consumption as have automobiles and washing machines. Some of the students who take courses based on the Amherst Project materials cast in a framework to teach for critical thinking will be developers of information and, as such, will hopefully draw on good research skills. If not historians, some may become journalists. But the majority of students will be consumers, not developers of information. Isn't the use of such research skills beyond what we would normally be expected to do as consumers? How do these skills help us to be better critical consumers?

This is an important and a complex question. Certainly good critical consumers should know what type of research backs up claims made in a field like history, and they should be sensitive to the way that the point of view of the historian can shape the presentation of history. The critical consumer of history will have a questioning attitude towards what he or she reads, just as the students using the Amherst Project materials are prompted to question the accuracy of both Samuel Steinberg's and Winston Churchill's rendering of the first shots at Lexington. The way we relate to the writings of historians from the outside can be transformed by an exploration inside history. There is an intimate connection here. Students who do the type of research involved in this example have as solid a base as they need to think about history as consumers.

But this may not be enough. Surely as consumers, it is not just history books that we must adopt a good critical stance towards. It is also—and in fact especially—*present* history that we must relate to in this way: newspaper reports, news items on TV, and even oral reports by our neighbors about happenings in the neighborhood. What are the sources of this information? Do they stand up to critical scrutiny? Here a more acute issue of transfer arises. One of our goals concerning students as consumers of information should be that we impact on their thinking attitudes, skills, and practices with regard to this stuff of their daily lives. Is it asking too much of the teacher of history to adopt means to achieving this goal as well? And what means are at our disposal?

Teachers who are concerned about this issue have adopted an approach that involves an extension of the techniques that I have emphasized as useful in impacting on the transfer of critical thinking skills *within* history. Material that is consumer oriented can be brought directly into the classroom for critical examination. For example, some teachers have used newspaper articles, broadsides, and the like and set them in a context in which students are asked to adopt the stance of consumers for this purpose. The very same principles relating to the reliability of sources that were exposed in thinking through examples like the Battle of Lexington can be brought to bear on these items as well, and they can serve as further examples for students to focus on to gain practice in using these principles. Surely, what we have here is a continuum and the good history teacher can exploit this fully in ways that draw on good techniques at teaching for critical thinking. Techniques that *motivate* student questioning, that involve students in *using* the critical thinking skills we are concerned with, and that put them in the position of *reflecting upon and understanding* these skills and the principles of their use are all relevant. Extending teaching to effect this kind of transfer to contexts that impact on the lives of all students as consumers of information is well within the reach of any history teacher.

McPECK ON THE NONTRANSFERABILITY OF CRITICAL THINKING SKILLS

I have argued that explicit teaching for transfer *within* a field like History is manageable. But are the skills that history students develop when they are taught using the Amherst Project materials in the ways I described previously the same skills that we use in other fields; are they *transferable* to the other academic subjects in which we immerse our students? This is different from asking: *Do* these skills transfer? The latter is an empirical question about whether students actually do make use of any thinking skills that they might hone through their study of history in other fields of study. Even if they do not, the reason may be because of the educationl practices that the students experience, and not because these skills are *inapplicable*.

The importance of distinguishing and thinking about both of these questions cannot be stressed enough. The question of *transferability* is, however, a question that should be thought through first. To answer that question, we will be trying to answer a question of the scope of the particular critical thinking skills that we may wish to help students develop in a field like history. What we do in other fields, and in our teaching in general, will be determined by how we answer this question.

In his book, *Critical Thinking and Education,* John McPeck argues that the expectation that good critical thinking skills in history will transfer to other fields is bound to be frustrated (McPeck, 1981, p. 31). Critical thinking does *not* involve the use of general critical thinking skills that cut across the traditional disciplines. Rather, he claims, because *the logic* of each academic discipline is different from the logic of any other, critical thinking is *subject-area specific.* Historians, he suggests, use different critical standards and techniques from those employed in the natural sciences, and from literary critics. These standards and techniques ought to be learned when we learn the different subjects. The only way we can become proficient critical thinkers is through a broad exposure to *all* of the academic subjects.

McPeck's arguments here are not convincing. McPeck cannot mean that for each academic field there is a different system of formal logic that represents the set of principles of deduction that is used in that field and no other. Deductive logic is not subject, or content, specific, except insofar as the particular system keys into specific relationships that derive from the use of special terms or connectives like *If . . . then, or,* etc. The logical import of these terms does not vary from subject area to subject area. Propositional logic, the more emcompassing quantificational logic, or even the different systems of modal logic cut across different subject areas. *Modus ponens* is the same in science as in history.

Perhaps McPeck means that the *epistemologies* of the different fields of study are different; that is, perhaps the standards of knowledge and rational belief and the ways that knowledge is gathered and used vary from field to field. Indeed, there is a point to be made here. Even between such broad category distinctions as the natural sciences and the social sciences, there is a variability in the ways that knowledge is gathered and used. For example, the rigorous use of controlled experiments in the social sciences is far more restricted than in the natural sciences, and reliance on such experimentation is more central in the natural sciences than in the social sciences.

That there is such variation in the role of certain practices in accumulating knowledge in the different fields in no way implies that the notion of a controlled experiment in the social sciences is different from that in the natural sciences. Similarly, this variation in no way implies that standards relating to developing such skills as those involved in accurate observation vary from the natural sciences to the social sciences. There still may be—indeed there are—common practices and common skills relating to knowledge and rational belief that cut across these broad disciplinary boundaries, just as there are common types of deductive inference that cut across these boundaries. This is not to say that there may not be some idiosyncratic skills related to the separate disciplines. It *is* to say that McPeck's argument, developed to show that the *only* skills we find used in the separate disciplines are idiosyncratic, is not convincing.

On the other hand, there is good reason for thinking that what we should do in thinking critically can vary depending on what we think about. The standards of evidence, methodology, and skills involved in assessing general *causal* claims, for example, are different from those involved in investigating and assessing simple claims about the past or about the reliability of witnesses. Hence, there is a sense in which developing one set of critical thinking skills, like those involved in distinguishing reliable from unreliable sources, will not be useful in certain other contexts calling for critical thinking. This does imply that critical thinking instruction should be multidimensional in that it should concentrate on the array of different skills involved in thinking critically. But this variability does not map onto the different *subject areas* of instruction, as McPeck claims. It still could be that there are common skills used in thinking critically, like those involved in assessing the reliability of sources of information, or those used in thinking critically about causal hypotheses that cut across traditional disciplinary lines.

Still, McPeck's point about the *locus of instruction* in critical thinking, i.e., the traditional academic disciplines, is a forceful one. His message builds on the traditional compartmentalization of the curriculum by fields with which we all have to live, and the ready-made basis for integrating teaching for critical thinking that we find in the research methodology of the separate disciplines. The example I presented from American History illustrates how rich this way of infusing teaching for critical thinking can be. Similar practices can be initiated in science, and indeed have been: The "Process Science" approach developed at the University of Warwick in England and the new K–12 Science Curriculum Framework adopted by the State of California similarly reshape teaching traditional content in science based on the infusion of teaching for critical thinking derived from a taxonomy of skills directly related to the active research traditions in science. It makes sound *educational* sense to base teaching for critical thinking on the epistemology of the separate fields of study, although we may reject McPeck's stronger conclusion that critical thinking skills used in the separate fields of study are radically different from field to field.

There are dangers of excessive fragmentation, however, in adopting a discipline-by-discipline approach to teaching critical thinking. Confusion can be are caused by the use of different terminology for the same thinking skills and processes, for example. Difficulties in students grasping the application and use of the same basic critical thinking skills that cut across the different disciplines may result. These difficulties underscore the need to address the question of teaching for the transfer of these skills across different disciplinary areas. A discipline-by-discipline approach should be based on a common agreement among teachers in the same school or school system on a common vocabulary for the same skills whose use recurs in the different fields of study. I also suggest cross-referencing in the classroom, where teachers point out to, or ask, students to draw analogies between the critical thinking activities they engage in across subjects like history and science. The two strategies I mentioned earlier that were directed at transfer *within* a field of study can be used to some extent, drawing out some of the general principles of causal inference, for example, and helping students to see connections between the examples that they initially focus on in using these skills and other examples from other fields.

Teaching for thinking within a field of study based on its research tradition is something many teachers feel they already practice. To what extent this is presently practiced is largely a matter of speculation. But this is not enough.

If we are concerned that the thinking that students do within a field of study be integrated into their lives, this teaching must be enhanced in ways that impact on its transfer potential. Activities that involve more reflection on the sort of thinking that is important in certain contexts (metacognition) and repeated practice in doing this thinking reflectively are crucial if we want to realize this potential.

SOME PRINCIPLES ABOUT CRITICAL THINKING

What is the concept of critical thinking involved in this approach to teaching? We can glean five important principles from our discussion so far.

1. What we want to encourage in helping our students to think more critically grows out of procedures and standards that are useful in acquiring knowledge, or, better, in providing good reasons for belief, disbelief, or suspension of judgment, and for decision making and action.

The principles of critical thinking are not *just* the principles of logic. It is epistemology to which we must turn for the study of critical thinking; logic can at best only give us a partial set of principles dealing with the internal structure of reasoning. The sources of information that our reasoning proceeds from and their *authority* must be part of the expanded locus for the principles of critical thought.

2. Standards for thinking about things critically vary depending on the epistemological type that the claim we are considering represents. If we are considering present observations, the past, causal claims, and value claims what counts as good reasons will vary.

There are two important consequences of this principle. First, being a critical thinker includes having a cluster of different thinking skills ready for use, and teaching no one of these will be sufficient to assure the development of the others. These skills involve the efficient use of standards relating to the credibility or lack of credibility of the particular claim in question. Sorting out what these skills are and organizing a comprehensive critical thinking skills list can be an important step in establishing goals for critical thinking instruction.

The second upshot of this principle is that this variability does not mean that critical thinking skills vary from traditional discipline to traditional discipline. There may be critical thinking skills that are useful in some or, indeed, all the traditional disciplines.

Disciplinary-oriented critical thinking instruction, therefore, should be undertaken with this in mind. One key issue in developing principles for critical thinking that can serve as the basis for instruction in the disciplines is whether there is some simple way of systematizing and categorizing these different standards and principles that, at the same time, shows their usefulness in different disciplines.

3. Nothing is immune from critical thinking. Even our most deeply ingrained beliefs fall within the range of subjects for critical thought, as do questions about what the standards of critical thought are, together with the multitude of specific questions that arise day to day concerning both everyday beliefs and more specialized claims in the traditional fields of human enquiry. Nothing is immune from the search for good reasons.

This does not mean that scepticism follows from an endorsement of critical thinking or that critical thinking is always the search for reasons for rejecting beliefs. Good critical thinking can alleviate doubt and provide us with good reasons for beliefs and decisions, not just raise questions.

Any educational system that truly adopts teaching for critical thinking as a goal must do so with the full awareness that this carries with it a commitment to a *spirit* of questioning that exposes everything to the demand for good reasons, not just to practicing certain mechanical procedures of evaluation. How this plays itself out in the classroom, however, may be subject to constraints of time and good sense that avoid turning a classroom into a forum for never-ending Socratic dialogue.

4. Critical thinking skills—and indeed thinking skills in general—are not just another set of skills added to our list of basic skills (reading, writing, and computing). They are fundamental skills that permeate the effective development of the other so-called basic skills. Effective writing cannot go on without effective thinking, nor can effective computing, or reading.

This implies that just as a focus on these traditional basic skills must permeate the teaching of content in education, teaching thinking must be fused with these basic skills, not taught apart from their practice. Critical writing, reading, and problem solving in mathematics must permeate the development of these skills.

5. Finally, whereas effective thinking is something we can accomplish, it is the product of attitudes that are equally important to encourage in the classroom (attitudes of appropriate questioning, wondering, puzzlement, openness, etc.). The relation between promoting these attitudes in our classrooms and modeling them in situations in which we, as teachers,

genuinely have questions, are puzzled, are open to criticism, etc. cannot be stressed enough. The tendency to think of teaching for critical thinking as simply adding another subject in which the teacher retains the traditional authoritarian role will be combatted only if this point is fully embraced.

GENERAL PROGRAMS IN CRITICAL THINKING

A chart entitled, "The Universe of Critical Thinking Skills," circulated by the California-based *Project Impact* representing the basis for its new critical thinking program, is shown in Fig. 16.1 (Winocur, 1982). This program is based on an implicit rejection of the position adopted by McPeck concerning the subject specificity of critical thinking skills (a position that I have argued against earlier in this chapter). In fact, this program can be viewed as attempting to base a critical thinking curricu-

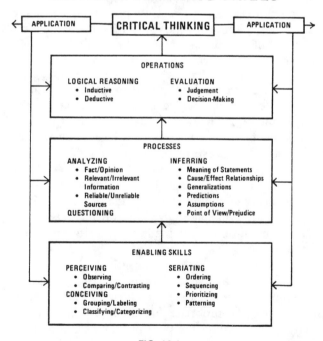

FIG. 16.1

lum on a synthesis of the common activities involved in critical thinking that cuts across the different areas of human concern. I call the approach to critical thinking that underlies the program a *general-skills approach.* This attempt at a general characterization of critical thinking has its roots in a number of classical works in the field, especially those of Robert Ennis (see Ennis, 1962). Ennis, in fact, is the main proponent of the view that McPeck argues against in *Critical Thinking and Education* (McPeck, 1981, Ch. 5). Our rejection of McPeck's main thesis makes a return to the Ennis approach to critical thinking important to examine. *Project Impact* represents the only major attempt to date to base a published curricular program on this general approach.

Adopting this approach does not dictate exactly how the goal of enhancing critical thinking will play itself out in the curriculum. The skills list in Fig. 16.1 could serve as the basis for the kind of restructuring of the curriculum in each subject area to teach for critical thinking that I described in connection with the Amherst Project material and American History. But *Project Impact* adopts a variant of a different and more traditional way of bringing new material into a classroom; it contains a packet of curriculum materials that are designed to be *added onto* the regular curriculum. For *Project Impact,* however, this does not mean the addition of a whole, integrated, stand-alone program in critical thinking, like a critical thinking course. Rather, the *Impact* approach is to integrate appropriate lessons on specific critical thinking skills at appropriate times and places in the curriculum, to be determined by the individual teacher. Lessons designed to focus on each of the skills in "The Universe of Critical Thinking Skills" are included in the *Impact* program. Among unified programs to teach critical thinking, *Project Impact* is at one end of a continuum that has, at the other end, structured and separate critical thinking courses that use single integrated textbooks on critical thinking.

Project Impact brings an approach to teaching critical thinking into schools that is used by a multitude of other more general thinking skill-oriented programs, even though there are basic differences between the content and structure of these programs. The basic notion underlying the development of these programs is that there are many identifiable and discrete skills that we all can and should develop to become good thinkers that cut across different subject areas. The curricular approach is to abstract these out of specific curricular contexts and make them the subject of a separate program where thinking skill development can take place. *Project Impact* is a specialized program focusing only on *critical* thinking skills. Such programs as *Strategic Reasoning* (Glade & Rossi, 1983), *Project Intelligence* (Adams, 1983), and *Philosophy for Children* (Lipman, 1972) are different from *Project Impact* in their scope, the type of thinking, and the skills they focus on. But they too detach teaching

these skills from the regular curriculum. This approach is also characteristic of a great many critical thinking textbooks, including *Critical Thinking*
by Anita Harnadek, a series designed to be used in K–12 instruction
(Harnadek, 1981).

To capture the flavor of *Project Impact,* I include a sample lesson from
the packet (Fig. 16.2). I have chosen a lesson in the skill category
corresponding to the skill category we focused attention on in our
exploration of a way to use Amhert Project material in American History
to teach for critical thinking: reliable/unreliable sources of information.
The *Impact* lesson is aimed at the upper elementary grades. It demonstrates how teaching for the same critical thinking skill that was used in
the American History activities I described earlier can occur at a different
grade level and with different content. However, notice that the activities

---

"Who Knows?"
Study Sheet 1

Directions: There has been a serious plane crash in which a light plane clipped
the right wing of a jumbo jet. A Government Commission has been set up to
investigate the accident. As a clerk for the committee, it is your job to sift
through a list of those who wish to appear before the committee to give
evidence, and decide which ones should be called to give reliable data to the
Commission.

I am going to give you a list of witnesses and the location of the witnesses at
the time of the accident. I would like you to circle the names of those sources
whom you believe could supply the most reliable data. Beside each name on the
list, give reasons why you chose or did not choose that person.

List of Sources
1. Captain of the jet's flight crew.
2. Pilot of the small plane (bailed out prior to impact).
3. Steward on jet (was in the galley preparing food during impact).
4. Passenger No. 1 (was sitting on the left front side of jet).
5. Passenger No. 2 (was sitting over the left wing).
6. Air Traffic Controller.
7. Airline Official in the terminal.
8. Manufacturer of light plane.
9. Widow of man who was killed in the crash.
10. Representative of the aircraft insurance company.
11. F.C.C. official who inspected both aircrafts after crash.
12. Pathologist who performed autopsy on dead passenger.
13. Farmer who was ploughing his field below the site of the crash.
14. Steward (was in the cockpit at the time of the crash).
15. Film crew from a local TV crew who shot film of the crash from their
    helicopter.

© 1981 OCDE
All right reserved.

FIG. 16.2

I described based on the *Amherst Project* involved *restructuring* the use of traditional content material, a textbook account of the Battle of Lexington, to teach for critical thinking. By contrast, the *Project Impact* lesson uses a contrived real-life situation relating to eyewitnesses to a plane crash, developed by the lesson designer to focus students on the use of the skills in question. This lesson, then, becomes a supplement to regular curriculum materials used in the school classroom.

Individual lessons keyed into each specific skill on the *Impact* list will give us a total package of materials that can bring a comprehensive critical thinking program into a school system.

CRITICAL THINKING SKILLS FOR GENERAL USE

The Universe of Critical Thinking Skills, as a representation of the conceptual basis of *Project Impact,* serves as a goals checklist that is used to determine the critical thinking focus of specific lessons like the plane-crash lesson. It implies that critical thinking is the use of an identifiable set of skills—in fact this chart presents us with an attempt at a comprehensive and exhaustive list of such skills. Hence, the development of critical thinking involves the development of these skills. (This approach to critical thinking—as the use of a special set of skills—has become a common approach since this chapter was delivered, with numerous other critical thinking skills taxonomies being developed in the same spirit.) We should note that the *Impact* list contains reference only to skills, not to critical thinking attitudes.

This list attempts to capture the broader epistemological orientation of critical thinking we found in the subject-area approaches I discussed earlier in this chapter. Assessing the credibility of statements and claims is its focus, and the skills listed are all supposed to be involved in doing this well. They include such skills as distinguishing the reliability and unreliability of basic sources of information, and not just skills at inference. *Impact* claims to derive this conception of critical thinking directly from the works of Ennis (Winocur, 1982, pp. 2–3), although the set of skills contained in the *Impact* list as well as its structure diverges from Ennis' listing.

This being the case, the cash value of the *Impact* list, insofar as it is a list of *critical* thinking skills, will be in the normative principles that *Project Impact* promotes, which we use in each of these skill areas. These should be exposed to gain a full understanding of the content of *Project Impact* as a critical thinking program. Merely listing categories like *cause/effect* does not yet reveal what specific skills are being promoted in these categories. Moreover, that an activity is about cause and effect is not enough to make that activity a good critical thinking activity. This will be true of any critical thinking skill taxonomy and/or program.

For example, it is often claimed that certain ways of supporting claims about causes and effects (e.g., the evidence of repeated controlled experiments) are *better* than others (e.g., the evidence of one event occuring after another) in that they *justify* such claims. This is a prescriptive principle and not simply descriptive of how people *do* justify such beliefs. The critical thinking skills one learns with regard to causal inference will involve thinking in accordance with such normative principles, and lessons about cause and effect that are critical thinking lessons should involve their use. The basis of *these* principles lies in the general philosophical study of rational belief, just as the basis of the principles that lie behind the subject-specific approaches I considered in the first part of this chapter is the philosophy of knowledge and rational belief implicit in the research traditions of the academic disciplines.

It is also important to note that the *Impact* list is not *just* a list of critical thinking skills. It is structured to represent certain relationships between these skills. In this case, its organization is *heirarchical:* the skills at the bottom of the list are presupposed by, and subsumed under, the skills higher up. In this respect, it is similar to Bloom's famous taxonomy of thinking skills, although it is a more finely tuned listing of skills than Bloom's and no implication is carried that the skills at the higher end of the continuum reflect higher order functions in any sense other than that they presuppose the skills at the lower end.

We should note that setting out these skills in a heirarchy of this sort is not yet setting them out *developmentally*. It involves a further overlay of psychological theory not yet implied in the heirarchical structure of the *Impact* list to say that children develop through stages in which only certain of these skills are manifested. This stronger idea is more problematic. The heirarchical nature of the *Impact* list, therefore, presents us with an important feature that may have implications about whether and how we should structure and sequence a program that brings critical thinking into the classroom. But it does not contain the constraints of matching this sequence with ages and grade levels sometimes taken as an implication of Piagetian developmental theory.

These reflections generate a set of *adequacy conditions* for the conceptual basis of programs like *Project Impact*. Does each skill category represent a discrete skill? Is the list of skill areas and principles *complete?* Are the skills listed *cognitively ordered* in the way represented? Are the principles of critical thought that stand behind each skills area *philosophically defensible?* Finally, are there items other than skills that should be included in such a characterization of critical thinking (e.g., attitudes, dispositions, and strategies)?

The health of the new critical thinking movement in education depends on *our* use of good critical skills in addressing these questions about the conceptual basis of programs like *Project Impact*. Insofar as the *Impact* list represents the goals of a critical thinking program, we should be sure that it is a set of goals we can embrace. If not, we should be prepared to defend any modifications we wish to make. After all, if we want our students to assimilate and use the skills that we teach them when critical thinking is called for, we must make sure that we are teaching them the right ones and that we have them all.

A CRITICAL THINKING SKILL LESSON

The plane-crash lesson is supposed to work in the following way. Students are asked to think about the reliability of certain potential witnesses to the plane crash. They make their choices based on the use of certain criteria. For example, they might rule in the pilot of the jet and rule out the farmer plowing his fields below the crash. The students are also asked to state the reasons for their choices. They might say that the pilot was probably in full view of the oncoming light plane, whereas the farmer was probably attending to his plowing and not looking up into the air. Here they must bring to consciousness the basis for their decisions, a clear metacognitive activity. They already have been told that they are considering the reliability or unreliability of witnesses, an important critical thinking skill. Involvement of the students in thinking through this issue, therefore, is supposed to lead to the acquisition and an understanding of this skill through a combination of its use, and an awareness of what the skill is that they are using.

The plane-crash lesson represents a paradigm example of a particular approach to bringing teaching for a specific critical thinking skill into the classroom. The content of the lessons is created as a locus for the use of a specific skill in a more or less natural setting. In the plane-crash lesson it is calling up witnesses that raises the issue of the reliability of these witnesses as sources of information. The content of the lesson could be different and the same skill goals accomplished: Instead of a plane crash, the example could have involved an automobile accident, or simply an event of interest that a number of different people observed, like the President coming to town. Furthermore, the skill goal of the lesson could also be different although the same overall content might remain the same. The same plane crash could be the basis of a lesson about explanatory inference: What caused the crash? Three considerations on the part of the lesson designer are necessary here: a decision about which skill will be the dominant goal of the lesson, a sensitivity to natural contexts in which the use of this specific critical thinking skill is appropriate, and how it is used.

When students do similar activities designed specifically to incorporate the other skills on the *Impact* list, they will similarly acquire all the other skills necessary to make them good critical thinkers, according to *Impact*. They will be able to engage in well-founded causal inference and predictions, for example, uncover and assess assumptions, and engage in sophisticated deductive reasoning. In the spirit of *Project Impact* as a general skills-oriented program, this is accomplished in a way not tied to any specific academic discipline or disciplinary content.

TEACHING CRITICAL THINKING SKILLS FOR TRANSFER

Just as in the subject-specific approaches, such teaching may be too particularized and students may not integrate the skills they develop into more general patterns of thinking. The transfer of these skills to other appropriate examples may be minimal. The published lessons in *Project Impact* contain the seeds of strategies that can be used to avoid too narrow a focus on specific examples like the plane crash. In the hands of teachers who are sensitive to this problem, the plane-crash lesson can be enhanced to teach for transfer using techniques quite similar to those I described earlier.

For example, asking students to give the reasons for their choices provides raw material that gives a teacher a chance to reflect with the students about good standards to use in making such choices, and it can lead to the formulation of some tentative principles about the reliability and unreliability of witnesses. But rather than stop there, to teach for transfer a teacher might then ask students to think about other cases in which the reliability of witnesses is an issue. The students could be asked to describe cases from their own experience, or the teacher could provide a number of others herself or himself and ask the students to bring the principles they develop to bear on these cases. The important thing in these activities will be to engage students actively in using the general standards they develop to make decisions about these new examples, while using these other examples to test and perhaps modify these principles. Active thinking of this type can be engaged in in a true philosophical spirit, in which even the standards of critical thought are subjected to careful critical scrutiny.

Even more can be done to promote assimilation and transfer. Programs that split complex operations like solving problems in mathematics into a number of discrete skills and teach these skills piecemeal have always run the risk of not helping students gain practice in using clusters of these skills together in appropriate combination to solve the types of complex problems they began with. Splitting apart critical thinking into discrete skills and developing individual lessons to teach for these skills runs the risk of missing the importance of helping students develop a realistic sense of contexts in which such skills are appropriately used in combination in thinking through important issues.

Perkins (Perkins, Allen, & Hafner, 1983) has argued for the need for a model of good reasoning construed in this broad way. Perkins uses the particular case of the issue of requiring a deposit on bottles and cans to provide a paradigm in which particular skills are used in a broader reasoning context. He then develops a model for good reasoning that involves the systematic interplay between considerations pro and con this issue. He suggests that we will capture the notion of informal reasoning better by looking at the *dialectical* movement of thought, stimulated by a kind of internal questioning, in which relevant information is retrieved and brought to bear on an issue, and new information is sought through adequate investigative procedures, while we consider carefully the pros and cons of the various different solutions in a problem situation from multiple points of view. Skills related to the reliability of basic sources of information play a role on this model in that they are appropriate when certain types of questions arise about the premises or basic evidence in an argument. Other skills are appropriate at other points in the reasoning process. What Perkins promotes is that we teach broad *frameworks of reasoning*. These will provide frameworks within which we can broaden the transfer potential of the skills developed in critical thinking programs like *Project Impact*.

The seeds of this are present in *Impact* lessons like the plane-crash lesson, but more systematic supplementary work is called for. (For an argument linking transfer to the development of critical *attitudes*, see A. Swartz, 1985.)

CRITICAL THINKING ACROSS THE CURRICULUM

Although *Project Impact* is by no means designed as a separate integrated critical thinking course, lessons like the plane-crash lesson, as a paradigm of an individual lesson constructed to teach for specific critical thinking skills, are lessons themselves that remain outside of mainstream curricular content.

The danger of relying only on activities of this sort to teach critical thinking skills should be clear. Suppose, for example, that when issues about the reliability of textbook accounts, or about possible bias in textbooks, or even in firsthand accounts of events are appropriate in a History or Social Studies classroom they are *not* raised. Rather, the material is taught in a traditional teacher-and-textbook-to-student way. We run the risk of undoing what we are trying to accomplish in using the *Project Impact* approach to bring critical thinking into the classroom. These conflicting practices will give students a serious mixed message. Without a major reshaping of the standard curriculum in a school to *infuse* teaching for critical thinking into mainstream instruction, the effectiveness of lessons like the plane crash—however interesting they may be—may be minimal.

I have argued that teaching for critical thinking using a subject-by-subject approach runs the risk of fragmentation and confusion. A unifying conceptual framework for critical thinking that cuts across these different subject areas is needed. It should be clear that a separate critical thinking program or course, or the use of specially contrived lessons like the plane-crash lesson in *Project Impact,* without the integration of teaching for critical thinking into the rest of the curriculum, may be ineffective. Both together, on the other hand, provide a powerful route to the goal of creating good thinkers through our system of education. Lessons like the plane crash can be used as "warm-up"lessons to others that involve restructuring traditional academic content to teach for the same skills (O'Reilly, 1985, uses this combined strategy in many of the lessons he developed for critical thinking in American History). Or they can be used as follow-up lessons to show connections between the application of skills related to the reliability of basic sources of information to "real-life" examples. Whether one or both of these combined strategies is used, good teachers can integrate the two through the use of a thoughtfully developed and comprehensive critical thinking skills inventory, modeled perhaps on the *Impact* "universe of critical thinking skills," which can be the basis for *both* types of lessons. In fact, it can provide the unifying thread that can tie together an integrated and systematic approach to teaching for critical thinking through a whole school, school system, or school district.

(Since this chapter was presented, a number of schools and school systems from the K–4 Coolidge Elementary School in Shrewsbury, Massachusetts to the Irvine Unified School District in Southern California have developed their own skills taxonomy, some similar, some more elaborate and differently structured than the *Impact* list. The comprehensive new "Goals for a Critical Thinking/Reasoning Curriculum" by Ennis, 1985, should also be mentioned. These are all being used typically on the

Impact model, as a set of goals that determine the character of individual lesson development. *Both* "cooked up" lessons of the type that are found in *Impact* have been developed by teachers in these systems, and lessons that restructure traditional material like basic readers or history textbooks to teach for critical thinking. In fact, such critical thinking skills inventories *are* being used as the basis for infusing critical thinking *across* the curriculum in these schools and school districts.)

SUMMARY AND A LOOK AHEAD

The problem of the transfer of critical thinking skills is a key problem that must be addressed if the new emphasis on bringing critical thinking into classroom instruction is to be effective. There are multiple skills that we must acquire to become proficient at critical thinking. We must help students not only to acquire the skills of a good critical thinker but to develop facility in using them in all appropriate contexts. Hence, we must teach for transfer. There are various levels of transfer to which we must attend: transfer *within* a restricted field of study to new examples within that field, transfer *across* disciplinary boundaries, and transfer *into* the thinking practices in which we engage in our everyday reasoning. We must also develop a "spirit of critical thinking" (good thinking attitudes and dispositions that prompt us to use these skills).

I reject the idea that critical thinking skills are subject-specific in that they vary from academic discipline to academic discipline. This prompts a look at a more comprehensive critical thinking program based on a more comprehensive inventory of critical thinking skills. To use such a comprehensive approach requires that we not just develop new lessons that exemplify the use of the skills we wish to teach in teaching for critical thinking. We must also infuse teaching for critical thinking into mainstream instruction by restructuring traditional curricular content. Indeed, this should be our central goal.

The implications of embracing this goal go well beyond the practices of individual teachers. The kinds of changes that must be made in school structure, in the way in-service programs are run, in preservice teacher education, in the ways students are taught, and in the way we evaluate them in order to bring effective teaching for critical thinking into the classroom must all be undertaken with the care a good critical thinker should put into his or her task. Not doing this now, when these changes are possible, we may well be missing an opportunity to realize one of our most cherished educational ideals that we will not have again in our lifetimes.

REFERENCES

Adams, M. J. (1983). *Project intelligence.* Republic of Venezuela: Ministry of Education.

Bender, D. L. (1982). *The arms race: Opposing viewpoints.* St. Paul, MN: Greenhaven Press.

Brown, S. (1970). *What happened on Lexington Green: An inquiry into the nature and methods of history.* Menlo Park, CA: Addison–Wesley.

Churchill, W. S. (1957). *A history of the English speaking peoples: The age of revolution* (Vol. 3). New York: Dodd, Mead.

Dewey, J. (1933). *How we think.* Boston, MA: Heath.

Ennis, R. (1962). A concept of critical thinking. *Harvard Education Review, 32,* 81–111.

Ennis, R. (1985). Goals for a critical thinking curriculum. In A. Costa (Ed.), *Developing minds.* Alexandria, VA: ASCD Publications.

Feuerstein, R. (1979). *Instrumental enrichment.* Baltimore: University Park Press.

Glade, J., & Rossa, F. (1983). *Strategic reasoning.* Stamford, CT: Innovative Sciences.

Harnadek, A. (1981). *Critical thinking.* Pacific Grove, CA: Midwest Publications.

Lipman, M. (1970). *Harry Stottlemeyer's discovery.* Montclair, NJ: First Mountain Foundation.

McPeck, J. (1981). *Critical thinking and education.* New York: St. Martin's Press.

O'Reilly, K. (1985). *Critical thinking in American History.* Beverly, MA: Critical Thinking Press.

Paul, R. (1984, September). Critical thinking: Fundamental for education in a free society. *Educational Leadership.*

Perkins, D., Allen, R., & Hafner, J. (1983). Difficulties in everyday reasoning. In W. Maxwell (Ed.), *Thinking: The expanding frontier.* Philadelphia: The Franklin Institute Press.

Steinberg, S. (1963). *The United States: Story of a free people.* Boston: Allyn & Bacon.

Swartz, A. (1985). *Critical thinking attitudes and the transfer question.* Unpublished paper.

Winocur, S. L. (1982). *Project Impact.* Costa Mesa, CA: Orange County Board of Education.

Wright, I. (Ed.). (1980). *Values reasoning series.* Toronto: Ontario Institute for Studies in Education.

17 Transfer and Teaching Thinking

D. N. Perkins
Harvard Graduate School of Education

Gavriel Salomon
University of Tel Aviv

TWO PARADOXES OF TRANSFER

In the years 1931–1932, the noted Russian psychologist Alexander Luria conducted a study of the impact of literacy on village and farm folk in Uzbekistan and Kirghizia (Luria, 1976). The occasion was ideal for such an inquiry, because an all-out effort was underway to make the population literate. Some individuals had virtually no schooling, others had some, others quite a bit. Luria and his colleagues administered a number of tests probing for abilities to reason and categorize. Many of these tasks had an academic quality, some a more everyday character involving arithmetic word problems, curiosity and question asking, and self-reflection. Luria reported a dramatic impact of literacy on the population: Those more exposed to literacy performed better on these tests, and those who had more schooling performed better yet. This study stands as evidence of the impact a symbolic vehicle like writing can have on the human mind.

During the period 1973 to 1978, the psychologists Sylvia Scribner and Michael Cole conducted a study of a somewhat different kind of literacy in another rural population, with radically different results (Scribner & Cole, 1981). Their investigation concerned the Vai, a Liberian tribe that had evolved its own written language. Some Vai learned this script whereas others did not. Many Vai were Muslims and some of these learned Arabic also. Scribner and Cole investigated the impact of literacy on the mental functioning of the Vai, contrasting Vai script literates,

Arabic literates, and illiterates. As with Luria before them, Scribner and Cole used a wide variety of instruments. But, unlike Luria, these investigators found hardly any cognitive contrasts among the groups.

The computer language Logo was devised around 1970 as an accessible programming language through which youngsters could explore the nature of formal procedures and concepts from mathematics (Feurzeig et al., 1971; Feurzeig, Papert, Bloom, Grant, & Solomon, 1969). Many scholars have argued for the potential in principle of Logo and other programming languages to teach powerful mathematical and metacognitive lessons (e.g., Feurzeig, Horwitz, & Nickerson, 1981; Linn, 1985; Papert, 1980; Salomon & Perkins, in press). The planning and precision demanded by programming, the application of notions like a program and a "bug" to nonprogramming contexts such as athletic or study skills, the manner in which programming makes concrete certain Piagetian notions such as taking all possible combinations of something, and many other latent lessons constitute the hidden message carried by the medium of a programming language.

Investigators at Bank Street College of Education set out to determine whether Logo delivered on these potentials, with disappointing results. Students with programming experience performed no better on a planning task than those without (Pea & Kurland, 1984a, b). The programming students also did no better on a task designed to have a programming character. Indeed, the students performed rather poorly on tests of programming in Logo, when those tests gauged performance in ways related to the possession of planful top-down programming skills. In contrast, Clements and Gullo have reported a significant impact of Logo instruction on tasks and abilities not specific to programming (Clements, 1985; Clements & Gullo, 1984). In two separate studies involving children in early primary school, the authors found positive impact on measures of reflectivity, divergent thinking, and comprehension monitoring, a metacognitive ability originally studied by Markman (1977, 1979).

Abundant differences appear among these cases—from Uzbekistan to Liberia, from literacy to computer literacy, from tests of planning to comprehension monitoring. But which of these factors or what others led to transfer in some cases and not in others? The conditions for transfer of learning have become a crucial issue in contemporary efforts to understand the causes of skilled thinking and to foster such thinking through education. "No transfer" has been a discouraging refrain in study after study. In this chapter, we offer a perspective on transfer that explains the conflicting findings just mentioned and defines tactics that should promote transfer in the teaching of thinking skills or other knowledge and know-how.

TRANSFER AS A SIDE EFFECT

A look at the meaning of transfer is a necessary step toward examining its psychology. Broadly speaking, transfer of learning is a side effect, a fringe benefit: You learn A and find that performance B improves as well. For example, you learn to drive a car and discover that you have some ability to drive a truck. You learn one videogame and note that the reflexes developed there help you with another similar game.

Whereas these examples illustrate positive transfer. psychologists also recognize another pattern, *negative transfer,* where learning A impairs performance on B. For example, having learned one language in some respects impairs your learning of another, at least initially, because of interference effects between the vocabulary and syntax of the original and new language. Psychologists also distinguish between horizontal and vertical transfer. In horizontal transfer, A and B are somewhat different tasks, whereas, in vertical transfer, A is a part of B. For instance, A might be addition and B long division. Improving your addition would enhance your long division by improving the addition part of it. With these variations mentioned, we focus on positive, horizontal transfer, the type most germane to the teaching of thinking skills.

Transfer varies in other ways as well. "How much does a certain gain in performance A improve performance B" asks about *amount* of transfer. "How remote is performance B from A in its character and context" asks about *distance* of transfer. For some examples of the latter, driving a car has many features in common with driving a truck, so transfer from car to truck driving is "near transfer." In contrast, "far transfer" would occur if studying higher mathematics improved your bridge game, because the two lack the many common elements obvious in the case of car and truck driving. Often in teaching thinking, far transfer is the aim because we hope to empower students over a wide range of intellectual challenges.

How does learning A enhance performance on B? This question about the mechanism of transfer also allows a variety of answers, and which answer applies in a particular case is often far from obvious. Perhaps A and B share component processes—gear shifting or guiding the vehicle with a steering wheel in the case of cars and trucks. Characteristics of cognitive style might figure in transfer, the habit of precision learned in higher mathematics carried over to bridge play, without any common components. Possibly A exercises certain low-level information-processing operations of categorization and memory retrieval that apply not only to B but to a wide range of other performances. Perhaps high-level strategies such as "divide the problem into subproblems" acquired for A help with B as well. All these mechanisms are assumed in one or another approach to teaching transferable thinking skills.

The concept of transfer has many rough edges. By what yardstick do we measure the "distance" between A and B, for example? Or if car driving transfers to truck driving, do we also say that standard shift driving transfers to automatic transmission driving, and then that Ford driving transfers to Chrysler driving? By what standard do we draw the line between transfer and mere learning, between A and B being "the same performance," and A and B being "different performances?" Having acknowledged these rough edges, we simply keep away from them in this discussion. Fortunately, the viewpoint advanced here does not depend on precise measures of distance from A to B or exact discriminations between "same" and "different" performances. Some further discussion on these points appears in Salomon and Perkins (1984).

LOW ROAD TRANSFER

The key to understanding the nature of transfer and the conflicting findings mentioned earlier is the recognition that transfer is not one phenomenon; transfer can occur in radically different ways. We distinguish between two broad types of transfer, *low road* and *high road*. Low road transfer occurs as the automatic consequence of varied practice. High road transfer, in contrast, reflects deliberate mindful efforts to represent principles at a high level of generality, so that they subsume a wide range of cases. Let us consider the mechanism of low road transfer first.

Low road transfer is by far the most common route by which learning generalizes. The cases of transfer from car to truck driving, or from skill in one videogame to another, illustrate its character. When you sit for the first time in the driver's seat of a truck, you do not have to think to yourself, "How do I turn *this* steering wheel in order to direct the truck?". You know. You are used to a standard car transmission, so you will find the truck transmission with its greater number of gears more challenging. But the rhythm and feel of gear shifting will carry you along to a considerable extent. When you back up the truck, if it has a separate cab and body, you are in for a surprise. As you back the cab leftward, the body swings rightward. This negative low road transfer of your expectations needs to be overcome before you can manage backing well.

As suggested by the example of the truck, low road transfer occurs intuitively and automatically. The learner needs to think and attend with care only to those aspects of the task that go beyond the preparation afforded by prior experience. Thus, the new gears require concentration, but not so much the rhythm of shifting. Negative transfer, as with the backing problem, recruits the full cognitive capacities of the individual, who must override with deliberate control the misleading message of habit. Far from being the mechanism of low road transfer, focused attention adjusts and repairs the results of low road transfer to suit the novel circumstances.

Extensive practice is one condition for low road transfer. As a performance becomes automatic, it runs off more rapidly and smoothly in response to the stimuli that evoke it (Schneider & Shiffrin, 1977; Shiffrin & Schneider, 1977). Transfer effects depend on the consolidation of representations (Fiske & Dyer, 1985; Hayes-Roth, 1977), the gradual spread of patterns of behavior that depend on context-specific memory traces (Kolers & Roediger, 1984; see also Kolers, 1973, 1975), and, according to the view of MacKay (1982), on the gradual development with practice of priming of "next steps" while one step at a high level in a behavior hierarchy is being executed. Until such fluency occurs, other related situations are not likely to trigger the performance in question.

Extensive practice alone, however, tends to make a performance context bound (Kolers & Roediger, 1984; Langer & Imber, 1979; Mayer, 1976, 1981). As in Anderson's model of learning, aspects of the performance that initially have a general character become particularized to the exact task demands (Anderson, 1983). Although some transfer will always occur to very similar circumstances, it will not have great range. Accordingly, *varied* practice that samples tasks widely from the range of desired transfer provides the additional condition for substantial far transfer via the low road.

There is a catch, though: Varied practice and other manipulations to promote transfer may sometimes lead to somewhat weaker performance in the most conventional instances, which consequently receive less intensive practice. Mayer, for instance, found such effects in a teaching experiment in programming. The students who were taught in a way that fostered the development of a good mental model of the computer performed much better on novel problems than students who were taught in a more rote manner; but they did a little worse on problems similar to those used in practice (Mayer, 1976, 1981).

Varied practice yields far transfer through a chain of near transfers. It is easy to illustrate how this might occur in terms of some potentially very general cognitive style trait, such as precision (Baron, 1985b). Suppose a particular teacher emphasizes precision in arithmetic. Responding, Johnny develops skills of self-monitoring and checking in addition. As the academic year advances, he spontaneously carries these over to multiplication and addition. The class also commences to study grammar. A flood of red marks on Johnny's first exercise sheets reminds him of his early arithmetic papers and triggers the self-monitoring and checking practices he learned there. Of course, Johnny cannot check grammar in just the same way as arithmetic. The arithmetic-checking skills gets adapted to grammar through reinforcement mechanisms and/or deliberate attention. This stretching process as a matter of course generalizes some aspects of the self-monitoring and checking skills. When Johnny tackles spelling, low road transfer will occur all the more readily, stretching the skill again and generalizing it more yet. By incremental extensions, Johnny is developing a pervasive cognitive style of precision.

Of course, this is an ideal scenario. If the gap from arithmetic to grammar is too large, Johnny's arithmetic precision habits may not bridge it. If Johnny's teacher does not press him enough in arithmetic over a sufficient period of time, Johnny may not develop an automatized habit of precision in arithmetic that affords low road transfer. If Johnny's teacher badgers him too much, he may become rebellious or indifferent, also to no effect. Especially at the beginning, low road transfer can go wrong in many ways. If all goes right, however, a skill can start small and, through extensive varied practice, extend over a wide range of circumstances.

The character of low road transfer explains the conflicting findings of Luria (1976) and Scribner and Cole (1981). Note that as people become literate and schooled, they do not normally receive direct instruction in problem solving, logical reasoning, or categorizing techniques, although they do receive some practice. Nor can people readily give explicit accounts of the strategies they use for such tasks. Accordingly, low road transfer accounts for whatever ripple effects literacy and schooling may have. What, then, can be said about the conditions for low road transfer in the settings investigated by Luria and by Scribner and Cole?

In Luria's setting, literacy occurred in company with schooling. Reading figured in a variety of subject matters. As literacy became a part of the culture, applications of importance outside of school also evolved. The circumstances met the conditions of extensive, varied practice. Scribner and Cole, however, describe quite different circumstances among the Vai. Vai literacy, either in the Vai script or in Arabic, played a very limited and marginal role in the Vai culture. There was no schooling as such. Those Vai that learned the script used it primarily for letter writing and family record keeping; the learners of Arabic mainly read the Koran. Mastery of either literacy certainly required extensive practice, but not *varied* practice in domains of activity where success counted.

HIGH ROAD TRANSFER

High road transfer proceeds in a very different way from low road, through the mindful abstraction and application of principles. For example, suppose that, in playing twenty questions, you learn the rule "Ask a question that will divide the set of possibilities roughly in half." You formulate this principle generally, not just for twenty questions, wondering whether it might find uses elsewhere. Later, you are trying to find your place in a book you read part way through awhile ago and set aside. Remembering the principle, you turn to the middle of the book, read a little, and ask yourself, "Have I read this yet?" If not, you turn to about one-quarter way through the book and ask the same question. After a few cycles, you have narrowed down where you left off to a single page.

Many kinds of knowledge lend themselves to this pattern of abstraction and application. Bluffing tactics developed in card play may suit a military situation. Memory tricks learned for school quizzes may help you to recall the names of new acquaintances. Patterns of argument studied in math or philosophy may inform forays into the stock market. Whatever the content, high road transfer requires the learner to recognize a principle and formulate it in a symbol system that affords generality (language, diagrams, or formulas, for instance). The abstract representation forms a bridge between the learning context and the application. Whereas low road transfer occurs through gradual stretching, high road transfer happens via a generalization that subsumes a range of cases.

Like low road transfer, high road transfer requires the right conditions. Broadly speaking, high road transfer calls for great mindfulness in the processing of information (Chanowitz & Langer, 1980; Langer, 1984; Langer, Blank, & Chanowitz, 1978; Salomon, 1983). The abstraction required takes a strong sense here, entailing genuine understanding of the principle and its relation to particular cases, and a grasp of the conditions under which the principle might apply. The abstraction need not be devised by the learner; a teacher or book may provide it. But all too often learners gain from teachers or books merely what might be called a *nominal abstraction,* a ritual formula without any sense of its connection to examples, as amply demonstrated by studies of discovery learning (e.g., Haslerud & Meyers, 1958; Kersh, 1958, 1962; McDonald, 1964). This weak sense of abstraction does not afford transfer.

High road transfer, like low road, can proceed by different routes. In the twenty questions example aforementioned, the learner abstracts a general principle without a target application in mind. For a contrasting case, suppose you are a student of archeology taking a standard course in statistics. Throughout your statistical work, which mentions nothing about archeology, you think about the potential applications: Might tests of statistical reliability be relevant to discriminating social class differences based on data from burial site artifacts? Might such tests detect infiltration of a new agricultural practice into an ancient culture? By the time you begin to do some archeology on your own, your statistical knowledge is well primed for application.

Also, high road transfer can begin with events in the application domain and reach back toward the learning domain. Suppose you want to find your place in the neglected book. Feeling thoughtful, you puzzle over the problem. "How can I locate my place? Well, how can I narrow it down? What do I know about narrowing down? Where else do I narrow down? Aha! Twenty questions. I do have a strategy there—asking questions that divide the possibilities in half. Can I generalize that strategy and apply it to the book problem?" In this case, instead of abstracting a principle from A at the outset, the learner abstracts a key question from B and uses it to search A, find a candidate principle, and *then* abstract and apply it to B. Not only these but other patterns of abstraction and application can lead to high road transfer, always via one or more representations in a symbol system affording abstraction that bridges between the contexts in question.

The concept of high road transfer aids in understanding the second pair of conflicting findings mentioned at the outset: In two studies conducted by Pea and Kurland students showed no transfer, but in two conducted by Clements and Gullo they did. Pea and Kurland (1984a,b) organized their teaching experiments in the manner suggested by Papert (1980), with minimal intervention by the teachers. Logo was treated as a cognitive sandbox, one might say. In contrast, the teaching experiments of Clements and Gullo involved considerable one-on-one guidance by the instructors, with a high teacher–student ratio and the provision of cognitive props. For instance, the students were urged to respond to bugs by thinking aloud answers to such questions as, "What did you tell the turtle to do? What *did* it do? What did you *want* it to do? How could you change your procedure?" (Clements, 1985, p. 8). The experiences of the students in the Clements and Gullo interventions seem somewhat akin to the highly "scaffolded" learning episodes provided by the LISP tutor developed by Anderson and Reiser (1985), the interactive clinical interviewing technique used by Perkins and Martin (1986), or the reciprocal tutoring method described by Palincsar and Brown (1984). Although many differences appear among these methods, all offer considerable high-level moment-to-moment support of the student's problem management.

To summarize the circumstances, the concepts involved in Logo (and, to some extent, in other programming languages) plainly invite high road transfer (Salomon & Perkins, in press). "Bug," for example, is a notion readily and usefully applied to many sorts of human behavior: Schoolchildren have bugs in their arithmetic "programs" (Brown & VanLehn, 1980; VanLehn, 1981). More advanced scientific and mathematical reasoning is plagued with a variety of bugs (Davis, 1984; Lochhead & Clement, 1979). Numerous bugs in probabilistic inference give people trouble (Kahneman, Slovic, & Tversky, 1982; Nisbett & Ross, 1980). The purely qualitative reasoning characteristic of much real-life decision making also suffers from a number of fallacies (Perkins, 1985;Perkins, Allen, & Hafner, 1983). But Logo instruction as prescribed by Papert and studied by the Bank Street investigators involves a hang-back philosophy that results in no instruction in general principles nor any strong press for youngsters to abstract principles themselves. The learners typically do not devleop the principles in question even within the context of Logo itself.

Of course, one might hope for low road rather than high road transfer from Logo. But this requires practice extensive, varied, and consequential enough to foster good learning of Logo and to reach beyond its boundaries. Most Logo instruction involves students only for an hour or two per week and does not get beyond turtle graphics. If schools would provide the time and resources, much better results could be possible. In fact, note that no either/or obtains between low road and high road transfer. Varied practice and mindful abstraction can co-occur. In our estimate, an instructional approach that is designed to take both roads at once could yield positive results for Logo and for many other approaches to fostering thinking as well.

TRANSFER AND INTELLIGENCE

Any effort to teach thinking has its tacit or explicit theory about intelligence, taking the term broadly to mean whatever basis cognitive competence has, not IQ specifically. In this rapidly expanding field, the instructional approaches and their accompanying theories present a bewildering variety, as recent surveys and compendia make apparent (Chipman, Segal, & Glaser, 1985; Lochhead & Clement, 1979; Nickerson, Perkins, & Smith, 1985; Segal, Chipman, & Glaser, 1985). How does the view of transfer recounted here relate to these theories and what does that imply about the prospects for teaching cognitive skills?

Although we cannot review here the many extant conceptions of intelligence nor decide among them, two general points can be made: (1) Different theories of intelligence entail different opportunities for and limits to transfer; (2) any theory makes room either for low road or high road transfer, sometimes both.

Intelligence as Power

It is useful to discuss intelligence under four broad headings, as power, expertise, tactics, or cognitive style. A power model sees intelligence as speed and accuracy at the "hardware" or neurological level of the mind. The classical power model is, of course, g for general intelligence. Arthur

Jensen, among others, has recently articulated a case for the central and relatively unmodifiable character of intelligence in this sense (Jensen, 1983, 1984, this volume). However, several other power models describe multiple powers. Cattell's distinction between fluid and crystallized intelligence is one case in point (Cattell, 1963; Horn & Cattell, 1966). Another contemporary view proposes that there are some seven distinct intelligences, corresponding roughly to areas of endeavor such as language use, logical-mathematical skill, musical skill, kinesthetic skill, and others (Gardner, 1983, this volume). The number of distinct powers runs much higher in Guilford's "Structure of Intellect" model, which posits no fewer than 120 distinct factors (Guilford, 1967; Guilford & Hoepfner, 1971).

The question of initial learning for power models should not be confused with the question of transfer. The models mentioned take quite different stances on the prospects of initial improvement. Jensen sees little chance of significant modification. Guilford views his factors as modifiable, as in the Structure of Intellect Institute's training program (Meeker, 1969). Gardner (1983, this volume) believes that one's initial endowment strongly influences what one will learn under normal circumstances of exposure and instruction, but that unusually effective contexts of learning may yield exceptional achievement in individuals not especially talented. The Suzuki violin method is a case in point. Cattell holds fluid intelligence to be more basic and less subject to modification than crystallized intelligence, which depends more on acquired knowledge and skill (Cattell, 1963; Horn & Cattell, 1966).

Given initial learning, transfer takes the same form in all power models: Improvement of a power would transfer automatically to all contexts where the power is called on, just as a muscle strengthened in one context automatically functions more strongly in others. Extensive practice would be required to improve the power in question, varied practice to ensure that the power itself, not some narrow performance, gained. The consequence of exercise rather than mindful abstraction is low road transfer. High road transfer may occur, of course, and may enhance cognitive competence somewhat, but a power theory of intelligence would view such effects as peripheral; intelligence lies in the power of computational mechanisms rather than in explicit knowledge.

Can intellectual power be improved? The question is difficult to answer straightforwardly. Certainly performance on intelligence tests can be improved; the literature includes a number of such cases (Berrueta-Clement, Schweinhart, Barnett, Epstein, & Weikart, 1984; Garber & Heber, 1982; Ramey, MacPhee, & Yeates, 1982; Whimbey, 1975). The most dramatic gains, some 25 IQ points, reflected 5 years of special treatment (Garber & Heber, 1982). Moreover, such gains do not always reflect instruction directly to the test and are sometimes accompanied by better school performance generally. This suggests a general intellectual improvement of some type.

On the other hand, after a few years without special treatment, the advantage on test performance has faded away, although some advantages of attitude and character persist (Berrueta-Clement et al., 1984). This does not deny that there was a power gain but argues against its persistence without continuing treatment. In addition, it is easy to doubt that the general effects were really on precision and efficiency of information processing at the neurological level. Instead, the treatments perhaps led to changes in cognitive style or other aspects of intellectual ability that would impact on test and school performance. Jensen (1983) argues just this, acknowledging a temporary effect on performance for some school subjects but not those most indicative of general intelligence. Given the complexity of the circumstances, the conservative conclusion is that performance on power-oriented measures of intelligence can be improved temporarily without teaching directly to the test and with associated gains in some school performances. As to the mechanism of transfer, most of these efforts were practice intensive and most did not involve the explicit teaching of high-level strategies. This picture fits the profile of low road transfer well.

Intelligence as Expertise

In recent years, evidence has accumulated that able intellectual performance characteristically requires a large repertoire of knowledge and skill specific to the performance in question. For instance, Simon and Chase (1973) have presented evidence that master chess players depend on a repertoire of some 50,000 configurations of play, most consisting of just a few pieces in a pattern that frequently recurs, accumulated over years of play. Researchers investigating problem solving in physics and mathematics have argued that effective problem solving draws on a number of problem-solving schemata specific to the disciplines in question (Chi, Feltovich, & Glaser, 1981; Chi, Glaser, & Rees, 1982; Larkin, McDermott, Simon, & Simon, 1980; Schoenfeld & Herrmann, 1982). Some urge that cognitive competence is largely a matter of context-specific knowledge and skill (Carey, 1985).

This view implies that opportunities for transfer are far more limited intrinsically than one might hope, but transfer of course can still occur. The low road to transfer would not lead very far: In practice-intensive situations, the learning would not generalize very much beyond the context of practice; varied practice would not stretch it far. The high road by way of abstraction might lead far but would not carry much weight: One can abstract general principles and apply them in other contexts, but, according to the expertise perspective, such general principles are not very powerful compared to context-specific knowledge and skill.

This stance still leaves room for teaching intelligence in a sense, but primarily context by context: problem solving in physics, problem solving in mathematics, problem solving in poetry writing, and so on. The challenge of transfer contracts to one within rather than across subject matters: how to teach so that low road and high road transfer at least improve mathematical problem solving in general, or problem solving in physics in general. We note one very successful effort along these lines. Alan Schoenfeld has achieved excellent gains in mathematical problem solving at the college level with 1 month of intensive instruction. This is not to say that Schoenfeld advocates an extreme expertise model, but only that his results are consistent with one (Schoenfeld, 1982; Schoenfeld & Herrmann, 1982).

Intelligence as Tactics

Yet another view of intelligence locates it in a repertoire of rather general and far-reaching heuristic strategies, often metacognitive in nature. The great majority of the better known efforts to enhance cognitive competence depend at least in part on this notion, including the heuristic approach to mathematical problem solving (e.g., Polya, 1954, 1957; Schoenfeld, 1980; Wickelgren, 1974), general strategies for problem-solving and inventive thinking (e.g., Bolt, Beranek, & Newman, 1983; Covington, Crutchfield, Davies, & Olton, 1974; de Bono, 1970, 1973–75, 1983; Hayes, 1981), and learning skills (e.g., O'Neil, 1978; O'Neil & Spielberger, 1979; Palincsar & Brown, 1984; Perkins, 1986). Many of these and other programs are reviewed in Nickerson, Perkins, and Smith (1985) and in Segal, Chipman, and Glaser (1985).

Heuristic instruction characteristically stresses high road transfer. General principles are abstracted from experience or taught as such and related to experience. Sometimes transfer itself becomes a focus of mindful attention. As to evidence of success, many such programs yield performance gains on the tasks directly addressed, but far transfer often cannot be assessed on the basis of the instruments used. One exception is Project Intelligence, a year-long course addressing a number of thinking skills, which employed some broad-spectrum instruments and showed modest gains on them and larger gains on instruments gauging performance on the tasks directly addressed (Bolt, Beranek, & Newman, 1983). Palincsar and Brown (1984) obtained transfer to tasks somewhat unlike the training tasks in a strategic approach to remedial reading. Schoenfeld (1982), although working entirely within mathematics, achieved transfer of problem-solving skills to problems quite different from those stressed in the instruction.

Belmont, Butterfield, and Ferretti (1982) review seven studies of efforts to teach retardates metacognitive skills for simple memory and other performances. The authors stress that in six of the seven studies the students were taught not only to exercise certain strategies but to monitor and manage their own behavior in doing so. Lack of such management and monitoring instruction accounted for lack of transfer in several other similar studies. All seven studies showed good transfer of the skills learned to other contexts. In one particularly striking study, retardates studied a memory strategy for a list-learning problem and exhibited improved performance 1 year later with a prose recall problem (Brown & Barclay, 1976; Brown, Campione, & Barclay, 1979). These and a few other examples provide existence proofs that heuristic instruction can yield transfer at least some of the time.

Intelligence as Cognitive Style

Baron advances the view that intelligence is best construed as cognitive style (Baron, 1985a,b, this volume). Roughly speaking, a cognitive style is a pattern of attitude and information processing that pervades an individual's behavior. Some people are precise at nearly anything they do, some exploratory, some efficient, some all these, to mention a trio of cognitive styles Baron thinks to be important (Baron, 1985b). Taken together, different writers on cognitive style have proposed a bewildering array of styles whose relations to one another are not entirely clear (see, e.g., Guilford, 1980; Kagan & Kogan, 1970; Messick, 1984; Witkin, 1976). Many of the styles seem closely related and may reduce to only a few "core" styles that occur in various combinations.

Although there is no need to review the literature on cognitive style, the relation between cognitive styles and transfer must be examined. As pervasive habits that recur spontaneously throughout the range of a person's behavior, cognitive styles bear the earmarks of low road transfer. Indeed, in an earlier section, we recounted how a style of precision might develop through a propitious sequence of practice-based extensions from arithmetic to grammar to other subject areas. However, it is also true that individuals may deliberately adopt styles with strategic intent, as when one directs oneself to concentrate, be careful, or loosen up. Such calculated marshalling of styles would be subject to high road transfer.

As to applications of this approach, the work of Reuven Feuerstein with marginal retardates deserves mention (Feuerstein, 1980). Although not talking the language of cognitive style, Feuerstein has developed a method called instrumental enrichment that seeks to build a number of information-processing habits that the marginally retarded individual typically lacks. Feuerstein's approach has met with at least some success (Feuerstein, 1980; Nickerson, Perkins, & Smith, 1985).

TEACHING FOR TRANSFER

The general theory of transfer presented here is consistent with all four construals of intelligence: as power, expertise, tactics, and cognitive style. We should add that in our view all four are right to a degree. It would be surprising to find that mental powers, context-specific knowledge, general strategic knowledge, or cognitive style played only a slight role in cognitive competence generally. Indeed, a view of intelligence such as Sternberg's incorporates aspects of all four (Sternberg, 1985, this volume). Given this premise, despite the diversity of views on intelligence there is an immediate implication for teaching for transfer: Do everything you can, low road and high.

Consider the risks of omission. A power model entails mostly low road transfer, but because strategic knowledge may also be significant, mindful abstraction of principles should not be neglected. An expertise model implies that transfer beyond the general subject area will not be significant, but transfer within the subject area, both high road and low road, still needs attention; and, to the extent that the power and strategic perspectives have some truth in them, transfer beyond the subject area may be found. The tactical perspective has its blind spot too: Instruction in this vein often neglects practice and deals in what we earlier called *nominal* abstractions. Accordingly, attention to the low road as well as to the high is imperative. Finally, a focus on cognitive style not only may neglect tactics but may fall short of sufficient varied practice to yield a truly general stylistic change.

Toward designing instruction to make the most of the opportunities for high road and low road transfer, we offer the following list of pitfalls and remedial tactics implied by the present theory of transfer:

Pitfall: According to our model, sheer practice can actually undermine mindful abstraction and thus limit far transfer.

Tactic: Highlight mindful abstraction and application of principles.

Pitfall: Practice may address a narrow range of cases thoughtlessly taken as representative.

Tactic: Vary practice, keeping in mind the desired range of transfer.

Pitfall: Nominal generalizations that sound powerful but that the learner cannot apply.

Tactic: Take care that learners can connect principles to cases in point.

Pitfall: Brief practice of general principles, even if understood.

Tactic: Provide plenty of practice, to gain the benefits of low road and high road transfer.

Pitfall: Neglecting students' mindful attention to the problem of transfer itself.

Tactic: Teach metacognitive self-monitoring strategies that promote deliberate transfer.

Pitfall: Focused instruction may yield better results on a narrow range of tasks than teaching for transfer.

Tactic: Except in special situations, this is a Phyrric victory. Teach for transfer.

ACKNOWLEDGMENTS

First authorship was determined by the flip of a coin. The authors gratefully acknowledge support from the John and Mary R. Markle Foundation to Gavriel Salomon, from National Institute of Education grant number NIE-G-83-0028, *Learning to Reason,* to David Perkins, and from the NIE-sponsored Educational Technology Center at the Harvard Graduate School of Education. The views expressed here do not necessarily reflect the position or policy of the supporting agencies.

REFERENCES

Anderson, J. R. (1983). *The architecture of cognition.* Cambridge, MA: Harvard University Press.

Anderson, J. R., & Reiser, B. J. (1985). The LISP tutor. *Byte, 10* (4), 159–175.

Baron, J. (1985a). *Rationality and intelligence.* New York: Cambridge University Press.

Baron, J. (1985b). What kinds of intelligence components are fundamental? In S. S. Chipman, J. W. Segal, & R. Glaser (Eds.), *Thinking and learning skills, Volume 2: Current research and open questions* (pp. 365–390). Hillsdale, NJ: Lawrence Erlbaum Associates.

Belmont, J. M., Butterfield, E. C., & Ferretti, R. P. (1982). To secure transfer of training instruct self-management skills. In D. K. Detterman & R. J. Sternberg (Eds.), *How and how much can intelligence be increased?* (pp. 147–154). Norwood, NJ: Ablex.

Berrueta-Clement, J. R., Schweinhart, L. J., Barnett, W. S., Epstein, A. S., & Weikart, D. P. (1984). Preschool's long-term impact: Summary of the evidence. Chapter VI in *Changed lives: The effects of the Perry preschool program on youths through age 19.* Ypsilanti, MI: The High/Scope Press.

Bolt, Beranek, & Newman. (1983). *Final report, Project Intelligence: The development of procedures to enhance thinking skills.* Cambridge, MA: Author.

Brown, A. L., & Barclay, C. R. (1976). The effects of training specific mnemonics on the metamnemonic efficiency of retarded children. *Child Development, 47,* 70–80.

Brown, A. L., Campione, J. C., & Barclay, C. R. (1979). Training self-checking routines for estimating test readiness: Generalization from list learning to prose recall. *Child Development, 50,* 501–512.

Brown, J. S., & VanLehn, K. (1980). Repair theory: A generative theory of bugs in procedural skills. *Cognitive Science, 4,* 379–426.

Carey, S. (1985). Are children fundamentally different kinds of thinkers and learners than adults? In S. F. Chipman, J. W. Segal, & R. Glaser (Eds.), *Thinking and learning skills, Vol. 2: Research and open questions* (pp. 485–517). Hillsdale, NJ: Lawrence Erlbaum Associates.

Cattell, R. B. (1963). Theory of fluid and crystallized intelligence: A critical experiment. *Journal of Educational Psychology, 54,* 1–22.

Chanowitz, B., & Langer, E (1980). Knowing more (or less) than you can show: Understanding control through the mindlessness–mindfulness distinction. In J. Garber & M. E. P. Seligman (Eds.), *Human helplessness: Theory and applications* (pp. 97–129). New York: Academic Press.

Chi, M. T. H., Glaser, R., & Rees, E. (1982). Expertise in problem solving. In R. Sternberg (Ed.), *Advances in the psychology of human intelligence* (pp. 7–75). Hillsdale, NJ: Lawrence Erlbaum Associates.

Chi, M., Feltovich, P., & Glaser, R. (1981). Categorization and representation of physics problems by experts and novices. *Cognitive Science, 5*, 121–152.

Chipman, S. F., Segal, J. W., & Glaser, R. (Eds.). (1985). *Thinking and learning skills, Volume 2: Research and open questions.* Hillsdale, NJ: Lawrence Erlbaum Associates.

Clements, D. H. (1985, April). *Effects of Logo programming on cognition, metacognitive skills, and achievement.* Presentation at the American Education Research Association Conference, Chicago.

Clements, D. H., & Gullo, D. F. (1984). Effects of computer programming on young children's cognition. *Journal of Educational Psychology, 76* (6), 1051–1058.

Covington, M. V., Crutchfield, R. S., Davies, L., & Olton, R. M. (1974). *The productive thinking program: A course in learning to think.* Columbus, OH: Merrill.

Davis, R. B. (1984). *Learning mathematics: The cognitive science approach to mathematics education.* Norwood, NJ: Ablex.

de Bono, E. (1970). *Lateral thinking: Creativity step by step.* New York: Harper & Row.

de Bono, E. (1973-75). *CoRT thinking.* Blandford, Dorset, England: Direct Education Services Limited.

de Bono, E. (1983). The cognitive research trust (CoRT) thinking program. In W. Maxwell (Ed.), *Thinking: The expanding frontier* (pp. 115–127). Hillsdale, NJ: Lawrence Erlbaum Associates.

Feuerstein, R. (1980). *Instrumental enrichment: An intervention program for cognitive modifiability.* Baltimore: University Park Press.

Feurzeig, W., Horwitz, P., & Nickerson, R. (1981). *Microcomputers in education* (Report no. 4798). Cambridge, MA: Bolt, Beranek, & Newman.

Feurzeig, W., Lukas, G., Faflick, P., Grant, R., Lukas, J., Morgan, R., Weiner, W., & Wexelblat, P. (1971). *Programming languages as a conceptual framework for teaching mathematics* (BBN report #2165). Cambridge, MA: Bolt, Beranek, & Newman.

Feurzeig, W., Papert, S., Bloom, M., Grant, R., & Solomon, C. (1969). *Programming languages as a conceptual framework for teaching mathematics* (BBN report #1889). Cambridge, MA: Bolt, Beranek, & Newman.

Fiske, S. T., & Dyer, L. M. (1985). Structure and development of social schemata: Evidence from positive and negative transfer effects. *Journal of Personality and Social Psychology, 48*, 839–852.

Garber, H., & Heber, R. (1982). Modification of predicted cognitive development in high-risk children through early intervention. In D. K. Detterman & R. J. Sternberg (Eds.), *How and how much can intelligence be increased?* Norwood, NJ: Ablex.

Gardner, H. (1983). *Frames of mind.* New York: Basic Books.

Guilford, J. P. (1967). *The nature of human intelligence.* New York: McGraw-Hill.

Guilford, J. P. (1980). Cognitive styles: What are they? *Educational and Psychological Measurement, 40*, 715–735.

Guilford, J. P., & Hoepfner, R. (1971). *The analysis of intelligence.* New York: McGraw-Hill.

Haslerud, G. M., & Meyers, S. (1958). The transfer value of given and individually derived principles. *Journal of Educational Psychology, 49*, 293–298.

Hayes, J. R. (1981). *The complete problem solver.* Hillsdale, NJ: Lawrence Erlbaum Associates.

Hayes-Roth, B. (1977). Evolution of cognitive structure and processes. *Psychological Review, 84,* 260–278.

Horn, J. L., & Cattell, R. B. (1966). Refinement and test of the theory of fluid and crystallized intelligence. *Journal of Educational Psychology, 57,* 253–270.

Jensen, A. R. (1983). The nonmanipulable and effectively manipulable variables of education. *Education and Society, 1* (1), 51–62.

Jensen, A. R. (1984). Test validity: *g* versus the specificity doctrine. *Journal of Social and Biological Structures, 7,* 93–118.

Kagan, J., & Kogan, N. (1970). Individuality and cognitive performance. In P. Mussen (Ed.), *Carmichael's manual of child psychology* (Vol. 1). New York: Wiley.

Kahneman, D., Slovic, P., & Tversky, A. (Eds.). (1982). *Judgment under uncertainty: Heuristics and biases.* Cambridge, England: Cambridge University Press.

Kersh, B. Y. (1958). The adequacy of "meaning" as an explanation for the superiority of learning by independent discovery. *Journal of Educational Psychology, 49,* 282–292.

Kersh, B. Y. (1962). The motivating effect of learning by directed discovery. *Journal of Educational Psychology, 53,* 65–71.

Kolers, P. A. (1973). Remembering operations. *Memory & Cognition, 1* (3), 347–355.

Kolers, P. A. (1975). Memorial consequences of automatized encoding. *Journal of Experimental Psychology: Human learning and memory, 1* (6), 689–701.

Kolers, P. A., & Roediger, H. L. (1984). Procedures of mind. *Journal of Verbal Learning and Verbal Behavior, 23,* 425–449.

Langer, E. (1980). Rethinking the role of thought in social interaction. In J. Harvey, W. Ickes, & R. Kidd (Eds.), *New directions in attribution research* (Vol. 2). Hillsdale, NJ: Lawrence Erlbaum Associates.

Langer, E. J. (1984). Playing the middle against both ends: The influence of adult cognitive activity as a model for cognitive activity in childhood and old age. In S. R. Yussen (Ed.), *The development of reflection.* New York: Academic Press.

Langer, E. J., Blank, A., & Chanowitz, B. (1978). The mindlessness of ostensibly thoughtful action: The role of "placebic information" in interpersonal interaction. *Journal of Personality and Social Psychology, 36,* 635–642.

Langer, E. J., & Imber, L. E. (1979). When practice makes imperfect: Debilitating effects of overlearning. *Journal of Personality and Social Psychology, 37,* 2014–2024.

Larkin, J. H., McDermott, J., Simon, D. P., & Simon, H. A. (1980). Modes of competence in solving physics problems. *Cognitive Science, 4,* 317–345.

Linn, M. C. (1985). The cognitive consequences of programming instruction in classrooms. *Educational Researcher, 14,* 14–29.

Lochhead, J., & Clement, J. (1979). *Cognitive process instruction.* Hillsdale, NJ: Lawrence Erlbaum Associates.

Luria, A. R. (1976). *Cognitive development: Its cultural and social foundations.* Cambridge, MA: Harvard University Press.

MacKay, D. G. (1982). The problems of flexibility, fluency, and speed-accuracy trade-off in skilled behavior. *Psychological Review, 89,* 483–506.

Markman, E. M. (1977). Realizing that you don't understand: A preliminary investigation. *Child Development, 48,* 986–992.

Markman, E. M. (1979). Realizing that you don't understand: Elementary school children's awareness of inconsistencies. *Child Development, 50,* 643–655.

Mayer, R. E. (1976). Some conditions of meaningful learning for computer programming: Advance organizers and subject control of frame order. *Journal of Educational Psychology, 68,* 143–150.

Mayer, R. E. (1981). The psychology of how novices learn computer programming. *Computing Surveys, 13* (11), 121–141.

McDonald, F. J. (1964). Meaningful learning and retention: Task and method variables. *Review of Educational Research, 34,* 530–544.

Meeker, M. N. (1969). *The structure of intellect: Its interpretation and uses.* Columbus, OH: Charles E. Merrill.

Messick, S. (1984). The nature of cognitive styles: Problems and promise in educational practice. *Educational Psychologist, 19,* 59–74.

Nickerson, R., Perkins, D. N., & Smith, E. (1985). *The teaching of thinking.* Hillsdale, NJ: Lawrence Erlbaum Associates.

Nisbett, R., & Ross, L. (1980). *Human inference: Strategies and shortcomings of social judgment.* Englewood Cliffs, NJ: Prentice–Hall.

O'Neil, H. F. (Ed.). (1978). *Learning strategies.* New York: Academic Press.

O'Neil, H. F., & Spielberger, C. D. (Eds.). (1979). *Cognitive and affective learning strategies.* New York: Academic Press.

Palincsar, A. S., & Brown, A. L. (1984). Reciprocal teaching of comprehension-fostering and comprehension-monitoring activities. *Cognition and Instruction, 1,* 117–175.

Papert, S. (1980). *Mindstorms: Children, computers, and powerful ideas.* New York: Basic Books.

Pea, R. D., & Kurland, D. M. (1984a). On the cognitive effects of learning computer programming. *New Ideas in Psychology, 2* (2), 137–168.

Pea, R. D., & Kurland, D. M. (1984b). *Logo programming and the development of planning skills* (Report no. 16). New York: Bank Street College.

Perkins, D. N. (1985). Post-primary education has little impact on informal reasoning. *Journal of Educational Psychology, 77,* 562–571.

Perkins, D. N. (1986). *Knowledge as design.* Hillsdale, NJ: Lawrence Erlbaum Associates.

Perkins, D. N., Allen, R., & Hafner, J. (1983). Difficulties in everyday reasoning. in w. Maxwell (Ed.), *Thinking: The frontier expands* (pp. 177–189). Hillsdale, NJ: Lawrence Erlbaum Associates.

Perkins, D. N., & Martin, F. (1986). Fragile knowledge and neglected strategies in novice programmers. In E. Soloway & S. Iyengar (Eds.), *Empirical studies of programmers* (pp. 213–229). Norwood, NJ: Ablex.

Polya, G. (1954). *Mathematics and plausible reasoning* (2 vols.). Princeton, NJ: Princeton University Press.

Polya, G. (1957). *How to solve it: A new aspect of mathematical method* (2nd ed.). Garden City, NY: Doubleday.

Ramey, C. T., MacPhee, D., & Yeates, K. O. (1982). Preventing developmental retardation: A general systems model. In D. K. Detterman & R. J. Sternberg (Eds.), *How and how much can intelligence be increased?* Norwood, NJ: Ablex.

Salomon, G. (1983). The differential investment of mental effort in learning from different sources. *Educational Psychologist, 18,* 42–50.

Salomon, G., & Perkins, D. N. (1984, August). *Rocky roads to transfer: Rethinking mechanisms of a neglected phenomenon.* Paper presented at the Conference on Thinking, Harvard Graduate School of Education, Cambridge, MA.

Salomon, G., & Perkins, D. N. (in press). Transfer of cognitive skills from programming: When and how? *Journal of Educational Computing Research.*

Schneider, W., & Shiffrin, R. M. (1977). Controlled and automatic human information processing: I. Detection, search, and attention. *Psychological Review, 84,* 1–66.

Schoenfeld, A. H. (1980). Teaching problem-solving skills. *American Mathematical Monthly, 87,* 794–805.

Schoenfeld, A. H. (1982). Measures of problem-solving performance and of problem-solving instruction. *Journal for Research in Mathematics Education, 13* (1), 31–49.

Schoenfeld, A. H., & Herrmann, D. J. (1982). Problem perception and knowledge structure in expert and novice mathematical problem solvers. *Journal of Experimental Psychology: Learning, Memory, and Cognition, 8,* 484–494.

Scribner, S., & Cole, M. (1981). *The psychology of literacy.* Cambridge, MA: Harvard University Press.

Segal, J. W., Chipman, S. F., & Glaser, R. (Eds.). (1985). *Thinking and learning skills, Volume 1: Relating instruction to research.* Hillsdale, NJ: Lawrence Erlbaum Associates.

Shiffrin, R. M., & Schneider, W. (1977). Controlled and automatic human information processing: II. Perceptual learning, automatic attending, and a general theory. *Psychological Review, 84,* 127–190.

Simon, H. A., & Chase, W. (1973). Skill in chess. *American Scientist, 61,* 394–403.

Sternberg, R. J. (1985). *Beyond I.Q.: A triarchic theory of human intelligence.* New York: Cambridge University Press.

VanLehn, K. (1981). *Bugs are not enough: Empirical studies of bugs, impasses and repairs in procedural skills.* Palo Alto, CA: Cognitive and Instructional Sciences Group, Palo Alto Research Center, Xerox.

Whimbey, A. (1975). *Intelligence can be taught.* New York: E. P. Dutton.

Wickelgren, W. A. (1974). *How to solve problems: Elements of a theory of problems and problem solving.* San Francisco: W. H. Freeman.

Witkin, H. A. (1976). Cognitive style in academic performance and in teacher–student relations. In S. Messick & Associates (Eds.), *Individuality in learning.* San Francisco: Jossey–Bass.

18 Empathy, Reason, and Imagination: The Impact of Their Relationship on Education

Delores Gallo
University of Massachusetts/Boston

ABSTRACT

After questioning the traditionally held relationship between thought and feeling, specifically the relationship between reason, imagination and empathy, this paper advances the thesis that empathy fosters effective critical and creative thinking and that its enhancement should be adopted as an important educational goal. A subsidiary thesis that critical and creative thinking are much more integrated processes than is often supposed is also offered along with a discussion of role taking strategies as generative of empathy and remediative of ineffective reason and imagination.

INTRODUCTION

The humanities are valued for the humanizing effect that they purport to have upon the individuals who encounter them. Presupposing some validity to this view, one must ask what is meant by this humanizing influence and what aspect of such study might account for it.

In addition to exposing the individual to a rich body of knowledge in literature, history and the arts, the humanities are charged with the development of essential human competencies: a facility for dealing meaningfully with complexity and the development of clear personal expression. The manifestation of these competencies rests upon possession of a broad knowledge base, clear and resourceful thinking, and the *will* to speak. Thus the goal of the humanities might be stated as the cultivation of open-minded human understanding and response.

Genuine open-mindedness is multifacted, at times a seeming paradox, for it is marked by a disposition of distanced engagement and persistence that is free to relinquish. It requires engagement with the issue and investment in achieving a sound understanding that will permit action, while nonetheless demanding distance from any one perspective which might distort perception of the meaning and value of others. It is identified by an ability to probe persistently, yet regularly to relinquish conceptions in the service of seeing things afresh. It is a posture of chosen commitments held concurrently with a willingness to be shown wrong. It is a capacity to gather information disinterestedly, sensitive to its limits and missing elements; a capacity to revise one's position to accommodate compelling new evidence and questions, or new perspectives on extant knowledge. These abilities require a high degree of awareness—awareness of self, of the vantage point from which knowledge is constructed, of the variety of sound assessments available when information is judged against differing criteria and value systems. The exercise of these abilities rests upon personal dispositions and motivations, upon a tolerance for ambiguity, complexity, and deferred judgment, along with a capacity for focused inquiry, sustained investigation, and a drive for problem resolution and task completion. Importantly, these contrasting abilities are predicated on a capacity to function with cognitive and personal flexibility and with an acceptance of the concomitant risks. Thus, fundamentally, the goal of the humanities is the cultivation of the requisite antecedent traits and values: self esteem and courage, a valuing of the pursuit of truth and the comprehensive, elegant address of complex problems. Therefore, the humanities bear a special responsibility for the development of the whole individual, values and voice, disposition and capacity to imagine and to reason well.

The process by which this development occurs is the maturing process afforded by vicarious experience and the empathic identification with both familiar and remote ideas, events and persons. To elaborate, what seems essential to the process is not merely intellectual exposure to a variety of culturally identified truths, beliefs, or procedures but empathic engagement with them and with their human sources. This explanation suggests that the longstanding belief that empathy as an emotion can have no positive influence on reason as a distinct mental faculty is mistaken.

THE RELATION OF THOUGHT
AND FEELING RECONSIDERED

There is a long tradition in both philosophy and psychology that distinguishes thought from feeling, maintaining that the two are fundamentally different in nature, in the capacity to be controlled, and in their value to rationality and moral action. There are now reasons to challenge this tradition. Reflection suggests that all feelings are not by nature more weak, transitory, or capricious than rational thought and that the cognitive component in affective response or the intertwining of affect and cognition, in social understanding at the least, is no longer unclear. Further, the specific emotions, often called the altruistic emotions or empathy, may actually have a positive effect on reasoned judgment in a variety of contexts.

It is the purpose of this paper to question the relationship between thought and feeling, specifically the relationship between reason, imagination and empathy, and to advance the thesis that empathy fosters critical and creative thinking and that its enhancement should be adopted as an important educational goal. Following a clarification of terms, the paper offers a subsidiary thesis that critical and creative thinking are much more integrated processes than is often supposed. Evidence, first theoretical then empirical, to support that empathy can have a positive effect on the exercise of both reason and imagination is considered. Although the theoretical evidence draws solely on material from philosophers and psychologists who consider moral reasoning, the empirical evidence establishes that it is not just moral reasoning but reasoning generally which benefits from the empathic understanding. Following an overview of reasoning from a psychological perspective, patterns of successful reasoning and impediments to it are identified and related to empathy. Next the role that empathy plays in successful creative thinking is examined and explained. Finally, role taking strategies are discussed as generative of empathy and remediative of ineffective reasoning and imaginative thinking processes.

Before defining terms, a presupposition relevant to the topic should be identified: it is that thought and action are most meaningfully and comprehensively understood as having both cognitive and affective contributing factors and that these factors are as inseparable as the denotation and connotation of a spoken word. Further, these intellectual and behavioral events occur in a personal and social context and are therefore influenced by factors of disposition and motivation. Given this, it follows that a probing of the contribution of cognitive, affective, motivational factors and their interaction is necessary to the understanding of effective thinking.

EMPATHY, REASONING AND IMAGINATION DEFINED

Since this paper attempts to draw connections across different bodies of literature, the terminological problems faced are enormous; some precision must necessarily be sacrificed for the sake of the attempted synthesis.

As I use the term, an empathic response is one which contains both a cognitive and an affective dimension. In the field of social psychology, one can find the term empathy used in at least two ways: to mean a predominantly cognitive response, understanding how another feels, or to mean an affective communion with the other. In the latter instance, it may refer to putting oneself in the place of another and anticipating the behavior of the other. Or it might suggest a still more dramatic transformation, the imaginative transporting of oneself into the thinking, feeling and actions of another.

Empathy is often equated with role-taking, the capacity to take the role and perspective of the other. (I later develop the educational opportunities which this suggests.) Empathy is sometimes used interchangeably with and sometimes distinguished from social sensitivity, intuition, altruism, and projection. Some researchers require that empathy refer to an internal disposition or trait; others that it name a response to external situational circumstance. For this paper, I adopt Carl Rogers' definition of empathy: "the state of empathy or being empathic, is to perceive the internal frame of reference of another with accuracy and with the emotional components and meanings which pertain thereto as if one were the person, but without ever losing the 'as if' condition (Rogers, 1975, pp. 2-10). Thus, it is a condition with both a cognitive and an affective dimension; it includes the ability accurately to perceive and comprehend the thoughts, feelings and motives of the other to the degree that one can make inferences and predictions consonant with those of the other, while remaining oneself.

One last point requires clarification: often when emotion or its influence is studied, it is the attribute of intensity on which researchers focus. They frequently point out that intense emotion narrows the perceptual field and clouds the judgment. Empathy expands the breadth of perception or range of emotional experience. Empathy does not intensity emotional response; it broadens it.

The terms reasoning, logical thinking, logical problem-solving and critical thinking will be used interchangeably. The salient characterizing feature of the set is the underlying convergent processing which predominates when any of these functions is operating. (To say that convergent processing predominates is not to say that it is used exclusively). From a psychological perspective, the cited operations are identified by the selection and concentrated processing of a few, highly related, task-relevant pieces of data or experience, by an ease of coding and by the infrequent modifying of codes. The process is marked by a focusing or converging on factors that have been determined relevant to the given situation; it moves toward a single, uniquely determined response, highly dependent upon the reproduction of the previously learned and upon the categorization of new experiences as examples of familiar ones. It requires a context of low error-tolerance for optimal performance and is the criterion evaluated by traditional tests of intelligence.

Philosophers often describe critical thinking as the ability to analyze, criticize, advocate ideas, to reason inductively and deductively, to reach judgments and conclusions based upon sound inferences from statements of tested truth or the ability to identify the failure of any of the foregoing processes. Thus they also emphasize the convergent processes of inference and evaluation against articulated standards.

I use interchangeably the terms imaginative thinking, imagination, creative thinking, and creative problem-solving. The salient characterizing feature of this set is the underlying divergent processing which is required and predominates when any of these processes is operating. Divergent processes emphasize highly flexible intellectual functioning, capable of rapid, often drastic changes in problem representation. Less direct than convergent thinking, divergent thinking describes a process of ranging flexibly in the search of relevant factors in connection with a specific task. It is marked by the generation of questions, alternatives, hypotheses, and problem statements; it leads to the production of large numbers of varied responses and to the construction of original ideas and logical possibilities. It requires a context of high error-tolerance for optimal functioning. It is the criterion elicited by the popular Torrence Tests of Creative Thinking. Philosophers often prefer to describe creative thinking as imagination and frequently attend to the contribution of intuition to its occurrence.

THE RELATIONSHIP BETWEEN REASONING AND IMAGINATION

The common polarizing differentiation made between critical thinking and creative thinking is deceptive, since it often leads one to see creative thinking as the discrete opposite of rational thought. It minimizes the contribution of necessary evaluative, convergent, critical processes to effective creative production, and similarly, obscures the import of the speculative, divergent, imaginative processes to effective critical thought. While reasoning and imagination do differ, the difference appears not to be accounted for by the operation of discrete functions, but rather by the contribution of the same operations, both divergent and convergent, in differing proportions and in different positions in the sequence of intellective events that constitute addressing the task. Highly well-defined tasks may be approached convergently and may require the minimal or delayed contribution of divergent operations. Highly ill-defined tasks will demand the immediate operation of divergent processing for the construction of possible problem representations prior to the enactment of the selective mode and the establishment of a problem definition. These tasks will likely require the repeated intermittent use of both the generative and evaluative modes to identify possible appropriate rules and operations, then rules to be enacted, possible problem goals, then selected outcomes sought. Allow two brief concrete examples to clarify the description. Asked the mode required for an effective critique of a news article, most persons would cite the evaluative mode, critical thinking, and indeed this does operate in the expected ways to assess the givens and the logical relationships presented. However, a thorough critique requires the operation of divergent processes, as well, to generate new and appropriate tests of plausible explanations of the given elements, to raise questions about absent elements appropriate to the issue, and to identify hidden assumptions and presuppositions that demand scrutiny. Similarly, a task such as the development of a product advertisement, which most would describe as a creative thinking activity, also depends on the operation of evaluative processes intermittently with speculative ones to define audience, goal, appropriate materials and themes, and to assess the most elegant or fit response to the task.

The philosopher John Passmore, addressing the issue from another perspective, concurs with this conception of the dual nature of effective thought. In "On Teaching To Be Critical," he introduces the term "critico-creative" thinking as a learner's goal, "because critical thinking may suggest nothing more than the capacity to think up objections. Critical thinking as it is used in the great traditions conjoins imagination and criticism in a single form of thinking (Passmore, 1980, p. 168).

REASONING: THEORETICAL PERSPECTIVES

There are several perspectives from which to argue that empathy can have a positive effect on reasoning. To do so, however, requires that one re-examine and depart from longstanding traditions in philosophy and psychology. Several notable scholars in both fields have begun such a reexamination: two among them are Larry Blum and Carol Gilligan, who have focused their attention on moral reasoning. I propose to offer evidence from their work and arguments from others who have studied critical thinking on a range of issues to support my hypothesis that empathy can have a positive effect on reasoning.

In the *Crito,* Socrates advises that to make a sound decision, in this instance a moral decision, one must use reason and avoid the influence of the emotions. This view may be understood as the legacy of the shift from matrilineal to patrilineal socio-political structures and religious beliefs, and of the consequent devaluation of attributes connected to female entities. Whatever its origin, Socrates' advice produced a significant and enduring impact on perceptions of the relationship between the emotions and sound reasoning. It implied that, uniformly, the emotions will have a negative effect on reasoned judgment. It is time to question this advice.

In Friendship, Altruism and Morality, Larry Blum argues that contemporary moral philosophy in the Anglo-American tradition has paid little attention to what he terms the altruistic emotions of compassion, sympathy and human concern (Blum, 1980). Since compassion is defined as fellow-feeling, or the suffering together with another, and empathy is defined as the entering into the experience of or understanding the emotions of those outside the self, I shall consider Blum's statements about compassion as relevant to empathy as studied here. In assessing the powerful traditions of thought and philosophic orientation that have militated against giving the altruistic emotions a substantial role in the moral life, Blum focuses on the Kantian view. According to this view, "Feelings and emotions are entirely distinct from reason and rationality. They do not yield knowledge, and can in fact divert us from morally-directed thinking and judgment. . . . In order to obtain a clear view of the rights and wrongs in a situation, we must abstract and distance ourselves from our feelings and emotions, (since these) are transitory, changeable, capricious (and) week" (Blum, 1980, p. 2). According to the Kantian view, if an action is based purely on a *feeling* of altruism, then it has no moral value: for that, the agent must act from a reason-based *duty* to act altruistically. Actions based on altruistic feelings lack the defining features of universality, impartiality and obligation which characterize morality which "is first and foremost an enterprise of reason and rationality" (Blum, p. 3). Blum continues,

> Taken together, the Kantian view of feelings and emotions and its view of morality constitute a powerful and influential tradition of thought, which would deny a substantial role to sympathy, compassion, and concern in morality and moral motivation. It is important to see that these lines of thought do not spring solely from explicit philosophical thought. Rather, they have roots in our own moral culture. The Kantian view has affinities with a definite Protestant tradition of morality—the emphasis on subjection to duty, on control of feelings and inclinations from one's selfish lower

nature, on conscientious action on principle, rather than on emotional spontaneity. That tradition has deeply affected the moral thinking and experiences of Anglo-Americans. (p. 3)

Offering an argument strongly refuting the Kantian and Protestant view and asserting the moral significance of the altruistic emotions, Blum states, "The emotion itself is often part of what makes the act the morally right or appropriate one in the situation" (Blum, p. 142). He continues, "Good judgment is in no way guaranteed by sympathy, compassion, or concern. But neither is it in any way antagonistic to them" (Blum, p. 155). Agreeing that empathy in no way guarantees effective functioning, I would suggest that it can predispose the individual to more effective reasoning by increasing one's engagement with the issue and one's motivation for producing a fair judgment.

A second call for the reconsideration of the value of emotion and caring in arriving at sound judgments, again in this instance moral judgments, comes from Carol Gilligan. She asserts that psychological developmental theory has not given adequate expression to the concerns and experiences of women, that the contractual conception of justice is seriously limited, and that a model of an ethical adulthood that encourages becoming principled at the expense of being caring is to be rejected (Gilligan, 1982). In so doing, she argues indirectly for the recognition of the value of caring, an altruistic emotion, in arriving at sound ethical judgments.

Having reviewed these theoretical perspectives from which empathy, as an altruistic emotion, can be newly appreciated in its relationship to sound judgment, I will turn to the evidence for this view found in the empirical literature.

REASONING: EMPIRICAL PERSPECTIVES

In looking empirically at the process of reasoning, it is necessary to distinguish among the individual's information and theories, the processes used to generate these (where available), and the individual's inferential and predictive performance. Cognitive psychologists frequently identify beliefs and theories as knowledge structures, defining them specifically as "pre-existing systems of schematized, abstracted knowledge" (Flavell & Ross, 1981). They distinguish these knowledge structures from the methods used to process information often called judgmental heuristics; these general cognitive strategies are the processes used in ordinary perception and problem solving; they allow us to make sense of the flux of experience with speed and little effort.

Two strategies that seem especially important in this endeavor are the "representative heuristic" by which we sort new experience into pre-existing categories by matching salient features of the two, and the "availability heuristic . . . through whose application objects or events are judged probable or casually efficacious to the extent that they are cognitively and/or perceptually 'available' " (Ross, 1982, p. 15). How and why a sound of a particular frequency may be categorized, for example, as an infant's cry, a cat's wail, or an oboe's lament is not well understood, but the categorization occurs through the interaction of schema recruitment, representativeness and availability heuristics.

Adopting a model of the adult lay person as "intuitive social scientist," Lee Ross in reviewing selected relevant research on reasoning offers several interesting observations about its effective and ineffective operation. He notes that when persons reason to sound and unsound conclusions the methods that they employ are not significantly different. Among the factors that appear to differentiate successful from less successful critical thinkers are the initial codings of data, sensitivity to sample size and possible bias in assessing the generalizability of data, and factors affecting belief perserverance; these factors are co-variation assessment, causal assessment and prediction, and the testing and revising of theories. Less effective critical thinkers have difficulty detecting and assessing empirical co-variations (Ross, 1982, pp. 7–13). Ross, summarizing his own studies and those of Amabile, Jennings and others notes, "Even relatively powerful empirical relationships are apt to go undetected, or to be assessed as trivial in their magnitude, if they could not be predicted from the intuitive scientist's prior theories and preconceptions" (Ross, p. 10). With respect to causal judgments, one important source of error has to do with "notions of parsimony"; once an individual has discerned one satisfactory explanation or cause of a phenomenon, he essentially stops looking and/or may fail to recognize other equally sufficient causes (Ross, 1982, p. 32). Factors of disposition and motivation clearly enter in here.

Studies of belief perseverance are particularly important to an understanding of open-mindedness and critical thinking. Reviewing work on belief perserverance, Ross notes that theories and beliefs are tenacious; assimilation of new data to pre-existing beliefs endures even when the accommodation of those theories is more appropriate. Less effective reasoners exhibit greater rigidity than their more successful counterparts. When subjects were exposed to information that was ambiguous with respect to their current values, they tended to accept the information at face value and to shift their attitudes in the direction of strengthening their existing beliefs (Ross, 1982, p. 12). "When the information ostensibly opposes their beliefs, they evaluate it more critically. They seek to formulate alternative, less damaging interpretations and tend to shift their beliefs only slightly" (Ross, 1982, p. 12). Such belief perserverance occurs not only in response to added, new evidence but also in response to the discrediting of old evidence. Many studies reveal that "theories about functional relationships in the world can survive even the most logically compelling of challenges to the evidence that initially gave rise to such beliefs" (Ross, 1982, p. 12).

Perkins in "Difficulties in Everyday Reasoning," a study of broad scope whose subjects ranged from ninth graders to fourth-year doctoral students and older adults with and without college degrees, found that the vast majority of difficulties in reasoning demonstrated across this diverse population was not logical fallacies or other problems of a formal nature but rather what might be called problems resulting from the subjects' under-utilization of available information. Assessing subject performance in situations in which subjects were required to generate and judge their own arguments rather than assess given information, he summarizes,

> As to the difficulties subjects encountered in making sound arguments, the analysis of the objections disclosed that only about a quarter concerned problems of a formal character. The rest reflected what might be called inadequate model-building—various failures to use available knowledge in constructing a more elaborate and realistic analysis of the situation under consideration. For instance, overlooking a counterexample, one of the most common lapses, is not an error of deductive or probabilistic inference from givens, but one of failing to retrieve relevant information. (Perkins, 1982, p. 4)

Perkins suggests that the naive reasoner has a "makesense epistomology", while the sophisticated reasoner has "a critical epistomology" which includes skills for challenging and elaborating models of a situation. He provides evidence that these skills can be taught (Perkins, 1982, p. 36).

Several patterns emerge from these studies of reasoning. Successful reasoning requires an alternation between probing persistence and open-minded flexibility. Various impediments to successful reasoning may be identified and affect different stages of the reasoning process: perception and belief construction, belief maintenance, and the continuance of motivational attitudes and dispositions. Poor reasoners exhibit a pattern of superficial, narrow, undifferentiated, or unelaborated perception of the problem and its elements (e.g., specific datum, quality of sample, or structure of the problem). Often this cannot be attributed to the unavailability of data or knowledge of sound empirical procedures. In these instances, the lack of probing persistence appears to be the source of the difficulty and to be rooted in dispositional factors: an unwillingness to invest in the enterprise, a desire for immediate and simple solutions, a contentment with easily available if flawed outcomes. I believe that these attitudes, which impede sustained inquiry, are rooted in a low tolerance for ambiguity and complexity.

The second impediment to effective reasoning is inappropriate belief perserverance. This factor is complex, for some pattern of belief maintenance is necessary not only to learning but also to the individual's mental health. To see all as ineluctable flux is immobilizing, if not maddening. In addition, for all, theory change comes slowly; Thomas Kuhn in tracing the history of scientific revolutions documents the fact that significant, cultural theory change often requires evidence accumulated over centuries, evidence which is often "not seen" by those well-schooled in the scientific method (Kuhn, 1970). Given this, one nonetheless recognizes that what separates the less successful reasoner from the more successful one is the rigidity with which beliefs are held and maintained. I believe that the cognitive flexibility needed to modify beliefs and theories will not be available unless supported by a tolerance for deferred judgment and ambiguity.

The third impediment to effective reasoning is the absence of the necessary underpinnings, the appropriate dispositions and motivation. Some of these factors have already been introduced in relation to belief construction and maintenance. While a valuing of the enterprise of reasoning well and tolerances for deferred judgment, ambiguity and complexity are especially important to successful reasoning, several other attributes and their relationships deserve mention.

Curiosity, wonder and a desire to understand deeply are also fundamental dispositions for successful thinking. Highly important, too, is the capacity for a modestly skeptical and independent approach to judgment—a capacity whose roots lie in self-esteem and courage, since its exercise requires a self-trusting standing-apart, in which one risks the consequences of self-initiated questioning and challenging.

It is clear that these attitudes would be especially difficult to exhibit genuinely during adolescence, when peer approval is a prime goal and motivator. But the doubting, the taking of initiative and risk remain difficult for the adult as well, since genuine skepticism and probing inquiry uproots the individual from the comfort of an accepted world view. As it often produces temporary confusion, independent reasoning is unsettling and disorienting not only in relation to others (e.g. society and authority), but in relation to *oneself*. Some discomfort and stress and the courage and will to endure them, must be recognized as part of the successful critical process. Programs for developing sound reasoning must attend to the cultivation of the attitudes and dispositions necessary for the manifestation of the target cognitive performances. To neglect this is to fling potent, costly seeds into desiccated, unplowed soil.

CREATIVE THINKING: A NETWORK OF PERSPECTIVES

There are many perspectives from which to see a relationship between empathy and imaginative production. Traditional biographical sources, and recent empirical studies all suggest that the creative individual possesses unusual perceptual and personal openness, and a marked capacity for empathic identification with the other. In the extreme, this produces a condition in which the individual's self-perception is that of egoless vehicle, the instrument of the creative product. Flexible ego-control and low defensiveness indicate a desire and a capacity in the creative person to react beyond the boundaries of self, traits identical to those characteristic of the empathic disposition. Reported research indicates that, although there are some differences in the observable behavior of highly imaginative persons in diverse fields, creative members of the studied professions are more alike than dissimilar. Prominent researchers concur, as Barron states, that the dominant "cross disciplinary correspondences allow one to comment validly on the nature of the creative person across fields" (Gallo, 1973, p. 60).

Openness is a salient trait of the creative individual. Grounded in self-trust, personally-determined values and independence, the original person's perceptual style is characterized by child-like receptivity, a sense of wonder, and a capacity for non-judgmental spontaneous response. Providing a succinct account of the traditional view in "Tables Turned," Wordsworth characterizes the creative perceptual style as a condition of attunement, as "a heart that watches and receives". In "Expostulation and Reply," he summarizes the condition when stating,

> The eye—it cannot choose but see;
> We cannot bid the ear be still;
> Out bodies feel, where'er they be,
> Against or with our will.

> Nor less I deem that there are Powers
> Which of themselves our minds impress;
> That we can feed this mind of ours
> In a wise passiveness. (Gallo, 1973, p. 68)

Empirical research confirms that a Wodsworthian "wise passiveness" is a prominent characteristic of creative individuals, although the terms denoting the quality vary. Crutchfield calls the attitude an "openness to full contact with reality," while Bruner and Wallach associate the quality with an open cognitive style. Rogers labels it "permeable boundaries" and Maslow "a bold and free perspicuity." Guiford and Torrance refer to the trait as "sensitivity," while Abelson and Brown incline to descriptions like "proceeding with curiosity and an inquiring mind." Mednick and Maltzman identify a pattern of "freedom from pre-existing sets." Mac-Kinnon states succinctly, "The creative person approaches life with perceptual openness" (Gallo, 1973, pp. 60–73). Thus, the consensus may be captured by Henry James' observation that the creative person is "one on whom nothing is lost" (Gallo, 1973, p. 73).

Along with perceptual openness and a concomitant tolerance for ambiguity and penchant for complexity, the creative person exhibits flexible ego-control, which in the extreme may be described as possession by the task or object. MacKinnon asserts that, confident of his ability to manage his ego, the creative person can relax his control and release himself from his role without fear of being unable to return to it (Gallo, 1973, p. 68). In "Ego Diffusion and Creative Perception," Barron reports that in an atmosphere of psychological safety, the creative person can forego "the project of the ego," and can experience no distinctions between self and not-self; instead he can relinquish himself to a fusion with all things that nurture a productive harmony (Gallo, 1973, p. 12).

Further, the imaginative individual is spontaneous and eschews impulse control through the defense mechanisms of repression. Barron has reported "that creative males score higher on impulsivity scales and score in the direction of undercontrol on an Ego Control scale" (Gallo, 1973, p. 70). These and other measures suggest low levels of repression or defensiveness. Low definsiveness is related to the creative individual's receptivity to the non-rational in himself and in the world. Assessed by the Myer-Briggs Type Indicator, which classifies a subjects' perceptual-cognitive style (using the categories of Intuitive vs. Sensory, Perceiving vs. Judging, Feeling vs. Thinking, Introversion vs. Extroversion), the creative person is found to perceive rather than judge, to respond with feelings as well as thinking. . . . Most striking is the datum that when only 25 percent of the general population rate as intuitive, Barron and MacKinnon found 100 percent of their creative architects and 92 percent of the studied creative writers preferred an intuitive mode (Gallo, p. 70).

Paralleling the ability to be possessed by the nonrational within is the creative individual's ability to be possessed by task or product. Bruner calls the condition "an ability to be dominated by the object." Keats terms it "negative capability" (Gallo, 1973, p. 71). The poet describes it as a state of "being in uncertainties, mysteries, doubts without any irritable reaching after fact or reason," for he maintains, the creative character "has no self—it is everything and nothing." This view of the "ego-less" involvement of the artist coincides with the traditional view derived from journals and personal reports; these documents portray the artist as the instrument of the work, the vehicle of its production through insight. In his preface to *The Ambassadors*, Henry James describes his domination by his "fable" and the automatic, involuntary service he rendered it. He records,

> The steps, for my fable, placed themselves with prompt and as it were, functional assurance—an air quite of readiness to have dispensed with logic had I been in fact too stupid for my clue. . . . These things continued to fall together, *as by the neat action of their own weight and form,* even while their commentator scratched his head about them; he easily sees that they were always well in advance of him. As the case completed itself he. . . . [was] breathless and a little flurried. (Gallo, 1973, p. 71; italics added)

This is just one of many such accounts of the creative artist's possession by his task. (The reader is referred to Ghiselin's *The Creative Process* for others.)

Thus, the perceptual openness and flexible ego-control characteristic of empathy clearly correlate with the attributes of highly creative individuals. A capacity for spontaneous response is also important. Several relevant attitudinal factors can be identified; important among them are high self-esteem and task motivation, a great tolerance for disorder, ambiguity and complexity, the courage to deal with the cognitive and personal disorientations and risks created by the process and an enormous valuing of the creative enterprise. In comparing these traits to those of successful reasoners, one finds significant similarity. If one accepts the asserted conception of the dual nature of both critical thinking and imagination, this finding is not surprising.

ROLETAKING: A STRATEGY FOR DEVELOPING REASONING, IMAGINATION AND EMPATHY

The practice of empathic role taking from multiple perspectives followed by evaluative reflection on the experience can facilitate the development of an individuals' reason and imagination.

As I conceive it, a roletaking experience has these features. It begins with a presented or learner-generated issue or problem; each participant adopts a role which, when enacted, produces a definition, a detailing and a resolution of the problem or issue. Roles are rotated among participants, or new roles are generated and enacted. Each participant works through the issue from at least three contrasting perspectives. The practice of having several concurrent groups, working without audience is recommended in order to provide maximum student involvement, to use instructional time efficiently, and to decrease the psychological threat of the activity. Topics and problems evolve from the more immediate and familiar to the more abstract and remote; the issues of any subject area can be used. Following the series of roletakings, participants engage in a reflective, evaluative discussion in which the issue is defined and detailed from several viewpoints; then these perspectives are incorporated into an elaborated model of the problem. Resolutions and their multiple consequences are evaluated against articulated criteria. Many expository and imaginative writing tasks flow naturally from such experiences and are encouraged, because they provide for the further persistent probing of details, comparisons, conclusions, and consequences, as well as the participants' engagement with them.

It has already been shown that successful and poor reasoners differ from each other in three aspects of their performance: in belief construction, belief maintenance, and the dispositions and attitudes that influence these events. I shall argue that practice with empathic role taking fosters behaviors and attitudes like those exhibited by successful reasoners.

First, role taking, as described, will facilitate the development of elaborated models of problems and issues. At least temporarily, it will modify the individual's original perception of the issue and its components, for the sustained examination of the issue from contrasting perspectives will yield more relevant data, will be likely to produce counterexamples to items generated from different vantage points, and will eventuate in several problem definitions, and their subsequent incorporation into one or more elaborated problem models. The activity will raise questions about the meaning of specific data and about the quality of evidence and samples. The activity invites and practices the concurrent consideration of an increasing number of factors and thus faciitates what Piaget calls development from centration to decentration. Regular practice will foster increased participant tolerance for complexity, ambiguity, and deferred judgment.

Something deeply important in human understanding occurs here. I propose that when successful empathic role taking occurs, it produces from each perspective not only additional, and new knowledge, as well as the discrediting of some earlier knowledge, but it produces a new organization of information, a new or variant knowledge structure, with both intellective and feeling-state components. It is the creation of this new or variant structure and the self-generated nature of the new and discredited information that account for the impact of the process, an increase in human understanding.

Secondly, there are two ways in which empathic role taking will tend to increase the flexibility with which beliefs are held. First, the process requires that the participant not only hear but generate views different from his own; as one's own construction, these views will typically be attended to with openness and "taken seriously," if only temporarily.

Also, the regular shifting of perspective will produce some consequent distancing from any one view and provide some greater engagement with perspectives which were originally remote. Thus it will tend to reduce the salience of the original perspective of the self, while increasing the viability of other views. In this way, it will promote development from egocentrism to non-egocentrism, a movement which correlates with more effective formal operational thought (Higgins, 1982, pp. 144–148).

Lastly, role taking nurtures the attitudes and dispositions supportive of effective reasoning. It fosters interest in the activity of reasoning, a positive attitude toward the enterprise; it supports the development of initiative, risk-taking and courage and a tolerance for complexity, ambiguity and independent judgment. From the evidence of my own teaching experience, I find that role taking has significant influence on motivation and attitude toward critical inquiry. Role taking tends to be intrinsically motivating because it involves the whole person, requires initiative, and accords the participant both responsibility and power, or fate control in the learning situation. It is an established principle of learning that active involvement and fate control are motivating factors to child and adult learners and that behavior needs an opportunity to manifest itself.

Beyond the investment of time and effort that genuine critical thinking requires, it is a costly and dangerous activity in that it requires one to separate oneself from comfortable and familiar beliefs held to be right, and deliberately and systematically attempt to prove oneself in error, in the service of making oneself correct according to a more rigorous and valuable set of standards. The threats are clear. Role taking fosters a positive attitude toward critical inquiry and nurtures courage, because it allows one earnestly to take the risks, but in a condition of personal distance and reasonable psychological safety. The naturalistic setting of the role taking situation may add some of the comfort of the familiar to the complex, ambiguous task.

Thus, having argued that as an altruistic emotion empathy is not to be avoided by those who would reason well, but more likely should be cultivated through role taking as a facilitator of sound critical judgment, I identify some ways in which empathic role taking relates to effective creative thinking. (This discussion is briefer, since the relationship between these is widely recognized in the fields of psychology and education.)

Creative thinking as here discussed is supported by perceptual openness, flexible ego-control, and a capacity for immersion in the task, for spontaneous response, and for seeing connections between apparently unrelated elements. Role shifting both practices and nurtures flexible ego-control and a capacity to see the same event afresh and with openness from different vantage points. It invites immersion in the task by requiring absorption in each role, so that one can effectively analyze, infer, predict, and act in ways consonant with it. In so doing, it fosters spontaneous and original response. Importantly, the procedure of developing what I have called variant knowledge structures, with both affective and cognitive dimensions, and then evaluating them reflectively produces an optimal situation for the finding or constructing of remote associations, or novel connections between formerly unrelated elements. Thus empathic role taking fosters imagination by providing opportunities for immersive, holistic, spontaneous, and novel responses to problems that are engaging and complex. In so doing, it exercises and nurtures intrinsic motivation for tasks requiring imagination, a tolerance for complexity and ambiguity, as well as self-esteem and courage.

CONCLUSION

In this paper, I have argued that the attributes which characterize empathy correlate with those of effective critical thinking and imagination. Of course, this correlation makes no causal claim: to suggest that the attributes of the empathic, the creative and the rational individual overlap is to suggest that these qualities appear to be significant among a set of conditions necessary for the demonstration of empathy, rationality, or creativity. It in no way suggests that they form a set that is both necessary and sufficient.

Nonetheless, the correlation yields significant insights and holds important educational implications. First, it reveals that an affective component can have a positive effect on both rational and imaginative thought. Second, it suggests that empathy is the emotion or affective disposition to cultivate, since it develops emotional range which is essential to multiple perspective-taking and genuine open-mindedness. Third, in educating for these goals, role taking is a strategy of promise, since it has a positive influence on problem perception, on belief maintenance, and on relevant attitudes and dispositions. Role taking discourages hasty and superficial problem examination and facilitates the construction of more fully-elaborated, possibly novel, problem models. It discourages belief rigidity and the salience of the perspective of the self and encourages cognitive and personal flexibility. It practices persistent, probing, engaged examination of an issue in alternation with flexible relinquishment and reflective distance. Thus, the strategy has potential for addressing all three of the documented impediments to sound reasoning while practicing the perceptual openness, flexible ego-control and spontaneity so important to originality. By conjoining and practicing both openness and commitment, flexibility and persistence, empathic role taking can foster the cognitive and affective patterns that charcterize effective reasoning and imagination, and can promote open-mindedness and the humanistic response.

REFERENCES

Blum, L. (1980). *Friendship, altruism and morality*. Boston: Routledge and Paul.
Gallo, D. (1973). *The traits and techniques of creative production*. Unpublished doctoral dissertation. Harvard University.
Gilligan, C. (1982). *In a different voice: Psychological theory and women's development*. Cambridge: Harvard University Press.
Higgins, E. (1982). Role taking and social judgment: Alternative developmental perspectives and processes. In *Social cognitive development: Frontiers and possible futures*, J. H. Flavell, & L. Ross (Eds.). Cambridge: Cambridge University Press.
Kuhn, T. (1970). *The structure of scientific revolutions*. Chicago: University of Chicago Press.
Passmore, J. (1980). On teaching to be critical. In *The philosophy of teaching*, J. Passmore. Cambridge: Harvard University Press.
Perkins, D. (1982). *Difficulties in everyday reasoning and their change with education*. Cambridge: Harvard Project Zero, Final Report to the Spencer Foundation, November.
Rogers, C. (1975). Empathic: An unappreciated way of being, *Counseling Psychologist, 5*, 2-10.
Ross, L. (1982). The "Intuitive Scientist" Formulation and its developmental implications. In *Social cognitive development: Frontiers and possible futures*, J. H. Flavell, & L. Ross (Eds.). Cambridge: Cambridge University Press.

19 Creativity and Skill

Sharon Bailin
University of Manitoba

It is frequently maintained, particularly in contemporary educational circles, that creativity necessarily involves going beyond or breaking rules, and that this is, in fact, the defining characteristic of creativity. Theories such as these generally hold that creativity involves an essentially free activity, and they tend to view rules as constraining and skills as inhibiting. Arthur Koestler (1964) offers an eloquent statement of this point of view:

> Matrices vary from fully automatized skills to those with a high degree of plasticity; but even the latter are controlled by rules of the game which function below the level of awareness. These silent codes can be regarded as condensations of learning into habit. Habits are the indispensable core of stability and ordered behaviour; they also have a tendency to become mechanized and to reduce man to the status of a conditioned automaton. The creative act, by connecting previously unrelated dimensions of experience, enables him to attain to a higher level of mental evolution. It is an act of liberation—the defeat of habit by originality. (p. 96)

Because of the pervasiveness of this type of view, attempts to foster creativity have resulted in a pedagogical practice that places primary emphasis on encouraging flexibility, spontaneity, divergent thinking, and nonevaluative generation, whereas the skills and rules of specific disciplines are downgraded.

This view of the nature of creativity rests on two main assumptions. The first is that the spontaneity involved in creativity precludes skills and technique because these can operate only within the context of a preconceived end. The second assumption is that skills are simply habits. Both these assumptions can, I believe, be questioned. It is argued here that skills and rules play a central role in creativity.

For purposes of this discussion, the examples are drawn primarily from the arts. However, many of the points made are also applicable in other spheres in which creativity is manifested.

The first question addressed is whether creativity does indeed necessarily involve going beyond or breaking rules. This rule-breaking model does not seem to be an accurate characterization of all creative activity, at least in the arts. Most artistic work is not revolutionary but rather takes place within the confines of a framework and is characterized by adherence to the rules dictated by a tradition, a school, a style, or a genre. The painter is directed by the rules of style and technique of the school of painting to which he or she adheres. The poet is subject to the traditional limitations of form and language. The dancer's work is limited by the forms and conventions of the relevant style of dance. A classical ballet dancer, for example, will abide by the principles of classical ballet and try to master the techniques that are consequent to them. A poet composing a sonnet is constrained by the sonnet form and must produce a poem with 14 lines, a specified metre, rhyme scheme, mood, division of ideas, and so on, in order for it to be evaluated as a successful sonnet. Indeed, one may contend that the genius of many outstanding artists lies not so much in their innovative departures, but rather in the excellence of their achievements within the limits set by these rules.

It is true, however, that not all artistic endeavor takes place within the confines of strict adherence to a framework. Art develops and changes by the creation of novel works that depart from existing frameworks, and some rules of the framework are broken or repudiated in the process. This may involve the rejection of explicitly formulated doctrines or the unearthing of presuppositions that had been implicit, the recognition of them as conventions, and thus their rejection. An example of the first type might be the rejection of some conventions of form such as traditional metre, rhyme, stanza form, punctuation, or capitalization on the part of many modern poets. An example of the latter would be the recognition by absurdist dramatists of realism as a convention in theatre, and its subsequent rejection in favor of other possibilities. Thus, the very existence of works of art that depart from the rules of a framework and that, at least temporarily, are not completely subsumed under any existing framework demonstrates one way in which artistic creation is not totally determined by these types of rules. Artistic creation can involve breaking or going beyond rules.

Even in such cases, however, not all rules are broken. An innovation is meaningful only because the innovator continues to operate within the context of rules that are substantially unchanged. Artistic creation, even of a revolutionary kind, is usually less radical a departure from the existing framework than we tend to believe. Thus, the view of creativity in question underestimates the importance of adherence to the rules of specific frameworks in creative enterprises.

Let us turn to an examination of other types of rules—the internal rules governing thought and performance, namely competencies, techniques, and skill. Do such skills inhibit creativity?

There is a long-standing debate concerning this issue in the realm of art that goes back at least to the Greeks. On the one side, there is the view that the essence of art is inspiration, and that the artist does not really understand what he is doing or how he does it. Artistic creation is seen as essentially irrational. Plato, for example, has Socrates say in the *Ion* that: "all the good poets who make epic poems use no art at all, but they are inspired and possessed when they utter all these beautiful poems . . . Not by art, then, they make their poetry, but by divine dispensation" (533c–534c).

The opposed view sees art mainly in terms of the perfection of skills and the essence of art as technique. "Techne' is, in fact, a central concept for Aristotle's theory of art, which he views as "a productive state that is truly reasoned" (Nichomachean Ethics, IV, 1140a5). The skills, the technique, the "art" (in Plato's sense) involved are part of what we generally think of as craft, and so this issue of the role of skills in art is connected with the nature of the distinction between art and craft and the role of the latter in the former. The two views presented exemplify opposing positions concerning this relationship. The view of divine inspiration excludes craft from the realm of art whereas the techne view reduces art to craft.

The reluctance of contemporary theorists to admit skill into the realm of creativity is connected with this Platonic vision of the act of creation as mysterious, inexplicable, and unanticipated. This can be demonstrated by looking at Collingwood's characterization of art and craft. Collingwood draws a sharp distinction between the two and sees the essence of art as lying in the way in which it is different from craft. The main characteristics of craft that he outlines are that it involves (a) a means–end relationship, (b) a distinction between planning and execution, (c) a progression from raw material to finished product, and (d) an imposition of form on matter. Art, on the other hand, cannot display any of these characteristics. It does not involve, on the part of the artist, a preexisting goal or idea that he then consciously works toward by means of his medium, transforming some raw material into a finished work by imposing a form on some preexisting matter. For Collingwood, the essence of art lies in the fact that the end does not really exist until the work is completed. It involves, essentially, the expression of emotions, and this is achieved only in the course of the execution of a work. If this is the case, then the essence of art cannot lie in the perfection of technique. Making something purely technically is a feature of craft and implies a preconceived end; but Collingwood (1974) states that, in art "the end is not something foreseen and preconceived to which appropriate means can be thought out in the light of our knowledge of its special character. Expression is an activity of which there can be no technique" (p. 111).

This type of claim about the impossibility of foreknowledge is frequently made in art theory (Tomas, 1964, p. 285; Hausman, 1975, pp. 10–11) and has something in common with the divine inspiration view. The main point of this kind of claim is that creativity necessarily involves spontaneity, imagination, and the generation of novelty, but that these are a logical impossibility if the end is conceived beforehand. Thus, the creative process retains an element of the unexpected, the unforeseen, the mysterious.

The basic problem with such a view, however, is that it becomes difficult, if not impossible, to explain how the artist exercises control in creating his work of art (Maitland, 1976, p. 397). Howard (1982) describes this as the creativity paradox: "that the artist both knows and does not know what he is up to, that he directs without foresight or preconception" (p. 118).

There have been some attempts to explain how control is possible given this account, but they are, on the whole, unsatisfactory. Collingwood asserts that art involves the expression of an emotion, and that the artist does not know what this emotion is until he or she has expressed it by creating his or her work of art. Thus the artist discovers and clarifies his or her emotions in the course of executing the work, and therein lies the element of control. The weaknesses of Collingwood's view have been pointed out frequently (Beardsley, 1968, p. 58; Howard, 1982, p. 119). Although creating a work of art may sometimes involve, for the artist, a process of discovering his or her emotions, there seems no reason to believe that this need always be the case. The artist's emotions may be relatively clear at the outset, and he or she may not have to discover them. In addition, emotions may simply be irrelevant to the creation of some works. Tomas's view of control as manifested by inspiration "kicking" the artist through inner twinges seems to be similarly plagued with difficulties. It does not go very far towards explaining the critical nature of the control and ignores the goal in light of which judgments are made (Maitland, 1976, p. 399). The failure of these types of theories points to the conclusion that the question of foreknowledge is really a spurious issue. There is a considerable variety of starting points from which an artist may begin a work of art, and no one of them is privileged. The artist may begin with a well-worked-out plan, a definite goal, or a strong, well-defined image; he or she may begin with only a hazy vision, subtle impression, or inarticulate feeling; or he or she may begin with hardly any advanced vision but with a desire to experiment in the medium. There seems to be no good reason to deny the status of art to any work because of its mode of inception.

That there can be this range of starting points for works of art indicates that the creative process cannot be characterized in terms of a necessary lack of foreknowledge (Howard, 1982; Maitland, 1976). The control that is exercised in the process of creating a work of art is a product of a variety of factors including what the artist knows when he or she begins and the state of the work of art at any given moment. Moreover, this control is not rigid and deterministic but is flexible or plastic, as Briskman (1980) points out:

> Clearly, if the control of either the background or the problem were 'cast-iron' it would be impossible for the creator to loosen their control over his generation and selection of variants. In other words, the *plasticity* of the control is crucial to the possibility of creativity, but so is the *control itself*. (p. 101)

Where does this discussion leave us in our initial question about the role of skills and of craft in art? It has, I think, been demonstrated that there is little support for a view that would exclude craft from art. There is critical control maintained in the production of a work of art, and skills are involved in exercising this type of judgment. Thus, the creativity evident in works of art that conform to existing frameworks certainly involves skill. The question remains, however, as to whether skills might still be inhibiting to innovation.

We come to the second main assumption that underlies the contemporary view that skills and rules are necessarily inhibiting to creativity—that skills are simply habits. This assumption is based on the idea that skills, once learned, become automatic, operating below the level of consciousness, and fixing predetermined ways of seeing and behaving. Once in the grip of these unconscious constraints, it is thought that we are no longer aware that they operate nor that our action is rule bound; thus it becomes extremely difficult, if not impossible, to go beyond the rules and to innovate. Koestler (1964) expresses this point of view:

> The force of habit, the grip of convention, hold us down on the Trivial Plane; we are unaware of our bondage because the bonds are invisible, their restraints acting below the level of awareness. They are the collective standards of value, codes of behaviour, matrices with built in axioms which determine the rules of the game, and make most of us run, most of the time,

in the grooves of habit—reducing us to the status of skilled automata which Behaviourism proclaims to be the only condition of man. (p. 363)

In views such as these, skills are seen as identical with habits—as rigid, unthinking, and inflexible. Indeed, William James (1908) saw such habits as pervading all our behavior and constituting the mainstay of our activity.

Habit is thus a second nature . . . at any rate as regards its importance in adult life; for the acquired habits of our training have by that time inhibited or strangled most of the natural impulsive tendencies which were originally there. Ninety-nine hundredths or, possibly, nine hundred and ninety-nine thousandths of our activity is purely automatic and habitual. (p. 64)

This portrayal of skills as habits does not seem accurate, however. A number of philosophers, including Ryle, Scheffler, and Howard, have taken great pains to point out how skills and habits differ. If a habit involves the performance of an action blindly, without thought, a true skill can be seen to involve just the opposite. Ryle (1949), for example, states: "When we describe someone as doing something by pure or blind habit, we mean that he does it automatically and without having to mind what he is doing. He does not exercise care, vigilance, or criticism" (p. 42). For Ryle, however, care, vigilance, and criticism must be involved in a skill. He continues: "A person's performance is described as careful or skilful if in his operations he is ready to detect and correct lapses, to repeat and improve upon successes, to profit from the examples of others and so forth" (pp. 28–29).

The main point here is that, in terming an action skilled, we are emphasizing just this critical, careful aspect. A skilled performance is one that is not purely automatic and totally inflexible but is one that is able to adjust to changing circumstances. A habit is acquired deliberately or inadvertently by continual repetition of an action and may be either desirable or undesirable—there are good and bad habits. In the case of skill, however, one deliberately sets out to learn, and it is acquired, not through mere repetition, but through training. A person can continually improve on a skill and eventually attain mastery and hence freedom, in the sense that what a person wants to do he or she can do. The notions of proficiency or mastery do not apply to habits.

There are, of course, certain habitual elements that constitute a part of most skills. The ability to spell for writing or manual dexterity with scales for playing the piano are examples. But there is more involved in a skill than such routine and automatic facilities. A skill also involves judgment. It involves applying the ability in a variety of circumstances and making changes when appropriate. A painter is skillful not only in terms of the brush strokes employed, but also in how he or she uses them in a specific work (how the painter makes adjustments according to the way the work is progressing). A pianist's skill goes beyond technical proficiency at the keyboard to involve, as well, his or her judgments as to tempo or volume.

The distinction between habit and skill is parallelled to some extent by that between drill and training. Drill involves continual repetition and what is inculcated by drill will be a habit. A skill, on the other hand, is learned through training that may contain some elements of drill but will involve more than this. Training involves the development of critical skill and must involve some degree of understanding. Scheffler (1965) provides an account of skill development that emphasizes this distinction, as follows:

> critical skills call for strategic judgment and cannot be rendered automatic. To construe the learning of chess as a matter of drill would thus be quite wrong-headed in suggesting that the same game be played over and over again, or intimating that going through the motions of playing repeatedly somehow improves one's game. What is rather supposed, at least in the case of chess, is that improvement comes about through development of strategic judgment, which requires that such judgment be allowed opportunity to guide choices in a wide variety of games, with maximal opportunity for evaluating relevant outcomes and reflecting upon alternative principles and strategy in the light of such evaluation. (p. 103)

Howard (1982) goes even farther than this to contend that even drill cannot be construed as mere mindless repetition. He argues that practice of any kind involves an effort to improve according to some standard, and thus some thought and judgment. Of the practice of advanced musicians, for example, he states: "Rather than mechanically duplicating a passage, one strives for particular goals, say, of fluency, contrast, or balance. Successive repeats reflect a drive toward such goals rather than passive absorption of a sequence of motor acts" (p. 162).

The reason why skills have been assimilated to habits by some theorists is related to the fact that skills, like habits, frequently operate below the level of awareness, Koestler's "invisible bonds." This being so, it is assumed that the element of control cannot be present and that skills must be blind and thoughtless. This certainly need not be the case, however. There are many skills that are routine and of which we are not consciously aware, but over which we still exercise control. The skill of driving a car is a good example. An experienced driver is fully in control, although he or she is not conscious of the skills deployed in manipulating the vehicle through traffic. He or she makes adjustments according to the changing traffic conditions and is, in fact, in control because of and not despite these skills. Thus, the lack of explicit awareness does not seem to preclude the possibility of control.

The skills that are manifested in the arts certainly demonstrate this type of implicit knowledge. As an artist becomes more and more skilled, it is not only his technical expertise but also his judgments that become assimilated into physical responses. Gilson (1957) says: "Man does not think *with* his hands, but the intellect of a painter certainly thinks *in* his hands, so much so that, in moments of manual inspiration, an artist can sometimes let the hand do its job without bothering too much about what it does" (p. 31).

This does not imply that such skills, which operate to some extent below the level of awareness, are automatic and lacking in judgment, but rather that some judgments can be executed without conscious attention. They are, however, still judgments. Critical skills cannot, however, be totally reduced to routine performances, for they involve making choices according to changing circumstances.

Nonetheless, some aspects of critical skills can be improved with practice, and an individual can reach the stage where he or she can accomplish them with speed, accuracy, finesse—and seeming effortlessness. This is part of what is involved in doing something well. The proficiency in certain more fundamental aspects of a skill is what allows one to achieve higher levels. The mastery of a certain level of skill is what allows one to go on, and the possibilities for further development seem unlimited. Thus, new ground is broken in a field by critical judgment, but this judgment is itself based on a repertoire of acquired and assimilated skills in the discipline.

It is now time to return to the question with which we began, the question of whether or not rules and skills are inhibiting to creativity. We have seen that the acquisition of certain types of skills is often connected with a high level of achievement in a discipline. Nonetheless it might still be asked whether skills might not, at times, inhibit creativity by fixing a predetermined way of seeing and operating, and thus limiting the possibilities for innovation. It could be pointed out that even those with a great deal of technical proficiency in an area can and sometimes do perform in a mechanized, unthinking manner. What, then, is the difference between instances where skills manifest creativity and those where they do not? Moreover, it might be claimed that there is a difference between doing something well according to certain rules and going beyond or changing those rules; and that the acquisition of skills is an aid only to the former, but is, in fact, a hindrance to the latter.

The response to these questions have been indicated in the course of this chapter. With reference to the latter issue, I would claim that there is not a real discontinuity between achieving highly within the rules of a discipline and achieving highly when it entails going beyond or changing some rules. The latter is, rather, an extension of the former. It would be incorrect to view any discipline or creative activity as taking place within rigid boundaries and being totally delimited and defined by rules. Instead, the possibilities for what can be achieved are really open ended. Furthermore, one never breaks all the rules because to do so would be to abandon the discipline. And when a master of a discipline does break some, it is usually because he or she is at such an advanced stage in the discipline that he or she can see the point in doing so. One difference between creative and uncreative performances might relate to having a real understanding of the discipline in which one is engaged, and knowing what it is about. If, for example, a musician were technically proficient but nonetheless played mechanically, we might suspect that he or she does not really understand what music is about. The skills in question would be of a rather limited type, encompassing only technical expertise but not highly developed judgment. If, however, an artist is highly skilled and at the cutting edge of the discipline and has a real understanding of what the discipline is trying to achieve, then he is in a position to go beyond or change rules if this seems necessary in order to further the ends of the discipline.

The question may arise at this point as to what the implications of this view are for pedagogy. What, if anything, can the educator do so that the skills taught are not reduced to uncreative proficiency? My response to this has two parts, the first having to do with the manner in which skills are taught. As we have seen, skills are not mere habits but involve critical judgments applied in a variety of changing circumstances. Thus, the teaching of skills as flexible abilities related to ends that may vary might obviate the possibility of rigidity and mechanization.

Students too often are taught skills in isolation, without gaining a sense of their place within the broader context of the discipline as a whole. The possibility for creativity rests, however, on being able to see beyond the specific problem or issue with which one is dealing and having a real understanding of the methods and procedures of the discipline and the principles and goals that lay behind them. Furnishing such a context can be one goal of the educator. Another can be attempting to convey a sense of a discipline not as a static body of knowledge and procedures, but rather as very much alive, active, and in flux. In terms of fostering creative outcomes, students must realize that there are open questions, areas of controversy, and live debates within a discipline.

This sense that a discipline is alive and active relates also to the second part of my answer, which concerns attitudes. The attitude that I think is most conducive to creativity is one that has been characterized by McKellar (1957) as "discriminating receptivity" (p. 116); that is, the attitude of taking seriously what one learns but being unwilling to accept it as final; the attitude of attempting to understand what has transpired in a discipline and why, and attempting to do better. This avoids both the extremes of blind obedience to authority and tradition, which can only result in stagnation, and that of wholesale rejection of a tradition, which can lead nowhere. It advocates, rather, taking the skills seriously that one learns and being open to change should the need arise.

The point that I want to stress is that learning skills is important for creativity. This is in contrast to the view that skills are mere habits that lock one into an established way of seeing and prevent one from going beyond the rules. First, some pure habits are necessary and vital for creating. Habits such as spelling or manual dexterity at the keyboard are the foundation for more complex skills, and no high-level creativity would be possible without them. The second point is that many skills are not reducible to habits but involve critical judgment and adjustment to changing circumstances. Thus, they do not lock one into one way of seeing and are not incompatible with the possibility of changing rules, if necessary. One is, in fact, more likely to be in a position to go beyond or change rules, to make a breakthrough and advance a discipline, if one is working at an extremely highly skilled level at the peak of the discipline.

ACKNOWLEDGMENTS

I would like to acknowledge the assistance of a fellowship from the Social Sciences and Humanities Research Council of Canada.

REFERENCES

Aristotle. (1947). Nichomachean ethics. In R. McKeon (Ed.), *Introduction to Aristotle.* New York: Modern Library.
Beardsley, M. (1968). On the creation of art. In L. A. Jacobus (Ed.), *Aesthetics and the arts.* New York: McGraw–Hill.
Briskman, L. (1980). Creative product and creative process in science and art. *Inquiry, 23,* 83–106.
Collingwood, R. G. (1974). *The principles of art.* London: Oxford University Press.
Gilson, E. (1957). *Painting and reality.* Princeton: Princeton University Press.
Hausman, C. (1975). *Discourse on novelty and creation.* The Hague: Martin Nijhoff.
Howard, V. (1982). *Artistry: the work of artists.* Indianapolis: Hackett.
James, W. (1908). *Talks to teachers on psychology.* New York: Henry Holt.
Koestler, A. (1964). *The act of creation.* New York: MacMillan.
Maitland, J. (1976). Creativity. *Journal of Aesthetics and Art Criticism, 34,* 397–409.
McKellar, P. (1957). *Imagination and thinking.* London: Cohen & West.
Plato. (1956). *Ion.* In E. Warmington & P. Rouse (Eds.), *Great dialogues of Plato.* New York: Mentor Books.
Ryle, G. (1949). *The concept of mind.* London: Hutchinson of London.
Scheffler, I. (1965). *Conditions of knowledge.* Glenview, IL: Scott, Foresman.
Tomas, V. (1964). Creativity in art. In W. E. Kennick (Ed.), *Art and philosophy.* New York: St. Martin's Press.

20 Mapping the Cognitive Demands of Learning to Program

D. Midian Kurland
Catherine A. Clement
Ronald Mawby
Roy D. Pea
Bank Street College of Education

Introduction

Vociferous arguments have been offered for incorporating computer programming into the standard precollege curriculum (Luehrmann, 1981; Papert, 1980; Snyder, 1984). Many parents and educators believe that computer programming is an important skill for all children in our technological society. In addition to pragmatic considerations, there is the expectation among many educators and psychologists that learning to program can help children develop general high-level thinking skills useful in other disciplines, such as mathematics and science. However, there is little evidence that current approaches to teaching programming bring students to the level of programming competence needed to develop general problem-solving skills, or to develop a model of computer functioning that would enable them to write useful programs. Evidence of what children actually do in the early stages of learning to program (Pea & Kurland, 1983; Rampy, 1984) suggests that in current practices programming may not evoke the kinds of systematic, analytic, and reflective thought that is characteristic of expert adult programmers (Kurland, Mawby, & Cahir, 1984).

As the teaching of programming is initiated at increasingly early grade levels, questions concerning the cognitive demands for learning to program are beginning to surface. Of particular interest to both teachers and developmental psychologists is whether there are specific cognitive demands for learning to program that might inform our teaching and tell us what aspects of programming will be difficult for students at different stages in the learning process.

In the first part of this chapter, we explore factors that may determine the cognitive demands of programming. In the second part, we report on a study of these cognitive demands conducted with high school students learning Logo. The premise for the study was the belief that in order for programming to help promote the development of certain high-level thinking skills, students must attain a relatively sophisticated understanding of programming. Therefore, we developed two types of measures: measures to assess programming proficiency, and measures to assess certain key cognitive abilities that we hypothesized to be instrumental in allowing students to become proficient programmers. The relationship between these two sets of measures was then assessed.

Issues in Determining the Cognitive Demands of Programming

One of the main issues in conducting research on the cognitive demands of programming is that the term *programming* is used loosely to refer to many different activities involving the computer. These activities range from what a young child seated in front of a computer may do easily using the immediate command mode in a language such as Logo, to what college students struggle over, even after several years of programming instruction. Contrary to the popular conception that young children take to programming "naturally" whereas adults do not, what the child and the adult novice are actually doing and what is expected of them is radically different. Clearly, the cognitive demands for the activities of the young child and the college student will also differ. Thus, what is meant by programming must be clarified before a discussion of demands can be undertaken.

Defining programming and assessing its cognitive demands is problematic because programming is a complex configuration of activities that vary according to what is being programmed, the style of programming, and how rich and supportive the surrounding programming environment is (Kurland et al., 1984; Pea & Kurland, 1983).

One consequence of the fact that programming refers to a configuration of activities is that different combinations of activities may be involved in any specific programming project. These activities include, at a general level, problem definition, design development and organization, code writing, and debugging (Pea & Kurland, 1983). Different combinations of activities will entail different cognitive demands. For example, a large memory span may facilitate the mental simulations required in designing and comprehending programs. Or analogical reasoning skill may be important for recognizing the similarity of different programming tasks and for transferring programming methods or procedures from one context to another. An adequate assessment of the cognitive demands of programming will depend on analyses of the programming activity and examination of the demands of different component processes.

Specifying Levels of Programming Expertise

In assessing the cognitive demands of programming, specifying the intended level of expertise is essential. Different levels of expertise will entail different cognitive demands. In many Logo programming classrooms, we have observed children engaging in what we term *brute-force paragraph* programming, or what Rampy (1984) has termed *product-oriented* programming. This style is analogous to so-called spaghetti programming in BASIC. When programming, students decide on desired screen effects and then write linear programs, lining up commands that will cause the screen to show what they want in the order they want it to happen. Students do not engage in problem decomposition or use the powerful features of the language to structure a solution to the programming problem. For example, if a similar shape is required several times in a program, students will write new code each time the effect is required, rather than writing one general procedure and calling on it repeatedly. Programs thus consist of long strings of Logo primitives that are nearly impossible to read, modify, or debug, even for the students who have written them. Although students may eventually achieve their goal, or at least end up with a graphics display with which they are content, the only "demands" we can imagine for such a linear approach to programming are stamina and determination.

Thus, as a first step in determining what the cognitive demands are for learning or doing programming, we need to distinguish between *linear* and *modular* programming (or between learning to program elegantly and efficiently, and a style that emphasizes the generation of effects without any consideration of how they were generated).

The beginner's linear style of constructing programs, whether in Logo or BASIC, contrasts with modular programming (a planful process of structured problem solving). Here, component elements of a task are isolated, procedures for their execution developed, and the parts assembled into a program and debugged. This type of programming requires a relatively high-level understanding of the language. Modular programming in Logo, where programs consist of organized, reusable subprocedures, requires that students understand the flow of control of the language, such powerful control structures as recursion, and the passing of values of variables between procedures. The cognitive demands for this kind of programming are different from the demands for linear programming, as are the potential cognitive benefits that may result from the two programming styles.

Distinguishing Between Product and Process

In assessing the demands for different levels of expertise, however, it is important not to equate level of expertise with the effects the students' programs produce. We must distinguish product from process (Werner, 1937). We have seen very elaborate graphics displays created entirely with brute-force programming. One characteristic of highly interactive programming languages such as Logo and BASIC is that students can often get the effects they want simply by trial and error—without any overall plan, without fully understanding how effects are created, without the use of sophisticated programming techniques, and without recognizing that a more planful program could be used as a building block in future programs.

Furthermore, in school classrooms students borrow code from each other and then integrate the code into their programs without bothering to understand *why* the borrowed code does what it does. Students therefore can often satisfy a programming assignment by piecing together major chunks imported from other sources. Although such "code stealing" is an important and efficient technique widely employed by expert programmers, an overreliance on other people's code that is beyond the understanding of the borrower is unlikely to lead to deeper understandings of programming. Therefore, if we simply correlate students' *products* with their performance on particular demands or programming proficiency measures, we are likely to find the correlations greatly attenuated.

Compensatory Strategies

This point suggests another important factor that complicates the identification of cognitive demands of programming. Any programming problem can be solved in many ways. Different programmers can utilize a different mix of component processes to write a successful program. This allows for high levels on some abilities to compensate for low levels on others. For example, a programmer may be deficient in the planning skills needed for good initial program design but may have high levels of skills needed to easily debug programs once drafted. Thus, it will not be possible to identify the unique set of skills that are necessary for programming. Instead, different programmers may possess alternative sets of skills, each of which is sufficient for programming competence.

The Programming Environment

The features of the programming environment may also increase or decrease the need for particular cognitive abilities important for programming. We cannot separate the pure demands for using a programming language from the demands and supports provided by the instrumental, instructional, and social environments. For example, an interactive language with good trace routines can decrease the need for preplanning by reducing the difficulty of debugging. Similarly, implementations of particular languages that display both the student's program and the screen effects of the code side by side in separate "windows," such as Interlisp-D, can reduce the difficulty in understanding and following flow of control.

In learning to program, the instructional environment can reduce certain cognitive demands if it offers relevant structure, or it can increase demands if it is so unstructured that learning depends heavily on what the students themselves bring to the class. For example, understanding the operation of branching statements of the IF–THEN–ELSE type requires an appreciation of both conditional logic and the operation of truth tables. If students have not yet developed such an appreciation, doing programs that require even simple conditional structure can be very confusing. However, with appropriate instruction, an understanding of how to *use* conditional commands in some limited contexts (such as conditional stop rules to terminate the execution of a loop) can be easily picked up by students. Thus, in the absence of instruction, conditional reasoning skill can be a major factor in determining who will learn to program. However, with instructional intervention, students can pick up enough functional knowledge about conditional commands to take them quite far.

Instruction is important in other ways also. It has been our experience that students are very poor at choosing appropriate programming projects that are within their current ability, yet which will stretch their understanding and force them to think about new types of problems. They are poor at constructing for themselves what Vygotsky would describe as the *zone of proximal development* (Rogoff & Wertsch, 1984). Consequently, too little guidance on the part of the teacher can lead to inefficient or highly frustrating programming projects. On the other hand, too much teacher-imposed structure can make projects seem arbitrary and uninteresting, with the result that they are less likely to evoke students' full attention and involvement. Finding the right balance between guidance and discovery will have a major impact on the kinds of cognitive abilities students will have available to them when engaging in programming tasks.

Finally, the social context can mediate the demands placed on an individual for learning to program because programming—particularly in elementary school classrooms—is often a collaborative process (Hawkins, 1983). The varying skills of student collaborators might enable them to create programs that any one of them alone could not have produced. Although teamwork is typical of expert programmers, it raises thorny assessment problems in an educational system that stresses individual accountability.

In summary, several factors complicate the identification of general cognitive abilities that will broadly affect a child's ability to learn to program. In asking about demands, we must consider level of expertise, the impact of supportive and/or compensatory programming environments, and the role of instructional and social factors that interact with children's initial abilities for mastering programming.

ANALYSIS OF THE COGNITIVE DEMANDS OF MODULAR PROGRAMMING

Two central motivations for teaching programming to precollege students are to provide a tool for understanding mathematical concepts and to develop general problem-solving skills. But achieving these goals requires that students learn to program extremely well (Mawby, 1984). To use a language like Logo to develop an understanding of such mathematical concepts as variable and function requires that students learn to program with variables and procedures, generate code that can be reusable, and understand the control structure of the language. Students must also become reasonably good modular programmers before Logo can be effective in teaching problem solving or planning. A rational analysis of the cognitive requirements of designing and comprehending modular programs suggests that students will first need to be skilled in *means–ends procedural reasoning* and in *decentering*.

Procedural reasoning ability is one of the important skills underlying the ability to program, because programmers must make explicit the antecedents necessary for different ends and must follow all the possible consequences of different antecedent conditions. Designing and following the flow of control of a program necessitates understanding different kinds of relations between antecedent and consequent events, and organizing and interrelating the local means–end relations (modules) leading to completion of the program. Procedural reasoning thus includes understanding conditional relationships, temporal sequencing, hypothetical deduction, and planning.

Decentration also may be an important skill in programming because programmers must distinguish what they know and intend from what the computer has been instructed to execute. This is important in both program construction and debugging: In the former, the program designer must be aware of the level of explicitness required to adequately instruct the computer; in the latter, he or she must differentiate between what the program "should" do from what it in fact did. We have found that such decentering is a major hurdle in program understanding at the secondary school level (Kurland & Pea, 1985).

On the basis of this rational analysis, we designed a study to investigate the relationship of measures of procedural reasoning and decentering to the acquisition of programming skill.

METHOD

To investigate the relationship between these cognitive abilities and programming competence, we studied novice programmers learning Logo. Logo was chosen because of the high interest it has generated within the educational community, and because the Logo language has specific features that support certain important thinking skills. For example, the strategy of problem decomposition is supported by Logo's modular features. Logo procedures may be created for each subpart of a task. The procedures may be written, debugged, and saved as independent, reusable modules and then used in combination for the solution of the larger problem. Efficient, planful problem decomposition in Logo results in flexibly reusable modular procedures with variable inputs. Whereas the same can be true of languages such as BASIC, the formal properties of Logo appeared to be more likely to encourage students to use structured programming.

Participants and Instructional Setting

Participants in the study were 79 eighth- to 11th-grade female high school students enrolled in an intensive 6-week summer program designed to improve math skills and introduce programming. The goal of the program was to improve students' mathematical understanding, while building their sense of control and lessening their anxiety about mathematics. (See Confrey, 1984, and Confrey, Rommney, & Mundy, 1984, for details about the affective aspects of learning to program.) Those admitted to the program were generally doing very well in school and had high career aspirations, but they were relatively poor in mathematics and, in some cases, experienced a great deal of math-related anxiety.

Each day the students attended two 90-minute mathematics classes, as well as lectures and demonstrations on how mathematics is involved in many aspects of art and science. Each student also spent 90 minutes a day in a Logo programming course. The teachers hoped that the programming experience would enable students to explore mathematical principles and thus lead them to new insights into mathematics. The guiding philosophy of the program, which influenced both the mathematics and Logo instruction, was constructivist. This Piagetian-inspired philosophy of instruction holds that a person's knowledge and representation of the world is the result of his or her own cognitive activity. Learning will not occur if students simply memorize constructions presented by their teachers in the form of facts and algorithms. Thus, students were expected to construct understandings for themselves through their direct interactions with and explorations of the mathematics or programming curricula.

The Logo instruction was given in small classes, with the students working primarily in pairs, that is, two students to a computer. There was a 6:1 student–teacher ratio, and ample access to printers and resource materials. In order to provide structure for the students' explorations of Logo, the program staff created a detailed curriculum designed to provide systematic learning experiences involving the Logo turtle graphics commands and control structures. Although the curriculum itself was detailed and carefully sequenced, the style of classroom instruction was influenced by the discovery-learning model advocated by Papert (1980). Thus, students were allowed to work at their own pace and were not directly accountable for mastery of specific concepts or commands. The instructors saw their primary role as helping students to develop a positive attitude towards mathematics and programming. In this respect, the program seemed by our observations to have been very successful.

The emphasis of the course was on learning to program. The teachers repeatedly called attention to the underlying mathematical principles at work in the assignments and, at the same time, tried to bring students to an adequate level of programming proficiency. Thus, the curriculum was designed around a series of "challenges" (i.e., worksheets) that the students were to work through in a systematic order. These challenges included creating graphics using Logo primitives, unscrambling programs, predicting program outcomes, and coordinating class projects to produce large-scale programs. It was assumed that the students would find the challenges and the opportunity to work at the computer enjoyable and would as a result be largely self-motivated.

MEASURES

We were interested in how the students' level of programming proficiency would relate to the specific cognitive abilities that our earlier analysis had indicated to be potentially important. We therefore developed the following measures of cognitive performance and programming proficiency.

Cognitive Demands Tasks

Two cognitive demands tasks were developed and administered to students at the beginning of the program. The first, *procedural flow of control task,* was designed to assess students' ability to use procedural reasoning in order to follow the flow of control determined by conditional relations. In this task, students had to negotiate a maze in the form of an inverted branching tree (see Fig. 20.1). At the most distant ends of the branches were a set of labeled goals. To get to any specific goal from the top of the maze, students had to pass through "gates" at each of the branching nodes. The conditions for passage through the gates involved satisfying either simple or complex logical structures (disjunctive or conjunctive). Passage through gates was permitted by a set of geometric tokens with which the student was presented at the beginning of each problem. Each gate was marked with the type or types of tokens that were required to gain passage. For example, a circle token allowed students to pass through a circular gate, but not through a square gate. If they had both a square and a triangle token, they could pass through a joint square–triangle gate, but not through a joint square–circle gate.

The task consisted of two parts. In the first, students were presented with five problems in which they had to find paths through the maze that did not violate the conditions for passage through the gates. They were given a set of tokens and asked to discover all the possible goals that could be reached with that set.

In the second part of the task, we designed two problems, based on a more complex maze, to add further constraints and possibilities for finding the optimal legal path to the goals. Unlike part one, at a certain point in the maze students could choose to trade one kind of token for another. As they passed through each gate, they forfeited the token that enabled them to get through it. This feature introduced additional planning and hypothetical reasoning requirements because the students had to foresee the sequential implications for choosing one path over other possible paths. This task allowed for several possible solutions that met the minimum requirements of the task (i.e., reaching a specified goal). However, some solutions were more elegant than others in that they used fewer tokens. Thus, it was of interest to see whether students would choose to go beyond an adequate solution to find an elegant one.

The task was designed using non-English symbolisms so that verbal ability and comprehension of the IF–THEN connectives would not be confounding factors. In natural language, IF–THEN is often ambiguous,

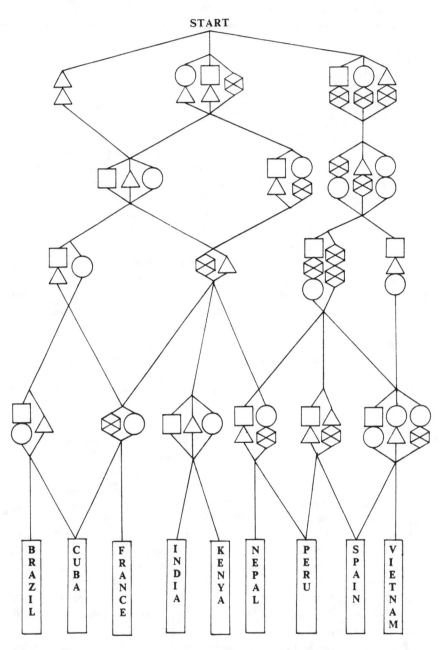

FIG. 20.1 Procedural flow of control task to assess students' ability to use procedural reasoning.

its interpretation depending on context. We therefore did not include standard tests of the IF–THEN connective in propositional logic because computing truth values, as these tests require, is not strictly relevant to following complex conditional structures in programming.

The procedural flow of control task, therefore, involved a system of reasonable, although arbitrary and artificial, rules, not easily influenced by the subjects' prior world knowledge. The nested conditional structure of the tree and the logical structures of the nodes were designed to be analogous to the logical structures found in computer languages.

The second cognitive demands task was designed to assess decentering as well as procedural and temporal reasoning. In this *debugging task* students were required to detect bugs in a set of driving instructions that has supposedly been written for another person to follow. Students were given the set of written directions, a map, and local driving rules. They were asked to read over the directions and then, by referring to the map, catch and correct bugs in the directions so that the driver could success-fully reach the destination. In order to follow the instructions and deter-mine their accuracy, students had to consider means–ends relationships and employ temporal reasoning. They had to decenter by making a distinction between their own and the driver's knowledge. The kinds of bugs students were asked to find and correct included:

Inaccurate information bug: Instructions were simply incorrect (e.g., telling the driver to make a righthand turn at a corner instead of a left).

Ambiguous information bug: Instructions were insufficiently explicit to enable the driver to make a correct choice between alternative routes (e.g., telling the driver to exit off a road without specifying which of two possible exits to use).

Temporal order bug: One line of instruction was given at the wrong time (e.g., telling the driver to pay a token to cross a toll bridge before indicating where to purchase tokens).

Bugs due to unusual input conditions, and *embedded bugs* in which obvious corrections failed because they introduced and/or left a bug (e.g., telling the driver to make a detour in response to a rush hour traffic rule, but failing to note that the obvious detour violates a second traffic rule).

Programming Proficiency Tasks

In order to determine skills in modular programming, we developed measures for three aspects of programming proficiency: flow of control, program decomposition, and reusability of code. In designing the test, we were concerned less with the students' knowledge of individual commands than with assessing their comprehension of the overall structure of the language and the pragmatics of programming. The test consisted of three parts: one production task and two comprehension tasks.

Production Task.   The production task was a paper-and-pencil test designed to assess students' skills in planning, problem decomposition, and features of programming style such as the conciseness and generality of procedures. Students were shown a set of seven geometric figures, represented in Fig. 20.2.

The students were instructed to select five of the seven figures and write Logo programs to produce them. The task called for students first to indicate the five figures they would write programs for, and then to number them in the order in which the programs would be written. It was hoped that this instruction would encourage the students to plan before writing their programs. Students were free, however, to alter the choice and/or order of their figures once they began to code. For each of their five programs, they were to write the code and give the run command needed to make the program produce the figure.

The task sheet included an area labeled *workspace,* analogous to the Logo workspace, in which students could write the procedures to be called by their programs. The layout of the task sheet, two sample problems, and explicit instructions made it clear that, once written in the workspace, the procedures were available to all programs.

The task was designed to encourage planning for modular procedures that could be reused across programs. In fact, figures B, C, E, F, and G could be programmed by writing three general-purpose procedures. An optimal solution would be to write a procedure with two variable inputs to produce rectangles, a "move over" procedure with one input, a "move up" procedure with one input, and then to use those three procedures in programs to produce figures B, C, E, F, and G. Figures B and G could be most efficiently produced using recursive programs, although recursion was not necessary.

Figures A and D were included as distractor items. Unlike the other five figures, they were designed *not* to be easily decomposed and could not be easily produced with code generated for any of the other figures.

The task could be solved by planful use of flexible modules of code. It could also be solved in many other ways, such as writing low-level, inelegant "linear" code consisting of long sequences of FORWARD, LEFT, and RIGHT commands, thereby never reusing modules of code. We were particularly interested in this style dimension because a linear solution gives no evidence that the student is using the Logo constructs that support and embody high level thinking.

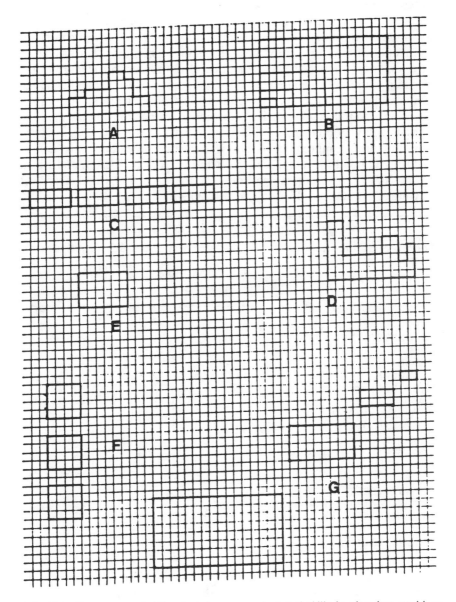

FIG. 20.2 Program production task to assess students' skills in planning, problem decomposition, and features of programming styles.

Comprehension Tasks.   Each of the two comprehension tasks presented four procedures: one superprocedure and three subprocedures. The students were asked first to write functional descriptions of each of the procedures, thus showing their ability to grasp the meaning of commands within the context of a procedure. Then they were asked to draw on graph paper the screen effects of the superprocedure when executed with a specific input. To draw the screen effects, students had to hand-simulate the program's execution, thus providing a strong test of their ability to follow the precise sequence of instructions dictated by the program's flow of control.

In the first comprehension tasks, the superprocedure was named TWOFLAGS and the subprocedures were CENTER, FLAG, and BOX. Figure 20.3 presents the Logo code for the procedures and a correct drawing of the screen effect of TWOFLAGS 10.

Logo Prodedures   Drawing of Screen Effects

                                   TWOFLAGS 10

```
TO CENTER
  PENUP
  HOME
  PENDOWN
END

TO FLAG :X
  FORWARD 15
  BOX :X
  CENTER
END

TO BOX :SIDE
  REPEAT 4 [FORWARD :SIDE RT 90]
END

TO TWOFLAGS :X
  CENTER
  FLAG 15
  PENUP
  RT 90 FORWARD 20 LT 90
  PENDOWN
  FLAG :X
END
```

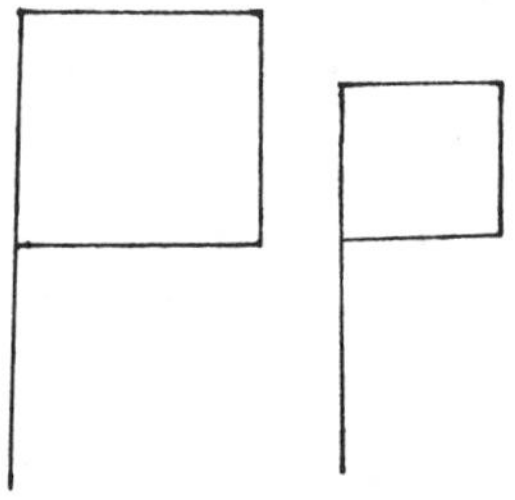

FIG. 20.3   First Logo comprehension task with correct drawing of the resulting screen effects.

The second comprehension task included procedures with two inputs and a recursive procedure with a conditional stop rule. The task was designed to make the master procedure progressively harder to follow. The superprocedure was named ROBOT, and the three subprocedures were called BOT, MID, and TOP. Figure 20.4 presents the Logo code and correct drawing of the screen effects of ROBOT 30 25.

Both programming comprehension tasks were designed as paper-and-pencil tests that did not require the use of the computer. Students were given a sheet that listed the programs, a sheet on which to write their descriptions of what each procedure would do, and graph paper on which to draw their predictions of what the program would do when executed.

Logo Procedures

Drawing of Screen

Effects of ROBOT 30 25

```
TO BOT :X :Y
  FORWARD :X
  RT 90
  FORWARD :Y
END

TO MID :X :Y
  BOT :X :Y
  RT 90
  BOT :X :Y
END

TO TOP :X
  IF :X 5 RT 90 BACK 10 STOP
  REPEAT 4 [FORWARD :X RT 90]
  FORWARD 5 LT 90
  TOP :X - 10
END

TO ROBOT :X :Y
  HT
  MID :X :Y
  BACK 15 LT 90
  BOT :X - 10 :Y - 15
  RT 90 PU FORWARD 50 PD
  TOP ;Y - 10
END
```

FIG. 20.4 Second Logo comprehension task with correct drawing of the resulting screen effects.

PROCEDURE

The cognitive demands measures were administered to the students on the first day of the program, along with a number of mathematics, problem-solving, and attitude measures (see Confrey, 1984, for a discussion of the attitude measures). The students were tested together in a large auditorium. Instructions for each test were read by the experimenters, who monitored the testing and answered all questions. Students were given 17 minutes for the procedural reasoning task and 12 minutes for the debugging task.

In the final week of the program, the students were administered the Logo proficiency test. Testing was done in groups of approximately 30 students each. Again the experimenters gave all the instructions and were present throughout the testing to answer students' questions. Students were given 30 minutes for the production task and 15 minutes each for the comprehension tasks.

RESULTS

Programming Proficiency Tasks

To use Logo as a tool for high-level thinking, one must employ relatively sophisticated Logo constructs, such as procedures with variable inputs and superprocedures which call subprocedures. To write and understand Logo programs using these language constructs, one needs to understand something about the pragmatics of writing programs and also have a good grasp of Logo's control structure, that is, how Logo determines the order in which commands are executed. The empirical question addressed is whether students develop such an understanding as the result of 5 weeks (approximately 45 hours) of intensive Logo instruction.

Comprehension Tasks.   The assessments of Logo proficiency given at the end of the course indicated that mastery of Logo was limited. On the TWOFLAGS task, 48% of the students correctly drew the first flag, which required simulating the execution of TWOFLAGS through its call to FLAG in line 2. But only 21% correctly drew the second flag, with 19% of the students correct on both flags (showing that in almost all cases performance was cumulative).

A third of the students were partially right on the second flag. Analysis of errors on this flag indicated that more students had trouble following the flow of control than had difficulty keeping track of the values of the variables. An error in *place* on the second flag suggests that the student's simulation did not execute all the positioning lines of code, especially the call to CENTER in the last line of FLAG. This reveals an error in flow of control. An error in *size* on the second flag suggests that the student did not correctly pass the variable from TWOFLAGS to FLAG to BOX.

On the ROBOT task, 65% of the students correctly drew the body of the robot, which involved simulating the execution of ROBOT through its call to MID. Thirty-seven percent correctly drew the leg, which involved following the execution through ROBOT's call to BOT in line 4. TOP is a recursive procedure with inputs to ROBOT of 30 25; it executes three times. The first time TOP draws the head, the second time it draws the nose, and the last time it draws the mouth and then stops. Sixteen percent of the students correctly drew the head, 13% succeeded with the nose, and only 2% were able to follow the program execution all the way through to the mouth. The cumulative percentages are within 3% of these absolute percentages.

Analysis of the errors of students who were partially correct showed that more of them correctly passed the values of variables than followed the flow of control. In partially correct drawings, the parts of the robot were more often sized correctly than placed correctly.

The students' written descriptions of the procedures in both the TWOFLAGS and ROBOT tasks showed that many had a general, albeit vague, understanding of the procedures. Often students understood the code in that they gave adequate glosses of individual lines. But when tested by the drawing task, many revealed that they did not understand Logo's control structure well enough to trace the program's execution. This was especially clear when the order of the lines in a listing of the program differed from the order in which the lines were executed.

Some students failed to grasp the fact that, because variable values are local to the procedure call, values can be passed among procedures under different names. Even more failed to understand the most basic fact of flow of control: After a called procedure is executed, control returns to the next line of the calling procedure.

Production Task. In the production task, students made very little use of variables and reusable subprocedures. Although most were able to generate the figures, many did so following the linear programming style. Only 21% of the students avoided both distractor items. An additional 35% avoided either A or D singly. Thus, 44% of the students wrote programs for both A and D. Given a low level of programming proficiency, choosing the distractors was reasonable because, by design, linear programs for the distractors were easier than linear programs for figures B and G (and comparable to C and F).

Among the possible approaches to the task are *analytic* and *synthetic* decomposition. By analytic decomposition, we mean analyzing a single figure into component parts, writing procedures for the parts, and having the program call the procedures. By synthetic decomposition, we mean decomposition of the entire problem set into components, writing procedures for the parts, and then having each of the five programs call the appropriate modules of code. Note that although the five nondistractor figures contain only rectangles, the rectangles are of different sizes. Thus, high-level synthetic decomposition, unlike analytic decomposition, requires a general procedure with variable inputs for producing the rectangles.

Students were much more likely to use analytic than synthetic decomposition. In fact, 88% wrote, used, and reused a procedure at least once, giving evidence of some analytic decomposition. However, only 20% of the students gave evidence of synthetic decomposition by using a procedure for more than one program.

Figure 20.5 and Table 20.1 provide more detail on the features used by Logo students to produce the individual figures. In the analysis represented by Fig. 20.5, we wished to know, for each figure, whether students could write code to produce it and whether they could correctly use REPEAT, variables, and recursion. The REPEAT command is the simplest modular feature in Logo. Variables go further in transforming

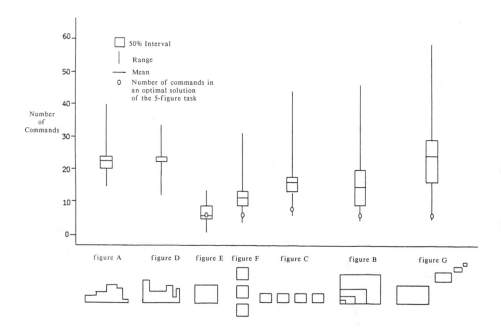

FIG. 20.5   Performance of students on program production task.

TABLE 20.1
Performance of Students on Program Production Tasks

Performance (percentages)	Figures						
	A	B	C	D	E	F	G
% who did it	73	60	96	51	91	91	31
Workable program	86	47	85	90	91	80	48
Variables used	5	43	10	2	14	12	40
Repeat used	8	49	65	2	49	84	78
Recursion used	0	4	0	0	0	0	8

procedures into reusable *functions,* making the procedures more general, and hence more useful. Recursion is an extremely powerful Logo construct in which a procedure can call on copies of itself from within other copies. These features of Logo make modular code possible and thus support problem decomposition strategies.

The number of commands used to produce the program is a good summary indicator of style. For these tasks, elegant programs use few commands. We counted each use of a Logo primitive as one command. Each procedure call was counted as one command and, on the first call to a procedure, the commands within the procedure were counted. On subsequent calls to that procedure, only the call itself was counted.

The graph at the top of Fig. 20.5 displays several statistics concerning the number of commands used: the range, the mean, and the region containing the middle 50% of the scores. For comparison, we also include the number of commands used in an optimal solution of the task as a whole. This particular optimal solution "synthetically" decomposes the five rectangular figures with three subprocedures and produces the programs in the order E, F, C, B, G.

The figures fall into three groups: the distractors A and D; C, E, and F; and B and G. As noted, nearly half the students chose figures A and D, and 90% of the students who chose these figures were able to write a Logo program to produce them. As expected from the design of the figures, less than 10% of these programs used variables or REPEAT. Most of the code was low-level, brute-force style, which could not be reused in other programs. Thus, whereas the students wrote programs to produce the figure, their programming style gave no indication that they were engaged in the high-level thinking that Logo can support.

The group of figures C, E, and F was chosen by more than 90% of the students, and nearly 90% of these students wrote workable programs.

More than half the students correctly used REPEAT, Logo's simpler, within-procedure modular construct. Less than 15% of these programs correctly used variables. This more elegant, across-program construct was largely ignored. As a result, most students needed more than the optimal number of commands to write programs for figures F and C.

Figures B and G were chosen by the least number of students (60% and 31%, respectively) and proved to be the most difficult because only half the students wrote workable programs. These programs used REPEAT and variables relatively often (REPEAT: 49% in B, 68% in G; variables: 43% in B, 40% in G). Thus, it seems that the skilled students who chose these figures did quite well. Of the other students who chose these figures, about half did not attempt to use variables, and half used variables incorrectly. Again, because few students did synthetic decomposition, most programs had more than an optimal number of commands.

No one tried to write a recursive program for any of the figures except B and G, and fewer than 10% of the students who chose figure B or G wrote correct recursive programs. This powerful Logo construct was conspicuous in its absence.

What factors may have kept these students from using the powerful and elegant features of Logo? It is unlikely that students did not notice the geometrical similarity among, for instance, figures C, E, and F. But in order to do a synthetic decomposition of the task, it is necessary to write procedures with variables. Moreover, coordinating subprocedures in a superprocedure requires a good understanding of Logo flow of control. Performance on the comprehension tasks showed that students had a fair understanding of individual lines of Logo code but had difficulty in following program flow of control.

Cognitive Demands Tasks

There was a fairly broad range of performances on the cognitive demands tasks. Many students showed moderate or high levels of reasoning skills as assessed by these tasks, and a few found the tasks fairly difficult.

Procedural Flow of Control Task.

The two parts of this task were examined individually. The first part included a series of problems for students to solve, each of which posed a different set of constraints and/or goals for going through the maze. Difficult problems required a more exhaustive testing of conditions than did the others (i.e., the given tokens satisfied many nodes early on). Some problems were best solved using alternate strategies, such as searching from the bottom up rather than from the top down. Performance was relatively low on the more difficult problems (30–40% correct, as opposed to 55–70% correct on the less complex problems). This indicated that when many possibilities had to be considered, and there were no easy shortcuts to reduce the number of possibilities, students had difficulty testing all conditions.

In the second part, there were three levels of efficiency among correct routes corresponding to the number of tokens required to successfully reach the goal. Only 14% of the students on the first problem and 21% on the second problem found the most efficient route, whereas 41% of the students on the first problem and 79% on the second problem were unable to reach the goal at all. Few students tested the hypotheses needed to discover the most efficient route.

Debugging Task.   Table 20.2 shows the percentage of students detecting and correcting each of the four types of bugs in the task. As shown, inaccurate information and temporal bugs were easiest to detect and correct (72–91% success). Students found it more difficult to successfully correct the ambiguous instructions. Only 48% were able to write instructions that were explicit enough for a driver to choose correctly among alternate routes. For the lines with embedded bugs, only 21% fully corrected the instructions; 40% caught and corrected one bug but not the other.

Results indicate that students had little difficulty detecting first-order bugs and correcting them when the corrections were simple; for example, changing a number or a direction to turn. However, when students had to be explicit and exhaustively check for ambiguity and for additional bugs, they were less successful.

TABLE 20.2
Debugging Task

	Task			
Bug Type	No Change	Catch No Fix	Catch Some Fix	Catch & Fix
	% of students (n = 70)			
Wrong instruction	3	6	na[a]	91
Ambiguous instruction	11	41	na[a]	48
Temporal order bug	16	11	na[a]	73
Embedded bugs	29	10	40	21

[a]not applicable

Relationship of the Cognitive Demands Measures to Programming Proficiency

Analysis of the relationship between these cognitive demands tasks and the assessments of programming proficiency yielded an interesting set of results. As can be seen in Table 20.3, the cognitive demands measures correlated moderately with composite scores on both tests of programming proficiency.

Examination of correlations with subscores on the programming production task showed that students' ability to write an adequate, runnable program was less highly correlated with cognitive demands measures than were appropriate use of variables, the use of subprocedures within programs, or the use of a minimum number of commands to write programs (one indication of program elegance).

Other subcomponents of the production task that we assumed would correlate highly with the cognitive demands measures (in particular, whether students reused procedures across several programs or used recursion) were not highly correlated. However, so few students engaged in either of these forms of programming that a floor effect may have masked this correlation. Interestingly, although few students used the more advanced programming techniques, many seemed to manifest sufficiently high levels of reasoning skills on the cognitive demands measures.

TABLE 20.3
Correlations of Demands Measures with
Measures of Programming Proficiency

Demands Measures		Measures of Programming Proficiency						
		A	B	C	D	E	F	G
		($n = 70$)						
Procedural reasoning part 1	A	—	—	—	—	—	—	—
Procedural reasoning part 2	B	.34b	—	—	—	—	—	—
Debugging task	C	.38c	.27b	—	—	—	—	—
Math level	D	.51c	.38c	.42c	—	—	—	—
Production proficiency	E	.45c	.19a	.39c	.38c	—	—	—
Comprehension proficiency	F	.54c	.50c	.45c	.59c	.26b	—	—
Teacher rating	G	.30b	.20a	.22a	.37c	.26b	.54c	—

[a]$p < .05$
[b]$p < .01$
[c]$p < .001$

Perhaps other knowledge specific to the programming domain is required in addition to the underlying cognitive capacity to reason in the ways we assessed.

In general, the correlations of the cognitive demands measure were higher with programming comprehension than with programming production. The design of the production task may have contributed to these findings. Students could write linear programs and still succeed on the task, and most did so. This was true even for those who at times in their class projects had utilized more advanced programming techniques. In contrast, the comprehension task required students to display their understanding of sophisticated programming constructs. Thus, although the comprehension task was better able to test the limits of programming novices' understanding of the language, a production task such as the one we employed may prove the better indicator of programming proficiency for students once they attain a more advanced level of ability.

We examined the relation between math achievement level (assigned on the basis of grade-point average, courses taken in school, and scores on math tests administered on the first day of the program) and Logo proficiency. Math level was as good a predictor of programming proficiency as the specific cognitive demands measures taken individually. However, when math level was partialled out of the correlations, they all remained significant at the .01 level or better, with the exception of the correlation between part two of the procedural reasoning task and program production proficiency. Thus, our cognitive demands measures appear to tap abilities that are independent of those directly tied to mathematics achievement.

When both mathematics achievement and performance on our demands measures were entered into a multiple regression analysis, with Logo proficiency as the dependent variable, the multiple correlations were .71 and .52 for programming comprehension and production, respectively. Thus, a quarter to one half of the variability in tested programming proficiency was accounted for by mathematical understanding and specific cognitive abilities bearing a rational relationship to programming.

DISCUSSION

The present study was aimed at identifying the cognitive demands for reaching a relatively sophisticated level of programming proficiency. We examined students learning Logo in an instructional environment that stressed self-discovery within a sequence of structured activities, but with no testing or grading. Given this setting and the amount of instruction, we found that for the most part students managed to master only the basic turtle graphics commands and the simpler aspects of the program control structure. Although they gained some understanding of such programming concepts as procedures and variables, most students did not develop enough understanding of Logo to go beyond the skill level of "effects generation." Thus, for example, although they used variables within procedures, they seldom passed variables between procedures, used recursion, or reused procedures across programs. There was little mastery of those aspects of programming requiring a sophisticated understanding of flow of control and the structure of the language. Without this understanding, students cannot use the powerful Logo constructs that engage and presumably encourage the development of high-level thinking skills.

Nonetheless, we did find moderate relationships between the ability to reason in ways that we had hypothesized would be critical for advanced programming, and performance on our measures of programming proficiency. The magnitude of the correlations indicated that the students who developed most in programming were also those who tended to perform better on tests of logical reasoning. However, our observations of the students during the course of their instruction and their performance on the Logo proficiency measures suggest that, for many students, the actual writing of programs does *not* require that they use formal or systematic approaches in their work. Programming can invoke high-level thinking skills, but such skills are not necessary for students to generate desired screen effects in the early stages of writing programs.

CONCLUSIONS

The field of computer education is in a period of transition. New languages and more powerful implementations of old ones are rapidly being developed, and more suitable programming environments are being engineered for both the new and established languages.

We can best assess the cognitive demands of programming when we are clear about our goals for teaching programming and about how much we expect students to learn. However, to understand the cognitive demands for achieving a particular level of expertise, we must consider the characteristics of a specific language (such as its recursive control structure), the quality of its implementation, the sophistication of the surrounding programming environment (the tools, utilities, and editors available), and the characteristics of the instructional environment in which it is being presented and learned.

Our results indicate that certain reasoning abilities are linked to higher levels of achievement in learning to program, but that most students opt for a programming style that negates the need for engaging in high-level thinking or planful, systematic programming. Thus, the cognitive demands issue remains clouded by the inherent characteristics of interactive programming languages, which promote the use of a trial-and-error approach to program production, and the particular characteristics of the instructional environment in which learning occurs.

In conclusion, we have argued that uncovering the cognitive demands of programming is far from simple. On the one hand, programming ability of one form or another is undoubtedly obtainable regardless of levels of particular cognitive skills. On the other hand, if by "learning to program" we mean developing a level of proficiency that enables programming to serve as a tool for reflecting on the thinking and problem-solving processes, then the demands are most certainly complex and will interact with particular programming activities and instructional approaches.

Programming can potentially serve as a fertile domain in which to foster the growth and development of a wide range of high-level thinking skills. However, if this potential is to be realized, studies are needed on two fronts.

First, more work is needed to discover what kinds of instructional environments and direction are best suited for achieving the many goals educators have for teaching programming to children of different ages. We are only beginning to understand how to teach programming. Indeed, many parents and educators who read *Mindstorms* (Papert, 1980) too literally are surprised that programming has to be taught at all. But the unguided, free exploration approach, although effective for some purposes, does not lead all students to a deeper understanding of the structure and operation of a programming language and thus does not lead them to see or develop high-level thinking skills such as problem decomposition, planning, or systematic elimination of errors.

Second, our ability to design effective instruction will depend in part on further experimental work to tease apart the roles various cognitive abilities play in influencing students' ability to master particular programming commands, constructs, and styles. A better understanding of the cognitive demands of using a programming language should help us to focus our instruction and identify those aspects of programming that will be difficult for students. Whereas this study demonstrated a relation between conditional and procedural reasoning ability and programming, we conjecture that, at a more fundamental level, these tasks correlated with programming proficiency because they required the ability to reason in terms of formal, systematic, rule-governed *systems,* and to operate within the limitations imposed by such systems. This may be the major factor in determining whether students will obtain expert levels of proficiency. What remains to be determined is whether extended programming, at proficiency levels below that of the expert, require and/or help to develop high-level cognitive skills and abilities.

ACKNOWLEDGMENT

The work reported here was supported by the National Institute of Education (Contract No. 400–83–0016). The opinions expressed do not necessarily reflect the position or policy of the National Institute of Education and no official endorsement should be inferred.

REFERENCES

Confrey, J. (1984, April). *An examination of the conceptions of mathematics of young women in high school.* Paper presented at the meeting of the American Educational Research Association, New Orleans.

Confrey, J., Rommney, P., & Mundy, J. (1984, April). *Mathematics anxiety: A person-context-adaptation model.* Paper presented at the meeting of the American Educational Research Association, New Orleans.

Hawkins, J. (1983). *Learning Logo together: The social context* (Tech. Rep. No. 13). New York: Bank Street College of Education, Center for Children and Technology.

Kurland, D. M., Mawby, R., & Cahir, N. (1984, April). *The development of programming expertise.* Paper presented at the meeting of the American Research Educational Association, New Orleans.

Kurland, D. M., & Pea, R. D. (1985). Children's mental models of recursive Logo programs. *Journal of Educational Computing Research.*

Luehrmann, A. (1981). Computer literacy: What should it be? *Mathematics Teacher, 74.*

Mawby, R. (1984, April). *Determining students' understanding of programming concepts.* Paper presented at the meeting of the American Educational Research Association, New Orleans.

Mawby, R. Clement, C., Pea, R. D., & Hawkins, J. (1984). *Structured interviews on children's conceptions of computers* (Tech. Rep. No. 19). New York: Bank Street College of Education, Center for Children and Technology.

Papert, S. (1980). *Mindstorms: Children, computers, and powerful ideas.* New York: Basic Books.

Pea, R. D., & Kurland, D. M. (1983). *On the cognitive prerequisites of learning computer programming* (Tech. Rep. No. 18). New York: Bank Street College of Education, Center for Children and Technology.

Rampy, L. M. (1984, April). *The problem solving style of fifth graders using Logo.* Paper presented at the meeting of the American Educational Research Association, New Orleans.

Rogoff, B., & Wertsch, J. V. (Eds.). (1984). Children's learning is the "zone of proximal development." *New Directions for Child Development* (No. 23). San Francisco: Jossey-Bass.

Snyder, T. (1984, June). Tom Snyder: Interview. *inCider* (pp. 42-48).

Werner, H. (1937). Process and achievement. *Harvard Educational Review, 7,* 353-368.

21
Proficiency Conditions for the Development of Thinking Skills Through Programming

Ronald Mawby
Bank Street College of Education

The claim that computer programming is a fertile environment for the growth of thinking skills has an intuitive appeal. Plausible arguments, sometimes presented with persuasive rhetoric, have been offered in support of the claim (e.g., Nickerson, 1982; Papert, 1980).

However, to date there has been little solid evidence that programming leads to the development of general thinking abilities. Despite the lack of evidence, the advent of affordable computers in the classroom, the dearth of alternative ideas about what to do with them, and the untested arguments for the general cognitive benefits of programming have converged to promote computer programming as *the* way to use computers in the precollege curriculum (Becker, 1982).

My purpose is to examine one aspect of what will be required for programming to serve as a catalyst for the growth of thinking skills. The first part of the chapter describes how thinking skills might develop through programming. The argument assumes that if a thinking skill is to develop *through* programming it first must develop *within* the programming domain. A consequence is that there are proficiency conditions for the development of thinking skills through programming.

The second part of the chapter presents evidence from two studies that indirectly address the question: How much computer programming experience is required to attain the proficiency conditions? A study of novices learning Logo and a study of six expert programmers under the age of 14 suggest that the proficiency conditions are not easily or quickly met.

The conclusion offers a few guidelines for programming instruction, focusing on the programming knowledge needed to meet the proficiency conditions.

Developing Thinking Skills Through Programming

When we speak of developing thinking skills through programming, what type of thinking do we have in mind? Although the computer supports many symbolic manipulations, and thus many kinds of thought, programming per se is best thought of as a design activity. Design, as used here, means devising a course of action leading to a desired result (Simon, 1981).

When discussing the development of thinking skills through programming in this chapter, I restrict the meaning of thinking to intellectual design. In general, thinking should not be equated with design, nor is design the only kind of worthwhile thinking. But there may be an element of design in all our thought and expression, and design plays such a large role in our lives that design skill is worthwhile to develop.

I discuss programming as a design activity and describe some particular design skills involved in programming. Then, using the theories of John Anderson and Jean Piaget, I discuss how general design skills could develop through the practice of programming.

Programming as Design

If the general thinking skills involved in programming are design skills, how should programming be described as design activity?

The programmer's task can be seen as one of transforming a representation of a problem into lines of code that represent a solution. The program code—the solution to the design problem—represents a sequence of computations that leads to the desired result. Thus, a programming language is a medium of expression for computational solutions to design problems.

We may distinguish four phases of the programming process: problem representation, program design, coding, and testing/debugging (Pea & Kurland, 1983; Pennington, 1982). The phases are analytic ones, not temporal steps in a linear sequence. They correspond to Polya's (1957) four stages in problem solving: understanding the problem, planning a solution, carrying out the plan, and looking back over the result.

The first phase is problem representation, in which the original problem statement is made explicit. Problem representation may be done by explicating the initial problem statement in terms of (a) goals, or (b) data objects and operations on them, or (c) sequences of actions. Whereas any of the three may be put in the foreground, each one implies the others in the background.

The second phase is program design proper, in which the program structure is planned. In this phase the task may be decomposed into subtasks, algorithms for solving the subtasks found, and the proper organization of the parts formulated. Problem decomposition and problem-solving strategies may be employed, iteratively, until the program design is in a form that can be coded into a particular programming language.

The third phase is coding, in which the program as designed is represented in a programming language.

The fourth phase involves testing the program, debugging if necessary, and, ideally, documenting the program.

These four phases are not temporal stages, in the sense that earlier phases must be completed before later phases are begun. Work on aspects of a later phase may shape the development of an earlier phase. Nor are the phases clearly distinct. Problem representation shades into design, and design shades into coding. Programmers may plan in action, revising their design as they go.

Anticipations of later phases, and actual work on later phases, may also affect the execution of earlier phases. In particular, notice the possible influence of the programming language in which the code will be written on the process of program design. Each programming language has features that make certain decompositions, or certain algorithms, or certain flows of control, more or less straightforward to code. A programmer who knows the language will anticipate the coding phase and design the program to fit the language.

Programming is a design process with several phases in which a problem is transformed into a determinate solution. The first three phases may be seen as activities at different levels of specificity, with the testing/debugging phase influencing revisions at any of the levels.

Design Skills and Their Development

What design skills are involved in each of the phases of programming? Problem representation requires skills for specifying the problem and choosing an appropriate problem representation. Because "a well-framed problem is half solved," and a good problem representation can markedly affect the ease of finding a solution, these skills are important. Coding demands skills in giving clear expression to a design in a computational language. Because the language is intended to "communicate" with a computer, and the computer pays attention only to what is said, never what is meant, coding puts a premium on clarity and explicitness. Testing and debugging demand skills in systematically formulating and testing hypotheses.

In the phase of program design proper lie perhaps the most important general design skills. These include planning and problem-solving heuristics such as problem decomposition, means–end analysis, and use of analogous problems with known solutions. These design principles have wide application and I henceforth restrict my discussion to them.

What are the conditions for developing these design skills through programming? The conditions may be stated in two steps. First, there are conditions for the skills to be developed *within* programming. If the skills are not developed within programming, we will hope for the transfer of skills that do not exist. Second, the skills, once developed within programming, must be represented in such a way that they can be applied to other domains. The program design skills must be given an effective general representation.

Development of Design Skills Within Programming

For design skills to be securely developed within programming they must be used and practiced within programming. If, as often happens in schools, "programming" is strictly synonymous with "coding," program design strategies will not be used. If no program designing occurs, then we have no reason to expect design skills to develop.

Here we may be misled by assuming that all programming resembles expert programming. Professional programmers report spending much more time planning, designing algorithms, and searching for old code to exploit, than they spend in coding (see, e.g., Brooks, 1980; Kurland, Mawby, & Cahir, 1984). For the professional, programming centers on the program design phase.

This is in contrast with novice programmers, who are more likely to identify programming with coding. Programming tasks set for novices often do not require a program design phase distinct from coding (Dalbey & Linn, 1984). The design task is either trivial, or, when the design is given to the student, nonexistent. The task demands are for coding, not for designing.

Of course, before students can be expected to complete (i.e., design, code, and debug) nontrivial design problems, they need to have learned the language well enough so that they can code a program once it is designed. A certain level of coding proficiency must be obtained before it is reasonable to set tasks that demand significant design skills. The coding knowledge that allows a novice to represent a linear sequence of steps in a simple design will often be inadequate for coding more complex designs. Only after a student becomes a proficient coder and has been set complex design tasks should we expect design skills to be practiced.

Suppose, then, that a programmer is a good coder and has been set tasks that require a design phase. Suppose further that the programmer has developed some design skills by practicing them within programming.

What more is needed to make the design skills general, applicable beyond the programming domain?

Development of Design Skills Applicable Beyond Programming

General Principles and Specific Skills.   Here we need to pause and consider our terms. The way I am using terms, *general skills* is almost a contradiction. A skill is an ability to perform a task. Skillful performance involves domain-specific knowledge (Waldrop, 1984). A general skill would seem to be a general *principle* applied and integrated into many specific knowledge domains.

Consider, for example, Anderson's theory of the acquisition of cognitive skill (Anderson, 1982). In his theory there are two stages in skill development. In the first stage performance is controlled by interpretive procedures that use declarative or propositional knowledge about the skill domain. In the second, more developed stage, performance is controlled by domain-specific procedural knowledge represented as condition-action production rules. The second stage is attained through a process of *knowledge compilation*, in which propositional knowledge is embedded in productions, and sequences of productions are collapsed into single productions. The generality of declarative knowledge is sacrificed in favor of domain-specific procedural skills that control action directly, quickly, and, within the domain, effectively.

Thus, in Anderson's view a developed skill is domain-specific procedural knowledge. The interpretive procedures of the first stage may use general principles, represented as propositions. These principles are weak methods for a wide range of cognitive tasks. Specific well-developed cognitive skills are strong methods for a narrower range of tasks.

This leads to a sort of paradox. In order to develop general design skills through programming, one must become skilled within programming. But the programming skill then becomes domain specific. The skill becomes effective in controlling performance in part by being integrated with the other phases of the programming process, such as coding, which are totally domain specific. How can procedural expertise in one domain aid performance in another?

A domain-specific cognitive skill might be generally useful if it can be represented as an instance of a general principle. Then, in a new domain, during the first stage of skill acquisition, the interpretive procedures could employ the general principle. The principle, in the absence of domain knowledge, would not directly generate skilled performance. However, using the principle may help speed the acquisition of skills in the new domain. The principle would work as an organizer for the learning process. A general principle defines a goal (e.g., "decompose the problem" or "compare the current state and the goal state") and thereby directs learning. Thus, even though design skills in the full sense are domain specific, general principles of design may be useful for acquiring skills in many domains.

Consider the following example. Suppose one writes programs using modular subroutines. Using modular subroutines is an instance in programming of the general principle of problem decomposition. In a novel domain, one might not immediately be able to apply the advice "break down problems into simpler subproblems." Finding the right problem decomposition may depend on domain-specific knowledge. But trying to apply the principle would direct the search for decomposable parts of the problem. The principle sets a goal and thereby orients learning in the new domain. Consequently the domain-specific knowledge and skills may be acquired faster.

This account implies that general design principles, as such, affect the learning process rather than directly generating skilled performance. It is consistent with the importance of general thinking principles and with the large amount of domain-specific knowledge that underlies expert performance.

Representation of Skills as Instances of Principles.

Resuming the main line of argument, we are supposing that a student has developed some skill in program design, and asking, what is needed for this skill to be represented as an instance of a general design principle?

Piaget's concept of *reflective abstraction* provides one way to think about the process (Piaget, 1976). In reflective abstraction a skill or practical know-how becomes the object of reflection. The principle of organization underlying the skill is abstracted and represented in propositional form. In this way procedural knowledge becomes conceptualized in general terms and so becomes available for use by interpretive procedures in other domains. Reflective abstraction allows one to know propositionally what one knows procedurally. Thus, it is a means of self-awareness or *cognizance*, Piaget's term for becoming aware of one's own actions (Piaget, 1976).

Applying the reflective abstraction notion to programming, we expect skilled program designers to be able to reflect on their own design activities, abstract the general principles they use, and represent these principles in general propositional form. For example, after skillfully *using* problem decomposition strategies, a programmer would come to reflect on his or her use of the strategies and then represent the general concept of problem decomposition. This general concept could then guide his or her design activities in nonprogramming domains.

If we accept the foregoing as plausible, we must ask about the relevant features of reflective abstraction. There are three.

First, the practical know-how that is reflected on must be moderately well developed. Only when the skilled action can be undertaken more or less automatically will there be cognitive resources available for reflection on it. Reflection must not cause cognitive overload. If the first-order performance requires constant attention, the second-order reflection upon it will not proceed.

Consequently, we should expect reflective abstraction to occur in programming only for those programmers who are reasonably well skilled. This lends converging support for the importance of proficiency conditions.

Second, reflective abstraction is not a simple, one-step process of mirroring. Reflection is not a mirror held above action sending its image directly into propositional knowledge. Piaget emphasizes that cognizance of one's actions involves a conceptualization that is arduous rather than automatic. Skill in the performance often precedes an adequate propositional representation of it. For example, Piaget asked adults to walk on all fours and then report the sequence of arm and leg movements they used to do so. Not everyone succeeded in the reflective abstraction, although everyone had been skilled at the action since infancy (Piaget, 1976). Thus, even for well-developed, observable patterns of action, an adequate declarative representation may not be immediately attainable.

This point tells us that programming proficiency may not be sufficient for reflective abstraction to occur. There is no automatic process by which skills become represented as propositional knowledge.

Third, Piaget argues that cognizance of one's action proceeds "from the periphery to the center." The periphery in this sense is the goal and result of an action. The center is the process or means used to attain the goal, or more centrally still, the organization of the process or means. Thus, awareness first is directed to the goal and the action's success or failure. Then, often due to an action's failure, attention is directed to the means. Finally, cognizance of more central organizing principles may occur.

What would the path of cognizance be in programming? First, students would be focally aware of the program goal and its success or failure. Second, they would become cognizant of the program's internal structure that leads to the result. Next, they would become cognizant of their own design activities that produced the program's structure. And finally, they may reflectively abstract the principles underlying good program designing.

There are proficiency conditions within programming for the development of design skills through programming. These conditions include skill in coding and skill in program design. Development of these skills would be a necessary, though not a sufficient, condition for reflective abstraction of general design principles.

Given this sketch of the design skills involved in computer programming, what evidence is there that novices, after an introductory programming course, attain enough proficiency to develop design skills? How much programming expertise is needed for students to become proficient enough for the model outlined here to be applicable?

HOW MUCH PROGRAMMING IS NEEDED
FOR PROFICIENCY?

I now describe aspects of two studies that have been reported more fully elsewhere (see Kurland, Clement, Mawby, & Pea, 1984; Kurland, Mawby, & Cahir, 1984; Mawby, 1984). Both studies, conducted at Bank Street College under the direction of Midian Kurland, indirectly provide evidence for the amount of programming experience needed to become proficient.

Study 1: Novice Logo Programmers

The first study asked whether high school students, after an initial course in the Logo programming language, actually used any of the language features that indicate skill in design.

Logo has specific features that support certain design skills. For example, the design strategy of problem decomposition is supported by Logo's modular features. Logo procedures may be created for each subpart of a task. The procedures may be written, debugged, and saved as independent, reusable modules and then used in combination for the solution of the larger problem. Efficient, planful problem decomposition in Logo results in flexible, reusable modular procedures with variable inputs.

To use Logo in this way as a tool for design one must use relatively sophisticated Logo constructs, such as procedures with variable inputs and master procedures that call subprocedures. To write and understand Logo programs using these language constructs, one needs a good grasp of Logo's control structure; that is, how Logo determines the order in which commands are executed. Thus, for design skills to be used within Logo, students need to understand the control structure of Logo.

The empirical question of this study was whether 79 novice high school students gained enough proficiency in Logo after 45 hours of instruction to use the Logo constructs that support design skills. (For details of the tasks and results, see Mawby, 1984.)

Students were given a program production task that was designed to encourage, without requiring, planful problem decomposition leading to reusable modular procedures. Students were asked to select five geometric figures from a set of seven and write Logo programs to produce them. Two of the seven figures were included as distractor items. Unlike the other five, they were designed *not* to be easily decomposed and could not be easily produced with code generated for the other figures.

The task could be solved in many different ways. At the lowest level of proficiency, it could be solved by writing linear, *brute-force* code and never reusing modules of code. A brute-force solution gives no evidence that the student is using Logo as a tool for supporting design skills.

A better approach would be to analyze a figure into component parts, write procedures for the parts, and have the program call the procedures. This *analytic* approach shows some modular designing.

An even better approach would be to decompose the entire problem set into components, write procedures for the parts, and then have each of the five programs use the appropriate modules of code. This *synthetic* decomposition shows careful planning for modularity in program design.

The results show that nearly half the students chose the distractor figures that could only be programmed in brute-force style. Although almost all students gave evidence of at least one analytic decomposition, only 20% of the students gave any evidence of synthetic decomposition by using a given procedure for more than one program. In general, students took little advantage of Logo's modular features that make code reusable.

What may have kept these students from using the powerful and elegant modular feature of Logo? To *code* a synthetic decomposition of the task one must write procedures with variables. Moreover, coordinating subprocedures within a master procedure demands a good understanding of Logo's flow of control. Thus, to code Logo programs that reflect the use of modular design strategies, one needs to comprehend Logo variables and flow of control.

Students' understanding of these aspects of Logo was assessed through two program comprehension tasks that focused on variables and flow of control.

Each comprehension task presented four procedures: one master procedure and three subprocedures. The students first wrote functional descriptions of each of the procedures, thus showing their ability to grasp the meaning of commands within the context of a procedure. Then the students were asked to draw on graph paper the screen effects of the master procedure when executed with a specific input. To draw the screen effects students had to hand simulate the program's execution. This provided a strong test of their ability to follow the program's flow of control.

The student's functional descriptions showed that many had a vague, general understanding of the procedures. They gave adequate glosses of individual lines, showing that they understood the Logo primitives involved. But only two-thirds of the students were able to correctly hand simulate execution of the master procedures even through the first call to a subprocedure. Only 20% of the students successfully simulated the execution of the simpler master procedure, and only 2% succeeded on the more difficult one. Most of the errors arose from difficulty with passing variables and, especially, following flow of control.

Given the students' problems comprehending Logo control structure and variables, it follows that they would have trouble writing and coordinating flexible and reusable subprocedures. This helps to explain why many students used only the lowest level Logo constructs in the production task.

It also illustrates how inadequate coding knowledge can restrict design thinking in programming. Even if these students had performed a synthetic modular task decomposition as part of the design phase, they would be unable to correctly code the resulting design. Therefore, there would be no reason for these students, at their current level of proficiency, to attempt any sophisticated thinking in the design phase.

In summary, these results show that after 45 hours of Logo instruction many high school students lack an adequate understanding of Logo variables and control structure. Without this understanding they cannot use the powerful Logo constructs that engage and support high-level design skills, such as problem decomposition.

Study 2: Young Experts

The second study was of expert programmers under the age of 14. As part of an attempt to elucidate the developmental course and end-state characteristics of expert programmers, we examined young programmers with some attested expertise. (For details of this study, see Kurland, Mawby, & Cahir, 1984.) Of interest here were the conditions under which they had attained a level of proficiency at which design skills are required.

The young experts were not easy to find. Several purported experts were, in fact, children from computer-rich environments who were frequent computer users but rank novices as programmers. However, we did find six children with some claim to programming expertise.

We based assessments of their expertise on several types of data. They were given program comprehension and production tasks in their language of greatest proficiency. They filled out a questionnaire on their programming history, knowledge, environment, projects, and style. We supplemented the questionnaire with a clinical interview. Finally, we asked them to bring in and explain to us a sample of what they considered their best programming work.

All six were good coders in at least one language. Each had written large programs (e.g., communications systems, Monopoly simulations, programming utilities) in which some planning was clearly required. Thus, for these boys, the hypothesized proficiency conditions for developing thinking skill through programming had been met. The point of interest here is the amount of time these young experts had invested in programming to become this proficient.

We asked each subject for a detailed estimate of how many hours in his whole life he had spent programming. The responses ranged between 500 and 3,850 hours. Even our youngest expert, a 9-year-old, had spent 1,250 hours programming. We compared rough ratings of expertise with hours spent. The relation was clear and unsurprising: the more time, the more expertise.

Consider what this many hours of programming means. Suppose you take up programming in college, go to a class that meets three times a week for an hour, and spend 2 hours outside of class studying for every 1 hour spent in class. That yields about 10 hours a week. If the semester lasts 15 weeks, you would spend 150 hours per semester in programming. Thus, our 9-year-old with 1,250 hours had the time equivalent of 8 semester's of computer programming classes. The 14-year-old with 3,850 hours had the time equivalent of 25 semesters. After this much time we expect expertise.

The findings from these two studies are not conclusive, but they do suggest how much time may be needed to meet the proficiency conditions. Contrary to popular opinion, children do not easily master programming. Becoming skilled enough as a programmer to develop thinking skills through programming is no simple task. The investment of time is considerable. Although attainment of the proficiency conditions will vary with many factors, it is unlikely that students will meet them after one or two courses in programming. If we think realistically about programming as a way to develop design skills, we must live with the fact that there is no royal road to programming skill.

CONCLUSIONS

I want to sketch some consequences of the preceding arguments for programming instruction. The arguments lead to the conclusion that general thinking skills will emerge from the practice of programming only after students become proficient. Thus, their initial enthusiasm for computing must be maintained until they become proficient. This is the most difficult practical aspect of teaching programming. Enthusiasm can wane once students begin to find that producing interesting programs requires a good deal of precise knowledge. The situation in programming may be the same as in many other fields: The activities that are initially most engaging are often least educational, and the activities that are most educational are often least engaging. As Whitehead (1929) remarks, the challenge for teachers is to create a rhythm between the "stage of romance," which excites interest and promotes initiative, and the "stage of precision," which yields exact knowledge with some cost to spontaneity. The ideal outcome is a "stage of generalization," in which enthusiasm is strengthened by an enlarged vision and detailed knowledge (Whitehead, 1929).

Unfortunately, I have no special insight into how a productive rhythm can be generated in programming courses. The following observations concern important features of the content of programming instruction, rather than method or style.

In our experience, students tend to focus on producing screen effects. The "romance" of programming seems to lie in making things happen on the screen. This corresponds in Piaget's model of reflective abstraction to focus on the "periphery." Proficiency requires *comprehending* the language. If instruction can make students focus on *how* the program produces the screen effects, it will shift students' awareness toward more central factors. This shift in direction leads students to the principles of the language that must be mastered for the proficiency conditions to be met. Instruction should balance the students' tendency to center on production by insisting on comprehension.

In our studies of Logo we find that the key weakness in comprehension is inadequate knowledge of flow of control. Mapping the organization of a program design into code requires a flow of control model of the language. If one cannot map the organization of design modules, then only low-level linear solutions to problems will be designed. We see this in the Logo programs of novices. They have inadequate Logo knowledge to support use of design skills. Flow of control should be explicitly taught. This will help students make connections between the phases of program design and coding.

Furthermore, principles of good design should be taught directly as part of programming. There is no reason to force each generation of students to discover on their own principles that could be taught. This is not to advocate passive learning. Students still must make the principles their own by actively turning them into skills.

Finally, if we want students to transfer design principles to other domains, we must help students represent the design skills in general terms. The difficulties Piaget cites with reflective abstraction should make us skeptical about spontaneous generalization of skills into principles.

Programming may be a fertile field for the growth of thinking. For it to yield a harvest, students must become proficient programmers. Proficiency is not easily acquired. Ample time, enduring motivation, instruction in high-level language features, and explicit teaching of design principles will be needed for programming to be fruitful.

ACKNOWLEDGMENTS

The research reported here was supported by a National Institute of Education grant (Contract #400-83-0016; Principal Investigator, D. Midian Kurland). The opinions expressed do not necessarily reflect the position or policy of the National Institute of Education and no official endorsement should be inferred. I would like to thank Catherine Clement, Midian Kurland, and Warren Simmons for helpful comments on earlier drafts of this chapter.

REFERENCES

Anderson, J. R. (1982). Acquisition of cognitive skill. *Psychological Review, 89*(4), 369–406.

Becker, H. J. (1982). Microcomputers in the classroom: Dreams and realities. *Report No. 310. Center for Social Organization of Schools,* Johns Hopkins University, Baltimore.

Brooks, R. E. (1980). Studying programmer behavior experimentally: The problems of proper methodology. *Communications of the ACM, 23,* 207–213.

Dalbey, J., & Linn, M. (1984, April). Making precollege instruction in programming cognitively demanding: Issues and interventions. In K. Sheingold (Chair.), *Developmental studies of computer programming skills.* Symposium conducted at the meeting of the American Educational Research Association, New Orleans.

Kurland, D. M., Clement, C. A., Mawby, R., & Pea, R. D. (1984, April). The development of reasoning skills in relation to learning Logo programming. In K. Sheingold (Chair.), *Developmental studies of computer programming skills.* Symposium conducted at the meeting of the American Educational Research Association, New Orleans.

Kurland, D. M., Mawby, R., & Cahir, N. (1984, April). The development of programming expertise. In K. Sheingold (Chair.), *Developmental studies of computer programming skills.* Symposium conducted at the meeting of the American Educational Research Association, New Orleans.

Mawby, R. (1984, April). *Determining students' understanding of programming concepts.* Paper presented at the meeting of the American Educational Research Association, New Orleans.

Nickerson, R. S. (1982). Computer programming as a vehicle for teaching thinking skills. *Thinking: The Journal of Philosophy for Children, 4,* 42–48.

Pea, R. D., & Kurland, M. D. (1983). *On the cognitive prerequisites of learning computer programming.* (Technical report No. 18). New York: Center for Children and Technology, Bank Street College of Education.

Pennington, N. (1982). *Cognitive components of expertise in computer programming: A review of the literature* (Technical Report No. 46). Ann Arbor: University of Michigan Center for Cognitive Science.

Piaget, J. (1976). *The grasp of consciousness* (S. Wedgwood, Trans.). Cambridge, MA: Harvard University Press. (Original work published 1974)

Polya, G. (1957). *How to solve it.* New York: Doubleday–Anchor.

Simon, H. A. (1981). *The sciences of the artificial* (2nd ed.). Cambridge, MA: MIT Press.

Waldrop, M. M. (1984). The necessity of knowledge. *Science, 223,* 1279–1282.

Whitehead, A. N. (1929). *The aims of education and other essays.* New York: Macmillan.

22 Critical Thinking and the Critical Person

Richard W. Paul
Sonoma State University

Education is training in HOW to think rather than in WHAT to think; it is a confrontation, a dialogue between ways of assessing evidence and supporting conclusions. It implies that the teacher's primary job is that of making explicit the standards by which he separates facts from fancies, and the ways in which he discovers and selects his ultimate norms . . . This concept of teaching . . . requires that the purported facts be accompanied by the reasons why they are considered the facts. Thereby the teacher exposes his methods of reasoning to test and change. If the facts are in dispute . . . then the reasons why others do not consider them to be facts must also be presented, thus bringing alternative ways of thinking and believing into dialogue with each other.

—Emerson Shideler

INTRODUCTION

As the clarion call for critical thinking instruction from kindergarten to graduate school grows louder, it is natural that those responsible for classroom instruction, heavily overworked as typically they are, should look for simple answers to the question, "What is critical thinking?," answers that generate routine and simple in-service strategies. There is a low level of awareness of, and indeed a high degree of resistance to, recognizing how much of what is deeply ingrained in standard school and classroom procedures and mirrored in deep-seated ways of thinking about instruction on the part of teachers and administrators is in need of significant reformation, if students truly are to become critical thinkers in their daily personal, professional, and civic lives.

The purpose of this chapter is to clarify and develop some of the theoretical and practical implications of the concept of critical thinking. I touch base with the work of some of the leading critical thinking theorists. Some points of contrast are also developed with the general approach of cognitive psychologists. Social studies are used throughout the chapter as one major example of the problem. However, much of the explication is comprehensive in nature and consequently many of the more domain-specific questions of the reader are not addressed. I, along with most critical thinking theorists, believe that global insights into the multifaceted obstacles to critical reflection, critical inquiry, and critical discussion on the part of students, teachers, and people in general are crucial to sound design of critical thinking instruction. Such insights are severely limited to the degree that the "big picture" is not clearly and coherently grasped. For example, it is rare that any significant attention is given to John Passmore's claims that "being critical can be taught only by persons who can themselves freely participate in critical discussion" and that "In many systems of public instruction . . . it is a principal object of teacher training to turn out teachers who will firmly discourage free critical discussion."[1] It is certainly rare that teachers grasp where and when "free critical discussion" is essential, what it means to conduct it, and what is required to empower students to pursue it with understanding and self-command. What follows, I hope, contributes something to those foundational understandings, to the insights on which successful critical thinking instruction depends.

RATIONAL AND IRRATIONAL LEARNING

All rational learning presupposes rational assent. And, though we sometimes forget it, all learning is not automatically or even commonly rational. Much that we learn in everyday life is quite distinctively irrational. It is quite possible—and indeed the bulk of human learning is unfortunately of this character—to come to believe any number of things without knowing how or why. It is quite possible, in other words, to believe for irrational reasons: because those around us believe, because we are rewarded for believing, because we are afraid to disbelieve, because our vested interest is served by belief, because we are more

---

[1] John Passmore, "On Teaching to be Critical," included in *ThConcept of Education*, Routledge & Kegan Paul, London: 1967, pp. 192-211.

comfortable with belief, because we have ego identified ourselves, our image, or our personal being with belief. In all these cases, our beliefs are without rational grounding, without good reason and evidence, without the foundation a rational person demands. We become rational, on the other hand, to the extent that our beliefs and actions are grounded in good reasons and evidence; to the extent that we recognize and critique our own irrationality; to the extent that we are not moved by bad reasons and a multiplicity of irrational motives, fears, desires; to the extent that we have cultivated a passion for clarity, accuracy, and fairmindedness. These global skills, passions, and dispositions integrated into a way of acting and thinking are what characterize the rational, the educated, and, in my sense, the critical person.[2]

No one on this view is ever *fully* educated. Hence, we should view rational learning not as something completed by schooling but as something struggling to emerge against deep-seated, irrational, and uncritical tendencies and drives. It is quite possible for schooling to be structured in order to foster belief without regard to rational justification. To make rational belief a probable outcome of schooling requires special design and distinctive commitment.

THINKING CRITICALLY IN THE "STRONG" SENSE

It is not possible to develop a coherent concept of critical thinking without developing a coherent concept of rationality, irrationality, education, socialization, the critical person, and the critical society, as they bear on and mutually illuminate one another. This holistic approach distinguishes the mode of theorizing of most philosophers working on the concept of critical thinking from that commonly used by most cognitive psychologists concerned with the nature of thinking. There is a tendency among cognitive psychologists, for example, to treat cognitive processes and their "pathology" separate from any consideration of the affective, social, or political life of the thinker. Rarely are the research findings of clinical and social psychologists concerned with self-deception, egocen-

---

[2]For a sense of the dimensions in which critical thinking is called for, see the Phi Kappa Phi *National Forum* special issue on *Critical Thinking,* edited by myself, and including articles by Neil Postman, Sabini and Silver, Matthew Lipman, Edward Glaser, Robert Ennis, Michael Scriven, Ernest Boyer, and myself. Winter 1985.

See also my "Critical Thinking: Fundamental to Education For a Free Society," *Educational Leadership,* September 1984; "Teaching Critical Thinking in the Strong Sense," *Informal Logic,* 1982, Vol. *4,* p. 3; and "Bloom's Taxonomy and Critical Thinking Instruction," *Educational Leadership,* May 1985.

tricity, or ethnocentricity of thought integrated into the problem definitions of conclusions of cognitive psychology. This has the consequent[3]
that cognitive psychologists rarely focus on messy real-life multilogical
problems that cross disciplines and tend instead to restrict their attention
to artificial or self-contained monological problems, problems whose
solutions can typically be found in a dominant, field-specific conceptual
framework without reference to major personal or social bias. The more
basic and difficult human problems, for whose solutions there are competing frameworks, and in which the problem of bias and vested interest
bulks large, are routinely ignored.

It is hard to go very far into the core concept of the critical person,
however, without recognizing the centrality of multilogical thinking, the
ability to think accurately and fairmindedly within opposing points of
view and contradictory frames of reference. Multilogical problems,
whose fairminded treatment requires that we attempt to suspend our
egocentric tendency to confuse the framework of our own thinking with
"reality" and reason within opposing points of view, are among the most
significant human problems and among those most resistant to human
solutions. The problems of human understanding, of war and peace, of
economic, political, and social justice, of who our friends and who our
enemies are, of what we should accept as the most basic framework of our
thinking, of our own nature, our goodness and our evil, our history and
that of those we oppose, of how we should interpret our place in the
world, and how to best satisfy our needs and critically assess our
desires—all such problems are at the heart of the basic frustrations and
conflicts that plague human life and all require multisystem thinking. We
cannot justifiably assume that any one frame of reference or point of view
is preeminently correct, as the perspective within which these basic
human problems are to be most rationally settled. Schooling should
heighten the student's ability to distinguish monological from multilogical
problems and to address each as they impact on the conduct of everyday
life.

On this view, we distinguish two important senses of critical thinking,
a *weak* sense and a *strong* one. A person who thought critically only with
respect to monological issues and, as a result, attacked multilogical issues
with a pronounced monological bias would be understood as merely
having mastered the art of weak sense critical thinking. He would lack the
ability, and presumably the disposition also, to critique his own most

---

[3]"Dialogical Thinking: Critical Thought Essential to the Acquisition of Rational Knowledge and Passions," delivered at the *Connecticut Thinking Skills Conference*, March 11–13,
1985, forthcoming in *Teaching Thinking Skills: Theory and Practice*, W. H. Freeman, New
York, edited by Joan Baron and Robert J. Sternberg.

fundamental categories of thought and analysis. He would, as a result, lack the ability to enter sympathetically into, and reconstruct, the strongest arguments and reasons for points of view fundamentally opposed to his own. When the root cause of his monological thinking was a result of an unconscious commitment to a personal point of view, his thinking would be egocentric; when the result of an unconscious commitment to a social or cultural point of view, his thinking would be ethnocentric. In both cases he would think more or less exclusively within his own frame of reference. He might use the basic vocabulary of critical thinking with rhetorical skill; his arguments and reasons might be impressive to those who already shared his framework of thought; but he would lack the basic drives and abilities of what I call *strong sense* critical thinking: (a) an ability to question deeply his own framework of thought, (b) an ability to reconstruct sympathetically and imaginatively the strongest versions of points of view and frameworks of thought opposed to his own, and (c) an ability to reason dialectically (multilogically) in such a way as to determine when his own point of view is at its weakest and when an opposing point of view is at its strongest. A strong sense critical thinker is not routinely blinded by his own point of view. He knows that he *has* a point of view and therefore recognizes on the basis of what framework of assumptions and ideas his own thinking is based. He realizes the necessity of putting his own assumptions and ideas to the test of the strongest objections that can be leveled against them. If he is a proponent of a socialist economic system, to use a political example, he is able to analyze economic events from the perspective of an insightful proponent of capitalism. If he is a proponent of a capitalist economic system, he is able to analyze economic events from the perspective of an insightful proponent of socialism. This implies, by the way, that when economics is taught it should not be taught in order to presuppose capitalism, socialism, or any other economic system as *the* correct one. To put it another way, the issue as to what economic system is most justified is a multilogical issue. In a related way, a strong sense critical thinker's thought is disciplined to avoid confusing concepts that belong in different categories. For example, he does not confuse "democracy," a political concept, with "capitalism," an economic concept. He realizes that if there is an important connection between democracy and capitalism it must be argued for, not assumed, that *free enterprise* ought not to be routinely injected into U.S. social studies texts as a neutral synonym for *capitalism,* any more than people's *democracy* ought to be routinely injected into Russian social studies texts as a neutral synonym for Russian communism. If he reads a school text he recognizes when terms are being used in this question-begging way. A teacher who values strong sense critical thinking fosters these abilities.

The importance of strong sense critical thinking has been underscored, each in his own terms, by most leading critical thinking theorists: Robert Ennis[4], Harvey Siegel[5], Israel Scheffler[6], Michael Scriven[7], Matthew Lipman[8], R. S. Peters[9], John Passmore[10], Edward Glaser[11], Ralph Johnson[12], J. Anthony Blair[13], and others. I exemplify the point briefly with four of them: Ennis, Siegel, Scriven, and Peters.

Robert Ennis defines critical thinking as "reasonable reflective thinking that is concerned with what to do or believe." He argues that the various component cognitive skills essential to critical thinking cannot be effectively used to achieve genuine "rational reflective thinking" unless they are used in conjunction with, as the driving manifestations of, a complex of dispositions. For example, in and of themselves the component cognitive skills of critical thinking can be used to serve either closed-mindedness or open-mindedness of thought. If the student has developed genuine open-mindedness, Ennis claims, he will: (a) Consider seriously

---

[4]Robert Ennis heads the Illinois Critical Thinking Project, co-authored the Cornell Critical Thinking Tests, and has written many seminal articles on critical thinking, beginning with his "A Concept of Critical Thinking," *Harvard Educational Review*, 1962, Vol. *32* (1), 81-111.

[5]Harvey Siegel has developed a number of ideas implicit in the writings of Israel Sheffler. Most important for critical thinking theory of Siegel's contribution is his "Critical Thinking as Educational Ideal," *The Educational Forum*, November 1980, pp. 7-23.

[6]See Israel Scheffler's *Reason and Teaching*, Bobbs–Merrill, New York: 1973; and *Conditions of Knowledge*, Scott Foresman, Chicago: 1965.

[7]See Scriven's "Critical For Survival" in the *National Forum*'s special issue on critical thinking and his textbook, *Reasoning*, McGraw-Hill, New York: 1976.

[8]Matthew Lipman has developed a multitude of innovative instructional strategies for bringing critical reflection into classroom discussions, third through twelfth grades, in the process of creating the *Philosophy for Children Program*.

[9]See R. S. Peters' *Reason and Compassion*, Routledge & Kegan Paul, London: 1973.

[10]Passmore, op. cit.

[11]Edward Glaser is one of the founding fathers of the critical thinking movement in the United States. Its early stirrings can be traced back to his *An Experiment in the Development of Critical Thinking* (1941) and his development with Watson of the *Watson-Glaser Critical Thinking Test* (1940).

[12]Ralph Johnson and J. Anthony Blair have been the major Canadian leaders in the Informal Logic/Critical Thinking movement. They have organized two major international conferences at the University of Windsor, have written many important papers in the field, and they edit *Informal Logic* (the major journal for those working on the theory of critical thinking) and have written an excellent text, *Logical Self-Defense*, McGraw-Hill, Toronto: 1977.

[13]Ralph Johnson and J. Anthony Blair have been the major Canadian leaders in the Informal Logic/Critical Thinking movement. They have organized two major international conferences at the University of Windsor, have written many important papers in the field, and they edit *Informal Logic* (the major journal for those working on the theory of critical thinking) and have written an excellent text, *Logical Self-Defense*, McGraw-Hill, Toronto: 1977.

other points of view than one's own ("dialogical thinking"); (b) reason from premises with which one disagrees—without letting the disagreement interfere with one's reasoning ("suppositional thinking"); (c) withhold judgment when the evidence and reasons are insufficient.[14]

Harvey Siegel argues that students will not develop into genuine critical thinkers unless they develop "the critical spirit," and that students will not develop the critical spirit unless they are taught in "the critical manner":

> The critical manner is that manner of teaching that reinforces the critical spirit. A teacher who utilizes the critical manner seeks to encourage in his or her students the skills, habits, and dispositions necessary for the development of the critical spirit. This means, first, that the teacher always recognizes the right of the student to question and demand reasons; and consequently recognizes an obligation to provide reasons whenever demanded. The critical manner thus demands of a teacher a willingness to subject all beliefs and practices to scrutiny, and so to allow students the genuine opportunity to understand the role reasons play in justifying thought and action. The critical manner also demands honesty of a teacher: reasons presented by a teacher must be genuine reasons, and a teacher must honestly appraise the power of those reasons. In addition, the teacher must submit his or her reasons to the independent evaluation of the student. Teaching in the critical manner is thus teaching so as to develop in the students skills and attitudes consonant with critical thinking. It is, as Scheffler puts it, an attempt to initiate students into the rational life, a life in which the critical quest for reasons is a dominant and integrating motive.[15]

The point that Siegel is making is to say that in order for the student to develop the passions of a strong sense critical thinker (the passion for accuracy, clarity, and fairmindedness), it is necessary for the teacher continually to model those passions in his manner of teaching. The component microskills of critical thinking (such as the ability to clarify an issue, to distinguish evidence from conclusion, to recognize assumptions, implications, and contradictions, and so forth) do not become the skills of a (strong sense) critical thinker, except to the degree that they are integrated into "a life in which the critical quest for reasons is a dominant and integrating motive."

Michael Scriven represents (strong sense) critical thinking skills as not only requiring "a whole shift of values for most of us"[16] but also as essential for "survival" in a world in which "the wrong decision can mean

---

[14]Ennis, "Critical Thinking," a handout developed in July 1985, *Illinois Critical Thinking Project,* University of Illinois/Champaign.

[15]"Critical Thinking as Educational Ideal," op. cit., p. 11.

[16]*Reasoning,* op. cit., p. ix.

injury or long-term commitment to a disasterous form of life such as addiction or criminality or resented parenthood."[17] If we want students to "transfer" their critical thinking skills to situations such as these, we need to exercise them in a fairminded way on controversial (multilogical) issues:

> the real case, in dealing with controversial issues is the case as put by real people who believe in what they are saying. But the schools—and to a varying but often equal extent the colleges—are not willing to let there be that kind of serious discussion of the argument on both sides of controversial issues. Of course, they don't mind having the bad guys' position represented by someone who doesn't agree with it, in the course of dismissing it. But only the completely naive would suppose that such a presentation is likely to make the best case for the position. The notions of a fair hearing, or of confronting your accuser which are so deeply entrenched in our system of justice obviously transfer immediately to the intellectual sphere. If you want to hear the arguments for a political position other than those of the majority parties, for example the political position that the largest countries on earth espouse, you cannot possibly assume that it will be fully and fairly represented by someone to whom it is anathema.[18]

Unfortunately, it is natural to expect a good deal of fear in many teachers who are faced with the prospect of highlighting controversial issues in the classroom. It is fair to say, I believe, that most teachers have little or no background experience working with such issues. Many are familiar only with processes for laying out and testing for "right" answers, not with processes by which contradictory arguments are assessed in terms of their relative strength in dialogical or dialectical settings. There are, in other words, both affective and cognitive obstacles to the genuine fostering of fairmindedness. Some of the affective obstacles are in educators themselves.

R. S. Peters has developed the significance of the affective side of reason and critical thought in his defense of the necessity of "rational passions":

> There is, for instance, the hatred of contradictions and inconsistencies, together with the love of clarity and hatred of confusion without which words could not be held to relatively constant meanings and testable rules and generalizations stated. A reasonable man cannot, without some special explanation, slap his sides with delight or express indifference if he is told that what he says is confused, incoherent and perhaps riddled with contradictions.

---

[17]"Critical For Survival," op. cit., p. 9.
[18]Ibid.

. . .

Reason is the antithesis of arbitrariness. In its operation it is supported by the appropriate passions which are mainly negative in character—the hatred of irrelevance, special pleading and arbitrary fiat. The more developed emotion of indignation is aroused when some excess of arbitrariness is perpetuated in a situation where people's interests and claims are at stake. The positive side of this is the passion for fairness and impartial consideration of claims.

. . .

A man who is prepared to reason must feel strongly that he must follow the arguments and decide things in terms of where they lead. He must have a sense of the givenness, of the impersonality of such considerations. In so far as thoughts about persons enter his head they should be tinged with the respect which is due to another who, like himself, may have a point of view which is worth considering, who may have a glimmering of the truth which has so far eluded himself. A person who proceeds in this way, who is influenced by such passions, is what we call a reasonable man.[19]

What implications does this have for students and teachers? It entails that the affective life of the student must be brought into the heart of classroom instruction and dealt with in the context of the problem of thinking in a fairminded way. Students must come to terms not only with how they feel about issues both inside and outside the curriculum, but also with the extent to which those feelings are irrational. The teacher, on the other hand, must model rational passions and set the example of showing no favoritism to particular positions on those issues. The students must become convinced that the teacher is playing the role of a fair and reasonable referee and is, in other words, an expert in nurturing the process by which truth and understanding is sought, not an authoritative judge of what actually is true or false. Questions rather than assertions should characterize the utterances of the teacher. The classroom environment should be structured so that students feel encouraged to decide for themselves what is and is not so. The teacher should treat no idea or point of view as in itself absurd, stupid, or "dangerous," irrespective of his or her personal views or those of the community. The teacher should shield his or her students from the pressure to conform to peer group or community. Free and open discussion should be the sacred right of all classrooms.

It should be clear that strong sense critical thinking is embedded in a personal, social, and educational ideal. It is not simply a complex of atomistic cognitive skills. To think critically in this sense requires, as

---

[19]*Reason and Compassion,* op. cit., p. 79.

Passmore points out, "initiative, independence, courage, (and) imagination."[20] Let us now look briefly at the historical foundation for this concept.

CRITICAL THINKING AND THE SOCRATIC IDEAL

The concept of strong sense critical thinking, of critical thought integrated into the personal and social life of the individual, is not a new one. It was introduced into Western intellectual tradition in the chronicles of the life and death of Socrates (470–399 BC), one of the most important and influential teachers of ancient Greece. As a teacher he was committed to the importance of ideas and their critique in the conduct of everyday human life. It is to him that the precept "the unexamined life is not worth living" is attributed. It is in him that the ideal of conscientious civil disobedience and critical autonomy of thought is first to be found. He illustrated the possibility and the value of sharpness of mind, clarity of thought, and commitment to practical insight based on autonomous reason. He championed reason, the rational life, and a rationally structured ethic, the intimate fusion of reason and passion. He disclaimed authority on his own part but claimed the right to independently criticize all authoritative beliefs and established institutions. He made it clear that a teacher cannot be an educator in the fullest sense unless he is capable of criticizing the received assumptions of his social group and is willing to nurture a climate of questioning and doubt among his students. He demonstrated the intimate connection between a passionate love of truth and knowledge, the ability to learn through the art of skilled questioning, and the willingness to expose and face personally and socially embarrassing truths. He was quite conversant with persons who had a sophistic (weak sense) command of critical thinking skills, who could through their skills of persuasion and knowledge of the vulnerabilities of people make the false appear true and the true false.

Socrates taught by joining in a discussion with others who thought they knew or understood a basic or important truth, for example, what justice is, or knowledge or virtue. When questioned by Socrates—who probed the justification and foundation for the belief, examining its consistency or inconsistency with other beliefs—it became clear that his discussants did not know or understand what they at first thought they did. As a result of Socrates' mode of question, his "students" became clear that they lacked fundamental knowledge. Of course not all of Socrates' discussants appreciated the discovery. But for those who did a new drive to seek out

---

[20]Op. cit., p. 198.

knowledge was engendered. This included an appreciation of dialectical thinking, a recognition of the need to subject putative knowledge to probing questioning, especially from the vantage point of opposing points of view. Socrates' students became comfortable with and adept in the art of dialectical questioning. All beliefs had first to pass the test of critical scrutiny through dialectical challenges before they were to be accepted.

The social reaction to Socrates' mode of teaching through probing questions illustrated the inevitable antagonism between schooling as socialization into accepted beliefs and practices and schooling as education in the art of autonomous thought. Although he did not foster any doctrines of his own (other than the values of intellectual integrity and critical autonomy), he was executed for "not believing in the gods the state believes in . . . and also for corrupting the young" (see Plato's *Apology*).

Socrates' practice laid the cornerstone for the history of critical thought. He provided us with our first historic glimpse into the fact that the organizing concepts by which humans live their lives often do not reflect the organizing concepts through which they express their thoughts publicly. It is essential that we keep his example in mind when we conceptualize and elaborate the problem of learning to think critically. If we do, we certainly will not conceive of critical thinking in narrow intradisciplinary terms, nor will we ignore the significance of the affective dimensions of thought. It is intriguing to imagine classrooms in which the example of Socrates is highlighted and encouraged as a model of what school is all about.

THE EGOCENTRICALLY CRITICAL PERSON

Piaget's basic model for the egocentric mind, which he developed in studying the thinking of children, has significant application, with appropriate translation, to much adult thinking and therefore significant application for the design of critical thinking instruction. Rarely are adults practiced in reciprocal critical thought, able, that is, to place themselves or reason within their antagonists' point of view. Rarely are they experienced in making conscious the structure of their own thought. Rarely are they able, as Socrates unhappily discovered, to explain intelligibly how they came to their beliefs, nor to provide rational justifications for them.

The egocentrism of most adult thought is perfectly analogous to the egocentrism of childish thought, as Piaget characterizes it in *Judgment and Reasoning in the Child:*

'egocentrism of thought necessarily entails a certain degree of unconsciousness' (137) with the egocentric thinker 'in a perpetual state of belief', 'confident in his own ideas', 'naturally . . . (untroubled) about the reasons and motives which have guided his reasoning process', 'only under the pressure of argument and opposition . . . (seeking) to justify himself in the eyes of others . . .', '. . . incapable either by introspection or retrospection of capturing the successive steps . . . (his) mind has taken' (137/138) '. . . not conscious of the meaning which they assign to the concepts and words they use . . .' (149) suffers from 'illusions of perspective' (165), '. . . being ignorant of his own ego, takes his own point of view to be absolute, and fails to establish . . . that reciprocity which alone would ensure objectivity' (197) '. . . intelligent without being particularly logical', 'thought . . . at the service of desire', 'experience undeceives him only on very special technical points', 'simply believes . . . without trying to find the truth' (203), 'assimilates everything he hears to his own point of view' (208). 'He does not try to prove whether such and such of his ideas does or does not correspond to reality. When the question is put to him, he evades it. It does not interest him, and it is even alien to his whole mental attitude.' (p. 247)[21]

There is a natural tendency in the human mind to think egocentrically, especially in domains of significant personal or social interests. Egocentrism is, in some sense, as typical of adult as childish thought. It takes a special cultivated discipline to recognize and attempt to correct for it. This becomes apparent when one formulates basic safeguards against egocentrism of thought and attempts to cultivate an interest in students or people in general in utilizing them. Consider, for example, the platitude "one cannot disagree with a position one does not understand," that in other words "judgment presupposes understanding." Cultivating it as a critical principle involves taking steps to ensure one has a clear sense of what someone else is saying before one "disagrees" with that person. My experience is that most people, including some with a good deal of schooling, tend uncritically to assume understanding when they have done little or nothing to test their understanding and, as a result, are much too quick to "disagree." Most people are surprised if after they disagree with something said, a person says, "What exactly did you take me to be saying that you are disagreeing with?" Often they will be puzzled and say, "Well, perhaps you had better state your position again," or words to that effect.

---

[21]Piaget, *Judgment and Reasoning in the Child*, Littlefield, Adams, Totowa, NJ: 1976. Compare R. S. Peters: "The connection of being unreasonable with egocentricity is obvious enough. There is lacking even the stability in behavior that comes from acting in the light of established beliefs and practices. Beliefs tend to be infected with arbitrariness and particularity. Little attempt is made to fit them into a coherent system. A behavior is governed largely by wants and aversions of an immediate, short-term character. Little account is taken of the viewpoint or claims of others. Indeed, the behavior of others is seen largely in a self-referential way as it impinges on, threatens or thwarts the demands of the greedy, restless ego . . . ," op. cit., p. 97.

Or consider a more profound safeguard against egocentrism of thought, an attempt to probe the justification for one's belief by formulating sympathetically the strongest arguments for rejecting that belief from opposing points of view. Rarely after confidently stating a belief can most adults summarize strong arguments and reasons that have persuaded intelligent, rational others to believe in opposing positions. The egocentric person, or better, all of us to the extent that we are egocentric, spontaneously thinks along lines that serve to justify his or her fears, desires, and vested interests. Few people have developed a "Socratic" character. As a result, a good deal of everyday critical thought is egocentric in nature. We unconsciously tend to think in the following way: "Your thinking is well founded and insightful to the extent that it agrees with or supports my own. If it does not, then, as a matter of course, it is 'wrong' and I am obliged to criticize it." It is important to see, to rephrase the point, that much "critical" thought on the part of adults is not fairminded but rather is egocentrically motivated and structured, lacking fairmindedness at it is very core. Is it not also accurate to say that most adults had few opportunities in their schooling to grapple with their own tendencies to think irrationally?

THE SOCIOCENTRICALLY CRITICAL PERSON AND THE IDEAL OF A CRITICAL SOCIETY

In my view, Piaget rightly identifies uncritical thought with a tendency toward egocentrism, and critical thought with a tendency toward reciprocity. He is aware of but nowhere develops the recognition that egocentrism of thought tends to develop into and partially merge with sociocentrism of thought:

> The child begins with the assumption that the immediate attitudes arising out of our own special surroundings and activities are the only ones possible. This state of mind, which we shall term the unconscious egocentricity (both cognitive and affective) of the child is at first a stumbling-block both to the understanding of his own country and to the development of objective relations with other countries. Furthermore, to overcome this egocentric attitude it is necessary to train the faculty for cognitive and affective integration; this is a slow and laborious process consisting mainly in efforts at 'reciprocity,' and at each new stage of the process, egocentricity re-emerges in new guises farther and farther removed from the child's initial center of interest. There are the various forms of sociocentricity—a survival of the original egocentricity—and they are the cause of subsequent disturbances or tensions, any understanding of which must be based on an

accurate analysis of the initial stages and of the elementary conflicts between egocentricity and understanding of others (Reciprocity).[22]

One manifestation of the irrational mind is to uncritically presuppose the truth of beliefs and doctrines embedded in social life or values. We intellectually and affectively absorb, like plankton, common frames of reference from the social settings in which we live our lives. Our interests and purposes find a place within a socially absorbed picture of the world. We use that picture of the world to test the claims of contesting others. We imaginatively rehearse situations within portions of that picture. We rarely, however, describe that picture as a picture, as an image constructed by one social group as against that of another. It is difficult, therefore, to place that picture at arm's length, so to speak, and, for a time, suspend our acquiescence to it. That our thought is often disturbed and distorted by ethnocentric tendencies is rarely an abiding recognition. At best, it occurs in most people in fleeting glimpses, if we are to judge by the extent to which it is recognized explicitly in everyday thought.

Although there is a good deal of talk about and research into ethnocentrism or sociocentrism as a problem for education, there has yet to be devised a reasonably effective means of combatting it. The tendency for institutions and beliefs to become "sacred" and "cherished" and the thinking that critiques them conceptualized as "dangerous," "subversive," or at least "disturbing" and "unsettling," is probably as strong as ever it has been. Habits, customs, and faiths become deeply embedded in how we define ourselves, and intolerance, censorship, and oppression never seem to be such by those who carry them out in the name of "true belief."

Socrates is not the only thinker to imagine a society in which independent critical thought became embodied in the concrete day-to-day lives of individuals; others, including William Graham Sumner, America's distinguished conservative anthropologist, have formulated the ideal:

The critical habit of thought, if usual in a society, will pervade all its mores, because it is a way of taking up the problems of life. Men educated in it cannot be stampeded by stump orators and are never deceived by dithyrambic oratory. They are slow to believe. They can hold things as possible or probable in all degrees, without certainty and without pain. They can wait for evidence and weigh evidence, uninfluenced by the emphasis or confidence with which assertions are made on one side or the other. They can resist appeals to their dearest prejudices and all kinds of cajolery. Educa-

---

[22]Piaget, from "The Development in Children of the Idea of the Homeland and of Relations with Other Countries," *The International Social Science Bulletin,* Vol. III, no. 3, 1951, pp. 561–578.

tion in the critical faculty is the only education of which it can be truly said that it makes good citizens.[23]

Until critical habits of thought come to pervade our society, however, there will be a tendency for schools as social institutions to transmit the prevailing world view more or less uncritically, and, of course, to transmit it as reality, not as a picture of reality. Our ability to solve social and international problems becomes constrained by the solutions that are credible and plausible within the prevailing ideas and assumptions of our world view. When solutions are suggested from the vantage point of contrary world views, they will appear patently false to us because they will appear to be based on false ideas; that is, ideas that don't square with "reality" (more accurately, with our own ideas of reality). Of course, those who live in societies with divergent world views will themselves experience the frustration of interpreting our proposed solutions as patently false because they will appear to them to be based on false ideas; that is, ideas that don't square with reality (more accurately, with their ideas of reality). Hence, one society's freedom-fighters are another society's terrorists, and vice versa. Each is outraged at the flagrant propaganda of the other and is forced to conclude that the other must knowingly be distorting the facts, and hence is evil to the core. If a citizen in any country questions the prevailing labels, it is common for his or her patriotism to be questioned.

Ideas, in other words, do not enter into school life in socially neutral but rather in socially biased ways. To entertain the concept of students thinking critically entails developing their ability to recognize and so to question this process.

The sociocentrically critical person may use the vocabulary of critical thinking. He may develop facility in its microskills. But he will inadvertently function as an apologist for the prevailing world view nevertheless. He will doubtless conceive of himself as a hard-headed realist, fundamentally beyond "ideology" or naive "idealism," but there will be little reciprocity in his thought.

A critical society will emerge only to the extent that it becomes socially unacceptable routinely to presuppose rather than explicitly identify and argue for one's fundamental ideas and assumptions. In the schools of a critical society, both teachers and students would recognize multilogical issues as ones that demand dialogical rather than monological treatment. Reasoning within opposing points of view would be the rule, not the rare exception. Social studies instruction in particular would play a significant

---

[23]William Graham Sumner, *Folkways,* originally 1906, reissued by Dover Publications, New York: 1959, p. 633.

role in fostering reciprocal multilogical thinking and so would contribute in a special way to the nurturing in the citizenry of values and skills essential to the conduct of everyday life in a critical manner.

SOCIAL STUDIES AND THE FOSTERING OF RATIONAL BELIEF

We can assess any school program for its educative value, on this view, by determining the extent to which *rational* as against *irrational* belief formation is fostered. To the extent that students are merely memorizing what is said by the teacher or textbook, or presupposing the correctness of one point of view, and so developing no appreciation for the nature of the evidence required to justify rational belief in the area of their learning, to that extent the school is fostering irrational learning and irrational belief.

Social studies instruction is an excellent area to canvas in this regard because there is a pronounced and natural tendency in it to inculcate an uncritical monological nationalistic perspective, despite the fact that all the major issues in the field are by nature multilogical. The tendency is natural because it is natural, as pointed out earlier, for people within a country or culture to ego identify with it and hence to assume rather than question the policies of its leaders. The result is that the history of those policies and of the social representation of them gravitates continually in a self-serving direction. Reason is inadvertently made to serve an intellectually dishonorable function: the rationalization of the prevailing structure of power and the idealization of the national character. This is what Karl Mannheim identified as the inevitable development of *ideology*.[24] Louis Wirth suggests the practical problems for thought that it engenders: "Even today open, frank, and 'objective' inquiry into the most sacred and cherished institutions and beliefs is more or less seriously restricted in every country of the world. It is virtually impossible, for instance, even in England and America, to enquire into the actual facts regarding communism, no matter how disinterestedly, without running the risk of being labelled a communist" (p. XIV, preface).[25]

At the same time, the field is clearly multi logical; that is to say, there are inevitably multiple perspectives through which the issues in the field may be intellectually defined, analyzed, and "settled." There are inevitably—to put it another way—*schools* of social thought. Whether one looks

---

[24]See Karl Mannheim's magnificent classic *Ideology and Utopia,* a seminal work whose contribution to theory of critical thinking has yet to be absorbed.

[25]Ibid., Louis Worth in his preface to Mannheim's *Ideology and Utopia.*

at the classic theorists (Durkheim, Weber, Marx, Mannheim, Sumner, etc.) or one examines those more recent theorists (Sorokin, Parsons, Mills, Merton, Presman, Garfinkel, Berger, etc.), it is clear that there is no ultimate agreement about the frame of reference by means of which social behavior is to be represented and understood. Those with a more "conservative" slant on the world inevitably come to different fundamental conclusions about people and world events than those with a more "liberal" slant, and there is no way to abstract all discussion and study from foundational disputes derivative of conflicting frames of reference. If students are to have a shot at a rational understanding of social events, they need not only recognize this but also enter the debate actively. They need to hear and themselves make the case that can be made for a variety of conservative, liberal, and radical interpretations of events. They need to develop the critical tools for assessing the differences among these views. These skills develop only with practice.

When students cover a conflict between two countries—especially when one of those countries is their own—they need to hear the case that can be made, not just from one but from both countries' perspectives. Often, other perspectives are relevant as well. American text book writers canvassing the Cold War, for example, do not identify themselves as arguing for one selective representation of it. They do not identify themselves as having a pro-American bias. They do not suggest that they represent only one out of a number of points of view. They suggest rather an "objective" account is being presented, as if the issues were intrinsically monological in nature and so settleable by considering merely one point of view. They imply that there is no need for the reader to consider other points of view on the *Cold War*. They imply that the facts speak for themselves and that they (the textbooks) contain the facts, all the facts, and nothing but the facts. There is nothing dialogical about their modes of canvassing the material nor in the assignments that accompany the account the student is inevitably led to believe.

The fact that some of the most distinguished historians have concluded that the United States bears a large share of the blame for the Cold War is never, to my knowledge, even casually mentioned. It would be unintelligible to most American students and their teachers to hear a distinguished historian like Henry Steele Commager speak of the Cold War as follows: "How are we to explain our obsession with communism, our paranoid hostility to the Soviet Union, our preoccupations with the Cold War, our reliance on military rather than political or diplomatic solutions, and our new readiness to entertain as a possibility what was long regarded as unthinkable—atomic warfare."[26] The notion that Americans might be

---

[26]Commager, *The Atlantic*, March 1982.

subject to an "obsession" or be a victim of "paranoid hostility" is entirely inconsistent with the way American textbooks characterize the country, its philosophy, behavior, and values.

Or consider Arnold Toynbee's characterization:

> In examining America's situation in the world today, I can say, with my hand on my heart, that my feelings are sympathetic, not malicious. After all, mere regard for self-interest, apart from any more estimable considerations, would deter America's allies from wishing America ill . . . (But) today America is no longer the inspirer and leader of the World Revolution . . . by contrast, America is today, the leader of a world-wide, anti-revolutionary movement in defense of vested interests. She now stands for what Rome stood for. Rome consistently supported the rich against the poor in all foreign communities; and since the poor, so far, have always been far more numerous than the rich, Rome's policy made for inequality, for injustice, and for the least happiness of the greatest numbers. America's decision to adopt Rome's role has been deliberate, if I have gauged it right.[27]

These views would shock the average American. Their schooling has given them no inkling that America's and Britain's most distinguished historians could have such a low estimation of America's policies. What they would understand is the recent California State Assembly resolution, which was endorsed on a vote of 52–0, that held that the Vietnam war was waged for a noble purpose.

Similar points can be made about every major issue in history and Social "Science." They are all approachable from more than one point of view. All history, to put it another way, is history-written-from-a-point-of-view, just as all social perception is perception-from-a-point-of-view. There are, inevitably, different philosophies of history and society based on different presuppositions about the nature of people and human society. Different organizing concepts and root metaphors are inevitably used by different schools of historical and social research.

The result is that a rational approach to historical, sociological, and anthropological issues needs to reflect this diversity of approach. Just as in a jury trial we insist on hearing both the pro and con cases before we come to a judgment, irrespective of the strength of the case that can be made for either. So, too, must we insist as rational students of history and human society to hear the case made for more than one interpretation of key events and trends so that our own view may take into account this relevant evidence and reasoning. Intellectual honesty demands this and education requires it. It is irrational to assume a priori the correctness of

---

[27]Toynbee, *America and the World Revolution,* Oxford University Press, New York and London: 1962, p. 92.

one of these perspectives and intellectually irresponsible to teach in order to make fundamental frame of reference decisions for our students. Once students are exposed to different conflicting perspectives, they need to experience the process of actually arguing the case for them, of role playing the thought of those who insightfully hold them. This requires that students learn how to collect the "facts" that each side marshals in defense of its views and their divergent analyses of the key terms used. For example, what exactly is the difference between groups we label *freedom fighters* and those we label *terrorists?* How are we to define them without presupposing the truth of someone's ideology. These crucial terms and many others that are current in social disputes are often used in self-serving ways by nations and groups, begging most of the crucial social and moral issues. Students need skills in breaking down ideologically biased uses of them. This requires that they develop concepts that do not presuppose specific national ideological slants. This, in turn, requires that they engage in the argumentation for and against their application in key cases.

Unfortunately, even when critical thinking is made into an explicit instructional objective and significant attention is given to formulation of curriculum, unless teachers and curriculum specialists have internalized the concept of strong sense critical thinking, it is not unusual for sociocentrically weak sense critical thinking skills to be fostered, at the expense of potential strong sense skills.

Consider the following critical thinking writing prompts that are part of a series of similarly constructed items for inclusion in a State Department of Education state-wide testing program:

Critical Thinking Writing Prompt
History-Social Science

THE COLD WAR: CUBAN MISSILE CRISIS

In 1962 an international crisis erupted when the Soviet Union installed missile-launching equipment in Cuba. Cuba is only 90 miles from the United States and many Americans felt threatened by the missile bases. Others felt that providing Cuba with such powerful weapons would upst the balance of power in the western hemisphere.

Directions: Based on this information and the information in your textbook about the Cuban Missile Crisis (you may use your

textbook during this assignment), write a letter to President
Kennedy. In the letter, explain YOUR position on the Cuban
situation. Convince him to take a particular course of action
and explain why you want him to pursue that course.

• State your position clearly.
• Support your position with facts and examples.

John F. Kennedy
President of the United States

Dear Mr. President:

_____

_____

_____

_____

_____

_____

_____

_____

_____

_____

_____

Critical Thinking Writing Prompt
History-Social Science

THE COLD WAR: CUBAN MISSILE CRISIS

Directions: Read the conversation below that might have taken place
between two United States citizens during the Cuban missile
crisis in 1962.

Speaker 1: "These photographs in the newspaper show that beyond a doubt that Russians are building missile bases in Cuba. It's time we took some strong action and did something about it. Let's get some bombers down there."

Speaker 2: "I agree that there are Russian missiles in Cuba, but I don't agree with the solution you suggest. What would the world think about America dropping bombs on a neighboring small island?"

Speaker 3: "I think the only way to deal with the threat of force is force. If we do nothing, it's the same as saying it's okay to let them put in missiles that will threaten the whole hemisphere. Let's eliminate those missile bases now with military force."

Speaker 2: "The solution you propose would certainly eliminate those bases, but innocent people might be killed, and world opinion might be against us. What if we try talking to the Russians first and then try a blockade of their ships around Cuba, or something like that?"

Speaker 1: "That kind of weak response won't get us anywhere. Communists only understand force."

Speaker 2: "I think we should try other less drastic measures that won't result in loss of life. Then, if they don't work, use military action."

Imagine that you are a concerned citizen in 1962. Based on the information above, write a letter to President Kennedy about the missile crisis. Take a position and explain to President Kennedy what you think should be done about the missiles in Cuba and why.

• State your position clearly.
• Use information from the conversation above and from what you know about the missile crisis to support your position.

Critical Thinking Writing Prompt
History-Social Science

Directions: Read the information below and answer the questions that follow.

THE COLD WAR: CUBAN MISSILE CRISIS

In 1962 an international crisis erupted when the Soviet Union installed missile-launching equipment in Cuba. Because Cuba is only 90 miles from Florida, many Americans felt threatened by the missile bases. On October 26, 1962, President Kennedy sent the following letter to the Soviet Union's premier, Nikita Khrushchev:

"You would agree to remove these weapons systems from Cuba under appropriate United Nations' supervision . . . the first ingredient is the cessation of work on missile sites in Cuba. . . ."

Nikita Khrushchev responded in a letter shortly thereafter by saying:

"We accept your proposal, and have ordered the Soviet vessels bound for Cuba but not yet within the area of American warships' piratical activities to stay out of the interception area."

1. Based on the information above about the Cuban missile crisis, what do you think the central issue or concern is?

_____

_____

2. List two facts in the information about the missile crisis.

_____

_____

3. Do you see any words in either President Kennedy's or Premier Khrushchev's letters that might be considered biased or "loaded"? Find which one or ones are "loaded" and list why they are "loaded."

_____

_____

_____

4. Based on the information above, which side do you think is the aggressor? Why?

_____

_____

_____

5. Khruschev had spoken earlier of the need for "peaceful coexistence" between the U.S. and USSR. Is arming Cuba with missiles CONSIST-ENT with his statement about peaceful coexistence? Why or why not?

_____

_____

_____

6. If you had an opportunity to interview Khrushchev in 1962, what question would you ask to find out why he placed missiles in Cuba?

_____

_____

_____

7. President Kennedy was convinced that there actually were missile bases in Cuba. If you were President Kennedy in 1962, what information would YOU need to conclude that missile bases actually existed in Cuba?

_____

_____

_____

8. If Cuba had been permitted to install missile bases, what affect would this have had on Cuba's relationships with other countries?

_____

_____

_____

_____

Critical Thinking/Writing Prompt
History-Social Science

THE COLD WAR: CUBAN MISSILE CRISIS

Directions: Read the information below about missiles in Cuba and answer the questions that follow.

In 1962 an international crisis erupted when the Soviet Union installed missile-launching equipment in Cuba. Some of the facts relating to the incident are:

1. Photographs of Cuba taken by United States planes show missile sites under construction in Cuba.

2. Long-range missiles are observed near the sites.

3. Russian supply ships are bringing missile base equipment and technicians to Cuba.

4. Cuba is only 90 miles from the United States.

5. The President's military advisers recommend that the missiles be removed.

1. What is the central issue?

_____

_____

2. Write one question you might want to ask the United States military advisers.

_____

_____

3. Write one question you might want to ask Soviet Premier Khruschev.

_____

_____

4. What does the United States assume that Cuba will do with the missiles?

_____

_____

5. List two actions the United States might have taken in response to this crisis.

_____

_____

_____

6. List two facts that support one of the actions identified in item 5.

_____

_____

_____

7. Imagine are a concerned citizen who has been following the above events with great interest. You decide to write a letter to the editor of the local newspaper. Write your letter on this sheet of paper. In your letter, take a stand on the situation in Cuba and clearly explain your reasons.

- State your position clearly.
- Use information from the list and from what you know about the missile crisis to support your position.

Editor
Daily Bugle
Yourtown, USA

Dear Editor:

_____

_____

_____

_____

_____

_____

_____

_____

_____

_____

_____

In every case, the student is provided with *none* of the facts to which a Russian might call attention, nor given any sense of how a Russian might develop an opposing line of reasoning, based on those facts.

Imagine, in contrast, a test item that provided a list of facts to which Americans might allude (such as those preceding), followed by a list of facts to which Russians might allude, including in the latter such facts as: (a) the United States had already placed many of its own missiles within 90 miles of the Soviet border; (b) Cuba is a sovereign country; (c) The United States previously rejected Russian complaints that America was putting missiles too close to their borders with the claim that the countries within whose borders the missiles were placed were sovereign countries.

After the two lists of facts were provided, short arguments in favor of the opposed positions might be provided. Then the students might be asked to answer the same kinds of questions as aforementioned. Other contrasting lists of facts could be provided, including all the key facts each side would marshall for interpreting many of the tense situations that have characterized the Cold War, and the students would be given a variety of dialogical writing and role-playing assignments. Through such assignments the students could come to understand how Russians actually reason about the conflicts and tensions that have characterized the history of the two countries. They would learn not to presuppose that their country is always right. They would develop a much more realistic sense of how governments of all kinds of national backgrounds often act in ways in which they themselves (the various governments) would disapprove were "the enemy" to do what they do.

One of the major ways in which sociocentric bias is introduced into social studies texts is through the fostered illusion of "scientific" objectivity. The reader is led to believe either that the textbook writers are not taking a position on issues about which reasonable people could disagree, or alternatively, that the textbook writers are taking such a position only when they claim to be.

The textbook *American Democracy In World Perspective,*[28] written by four professors at the University of California for use in college Political Science courses, is an exemplary case in this regard. Virtually everything in its some 700-plus pages is oriented toward persuading the reader that the United States has the best form of government, comes closest to "perfect" democracy, and that the fate of freedom in the world depends on the United States: "As democracy fares in the United States, so will it, in the long run, fare throughout the world."

All governments are divided in the text into two basic types, demo-

---

[28]Eberstein, Pritchett, Turner and Mann, *American Democracy in World Perspective,* Harper & Row, New York: 1967, all quotes pp. 3–5.

THE WORLD POLITICAL
SPECTRUM

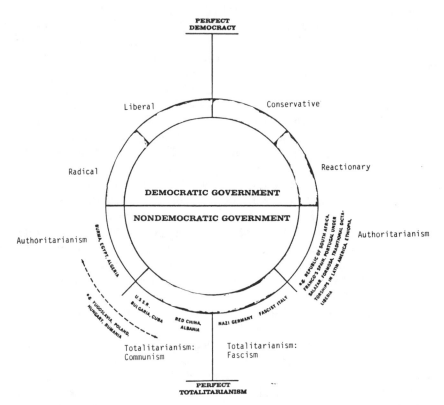

cratic and nondemocratic, the nondemocratic ones divided into authoritarian and totalitarian ones, in accord with the following chart:[29]

There are a number of features that stand out in this chart. *Democracy* is a term that we apply to ourselves (a *positive* term with which virtually all people around the world identify). *Authoritarian* and *totalitarian* are *negative* terms with which virtually no one identifies. The United States is characterized by a term that expresses an ideal, whereas its enemies, the USSR and its allies, are characterized by terms that in effect condemn them. The chart, presented as if purely descriptive, obscures its tendentious character. By the same token, the distinction between authoritarianism and totalitarianism provides, under the guise of pure description, a

---

[29]Op. cit., chart printed on inside covers.

means whereby support of dictators by the United States can be justified as the "better" of two evils. It does not take too much imagination to reconstruct how an equally tendentious chart might be fabricated for a "neutral" Russian social studies text:

THE WORLD POLITICAL
SPECTRUM

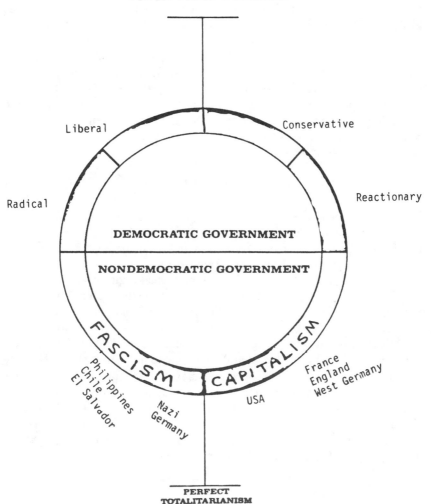

The textbook writers also imply that most Americans believe in *reason and experience,* whereas Communists believe in *dogmatism:* "By using reason and experience, man has scored impressive advances in the mastery of nature . . . Democrats believe that reason and experience can also be fruitfully used in the understanding and harmonious adjustment of human relations . . . In contrast, dogmatists (such as Communists or Fascists) reject this belief in reason and experience.[30] At the same time, lip service is given to the need for a free discussion of issues in social studies: "In trying to present a fair and balanced picture of American democracy, we have not sought to avoid controversial issues. The United States owes its existence to controversy and conflict, and throughout its history, as today, there has never been a dearth of highly controversial questions.[31]

I know of no textbook presently in use in a large public school system that focuses on the multilogical issues of social studies or highlights the importance of strong sense critical thinking skills. Monological thinking that presupposes an American world view is clearly dominant. At the same time, students do not recognize that they are learning, not to think, but to think like "Americans."

CONCLUDING REMARKS: THE CRITICAL TEACHER

To be in the best position to encourage critical thinking in her or his students, a teacher must first value it highly in her or his personal, social, and civic life. A teacher of critical thinking must: be a critical person, a person comfortable with and experienced in critical discussion, critical reflection, and critical inquiry; be willing to make questions rather than assertions the heart of her or his contribution to student learning; explicitly understand her or his own frame of reference and that fostered in the society at large; be willing to treat no idea as intrinsically good or bad; have faith in reason, evidence, and open discussion; deeply value clarity, accuracy, and fairmindedness; and be willing to help students develop the various critical thinking microproficiencies in the context of these values and ideals. To do so, a teacher must be a student of human irrationality, egocentricity, and prejudice. Her or his interest must be both theoretical and practical. She or he must experience (recognize) irrational drives and behavior in herself or himself as well as others. A teacher must be patient and capable of the long view, for people, schools, and society change only

---

[30]Op. cit., p. 5.
[31]Ibid.

in the long run, never quickly, and always with some frustration, conflict, and misunderstanding.

At present there is as little recognition that the critical teacher is rare as that the bulk of the critical thinking cultivated in students today is, at best, monological and technical, and, at worst, sociocentric and sophistic. The concept of strong sense critical thinking skills—of what it is to live, and if a teacher to teach, in a critical manner—has as yet exerted little perceptible influence on schools as a whole. If in our haste to bring critical thinking into the schools, we ignore the need to develop long-term strategies for nurturing the development of teachers' own critical powers and passions, then we shall truly make the new emphasis on critical thinking into nothing more than a passing fad, or worse, into a new, more sophisticated form of social indoctrination and scholastic closed-mindedness.

23 "Upwards and Across": An Essay on Cross-Disciplinary Thinking

Oscar van Leer
Bernard van Leer Foundation
Amstelveen, The Netherlands

Cross-disciplinary thinking, whatever else it may amount to, is first and foremost a form of thinking. Hence, it is only fitting to start with a rough definition of the general species. Thinking is the process of searching for, ultimately discovering, and thereby creating, structures of and relations between existing elements. This amounts to increasing the order and so decreasing the entropy of bodies of knowledge. Given that an aim of thinking is to create structures of and relations between more and more of what is known, part of this process must be to find and use all of the ways and means that may help. Cross-disciplinary thinking is one type of help. It can be defined as the use of structures and relations found within the framework of one discipline as points of departure for discovering or confirming similar structures and relations in other disciplines.

To bring this about, it follows logically that cross-disciplinary thinking must begin with "ascendent thinking," whereby thoughts are generalized, decontextualized, that is, translated into more general and fundamental concepts that treat the conclusions already obtained merely as special cases. From there, cross-disciplinary thinking can proceed to identify specifics of that same fundamental in other disciplines and then try to apply whatever conclusions have been reached within the initial discipline. This also involves a relation of ascendency.

Cross-disciplinary thinking is but a particular client of the more general and fundamental mode ascendent thinking, in which as many concepts as possible are seen from a higher level as specifics of more fundamental concepts. This not only discloses particular connections but also advances the cause of thinking generally, by identifying encompassing

405

concepts that cut across disciplines that previously appeared unrelated. Thereby further structures of and relations between them, whereas inconceivable before, are now in line to be discovered. This clearly increases the order and reduces the entropy of existing knowledge.

Such an aid to the creation of more of what thinking is after cannot be considered anything but a material and probably indispensable tool of the thinking process. Still, this aid does not come easily because cross-disciplinary thinking is severely obstructed by the irresistible and irreversible growth of knowledge. Look at the dimensions of that growth. It is knowledge that begets knowledge. New knowledge consists in large part of combinations of known elements of knowledge, combinations that reveal new emergent meanings. The formula relating the number of elements (n) to the number of combinations (x) that can be made of these elements is as follows: $x = 2^n - (n + 1)$. Applying the formula, one can create out of 3 known elements of knowledge 4 new combinations, and, out of these 4 new combinations themselves taken as elements, 11. Then these 11 bits of newly acquired insight can give rise to another 2,036 combinations. To point out that from these 2,036 elements some 8×10^{612} new combinations can be culled would be pushing the point beyond credibility. Of course, nowhere near all possible combinations will be either discovered or meaningful, but when only some of them are, considering the astronomical numbers involved, it is still a euphemism to characterize this kind of growth merely as exponential. Knowledge, begetting knowledge, multiplies in a way that puts the proverbial rabbits to shame. So much for the theoretical rate of growth of knowledge. Even if the actual rate of growth only constitutes a fraction of the theoretical limit, we are in trouble.

It is both evident and unavoidable that such a rate of growth of knowledge must lead to specialization. There is so much to know about the tiniest segment of the totality of knowledge that we humans have gathered since we ceased to walk on all fours that specialization for many of the practical purposes of life has become a dire necessity. Still, as a physician once said, we will yet see "specialists of the left nostril," with little knowledge and even less interest in the right one. Who knows, one day so much may be known about the left nostril alone that the human brain will be hard put to take it all in, and a human life may not be long enough for a person to develop the skills needed to put all the person has learned about it into practice.

If specialization is the unwanted child of the exponential growth of knowledge, it has also improved on the family tradition and begotten two unwanted children of its own. These are, first, the water- and thought-tight partitions built around each specialty, and, second, the professional jargon that is the proprietary code-language of each specialization. These two children have conspired to render each specialty virtually inaccessible to all but the initiated and thereby to give specialization two inseparable companions: compartmentalization and fragmentation.

With its misbegotten sons and grandsons, the fast and ever faster growth of knowledge is indeed a formidable obstacle to cross-disciplinary thinking, and thereby an obstacle to we human beings attaining understanding of the world as one systemic whole and of the endlessly bifurcated network of mutual relationships between the countless components of reality. But without this understanding, we are bound to infringe unwittingly on, and at length perhaps destroy, these relationships, to the detriment of the components involved, including ourselves. Therein lies the vice inherent in the growth of knowledge.

To recognize an inevitable trend is to realize that, absent a real choice, it is only wisdom to cooperate with that trend and find ways and means to eliminate or neutralize its vices—the vices but for which it would be a blessing. Elimination is fine for simple vices. But inherent vices are the other sides of medals, or shadows that no object can possibly be kept from casting. They cannot be done away with. Those watertight partitions between specializations, sealed by the secret knowledge. They are inherent vices, here to stay.

Neutralizing rather than eliminating them, therefore, becomes the hope. We must learn to live with them, building and crossing bridges between the isolated disciplines. This endeavor should include a deliberate effort on the part of those who direct and who educate, and especially on the part of those who direct education, to promote the development of people's capacity to think in a cross-disciplinary way, passing through those watertight partitions as if they did not exist. Or, to mix in a yet a third metaphor, such an education would be deliberately designed to stimulate the courage and mental dexterity to widen the field of view and take in more of the landscape, encompassing an ever larger part of our intellectual, emotional, and material environment.

It should be clear by now that cross-disciplinary thinking is important, necessary, and has *very* formidable forces to overcome. For there to be any hope at all, we must ask what patterns of ascendent thinking might serve to do the job. Although this is no place for a treatise, by way of analogy and example we can explore that question.

There is some moral support to be garnered by thinking about cross-disciplinary thinking in analogy to this problem: How can one make two symmetrical figures lying in one common plane—say left and right footprints or handprints—coincident with one another? This is possible *only* by recruiting another, in this case a third, dimension. No matter how you maneuver the left figure in the plane, it will never coincide with the right. You must rotate the left figure through space to overlay it on the right one.

In this example, the crucial extra dimension is a dimension in the literal spatial sense. Generally, however, the introduction of an additional dimension in its broader more figurative sense greatly aids in solving problems or making them disappear altogether. It is a tool of ascendent thinking.

Let us look to a somewhat more concrete example. Once upon a time there was a deep-seated conflict between two nations, one a David, the other a Goliath, that from time to time broke into actual warfare. The background of the conflict extended too far into the past and too deeply into emotions and sentiments for the taking of sides by interested and observing nonbelligerents to be warranted. Still, a large group of such observers became partisan supporters of the David-like belligerent and did not fail to give clear and public expression to their feelings in the matter.

Then, once again, warfare broke out in a short and violent battlefield campaign, handily won by the David-nation. After the smoke had cleared, the large group of observers, which previously had sided with the David-nation, changed allegiance and clearly and openly shifted its sympathy to Goliath's camp. This unleashed among those who, for whatever reasons, had no choice but to remain faithful, a tidal wave of criticism and accusation, with "hypocritical turncoats" being the mildest phrase used.

Looking at this shift of attitude from a certain level, such accusations were undeniably justified. The earlier and later attitudes of the erstwhile David-supporters were in irreconcilable conflict—a symmetry of irreconcilable opposites just as with the left and right footprints on the plane. But suppose that one views the issue of allegiance from a higher vantage point afforded by a third dimension, that considers the feelings of any group toward certain nations no longer in terms of favoring a particular nation, but in terms of whether a nation does or does not belong to some class. The class in question might be called *underdog*. Before the eruption of open warfare, the David-nation was considered to be the underdog, whereas after the clash of arms Goliath came to hold that office.

From this viewpoint, the conflict between the observers' attitudes "before" and "after" disappears. Consistently, both before and after, they favored the underdog. With a shift of level of observation and more fundamental thinking, a conflict disappears and an inconsistency becomes a differentiation.

But enough of politics and ascendent thinking. Turn to the contexts of science and education and an example of explicitly cross-disciplinary thinking. Scientific inquiry affords a special opportunity for cross-disciplinary thinking. In the domain of the exact sciences, a scaffolding of concepts has been built more clearly and conclusively than in probably any other field of intellectual concern. This is so, in large measure, because of the technique of designing experiments and conducting them in controlled environments. By this method artfully exercised, answers emerge that are as specific and unqualified as answers to empirical questions will ever be. This is not to say that other disciplines cannot have their equivalent to science's tools. It stands to reason that among the most profitable applications of cross-disciplinary thinking would be those that map structures and relations uncovered in the exact sciences into kindred structures and relations hidden beneath the surface of other disciplines.

For example, assume that you are faced with a problem such as the Minister of Education in a developing country once encountered: a law was passed calling for the introduction of universal primary education, meaning that some 18 million children were instantly added to the primary school population. Suppose as was the case that this happened under circumstances, as that minister described, "of virtually having, so to speak, not a single teacher with whom to execute that law." Imagine you are faced with an immense, nearly astronomical increase in the need for teachers, where another 1 of 12 or even 100 additional teacher training institutes would not help significantly. Then imagine this course of thought:

You start to think in more fundamental terms and realize that education basically is "information transfer."

You peep into the storeroom of structures and relations discovered and created within the field of exact science, where you discover that part of this field also deals with information transfer.

You see the beginnings of a connection: Whereas the educational establishment is a chain of components serving information transfer, so are, in science and technology, amplifiers and loudspeakers components in a like chain.

You remember that, irrespective of the vast differences between the amplifier and its loudspeaker, experiment and theory both show that in order for information transfer to be effective and undistorted the "impedance" of amplifier and loudspeaker must match.

You then muse that so also in the educational chain of information transfer something would need to be matched in order for information transfer to be effective and undistorted.

After considerable mental scouting, you conclude that in the educational case this matching could well consist in establishing a relationship of "equality short of identity" between the ages and intellectual development of transferor and transferee.

So you arrive at the speculation that a system of peer-to-peer education, whereby whatever little teaching staff there is will be reinforced by the masses of pupils who will teach next to learn, may be—although it certainly has not yet been proven to be—the answer to the Minister of Education's prayers.

Eventually it may turn out that peer-to-peer instruction *is* this solution, and perhaps even a contribution to education in many other respects due to collateral advantages. If so, the discipline of education will owe such progress in part to the helping hand extended by analogy from the natural sciences, by way of cross-disciplinary thinking. Although no string of examples can be proof of a general concept, the illustrations of ascendent and cross-disciplinary thinking offered here at least should make more plausible the proposition that such thinking has an important contribution to make.

Perhaps I am saying things no different from what was meant by the rabbi of Sadagora, from the legend recorded by Martin Buber, when he taught that from modern inventions based on science there were worthwhile lessons to be learned outside their home fields, namely:

—from the train: that for being one minute late, all may be lost,

—from the telegraph: that every word is counted, and

—from the telephone: that what is spoken *here* is heard *there*.

And if someone would say to me, "You have spoken well. Now tell me what to do," I would answer like this. You should always seek, and cross-disciplinary and ascendent thinking will greatly help you to find: the universal in specifics, the fundamental in symptoms, the invariant in changes, the necessity in chance, the pattern in randomness, the grand design in incidents, the forest in trees, the potential in beginnings, and the theme in variations.

IV

DESIGNS FOR THE TEACHING OF THINKING

This section collects together chapters that suggest or assess specific systems or techniques for the teaching of thinking, whether in general or in specific subject areas. Margarita de Sánchez offers, in Chapter 24, a general model for the teaching of thinking processes and includes in her discussion some interesting assessment of the programs developed for use in Venezuela. Chapters 25 and 26 are studies of specific programs designed to improve thinking: Marcia Heiman reports on the "Learning to Learn" program and reflects on what she claims to be the advantages of the behavioral approach; John Edwards and Richard Bauldauf report on the results of the use of Edward de Bono's CoRT Program in primary schools in North Queensland. Francis Schrag discusses, in Chapter 27, a perennial problem for the teacher: can the requirements of achieving control in the traditional classroom be reconciled with the development of the spirit of "Socratic" inquiry that is needed if problem solving ability is to be enhanced? Chapter 28 offers useful advice from Richard Wertime about how undergraduates and college students may be encouraged to engage in Socratic inquiry in their essay writing in English literature. In Chapter 29, Jack Easley offers several provocative hypotheses developed from his own observations of teachers. He suggests that, if we value the development of children's thinking, then we may need to reshape the role of the teacher in some rather unexpected ways. Finally, in Chapter 30, Judah Schwartz and Michal Yerushalmy report on a particular example of the use of computer technology to enhance inventive learning.

24 Teaching Thinking Processes

Margarita de Sánchez
Caracas, Venezuela

Today in many settings there are efforts to teach thinking. But what is thinking, and what does one have to do to teach it? This chapter proposes general but practical answers to both these questions. Thinking is seen as based on mental operations that, once internalized, can be applied as instruments, strategies, or tools in problem solving, decision making, and learning. Teaching thinking involves imparting to the learner the mental operations in ways that ensure that the learner masters and transfers the operations. A general methodology is presented for analyzing a thinking skill and teaching it.

First we turn to the literature for a frame of reference to clarify the nature of thinking skills and their relationship to the learning of information about facts and concepts. We then deal with the problem of teaching thinking skills, underlining the need to adopt a special didactics for the purpose. Finally, the principles advanced are illustrated through a brief review of three rather different programs to teach thinking skills implemented in Venezuela in recent years.

The Nature of Skilled Thinking

The ability to think in an advanced way, according to Piaget's (1968) conception of cognitive development, involves the capacity to reason in terms of formal operations, which the individual achieves as the last stage of intellectual growth. Karplus and collaborators (1974) designed experiments for students of different ages in order to observe their intellectual

413

performance at various stages of development. Although, according to Piaget, adolescents should come to manifest formal operations, Karplus' research disclosed that the percentage of adolescents capable of realizing formal thought was low and that the percentage of those exhibiting creative thinking was even lower.

Another view of the nature of thinking comes from Gagné (1977). Gagné distinguished five types of human intellectual capabilities, three of which are related to the development of thinking skills as follows: intellectual skills that allow the individual to perform mental operations with symbols, such as identifying classes, relationships between concepts, and so on; acquisition and retrieval of verbal information, involving the capacity to store knowledge and reproduce it later without modification; and cognitive strategies that provide stages or steps guiding the act of thinking.

Although within different theoretical frameworks, both Piaget and Gagné stress that thinking involves *operations on content*. The ability to solve problems and to think critically and creatively requires the joint use of knowledge and skills—knowledge because it is the raw material from which further ideas are created and because it provides the individual with a context to which new ideas can be related, and skills because they are operational instruments of thinking that allow establishing relationships and generating new products.

The two complementary elements of skill and content both can be learned through systematic exercise and a conscious and deliberate effort. However, conventional education, whereas giving explicit attention to content, generally neglects the operational side of thinking. In contrast, Bruner (1971) urged that a methodology for the development of thinking skills must provide frequent opportunities for practice and the unfolding of originality and inventiveness, within an instructional framework that stimulates cognitive development and the *use* of knowledge. Ausubel (1968) also argued that learning must be significant, meaning that it must include cognitive structures that give it general value.

Teaching Based on Processes

If the process of thinking itself requires instructional attention, as the foregoing sources suggest, what principles should govern instruction designed to foster thinking processes? First and foremost, viewing thinking as a process means focusing our attention not just on content but on the *way* the thinker uses that content to generate new products by transforming the given information, which otherwise would only be stored and retrieved without substantial modifications. In somewhat mathematical terms, the processes are functions that are applied to content in order to generate results, as illustrated by Fig. 24.1. For instance, consider the process of classification and suppose we have information about a set of objects. We can apply the process to the set in order to map each object into a class.

Besides attention to the processes of thought, other principles must be respected too. Experience has shown that in order for a learner to manage a process effectively, the learner should not only understand how to execute the process but also should practice its application until the ability and habit of employing it naturally and spontaneously in a variety of meaningful situations develop; that is, to foster thinking skills, one must arrange for internalized learning and exercises that promote transfer and even transcendance. By transcendance we refer to that quality of consciousness in which one becomes aware that every concrete entity is experienced within a context of wider relationships and possibilities. No content or process is only what it appears to be here and now; there is a projection of its meaning and significance beyond the immediate possibilities based on previous experiences. Once such learning has occurred, the processes that have been acquired constitute flexible tools that facilitate decision making, problem solving, and other intellectual activities called for as individuals manage their interactions with their environments.

Another principle concerns the level on intellectual performance one can hope for with appropriate instruction. According to Ausubel (1976),

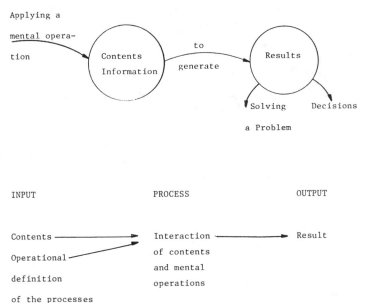

FIG. 24.1. Thinking in Terms of Processes.

problem solving "involves a process through which the learner discovers the way to combine rules previously learned and to apply them in the treatment of new situations." We suggest that the problem-solving process should allow for the possibility of generating new rules. Not only combining and reconstructing facts but producing new associations is an important and feasible objective. The teaching–learning process should stimulate the discovery of new ideas and relationships that restructure the existing pattern.

With these comments in mind, there remains the problem of how to specify a thinking process so that students may learn it. The teaching of thinking skills benefits from a knowledge of the internal structure of the thinking process, which in turn informs how the teaching should be conducted. Cybernetics has developed methods to control "black boxes" without knowing their contents, but the fact remains that the more transparent the box, the greater the possibility of controlling it!

A technique for analyzing a thinking process is to break it up into discrete elementary operations. These operations then can be organized into sequences for learning. Of course, such an analysis must consider the activities and conditions necessary for learning to take place and the operations themselves. To continue the example of classifying, suppose one wants to develop a classification for a set of objects with a certain purpose in mind (of course, we classify for many different reasons that influence the form our classification system take). One might break up the process of classification as follows:

1. Explore the objects to accumulate some experience of their nature.

2. Select observable dimensions.

3. Identify the characteristics that place an object along a specific dimension, for instance, degrees of brightness, hardness, complexity.

4. Compare the objects on the dimensions, identifying similarities and differences. Take one dimension at a time, determining whether it differentiates among the objects in a way relevant to the purpose of the classification. Repeat the operation until all the dimensions are considered.

5. Define classes in terms of an object having certain values along certain dimensions.

6. Assign objects to classes—group in each class all the objects having the attributes of the class.

7. Verify. All the objects should be assigned to classes and no object should fall into more than one class.

To be sure, there is no single unique way of breaking down classification or any other process into component operations. Different analyses are possible, some of which allow more naturalness and flexibility than others. It is important not to foment rigidity; one wants to generate strategies that will quicken the mind, favoring the development of organized, critical, and creative thinking processes relevant to academic and real-life situations. But an analysis need not be rigid; this is a matter of the craft of doing a pedagogically sound analysis.

A related problem of rigidity concerns the teaching of thinking "recipes" by leading students to memorize them. The act of learning cannot be reduced to inducing students to remember the thinking process that is to be applied. Rather, as emphasized earlier, students should come to apply the process as the result of internalization of the process and component operations, internalization achieved through instruction that emphasizes the habit of using processes and acts of building, reorganizing, and transferring patterns of thinking.

One of the great mistakes when teaching processes has been to try to apply standard techniques for teaching facts and concepts to be remembered to teaching cognitive skills and strategies. Much has been said about habits, about practice, about learning by doing, and so on; but it appears that these recommendations have dealt only with the levels of knowledge and comprehension. The teaching of process, so that knowledge will be viewed critically and used creatively, requires a didactics all its own.

Adoption of this idea means planning modifications of conventional curricula, not only as to content but as to approach and methodology also. Instruction in particular subject matters needs to be modified to make room for the teaching of relevant thinking processes with an appropriate didactics. Moreover, it seems desirable to include, besides the traditional subjects, one that concerns thinking processes specifically, also with instruction based on principles from a didactics appropriate for the teaching of skills. At the outset, students must be introduced to the difference between developing thinking skills and acquiring content, and throughout they must be guided in the integration of learning content and processes to foster their capacity for thinking in terms of more abstract and complex cognitive operations (Sanchez, Astorga, de Blanco, & de Griffin; 1983a, b).

An especially important principle governs such interventions: the intentionality of directing and optimizing the development of intellectual skills, an intentionality shared by both teachers and students. Contrast this with how people spontaneously react to learning situations, without the guidance of a deliberate purpose to improve thinking. To be sure, both are occasions of learning. But in the "natural" case there is no method or system to guide or monitor the thinking process or to verify progress in the development of a skill; instead, learners apply processes that often are products of chance, that cannot be reproduced in similar situations, and so that receive no critical scrutiny. With the intentional teaching of thinking comes an awareness of the process and the component operations; consequently, students' thinking processes, not just products, are subject to reproduction, evaluation, and guided improvement.

To summarize the foregoing principles, the teaching of thinking processes should involve:

A focus on the *way* thinking processes operate on content.

Practice, with attention to transfer and transcendance, leading to internalization and natural and spontaneous application in a variety of contexts.

Selection of processes that foster not just manipulating conventional ideas and relationships but discovering new ones.

Analysis of processes into discrete elementary operations in terms of which the students can learn the processes.

Avoidance of the trap of treating processes like content and simply having students memorize sequences of operations.

Explicit intentionality on the part of teachers and students to attend to, examine, evaluate, and improve processes.

These principles taken together provide several elements of a didactics of teaching thinking processes, a didactics that underscores the contrasting demands of teaching processes and teaching content for retention and retrieval.

A Concrete Case

Consider a specific example. Suppose an instructional objective is established: "The student will be able to analyze a cell." This performance involves at least two aspects: On the one hand, the student should know what is expected from him or her when required to analyze something; on the other hand, the student should be able to apply this skill to the examination of a particular object, in this case a cell.

In such a situation, students can fail for different reasons: because they do not know what analysis requires, because they have not practiced the process, or because they have no prior experience of the concept or object to be analyzed. Often, all these problems occur simultaneously. Frequently, the situation is even more unfavorable for the student because other processes, which have some bearing on analysis, are not included in the program of study either. Circumstances like this occur in innumerable cases in which the interaction between processes and content is required. Often the defect is concealed because *remembering* stands in for analysis; remembering an analysis of a cell takes the place of analyzing a cell. But this, of course, is not the intended objective at all. A student in such a situation has learned nothing functional about analysis.

What should one do instead? To answer this question, the teacher needs to decide on the type of analysis he or she is asking for. Analysis in general involves dividing into parts in some general sense. So the students need to have the skills to perform such discrete operations as observing the object—in this case the cell—identifying parts or elements, and verifying such identifications. But the conduct of the analysis depends on the purpose of the analysis. The teacher may be interested in asking the students to perform a "functional analysis," a "structural analysis," or an "operational analysis," for instance.

Take the first one, analysis of the cell, from the point of view of its functions. What is the whole in this case? It is a more abstract concept than the physical cell: The whole is the set of all the cell's possible functions. A student must be able to perform such operations as identifying functional dimensions (survival or reproduction, for instance), characterizing the cell's manner of achieving those functions, and verifying the accuracy of his or her ideas. If the students already have mastered such operations, they can learn functional analysis using them. Otherwise, it will be necessary to divide each step into substeps.

To generalize, when students need to analyze something, they should know: (a) the purpose of the analysis, (b) the sequence of operations to be performed in order to achieve the goal, (c) how to perform those operations, and (d) how to evaluate whether the goal has been achieved. The operations and their sequence will vary depending on the purpose of the analysis. All this demonstrates the complexity of some of the mental tasks we continually ask students to do without any type of previous training. Up to the present, schooling has not treated the development of thinking skills as a specific topic. Consequently, instructional time and effort have not been divided judiciously between the teaching of content and processes.

A Process-Oriented Model of Instruction

The foregoing example illustrates a general approach to planning instruction in thinking skills in terms of processes. This general approach involves the completion of two steps: definition of the process from two points of view, the conceptual and the operational, and definition of an appropriate instructional method to ensure learning.

The first step consists in analyzing the process in terms of its conceptual definition and searching for an operational definition that yields a procedure for executing the process. In the case of the process of analysis, the conceptual definition involved a division of the whole into parts. The operational definition involved deciding on the purpose of the analysis, selecting and executing various elementary operations, and evaluating the result. The elementary operations depended on the purpose of the analysis.

The second step consists in planning the actions required to teach the thinking skill as operationally defined. For instance, in the case of analysis, first the student should be taught conscious knowledge and understanding of: (a) the process of analysis, (b) the types of analysis that can be done, and (c) the steps to perform for each type of analysis and the expected results. Second, the student should follow a plan of practice of what will make fluent and habitual the execution of each of the skills required to analyze a situation. Third, the student should have the opportunity to apply the process to solve specific familiar and novel problems.

Table 24.1 provides a general map of the didactics suggested here, a map that encompasses more than the teaching of a single process. Reading across the page, one encounters a series of phases through which the process of teaching and learning should pass. The earlier phases involve the direct teaching of processes by means of operational analyses. However, the instruction also should be designed to make the learner more and more independent of the facilitator, so that eventually, in the late phases, the learner has learned to explore and acquire new thinking processes for himself or herself. The top row, entitled "actions of the learner," specifies the actions the learner must complete alone or with the help of a facilitator to acquire the process in question. The second row designates the achievements of the learner at each step along the way. The third row describes the actions that the facilitator must perform in order to guide the teaching–learning process

IMPLICATIONS FOR THE CONDUCT OF EDUCATION

So far, the discussion has emphasized an approach appropriate for the teaching of process. We suggest that such an approach should play a pervasive role in the conduct of education in general. At present, the instructional methods applied to the teaching–learning process focus mainly on the transmission of content. Such methods do not help students to carry out the complex mental processes that are needed for successful performance in academic and everyday situations.

What would a process-oriented education be like? In general, a change in the attitude and practices of teachers and designers of educational programs is required, so that learners are treated as individuals poten-

TABLE 24.1
Development of Skills for Thinking in Terms of Processes

ACTIONS OF THE LEARNER				
Receives information about the process and its operational definition, and about the purpose and importance of those.	Realizes intentional directed and deliberate practice.	Applies the mental operations spontaneously and naturally.	Acts according to internal motives.	Explains and analyzes his/her mental acts and actions.
		Applies the operations in a variety of situations and contexts.	Manages his/her own further learning.	Evaluates his/her own performances, considering both practical results and intellectual skills.
				Determines the improvements required.
				Uses others' points of view and experiences to achieve new learning.
				Executes actions to promote his/her growth.
				Interacts satisfactorily with the elements of his/her environment.

(Continued)

421

TABLE 24.1 *(Continued)*

ACHIEVEMENTS OF THE LEARNER	Understands the purpose and importance of the process and of its operational definition.	Applies the operations that constitute the procedure in a variety of situations and contexts.	Internalizes mental operations (appropriates them).	Acquires positive attitudes towards the thinking act, life, self, others.	Diagnoses, determines, and defines his/her own changes.
	Understands the procedure for applying the process by performing the operations.	Makes conscious his/her mental act.	Transfers the mental operations to situations in life, school, work, etc.		
FUNCTIONS OF FACILITATOR	Provides information about the process and its operational definition.	Promotes the interaction of the learner with objects and images and the application of thinking operations in specific situations.	Promotes the practice of mental operations in a variety of problem situations and contexts.	Promotes operations guided by internal motives. Assists transition between internal and external motivation.	Promotes the independence of the learner and promotes actions that stimulate his/her performance within a climate that provides security and confidence.
	Promotes the learner's exploration of the process and its operational definition.	Emphasizes the need to make conscious the process and its operational definition.	Guides the process of internalization and the transfer of thought patterns.	Stimulates the generation of positive attitudes towards the thinking act, self, life, and others.	Employs methods and rewards that stimulate the learner's initiative to find new paths, try alternatives, evaluate results, correct directions, change approaches, etc., without active and direct help of other people.

Emphasizes the usefulness of the process and the need to practice it.

Diagnoses the learner as a function of his/her mental development.

Applies correctives and stimulates self-development.

Creates conditions that will facilitate the clarification of values, the stimulation of creativity, independence, knowledge of self and others, constructive criticism and personal and social growth integrally and harmoniously.

tially capable of modifying their cognitive structures, of dealing with challenges, and of proceeding actively, openly, constructively, critically, and creatively when confronted with problematic situations.

This involves direct attention to thinking processes, as has been emphasized. In particular:

> A didactics must be applied that, without ignoring the informative role of education, enables learners to think in terms of processes and mental operations, free of the dependency that comes from the near total dominance of content.

> A curriculum is needed that attends not only to content but also directly to cognitive skills and strategies that improve symbolic communication, abstract thought, originality, and generally the capacity for problem solving and decision making.

> The consequent restructuring of curriculum must incorporate both new content and new teaching methods—new content about processes and their analysis into operations, and new teaching methods that are designed not just to convey such process knowledge but to foster its skilled spontaneous use and transfer to a diversity of appropriate contexts.

But mere technical attention to thinking processes will not be enough. A revisionary approach to education, besides addressing conventional content and thinking processes, should address the development of the personality with a strong emphasis on attitudinal, ethical, and moral aspects that have both intellectual and affective sides, in order to educate individuals not only intellectually equipped but appropriately motivated to confront the challenges of life in and out of school. In particular:

> The personal and social growth of the student should receive considerable attention, emphasizing self-diagnosis, the use of feedback, and the making of plans, as basic elements that help to build the capacity of the student to manage, consciously and deliberately, his or her own development.

> Pains should be taken to foster in individuals the sensitivity to recognize their potentials and limitations and to react positively and sensibly in any situation.

> The instructional process should strive to develop instrinic motivation that will generate changes and promote its own perpetuation.

SOME EXAMPLES OF PROGRAMS THAT DEVELOP THINKING SKILLS

The principles outlined here are exemplified in experience that has been accumulated by the author during 5 years of activity as director of the Venezuelan "Programs for the Development of Intelligence Directed at the Formal Educational System." These programs were planned and executed in Venezuela at the initiative of the State Minister for the Development of Intelligence during the period 1979–1983. Seven projects addressed the school populations at various levels of the educational system, programs designed to develop the intellectual potential of human beings through specific instruction in a separate course.

Three of the programs, "Learning to Think," "Project Intelligence," and "Instrumental Enrichment," have been thoroughly developed and subjected to summative evaluations. The information in Table 24.2 reveals that the interventions produced significant changes in favor of the experimental group of students in the majority of the variables examined.

These three projects illustrate the generality and flexibility of the methodology described here. The three had quite different intellectual origins, yet in each case, attention to the principles outlined earlier facilitated the process of design or adaptation and contributed to positive results. Consider the match between the projects and the principles for each project in turn.

Learning to Think

The project "Learning to Think" was based on the methodology of the CoRT thinking program developed by Edward de Bono (1973–1975, 1983). In the original, CoRT is a set of 60 lessons emphasizing two aspects of thinking: breadth and change. On the one hand, the program promotes thinking in ways that create a broader and more detailed perceptual map of situations. On the other, the program encourages lateral thinking, where people learn to explore paths different from the conventional or completely logical ones. An adaptation to the Venezuelan context was prepared. As indicated in Table 24.2, the evaluation of the program revealed a positive impact (de Sánchez et al., 1983a, b). A number of general principles characterize the course.

The key premise, of course, is that thinking as a skill can be improved by training. Effective application of thinking skills to solve problems and to make decisions is not a matter of spontaneous development but one of deliberate effort and systematic, continuous practice. Implementing such a plan calls for treating thinking as a regular school subject with no less

TABLE 24.2

Information about the Evaluations of the Projects Learning to Think, and Project Intelligence Instrumental Enrichment

Project	Population of Interest	Number of Subjects in the Sample		Applied Tests	Results
		Experimental	Control		
Learning to think	Elementary education Students—10, 11 and 12 years old.	322	275	Specific skills Barsit for Intelligence	Significant differences in favor of the experimental group in number of ideas, pertinence of the ideas and level of abstraction and of organization of ideas.
Project Intelligence	Secondary Education Students—13, 14, and 15 years old.	463	434	Olast Ottis Lennon Cattel General skills Target ability tests	Gain in all the tests in favor of the experimental group. Significant difference in general and specific skills; Cattel, Subtest 1, and Olsat.
Instrumental Enrichment	Elementary Education 10, 11, and 12 years old	787	216	Cattel Mastery in specific skills Language and mathematics Socioeconomic scale	Gain in favor of the experimental group in Cattel, Language, Mathematics and Mastery. Significant differences in Cattel subtest N 3, and in all the other tests.

than 2 hours per week devoted to the exercise and improvement of mental skills. "Learning to Think" places great emphasis on the development of metacognitive skills and on helping students to be conscious of their own thinking processes. Practice focuses on developing students' mental habits. The instruction seeks to create in them new patterns of thinking that they will be able to apply spontaneously every time they attempt to solve problems, make decisions, or engage in other sorts of thinking. Accordingly, the instruction places special emphasis on mental processes and operations. The aim is to separate process from content and from result, in order to promote students' attention to the way they think.

The role of the teacher is crucial in "Learning to Think." Teachers act as mediators and facilitators of learning, promoting the attainment of self-confidence, self-regulation, and a sense of freedom to think and act by oneself. Teachers need to be able to follow the students' progress and to stimulate them to be actively involved with thinking during most of the class time. The student–teacher interaction emphasizes the use of open questions inviting a variety of responses, and on teacher recognition of any effort to generate ideas. The exercises themselves are written to promote internalization and transfer of the mental operations. The usefulness of the thinking skills taught in "Learning to Think" for real-life problem solving and decision making depends on developing the habit of deploying these skills instantaneously at the right moment with proficiency. The superposition of these patterns of thinking on new circumstances only becomes possible when students have thoroughly internalized the patterns.

Project Intelligence

Project Intelligence comprises a set of 99 lessons in thinking in Spanish, the joint product of Harvard University, the Cambridge consulting firm Bolt, Beranek, and Newman, and the Venezuelan Ministry of Education. The materials were prepared for a 1-year course in thinking at the seventh-grade level and are also applicable to students both younger and older. An English language version of the Project Intelligence course, under the name Odyssey, exists as well (see Adams, Buscaglia, de Sánchez, & Swets, 1986, and other volumes). The evaluation of the course indicated in Table 24.2 can be found in Bolt, Beranek, and Newman (1983).

Project Intelligence proceeds from the assumption that thinking ability depends on the students' mastery of specific skills to perform certain elementary mental operations such as observation, comparison, classification, and ordering. As in "Teaching to Think" and the next project that is discussed, the instructional strategy emphasizes practice of the processes on problems drawn from a variety of situations ranging from everyday to academic. In designing such instruction, the project drew on a combination of several ways of conceptualizing thinking skills—as cognitive processes, a repertoire of heuristics, algorithmic procedures, and others.

The promotion of transfer is one of the most important features of the Project Intelligence course. There is a deliberate integration of the primary thinking operations already mentioned and taught in the first section of the course—Foundations of Reasoning—into later sections addressing language use, formal and informal reasoning, problem solving, decision making, and inventive thinking. Each additional section introduces opportunities for learning new thinking skills and applying the skills already mastered in a different context.

The same teaching methodology appears in each lesson in a systematic effort to achieve the instructional objectives of the course. Processes and strategies are carefully defined and demonstrated at the outset. Exercises are ordered to achieve introduction, practice, and consolidation of the mental operations taught. The teachers' materials lay out the teaching process in considerable detail, making the course easy to use for any teacher who follows the guide carefully.

Instrumental Enrichment

This program, developed by Reuven Feuerstein (1980), was implemented and evaluated in the Venezuelan setting without any modification except for translation into Spanish. The project was selected for study because of its consistency with the principles of the other programs especially written for or adapted to the general philosophy and setting, with the aim of comparing the effects of different alternatives for teaching thinking. The results of this experiment appear in de Sánchez, García, and de Singer (1983).

The particular approach of Instrumental Enrichment is to increase learners' cognitive skills and modifiability through a series of guided exercises and confrontation with academic and real-life experiences. The conceptual framework rests on four key themes analyzed by Feuerstein (1980): cognitive modifiability, deficient cognitive functions, the cognitive map, and cultural deprivation. The program proceeds through providing practice with 14 "instruments" that are designed to correct deficient cognitive functions. The instructional method is presented in a very structured way in the form of teacher and student guides.

Earlier, in Table 24.2, positive results for these three programs were reported. It is worth adding that, according to our informal observations, effects of a qualitative nature among the students of the experimental groups are apparent, including a positive attitude toward learning, self-criticism, improvement in discipline habits, greater openness and flexibility in analyzing viewpoints that are different from one's own and in confronting novel situations, and more practical approaches to academic and out-of-school tasks.

Likewise, some favorable changes were observed among teachers participating in experimental group instruction; improvements were apparent in their handling of the teaching–learning process and their attitude towards students. Parents and guardians often manifested approval of the methodology and pleasure because of changes of behavior they observed in their children.

The work done up to now and the results of the formal evaluations that have been conducted reveal that it is possible to integrate pedagogical and psychological theories to generate practical instructional approaches to teaching. The approach described here has proved appropriate for improving thinking skills, developing positive attitudes toward learning, and stimulating the integral growth of the individual.

ACKNOWLEDGMENT

I want to thank David Perkins for his valuable suggestions toward revising this chapter.

REFERENCES

Adams, M. J., Buscaglia, J., de Sánchez, M., & Swets, J. A. (1986). *Foundations of reasoning* (Vol. 1 of *Odyssey*). Watertown, MA: Mastery Education Corporation.

Ausubel, D. P. (1976). *Psicología educativa: un punto de vista cognoscitivo.* Méjico: Editorial Trillas.

Aususbel, D. P. (1968). Fostering creativity in the school. In D. W. Brison (Ed.), *Accelerated learning and fostering creativity.* Toronto: Ontario Institute for Studies in Education.

Bolt, Beranek, & Newman (1983). *Final report, Project Intelligence: The development of procedures to enhance thinking skills.* Cambridge, MA: Author.

Bruner, J. S. (1971). *The relevance of education.* New York: W. W. Norton.

de Bono, E. (1973–1975). *CoRT thinking.* Blandford, Dorset, England: Direct Education Services Limited.

de Bono, E. (1983). The cognitive research trust (CoRT) thinking program. In W. Maxwell (Ed.), *Thinking: The expanding frontier.* Hillsdale, NJ: Lawrence Erlbaum Associates.

de Sánchez, M. (1982). *Los procesos y el desarrollo de habilidades de pensamiento.* Presentation at the conference Primeras Jornadas Internacionales que se Realizan en Venezuela para el Desarrollo de la Inteligencia, Caracas, Venezuela.

de Sánchez, M., Astorga, M., de Blanco, E., & de Griffin, N. (1983a). *Proyecto aprender a pensar, estudio de sus efectos sobre una muestra de estudiantes venezolanos.* Caracas,

Venezuela: Ministerio de Educación y Ministerio de Estado para el Desarrollo de la Inteligencia.

de Sánchez, M., Astorga, M., de Blanco, E., & de Griffin, N. (1983b). *Projecto aprender a pensar: Extension y generalización: Informe de ejecución.* Caracas, Venezuela: Ministerio de Educación y Ministerio de Estado para el Desarrollo de la Inteligencia.

de Sánchez, M., Garcia, L., y de Singer, F. (1983). *Projecto enriquecimiento instrumental: Estudio de sus efectos sobre una muestra de estudiantes venezolanos.* Caracas, Venezuela: Ministerio de Educación y Ministerio de Estado para el Desarrollo de la Inteligencia.

Feuerstein, R. (1980). *Instrumental enrichment: An intervention program for cognitive modifiability.* Baltimore: University Park Press.

Gagné, R. M. (1977). *The conditions of learning.* New York: Holt, Rinehart, & Winston.

Gagné, R. M. (1980). Learning aspects of human thinking. *The psychology of teaching for thinking and creativity.*

Karplus, R. E., & Wolman, W. T. (1974). Intellectual development beyond elementary school IV: Ratio: The influence of cognitive style. *School, Science, and Mathematics, 74,* 476–482.

Ministeria de Estado para el Desarrollo de la Inteligencia. (1983). *La democratización de la ciencia.* Caracas, Venezuela: Ediciónes de la Presidencia de la República.

Piaget, J. (1968). *Six psychological studies.* New York: Vintage Books.

25 Learning to Learn: A Behavioral Approach to Improving Thinking

Marcia Heiman
Boston College

The Learning to Learn Thinking Improvement System provides students with a set of analytical thinking skills that result in statistically significant, long-term improvements in college students' grade-point averages and retention through graduation. Data supporting these claims has been validated by the U.S. Department of Education's Joint Dissemination Review Panel (JDRP), which subsequently approved Learning to Learn for national dissemination.[1] Learning to Learn is one of three college-level learning improvement programs that have met the JDRP's criteria for approval since the panel's inception in 1972; further, it is the *only* such program to achieve its effects solely through instruction in thinking strategies, without using any form of supplemental group or tutorial content-area instruction.

In this chapter I discuss the genesis of the Learning to Learn system, outline some of its principal components, and review research on the system. Finally, I place the Learning to Learn system in its theoretical framework: From inception through development, Learning to Learn is a behavioral approach to improving thinking. In my discussion of the behavioral origins of Learning to Learn, I suggest some of the advantages of using a behavioral framework for investigating the operations of human thought.

---

[1]The JDRP is a group of research and program design experts chosen by the Department of Education to identify exemplary new projects in education. Their approval is based on factors such as statistical significance, research design, and evidence of replicability.

HISTORY OF LEARNING TO LEARN

The first phase of Learning to Learn's development took place at the University of Michigan in the 1960s. A group of graduate students employed at the University's Reading Improvement Service used techniques of behavioral analysis to identify critical learning skills common to successful learners. The group worked under the direction of Dale M. Brethower, who came to Michigan in 1961 after working at Harvard with B. F. Skinner. Rather than focusing on the traditional techniques of diagnosis and remediation of unsuccessful students, the group sought to discover what was systematic and predictable about successful students' learning. By studying behaviors common to good learners, an attempt was made to isolate skills that could be taught to failing students in a relatively short period of time. These behaviors were identified by asking the successful students to make internal events external and explicit (to speak their thoughts out loud as they engaged in a variety of academic tasks).

The Michigan group found that successful students commonly use the following major learning tools:

• They ask questions of new materials, engaging in a covert dialogue with the author or lecturer, forming hypotheses, reading or listening for confirmation.

• They identify the component parts of complex principles and ideas, breaking down major tasks into smaller units.

• They devise informal feedback mechanisms to assess their own progress in learning.

• They focus on instructional objectives, identifying and directing their study behaviors to meet course objectives.

These skills were translated into a set of exercises that failing students could apply directly to their academic work. There are general learning skills exercises—which apply across the curriculum—and subject specific learning skills—a central focus of my own work.

I joined the Michigan group in 1967 and have been refining the system ever since, first as a doctoral candidate and later as director of several college learning centers. Significant aspects of the system that have been important to its current success were contributed by Joshua Slomianko, who has been my colleague since 1979. The system refinements have consisted in examining successful students' learning strategies in a wide variety of fields (there are different critical learning skills for different fields); sequencing the skills to provide for immediate feedback, such that the skills themselves are maximally reinforcing to the student; and collecting ongoing data on students' progress.

It is not within the scope of this chapter to review the entire Learning to Learn system, which is contained in nearly 300 pages of instructional materials (Heiman & Slomianko, 1979, 1980, 1984). However, I will examine some of the skills that are central to the system, and which reflect all four of the aforementioned learning strategies.

THE LEARNING TO LEARN SYSTEM

Learning to Learn contains general learning skills, which apply to all subject-matter areas, and subject-specific skills, which relate to the structure of complex academic disciplines, like economics of chemistry. Students begin using general learning skills by systematically generating questions from lecture notes and reading materials. They begin with lecture notes, which are often more accessible than texts to the poor reader/learner.[2] Students are asked to do simple "translations" of the materials in their lecture notes (to view the notes as a series of answers to implied questions and to generate those questions). At this stage they are not asked to be creative, but, rather, in their own words, to make explicit what is implied by the material. Pre and postexamples of this behavior in a second-semester freshman taking Inorganic Chemistry are illustrated here:

Before learning skills instruction:

After 4 hours of learning-to-learn instruction (1 hour a week for 4 weeks, with practice assignments given each week):

[2]In Learning to Learn, we are teaching students to generate questions, not to take notes. Better note taking results from the questions' improving students' ability to discriminate relevant information.

Later in the semester, students use questions they have been generating as the basis for constructing information maps and simplified flow charts. These maps show interrelationships among parts of the field under study. For example, the map shown next is a partial information map for a course in anthropology. Across the top are items that can be compared and contrasted. To the left is a column of questions (taken from the student's notes and readings), which can be asked about these items. As the course continues and the student understands the field better, more questions will be added to the column (and new maps will be constructed). These maps facilitate comparative analysis (the student will see relationships between comparable items in the field and will see the field as a whole in terms of the kinds of questions it raises).

	Tribesmen	Peasants	Indians	Groups Studied
What are the coming-of-age rites?				
How is the economy run?				
What is the role of the elders?				
etc. (other questions asked by the course)				

Finally, students learn to use this information in problem-solving situations, such as exams. Students must progress beyond the mere acquisition of information; they must learn to demonstrate their understanding in concrete, measurable terms. One of the skills we use to help students in this area is key-word diagramming, where students construct key-word diagrams from the materials they have devised in previous LTL exercises. These are used in home practice sessions, and later in classroom essay exams. As this skill illustrates, a critical part of academic learning is identifying and practicing the behavior required by the instructor. A sample key-word diagram answering the question, "Compare the domestic economic policies of Franklin Roosevelt, Richard Nixon, and Jimmy Carter," is illustrated following:

Franklin Roosevelt	Richard Nixon	Jimmy Carter
deficit spending; wage & price controls; antirecessionary	monetary controls; limited wage & price controls; antiinflationary	monetary controls; wage & price guidelines; antiinflationary

Of course, learning is more than committing to memory a set of facts, or even applying these facts to new circumstances. It implies the ability to see things in a new way. We have found that the application of the Learning to Learn system results in students' thinking more creatively. Thus, when initially failing students in an oceanography course learned to adapt LTL skills to their course work, they not only began to do well on exams; they also began to ask increasingly more complex questions about the field:

Before Learning to Learn Instruction

Student A: What is a mid-ocean ridge?
            What is a trench?
            What is the speed of continental drift?
Student B: How is a beach formed?
            What is a delta?
            What is a turbidity current?
Student C: How are sand bars formed?
            Name and describe the four types of dams.
            What is isostatic balance?

After Learning to Learn Instruction

Student A: Contrast water hitting hard rock with waves rolling up on a beach of sand.

            Contrast difference between waves that hit a beach straight on and those that fit at a particular angle.
Student B: How does the theory of "plates" relate to the age of the sea floor?
Student C: Give a short explanation of how we use knowledge to the earth's magnetic field reversal to explain sea floor drift.

As these examples illustrate, initially unsuccessful students moved from simplistic questions, requiring merely repetition of established information, to questions that were of a complex, problem-solving nature. They began to ask *the kinds of questions addressed by the field under study.*

The LTL system contains a number of skills that are subject specific, determined by a given field's structure, by the kinds of questions it raises, and by the kinds of behaviors and subskills required of the student. For example, both history and economics ask cause/effect questions. However, our work on the questions asked by differing fields suggests that history as a discipline often focuses on the effects of sequential events, whereas economics emphasizes the effects of simultaneous events. In order to clarify the interactions among simultaneous events, economics uses a variety of graphs. Thus, the structure of economics dictates the need for a subject-specific learning skill: teaching students to translate from prose to graphs, and back to prose. Again, the major principles in Learning to Learn form the basis of the strategies used: Students learn how to break down complex problems into component parts and to form ongoing questions about the material—in this case, about material presented in both prose and graphic form. *In sum, a determination of the relevant subject-specific LTL skills is not deduced from a general theory of cognition, but varies according to the explicit characteristics of the field under study.*

Learning to Learn is *not* a study skills system. Typically, study skills are a series of exercises that are designed to help the students make better use of their time and "beat the system." In study skills, students preparing for a multiple choice test may be taught that a distractor containing "always" is probably incorrect, that they should budget their time properly, outline their textbooks, etc. When students stop actively using most study skills, they stop benefitting them. In contrast, when students master Learning to Learn, they can *stop doing the exercises* and still perform well academically; they are learning how to think when doing academic work. The Learning to Learn exercises are overt forms of behaviors that good learners perform covertly. Once the behavior is well established, the student can stop performing it overtly and still be a good student; *the process of learning how to learn has been internalized.*

Thus, a key characteristic of LTL skills is that they become part of the learner's thinking. For example, I have noted that one of the general learning skills is generating questions from lecture notes—an overt behavior not found among good learners. However, good learners have covert dialogues with new material presented in lectures—they are constantly forming hypotheses and listening for confirmation. By performing exercises related to generating questions, unsuccessful students learn to practice behaviors that are implied by the terms *analysis* and *synthesis*. They do so by using a learning system developed by researchers who examined the behavior of students in relation to the structure of a given field, *not the structure of the mind.*

The research on the LTL system has been extensively reported elsewhere (Heiman, 1983; Heiman & Slomianko, 1983). In this chapter I report only the more recent data. At Boston College and Roxbury Community College, controlled studies were done comparing the academic performance of students introduced to the Learning to Learn system with comparable students unfamiliar with Learning to Learn.

Learning to Learn instruction was provided in classes of 15–20 students each. Classes met for an hour twice a week for 12 weeks. Each student received 30 minutes of individual help each week, when their application of the skills to academic course work was monitored. Much of this individual help was provided by trained peer tutors, who were good students before coming to the program or who became good students after receiving LTL training.

At Roxbury Community College, the control subjects received 2 or more hours of individual subject-matter tutoring each week. At Boston College, control subjects were wait-listed students who later received LTL instruction. The studies controlled for the following variables: college entrance test scores, previous semester's grade-point average, race, sex, year in school, and number of credits taken. The dependent variable was grade-point average.[3] Analysis of covariance was performed on data from both colleges. Results were as follows:

Fall, 1982
Boston College Liberal Arts Students

Experimental Subjects' Mean GPA:	2.44
Control Subjects' Mean GPA:	1.97
$N = 74$	
$F(1,76) = 4.616, p = .035$	
Credits completed by Experimental Subjects:	15.10
Credits completed by Control Subjects:	12.60
F-test significance: .001	

Fall, 1982
Roxbury Community College Students

Experimental Subjects' Mean GPA:	2.89
Control Subjects' Mean GPA:	2.22
$N = 62$	
$F = (1,56) = 5.939, p = .018$	
Credits completed by Experimental Subjects:	10.45
Credits completed by Control Subjects:	7.40
F-test significance: .001	

These studies were rigorously examined by the U.S. Department of Education's Joint Dissemination Review Panel and formed the basis of its formal recognition of Learning to Learn. They indicate that LTL students received significantly higher grades in college courses and completed significantly more academic credits than did non-LTL students.

Initial studies conducted with School of Management/LTL students at Boston College had different outcomes. Although experimental students completed significantly more courses than did controls (F-test: $p = .001$), their semester grade-point average was better, but not significantly better, than the controls'. We hypothesized that it might take longer for students to benefit from LTL if they were studying fields requiring new uses of symbols and language, like statistics and computer sciences. Both School of Management students' responses to questions on their continued use of

---

[3]Only grades in content courses were assessed; the Learn to Learn grade was not included in the data analysis.

LTL and their later academic performance support this hypothesis. When questioned about their continuing use of Learning to Learn, management students reported that they were better able to apply LTL techniques to technical courses a semester *after* taking the LTL course. Longitudinal studies summarized in the next section suggest that these students were accurately reporting.

Longitudinal Studies

Our longitudinal studies suggest that Learning to Learn has an enduring impact on students' learning and their ability to complete college. At Roxbury Community College, three semesters after completing Learning to Learn, 70% of the former LTL students were either still in college or had graduated, as compared with 40% for the college as a whole. Follow-up data on our original experimental groups at Boston College is even more striking, as the following table suggests. Three semesters after completing Learning to Learn, *all* the students in our experimental groups were either still at Boston College or had graduated from it. The groups' mean grade-point average continued to improve.[4]

Achievements of Disadvantaged Students in Fall, 1982 Experimental Group Three Semesters After Completing Learning to Learn (Spring, 1984)

Liberal Arts Students				School of Management Students			
% Minority	S.A.T. scores **	Spring '84 semester GPA	Retention	% Minority	S.A.T. scores **	Spring '84 semester GPA	Retention
75%	812	2.58	100%	76%	818	2.57	100%

(** Combined verbal and quantitative Scholastic Aptitude Test Scores.)

These results are particularly striking at an institution such as Boston College (a 4 year, private, selective Jesuit university). The average combined Scholastic Aptitude Test score for normally admitted freshmen at Boston College is 1,060; the majority of its students' parents are college educated; it is 90% white.

[4]The significance of continued grade-point average improvement is demonstrated by the fact that repeated measures analysis of variance shows that, for our disadvantaged students, there is a tendency to *decrease* in grade-point average in successive semesters *before* Learning to Learn is taken. We have reversed that trend for students enrolled in our program.

Replications

Replication studies suggest that the LTL program has become even more effective since our fall, 1982, studies. As I indicated earlier, besides 2 hours weekly of class, LTL students receive 30 minutes per week of individual monitoring. Most of this monitoring is done by trained college students. In 1983–84, after a year of LTL at Boston College, we were able to hire former LTL students. These students, still using LTL, suggested modifications of the skills to a wide variety of academic courses. In particular, LTL tutors who enrolled in the School of Management (one of whom moved from a 1.7 to a 3.70 GPA) were able to show us specific adaptations of the skills to some of the most demanding management courses: computer science, statistics, and accounting. The effects of these modifications are shown in a 1983 replication of the 1982 School of Management study.[5] Experimental students in the 1983 study were able to successfully apply LTL skills to complex management courses during the first semester that they used LTL; they received significantly higher grades than did wait-listed controls $F(1,46) = 8.750, p = .008$.

Further evidence of Learning to Learn's effectiveness has come from institutions adopting the system. For example, at the University of Lowell, LTL is being used with second-semester freshmen on academic probation. In the spring of 1985, 68 freshmen, all science and engineering majors, were given instruction in LTL after receiving D's (mean semester grade-point average = 1.09) during their first semester in college. Applying Learning to Learn strategies to their academic work, the students received mean second semester grade-point average of 2.62. The courses taken both semesters were standard academic courses, including courses in their major fields. These students, now juniors, have a mean cumulative GPA of 2.36 (through Fall, 1986); 76% are still in college—as compared with 50% for all students nationally in similar institutions, including students who performed well during their first semester in college.

Discussion

Student grade-point average in college courses is known for its resistance to remedial intervention. This is particularly true for interventions, like Learning to Learn, where content course instructors are unaware of

---

[5]In the replication study, only college entrance test scores and previous semester's grade-point averages were used as control variables. We did not control for effects of race, sex, year in school, or number of credits taken because all were found to have insignificant relationships to grade-point average in our three 1982 studies.

student participation in a special-help program; that is, the professor grades his or her students' papers "blindly." Because such professors do not know that a few of their students are taking advantage of an academic support program, they are not in danger of grading them less rigorously for effort without commensurate product. In such cases, there is a kind of external validation each time there is a significant improvement—otherwise unexplained—of students' performance on exams or papers.

These data suggest that there are very real, and lasting, effects produced in low-achieving students by the Learning to Learn system, and that the system greatly facilitates students' abilities to perform well on the complex intellectual tasks that are included in undergraduate curricula. The differences in student performance have prompted a confounding, yet predictable, response in many of my colleagues in the thinking skills movement: I am asked if I have finally renounced behaviorism, since behaviorists reputedly never examine anything as complex as thought.

In the remainder of this chapter, I provide a more balanced view, one that demonstrates that the study of thinking is consistent with applied behavioral analysis. I show that the tenets of behaviorism provide excellent working tools for studying thinking—perhaps more economical and systematic than those used in cognitive science.

Behaviorism as a Model for Improving Thinking

For a number of reasons, behaviorism has not been widely viewed as providing a fruitful theoretical basis for examining and improving thinking. First, most behaviorists have pursued research in areas of "lower level learning", and have not contributed to the literature on thinking. The paucity of behavioral research on thinking may be a legacy of the structure of American academia more than it is a reflection of the limitations of behavioral analysis. If they are on a tenure-track system, psychologists in academia must respond to the publish-or-perish dictum. Experiments must be conducted under controlled conditions and reported cleanly. However, the nature of behavioral research requires field work when human subjects are involved. To reduce extraneous variables, and also to reduce the cost of research (it is too expensive to pay adult learners to be subjects for the kind of field-based intervention required by behaviorism), most behaviorists have done human research with captive populations, such as patients of mental hospitals or people in schools for the retarded. Researchers with a different theoretical orientation have not had these restrictions. For example, much of the work of cognitive psychologists has been theory building around short-term lab work, as in experiments dealing with memory. Investigation of the thinking process by behaviorists has been done largely by persons who have spent most of their careers working in college-learning centers, where adult populations that are engaged in complex learning tasks have been readily available (e.g., Cohen et al., 1973; Heiman & Slomianko, 1983; Wark, 1970, in press; Wolters, 1983).

Another reason that behaviorism has been seen as peripheral to research on thinking stems from misunderstandings of the tenets of behavioral analysis; that is, behaviorism has been viewed as inherently opposed to the study of thinking. This view is significantly in error. The examination of thinking is integral to modern behavioral analysis. Skinner (1938) states: "The behavior to which [terms such as] 'will', 'cognition', 'intellect' . . . apply is naturally part of the subject matter of a science of behavior" (p. 441). Although few behaviorists have done research in this area, Skinner has written extensively on thinking for almost 50 years (Skinner, 1938, 1953, 1957, 1968, 1969, 1975, 1981, 1984, 1985).

Neither Skinner's writing on thinking nor research on thinking based on his theories is widely known or understood. In fact, there is a common misconception that behaviorism's only contribution to the study of complex verbal learning is programmed instruction, and that programmed instruction itself is limited to teaching factual knowledge.[6] It is true that programmed instruction has been used largely to promote efficient learning of specific material, and that learning information from a programmed text does not improve the student's general problem-solving strategies. As Skinner (1969) has said: "it is not the thing to do if we are interested in studying or in teaching problem solving" (p. 135). If we want to teach students how to solve problems, a more comprehensive process would be to teach them *how* to learn: "To the extent that students can be taught to study unprogrammed materials efficiently, instruction may be foregone" (p. 129).

One way to teach students how to learn is by modeling the process of programming through well-structured teaching and feedback systems. Thus, in his Personalized System of Instruction, (PSI), Keller proposes that an excellent way to teach students to "program" their own learning is through an individually structured system where students move through traditional texts at their own pace (Keller, 1966, 1968); that is, well-organized instructional systems help students see the parts of complicated ideas and obtain feedback on their learning. In the PSI classroom, each student demonstrates mastery of a given unit before moving on to new material; further, lectures and demonstrations are motivational

---

[6]There is no reason that programmed instruction must be limited to transmitting factual knowledge or basic perceptual skills. "The emphasis comes from the educational establishment, not from the nature of programming" (Skinner, 1968, p. 115). Students might be taught logical analysis or strategies for improving thinking through a step-by-step reinforcement of certain behaviors.

devices, not sources of information for testing. Keller suggests that students who have taken PSI courses develop strategies that facilitate their learning in traditionally structured courses (Keller, 1981). The students bring with them an increased awareness of the instructional objectives of their courses and are better able to direct their learning to meeting these objectives. Numerous replications of Keller's procedures and follow-up studies on student performance have borne out this suggestion (e.g., Conway, 1981).

We might further explore what is involved in improving students' thinking by defining what we mean by human thought. For the behaviorist, there is no magic "black box," no essential distinction between overt and covert thought. "We speak to ourselves as we speak aloud . . . we talk to ourselves while solving a problem" (Skinner, 1968, p. 124). "When we study thought, we study behavior" (Skinner, 1957, p. 451). Operant analysis does not treat thought as a "mystical cause or precursor of action, or an inaccessible ritual, but action itself, subject to analysis with the concepts and techniques of the natural sciences" (Skinner, 1957, p. 449). Problem solving may be defined as "any behavior which, through the manipulation of variables, makes the appearance of a solution more likely" (Skinner, 1953, p. 247). Students can learn to "clarify stimuli, change them, convert them into different modalities, isolate them, rearrange them to facilitate comparison, group or regroup them, or add other stimuli" (Skinner, 1968, p. 132). The student may adopt these behaviors through an initial trial-and-error search, followed by selective reinforcement by the environment (some methods result in problem solutions), or by being explicitly taught to adopt these strategies by an expert problem solver. Thus, parents who provide explanations when they tell their children what to do are providing *models* for their children: In talking aloud an action, the parent makes an overt, verbal translation of an event, seeking to help the child engage in a given action independently. For example, if a child has been given a name for an object and, while observing its action, has been instructed to watch certain dimensions of that action, these cues may serve as discriminative stimuli the next time he sees or plays with the object; he will be better equipped to make further discriminations about the object; better able to talk to himself about what it is he sees.

If overt and covert verbal behavior are the same kinds of behavior, "there is no reason why methods of thinking and of the teaching of thinking cannot be analyzed and made more effective" (Skinner, 1957, p. 449). We should begin our analysis by finding out what good thinkers do as they think. Identifying the critical skills used by good learners cannot be done effectively simply by asking such learners to introspect about what works for them when they solve problems: "Skillful thinkers may internalize their behavior to the point at which even the thinker himself cannot see what he is doing" (Skinner, 1968, p. 127). However, we can ask skilled learners to express their thinking overtly as they solve problems talking aloud their thoughts, drawing visualizations, writing mathematical or other symbols, many of which were initially learned at the overt level and later became shortcuts for expressing long chains of thought. In this way we can begin to have access to the learner's "intellectual self-management" (Skinner, 1968, p. 120) and determine which precurrent behaviors[7] the learner finds useful when solving problems. We may find that the learner uses certain identifiable strategies in problem solving. In executing a mathematical proof, for example, the learner might start with a conclusion, retracing the steps by which it was deduced from the original assumptions. The skilled learner may use such strategies quickly and covertly, no longer aware of the process that takes place during problem solving. However, once these behaviors have been identified in overt form, the problem of teaching thinking becomes clear: "The solution is simply to teach the behavior at the overt level" (Skinner, 1968, p. 124).

What are we doing when we teach students to adopt new strategies to improve their thinking? The behaviorist would say that we are teaching the student to construct discriminative stimuli. Constructing discriminative stimuli[8] makes it more possible to discern the relevance of new information to solving particular problems. These strategies may be ways of changing the environment so that the student is "more likely to respond to it effectively" (Skinner, 1968, p. 132). For example, an artist may rearrange the objects he wishes to paint, change the lighting, background, and his own distance from these objects. Or, he may alter his responses to the stimuli; he may "look back and forth to gauge distances, view from different angles, gesture or otherwise create supplemental stimuli which emphasize lines and curves" (Skinner, 1968, p. 127). In doing so, the artist is constructing discriminative stimuli—precurrent behaviors, or strategies, which will allow him to look at his still life in novel ways.

Not all problem solving has such obviously overt dimensions. In the absence of external stimuli, we can encourage students to generate novel ideas through teaching other precurrent behaviors, such as questioning.

---

[7]A precurrent behavior is a strategy, a sequence of behaviors arrived at accidentally, usually through trial-and-error search, which results in a solution to a problem. Because finding solutions to problems are generally inherently reinforcing to a problem solver, a precurrent behavior has a high probability of recurring the next time the problem solver faces a similar situation.

[8]Constructing discriminative stimuli is a matter of varying elements of one's environment until a recognizable pattern emerges.

Generating an hypothesis is a "relevant problem solving practice" (Skinner, 1969, p. 153). As Polya (1945) suggests, the kinds of questions teachers ask students are "equally useful to the problem solver who works by himself." Students who use such strategies are "learning how to learn" (Skinner, 1968, p. 127). They are learning "how to discover what they have to say—to tease out faint responses, and not only one response at a time but complex arrangements; not only the single analogical or metaphorical response, but a sentence, paragraph, chapter or book; not only the next best move in chess, but a whole strategy; not only one step in a proof, but a whole proof" (Skinner, 1968, p. 140).

LEARNING TO LEARN: AN EXAMPLE OF THE BEHAVIORAL ANALYSIS OF THINKING

Previously I have discussed the behavioral view of thinking, in which *thinking is itself a form of behavior, not some mysterious precursor to behavior.* In this section, I will show how Learning to Learn, the particular thinking-improvement system under investigation here, exemplifies the behavioral approach to the study of thinking.

First, the development of Learning to Learn is consistent with the dictates of behavioral theory. To the behaviorist there is no distinction between overt and covert thought, and teaching thinking is essentially a matter of teaching less successful thinkers the strategies (covert precurrent behaviors) of good thinkers. Thus, 20 years ago, when the core of the Learning to Learn system was developed, good learners were asked to talk aloud as they performed complex academic tasks.[9]

As indicated earlier, the Michigan group found that good learners generally use an identifiable set of learning strategies: They form hypotheses as they read or listen, engaging in a covert dialogue with the author or lecturer; they "program" their own learning, breaking complex ideas and tasks into components, and giving themselves ongoing feedback on their learning progress; they identify and direct their learning behavior to meet their courses' instructional objectives.

There are certain resemblances between these behaviors and the components of programmed instruction: ongoing feedback shapes the student's learning; the constituent parts of complex ideas are identified and analyzed; and the student is engaged in an active process of answer-

---

[9]This investigative approach is similar to that used by a number of field-based cognitive theorists in the last several years. The difference between our research and this more recent research may be one of the quantity of data. In identifying the critical learning skills in LTL, several hundred students were investigated each year over a period of 6 years (1964–1970). Development and expansion of LTL has been carried out for much of the last 16 years (1970–1986).

ing questions. The difference here is that the step size and questions asked are generated by the students: Students learn to "program" their own learning—they learn how to learn.

The critical skills that were found to be common to good learners are interrelated: A *question* becomes a discriminative stimulus for all new relevant information; analyzing the *components* of complex information, the learner asks subquestions (constructing more specific discriminative stimuli) and searches for *feedback* on accuracy, fit, step size (i.e., a given piece of information feedback tells the learner whether he needs to ask more subquestions and helps him adjust the breadth of his questions). All this is directed towards attaining the learner's original objectives, initially introduced by his questions.

These learning behaviors are common to all successful learning—in and out of the classroom. For example, the simple act of crossing a street in traffic involves using these skills. The pedestrian looks for feedback; he carries on an internal dialogue, as if asking himself questions such as "How far away are the cars and how quickly are they traveling?," "Will I make it safely across the street if I cross now, or should I walk to the corner and cross at the light?" In making this analysis, the pedestrian has identified the critical elements of the situation. Finally, his behavior is directed towards a specific objective: He wants to get across the street.

Just as there is no essential distinction between overt and covert thought, *there is no critical difference between verbal and nonverbal problem solving*. The "questions" that the pedestrian asks himself are a search for feedback: how can he get across the street without being hit by a car. Similarly, the auto mechanic, in repairing a transmission, tests out previously learned information (what has worked in the past). Finding solutions is a matter of responding to concrete, specific feedback. What works, what doesn't work is physically apparent: the car goes or it does not.

The mistake made by many educators and psychologists is imagining that there is something more complex involved in what is called "higher level" learning. In fact, identical elements are involved: The physicist and the prose writer are both responding to environmental feedback. Their questions are discriminative stimuli that allow them to obtain feedback from this covert environment. The physicist engages in an internal dialogue, raising and testing a series of hypotheses—the step-by-step consequences of his attempts to answer these questions provide feedback, shaping his further investigation. Similarly, the prose writer performs the same kinds of tasks: there is a continuing internal dialogue, and a search for feedback, where a series of questions and answers are often explicitly raised.

Although most children come to school with these behaviors—they are constantly raising and testing hypotheses about the world around them—they often cease applying their learning skills to school work. Active learning is punished, not reinforced, in far too many classrooms. The emphasis is on facts to be memorized, and other people's (usually teachers') questions to be answered. The apparent differences between academic and nonacademic learning are highlighted, and students come to see "book learning" as fundamentally different from other kinds of learning.

This distinction becomes stronger as academic learning becomes more complex. Most students have difficulty adapting learning strategies that are used outside the classroom to academic work: Novices in any field do not see the field in terms of the kinds of questions it asks; feedback on learning is not provided immediately, but rather at infrequent intervals; and, learning cannot be directed towards instructional objectives if students cannot discern those objectives.

Of course, these difficulties do not obtain for all students. However, because schools pay little or no attention to teaching children how to learn, it is most likely that those children who bring their learning skills to academic work do so because of appropriate reinforcement and modeling at home: For example, a parent talking aloud his or her responses to a picture book is modeling important learning skills for the child.

Children who come to school able to use their nonacademic learning skills (questioning, looking for feedback, seeing the parts of things) are "naturally" better students. Unfortunately, instead of finding out what it is (what learning behaviors they are using) that makes them effective learners, such students are usually seen as "gifted" relative to their peers. Their skills are seen as something mysterious, perhaps a reflection of good hereditary stock, rather than the product of a set of acquirable behaviors.

Most of the students we see at the Learning to Learn program have spent long years labeled *poor learners*. They are in college because of modified open enrollment programs that, despite worthy intentions, too often become revolving doors. It would seem that students with their academic histories could not survive, let alone perform, nearly as well as more gifted students. How is it possible for the Learning to Learn system to have such dramatic—and apparently permanent—effects on these students' learning the complex intellectual material presented at the university level? Perhaps they are able to succeed because they *already have the critical skills required for all learning:* they have been learning from the environment all their lives, generating hypotheses about how to negotiate the world around them, receiving feedback that shapes their learning. We are teaching them to apply these skills to academic subject matter, where questions asked and answered are in verbal or symbolic forms. With Learning to Learn, we are initially helping them to adopt these questioning/searching for feedback skills in an overt form; in time, they will begin to carry on an ongoing internal dialogue, as do those of us who have had more practice at being "good" thinkers.

Behaviorism and Cognitive Science

Thus far, I have shown, on both empirical and theoretical grounds, something of what behaviorism can offer to the examination and improvement of thinking. The nature of my work, and my findings, are consistent with some of the past decade's work in cognitive theory,[10] that is, in the past few years a number of cognitive theorists have developed models of prototypical good and poor problem solving. Their principle tool of investigation has been the method used by the Michigan behaviorists who developed the core of Learning to Learn system; that is, they have looked at the behavior of thinking by asking successful students to talk aloud their problem solving. Included in this group of researchers are Larkin (1977), who found that beginning physics students rely initially on formulae, whereas experts construct pictorial models of problems; Lin (1979), who has written about the difficulties in constructing good models of problem solving in novices and experts; and Greeno (1978, 1984), who has derived thinking-aloud protocols from both high school geometry students and children engaged in counting. Not all of this work has been confined to the *study* of thinking. For example, Whimbey and Lochhead (1981), working from expert-generated problem-solving protocols, have developed *intervention* procedures that help students think more systematically when engaged in academic problem solving.

The research and interventions in thinking improvement that are done by this group of investigators might be described in behavioral terms: as James G. Holland (1983), who worked with Skinner in the development of programmed instruction, has said, this work is "a form of task analysis, in the mainstream of behavioral research."

Although these researchers might resist a behavioral label, their tools of investigation are certainly more closely related to behavioral analysis than to the more traditional cognitive psychologists' emphasis on introspection and speculation on what and how a subject is thinking. Moreover, there is a clear disparity between their work and Piaget and Bloom, from whom many of these researchers trace their own theoretical origins.

For example, when Piaget was asked about the relevance of his work to improving the intellectual functioning of children, he responded that there was no such relevance; his work was intended to be descriptive, not prescriptive (Pines, 1967). And, Benjamin Bloom responded in a similar vein when he was asked about his reaction to Whimbey and Lochhead's (1981) analytical reasoning course, which is based on an original experiment by Bloom and Broder (1950). Bloom discounted the importance of this work, saying that he had not intended to create an instructional

---

[10]Although the 20-year history of Learning to Learn demonstrates that its development was independent of this more recent work.

system from that experiment (Bloom, 1982).

The argument can be made that when these contemporary thinking skills researchers did further empirical work exploring the hints left by Piaget and Bloom, they discovered reinforcers inherent in systematic thinking. Their contribution has been in the nature of a two-edged sword, however; the descriptions of their subjects' thinking behaviors have added much of importance to our understanding of thinking; yet, their explanations of these phenomena have often been less clear, resorting to newly invented terminology or inappropriate metaphors to "explain" their work.

It is this proliferation of new constructs, not the actual experimental and interventionist approaches, which puts the work of the new generation of cognitive theorists at odds with behaviorism. (Parenthetically, perhaps their work was discounted by Piaget and Bloom because it is *too* effective; it works too quickly to be adequately accounted for by cognitive stage theories.)

The new, field-based cognitive psychologists are looking at the data and have moved away from the introspective, the speculative. It is, in fact, the emphasis on the speculative that behaviorists have rejected—not the attempt to examine thinking. Behaviorists have difficulty with cognitive psychology when it speaks of mental entities, when it moves away from an observable data base. For example, imagining that there is such a thing as "motivation," which can be directly manipulated, may doom an intervention attempt to failure: A pep talk given in an effort to "motivate" potential school dropouts is not likely to increase their attendance at school if school is punishing for them. A behaviorist would translate that construct, *motivation,* into a description of the individual's history of reinforcement. Attempting to strengthen that constellation of behaviors that constitute motivation would be a matter of arranging the available contingencies, finding those that are strongly reinforcing to the individual.

The reification of mental constructs has important consequences for the teaching of thinking. As I have mentioned, a number of thinking-skills investigators are field based when examining students' learning strategies: They gather data on what learners do while talking aloud their problem solving. However, much of the recent works on thinking skills is neither field based nor open-ended. Rather than starting from observable data, it begins from a set of constructs that are seen as having their own reality. These constructs may become barriers to progress in research and pedagogy. Believing that mental states have some concrete reality may lead to the view that mental states are trainable entities. Feuerstein, for example, speaks of training students to abstract relevant aspects of a domain. He maintains that this and other thinking skills can only be adequately developed as content-free skills. For example, students trained in his system are asked to find geometric shapes in an apparently random field of dots. He (Feuerstein, 1980) maintains that this exercise gives students "practice in the projection of virtual relationships . . . [providing] opportunities for the performance of a number of cognitive operations: differentiation, segregation, organization by restructuring the field", etc. Later—perhaps months later—when students move with ease through such content-free exercises, a teacher may help a student apply a related academic strategy, like finding the main idea in a paragraph, to content-course learning. To a behaviorist, the central problem with this approach is that there is a kind of "magic" here; there is no direct evidence that training in the abstract transfers to concrete skill improvement.[11] The teachers in Feuerstein's system eventually construct content-related exercises where students use active learning skills; it is likely that the gains found from this direct instruction would obtain without the weeks and months of prior abstract, "conceptual" training.

The attempt by cognitive science to describe the brain as a kind of glorified computer has its own hazards. For example, when Estes et al. (1983) describe "information processing" as the "central activity involved in intelligent behavior" (Ibid) and computer science as "the foundation for understanding information processing systems" (Ibid), they appear to equate human learning with the operations of sophisticated machines. Is it good science to disregard what we know about how learning changes the organism behaviorally and physiologically? That is, might not an insistence on the computer science metaphor lead us away from what we know about learning, into a new kind of black box mythology?

It may be suggested that the theory motivating research in this area is irrelevant: What does it matter that terms such as *integrative reconciliation* or *cognitive structure* (Smith, 1984) are used, so long as those terms can be specified in a way generally understood by the community, and lead to useful findings about how people go about learning?

This is the crux of the problem. In current thinking skills research, much of the theorizing is done by researchers in direct response to their data as a kind of after-the-fact theorizing. Concepts are derived to fit certain apparent findings. There are real dangers in disregarding established findings in the study of human behavior.

First, replication may be difficult or impossible if researchers are not fully aware of the contingencies governing the responses of their subjects. Thus, some students may be judged "not ready" for given learning tasks or not sufficiently "motivated" when a given treatment fails a particular group of students. It may be that the successful interventions depend less

---

[11]Cognitive theorists who maintain that abstract processes are transferable to the learning of concrete content may well be right. However, they may have the sequence reversed: The abstract processes are possible only because of concrete learning experiences children acquire in the natural environment.

on qualities ascribed to the learner, and more on aspects of the environment in which the learner receives instruction.

Secondly, the researcher may go so far astray from established findings that solutions to learning problems are lost or discounted as too "simplistic," even when they are effective. A case in point is found in the teaching of science and math in this country. It has long been known that programmed instruction provides students with mastery in acquiring basic science and math competence—and does so more effectively than does conventional instruction, and in half the time (Skinner, 1968). However, classroom practices have not adopted this form of instruction, largely due to the commitment of the educational community to cognitive theories.

Discussing this point in a recent paper, Skinner (1985) notes that the "Report of the Research Briefing Panel on Cognitive Science and Artificial Intelligence" (Estes et al., 1983) disguises the notion of programmed self-instruction in language that unnecessarily complicates the issue (and makes the translation to classroom practice extremely difficult). The Panel (Estes et al., 1983) notes that:

> an intelligent tutoring system that can provide genuine help in educating a student in some well-understood domain, such as mathematics or science, must provide several components. (1) A powerful model of the task domain, so it can itself solve problems in that domain. (2) A detailed model of the student's current level of competence, encompassing both partial and erroneous competence as well as perfect competence. (3) Principles for interpreting the student's behavior, so as to be able to infer the student's knowledge and difficulties. (4) Principles for interacting with the student, so as to lead the student to a higher level of competence. (pp. 32–33)

Skinner (1985) suggests that these points can be conveyed "in many fewer words: to teach mathematics and science, we must (1) define our objectives, (2) find out what students already know, (3) present material to be learned in carefully designed steps, and (4) tell students immediately whether or not they have taken them successfully. Millions of students have suffered and are now suffering from the difference between those versions" (p. 19).

The quick and significant results of behavioral intervention are often dismissed by contemporary cognitive theorists, who believe that a behavioral approach, however successful, is somehow not "real," not deep enough to explain complex human behavior—especially in the realm of higher-level thinking. But how well is the study of human intelligence served by obscuring straightforward empirical results with an intricate overlay of newly invented terminology?

Philosophers have begun to notice this problem as well. Objections have been raised not only by philosophers like Quine, who are favorably disposed towards behaviorism, but also by some philosophers who are not behavioral sympathizers. For example, Putnam holds that "no set of mental events—images or more 'abstract' mental happenings and qualities *constitutes* understanding (Putnam, 1981, p. 20; Putnam's emphasis). That is, there is no doubt that we think and believe, but attempts to make mental models of thinking and believing which are intended to be more basic than the original, and to explain what they are in terms of abstract constructs, run into difficulty: there are infinite lists of such constructs (Putnam, 1985).

CONCLUSION

In this chapter I have presented a behavioral model of thinking improvement. I have shown the model to be empirically effective and have described its specific relation to a behavioral analysis of thinking. Finally, I have suggested that behavioral theory may have a more internally consistent explanation for the process of thinking than do other theoretical frameworks. All this does not necessarily mean, however, that behaviorism offers the best possible explanation of thinking. Indeed, such a claim could never be finally validated. However, by the criteria on which we judged scientific inquiry and theory, it is a good candidate; that is, a "best possible" theory is generally accepted as one that is fruitful (which helps investigators find solutions to important problems), and which predicts the maximal information with the most economical explanation. It appears that behaviorism, as exemplified by the Learning to Learn system, satisfies these criteria in the field of thinking improvement: It reliably predicts long-term, externally validated improvement in students' thinking across the spectrum of academic disciplines.

REFERENCES

Bloom, B. (1982, April). *Answer to audience question at a presentation of mastery learning*, American Educational Research Association Conference.

Bloom, B., & Broden, L. (1950). *Problem solving processes of college students*. Chicago: University of Chicago Press.

Conway, B. (1981). Math 800: The Keller Plan at a community college. *Journal of Learning Skills*, I, 18–22.

Cohen, R., King, W., Knudsvig, G., Markel, G. P. Patten, D., Shtogren, J., and Wilhelm, R. (1973). *Quest*. New York: Harcourt Brace.

Estes, W. K. Newell, T., Anderson, J. R., Brown, J. S., Feigenbaum, E. A., Greeno, J. Havs, P. S., Hunt, E., Kosslyn, S. M., Marcus, M., & Ullman, F. (1983). Report of the research briefing panel on cognitive science and artificial intelligence. *Research Briefings 1983*. Washington, DC: National Academy Press.

Feuerstein, R. (1979). *Instrumental enrichment*. Baltimore: University Park Press.

Greeno, J. G. (1978). A study of problem solving. In R. Glaser (Ed.), *Advances in instructional psychology* (pp. 13-73). Hillsdale, NJ: Lawrence Erlbaum Associates.

Greeno, J. G. (1984, January). Conceptual competencies and children's counting. *Cognitive Psychology, 16*, (1), 94-143.

Heiman, M. (1983). *Learning to learn*. Joint Dissemination Review Panel Submission, Washington, DC: National Diffusion Network, U.S. Department of Education.

———. (1985). Learning to learn. In A. Costa (Ed.), *Developing minds: A resource book on teaching thinking skills*. Washington, DC: Association for Supervision and Curriculum Development.

———. (1985, September). Learning to learn. *Educational Leadership, 43* (1), 20-24.

Heiman, M., & Slomianko, J. (1983). *Learning to learn: Some questions and answers*. Cambridge, MA: Learning Skills Consultants.

———. (1986), *Methods of inquiry*. Cambridge: Learning Associates.

Holland, J. (1983, Spring). Conversation with James G. Holland. *Journal of Learning Skills, 2* (3), 10-15.

Keller, F. S. (1966). A personal course in psychology. In R. Ulrich, T. Stachnik, & J. Mabry (Eds.) *Control of human behavior* (pp. 91-93). Glenview, IL: Scott Foresman.

Keller, F. S. (1968). Good-bye, teacher. *Journal of Applied Behavior Analysis, 1*, 79-89.

Keller, F. S. (1981, Fall). Conversation with Fred S. Keller. *Journal of Learning Skills, 1*, 12–17.

Larkin, J. H. (1979). Information processing models and science instruction. In J. Lochhead & J. Clement (Eds.), *Cognitive process instruction* (pp. 109-118). Philadelphia: Franklin Institute Press.

Pines, M. (1967). *Revolution in learning: The years from birth to six*. New York: Harper & Row.

Polya, G. (1945). *How to solve it*. Princeton: Princeton University Press.

Putnam, H. (1985). *Mind, language, and reality: Philosophical papers* (Vol. 2). Cambridge: Cambridge University Press.

———. (1981). *Reason, truth, and history*. Cambridge: Cambridge University Press.

Skinner, B. F. (1938). *The behavior of organisms*. New York: Appleton–Century–Crofts.

———. (1953). *Science and human behavior*. New York: The Free Press.

———. (1957). *Verbal behavior*. New York: Appleton–Century–Crofts.

———. 1968). *The technology of teaching*. New York: Appleton–Century-Crofts.

———. (1969). *Contingencies of reinforcement*. New York: Appleton-Century–Crofts.

———. (1975). *About behaviorism*. New York: Random House.

———. (1981). How to discover what you have to say: A talk to students. *Behavior Analyst, 4* (1), 1-7.

———. (1984). The shame of American education. *American Psychologist, 39* (9), 947-954.

———. (1985). Cognitive science and behaviorism. *British Journal of Psychology, 76*, 291-301.

Smith, M. (1984, Winter). Learning about learning. The contributions of Ausubel's assimilation theory to a teacher education program. *The Journal of Learning Skills*, (2).

Wark, D. (1970). Principles of self-reward for study skills (In C. A. Ketcham (Ed.), *Proceedings of the College Reading Assoc*. (Vol. 10, pp. 70–80).

——— (in press). Using imagery to teach study skills, *Society for Accelerated Learning and Teaching Journal*.

Whimbey, A. (1975). *Intelligence can be taught*. New York: E. P. Dutton.

———. (1982, Winter). Conversation with Arther Whimbey. *Journal of Learning Skills 1* (2), 14-22.

——— & Lochhead, J. (1985). *Problem solving and comprehension*. (4th edition). Hillsdale, NJ: Lawrence Erlbaum Associates.

——— & Lochhead, J. (1985). *Problem solving and comprehension* (3rd ed.). Hillsdale, NJ: Lawrence Erlbaum Associates.

Wilhelm, R. (1970). The power of immediate positive feedback. *Journal of Perceptual and Motor Skills, 3* (1), 337–338.

Wolters, T. (1983). *Student success*. New York: Holt, Rinehart.

26 The Effects of the CoRT-1 Thinking Skills Program on Students

John Edwards
Richard B. Baldauf, Jr.
*James Cook University
of North Queensland,
AUSTRALIA*

INTRODUCTION

Many claims and counterclaims have been made about the potential and actual effects of de Bono's CoRT materials on students. This chapter reports on an extensive study of the effects of de Bono's CoRT-1 materials on 67 Grade-7 students. Pre- and delayed posttreatment measures were taken in a range of areas including intelligence, creativity, self-concept as a learner, and achievement across subjects. The effects of parent and teacher reinforcement were also investigated. "Everyone thinks, therefore a course of thinking must be expected to show that it has improved thinking. Otherwise what is the point of devoting time to it? This is self-evident. But the trouble arises when we find that testing thinking is extraordinarily difficult and beset with pitfalls" (de Bono, 1976, p. 200).

This chapter addresses de Bono's dilemma. Many claims have been made by de Bono (1976) about the benefits of using his CoRT thinking materials (de Bono, 1981). At the same time, de Bono's ideas and materials have been strongly criticized by academics such as McPeck (1983). De Bono (1976) concedes that the studies reported to support his claims for the CoRT materials are unconvincing. However, a pilot study by the authors of this chapter, using CoRT-1 materials with Grade-10 students (Edwards & Baldauf, 1983), demonstrated positive effects for these materials on students' thinking skills. This study looks in greater detail at the effects of the CoRT-1 materials on Grade-7 students and examines some of the claims de Bono makes for the materials.

BACKGROUND TO THE STUDY

When thinking is used in its broader sense there is little agreement as to what thinking is (Anderson, 1965). No attempt is made in this chapter to tightly define thinking. Instead, we take as a starting point the range of claims made by de Bono for the "development of thinking skills," particularly as they are manifest in the CoRT-1 materials.

There is wide acceptance of the value of learning to think. As Taba (1962) says: "one scarcely needs to emphasize the importance of critical thinking as a desirable ingredient in human beings in a democratic society . . . people need to learn to think." Dienes and Jeeves (1965) see the major skill involved as: "how to encourage subjects to move from a strategy like the memory strategy, which is bound to fail when the information input reaches a certain load, to strategies which involve thinking."

Guilford (1967) with respect to his structure of intellect model suggests that appropriate teaching methods and techniques will promote the development of the different intellectual abilities. Torrance (1972) concludes that the most effective methods of training in creativity are those methods that give students opportunities for involvement, practice, and interaction with teachers and other children, and that include the deliberate teaching of the skills involved.

Maltzman (1960) reports success with teaching originality; Franklin and Richards (1977) report success with teaching divergent thinking; Covington and Crutchfield (1965) report success in improving skills, strategies, and attitudes towards problem solving; Rosenthal, Morrison, and Perry (1977) report success using CoRT materials to teach creativity; and Mansfield, Busse, and Krepelka (1978) report that most evaluation studies of creativity training programs support the view that creativity can be trained, while voicing serious methodological concerns. These studies strongly suggest that thinking and creativity are teachable skills.

With reference to measuring the effects of a thinking skills program, de Bono (1976) has discussed the difficulty of the problem: "Hard data are judged to be irrelevant or the result of teaching the test. Soft data in the form of teachers' comments are judged to be biased or subjective. These objections are valid" (p. 140). In our earlier study (Edwards & Baldauf, 1983), the anecdotal data from a wide range of students and teachers was overwhelmingly positive about the benefits of CoRT for students. The "harder" data gathered supported this position. However, the data gathered were limited in scope and the data quantification techniques were tentative.

In this study a wider range of both soft and hard data have been gathered in an attempt to present a more complete picture of the effects of CoRT-1 materials on students. The data gathered were focused on investigating some of the claims de Bono makes for his materials.

De Bono's (1976 and 1983) Claims for CoRT

1. "IQ tests manifestly require the exercise of thinking. But IQ tests are not a test of thinking. There should be no change in IQ after a course in training thinking skill. If such a change were to be measured this would automatically cast doubts on the validity of the IQ test as a measure of 'innate' intelligence" (1976, p. 201).

2. "Similarly the standard tests of verbal reasoning do not test the 'attention skills' developed in courses such as CoRT. All thinking involves an element of creativity, but a creativity test such as the Torrance test would be very unlikely to show a change after a course in thinking lessons" (1976, p. 201).

3. "Perhaps the most important aspect of the direct teaching of thinking as a skill is the self-image of a youngster as a 'thinker' " (1983, p. 708).

4. "There is evidence that it (CoRT) improves performance in other thinking areas (such as English essays), but in knowledge-bound subjects it is more difficult to show an effect" (1976, p. 141).

5. CoRT-1 "encourages pupils to look in a wider sweep round a situation instead of rushing off after the obvious, short-term, egocentric, pre-judged line of thought" (1976, p. 129).

6. "The transfer to situations outside school seems good" (1976, p. 217).

7. "Simply understanding the attention-directing devices is not enough . . . Understanding alone will never lead to use. Use can come only from habit and habit can come only from practice" (1976, p. 138).

These seven claims are taken as the major questions that are examined in this study.

Subjects and Procedures

The study was carried out using three Grade-7 classes in a small coeducational primary school in North Queensland (Australia), which had a total enrollment of 425 students. The average age of the 67 students used in this study at the start of the treatment was 12 years 2 months. The teachers used were the regular classroom teachers. Groups 1 and 3 had male teachers; Group 2 had a female teacher. Three 45-minute introductory sessions to CoRT were given to the group of three teachers on the rationale for CoRT, an introduction to each of the CoRT-1 sheets and demonstrations of their use. An opportunity was provided for each teacher to do some practice teaching using one of the sheets. Each of the three classes was given a different treatment.

Group 1 (28 students) were put through the CoRT-1 program and over the following 11 weeks the teacher occasionally reinforced the CoRT skills as part of the classroom teaching program. The reinforcement took the form of two planned applications of CoRT skills in each of language arts, social studies, and science, spread over the 11 weeks. Parents were invited to a series of three 2-hour parent education evenings and encouraged to be involved with their children in working with CoRT at home.

Group 2 (27 students) did the CoRT program and had teacher reinforcement the same as for Group 1, but no parent involvement was sought.

Group 3 (12 Grade-7 students in a composite class with 10 Grade-5 students) only did the CoRT program with no teacher reinforcement.

In each class, the treatment consisted of 10 CoRT-1 sessions, each lasting 45 to 55 minutes and spread over 4 weeks.

INSTRUMENTATION

The data presented and analyzed in this chapter represent the major portion of the data gathered in the study. The aim was to provide a coherent picture of the effects of CoRT-1 on the students, particularly in relation to the de Bono claims that were cited.

Pretreatment Data

All students were asked to complete the following measures:

1. Australian adaptation of the *Otis–Lennon School Ability Test—*Intermediate Form R (Otis & Lennon, 1982).
2. The *Torrance Test of Creative Thinking*—Verbal Test Booklet A (Torrance & Ball, 1984).
3. The *Self Concept as a Learner Scale* (Waetjen, 1967).

The first two were administered and scored by a trained research assistant, the third was administered by the classroom teacher and scored by the researchers.

The teachers completed a student achievement profile on each student. These were in the form of rating scales that were regularly used by the school for reporting student achievement to parents. Four subject areas were covered:

4. Language Arts.
5. Mathematics.
6. Social Studies.

7. Science.

8. Students also completed an essay on one of two topics:

    (a) "There has been a lot of stealing going on in school and you find out that a friend of yours is the thief, what would you do?", or

    (b) "If you wanted to earn some money in the holidays, what would you do?"

Half the students were allocated to each topic. The topics were taken from a set of topics designed by the Cognitive Research Trust for use in a current study comparing the performance of CoRT-trained and non-CoRT-trained students in the United Kingdom.

Delayed Posttreatment Data

Fifteen weeks later, that is, 11 weeks posttreatment, all the pretreatment measures were repeated. For the Torrance Test, Booklet B (a parallel form) was used. A cross-over procedure was used for the essays, with each student doing the alternative topic to their pretest.

Three extra measures were taken also:

9. Student recall of CoRT-1 was tested in class by the teacher asking: "I want you to write all you can remember about the CoRT program. Write the different thinking skills and what you can remember about them."

The students were then given time to write all they could remember.

10. A questionnaire was sent home to parents asking them to provide feedback on:

    how often they worked with their child on CoRT at home.

    how often their child spoke about CoRT at home.

    how often the child used CoRT terms at home.

    any changes they had noticed in their child's thinking as a result of CoRT.

11. For Group 1 the classroom teacher conducted individual interviews with each child seeking: their attitude to the CoRT-1 program; feedback on whether they had applied CoRT-1 in everyday life and, if so, in what ways; and general comments on strengths and weaknesses in CoRT-1.

DATA QUANTIFICATION

The data from each of the measures described in the previous section were quantified in the following manner:

1. Deviation IQ Scores were obtained from the Raw Scores by reference to the manual for the Australian adaptation (Otis & Lennon, 1982).

2. Three scores were obtained using the test scoring manual (Torrance, 1984)—a score for fluency, a score for flexibility, and a score for originality.

3. Scores were obtained on 4 subscales (Waetjen, 1967): motivation; task orientation; problem solving; and class membership; and an overall score for self-concept as a learner.

4. The language arts rating was given on a 1–5 rating for each of 9 subscales: reading with understanding; oral reading; legibility of writing; spelling; writing skills; written expression; listening for information; preparation and fluency of speech; library skills.

5. The mathematics rating was given on a 1–5 rating for each of three subscales: basic number facts; processes in arithmetic; and accuracy and application to everyday problems.

6. The social studies rating was given on a 1–5 rating scale for each of two subscales: research skills; and general factual knowledge.

7. The science rating was given on a 1–5 rating scale for each of two subscales: knowledge and understanding of subject matter; and process skill development.

8. These essays were marked by one of the researchers based on a marking scheme that was developed for use in a Cognitive Research Trust Project. Four major criteria were used: comprehensiveness, coherence, quality of argument, and creativity. An ideas count was also taken. Scoring was done on a blind basis, without reference to pretest, delayed posttest, class, or individual data.

9. The memory of CoRT was assessed on ability to recall and describe each of the 10 areas covered in CoRT-1. A composite percentage score was derived for each student.

10. The first three questions were rated by parents on a 1–3 scale, the last question was free response.

11. The recorded responses were transcribed and analyzed.

RATIONALE FOR THE RESEARCH DESIGN

The rationale for the research design of a study is rarely discussed in research papers on teaching thinking. This section has been included to give readers insight into the basis for our decisions. This should help readers focus on the strengths and weaknesses of the design, and provide a clear basis for interpretation of results.

Grade Level.   The decision to do the study at the Grade-7 level was based on both research findings and practicality. De Bono's experience with CoRT was a guide:

"Our experience is that children in the nine-to-twelve age group are ready to tackle just about any problem" (de Bono, 1976, p. 147).

"Youngsters in the middle grades really enjoy thinking, and motivation is very high. They have sufficient verbal fluency and experience to operate the thinking tools" (de Bono, 1983, p. 707).

Nicholls' (1978) work on children's concepts of ability also convinced us that children under 11 years of age would have difficulty in answering some of the questions we wanted to ask, particularly with respect to aspects of self-concept.

Grade 7 is the last year of primary school for Queensland children. The flexibility in primary curricula and school timetables was a practical advantage that made it relatively easy to do the study as part of the ongoing program of work during normal school hours.

Control Group.   Many studies have been cited (e.g., de Bono, 1976) using control groups. Results from these and our earlier study (Edwards & Baldauf, 1983) convinced us that the use of a control group would be of limited value because the large effects of the program have been clearly documented. It seemed more important to use our limited resources to try to assess treatment differences and to extend the range of variables examined and the statistical power of our tests of that data.

Hard Versus Soft Data.   Quotes from de Bono (1976) cited earlier in this chapter highlight the difficulties of measuring change in the area of thinking in any convincing way. In this study we have tried to use a mixture of well-accepted measures not specifically related to CoRT and specific measures related to CoRT objectives. Standardized measures such as IQ and Torrance's creativity, although rejected by de Bono as valid measures of outcomes of CoRT-1, provide hard data insights into the effects of the CoRT material. Use of Waetjen's Self-Concept as a Learner scale provides another hard measure that is essentially independent of a CoRT philosophy. We then move towards the soft data end of the spectrum with the teacher ratings of student achievement, the marked essays, and the memory of CoRT data, culminating in the soft anecdotal data provided by the parent questionnaires and the student interviews.

Use of IQ Tests.   De Bono (1976) claims that IQ test scores should not be affected by CoRT training. This is supported by Gray's (1972) claim that: "Results from the factor analytical studies of many researchers suggests that the ability to sense problem areas, to be flexible in each of several ways and to produce new and original ideas tend to have little relation to tests used to measure intelligence" (p. 237).

However, Chance (1981, p. 73) makes claims for IQ gains as a result of exposure to Feuerstein's Instrumental Enrichment materials.

What convinced us to use an IQ test was Anastasi's (1982) comment: "Research on the factors associated with increases and decreases in IQ throws light on the conditions determining intellectual development . . . the findings of this type of research point the way to the kind of intervention programs that can effectively alter the course of intellectual development in the desired directions" (p. 328).

The Otis–Lennon School Ability Test is an 80-item test of scholastic aptitude. The Intermediate Form R was used because it is the only form currently adapted for use in Australia. It comprises several types of verbal and nonverbal items intended to sample a wide variety of mental processes. Item content samples verbal, figural, and quantitative reasoning, and verbal comprehension ability.

Use of the Torrance Test of Creativity.   De Bono (1976) claims that effects of CoRT training should not show up on the Torrance test. However, when the structure of the Torrance Test of Verbal Reasoning is examined closely, this argument is hard to sustain. The test covers three areas: fluency—a measure of the number of relevant ideas that are produced; flexibility—the range of categories in which ideas are produced; and originality—the degree of commonality of the individual's ideas with the ideas that were reported in a sample of 500 student records. From the experience of the researchers, these areas fit well with the aims and practice of CoRT-1.

The activities in the test involve: asking questions about a drawing, making guesses about the causes of the event pictured, making guesses about the possible consequence of the event, producing ideas for improving a toy so that it will be more fun for children to play with, thinking of unusual uses for tin cans or cardboard boxes, asking provocative questions, and thinking of the varied possible ramifications of an improbable event.

Torrance (1972) reviewed 144 studies that were designed to teach children to think creatively or to improve their creative functioning. Of these, 71% were successful. This strongly suggests that creative thinking abilities are susceptible to development through educational experiences. The potential of CoRT in such a role is what we were investigating. In this study we are not concerned with the relationship between scores on the Torrance test and real-world creativity.

Teacher Rating Scales of Student Achievement.   Teacher judgments of student progress have also been included because de Bono

(1976) believes: "there is no doubt that a teacher would be in the best position to assess any improvement in thinking skills" (p. 206). The decision was made in this study to use the classroom teachers in an area where they had extensive experience, the assessment of student achievement in a range of subject areas: language arts, mathematics, social science, and science. We also used the achievement rating scale that the teachers commonly used for student reporting in an effort to get good inter and intrarater reliability.

Essays. The essays used here were on topics relatively familiar to the students, focusing on application to everyday life. Because they were designed by the Cognitive Research Trust, they could be seen as having the potential to discriminate between successfully and unsuccessfully trained CoRT students. The essays were marked according to criteria developed by one of the researchers based on suggestions in the CoRT-1 teachers manual. As such, they represent a direct measure of the supposed outcomes to be expected from the CoRT-1 program. To control for possible differences in the difficulty of the topics, half the students were tested on each essay in the pretest and a crossover was used for the delayed posttest.

Self-Concept as a Learner Scale. The Self-Concept as a Learner (SCAL) Scale was chosen as the most relevant scale available for measuring de Bono's concept of self-concept as a thinker, from a perusal of Buros (1978) and the literature on measuring aspects of self-concept. We are currently engaged in further study to look more closely at self-concept as a thinker, and how it is affected by CoRT-1 (Baldauf, Edwards, & Matthews, 1985).

SCAL is a 50-item written test on which the students rate themselves for each item on a 5-point scale from completely true to completely false. It takes 20 minutes to administer, and scoring provides an overall rating and scores on four rational subscales: motivation, task orientation, problem solving, and class membership.

Use of Different Treatment Groups. The use of the three different treatments was designed to reveal any effects of reinforcement and practice of CoRT-1 on students. De Bono's (1976) stress on the value of practice and of application and transfer to everyday life suggested that the treatment used here involve teacher and parent reinforcement.

The amount of reinforcement and practice provided was limited by curricular constraints, and the quantity of parent reinforcement is difficult to measure. However investigation of the relative effects of these treatments is important with respect to isolating the best ways of incorporating CoRT into existing school programs.

Delayed Posttesting.   Because many studies cited by de Bono (1976) of the pre-post control group type, and our earlier work (Edwards & Baldauf, 1983), had shown convincing evidence of the positive short-term effects of the CoRT-1 program, it was decided to use only a delayed posttest in this study. To have had both a posttest and a delayed posttest was not feasible within the constraints of the school situation. We were also concerned about the problem of overtesting students and the threat this would raise to the external validity of the study. These factors convinced us to use only a delayed posttest, 15 weeks after the pretest and 11 weeks after the posttreatment.

RESULTS

The presentation of results has been organized to primarily deal, in turn, with the seven claims by de Bono (1976, 1983), which form the research questions for this chapter.

Claim 1

De Bono (1976) argues that a thinking skills course should not change the results on a valid IQ test. The Otis–Lennon Manual (1982) reports: "research has shown Otis–Lennon scores on the average to be remarkably consistent over fairly long periods of time" (p. 11).

In Table 26.1 we see that IQ increased significantly (105.27 to 109.16:$p < .001$) over the 15-week period from the pretest to the delayed posttest. As these results are deviation IQ standard scores, the effects of maturation are controlled by the test. Also, no test–retest effect should be in evidence over a period of 15 weeks.

TABLE 26.1.
Analysis of Variance for Treatment by IQ ($N = 67$)

Source	SS	df	MS	F
Groups	1441.38	2	720.69	1.99
Error	23219.85	64	362.81	
Trials	508.36	1	508.36	19.84[a]
Groups x Trials	123.31	2	61.66	2.41
Error	1639.83	64	25.62	
Total	26932.73	133		

[a]$p<.001$

Trial Means	Pre	Delayed Post
	105.27	109.16

The pretest–delayed posttest correlation of .87 for the Otis–Lennon demonstrates the stability of the test over time. This high correlation suggests that the significant gains in IQ are a general phenomenon and are not the result of a few individual changes.

Claim 2

De Bono (1976) claims that results on a creativity test like the Torrance would be unlikely to show a change after a course in thinking. The overall pattern that was obtained in this study showed a significant increase in both flexibility and originality. There was also an increase in fluency, but not of sufficient size to be statistically significant. The changes for the individual groups were not uniform (see table 26.2 and Figure 26.1). Although most of the changes indicated an increase, Group 3's results declined in Fluency and Originality. Note that for all three Torrance subscales, groups were more divergent on the pretests and more homoge-

TABLE 26.2.
ANOVA for Torrance Subscales by Treatment ($N = 59$)

Source	SS	df	MS	F
FLUENCY				
Groups	6818.31	2	3409.15	2.16
Error	88235.11	56	1575.63	
TRIALS	277.16	1	277.16	0.93
Groups × Trials	2606.49	2	1303.25	4.38[a]
Error	16665.62	56	297.60	
Total	114602.69	117		
FLEXIBILITY				
Groups	30.48	2	15.24	0.11
Error	7628.13	56	136.22	
Trials	702.09	1	702.09	27.80[b]
Groups × Trials	195.06	2	97.53	3.86[a]
Error	1414.20	56	25.25	
Total	9969.96	117		
ORIGINALITY				
Groups	10918.21	2	5459.10	1.78
Error	171657.10	56	3065.30	
Trials	3129.16	1	3129.16	4.38[a]
Groups × Trials	6277.49	2	3138.74	4.39[a]
Error	40024.47	56	714.72	
Total	232006.43	117		

[a]$p < .05$.
[b]$p < .001$.

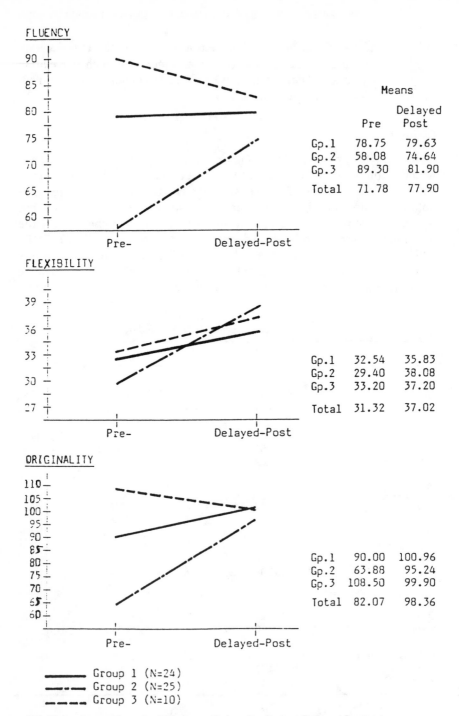

FIG. 26.1. Interactions for 3 Torrance Subscales Pretest-Delayed Posttest.

464

neous on the delayed posttests. This suggests that the pupils within groups may have learned and used a more homogeneous set of creative thinking strategies on the delayed posttest.

Pretest–delayed posttest (retest) correlations for the Torrance sub-scales were: .67 for Fluency, .68 for Flexibility, and .60 for Originality. These reliabilities fall within the lower range of test–retest reliability studies reported by Torrance (1984).

Claim 3

De Bono (1983) claims that the most important aspect of the direct teaching of thinking is the development of the child's self-image as a thinker. To examine this question students were administered Waetjen's SCAL. This is a 50-item test with four subscales: Motivation (13 items), Task Orientation (13 items), Problem Solving (13 items), and Class Membership (11 items). An item analysis suggested two items should be removed from Scale 1 and one from Scale 3. The resulting 47-item test was factor analyzed both at the scale and test level. No support could be found to justify the existence of the four rational subscales. Although the results for the subscales and the total test are presented in Table 26.3, the total results are those that are most psychometrically valid.

A one-way analysis of variance with repeated measures (Veldman, 1967) was used to examine the pretest–delayed posttest results by groups. The only differences found were for pretest and delayed posttest results for the Motivation ($p < 05$), Task Orientation ($p < .05$), Class Membership ($p < 05$) subscales, and for the overall SCAL score ($p < .01$). These results indicate that regardless of treatment type, there were positive changes in students' self-concept as a learner over time. In making this claim we have assumed that self-concepts are generally stable over the time period used in this study, unless specific intervention takes place.

Claim 4

De Bono argues that it is easier to show improvement in language-related areas (e.g., English essays) than in "knowledge bound" areas. De Bono has also argued that teachers are likely to be the best judges of student progress. The results were analyzed using a repeated measures ANOVA by group. No significant group differences or group by time interaction effects were found. In Table 26.4 the pretest–delayed posttest results of teacher judgments of student achievement are presented. Contrary to de Bono's claim, no pretest–delayed posttest differences were found in language arts whereas there were significant changes in mathematics (negative), social science (positive), and science (positive). In summary,

TABLE 26.3.
Summary of Waetjen's (1967) SCAL Data ($N = 67$)

Variable	k	Pre X̄	Delayed Post X̄	Pre Alpha	Delayed Post Alpha	Test Retest Rxx	ANOVA Analysis Proportion of Within Variance	F
1. Motivation	11	39.63	40.67	.27	.46	.63	.075	5.32[a]
2. Task Orientation	13	46.79	48.70	.79	.82	.66	.094	6.67[a]
3. Problem Solving	12	42.12	42.54	.83	.86	.79	.001	0.54
4. Class Membership	11	42.19	43.81	.80	.82	.44	.091	6.57[a]
Total	47	170.73	175.72	.90	.92	.79	.131	10.06[b]

[a] $p < .05$.
[b] $p < .01$.

TABLE 26.4
TEACHER Judgment Data ($N = 67$)

Content Area	k	Pre $\bar{X}$	Delayed Post $\bar{X}$	Test Retest R	Proportion of Within Variance	F
Language Arts	45	31.00	30.99	.94	0.0	0.002
Mathematics	15	10.39	9.97	.87	5.9	4.34[a]
Social Science	10	6.45	7.01	.78	15.4	11.67[b]
Science	10	6.39	6.81	.61	5.9	4.19[a]

[a] $p < .05$.
[b] $p < .01$.

this incoherent pattern of results suggests that, whatever effects CoRT-1 may have had on the subjects' thinking in the subject areas in question, the rating scales did not capture that impact but rather primarily reflected other factors in the educational situation.

Teacher judgments were stable with pretest–delayed posttest correlations of .94 for language arts, .87 for mathematics, .78 for social science, and .61 for science, across the 15 weeks.

Claim 5

De Bono claims that CoRT-1 improves students' approaches to answering questions. To test this claim students were given two CoRT essays in a crossover design described earlier. Each essay was scored holistically based on four major criteria and by an ideas count.

Table 26.5 presents the results by group, by pretest and delayed posttest, and by order of presentation using a complex Latin square design (Bruning & Kintz, 1977). No significant order of presentation effects were found. Significant differences were found between groups for pretest–delayed posttest results and for groups by pretest–delayed posttest. Using a scheffé test, we found that Groups 1 and 2 performed significantly better than Group 3, but an examination of the interaction means indicates that this can be explained by the significantly better pretest results for Groups 1 and 2. Overall performance declined from the pretest to the delayed posttest.

These results are confirmed by the ideas count on the same CoRT essays as presented in table 26.6. Again the significant interaction effect dominates.

Claim 6

The response rate to the questionnaire sent home to parents was 43%. Of these, 31% made no comment on changes in their child's thinking, 17%

TABLE 26.5
CoRT Essays by Groups, Pretest/Delayed Posttest, and Order of
Presentation

Source	SS	df	MS	F
Group	6071.61	2	3035.80	21.39[c]
PP × Order_b	51.02	1	51.02	0.36
PP × Order_b × Group_b	375.17	2	187.59	1.32
Error_b	7803.20	55	141.88	
Pre-Post	220.46	1	220.46	3.35[a]
Order	25.70	1	25.70	0.39
PP × Order_w	48.52	1	48.52	0.74
PP × Group	1188.40	2	594.20	9.04[b]
Order × Group	306.40	2	153.20	2.44
PP × Order_w × Group_w	13.94	2	6.87	0.10
Error_w	3419.58	52	65.76	
Total	19524.00	121		

[a] $p < .05.$
[b] $p < .01.$
[c] $p < .001.$

Means

	1	2	3
Group	64.5	60.79	45.58

	Pre	Delayed-Post
Trials	60.79	58.10

Groups × Trials

	Pre	Delayed-Post
1	69.22	59.78
2	60.27	61.32
3	42.75	48.42

reported no observable change, and 52% reported positive changes. The seven quotes listed represent a range of effects reported by parents:

"He now accepts that there is more than a single answer to a question."

"The program created an awareness that thought processes could be controlled and directed for problem-solving purposes."

"He now uses the methods to solve some personal and emotional problems.

"Has led to a more positive attitude to decision making."

TABLE 26.6
CoRT Essays Ideas Count by Groups and Pretest/Delayed Posttest

Source	SS	df	MS	F
Groups	439.84	2	219.92	18.70[a]
Error	693.84	59	11.76	
Pre-Post	26.20	1	26.20	2.28
PP ×				
Groups	219.10	2	109.55	9.54[a]
Error	677.32	59	11.48	
Total	2056.30	123		

[a]$p < .001$.

Means

	Pre	Delayed-Post	Total
Group 1	10.81	6.89	8.85
2	8.48	10.17	9.33
3	3.91	4.75	4.33

"More thought went into her project work . . . and she became more interested in the outcome of all our household discussions, e.g., furnishing our home, her father's future."

"She is a child with considerable problems at school with all aspects of her school work . . . there has been a considerable improvement mainly in improved confidence at tackling problems—this could be connected with the program."

"She is now prepared to work through a question rather than be told an answer."

The individual interviews of the children by the teacher of Group 1 revealed that: 58% of the students reported using CoRT in everyday life situations; 19% said they had not used it but planned to in the future; 15% said they had not used CoRT; and 8% made no comment. In the same interviews: 54% of the children thought the CoRT-1 program was good, helpful, or useful; 35% thought it was "O.K." or "all right"; whereas 4% believed it was "great," 4% thought it was bad or boring, and 4% thought it was very bad.

Claim 7

De Bono claims that practice and reinforcement should improve CoRT performance. This claim was tested in several ways. Firstly, a direct delayed posttest measure of memory of CoRT was analyzed by group and revealed results directly counter to de Bono's claim. Group 3, the treatment only group, displayed significantly better memory of CoRT than Groups 1 and 2, which had reinforcement. (see Table 26.7).

These results are supported by the spontaneous attitudes to CoRT that are expressed by students in their memory of CoRT statements. The attitudes that are expressed by members of Group 3 were 50% positive, 8% negative, compared to Group 1 (36% positive, 7% negative), and Group 2 (22% positive).

Secondly, a review of the data related to groups that are discussed in claims 1 to 6 shows few significant differences by group, or group by pre-delayed posttest interaction results. None of these results directly support the claim that reinforcement has positive measurable effects.

DISCUSSION

The results for IQ, creativity (flexibility and originality), and self-concept as a learner present a coherent picture. These are each areas where one would expect no significant overall change in a group this large over a 15-week period. Despite this, students showed a significant gain over time in each of the areas. The results for IQ and creativity (flexibility and originality) support the contentions of Anastasi (1982) and Torrance (1972), respectively, that each measure is open to systematic improvement through instruction. In this respect, CoRT-1 appears to be an effective mode of instruction. Because standard scores have been used for both measures, and there was a time lapse of 11 weeks posttreatment, the results are particularly convincing.

The evidence of improvement in self-concept as a learner as revealed by SCAL is supported by the generally positive attitude to CoRT-1 and its effect on their learning reported by the students. The responses from parents with respect to the effects of CoRT-1 on their children are again in

TABLE 26.7
Memory of CoRT by Group

Source	SS	df	MS	F
Groups	158998.53	2	79499.27	218.80[a]
Error	23253.21	64	363.33	
Total	182251.74			

[a]$p < .001$

Means

Group	1	2	3
	48.54	47.33	58.75

the same direction. Indeed, the anecdotal data from students and parents that was obtained and reported here are in keeping with the strong positive attitudes commonly reported for programs such as CoRT. This feedback also strongly supports de Bono's contention that CoRT skills transfer to outside situations.

Although a few effects related to groups emerged in the study, there was no consistent pattern and it is difficult to attribute any effect to treatment differences. Feedback from the parents revealed that the Group 1 students did, in general, get more parent reinforcement than the other groups, indicating that the treatment was implemented. At the same time, it should be pointed out that the amount of reinforcement and practice both at school and at home was limited. The study design also contains the confounding interaction of treatment and teacher personality or style. It may be that a closer analysis of this interaction could help explain some of the apparently counterindicative effects revealed in our data. Neither practice nor reinforcement had any consistent effect on CoRT performance.

The lower performance of the students on the delayed posttest CoRT essays was a surprising result. The large drop in performance for Group 1 masked the slight improvement for Group 2 and the larger improvement for Group 3. Given the results of previous research, it is unlikely that the CoRT-1 program would cause such a drop. No convincing explanation for this result was apparent from the data gathered.

Particular care needs to be taken in attributing changes in achievement across subjects to CoRT-1. Teacher "assessment-set" could vary at different times of the year and still produce reliable results. Although it is interesting to note that mathematics, the area where achievement declined, was the subject area where teachers found it hardest to apply CoRT and, in this study, gave no reinforcement, to attribute the decline to this cause would be premature. The teaching the students received in these subject areas across the 15 weeks could equally well explain the results. No impact of CoRT-1 one way or another is apparent in the pattern of results, which more likely reflects accidents of the curriculum and teacher "assessment-sets." However, the results obtained in this study do not support de Bono's contention that CoRT improves performance in language arts relative to performance in the "knowledge-bound" subjects.

CONCLUSION

For many, the anecdotal data gathered in the study would be enough to warrant the introduction of CoRT materials. To have students showing such positive attitudes to the materials and their usefulness, supported to a degree by parent feedback, 11 weeks after the intervention program and after only 8 hours of direct instruction and limited reinforcement, is convincing testimony.

Significant positive shifts in IQ, creativity (flexibility and originality), and self-concept as a learner occurred during the period of exposure to CoRT-1, encouraging those who favor implementation of CoRT materials.

The finding that practice and reinforcement revealed no measured effects on students with the instruments used in this study is important for those considering the mode of teaching with CoRT materials.

This study has taken a much more detailed look at the effects of CoRT-1 on students than previous studies. Further studies may reveal detailed insights into how such materials work, thereby enabling both improvement of materials and improvement of learning environments for students.

ACKNOWLEDGMENTS

This research was mainly funded by a special research grant from James Cook University of North Queensland. The authors also wish to acknowledge the research assistance of Barbara Watson, the help of Col Shepherd, Graham Buchan, Meredith Wenta, and Mick Hitchins, and the cooperation of the students and parents involved.

REFERENCES

Anastasi, A. (1982). *Psychological testing*. New York: Macmillan.

Anderson, R. C. (1965). Introduction. In R. C. Anderson & D. P. Ausubel (Eds.), *Readings in the psychology of cognition*. New York: Holt, Rinehart & Winston.

Baldauf, R. B., Jr., Edwards, J., & Matthews, B. (1985). The factorial validity of the Self-Concept as a Learner Scale (SCAL) *Educational and Psychological Measurement, 42 (3), 655–659*

Bruning, J. L., & Kintz, B. L. (1977). *Computational handbook of statistics*. IL: Scott, Foresman.

Buros, O. K. (1978). *The eighth mental measurements: Yearbook*. (Vol. 1). NJ: Gryphon Press.

Chance, P. (1981). The remedial thinker. *Psychology Today, 15* (10), 63–73.

Covington, M. V., & Crutchfield, R. S. (1965). Facilitation of creative problem solving: Experiments using P.I. for this purpose. *Programmed Instruction, 4* (4).

de Bono, E. (1976). *Teaching thinking*. London: Maurice Temple Smith.

de Bono, E. (1981). *CoRT thinking*. Sydney: Pergamon Press.

de Bono, E. (1983, June). The direct teaching of thinking as a skill. *Phi Delta Kappan*, 703–708.

Dienes, Z. P., & Jeeves, M. A. (1965). Thinking in structures. *Cognitive processes, (Vol. 1)*. London: Hutchinson Educational.

Edwards, J., & Baldauf, R. B., Jr. (1983). Teaching thinking in secondary science. In W. Maxwell (Ed.), *Thinking: The expanding frontier*. Philadelphia: Franklin Institute Press, 129–138

Franklin, B. S., & Richards, P. N. (1977). Effects on children's divergent thinking abilities of a period of direct teaching for divergent production. *British Journal of Educational Psychology, 47,* 66–70.

Gray, K. (1972). Thinking abilities as objectives in curriculum development. *Educational Review.* (E. A. Peel, Ed.), 24(3), 237-250.

Guilford, J. P. (1967). *The nature of human intelligence.* New York: McGraw-Hill.

Maltzman, I. (1965). On the training of originality. R. C. Anderson & D. P. Ausubel (Eds.), *Readings in the psychology of cognition.* New York: Holt, Rinehart & Winston.

Mansfield, R. S., Busse, T. V., & Krepelka, E. J. (1978). The effectiveness of creativity training. *Review of Educational Research, 48(4), 517–536.*

McPeck, J. E. (1983). A second look at de Bono's heuristics for thinking. In W. Maxwell (Ed.), *Thinking: The expanding frontier.* Philadelphia: Franklin Institute Press.

Nicholls, J. G. (1978). The development of the concepts of effort and ability, perception of academic attainment and the understanding that difficult tasks require more ability. *Child Development, 49,* 800–814.

Otis, A. S., & Lennon, R. T. (1982). Otis–Lennon School Ability Test: Intermediate Form R (Australian Adaptation). *Victoria: Australian Council for Educational Research.*

Rosenthal, D. A., Morrison, S. M., & Perry L. (1977). Teaching Creativity: A comparison of two techniques. *Australian Journal of Education, 1977, 21,* 226–232.

Taba, H. (1962). *Curriculum development: Theory and practice.* New York: Harcourt, Brace, & World.

Torrance, E. P. (1972). Can we teach children to think creatively? *Journal of Creative Behavior, 6(2), 114–143.*

Torrance, E. P., & Ball, O. E. (1984). *Torrance tests of creative thinking.* Scholastic Testing Service.

Veldman, D. (1967). *Fortran programming for the behavioral sciences.* Englewood Cliffs, NJ: Holt, Rinehart & Winston.

Waetjen, W. B. (1967). *Self-concept as a Learner Scale.* Cleveland State University: W. B. Waetjen.

27 The Classroom as a Place for Thinking

Francis Schrag
University of Wisconsin, Madison

This chapter examines the classroom as a social setting for engaging in thinking. I begin by explaining the apparent dominance of the recitation as contrasted with the Socratic pattern of verbal interaction. I then inquire into the nature of social settings that promote thinking outside school. I argue that such settings provide the problem solver with a degree of autonomy to which, given the need to preserve order, would be difficult to duplicate in the school. I conclude by discussing ways of reconciling the tension between social control and autonomy in school.

PREVALENCE OF THE RECITATION

Consider specimens of the two patterns:

1. T. Mark, when was Grover Cleveland president?
   M. Let's see, was 1890 . . . or something . . . wasn't he the one . . . he was elected twice, wasn't he?
   T. Yes . . . Gloria, can you get the dates right? (Sizer, 1984, p. 83).
2. T. Do you know why there is a sparse population in Tibet now?
   S. Because it's desert?
   T. No.
   S. No? I don't know. Oh you said it was mountainous.
   T. Very mountainous.
   S. So it isn't good farmland.

T. O.K. It's very tough to farm when you have mountains there. You only have valleys to farm in O.K. Now do you think it's very dense in Alaska?

S. No.

T. Why?

S. I would imagine because of the cold.

T. The cold climate. And why does a cold climate . . .? (Collins, 1977, p. 349).

Which interaction is more likely to occur in a high school classroom? We would not hesitate a moment before answering, the first. And we would, of course, be right. Before documenting the prevalence and stability of the first kind of exchange, however, notice two of its characteristic features: First, the teacher's question asks for a statement of simple fact; second, the teacher, having received an answer from one student, briefly evaluates it and immediately calls on a different student. This familiar pattern is sometimes called the recitation. The second excerpt of dialogue illustrates a pattern of questioning that may be called Socratic. It is characterized by an effort on the part of the teacher to encourage students to draw warranted inferences about conditions that are needed for population density, from the information they already have about where population is and is not sparse. The subject of the lesson is geography but the teacher's interest clearly goes beyond conveying information about population density to helping the student *think*, that is "figure out" *why* things are the way they are.

Studies of teacher behavior in the classroom reveal a striking stability (see Hoetker & Ahlbrand, 1969). The systematic observational studies of Arno Bellack (1965) and his co-workers that were published in the mid-1960's yielded generalizations that coincide with both earlier and more contemporary studies to a remarkable degree. Hoetker and Ahlbrand (1969) state:

> What Bellack observed, . . . was that his teachers, despite differences in the sizes, ability levels, and backgrounds of their classes, acted very much like one another. They talked between two-thirds and three-quarters of the time and their major activity was asking and reacting to questions that called for factual answers from students. (p. 148)

About 15 years later, researchers associated with John Goodlad's *A Place Called School* (1983) studied over 1,000 elementary and secondary classrooms. Kenneth Sirotnik (1983) reported the principal findings in a recent article. He also found that teachers " 'out-talk' students by a ratio of nearly three to one" (p. 20). Regarding the nature of verbal interchanges in the classroom, he reports,

Scanning the array of teacher-to-student interactions, we find that barely 5% of the instructional time is spent on direct questioning—questioning which anticipates a specific response like 'yes,' 'no,' "Columbus," or '1492'. Less than 1 percent of that time is devoted to open questions which call for more complex cognitive or affective responses. (Ibid)

It is safe to say that the Socratic pattern of questioning is extremely rare in elementary and secondary school classrooms. Why should this be? The answer is clearly *not* that pedagogy textbooks and professors endorse the recitation method, for it has been widely and consistently condemned. Nor is it very plausible to account for its prevalence by referring to the intellectual or psychological characteristics of teachers, for surely the range of such characteristics is greater than the range of classroom interaction patterns actually found.

SOCIAL CONTROL IN CLASSROOMS

In order to achieve a better understanding of the limitations of the school classroom as a place for thinking, a limitation reflected in the findings just cited, we need to understand the classroom environment from a sociological perspective. In particular, we need to understand its need for order or "social control." Why is order a problem? The vulnerability of the school and its classrooms to loss of social control depends on several obvious features of schools: (1) The students vastly outnumber the adults; (2) their attendance is coerced; (3) the physical setting is crowded enough for a single obstreperous student to disrupt the activities of all the others; finally (4) the activities to which the school is ostensibly dedicated are not those that would be chosen voluntarily by many or perhaps all the students were they given a choice. As sociologist Mary Metz (1978) notes, "Classroom order is fragile. One child intent upon his own purposes can easily destroy the concentration of thirty-six others. . . . Classrooms have the peculiar quality of being intimate yet compulsory settings" (p. 121).

To understand how teachers can maintain order, it is useful to examine the resources they have at their disposal. Even expulsion, the ultimate sanction, is sometimes welcome. The school has few penalties that constitute severe deprivation. A withholding of permission to participate in an extracurricular activity, such as athletics, may be perceived as severe, but only by students with at least some loyalty to the institution. Teachers and other staff do have personal influence over many students who can be urged to comply in return for the teacher's approval or acceptance (Dreeben, 1973, p. 459). But this too depends on at least some allegiance to the claims of the institution. Probably the most distinctive resource a teacher controls results from his or her responsibility for the allocation of grades.

Grades have a number of characteristics that make them quite unlike typical rewards outside school, such as money. It is rare for someone to value $5.00 over $100.00, but it is not at all rare for a student to value a D over an A. How is this possible? As a normative symbol, any grade above failing reflects a student's willingness to comply with the demands of the institution. For disaffected students, a low grade may become a badge of honor, a symbol of one's refusal to kowtow to the teacher's demands. Moreover, unlike money, the value of a particular grade depends to a large extent on the distribution of grades to *other* students. An A in a class where everyone gets A's is not usually perceived to be as valuable as an A when only 10% of the class get A's. If some students in a class are assured of an A, they have little incentive to comply. If some students expect to fail, compliance also loses its value for them. Grades then are a resource for maintaining control but they cannot be used to secure the compliance of *all* students *all* the time; and even one disruptive student is sufficient to create turmoil.

Grades are given for tasks such as tests, class participation, and homework. A course grade can be based on an "average" of many grades or based on the evaluation of a single task, such as a final examination. The tasks can vary from simple recall of factual information to the writing of a short story or the carrying out of an experiment in the science laboratory. Look at two dimensions of graded tasks (their frequency and nature) from the perspective of social control. If a teacher bases his or her entire grade on a single examination at the end of the course, there is little incentive to attend, much less to comply, during the bulk of the semester. The pressure will begin to build as the end of the term approaches, but a sense of urgency will probably be absent earlier. For the teacher, therefore, it is more rational to distribute tests or assignments with some frequency throughout the semester. In this way a poor performance at one point will not be so weighty as to jeopardize a final grade, and, by the same token, an outstanding performance early on will not preclude the need for continued effort.

If grades are to serve as means of social control, the tasks for which they are awarded (tests, assignments, and the like) must meet two criteria. They must be perceived as capable of being mastered with effort and perseverance, and they must be perceived as amenable to objective evaluation. If students felt that a decent grade is dependent primarily on their native gifts and talents rather than on the work they are willing to undertake, there would be no incentive for the untalented to comply. And if students felt that judgment of performance is a matter of personal bias, favoritism, or assessment based on relatively vague criteria, then again, compliance would be undermined. If the goal is maintaining order, it is rational for teachers to construct tests and assignments that require relatively low-level cognitive activities such as recall of information or routine application of procedures that are presented in class or in the textbook. Students will then be unlikely to interpret scores on tests and homework that are based on considerations other than objective performance. Every student may legitimately feel that if he or she "buckles down" to work he or she will do passably, if not commendably.

This mode of reasoning can be extended to embrace classroom procedures. Sociologist Robert Dreeben (1973) describes the teacher's situation in this way:

> Teacher's options for gaining attention and engagement are fairly circumscribed. They can command the front of the classroom and attempt to control the proceedings (both for instructional and management purposes) by doing most of the talking [lecturing, questioning and demonstrating] and by controlling pupil participation [presumably reducing its unpredictability] through rapid-fire questioning which limits pupils' engagement largely to occasions created by the teacher. (p. 466)

Socratic inquiry, on the other hand, is fraught with problems from the point of view of social control. Extended questioning of one student gives the *other* students more opportunity to pursue their own potentially subversive activities. It may be harder for the other students to follow the line of questioning because it goes beyond the overt lesson and it is harder to judge whether answers are "correct" or not because the teacher needs to press the student beyond what he is confident about. Finally, the open-ended nature of some of the questions, e.g., "why?," presents two dangers, which the request for factual information does not: The student may just invent something silly that will distract the class from the issue, or he or she may come up with a brilliant answer that the teacher had not anticipated. This could make the teacher look foolish in the eyes of the class, hence undermining his or her authority.

Granted that the recitation pattern is conducive to maintaining order, it might appear from what I've said that the teacher's concern with preserving order has absolute priority. In a sense it is. It may be that a degree of disorder is not inimical to the achievement of certain educational goals, but from the sociological perspective the point to stress is that an ability to control the class is *perceived by others* to be central to one's effectiveness as a teacher. As C. W. Gordon (1957) noted in his observation of a suburban high school about 25 years ago (Hudgins, 1971): "The duty of the teacher was to maintain order both as a condition for learning and because it symbolized his competence. Teaching competence was difficult to assess, but *disorder* was taken as a *visible sign of incompetence by colleagues, principal, parents and students"* (p. 15, italics added).

A very recent study of several high schools by Philip Cusick (1983) underlines the same point:

> The basic requirement for teachers was not that they instruct from some agreed-upon course of study. It was not even that they instruct. It was that they be capable of maintaining some state of moderate order among the students, and the proof that they could do that was that their students were neither running about the halls nor showing up in the office. (p. 56)

The use of the recitation pattern to maintain order is not only something that sociologists have explained; it is a pattern whose uses teachers have always understood. It is stated in Piaget (1957) that as early as 1658, for example, in his *Great Didactic,* Comenius urges that:

> The teacher . . . should give his attention first to one scholar, then to another, more particularly with the view of testing the honesty of those whom he distrusts. For example, if the scholars have to say a repetition lesson, he should call first on one pupil, then on another, first one at the top of the class and then one at the bottom, while all the rest attend. He may thus ensure that each one will be in readiness, since none can be certain that he will not be examined. (p. 68)

A recent study of four Wisconsin high schools by Linda McNeil (1983) demonstrates how teachers "maintain discipline by the ways they present course materials" (p. 114). The social studies teachers tended to reduce all topics to "disjointed pieces of information—lists" (p. 123). The teachers were, according to McNeil, "articulate in explaining their view of their jobs and their rationale for their instructional techniques" (p. 124).

> When filled with lists, the course content appears to be rigorous and factual. It makes teachers appear knowledgeable and gives students a sense of fairness in the grading: they know they have to memorize the lists. Lists and unelaborated items reduce the uncertainty for both students and teachers. For this reason, it is clearly the dominant mode of conveying information. (p. 124)

We have argued thus far that the disadvantage of the Socratic pattern in the struggle for survival in school classrooms lies in its tendency to undermine the one condition that the teacher must preserve at all costs—classroom order.

SETTINGS FOR THINKING

Although life in classrooms is dominated by lecture and recitation, those of us concerned with enhancing thinking should not assume that listening and answering simple questions constitute the only activities that *can* go on in school. Cannot thinking and problem solving also take place? Rather than focusing on the classroom, insight into this question may come from a different direction altogether. What kinds of social structures *outside* of school foster or support genuine problem solving? This question may appear virtually impossible to answer because genuine problem solving takes place in settings as diverse as consulting rooms and construction sites, but it becomes more manageable when we identify the impetus for solving problems in the first place. A remark by the late Gilbert Ryle (1979) is suggestive: "Thinking is trying to make up for a gap in one's education" (p. 67). What Ryle means is that if one already knew the answer, already knew what to do, there would be no need to stop and think. The work of "professional" problem solvers is best seen in contrast to the work of the people whose only task is to carry out a routine procedure or set of procedures. The contrast I am talking about is not the contrast between blue- and white-collar workers, for example, but between assembly line workers, typists, and telephone operators at one end of the spectrum and architects, attorneys, and auto mechanics at the other.

The work of those on the one end comprises a series of *identical* tasks. Because both the "input" and "output" are invariable, the task can be specified to such a degree that very little thinking is required. The tasks facing those on the other end resist such specification because either the input or the output or both vary from task to task. This is not to say that these tasks contain no repeatable elements. The auto mechanic may replace many spark plugs in his or her career, and replacing one set is not much different from replacing another, but he or she must first ascertain that new spark plugs are required. *Diagnosis* requires thinking and is required precisely because the mechanic cannot know at first glance (or hearing) what needs to be done. The architect or builder, to take another example, may be asked to build a house that is the virtual duplicate of one already built, but its location at a different site with distinctive characteristics will probably necessitate some adaptations at both the planning and implementation stages. Because the tasks carried out by those at this end of the spectrum have so many unpredictable characteristics, they require thinking.

Our interest centers on the relationship between the nature of the task and the nature of the social structure best suited to its performance.

Sanford Dornbusch and W. Richard Scott (1975) draw a useful contrast between delegations and directives: "an actor who is assigned a goal and allowed to make at least some nontrivial decisions regarding course of action has received a delegation. . . . By contrast, a directive presumes the previous selection of a path and tells the actor to carry out a prescribed course of action" (p. 72).

Dornbusch and Scott argue that there appears to be: "a relatively clear connection between the type of task to be performed and the work arrangements appropriate for regulating a task" (p. 82).

> Generally, in the interests of organizational effectiveness and efficiency, we would expect tasks which are high on clarity, predictability, and efficacy to be allocated by directive; tasks low on these three dimensions we would expect to be allocated by delegation. In its simplest terms, the argument is that, given high clarity as the objectives to be attained, high predictability of the resistance to be encountered, and established procedures for successfully handling this resistance, it is efficient to develop standardized, routine procedures which performers are directed to follow. (p. 82)

For tasks that are low on clarity, predictability, and efficacy, it is "more effective to allow the individual performer to assess the amount and type of resistance confronted at any particular point and to adjust the activities accordingly" (p. 84).

When tasks require problem solving, settings permitting a degree of worker autonomy are more likely to be found. The autonomy does not derive from the need to keep workers satisfied, or from our inability to schedule creativity, or the like. It has to do with the demands of the tasks themselves. Thus, the auto mechanic cannot anticipate exactly how much time will be needed for a particular job, or even if he or she can do it until a diagnosis is made. The autonomy I am alluding to carries no implication that the worker is unsupervised or is not operating within a rigid hierarchy. It is simply that the job cannot be done efficiently if the worker is not allowed a measure of flexibility in scheduling and carrying out his work. The service manager can rationally order the mechanic to work for 8 hours or to work on the 1982 Chevy first or to finish the job on the 1979 Ford before going on. He cannot rationally order the mechanic to repair the still undiagnosed Ford in 2 hours. Only the diagnosis will reveal how long the job will take. The process involves seeing whether the resources needed to repair the car are available, including the tools and spare parts, not just locating the problem.

I call your attention to two characteristic features of problem-solving activities. It is both rational and typical for problem solvers, whether physicians or auto mechanics, to consult with peers. Because of the innumerable variety of problems encountered, one worker may have specialized knowledge or experience needed by another. It is also typical for problem solvers to need access to more information than they can carry in their heads. The clinic, the law firm, the auto shop not infrequently have their own "libraries" in which practitioners can look up recent cases, recommended dosages, numbers of the parts that need ordering, and so on. Some of us have images of the professional thinker as a solitary man or woman sitting in his or her office for many hours at a time with only an empty pad of paper or a typewriter for company. Not even professional academics always fit this model (although there are occasions when they do); trips to the library and consultation with colleagues are part of the working day for the problem solver.

THINKING IN SCHOOLS

As far as teachers are concerned, they are treated like problem solvers, as we expect them to be. They are issued delegations rather than directives. Their work life is expected to include trips to the library, consultation with colleagues, and so on. Look at the school setting with a focus on the students. Students are generally issues *directives;* they are not permitted to collaborate with peers, they may not set their own work schedules, and they may go to the library only at appointed times, often only during "free periods." It is clear, then, that the social structure is not compatible with tasks that require genuine problem solving. Many writers have wittingly or unwittingly likened schools to factories. Regrettably, the tasks students are asked to perform in school are all too often like assembly-line tasks in their mindlessness. But it is a mistake to see this as resulting from a misguided ideology of education or from the needs of capitalists for docile workers. The social structures *most* congenial to problem solving are *least* conducive to the maintenance of social control.

By examining some apparent exceptions, we will find that the aforementioned generalization holds only if we make certain assumptions. Several exceptions come to mind: the law school classroom; the science laboratory, the art studio, the advanced seminar in college or graduate school, and the Montessori preschool classroom. Notice that all except the last are mostly voluntary rather than compulsory settings. This means that most of the students elect to take painting or torts or physics and are not forced to. Generally, these are students to whom grades are important because admission to college or medical or art school or a desirable firm is contingent on performance in the course. The advanced seminar and law school class are likely to feature more of the Socratic pattern of questioning or more open discussion. Students may be embarrassed or even humiliated by the law professor, but the threat of disorder is rarely present because the formal and informal sanctions against disrupting other students are perceived to be very potent. Moreover, these students believe that the dialogue in which they participate and observe is a model for subsequent interrogations by apellate judges in their professional practice. Contrast this with the high school student who may *want* to be kicked out of class or even, perhaps, out of school (See Philips, 1982).

Advanced seminars often feature significant amounts of desultory discussion or discussion that is inconclusive, yet disorder is never an issue because here again students are discussing topics in fields they have chosen and in which they have a good deal invested. But even in these instances, careful observation would show that attention often wanders, some students reading or snoozing while others are holding the floor; however, it would be considered extraordinarily bad form to manifest one's own lack of interest in such a way as to disrupt others.

Preschools present a different pattern. Here the division between work and play activities is not yet apparent, and the possibility of deliberate disruption or rebellion is not within the students' repertoire. The Montessori classroom does show us a unique possibility: It presents an environment that is enormously appealing to the preschool child, yet structured in such a way that it invites and even demands problem solving. Students here do not usually collaborate but they do select problems rather than have them handed to them, and they set their own pace of work. The materials themselves provide feedback relating to degree of success, so that the teacher is not involved in grading students according to some common standard (see Standing, 1962).

We must, therefore, qualify what I said earlier about the incompatibility of problem solving and social control. The generalization holds only in coercive settings, only if we assume the conventional technology of learning and teaching (that is, talk, books, paper and pencil, etc.), and only if we assume that students are aware of the possibility of deliberate disruption. Problem-solving activities *in school* can be compatible with social control if we either relax the constraint on compulsory attendance, or if we can invent alternative "technologies" of learning, as Montessori did. I see no prospect for relaxing the constraint on compulsory attendance. The current trend goes precisely in the opposite direction, toward an even longer period of compulsory attendance, toward lengthening the school day and the school year, and toward making every effort to prevent students from dropping out of school even when they gain nothing from "putting in their time," save a diploma. The current thrust toward raising requirements in the "academic" curriculum at the expense of vocational or arts-related courses will further reduce the minimal opportunities many students have of problem solving (see U.S. Department of Education, 1984). Students will be asked to abandon the auto shop, which requires genuine thinking, for the social studies or English classrooms in which they will be asked to memorize important dates or definitions of the parts of speech.

The potentialities of the new technologies are still unknown. Seymour Papert's (1980) work is inspiring. His conception of computers as new objects to promote thinking is in the Montessori tradition, though Papert makes no reference to Montessori's work. How far can we go in designing settings that are involving enough to deter disruption, demanding enough to require high-level thinking, yet flexible enough to permit the student the kind of autonomy that is needed for problem solving? We do not yet know. Simply creating open classrooms while maintaining the traditional technologies of learning and teaching is not sufficient. Computers may not be the answer, but their potential lies in the fact that, unlike the conventional learning materials found in classrooms modeled on the British Infant Schools, young people find them almost irresistable. If we consider thinking to be an important educational goal and activity, and we need not do so, we will need either to invent new technologies, new "objects" to think with, as Papert calls them, or to reverse the current trend toward standardized, compulsory curricula. If neither approach proves feasible, we shall need to explore locations for learning to solve problems outside of school classrooms.

REFERENCES

Bellack, A. et al. (1965). *The language of the classroom.* New York: Teachers College Press.

Collins, A. (1977). Processes in acquiring knowledge. In R. C. Anderson, R. J. Spiro, & W. Montague (Eds.), *Schooling and the acquisition of knowledge.* Hillsdale, NJ: Lawrence Erlbaum Associates.

Cusick, P. (1983). *The egalitarian ideal and the American high school.* New York: Longman.

Dornbusch, S. M., & Scott, W. R. (1975). *Evaluation and the exercise of authority.* San Francisco: Jossey-Bass.

Dreeben, R. (1973). The school as a workplace. In R. Travers (Ed.), *Second handbook of research on teaching.* Chicago: Rand McNally.

Etzioni, A. (1961). *A comparative analysis of complex organizations.* New York: Free Press.

Goodlad, J. (1983). *A place called school.* New York: McGraw-Hill.

Hoetker, J. E., & Ahlbrand, W. P., Jr. (1969). The persistence of the recitation. *American Educational Research Journal, 6,* 145-167.

Hudgins, B. (1971). *The instructional process.* Chicago: Rand McNally.

McNeil, L. M. (1983). Defensive teaching and classroom control. In M. Apple & L. Weiss (Eds.), *Ideology and practice in schooling.* Boston: Routledge.

Metz, M. H. (1978). *Classrooms and corridors: The crisis of authority in desegregated secondary schools.* Berkeley: University of California Press.

Papert, S. (1980). *Mindstorms.* New York: Basic.

Philips, S. V. (1982). The language socialization of lawyers: Acquiring the "cant." In G. Spindler, (Ed.), *Doing the ethnography of schooling*. New York: Holt.

Piaget, J. (Ed.), (1957). *John Amos Comenius: Selections*. Paris: UNESCO.

Ryle, G. (1979). *On thinking*. Totowa, NJ: Rowman & Littlefield.

Sirotnik, K. (1983). What you see is what you get—consistency, persistency, and mediocrity in classrooms. *Harvard Educational Review, 53*, 16-31.

Sizer, T. (1984). *Horace's compromise: The dilemma of the American high school*. Boston: Houghton Mifflin.

Standing, E. M. (1962). *Maria Montessori: Her life and work*. New York: Mentor.

United States Department of Education. (1984). *The nation responds*. Washington, DC: U.S. Government Printing Office.

28 Slowing Language Down: A Strategy for Systematically Getting at the Issues

Richard A. Wertime
Beaver College
Glenside, PA

The poet Wendell Berry (1980–1981) says that one of the functions of poetry is to "slow language down" and adds that this "slowing" process helps to protect us against glibness. Poetry, however, is not alone in performing this service: Any form of discourse that forces an uncommon degree of scrupulousness on the speaker will do the same thing.

Most of today's students—average and bright students—do not know how to slow language down in a way that makes them accountable for their every proposition. By virtue of this lack, they stand essentially at the mercy of good or ill fortune when they embark upon an inquiry: If a good idea occurs to them, they thrive; if not, they flounder. But rarely does the good idea, much less the poor or average one, result from their initiating a controlled, self-conscious search for reliably fresh notions.

The key words here are *self-conscious* and *reliable,* both referring to virtues that are absolutely critical to authentically principled thinking. It is axiomatic in studies of metacommunication (Wilden, 1972) that knowing how to know is vastly more important than the much simpler (and much chancier) business of merely knowing; yet the task of leading students into such metaknowledge seems as difficult as ever from the pedagogical point of view.

I propose a heuristic that involves brainstorming and the rigorous pursuit of some of the consequences of brainstorming that can help students articulate and develop the pertinent issues that are implicit in their thinking. I call this process "tethering an inquiry" because the particular type of brainstorming and the steps that follow it are "tethered" to a subject the student has already selected. It is knowing what to do with a subject once they have chosen it that distresses the majority of students most, not choosing a subject area. Students often sense that their subject is a good one and are quite right to do so; the spontaneous curiosity that led them to choose it is rich in intelligent, albeit tacit, understanding (Polanyi, 1983). But they simply do not know how to make conscious what is latent. So they get mired in commonplaces: They circle on themselves, loading their work with repetition; often they lose heart and give up altogether.

Many heuristics exist already that can help alleviate these problems: treeing; making grids and flowcharts; doing means–end analysis, drawing analogies; interviewing; etc. (Hayes, 1981). These heuristics do not, used singly, produce the result we yearn for. They do not abruptly upgrade the student's mental sophistication, nor do they open the secrets of metalevel cognition to the student. Why not? My guess is that the problem lies in the way in which we group these heuristics: It is often a democratic grouping that implicitly bestows the same power on all the heuristics. "Go window-shopping," we say, "and see which ones work for you." Such advice is misleading because it ignores two factors that have to be acknowledged when we use heuristics in our teaching: First, that heuristic strategies differ considerably in their power to help students achieve the more difficult objectives of thought; and second—a corollary—that the sequencing of heuristics has a great deal to do with their collective success or failure.

We must teach the hard stuff the hardest in order to move our students more quickly out of safe, pedestrian thought and into more difficult territory. The very kind of thought that students find overwhelming, that slow, precise groping and the painstaking unlocking of unfamiliar questions about familiar human matters, is exactly the kind of thought that can move them most quickly, as well as most reliably, into fresh and substantive insight. It is also what they most hunger for, and, at the same time, what they dread. To unlock an issue and pursue its deeper implications is what we mean, essentially, when we use the verb "to think." What follows is a neo-Socratic strategy to help students do the kind of thinking which, in fact, they are perfectly capable of, but often despair of undertaking.

Having described the heuristics in question, I explore their application and some of their implications in the following sections.

Methodology

The particular heuristics described here are most applicable once a student has selected a subject for an inquiry: an issue (abortion, capital punishment), a particular phenomenon (Beethoven's *Fifth Symphony,* Shakespeare's *Othello*), or a cluster of phenomena (the Italian Renaissance, Impressionist painting). When students try to define what subject they wish to study, they exhibit an initial diffuseness of interest; subsequently they tend to focus on the particular content of the subject they have chosen, rather than on the general problems that it raises or suggests. The student expressing an interest in writing on *Othello* (I use this example for the duration of this text) will answer my question, "What *about Othello* do you think you'd like to write about?," with the name of a character or a broad designation of some segment of the plot: "Well, Desdemona. I guess I'd like to look at Desdemona's behavior." And probed for a more specific answer, "What *about* Desdemona?," the student persists in the same vein: "Well, I want to look at the way she behaves toward Othello." The dialogue goes on:

Q. What *part* of her interaction with Othello interests you?

A. Well, like, you know, at the beginning of Act III, scene iii—she kind of pesters Othello to reinstate Cassio as Othello's lieutenant.

Q. Okay. And . . . ?

A. . . . And, well, we haven't *seen* that side of Desdemona yet. I mean, up till now, she's been obedient and—I don't know. *Goody*-goody, almost.

Q. What's she doing differently now?

A. [Sigh of exasperation.] Well, she's kind of testing her feminine power, I guess. Like, you know, marital *testing?* Just to see how much leeway she's got with her new husband.

Q. "Feminine power"? "Marital testing"? *Now* we're getting somewhere!

At this point the student has finally designated an *issue* or *cluster of interrelated issues* that serve to focus his or her interest and can fruitfully constitute the basis of meaningful inquiry. Until the student has designated such issues, his or her thinking can scarcely go beyond the discursive.

This is not fresh news but the simple rule of abstraction. Where the student will go next is what interests me. Even once the student has designated such issues, he or she may panic if pursued any further on these questions about *Othello* and may revert to citing examples from the plot: "What do I *make* of these issues? Well, look what *happens:* Othello gets angry, but good old Desdemona is so busy trying to get him to do what *she* wants that she can't even *see* how angry he's getting!"

Such junctures are signally frustrating for most students because they

reveal so sharply the thwarting disunion between the student's unarticu-
lated, latent understanding (which is rich, all the same, in intelligent
perception) and the student's lack of know-how for making such understanding conscious in a systematically articulate fashion. More specifically the student fails to understand that his or her "subject" has
suddenly become a good deal more than *Othello;* Shakespeare's play
becomes, for a time, little more than the focal instance or immediate
example of universal human issues—issues that are imbedded in the play
but not limited to the play. A turning of one's back on *Othello* is now
required while one examines the problem of what *the concepts of* "feminine power" and "marital testing" entail. It is time for the students to
"play" as well as to "think," in the sense that the exploration may not be
directed, at least for a while, toward any exact pragmatic end (Bruner,
1966).

Step I

The first step in thinking about such concepts is to see what adjacent or
allied concepts lie at hand. To facilitate this kind of preliminary brainstorming, students should compile a quick, loose word list of synonyms
and antonyms to surround the isolated concept with what I call a
conceptual environment. Because the concept of "marital testing" is but
an instance or subset of the concept of "testing" (the logically broader
category), the word list produced might look like the one following:

testing

antonyms	synonyms
accepting	experimenting
avoiding	confronting
retreating	examining
confirming	challenging
passivity	trial and error
acquiescence	venturing, foraying
status quo	defiance
	doubting
	effort
	exertion

Illustration 1.

Note that fairly strict synonyms and antonyms blend freely with casual
ones; the later terms on the lists are more associatively connected with

the parent term, *testing*, than logically so. In brainstorming generally, there is no "wrong" way; the student must be free to try options.

Such a bringing together of more or less related terms immediately awakens the student to the interrelationships among these terms—which, I remind the student, are being considered here *conceptually*, as abstract entities used to organize thought. To guard against the tendency toward reifying and toward reflexive exemplifying, I amend the list to look like this:

[the concept of] testing	
antonyms	synonyms
[the concept of] accepting	[the concept of] experimenting
[the concept of] avoiding	[the concept of] confronting
[the concept of] retreating	[the concept of] examining
etc.	*etc.*

Illustration 2.

The creation of this "conceptual environment" completes Step I.

Step II

The student is now invited to select a single pair of terms from within this environment. The sole criterion for choosing is that the two terms must be ones that the student finds *highly problematic* in relation to each other (even if the student isn't quite sure, yet, *what* is problematic about their relationship). In performing this step, students often choose a pair of neatly polar opposites (such as *avoiding* and *confronting*), which, as can be seen on a moment's reflection, are not really all that problematic in their relation. It's best to encourage students to choose two terms whose differences can be felt but are nonetheless hard to articulate; otherwise, there are no restrictions on the choice. The pair may consist of the pilot concept, *testing*, and one of the synonyms or antonyms; both terms may be synonyms, or both may be antonyms.

Because this inquiry was tethered at the outset to the question of marital testing in Act III, scene iii of *Othello,* and because the objective of the whole inquiry is ultimately to understand Shakespeare's play better, the student may want to select a pair of terms whose fuller exploration would visibly contribute to an enlarged understanding of marital testing per se. Pairs like *testing* and *challenging,* or *experimenting* and *confronting* might appeal to the student. But not necessarily; because curiosity is volatile and unpredictable in its nature, and because this procedure allows for play, and hence for detours, the student may suddenly seize on a pair of terms that, although richly problematic in conceptual relation to each other, are nonetheless tethered to the issue of testing by a rather longer leash than the pairs just cited.

But regardless of how the student chooses the pair of terms, the next objective is the same: to work through, slowly and carefully, the fine conceptual discriminations between the two terms (they are, after all, different words in our language) as a means of making tacit understanding become articulate. The student, now, is ready to begin the difficult process of exploring what he or she already latently knows about such matters as marital testing or testing more generally. Because we all know a great deal about such matters, the student is now ready to explore a minuscule portion of that reservoir of knowledge.

Step III

Step III consists of dialogic give-and-take governed by well-established rules. The objective of this dialogue is to *generate propositions* that articulate facets of the problematic relationship between the two terms that were selected in Step II. The referential base is not the student's understanding of Shakespeare's *Othello* but his or her wealth of human experience; the play, for a time, has to be relegated to a position of inconsequence because the present object of study is not an object at all, but a subject—the student's self: "What do *I* know about the ways in which testing and challenging relate to each other as concepts?"

For the purpose of the detailed illustrations that follow, *testing* and *challenging* is the pair that I use.

The Four Basic Rules.   The dialogue proceeds as a rigorous question-and-answer process. The student who acts as the answerer in this dialogue (as opposed to the questioner) must conform to four major rules in the discourse, and to three subsidiary rules. The three subsidiary rules are commonsense ones: (1 & 2) students must avoid undue ambiguity and grammatical incorrectness, and (3) they should offer only one proposition at a time, inasmuch as their offering more than one at a time makes the process of their accounting for implications unfeasible.

The four major rules concern the nature of the proposition that the answerer is called on to offer the questioner in response to his or her questions. Each proposition must meet these four criteria to constitute a valid addition to the dialogue, and hence a valid gain in systematic understanding:

1. It must be a *general* proposition, and not an exemplifying *instance*. It must be an assertion constructed of abstract terms whose objective is to elucidate some general aspect of the issue being explored.

2. It must answer *directly* and *exclusively* to the question just posed; it may neither introduce an irrelevant matter nor anticipate a question that the questioner might ask later. It must stick to the point.

3. It must avoid *circularity* and *redundancy:* It cannot constitute a mere rephrasing or a repetition of an earlier proposition.

4. It must succeed in holding up as a *true* proposition by which its speaker is willing to stand.

Students regularly find it hard to meet these four criteria in generating their propositions because the slow, painstaking groping that is called for is so unfamiliar to them. They are habituated to give examples rather than definitions, and their thought patterns largely consist of editorializing: the unsystematic, though not arbitrary, stringing together of familiar opinions. Because for the most part students do express these opinions in a propositional form, they are fit to have a place in genuine, connected argument; but no novel development takes place in students' thinking unless—or until—students begin to explore the implications imbedded in their opinions. As they "flesh out" such opinions, students are often appalled to discover how much is both implied by and presupposed in what they say. The firm ground beneath them abruptly turns into spongy swampland, and the bright sun of "fact" is suddenly dimmed by encroaching shadows.

I talk more later about the resistance that students manifest in the face of this process; for the moment, let us turn to the role that the questioner plays, a role students often find more difficult to play than that of the answerer or respondent. Because ultimately the student has to become self-sufficient as both the respondent and the questioner, the questions will grow out of a natural curiosity about the implications that the student discerns in a proposition. As they struggle to master this procedure, students are often stymied by the need to ask questions that are both *pertinent* and *fruitful:* It is as much the responsibility of the questioner to pose a question about the latest of the answerer's propositions as it is the answerer's task to stick to the question that the questioner has just asked; reminding students of this obligation helps to ensure that the questions posed will be pertinent ones.

Students are generally so poor at posing questions that they need to be reminded of the familiar journalistic repertoire: who? what? why? when? where? how? by whom? for whom? from whom? etc. The most basic question for pursuing the implications of any proposition is that pesky little two-word question, "So what?"—which, put more politely, asks, "What is the significance of the foregoing assertion?" This general, unfocused question can be invoked at any time that the student fails to think of a more directed question. On the other hand, in many cases, it is simply too vague and needs to be made more explicit before it can have any value.

Proper Conduct of the Dialogue.   I now give an example of the dialogue properly managed. Here, the student succeeds in abiding by the rules and in enlarging his or her conscious knowledge systematically:

Q. What are the essential differences between the concept of testing and the concept of challenging?

A. Testing and challenging both express a wish to learn, which is to say, curiosity; but challenging has a more adversarial quality than testing, at least in most cases.

Q. How so?

A. Well, to challenge something—something or someone—is to express a misgiving, an already formulated doubt; and to *have* such a doubt implies a conviction that the other point of view ought to be overturned. This will to overturn is what I call adversarial.

Q. Okay. So what?

A. Well . . .

Q. What assumption does the challenger, then, make about the adversary?

A. That the adversary is willing to defend his point of view and will be reluctant to give it up.

Q. So?

A. So challenging implies some sort of *confrontation,* whereas testing, all in all, deals more neutrally with *inquiry*—the elimination of doubt, but not necessarily of *disagreement.* A test, you might say, doesn't have to entail a quarrel.

Q. All right. What assumptions does a tester or challenger make about himself or herself?

A. Well, a challenger isn't very likely to offer a challenge if he or she doesn't feel up to the confrontation, true? The same—

Q. What do you mean by "up to," exactly?

A. Well, *sufficient,* I suppose. Challenging presupposes a certain self-confidence in the challenger.

Q. Don't we sometimes offer challenges that we know we're going to *lose?*

A. Sure. But even then, the challenger goes into it presupposing that, well, he's going to reap some *gain,* even if the gain doesn't consist of being the "winner."

And so forth. The student who persists in this type of inquiry with reasonable courage soon discovers that the simple issues of testing and challenging back up against a host of interesting issues that make the original issue of marital testing increasingly problematic. What the student is discovering in an experiential way is one of the fundamental rules of systematic inquiries: *Systematic inquiries, once begun, are indefinitely extendible.* Such inquiries never "end"; we simply curtail them because of exhaustion or lack of courage, or for purposes of convenience. Indeed, one of the virtues of tethering such open-ended explorations to a preestablished problem—here, Desdemona's marital testing in Act III, scene iii of *Othello*—is that it keeps the student from setting adrift amid a wash of endless abstractions. The student is still playing, or "shooting the bull," in William G. Perry's serious sense (Perry, 1965); but it is a *purposive* endeavor; the student is still "essaying" by however many detours in the direction of a richer, more fine-grained understanding of the issues in Desdemona's behavior. If the initial brainstorming described in Step I has produced a first enrichment of the conceptual territory within which marital testing rests, then the dialogic strategy exemplified here gives the student an even more detailed type of roadmap for selected portions of that territory. We use roadmaps only when we are uncertain of our route before embarking on a journey or have lost our way en route; roads that are entirely familiar to us are not problematic.

Improper Conduct of the Dialogue.   Look at the same dialogue interrupted by false turns and violations of the rules. For convenience, the questioner will explain the errors the answerer makes and suggest an appropriate remedy:

Q. What are the essential differences between the concept of testing and the concept of challenging?

A. Well, when Desdemona challenges Othello to reinstate Cassio—

Q. No, more generally, I mean [student has cited an *instance* instead of generating a *proposition*]: What are the essential differences between the two *concepts?*

A. Oh, okay. I get you. Well, let's see. Testing and challenging both express a wish to learn . . . curiosity, that is . . . but testing is a stronger word than challenging. Am I right?

Q. Let's see by following out the implications. *How* is testing stronger than challenging?

A. Personally, I don't like it when people test or challenge you. I just think its *rude*.

Q. That may or may not be [student, editorializing, has indulged in an irrelevancy]—but you're not sticking to the question: *How* is testing stronger than challenging?

A. How is testing . . .? Well, it's stronger because—well, *you* know! Like, it's scary to be tested.

Q. Scarier *in general* than it is to be challenged? It's scarier *in general* to test than to challenge? Again: *in general?*

A. Well, no . . . I guess not [student has seen the error of an earlier proposition]. [Pause.] Well. [Smile.] *Now* what?

Q. Let's go back to the source of the error. Which proposition can you see now is wrong?

A. The one about testing being stronger than challenging.

Q. Okay. Let's pick up there and try over again. We're really back to scratch—which, by the way, is all right. What are the essential differences between the concepts of testing and challenging?

A. Let's see . . . How about this? Challenging is generally a stronger word than testing because there's, well, something adversarial implicit in challenging.

Q. How so?

A. Well, challenging something—something or someone—expresses doubt and disagreement, whereas testing expresses uncertainty. But disagreement's a form of uncertainty, too.

Q. In what sense, exactly?

A. In order to disagree, you have to be uncertain of something.

Q. You've just said that [student's reasoning is *redundant*]. So I still don't understand.

This version of the dialogue is a good deal more lifelike than the earlier version; the student, here, has difficulty abiding by the rules and rather characteristically seeks to abandon accountability and to transpose the burdens of thinking and making decisions onto the teacher. ("Boy, is this *hard!*" one of my best students exclaimed.) The student speaking betrays a wish to retreat to islands of intellectual certainty (conventional opinions and familiar attitudes) and commits, early on, the most familiar violation, that of irrelevancy. Remedying such errors is simple enough, as one can see in the illustration: One simply backtracks to the point (often the previous assertion) at which the violation occurred and takes a different tack. Untrue propositions are the ones that may take some time to reveal themselves as errors and are therefore the most instructive errors because, in pursuing the implications of an untrue proposition, one may generate consequences that one *knows* to be false. Violations of the rules against irrelevancy, circularity, and instancing are relatively easy to spot, and hence to remedy.

Introducing the Heuristic Sequence to the Student. Because the heuristics described here are initially difficult for students to absorb and master, it is important to give students an abundance of guided practice. Generally, I introduce the method to an entire class and let students practice at it in small groups or pairs. One useful modification that I have tried consists of adding a third party to the dialogue. This third person acts as audience and referee, and his or her function is to encourage the other two—and to make sure that the answerer and questioner stick to their respective roles. The presence of a third party helps to keep the principals from getting bogged down and being unable to move.

The whole method becomes even more effective when the instructor takes the time to pursue it in conference with individual students. Because teachers, on the whole, are much more powerful questioners than students, the conference enables the instructor to intensify the process, inasmuch as little time is wasted on fruitless questions. But I emphasize that the process takes time; the student must be allowed a liberal amount of free space in which to grope and ponder answers. A period of from 50 minutes to an hour is ideal; the student is taxed but not overtaxed and often comes away in a state of exhilaration because he or she has made some authentic discoveries and has had his or her capacity to think reaffirmed. Sometimes, that capacity is affirmed for the first time in the student's career.

Implications and Applications

Earlier I mentioned that students essay by this method, both in the classic Montaignesque sense and in the more scriptorial sense. The are groping, as Montaigne did, to come to terms with their experience by taking care with words, and tentativeness of the type that one finds in the *Essais* is intrinsic to the process. But they are also *writing an essay* in the more pragmatic sense inasmuch as they are generating logically coherent prose. We can represent this process by means of an illustration that reveals how *all* coherent discourse logically works. In this illustration, (P) stands for each proposition offered in the form of an answer in the preceding two dialogues, whereas the question marks represent the *potential implications* that might be pursued for any given proposition and $(?)$ indicates which of the potential implications is *actually selected* as a bridge to the next proposition.

The underlying rule is that *any proposition implicitly responds to one or more antecedent questions, and the same proposition generates a host of successive questions that point the way toward its implications.* Systematic discourse occurs when the speaker chooses one of the questions raised by his previous proposition as the bridge that leads him to the next proposition, and so forth:

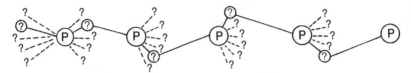

Illustration 3.

For each implication explored, one forfeits or defers a wealth of alternative implications because the potential number of implications for any given proposition is legion, if not limitless.

Which implications does one choose to pursue? It depends in part, although not exclusively, on the initial inquiry to which one remains tethered, and to the freer drift of one's curiosity. The most powerful use of this procedure occurs once the student has developed the habit of eschewing implications whose pursuit might be easy and asks instead, almost automatically, "What *don't* I know about these matters?" The process then slows, and the work becomes hard; but unsuspected implications quickly begin to come to light. The student gains confidence and succeeds in stretching considerably what I have called his or her *short-term courage span* (Wertime, 1979), which is the time that elapses between the assumption of a task and the moment at which it is abandoned.

That all systematic thinking is implicitly dialogic becomes strikingly evident if we simply omit—or render tacit—all the questions we have posed in the course of the interview, and bunch the answers together; the result is a logically coherent piece of prose of the kind we are accustomed to getting from practiced writers. Here is the first dialogue, with the questions deleted:

Testing and challenging both express a wish to learn—which is to say, curiosity; but challenging has a more adversarial quality than testing, at least in most cases. To challenge something—something or someone—is to express a misgiving, an already formulated doubt; and to *have* such a doubt implies a conviction that the other point of view ought to be overturned. This will to overturn is what I call adversarial. One of the assumptions that the challenger makes about the adversary is that the adversary is willing to defend his point of view and will be reluctant to give it up; so challenging implies some sort of *confrontation,* whereas testing, all in all, deals more neutrally with *inquiry*—the elimination of doubt, but not necessarily of *disagreement.* A test, you might say, does not have to entail a quarrel. One of the assumptions that a tester or challenger makes about himself is that he is up to the challenge; he feels sufficient. Challenging presupposes a certain self-confidence. Even if the challenger offers a challenge that he knows he is going to lose, he goes into it presupposing that he is going to reap some *gain,* even if the gain does not consist of being the winner.

Such prose is still rough-edged and needs a good deal of polishing—it isn't fully efficient yet, or perfectly consistent—but it is nonetheless coherent and constitutes valid thought.

Putting the matter in reverse, any piece of prose that has a coherent feel to it will be found, on inspection, to have imbedded in it a similar series of bridging questions that link the propositions together, even if such questions remain entirely unstated. One very useful way to show students how essential the question-and-answer format is to systematic thought is to give them a short piece of prose—a paragraph—and let them work at interpolating the unstated questions. Such interpolating constitutes educated guesswork of a parallel sort because there are always more than one potential question that might have served as the writer's bridge to the next utterance. The results (using the material of the preceding paragraph) might look like this:

> [What is the topic of this discourse? What distinctions separate testing and challenging?] Testing and challenging both express a wish to learn—which is to say, curiosity; but challenging has a more adversarial quality than testing, at least in most cases. [Why? How so?] To "challenge" something—something or someone—is to express a misgiving, an already formulated doubt; and to have such a doubt implies a conviction . . . etc.

Once the student has mastered the three-step heuristic described in this chapter and has used it to open some of his or her latent knowledge of the original issues identified as focal targets of inquiry, he or she is ready to return to the original problems: Why does Desdemona behave as she does in Act III, scene iii, and what are we, as readers, to make of such behavior? The student can now put this new knowledge to practical use. Its utility usually takes one of several forms. First, the student has overcome the problem of development because the nexus of issues that constitutes the problem's environment has made itself available for systematic elaboration. Second, the student is now equipped with a set of *guiding discriminations* that can be built into the essay (whatever form it takes: a formal paper, oral report, final exam, class discussion) in the alternative forms of controlling question, thesis statement, prefatory distinctions, or argumentative milemarkers interspersed throughout the essay to give it intellectual structure. Third and perhaps most importantly, the student has usually succeeded in pushing himself or herself farther away from self-evident ideas and has become more demanding of himself or herself for fresh thought. In a previous publication (Wertime, 1982), I addressed the question of how we might help students avoid the self-evident in their thinking, and my illustration shows why "slowing language down" is so powerful a strategy for leading students away from non-negotiably stale ideas. In any inquiry, we can distinguish among four zones of relative understanding by means of the following image:

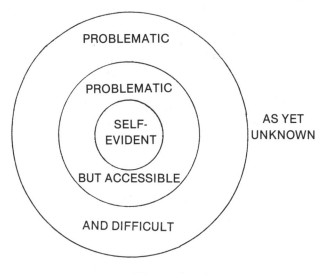

Illustration 4

The zone of the self-evident encompasses those things that can be taken for granted in a given inquiry and therefore need not be shared with others as though they were fresh news; indeed such matters can be left to the tacit understanding of all concerned. In writing a chapter like this, for example, I would not inform my audience that I am writing in good faith, or that as a teacher I find it important to try to help students grow, for all such simplicities are among the many "givens" that I and my audience accept as incontrovertible and nonproblematic "facts."

It is only as thought becomes problematic that it becomes worth sharing with other people at all; and it only becomes *seriously* worth sharing with others as it becomes seriously problematic. Thought becomes problematic only as one leaves the safety of ostensible "fact" and ventures into those areas where hypothesis and the testing of hypothesis reside. Problematic thought, inasmuch as it is governed by educated guesswork (by surmise, by conjecture, by hypothesis, what you will), is less judged by its correctness or rightness in a narrow right-or-wrong sense than by its philosophical power, its negotiability or fruitfulness. First we must move ourselves out to the very edge of our present conscious knowledge and then move *that* edge even further out as we bring into consciousness things we have tacitly known; or we must make, through fresh learning, altogether new discoveries.

If we draw a dotted line from the center of this graph to the edge of the largest circle, we effectively draw a line that encompasses all the knowledge that we can consciously lay claim to at any given moment in a particular inquiry:

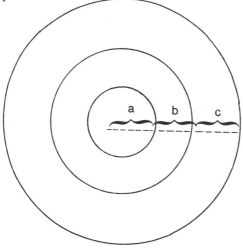

Illustration 5

Take *Othello* as the instance, or rather, one's understanding of it: Segment "a" of the line encompasses those things that in most adult situations are taken for granted: that *Othello* is a drama written by William Shakespeare; that such drama consists of words, *etc.*—the simplicities, again, that needn't be repeated as though they were fresh news. When students undertake to study *Othello*, they largely succeed in avoiding the baldest of such simplicities, unless they badly misjudge their audience and assume that audience to be abysmally ignorant.

Students run into problems when they try to negotiate their way as expeditiously as possible through the second of these zones, the "Problematic but Accessible," and make their way into the third, the "Problematic and Difficult." The first of these two latter zones (segment "b" on the dotted line) encompasses or describes that level of perception at which *some* conjectural power is required, but not very much. It is not strictly self-evident in *Othello*, for example, that Desdemona is engaging in some kind of marital testing in Act III, scene iii; all the same, any decently alert reader of Shakespeare would find it difficult to miss, and so the perception isn't likely to have much intellectual novelty. What the alert reader wants is something considerably more than preliminary observations. That "more" will consist of the more difficult and (it is likely) more hard-earned propositions that fall within the zone of the "Problematic and Difficult" (these are the kinds of perceptions that the heuristic sequence described in these pages is designed to elicit). What is it in Othello's complex vanity and defensiveness that makes him so intolerant of Desdemona's marital testing? What must one say, finally, about the nature of vanity generally, about its relationship to fragility and rigidity and bewilderment? Or about the finer distinctions, say, between jealousy and envy, so brilliantly expounded by Leslie H. Farber (1976)?

Questions of this magnitude, of this richness and intricacy, seem overwhelming at first, not only to students but also to us; and yet no authentically penetrating inquiry into *Othello* can afford to ignore such questions, which represent the inquirer's willingness to arrive at a principled understanding of the larger structures of human experience. Such understanding arises from a willingness to move away from the relative safety of the self-evident into the realm of vigorous hypothesis, and from there to the outer edge of what we can understand. The movement can be schematically condensed as follows:

the self-evident	the problematic but accessible	the problematic and difficult
factual "givens," concrete data	the need for simple conjecture	the need for complex conjecture and hypothesizing
concern for correctness, accuracy	concern for correctness and some fruitfulness	concern for correctness, coupled with intense need for fruitfulness or negotiability

Illustration 6

As we persist in enlarging our conscious understanding of what we tacitly know and in acquiring new knowledge, all three realms of knowledge are enlarged:

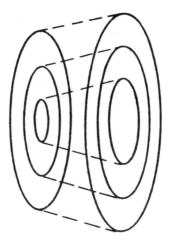

Illustration 7

To understand more is to find more and more self-evident, more and more problematic but accessible, and, too, more and more problematic and difficult; and the virtue of the heuristic described in Step III is that, for all its ostensible slowness, it moves the student expeditiously away from the self-evident and the minimally problematic into really serious questions, questions well removed from pat, familiar ideas. Our usual repertory of opinions (what I earlier called our *editorial* opinions) falls in the middle zone, the problematic but accessible; this is the deadening domain of commonsense pedestrian thinking which, as Suzanne Langer (1942) reminds us, has the power to produce only commonplace thought.

   Not only does the student, by means of this heuristic, substantially enlarge his or her domain of conscious knowledge and become more demanding of himself or herself; the student also assumes the presence of greater intelligence in the recipient of the inquiry, the "reader" or listener. It is woefully characteristic of too many students—and some of the teachers who pretend to enlarge them—that they make demeaning assumptions about the recipient's intelligence; they do so because they are simply unaccustomed to hearing or conducting high-level inquiry, and because they have trapped themselves in strategies for negotiating ideas that virtually condemn them to self-limiting thought. Even at this late date, in spite of a national "writing movement" that has sought to upgrade the quality of students' verbal expression, teachers often foist demeaning assumptions on their students; the two most deadly of these assumptions are: (1) "Assume that your audience is ignorant of your subject matter," and (2) "Back up everything you say with an illustration." One of my best students, a middle-aged woman, said recently after mastering the sequence of heuristics described in these pages: "I feel as though I've been asked to perform parlor tricks all these years!" Her bitterness was directed against the praise she'd received for what, as she could see now, had been altogether cautious and uninspiring thought; for her teachers had encouraged her to be merely *competent* instead of provoking her to strive for *brilliance,* which is the only legitimate aim of a liberal education. "But students have to be competent," I hear some of my colleagues saying, "before they can be brilliant!" To which I answer, "That may be. But to imagine that there is one set of strategies appropriate for achieving competency and another set for achieving brilliance is somewhat like teaching a novice to drive a car by saying, 'Okay: practice pushing in and letting out the clutch until you have *that* down perfect; and *then* you can use the gas pedal.' " Competency is merely an earlier way station one passes on the same journey, which is one of unending and ever-unfolding thought.

The reason why such teaching prescriptions as the pair I have cited are so deadly to rigorous thought is that they violate the relationship between articulate conscious knowledge and our fund of tacit knowledge. We leave undemonstrated or unjustified or unillustrated the larger share of what we say in our daily conversation, and this is as it should be because much of what we say (at least at the level of its propositional power; what it conveys in the way of ambiguous implication is quite another matter) is fairly unproblematic, and its affirmation can be left to our listener; it can be taken, again, for granted. We do not need to slow language down for commonplace thought; to pretend to such a need is to waste precious time that might be better spent attending to authentically serious matters. It is the first requirement of tact in the conduct of any inquiry that we address ourselves to others at a cognitive level appropriate to the others' training and intelligence; and because the training of an adult includes the richness of life's experience and all the accrued, if not yet awakened, understanding, the major business of the humanistic thinker is not really the offering of "proofs" at all but the pursuit of surprising and enriching implications. How simple this all is, in a sense: How can we expect to engage our own or another's interest with tired observations and well-trodden generalities? What excite us are the byways that lie off the major routes.

Earlier, I referred to the heuristic detailed here as a "neo-Socratic" one because it helps students recollect or put back together what they latently know through dialogic means that push them away from their conventional understanding. I promised to return to the issue of how students resist exercising their minds in such a vigorous fashion as the method I have described here calls for. It is an understatement to say that students do not always bear the stress of such work gladly; some become indignant; some cry; many panic. Any teacher will sympathize: We all get desolate when our props are removed.

But it is a central responsibility of the maturing intellectual to learn to confront one's ignorance and endure frustration. In one of his earliest publications (reported in Coles, 1970), Erik Erikson observed that Freud's classic rule for the conduct of therapy (keeping the patient constantly under the maximum degree of tolerable intellectual stress) applies equally well to the conduct of teaching. Socrates knew it as well as anybody, and called his method the *maieutic* or *midwiving* process because of its resemblance to helping someone give birth. Hard thought can be frightening labor. Even today, the spirit of Socrates remains a dangerous and threatening spirit. Socrates did not lack humility (Klein, 1977), but he did lack timidity, which, looked at with care, is but humility's distant cousin. Such absolute courage and inquisitive resoluteness as Socrates possessed are as rare today as they have always been.

More than a generation ago, William G. Perry, Jr. (1965) showed us how insidiously we represent cowardice as legitimate impatience when we condemn "shooting the bull" as irresponsible activity; and he demonstrated that the avoidance of healthy uncertainty rests on a foundation of intellectual despair. To be responsible for ourselves, as Wendell Berry tells us, is to stand by our words; and standing by our words involves our willingly bearing the birth pangs of the maieutic process. The teacher's role as midwife in this process is not an easy one; but the slow, hard labor by which ideas are brought to life keeps our world new and growing as nothing else does.

REFERENCES

Berry, Wendell. (1980–1981). Standing by Words. *The Hudson Review, XXXIII*(4), 498–521.

Bruner, J. S. (1966). *Toward a theory of instruction.* Cambridge, MA: Belknap Press of Harvard University Press.

Coles, R. (1970). *Erik H. Erikson: The growth of his work.* Boston: Atlantic-Little, Brown.

Farber, L. H. (1976). *Lying, despair, jealousy, envy, sex, suicide, drugs, and the good life.* New York: Basic Books.

Hayes, J. R. (1981). *The complete problem solver.* Philadelphia: The Franklin Institute Press.

Klein, J. (1977). *Plato's trilogy.* Chicago: The University of Chicago Press.

Langer, S. K. (1942). *Philosophy in a new key.* Cambridge, MA: Harvard University Press.

Perry, Jr., W. G. (1965). Examsmanship and the liberal arts: A study in educational epistemology. *Examining in Harvard College: A collection of essays by members of the Harvard faculty.* Cambridge, MA: Harvard University Press. Reprinted In A. M. Eastman, et. al. (Eds.), *The Norton reader: An anthology of expository prose* (Rev.). New York: W. W. Norton.

Polanyi, M. (1983). *The tacit dimension.* Magnolia, MA: Peter Smith.

Wertime, R. A. (1979). Students, problems and 'courage spans.' In Jack Lochhead and John

Clement (Eds.), *Cognitive process instruction: Research on teaching thinking skills.* Philadelphia: The Franklin Institute Press.

Wertime, R. A. (1982). Avoiding the self-evident: A heuristic device for teaching the nature of inquiry. *Problem Solving, 4*(4), 1–5.

Wilden, A. (1972). *System and structure: Essays in communication and exchange.* London: Tavistock Publications.

29

A Teacher Educator's Perspective on Students' and Teachers' Schemes

Jack Easley
University of Illinois at Urbana-Champaign

As Thomas Kuhn (1961) has pointed out, in physical science there comes a time when persistent anomolies and available new concepts require some fundamental changes in conventional assumptions. In math and science teacher education, we are approaching such a time now. There are deep discrepancies between conventional wisdom, now erupting in massive reports on what's wrong with education in the United States, and teachers' experiences, e.g., of the negative effects of increasing conflict on students and on themselves. Student indifference and teacher burnout are increasing at all levels as the pressure grows. New perspectives like symbolic interactionism (Bauersfeld, 1979; Brandau, 1985; Brandau & Easley, 1980) and constructivism (Davis, 1984; Driver, 1983; Petrie, 1981; Piaget and Garcia, 1983) offer us alternatives to conventional wisdom that better accommodate the perceptions of people in classrooms and the contents of children's thinking about scientific and mathematical topics.

I begin by identifying some of the key assumptions in mathematics and science education that need to be questioned and by pointing out alternative assumptions for each. I then summarize findings of field and clinical studies that have influenced my thinking, particularly about elementary school teaching. Finally, I look at some broader implications, stemming from recent philosophical developments and related practical experience in knowledge representation. In this chapter, I mean by "schemes" roughly what Kant and Piaget have meant: ideas, i.e., organizing structures, with or without precise definitions or labels, which become evident in the different responses people make to the same situations.

Assumption (1)

Teachers should regularly lead class discussions, presenting clear explanations and examples of basic concepts and/or asking questions so that students can piece together the principles desired. A great many elementary teachers in the United States can serve their pupils better by leaving most discussion of mathematics and physical science content to their pupils. Here are some reasons: (a) Clinical research shows that children between 5 and 10 years develop and test alternative schemes that authoritative exposition cannot readily displace; (b) the conflicts that arise between presentations by teachers or texts and the pupil's own math–science schemes can generate severe anxieties about mathematics and science in a few years; (c) open reflection on particular alternative schemes in the light of conflicts with standard schemes helps students develop useful revisions. Without such attention most of them persist; (d) it was the teachers' and parents' early anxiety-producing experiences with authority in mathematics and physical science that probably gave rise, in the first place, to their adopting an authoritative role with their students or children. Breaking these vicious cycles requires establishing teachers' and parents' faith in the greater long-range insights that children can accomplish on their own and in finding better ways for teachers to assist each other in the technical details of managing student thinking, such as problem presentations and moderateing debates between pupils. The new perspective of symbolic interactionism helps us understand the social, anxiety-producing messages that are received from teachers along with the factual information.

At the elementary level (especially K–4), most children still have enough confidence in their schemes that such indirect teaching works. Preliminary reports on turning over discussion to upper elementary and even to junior high school pupils suggest that they can often be convinced in this way they can accept scientific and mathematical theory as meaningful and nonthreatening.

Assumption (2)

All teachers need to master their subjects, as a prior condition to trying to teach them. I question whether or not it helps their pupils when teachers attempt to master the subjects of arithmetic and physical science to the level that they can avoid making errors in those subjects. When teachers attempt to master these subjects, they are likely to depend heavily on memorization (using mainly figurative schemes) because of their anxiety about their own operative schemes. That then encourages them to try to guide their pupils' thought toward the answers or procedures that they have memorized with three very likely consequences: (a) stifling of pupils' thought because of conflicts with their natural preconceptions; (b) misinterpretation by pupils because of their own schemes, and (c) misleading variations in presentation due to incomplete mastery.

It is probable that those few students who persist in mathematical or scientific subjects with clear and consistent knowledge employ a process of challenging authority, which only a few teachers are willing to undertake, even in their preservice training. This process can begin in all 5–10-year-olds, but more challenging problems at each grade than the textbooks provide for that grade are needed to encourage it. Finally, choosing sufficiently advanced problems is not likely if teachers feel thay they should have prior mastery of any problems that they introduce to pupils.

I have been greatly impressed with the learning that comes when primary teachers switch from presentation of subject matter to inviting children to do their own thinking in these areas. Children thinking together in heterogeneous groups appear to run little or no risk that they will go seriously astray in the long run. A common application of Assumption (2) is the belief that such indirect teaching requires an especially high level of subject-matter mastery. I have found it works well with elementary teachers having little knowledge of the subject and who are suppressing the scientific schemes they do have.

Assumption (3)

Teachers can and should transmit their knowledge to pupils. Knowledge is coming to be understood as a representation of experience that is constructed by the learner using his or her prior schemes and adapting them to subsequent experience. Controlling the pupils' experience has some effect on which mathematics and science schemes they use and how they are developed, but too little effect for teachers to develop confidence in their ability to transmit knowledge, if that is assumed to be their responsibility. Lack of confidence leads many sensitive teachers to doubts, discouragement, and burnout.

Assumption (4)

Teachers should, at first, present simple and easy problems and tasks, in order to build pupils' courage to tackle more difficult and unfamiliar tasks. If elementary school teachers tried to find the most interesting and challenging tasks they could get their pupils to work on seriously for an hour, and if they developed rather dramatic problem presentation, they could capture the interest of all their pupils. Easy problems or tasks are boring to students at all levels. Easy problems may occasionally be needed for particular students who may get lost in symbolic manipulations working on the harder ones, but presenting difficult problems at the outset could capture the interest of most students.

Assumption (5)

Teachers should give equal attention to all pupils. Even with very sophisticated knowledge of subject matter, pedagogy, and cognitive psychology, teachers cannot expect to regularly address each pupil's schemes directly in classes of more than about 12 pupils. When ideas clash, the conflict needs to be opened up quickly or pupil attention wanes.

What would happen, though, if teachers of regular elementary grade classes trained group leaders from their classes to monitor whether every member of their groups was interested and participating in a difficult but motivating problem and provide basic encouragement when needed? On a moment by moment basis, teachers of large classes can then supervise peer discussions from one level up. Group leaders in elementary grades (K–4), for example, can be trained to call on each group member for an opinion, thus keeping their interest alive. Teachers can also poll the class regularly, making sure every child's view is counted. One teacher who regularly uses peer groups for such dialogue calls it "individualization through groups" because the questions or ideas of every child are frequently responded to by someone.

Assumption (6)

Teachers should give quick feedback on pupils' work, indicating clearly what is wrong and why. What tends to go wrong when this advice is followed was identified in discussing Assumption (1). If, however, elementary teachers concentrated on moderating and supporting classroom communication in mathematics and science, instead of ruling on what is right and wrong, they would set an example for group leaders by providing an atmosphere in which ideas can be expressed without fear of being put down. They would be providing safe outlets for the emotional concomitants of pupil thinking. Even if the pupils did not reach a consensus on the problem or task at hand, they could all be gaining in courage to attack unfamiliar problems and in skill in the expression of their thoughts. Perhaps it is only these two metacommunication goals that require quick feedback.

Assumption (7)

Children should focus first on content and second on means of expression. If they do, the probability is high that their expressions will reveal misconceptions. In order to learn mathematics and science better, elementary children, working in heterogeneous groups, might first develop their oral and written expression by trying to convince each other through clear speaking and writing. They could be taught to say in advance what kind of contribution to the dialogue they are trying to make: an objection, an alternative view, a supportive point, etc. Once they have developed such skills, their learning from peer dialogue, which otherwise would remain hidden, can increase rapidly as the conflicts surface. These objectives, because they can be stressed over and over in different contexts, represent a metacurriculum with more hope of accomplishment than of teaching the particular facts and procedures of mathematics and science.

Assumption (8)

Children should strive to understand their teacher and the textbooks. The problem with this conventional advice, although perhaps useful in later educational emergencies like an impending examination in a little understood course, is that many children concentrate on reproducing teacher and text with superficial, figurative schemes. If pupils try to understand each other, because their physical and operative schemes are more similar to each other's than they are to teachers' figurative schemes, they may come to challenge their ideas creatively rather than give up in despair. Peer communication invites pupils to evaluate ideas critically because it does not involve the authoritative role of the teacher. The basic ideas of what knowledge is are socially constructed in the classroom, too often having to do with authority. The discovery of how one's own ideas build on and distort one's experience depends on sharing differing perspectives on the same problem or phenomenon.

How Field Studies Led Me to this View

I have been a participant–observer and research coordinator in several field studies involving school mathematics and/or science classes. The experience has influenced my perspective on teachers' and pupils' schemes more than I could express in the research reports.

The *Case Studies in Science Education* (Stake & Easley, 1978), were in-depth studies of 11 diverse United States senior high schools and their feeder schools (junior high and elementary), which explored the views of mathematics, science, and social science education held by people in the schools. Undertaken at the request of the National Science Foundation as a part of their program of status studies in 1977–1978, these studies led to several insights into the social task of teachers: Most teachers were expected to socialize children to general school norms, such as neatness, promptness, and working independently, and the three subject matters provided ready vehicles for doing so. Teachers were conscientious in attempting to provide equality of educational opportunity as they saw it. Teachers found most of their teacher training useless for these tasks in practice—both subject matter and professional courses (Easley, 1979a, Stake & Easley, 1978, ch. 16). So improvement seems unlikely to come through more course work and more requirements to meet.

Dialogues Between Teachers and Resource Persons.   I became convinced that teachers should be accepted as the persons who are effectively in charge of instruction and who can change only as their perceptions of their classrooms change. This can happen through dialogues in which there is respect for teachers, and where would-be reformers listen to the perceptions that teachers have built from their own experience (Brandau & Easley, 1980).

Promoting practical dialogues between teachers and resource persons in Kankakee, Illinois, a predominantly working-class town near Chicago with about 50% black population (Easley et el., 1980, supported by the Ford Foundation), it eventually became clear why communication of pedagogical ideas between the two professional groups was difficult. Technical ideas of the resource persons guided their thinking, even during demonstration lessons, in ways that teachers could not imitate, even if they saw them as effective. Using very different ideas, the teachers had to modify their thinking in small steps based on experience. Most of the teachers changed very little. The resource persons learned many detailed things from the teachers. For example, one particular thing we learned from a teacher was that children's counting schemes blocked the use of the place value scheme.

Rule-Dependent Socialization.   Aimee Grieb and I (1984), with support from the Ford Foundation and the Bureau of Educational Research at the University of Illinois, have analyzed teacher–pupil interactions in elementary math classes, uncovering a mechanism that can explain continuing gender and ethnic inequities in problem-solving confidence (Easley, 1983b). Our study of interactions with well-intentioned teachers (both black and white) shows that middle-class white boys who show problem-solving autonomy (whom we call "Pale Male Math Mavericks") are allowed to attain a significant degree of public independence in mathematical thought, whereas all others are held to strict accountability for using standard rules, thus limiting their opportunities for problem solving, i.e., working when they don't have sufficient rules to succeed mechanically.

Peer-Group Dialogues Between Pupils.   Kitamaeno Elementary School in Tokyo was chosen for study in 1981 because there was minimum involvement of pupils in extraschool tutoring (*juku*). My wife, Elizabeth, who speaks Japanese, and I (with the support of the University of Illinois) documented the introduction of adding and subtracting without counting (Easley, 1983a; Hatano, 1980). We also found that direct teaching was used little except for forming Japanese characters and Arabic numerals. Because these children, like their parents, were independent in spirit, teachers only presented the most challenging problems and used peer-group dialogues to support individual work (a practice in about 10% of Japanese classrooms, according to one estimate). Mathematics achievement was very high by American standards.

In Kitamaeno School, use of peer-group dialogues helped children from ages 6 to 12 to recognize their ideas as influencing their perceptions and to improve them. Organizing children into small working groups to assist on appropriately challenging tasks required group leaders with confidence and some training in what to do when things went wrong. Every child in the classroom was continually involved in active thinking, even with classes over 40. Teachers also reported that 8 or 10 good groups are much easier to manage than 40 individual pupils.

On our return, with the support of the Ford Foundation, we were participant observers with others introducing various Kitamaeno teaching priorities to teachers of American innercity elementary math classes (Easley & Easley, 1982, 1983) and providing them with 1 or 2 person-hours of support a week. The relatively few successes led me to conclude that teachers need a most unusual kind of support for permanent and effective implementation of such Kitamaeno practices as peer discussion of challenging problems. The problem was to help teachers shift their role in math and science teaching to an indirect one that they knew only in other contexts, not to develop a large repertoire of new technical schemes.

In our subsequent experience with teachers in this country, we found appropriately challenging problems starting from first grade, without obvious clue words, requiring two or three operations and perhaps including a number or two that are not needed. Suitable science tasks were inspired by the last 10 years of Piaget's work, where there is a well-documented account of children's progressively improved physics schemes from ages 5 to 12, based on typical childhood activities (see later). Other good resources are the reports of those researchers who, independently of Piaget, investigate the conceptions children have of math and science systems (see later). Some old textbooks such as Strayer and Upton (1933) contain good story problems that can be usefully adopted. Benezet's classic experiment (1935–1936), eliminating the teaching of computation for several years in several New Hampshire schools, deserves mention because the children were encouraged to work on story problems from *The Strayer–Upton Arithmetics,* to use numbers in telling time and making change, and apparently did much better on problem solving, language development, and computation than those taught to calculate first.

Pupil Changes.   Longitudinal case studies (Trumbull et al., 1985) were completed of five children going through elementary school mathematics, from kindergarten to sixth grade. The University of Illinois supported completing these studies including data from an earlier N.I.E. study of the same subjects (Lerch & Easley, 1978.) In children of varying ability and achievement, we documented progressive reductions in spontaneous, creative reasoning, an increasing dependence on teacher authority, and an increasing tendency by Grades 5 or 6 to reject both homework and classwork in arithmetic as boring and personally worthless. The absence of almost any way for these children at age 11 to understand arithmetic conceptually or to use it in everyday life was clearly evident. The teachers never saw it as their responsibility to support these pupils' own ideas. Teachers' ratings, based on recall of the pupils' creative motivation (Steinkamp, 1983), show a decline by the upper elementary grades, whereas responsive motivation generally increased. Now, we are following children who have experienced peer-group dialogue on advanced problems in third and fourth grade, to see how they cope with a more traditional program in Grades 5 and 6.

Teacher Change.   Two former graduate students studied cases of teacher change intensively. One of them, Brandau (1985), argues that a teacher who wants pupils to become independent thinkers and recognizes the limitations she is placing on them with traditional teaching may find it difficult to change because of the responsibility she feels to parents, other teachers, administrators, and the pupils, for keeping them on the "right track." The consequences of supporting pupils' nonstandard thinking, and the ways of helping them to develop standard ideas, are really unknown to most elementary school teachers. The other graduate student, Kau (1981), showed how a teacher's style during the whole school day tends to place constraints on what happens during the math period. From a variety of studies, I have learned that teachers functionally schematize the routines of running a math or science class. Changing those schemes may require something like a religious conversion, reminiscent of Kuhn's description of revolutions in physics.

An Informal Teacher-Support Network.   A network of 40–50 teachers and resource persons has developed over a period of 3 years involving some 20 persons in each category. Called "Dialogues in Methods of Education," it publishes a newsletter (DIME) and meets twice a year for 2 days at a time. Meetings now involve a few secondary school math teachers and include persons from three neighboring states. Discussion is always very lively and focuses mainly on promoting pupil dialogue in classes. It has spawned three local support groups that meet monthly.

Related Classroom Research.   Group learning in elementary schools has been found beneficial by Johnson and Johnson (1975) Slavin (1983) and Stodolsky (1983). Stenhouse (1983) gives a related theoretical rationale for peer-group dialogues in a high school humanities course. Brown and Walter (1983) describe, in an appendix, how to organize mathematics discussion groups. Lochhead has found two-person problem-solving teams successful. Work in England (Department of Education and Science, 1976) and in Italy (Cecchini and Peperno, summarized by Perret-Clermont, 1980, pp. 5–9), have also recommended peer-group dialogue over teacher–pupil discussion.

Individual Participant Observation.   Teachers have a high level of distraction to contend with when 25–30 pupils are losing patience over their confusions and ill-formed questions. When I participate by doing demonstration teaching, I have tried to attract children away from distracting me by posing more than usually challenging problems for them, but that too has its difficulties. Children who are used to being told ot shown precisely what to do, often panic when given so much responsibility too quickly, and they work hard to obtain any hints about the answer that they can.

I have personally been studying several elementary school teachers as they implement peer-group dialogues on challenging problems. Teachers regularly doing this have felt positive about it in terms of pupils' test scores, attitudes, and discipline. Teachers can see that, as children discover they have different solutions, different methods, different frameworks, they try to convince each other, or at least to understand each other, and revise their understanding in many small but important ways. One elementary grade teacher, after a year and a half of such experience, decided spontaneously to enroll in a mathematics course. (See Duckworth, 1983, the awakening of subject-matter interest on the part of elementary school teachers.)

Relevant Clinical, Cognitive Studies.

The most profound impression I have of hundreds of clinical studies of math and science reasoning is that children do make progress year-by-year toward more generally useful schemes, even on topics in physics in which they have had no instruction. Some of Piaget's early books (from his first decade, 1926, 1929, 1931) and some of his most recent books (from his last decade, Piaget, 1972a, b, 1973a, b, & c, 1976b, 1980, 1983; Piaget & Henriques, 1978, and more than 60 studies yet to appear as *Travaux sur la causalité*) provide evidence that children's schemes about aspects of the physical world with which they interact spontaneously, undergo a natural development from ages 5–12 in an educationally useful direction, even when inquiries made of schools revealed no instruction in physics at all. Although the middle four decades of Piaget's work, focusing centrally on logico–mathematical thinking, has drawn the almost exclusive attention of Anglo–American writers, both critics and supporters, *that* work seems least helpful to me. Writers who mention Piaget's untranslated causal studies include Gallagher and Reid (1981) and Driver and Easley (1978), but even books in English from the last decade, *The Grasp of Consciousness* (Piaget, 1973b), *Success and Understanding* (Piaget, 1976b), *Experiments in Contradiction* (Piaget, 1980), are quite different from those of Piaget's middle four decades. Take cognizance of Piaget's move away from logic and content-free forms of thought and toward content-specific schemes. In the preface to the first of these three books, Piaget explained at length (1973b, p. vi–vii) that his "reason for these new studies is that it was of more general importance to examine the nature and content of the subjects' conceptualizations" than the logical structures he had studied earlier.

Piaget and collaborators (Inhelder, Blanchet, Sinclair, & Piaget, 1975, Piaget, 1976a, 1977) have argued that the former emphasis placed on logical transformations, e.g., reversibility schemes, is not so central as they had earlier supposed. The commutability scheme (what is added corresponds bit by bit with what is taken away) provides a natural opening to conservation. This revision of Piaget's theory of logico–mathematical operations invites greatly reducing the significance that is attributed to logic in thinking, even in the heuristic way in which Piaget understood logic (Papert, 1963). I have argued (1978b, 1979b) that non-conservation of substance, number, and length can be understood better in terms of the general salience, for young children, of Piaget's overtaking scheme (1970), than as an absence of either commutability or concrete operations.

In 1980, Piaget called his new point of view "a logic of meanings" and explained the main difference between that and his previous concern with an extensional logic this way: "In a logic of meanings, the construction of extensions would be determined by the meanings and not vice versa. These extensions would thus be local and variable and not common to the set of all possible worlds" (p. 6).

A variety of viewpoints are possible (Easley, 1977), but studies by Ausubellians (Champagne & Klopfer, 1982; Driver, 1983; Novak, 1977) and other non-Piagetian cognitive researchers (Erickson, 1980, 1983; Hawkins, 1978; Nussbaum & Novak, 1976; Nussbaum & Novik, 1982) are helping to map the territory of elementary school science and mathematics, including both children's typical concepts and currently accepted ones. Piagetians like Denis-Prinzhorn and Grize (1966), M. Kamii (1981, 1982), C. Kamii and DeVries (1976), C. Kamii (1984), Doise, Mugny, & Perret-Clermont (1976), and Perret-Clermont (1980) have illuminated the social process of the development of children's mathematical thinking in practical ways. The question needing more fundamental research is: What is the educational potential of students' content-specific schemes (Easley, 1984)?

The Shrinking Role of Logic in the Philosophy of Science

It is no accident that the influence of Thomas Kuhn (1961) is felt in many of these discussions (as Driver, 1983, Driver & Easley, 1978, and Hanson, 1984, make clear), for cognitive processes are strongly involved in the social interactions of pupils with teachers. Piaget and Garcia (1983) also attempt to bring the Kuhnian chapter in philosophy of science to a more rational conclusion with their hypothesis of ideological determination of sharp shifts in schemes both in the history of science and in the individual development of Newtonian and modern mathematical concepts. The study of ideology and social interactionism can help teacher educators think about social influences on teacher thought (Easley & Kamara, 1983).

The Kuhnian revolution in philosophy of science was prompted by Kuhn's attack on one of the classic arguments about thinking and the teaching of thinking, i.e., the supposed necessity for external, syntactical criteria of thought—logic. Alternatives to a logical theory of inference are now actively sought (Feyerabend, 1978; Hanson, 1958; Lakatos, 1978).

In mathematics, there have been similar problems in what is called metamathematics. However, in mathematics and physics education, logic is still seen as essential by most writers. In 1963, Lakatos wrote, in the introduction to his now famous exposé of the fallibility of mathematical thought, *Proofs and Refutations:* "Since however metamathematics is a paradigm of informal, quasi-empirical mathematics just now in rapid growth, the essay, by implication, will also challenge modern mathematical dogmatism. The student of recent history of metamathematics will recognize the patterns described here in his own field" (p. 6). Lakatos' posthumous editors, Worrall and Zahar, disputed Lakatos' belief on this point, assuming that he had subsequently revised his view, without changing the text quoted, because (Lakatos, 1977) he had the "highest regard for formal deductive logic" (p. 138). But Davis and Hersh, in *The Mathematical Experience* (1981, p. 358), strongly supported Lakatos' statement.

Lakatos (1977) also wrote: "The history of mathematics and the logic of mathematical discovery, i.e., the phylogenesis and the ontogenesis of mathematical thought, cannot be developed without the criticism and ultimate rejection of formalism" (pp. 5–6).

The epistemological question about external formal syntax also reminds me of the "math wars" (De Mott, 1962), in which mathematicians 25 years ago attacked each other with surprising vehemence over the relevance of logic and sets for mathematics education. Patrick Suppes (1967) once told me that he had introduced the union of disjoint sets into primary school math as a model for addition, thinking that, as in the foundations of arithmetic, it would provide pupils with a semantic interpretation, only to find from observations in the classroom that pupils actually learned it "syntactically," i.e., in terms of rules of formation for strings of symbols.

Petrie illustrates a common simplifying of semantic relations in his interesting book (1981) on a cognitive process view of "enquiry and learning," by a story of his stepdaughter's math homework. Initially, she tried to follow a syntactical rule that every story problem on the page required that the two numbers contained in it should be multiplied. Through her stepfather's guidance, she switched to an understanding of somewhat subtle interpretations of key words contained in the last problem as meaning to divide. Even such semantic rules as those that interpret the "key words," to which many mathematics educators might react in horror, can constitute a conceptual improvement. Perhaps, in helping his stepdaughter, Petrie is using a Lakatosian approach to story problem solving, beginning with her conjectures, whatever they may be, and proposing exceptions to help her improve her rule, for Petrie is clearly in sympathy with the Lakatosian program (1978). Because school ideology has been focused on the formal properties of symbolic codes (syntax), key words are the starting framework for many pupils when they are challenged to think about the meaning of mathematics story problems. Physical situations escape these presuppositions. My hope is that, in dialogue with their peers, pupils' content-oriented semantic frameworks will also receive consideration.

Implications for Teacher Education

I work with in-service elementary school teachers on methods of mathematics and some physical science, and I teach preservice prospective elementary teachers methods of teaching science. I have had to learn that teachers have a lot on their minds when facing a room full of children, or even when just thinking about it. It is extremely difficult to guide teachers or teacher candidates in the development of sounder schemes of teaching because I cannot read their thoughts about teaching the subject at hand. I do not have the visible clues art teachers have for reading their students' thoughts about painting or athletic coaches have in reading their players' ideas about performing the play. Also, my lack of socialization as an elementary school teacher does not equip me to anticipate the schemes that teachers use and to address them in a way that is relevant to their developing understanding of the pupils' thought. I would also need a spontaneously functional understanding in two domains. When I do a demonstration lesson with primary grade children, if I have to deal with their authority or discipline problems (one domain), it is difficult for me to also think about the math or science schemes of the children (a second domain). However, I introduce problems in science and mathematics to teachers, and I ask that they try to present children with the same challenges. Then I can also discuss with them the phenomenon of children thinking, individually and in groups, with and without adult leadership. I can then invite them to explore that phenomenon and discover the art of teaching by listening to children think (Easley & Zwoyer, 1975).

Since The University of Massachusetts Conference on *Cognitive Process Instruction* (Lockhead & Clement, 1978), cognitively oriented researchers in math and science education have taken a variety of approaches to helping teachers work with their pupils' alternative frameworks, rather than just blindly running into conflict with them by standard presentations. A variety of approaches is needed to meet the diverse needs of teachers. Rather than review the pedagogical options that have been suggested, I have tried to look at more general questions, i.e., what does the existence and increasingly better understood functioning of pupils' and teachers' schemes mean for our concepts of education, educational goals, and behavioral objectives? What are the various roles teachers can assume, and what does it mean for students to learn and to understand a lesson?

The answers I am beginning to find build on the generalizing properties of schemes, which lie somewhere between those of general laws and particular facts, key elements of the old epistemology. When knowledge is thought of, as Piaget proposed, as a developmental product of the interaction of the infant's natural but flexible reflexes and the physical and social properties of the growing child's environment, then children's mathematics and physics emerge from the natural action schemes that the infant constructs at the sensory motor level. The dynamic properties of schemes energize solving problems (Piaget, 1981), so mathematical and physical knowledge schemes continue to develop, assimilating whatever they can to themselves in a naturalistic generalization (Stake & Trumbull, 1982) and accommodating to what doesn't initially work right in order to produce an explanation. Causal explanations are initially anthropomorphic, later involving more objective mechanisms.

Constructivism and Formal Education.   Knowledge can be communicated in written form only if schemes similar to the authors' can be evoked in one or more readers. It is appropriate schemes, not phonics, that form the prerequisite for reading. Therefore, transmission of knowledge through a textbook or by direct teaching is simply a misleading metaphor—an outmoded educational myth. One scheme competes with others in problematical situations until one wins out. There is always a limited generalization in each act of assimilation. The full ranges of the applicability or generalizability of schemes may never be experienced, even though they are limited in practice by competition with alternative schemes. Besides action-based schemes, however, those figural schemes of written or drawn patterns (even of sound patterns) permit a certain degree of reproduction of the material presented, but too often without the semantic schemes that give it meaning. Social interaction schemes are likely to be involved that interpret the social messages that accompany most factual communications (reading between the lines).

We need to abandon the quest for certainty implied in logical syntax and accept the inherent inaccuracies of a sociobiological model of knowledge (Easley, 1978a), so what counts is the quest for improvement of knowledge, not absolute certainty. That means the goal of education has to be thinking, and knowledge about how to stimulate others' thoughts. Two images may help us to be more tolerant of the inevitability of error along this road. Observing how often teachers make factual errors that some of their peers could catch, Stenhouse observed, that: "The archetypal effort to compress and present knowledge in accessible form, the encyclopaedia, encounters the same problem, for all the resources at the disposal of its editors" (p. 181).

A few years ago, working with a talented group of tutors, I proposed to them as a possible project, that we organize "master lessons" on familiar, but difficult, topics in math and science. Several of us started to work to prepare our lessons. We were surprised at the large number of hours we put into the preparation of single lessons, something like 50 each before we gave up, and we still weren't ready. These were familiar topics that we dealt with daily as tutors, and some of us had taught them as lectures in courses. The project fell through, but we learned how hopelessly inadequate are the available time and energy resources for a teacher who is expected to present any topic beyond criticism. In fact, lessons work because of the criticism of students.

The common assumptions that I outlined at the beginning of the chapter are wrong. The right idea is to stimulate thought. That does not require endless preparation for all eventualities, unless the students have already been too well "educated" to think for themselves.

REFERENCES

Bauersfeld, H. (1979). Hidden dimensions in the so-called reality of a mathematics classroom. *Critical Reviews in Mathematics Education, 9,* 109–136.

Benezet, L. P. (1935/1936). The story of an experiment. The teaching of arithmetic, I, II, & III. *The Journal of the National Education Association, 24* (8, Nov.), 241–244, (9, Dec.), 301–303, *25* (1, Jan.), 7–8.

Brandau, L. (1985). *Why one elementary teacher found it so difficult to encourage thinking in her mathematics classroom: A metaphorical analysis.* Doctoral dissertation, University of Illinois at Urbana-Champaign.

Brandau, L., & Easley, J. (1980). *Understanding the realities of problem solving in elementary school, with practical pointers for teachers.* Columbus, ERIC Clearinghouse for Science, Mathematics, and Environmental Education, The Ohio State University.

Brown, S. I., & Walter, M. L. (1983). *The art of problem posing.* Philadelphia: The Franklin Institute Press.

Champagne, A. B., & Klopfer, L. E. (1982). A causal model of students' achievement in a college physics course. *Journal of research in science teaching, 19,* 299–309.

Davis, P. J., & Hersh, R. (1981). *The mathematical experience.* Boston: Houghton–Mifflin.

Davis, R. (1984). *Learning mathematics: The cognitive science approach to mathematics education.* London: Croom Helm.

De Mott, B. (1962). The math wars. *The American scholar.* (Reprinted in R. W. Heath, (Ed.), *New curricula.* New York, Harper & Row, 1964.)

Denis-Prinzhorn, M., & Grize, J. B. (1966). La méthode clinique en pédagogie. In F. Bresson, & M. de Montmollin, (Eds.), *Psychologie et épistémologie génétiques.* Paris: Paris: Dunod.

Department of Education and Science (1976). Central Advisory Council for Education (England). *Children and their primary schools (Plowden report).* London: HM Stationery Office.

Doise, W., Mugny, G., & Perret-Clermont, A.-N. (1976). Social interaction and cognitive development: Further evidence. *European Journal of Social Psychology, 6,* 245–247.

Driver, R. (1983). *The pupil as scientist?* Milton Keynes, Open University Press.

Driver, R., & Easley, J. A., Jr. (1978). Pupils and paradigms: A review of literature related to concept development in adolescent science students. *Studies in Science Education, 5,* 61–84.

Duckworth, E. (1983). Teachers as learners. *Archives de psychologie, 51,* 171–175.

Easley, J. A., Jr. (1977). *On clinical studies in mathematics education.* Columbus, The ERIC Clearinghouse for Science, Mathematics and Environmental Education, The Ohio State University.

Easley, J. A., Jr. (1978a). Symbol manipulation reexamined—An approach to bridging a chasm. In P. Z. Presseisen, D. Goldstein, & M. H. Appel (Eds.), *Topics in cognitive development* (Vol. II). New York: Plenum.

Easley, J. A., Jr. (1978b). Four decades of conservation research: What do they mean for mathematics education? In J. McC. Gallagher, & J. A. Easley, Jr. (Eds.), *Knowledge and development, Volume 2: Piaget and education.* New York, Plenum.

Easley, J. A., Jr. (1979a). A portrayal of traditional teachers of mathematics in American schools. *Critical reviews in mathematics education (Materialien und studien)*. Band 9, 4–18.

Easley, J. A., Jr. (1979b). Mathematical foundations of 40 years of research on conservation in Geneva. *Focus on learning problems in mathematics*. *1* (4), 7–25.

Easley, J. (1983a). A Japanese approach to arithmetic. *For the learning of mathematics*. *3* (3).

Easley, J. (1983b). Reflections on tutoring minority undergraduates in mathematics and quantitative sciences. *Focus on Learning Mathematics, 5* (3 & 4), 79–94.

Easley, J. (1984). Is there educative power in students' alternative frameworks—or else, what's a poor teacher to do? *Problem Solving, 6* (2), 1–4.

Easley, J., & Easley, E. (1982). *Math can be natural: Kitamaeno priorities introduced to American teachers*. University of Illinois at Urbana-Champaign, Committee on Culture and Cognition (Report No. 24).

Easley, J., & Easley, E. (1983). What's there to talk about in arithmetic? *Problem Solving, 5* (3).

Easley, J., Grieb, A., Taylor, H., Stake, B., Chapelle, C., & Ruiz, I. (1980). *Pedagogical dialogues in primary school mathematics*. Bureau of Educational Research, University of Illinois at Urbana-Champaign.

Easley, J., & Kamara, A. I. (1983). An ecological model of change from authoritarian to inquiry-based elementary school science in Sierra Leone. In P. Tamir, A. Hofstein, & M. Ben-Peretz (Eds.), *Preservice and inservice training of science teachers*. Philadelphia: Balaban International Science Services.

Easley, J. A., Jr., & Zwoyer, R. (1975). Teaching by listening. *Contemporary Education, 47*, 19–25.

Erickson, G. L. (1980). Children's viewpoint of heat: A second look. *Science Education, 64*, 323–336.

Erickson, G. L. (1983, June). *Student frameworks and classroom instruction*. Paper presented at an international seminar of misconceptions in science and mathematics. Ithaca, NY: Cornell University.

Feyerabend, P. K. (1978). *Science in a free society*. London: New Left Books.

Gallagher, J. McC., & Reid, D. K. (1981). *The learning theory of Piaget and Inhelder*. Monterey, CA: Brooks/Cole.

Grieb, A., & Easley, J. (1984). A primary school impediment to mathematical equity: Case studies in rule-dependent soialization. In M. W. Steinkamp & M. Maehr, (Eds.), *Recent advances in motivation: Women in science*. Greenwich, CT: JAI Press.

Hanson, N. R. (1958). *Paterns of discovery*. Cambridge, MA: Cambridge University Press.

Hanson, R. K. (1985). Alternative theories in the classroom. In C. W. Anderson (Ed.), *Observing science classrooms: Perspectives from research and practice. 1984 Yearbook of the Association for the Education of Teachers of Science*. Columbus, ERIC Clearinghouse for Science, Mathematics and Environmental Education, The Ohio State University.

Hatano, G. (1980). Learning to add and subtract: A Japanese perspective. *Dokkyo University Bulletin of Liberal Arts, 15*, 84–110. (A shortened version appears in T. P. Carpenter, J. M. Moser, & T. A. Romberg (Eds.), *Addition and subtraction: A developmental perspective*. Hillsdale, NJ: Lawrence Erlbaum Associates.

Hawkins, D. (1978, Autumn). Critical barriers to science learning. *Outlook, 29* (3).

Inhelder, B., Blanchet, A., Sinclair, A., & Piaget, J. (1975). Relations entre les conservations d' ensembles d'éléments discrêts et celles de quantités continues. *Année Psychologie, 75*, 23–60.

Johnson, D. W., & Johnson, F. (1975). *Learning together and alone: Cooperation, competition, and individualization.* Englewood Cliffs, NJ: Prentice–Hall.

Kamii, C. (1984). *Young children reinvent arithmetic: Implications of Piaget's theory.* New York: Teachers College Columbia Press.

Kamii, C., & DeVries, R. (1976). *Piaget, children and number.* Washington: National Association for the Education of Young Children.

Kamii, M. (1981, October). Children's ideas about written number. *Topics in learning and learning disabilities.*

Kamii, M. (1982). *Children's graphic representation of numerical concepts: A developmental study.* Doctoral thesis, Harvard Graduate School of Education.

Kau, C.-V. J. (1981). *Growth of a teacher in a communication project.* Doctoral dissertation, University of Illinois at Urbana-Champaign.

Kuhn, T. S. (1961). *The structure of scientific revolutions.* Chicago: The University of Chicago Press.

Lakatos, I. (1977). *Proofs and refutations.* Cambridge, MA: Cambridge University Press. (Originally published serially in *The British Journal for the Philosophy of Science,* 1963, *14* (53–56, 1–25, 120–139, 221–245, 296–342.)

Lakatos, I. (1978). *The methodology of research programmes. philosophical papers* (Vol. 1) Cambridge: The University Press.

Lerch, H., & Easley, J. (1978). *Children's conceptions of number and numeral.* N.I.E. Project Final Report.

Lochhead, J., & Clement, J. (Eds.). (1978). *Cognitive process instruction.* Philadelphia: Franklin Institute Press.

Novak, J. (1977). *A theory of education.* Ithaca, NY: Cornell University Press.

Nussbaum, J., & Novak, J. (1976). An assessment of children's concepts of the earth utilizing structured interviews. *Science Education, 60* (4), 535–550.

Nussbaum, J., & Novik, S. (1982). *A study of conceptual change in the classroom.* Paper presented at the National Association for Research in Science Teaching.

Papert, S. (1963). Sur la logique Piagetienne. *Etudes d'épistémologie génétiques, 15,* 107–109.

Perret-Clermont, A.-N. (1980). *Social interaction and cognitive development in children.* London: Academic Press.

Petrie, H. G. (1981). *The dilemma of enquiry and learning.* Chicago: The University Press.

Piaget, J. (1926). *Judgment and reasoning in the child.* New York: Harcourt & Brace.

Piaget, J. (1929). *The child's conception of the world.* London: Routledge & Kegan Paul.

Piaget, J. (1931). *The child's conception of physical causality.* London: Routledge & Kegan Paul.

Piaget, J. (1970). *The child's conception of movement and speed.* London: Routledge & Kegan Paul.

Piaget, J. (1972a). *La transmission des mouvements.* (Vol. 27 of *Etudes d'épistémologie génétique*). Paris: Presses Universitaires de France.

Piaget, J. (1972b). *La direction des mobiles lors de chocs et de poussées.* Vol. 28 of *Etudes d'épistémologie génétique*). Paris: Presses Universitaires de France.

Piaget, J. (1973a). *La formation de la notion de force.* Vol. 29 of *Etudes d'épistémologie génétique*). Paris: Presses Universitaires de France.

Piaget, J. (1973b). *The grasp of consciousness.* Cambridge, MA: Harvard University Press.

Piaget, J. (1973c). *La composition des forces et le problème des vecteurs.* Vol. 30 of *Etudes d'épistémologie génétiques*). Paris: Presses Universitaires de France.

Piaget, J. (1976a). Correspondences and morphisms. *Newsletter of the Jean Piaget Society, 5* (3).

Piaget, J. (1976b). *Success and understanding.* Cambridge: MA: Harvard University Press.
Piaget, J. (1977). Some recent research and its link with a new theory of groupings and conservations based on commutability. *Annals of the New York Academy of Sciences. 291,* 350–358.
Piaget, J. (1978). *Recherches sur la généralisation.* Vol. 36 of *Etudes d'épistémologie génétiques).* Paris: Presses Universitaires de France.
Piaget, J. (1980). *Experiments in contradiction.* Chicago: University of Chicago Press.
Piaget, J. (1980, April). The constructivist approach. In L. Apostel, et al., *Construction and validation of scientific theories. Cahiers de la fondation archives Jean Piaget No. 1.* Geneva: Fondation Archives Jean Piaget.
Piaget, J. (1981). *Intelligence and affectivity, their relationship during child development.* Palo Alto, CA: Annual Reviews.
Piaget, J., & Henriques, G. (1983). *Travaux sur la causalité.* (3 volumes to appear, cited on p. 264 of Piaget & Garcia.)
Piaget, J., & Garcia, R. (1983). *Psychogenèse et histoire des sciences.* Paris: Flammarion.
Slavin, R. E. (1983). *Cooperative learning.* New York: Longmans.
Stake, R. E., & Trumbull, D. J. (1982). Naturalistic generalization. *Review Journal of Philosophy and Social Science, 7,* 1–2, 1–12.
Stake, R. E., & Easley, J. A., Jr. (1978). *Case studies in science education.* Washington: U.S. Government Printing Office.
Steinkamp, M. W. (1983). *The assessment of elementary schoolchildren's motivation in the classroom: An inventory of motivational behaviors.* Presented at the American Educational Research Association. Montreal.
Stenhouse, L. (1983). *Authority, education and emancipation.* London: Heinemann Educational Books.
Stodolsky, S. S. (1983). An ecological perspective for the study of instruction. In P. Tamir, A. Hofstein, & M. Ben-Peretz (Eds.), *Preservice and inservice training of science teachers.* Philadelphia: Balaban International Science Services.
Strayer, G. D., & Upton, C. B. (1933). *Strayer–Upton arithmetics.* New York: American Book.
Suppes, P. (1967). *Sets and numbers, books K–6.* L. W. Singer.
Trumbull, D. (Ed.), Easley, J., Smith, C., & Stake, B. E. (1985). *On the way to algegra: Longitudinal case studies in elementary school mathematics.* University of Illinois at Urbana-Champaign, Committee on Culture and Cognition (Report No. 25).

The Geometric Supposer: Using Microcomputers to Restore Invention to the Learning of Mathematics

30

Judah L. Schwartz
Massachusetts Institute of Technology
&
Harvard Graduate School of Education

Michal Yerushalmy
University of Haifa

WHAT PROBLEM WAS THE GEOMETRIC SUPPOSER DESIGNED TO SOLVE?

The GEOMETRIC SUPPOSER (Schwartz & Yerushalmy, 1985, in press-a) is a series of microcomputer-based programs that were designed to help students and teachers become makers of mathematics. Two lines of reasoning led to the development of the GEOMETRIC SUPPOSER. The first centers on the almost total absence of the making of conjectures by students (and teachers, for that matter) in the teaching of mathematics.

There is something odd about the way we teach mathematics in our schools. We teach it as if we expect that our students will never have occasion to make new mathematics. We do not teach language that way. If we did, students would never be required to write an original piece of prose or poetry. We would simply require them to recognize and appreciate the great pieces of language of the past, the literary equivalents of the Pythagorean theorem and the law of Cosines.

The nature of mathematics instruction is such that when a teacher assigns a theorem to prove, the student ordinarily assumes that the theorem is true and that a proof can be found. This constitutes a kind of satire on the nature of mathematical thinking and the way new mathematics is made. The central activity necessary to make new mathematics is the making and testing of conjectures. The GEOMETRIC SUPPOSER is designed to help the student become a potent and nimble conjecture maker. In order to make conjectures in geometry, it is helpful to be able to construct and manipulate geometrical "objects" in order to explore the relationships that do or do not hold among these objects. The need to explore such relationships leads us to the second line of reasoning that underlies the development of the GEOMETRIC SUPPOSER.

We do not have a reasonably accessible general notation scheme for geometric constructs in the way that we do for algebraic constructs. The kth term in a sequence can easily represent any term in the sequence. How can one draw a triangle that can represent any triangle without the particularity of the drawn triangle intruding? As a consequence of this difference between geometry and other branches of mathematics, in geometry we use representations of particular cases and infer from the particular to the general. That this procedure is not totally satisfactory is amply attested to by the fact that virtually everyone who has studied geometry has had the experience of being fooled by a diagram.

Because we do not have a general notation scheme for images in general and for geometric construction in particular, exploring conjectures becomes a matter of exploring particular cases in the hope of educing generality from the sequence of instances. Normally, this is a dismal prospect. But the GEOMETRIC SUPPOSER makes it possible to explore the consequences of one's constructions across an ensemble of equivalent diagrams, thereby reducing (although not eliminating) the dependence on the particular.

For example, remember the remarkable fact that the line segments joining the midpoints of adjacent sides of *any* quadrilateral form a parallelogram? Suppose one were to discover this in a particular case, say the isosceles trapezoid with base angles of 45 degrees. How might you convince yourself that it is true for other isosceles trapezoids, indeed true for any trapezoid, and in fact true for any quadrilateral? If you were obliged to carry out a large number of straight edge and compass constructions by hand, it is very likely that you would be willing to undertake the task.

In the normal course of events, it is not feasible to ask students (or anyone else) to do a great deal of construction for at least two reasons. First, accurate constructions are difficult to make, and second, because of the difficulty of making constructions, it is not reasonable to expect that people will be willing to repeat constructions over and over again in order to generate a repertoire of cases on which to base a conjecture.

The GEOMETRIC SUPPOSER allows users to make any construction they wish on a primitive structure (e.g., point and line, triangle, quadrilateral) of their choice. The program records that construction as a procedure that can then be executed on new exemplars of that primitive structure, including ones randomly generated by the SUPPOSER. As a

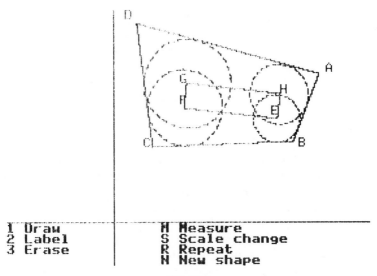

FIG. 30.1.

result, it becomes a simple matter to explore whether the consequences of a given construction on a given structure are dependent on some particular and peculiar property of that structure, or if there is the possibility of a more general result obtaining. In the example just cited, the program captures the actions of the user as he or she makes them on the particular quadrilateral ABCD and remembers the sequence

label midpoint of AB with the letter E
label midpoint of BC with the letter F
label midpoint of CD with the letter G
label midpoint of DA with the letter H
draw line segment EF
draw line segment FG
draw line segment GH
draw line segment HE

as a procedure that can be carried out on any quadrilateral ABCD. The user of the program may now proceed to execute this procedure on a wide variety of quadrilaterals and, in each instance, ascertain whether the newly formed quadrilateral EFGH is a parallelogram or not.

The possible constructions within the SUPPOSER include the construction of triangles and quadrilaterals and the drawing of segments, medians, altitudes, parallels, perpendiculars, perpendicular bisectors, angle bisectors, and inscribed and circumscribed circles. The user can measure lengths, angles, areas, and distances and call for arithmetic combinations of these measures such as the sum of two angles, the product of two lengths, or the ratio of two areas.

A program that merely provided extensive construction facilities to a student and/or a teacher would be useful in the learning of geometry by allowing accurate constructions to be made easily. But, in and of itself, that would not change either the intellectual or the pedagogic nature of the enterprise. The power of the GEOMETRIC SUPPOSER lies in its ability to remember and repeat constructions. As described previously, any construction on a primitive structure such as a quadrilateral that a user makes with the SUPPOSER may be repeated on a new quadrilateral of the user's construction, a previously used quadrilateral, or a random parallelogram, trapezoid, rhombus, rectangle, kite, or quadrilateral that may be circumscribed by or that can circumscribe a circle.

Neither possibility nor plausibility constitutes proof. Proof remains central to both the creating and the learning of mathematics. But conjecture, in this instance with the aid of the GEOMETRIC SUPPOSER as intellectual amplifier, can assume its proper role as the key activity in the making of mathematics. The fact that the SUPPOSER makes it possible to do constructions easily and quickly should not mean that the student is never asked to use a straightedge and compass to bisect angles or erect perpendiculars. Actual constructions with tangible straightedges and compasses are important for students. Indeed, it is only after some physical manipulations with these tools that the power of the SUPPOSER becomes apparent.

WHAT CAN STUDENTS (OF ALL AGES) DISCOVER WITH THE GEOMETRIC SUPPOSER?

A major purpose of the GEOMETRIC SUPPOSER is to reintroduce conjecture and invention into the teaching and learning of mathematics. Has the program helped to address these ends?

Using this facility, beginning geometry students have discovered that, if they draw a median in a triangle, the median bisects the area of the triangle; that seems to be true if they repeat the construction with triangles of all shapes and sizes. Having established the plausibility of this conjecture they are in a position to devise a proof with some conviction about what it is that they are trying to prove. Students have discovered for themselves that a midsegment in a triangle is parallel to the third side of the triangle, and that the three midsegments of the triangle partition the triangle into four triangles that are congruent to one another and similar to the original triangle. They have made discoveries about the ratios of perimeter and of areas that are frequently presented as theorems.

Perhaps, most striking of all, is the fact that a growing number of students are discovering new theorems. Consider the problem of dividing any triangle into N triangles of equal area? A 10-th grade student, who hitherto had not had a distinguished mathematical career in school, has just produced a novel solution to this problem.

The exploration that the SUPPOSER makes possible is not appropriate to high school students alone. What follows is an example of a conjecture that the authors have found, part of a family of conjectures about quadrilaterals for which we do not yet know a proof (Schwartz & Yerushalmy, in press-b). It is well known that one cannot inscribe a circle in an arbitrary quadrilateral ABCD, although one can inscribe a circle in any triangle. Consider then, the triangles ABC, BCD, CDA, DAB that are defined by the vertices of an arbitrary quadrilateral ABCD. These are the triangles formed by the sides of the quadrilateral and its diagonals. Suppose one were to inscribe circles in these triangles and label the centers E, F, G, and H, respectively. The following figures (Fig. 30.3) suggest that the quadrilateral EFGH might bear an interesting relationship to the quadrilateral ABCD.

In devising new mathematics in this way, students of all ages and degrees of intellectual engagement can choose to understand that making new mathematics is a continuing and exciting enterprise, and one that, with the right tools, is accessible to them.

THE GEOMETRIC SUPPOSER AND FORMAL PROOF

Many readers at this point may see the SUPPOSER as a mixed blessing. Specifically, one might suspect that a tool of this kind will weaken the already feeble appreciation of formal proof that many students have. After all, why bother to prove something if you can try out your assertion as often and as easily as you life?

One of the delightful side effects of the use of the SUPPOSER seems to be the realization on the part of the students that demonstration, even if one has accumulated a very large number of cases, is not tantamount to proof. Another anecdote supports this interpretation of the evolution of students' attitudes. During the 1984–1985 school year, one of the authors (MY) noticed a distinct shift in the nature of the students' requests to her when she came to visit the classroom. This shift took place over a 4 to 6-week period. At the beginning of that period students would ask her to "come look at my conjecture," whereas toward the end of the period, they would say "come look at my proof"! Rather than do away with the need for proof, using the SUPPOSER sharpens the students' perception of the need for proof.

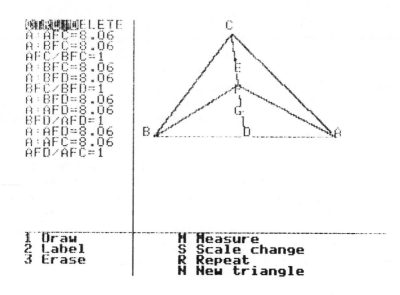

```
         ELETE
A:AFC=8.06
A:BFC=8.06
AFC/BFC=1
A:BFC=8.06
A:BFD=8.06
BFC/BFD=1
A:BFD=8.06
A:AFD=8.06
BFD/AFD=1
A:AFD=8.06
A:AFC=8.06
AFD/AFC=1
```

```
1 Draw            M Measure
2 Label           S Scale change
3 Erase           R Repeat
                  N New triangle
```

FIG. 30.2a.

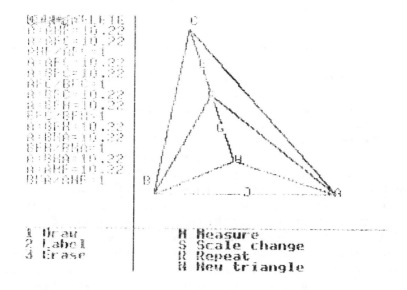

```
         ELETE
```

```
1 Draw            M Measure
2 Label           S Scale change
3 Erase           R Repeat
                  N New triangle
```

FIG. 30.2b.

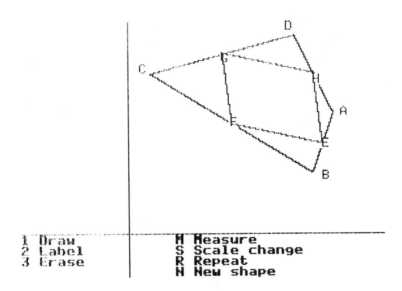

FIG. 30.3.

SOME DETAILS OF THE PROGRAM

Next, we describe the capability of the version of the SUPPOSER that works with triangles as the primitive structure. A similar set of capabilities obtains in the case of the quadrilateral, circle, and preSUPPOSER versions of the program.

The SUPPOSER allows users to construct a triangle of their own or to choose a random right, acute, obtuse, isosceles, or equilateral triangle as the shape on which they will make further constructions. If users opt to construct their own triangle, they are asked to specify how they wish to specify their triangle, i.e., by specifying SIDE–SIDE–SIDE or SIDE–ANGLE–SIDE or ANGLE–SIDE–ANGLE. They then specify the values of these quantities and can watch the SUPPOSER construct their triangle as one would with ruler and compass.

The GEOMETRIC SUPPOSER allows the user to draw on a repertoire of primitive constructions, each of which is classically possible with straightedge and compass. These include being able to draw:

a line segment between any two labeled points on the screen.

a circle, either circumscribed about or inscribed in a triangle of the user's choice, or one that is centered on any labeled point on the screen and whose radius is specified as a multiple of any line segment (drawn or undrawn) on the screen.

GEOMETRIC SUPPOSER QUICK REFERENCE CARD

Geometric Supposer Menus

1 DRAW	2 LABEL	3 ERASE	M MEASURE	S SCALE CHANGE	R REPEAT	N NEW TRIANGLE
1 Segment 2 Circle 3 Median 4 Altitude 5 Parallel 6 Perpendicular 7 Angle Bisect 8 Perpendicular Bisect 9 Midsegment 0 Extension	1 Intersection 2 Subdivide Segment 3 Reflection 4 Random Point	1 Segment 2 Label(s)	1 Length 2 Perimeter 3 Area 4 Angle 5 Distance Point-Line 6 Distance Line-Line 7 Adjustable Element(s)		1 On New Triangle 2 On Previous Triangle	1 Right 2 Acute 3 Obtuse 4 Isosceles 5 Equilateral 6 Your Own

☐ Main Menu

☐ Sub Menu

FIG. 30.4.

a median in any triangle, from any vertex.

an altitude in any triangle, from any vertex.

a parallel through any labeled point on the screen, parallel to any line segment (drawn or undrawn) and whose length is specified as a multiple of any line segment (drawn or undrawn) on the screen.

a perpendicular through any labeled point on the screen, perpendicular to any line segment (drawn or undrawn) and whose length is specified as a multiple of any line segment (drawn or undrawn) on the screen.

the bisector of any angle on the screen.

the perpendicular bisector of any segment on the screen.

a specified midsegment in any triangle on the screen.

and to extend any segment on the screen, from either end, by an amount whose length can be specified as a multiple of any line segment (drawn or undrawn) on the screen.

The GEOMETRIC SUPPOSER also allows the user to label the intersection of any two line segments, to subdivide any line segment into (up to 6) equal segments, to reflect a point or a line segment on a line, and to place a point at random on a line segment, and either inside or outside a specified triangle.

The measurement functions of the SUPPOSER include the ability to measure lengths, perimeters, areas, angles, distances from points to lines, and distances between lines. It is possible to measure directly the sums, differences, products, or ratios of any two similar quantities.

The SUPPOSER allows the user to move a cursor while monitoring the changing values of up to three angles, lengths, or distances. This facility makes it possible to do such things as locate the center of circumscribing or inscribed circles, or to erect equilateral triangles on line segments.

Finally, the SUPPOSER allows the user to repeat the construction that is on the screen on another exemplar of the primitive shape, in this instance, the triangle. As explained earlier, this feature of the SUPPOSER enables it to provoke the making of conjecture on the part of both students and teachers. It is very tempting to explore whether the newly discovered property of one's construction is true in general or is only an artifact of the specific case.

HOW HAS THE GEOMETRIC SUPPOSER BEEN USED?

Several middle school classes and a dozen or so high school classes, both public and private, have worked with various versions of the GEOMETRIC SUPPOSER. There is also at least one group of students in a vocational–technical high school that has used the GEOMETRIC SUPPOSER.

The middle school classes are working with the preSUPPOSER version of the program to explore a set of geometric ideas that would otherwise not be available to them. In one of these middle school classes, the teacher posed the problem of discovering exactly what a right triangle is to the children. Shortly afterwards two eager children were pleased to report that "a right triangle has three different angles!" This conclusion is understandable considering the fact that, although there are an infinite number of right triangles, the statement is true for all but one of them, the isosceles right triangle. The teacher showed the children an acute triangle that had three different angles and asked them about their definition. A discussion ensued of the question of how many of the properties of an entity have to be included in its definition in order for the definition to be adequate.

The high school geometry classes have used the triangles version and, to a lesser extent, the quadrilaterals version of the SUPPOSER to approach the traditional content of the geometry courses in a variety of ways. Some of these ways constitute rather modest departures from usual instruction in this area, whereas others are truly revolutionary in the manner in which they draw mathematics out of the students. A class in which students are sufficiently engaged in the enterprise to come to class with conjectures that they are willing to sign and post for all to see is a class in which mathematics is being cast in an unusual and exciting role.

In one SUPPOSER class, described as having students of average ability, the students who had not encountered midsegments prior to that time were given the following quiz;

> A midsegment in a triangle is the line segment joining the midpoints of two sides of the triangle. Make a list of all the things you believe are true about midsegments and triangles.

At the end of the hour the class concluded that in a triangle:

the midsegments are parallel to the sides of the triangle.

the midsegments partition the original triangle into four congruent triangles.

that each of these triangles is similar to the original triangle.

that the area of one of these triangles is equal to one fourth of the area of the original triangle.

that the perimeter of one of these triangles is equal to one half the perimeter of the original triangle.

Another example of geometry discovered by a student is the conjecture that in a triangle ABC, the length of the median AD drawn from A is less than the average of the lengths of the other two sides AB and AC. It is indeed rare for high school geometry students to engage the subtlety of eometric inequality.

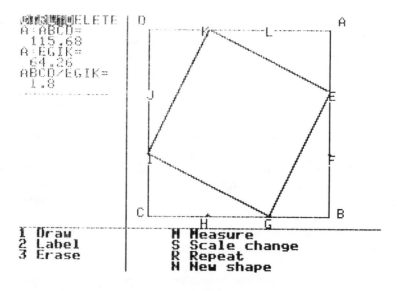

FIG. 30.5.

One final example: Consider the square ABCD and the points that trisect the sides of the square. The line segments joining appropriately corresponding such points form a new square whose area is $5/9$ of the area of the original square.

The students put forward the conjecture, proved it, generalized it to arbitrary subdivisions of the sides of the square, and were last seen trying to generalize the theorem to parallelograms.

The SUPPOSER has also been used in settings far from those of traditional geometry courses. In one vocational and technical high school, students worked with the GEOMETRIC SUPPOSER to augment their studies in drafting and design and to help develop a stronger set of spatial reasoning techniques. Some of the settings have been laboratory contexts in which a collection of microcomputers or terminals were available for class use. Other settings have been classrooms with only one microcomputer. Different teachers have evolved different styles of using the GEOMETRIC SUPPOSER in their teaching because of the constraints of hardware availibility. There is apparently no single most desirable arrangement, nor should there be.

AN AFTERWORD

The first version of the GEOMETRIC SUPPOSER was developed during the 1981–1982 school year. The early trials were exciting, challenging, and frustrating. Although we believed that we were engaged in an important endeavor in mathematics education, we were impatient with out inability to clarify issues and define things as crisply as we would have liked. At first, it was hard to explain to teachers what we were doing, and why we thought it was important.

In the intervening period we have gained much experience working with a wide variety of teachers and classroom settings. We are now more persuaded than ever that the GEOMETRIC SUPPOSER offers the mathematics teacher a new way to approach the teaching of geometry. We believe that the larger idea that underlies this program, namely that students can make their own mathematics, and that microcomputers can help them to do so, can change the way mathematics is taught and learned at all levels. Moreover, we think that the kind of use of the microcomputer that the GEOMETRIC SUPPOSER exemplifies can be extended beyond Euclidean plane geometry. Why not make such programs that work on constant-curvature non-Euclidean manifolds? Why restrict the dimensionality of the spaces in which such programs operate?

It is likely that this approach to the use of microcomputers in mathematics education can be extended beyond the study of geometry. The making and exploring of conjecture is clearly desirable throughout mathematics. It is quite likely that the approach we have taken with the SUPPOSER can be extended to other areas of intellectual inquiry, in which the exploration of the consequences of ones conjectures can be played out and the domain of their application investigated. Our greatest ambition for the impact the SUPPOSER might make is that perhaps this approach to using technology can help to engage the intellectual attention of a new generation of students.

REFERENCES

Schwartz, J. L., & Yerushalmy, M. (1985). *THE GEOMETRIC SUPPOSER; Triangles.* Sunburst Communications.

Schwartz, J. L., & Yerushalmy, M. (1985). *THE GEOMETRIC SUPPOSER; Quadrilaterials.* Sunburst Communications.

Schwartz, J. L., & Yerushalmy, M. (1985). *THE GEOMETRIC preSUPPOSER.* Sunburst Communications.

Schwartz, J. L., & Yerushalmy, M. (in press-a). *THE GEOMETRIC SUPPOSER; Circles.* Sunburst Communications.

Schwartz, J. L., & Yerushalmy, M. (in press-b). *The Geometric Supposer or The computer as intellectual prosthetic for the making of conjectures.* The College Mathematics Journal.

Author Index

Subject Index